PUBLIC OPINION AND POLITICAL CONTEST IN LATE MEDIEVAL PARIS

STUDIES IN EUROPEAN URBAN HISTORY (1100-1800)

VOLUME 60

Series Editors
Marc Boone
Anne-Laure Van Bruaene
Ghent University

Public Opinion and Political Contest in Late Medieval Paris

The Parisian Bourgeois and his Community, 1400-50

LUKE GIRAUDET

BREPOLS

Cover illustration: Louis II, duke of Anjou's entry into Paris. Paris, Bibliothèque nationale de France, fr. 2645, fol. 317v.

D/2022/0095/232
ISBN 978-2-503-59386-9
eISBN 978-2-503-59387-6
DOI 10.1484/M.SEUH-EB.5.122813
ISSN 1780-3241
eISSN 2294-8368

Printed in the EU on acid-free paper.

For Zoe

Contents

List of Illustrations

Figures

Abbreviations

Baye	Nicolas de Baye, *Journal de Nicolas de Baye, greffier du Parlement de Paris, 1400-17*, ed. by Alexandre Tuetey, 2 vols (Paris: Renouard, 1885-88)
BEC	*Bibliothèque de l'École des Chartes*
BNF	Bibliothèque nationale de France
Fr.	Fonds français
NAF	Nouvelle acquisition française
BSHP	*Bulletin de la Société de l'histoire de Paris et de l'Île-de-France*
Cordeliers	'Extrait d'une chronique anonyme pour le règne de Charles VI, 1400-1422' in *La Chronique d'Enguerran de Monstrelet en deux livres avec pièces justificatives, 1400-44*, ed. by Louis Douët-d'Arcq, 6 vols (Paris: Jules Renouard, 1857-62), VI (1862), pp. 191-327
Fauquembergue	Clément de Fauquembergue, *Journal de Clément de Fauquembergue, greffier du Parlement de Paris, 1417-35*, ed. by Alexandre Tuetey, 3 vols (Paris: Renouard, 1903-15)
Histoire de Charles VI	"Histoire de Charles VI, roy de France par Jean Juvénal des Ursins" in *Choix de chroniques et mémoires relatifs à l'histoire de France*, ed. by Jean Alexandre C. Buchon (Orléans: Herluison, 1875), pp. 323-573
Journal	*Journal d'un bourgeois de Paris, 1405-49 publié d'après les manuscrits de Rome et de Paris*, ed. by Alexandre Tuetey (Paris: Champion, 1881)
Monstrelet	Enguerrand de Monstrelet, *La Chronique d'Enguerran de Monstrelet en deux livres avec pièces justificatives, 1400-44*, ed. by Louis Douët-d'Arcq, 6 vols (Paris: Jules Renouard, 1857-62)
MSHP	*Mémoires de la Société de l'histoire de Paris et de l'Île-de-France*
Ordonnances des rois de France	*Ordonnances des rois de France de la troisième race*, ed. by Eusèbe Jacob Laurière & Denis François Secousse and others, 21 vols (Paris: Imprimerie royale, 1723-1849)
RSD	Michel Pintoin, *Chroniques du Religieux de Saint-Denys contenant le règne de Charles VI de 1380 à 1422*, ed. and trans. by Louis Bellaguet, 6 vols (Paris: Crapelet, 1839-52)

Note on conventions: Although the initial research for this book was based upon the creation of a new edition of the *Journal d'un bourgeois de Paris*, for the reader's reference and navigation I have elected to take all quotations from the last critical edition of the text, that published by Alexandre Tuetey in 1881. While serviceable, this edition is by no means perfect. Tuetey relied upon a second-hand transcription of the earliest surviving manuscript, Rome, Vatican Reg. Lat. 1923, which he supplemented with a fourth-generation copy of the Vatican manuscript, namely Paris, BNF Fr. 3480. In doing so, Tuetey overlooked other significant copies in the production of his edition, most notably the sixteenth-century Aix-en-Provence, Bibliothèque Méjanes MS 432 (316), which contains the most accurate copy of the material for 1438 missing from the Vatican manuscript, but only came to light as Tuetey's edition went to print. Lastly, in focusing upon the seventeenth-century BNF Fr. 3480, Tuetey also decided to include deviations, modernizations and additional content that he found in this manuscript, believing it to be a more complete first-hand copy of the lost original. Where necessary, these additions have been omitted to present a reading of the *Journal* in line with the Vatican manuscript.

With regards to the transcription of unpublished material, for the reader's convenience I have corrected u/v as appropriate throughout. I have included modern grammar such as commas and full stops where appropriate; abbreviations have been expanded and capitalization modernized.

Finally, although the *Journal d'un bourgeois de Paris* conformed to the medieval system of beginning the new year at Easter, all dates have been altered to correspond to the modern calendar. With regards to spelling in the book's text, French proper nouns and names have been retained, even in the case of accepted Anglicized forms. Unless otherwise stated, all translations of both primary and secondary material are my own, and I apologize for any errors that may result.

Acknowledgements

This book started life as a PhD thesis, completed at the University of York, where I had the pleasure of being a student and then an associate lecturer between 2011 and 2021. I owe a huge debt of gratitude to the various bodies that funded the research during this time, particularly the Wolfson Foundation for a generous doctoral grant, as well as York's Humanities Research Centre for granting me fellowships in 2019 and 2020.

I am also indebted to the hugely productive conversations held with numerous colleagues throughout the preparation of this book. My interest in the issues particular to late-medieval France, and the opportunity to study such a fascinating period, are due fundamentally to the outstanding seminars taught by Craig Taylor at the University of York. My sincere thanks to Professor Taylor, who has acted as a patient, encouraging and inspiring tutor, supervisor, and friend since 2014. I am also especially grateful to Tom Johnson, who very kindly gave his time to engage in productive conversations that profoundly shaped my thinking, both for this book and in the preparation of the projects that have followed since.

Numerous staff past and present at York also played vital roles in the evolution of my work. Linne Mooney's enthusiasm and delightful mentoring in the codicological analysis of the *Journal d'un bourgeois de Paris* was integral to getting this study off the ground. I am also deeply obliged to Lucy Sackville, Sarah Rees Jones and the late Mark Ormrod for readily discussing ideas and offering their support. Beyond York, I am appreciative of the numerous, rewarding and thought-provoking conversations and assistance provided along the way. Graeme Small's enthusiasm for this project, and insistence that it emerge as a monograph in some form, has been uplifting, and his comments on drafts of the work and further ideas have been essential to the development of the book's core themes. I would also like to thank Emily Hutchison, Erika Graham-Goering, Giacomo Valeri and Robert Grout for all of their comments and contributions.

I am grateful to the members of the Laboratoire de Médiévistique occidentale de Paris (Paris 1-Panthéon Sorbonne) for inviting me to participate in their seminars, providing me with the opportunity to reformulate my initial ideas and gradually trace the broader importance of Parisian journal writing in the fifteenth and sixteenth centuries. My thanks also to Xavier Rousseaux for his warm welcome to the *Centre d'histoire du droit et de la justice* at the Université catholique de Louvain in 2021, and for his incredible support in providing me with the time and space required to complete this book in its final stages. I am equally indebted to the reviewers and editorial team for the *Studies in European Urban History* series at Brepols for their support. My gratitude to Anne-Laure Van Bruaene and Marc Boone for their enthusiasm for this project and their insightful comments, and especially to Chris VandenBorre and Eva Anagnostaki for their invaluable assistance in perfecting the manuscript.

Of course, my deepest gratitude and affection goes to my parents, siblings and family members on both sides of the Channel for their unfailing encouragement throughout my studies. From a young age my grandparents (both French and British) have inspired my interests, and I am thankful for their wholehearted support. Finally, the greatest thanks of all go to Zoe Craig for her unique ability to help me see things clearly, her attentive engagement with my work, her calm patience and her love. Thank you.

Introduction

At dawn on the 19 August 1405, Paris awoke to unsettling news. The previous afternoon the sickly eight-year-old Dauphin Louis, duke of Guyenne, had been hurried from his chambers in the Hôtel Saint-Pol and extracted from the city by boat, en route to join his mother, the queen-consort Isabeau de Bavière and his uncle, Louis, duke of Orléans, at the fortress of Melun via Pouilly-le-Fort. The move had been undertaken surreptitiously following news that Jean sans Peur, duke of Burgundy was approaching the capital, and when the Burgundian duke learned of the Dauphin's departure in the early hours of the 19 August, he rode through the city in hot pursuit to the surprise of Parisian onlookers. Intercepting the Dauphin's entourage at Juvisy-sur-Orge, twenty kilometres south of Paris, Jean sans Peur approached the prince – his son-in-law following Louis' marriage to Marguerite de Nevers in August 1404 – and invited him to return to the capital in his company. Dismissing challenges from the Dauphin's escort, the Burgundian duke turned the litter around and headed back to Paris, where he was greeted by a large crowd of the city's joyous inhabitants.[1]

The events of August 1405 marked a total rupture in the relations between the French ducal houses of Orléans and Burgundy. The source of these tensions was found in the mental illness suffered by Charles VI of France (r. 1380-1422) who in July 1392 had first exhibited symptoms of a schizophrenic illness that would recur, in worsening bouts, throughout the remainder of his life. With the head of the French kingdom's body politic consequently incapable of ruling effectively, a power vacuum emerged that was ultimately contested by the house of Burgundy descended from Charles VI's uncle, Philippe II le Hardi (1363-1404), and the house of Orléans embodied by the king's brother Louis, duke of Orléans (1372-1407). When Jean sans Peur (1371-1419) then succeeded his father to the Burgundian duchy upon Philippe le Hardi's death in April 1404, he inherited a quarrel accentuated by the disparities between his own lack of influence at court and Louis d'Orléans' domination of the royal administration.[2]

---

1 This event, since known as 'l'enlèvement du Dauphin' (the kidnapping of the Dauphin), was described by several contemporary chroniclers, largely sympathetic to the duke of Burgundy. RSD, III, pp. 284-97; Monstrelet, I, pp. 108-13; *Histoire de Charles VI*, pp. 423-25; Baye, I, pp. 137-38; Cordeliers, p. 193. The *enlèvement* was analysed in detail by Léon Mirot, 'L'enlèvement du dauphin et le premier conflit entre Jean sans Peur et Louis d'Orléans (juillet-octobre 1405)', *Revue des questions historiques*, 51 (1914), pp. 329-55. Recently, Tracy Adams has proposed a reinterpretation of the events sensitive to the agency of Isabeau de Bavière. *The Life and Afterlife of Isabeau of Bavaria* (Baltimore, MD: John Hopkins University Press, 2010), pp. 166-92.

2 This early rivalry has been summarised in Richard Vaughan, *John the Fearless: The Growth of Burgundian Power*, Second Edition (Woodbridge: Boydell Press, 2005), pp. 29-48; Bernard Guenée, *Un meurtre, une société. L'assassinat du duc d'Orléans, 23 novembre 1407* (Paris: Gallimard, 1992), pp. 152-75.

The escalation in the tension between these princes led to one of the bloodiest and most divisive episodes in French history. In 1407, Louis d'Orléans' murder at the instigation of Jean sans Peur triggered a civil conflict that would last until 1435 and split France between two diametrically opposed factions, the 'Armagnacs' and the 'Burgundians'. Paris stood at the centre of this struggle. The capital was besieged by Armagnac forces in 1410 and 1411, was overwhelmed by radical protests in the Cabochien revolt of 1413, before being subjected to Armagnac rule until a Burgundian coup in May 1418 provoked a series of massacres and the flight of the then Dauphin Charles (future Charles VII, r. 1422-61). On 25 October 1415, Henry V of England (1386-1422) would take advantage of this French infighting to claim an against-the-odds victory at the Battle of Agincourt on 25 October 1415. A full-scale English conquest followed in 1417, culminating in the Treaty of Troyes concluded on 21 May 1420 that consolidated an Anglo-Burgundian alliance and designated Henry V as the regent and heir of France, destined to assume the French crown upon Charles VI's death and bring the two kingdoms of France and England together in a personal, Lancastrian union.[3] Ultimately, Henry V died two months before Charles VI, on 31 August 1422, leaving France divided between lands held for the infant Henry VI of England (1421-71) and his rival, Charles VII of France, Charles VI's last surviving son. As a result of the 1418 Burgundian coup, Paris was situated in the part of France that acknowledged Henry VI as monarch, and this acknowledgement was crucial to Lancastrian territorial ambitions, not least since the occupation of western Europe's largest city afforded the English regime significant spiritual, symbolic and political capital.[4] Henry VI's French regent and uncle, John, duke of Bedford (1389-1435), succeeded in maintaining these Lancastrian territories, including Paris, up until his death on 14 September 1435. A week later, the French and Burgundian factions were reconciled at the Congress of Arras, a moment that spelled the end of the Anglo-Burgundian alliance and the gradual decline of English power on the continent. On 17 April 1436 Paris was delivered to Charles VII, and by 1450 the English had been expelled from northern France altogether, save for Calais.

The events of 1405 also heralded the place that Paris and Parisian opinion would occupy in this contest between Burgundian, Armagnac, Lancastrian and Valois parties. The city's possession was crucial to claiming authority over the kingdom, providing direct access to royal institutions such as the Paris Parlement and, until 1422, control of Charles VI's person. As a relative political outsider, from 1405 Jean sans Peur rendered the cultivation of Parisian support a fundamental element in his strategic repertoire to challenge Louis d'Orléans. Integral to stability during times of unrest, the capital's support promised the financial and administrative resources necessary to securing Burgundian objectives. Two days after his return to the capital with the Dauphin Louis, on 21 August 1405, Jean sans Peur quickly set about justifying his intervention in royal politics. Through the carefully stage-managed delivery of a manifesto at the royal Palais on the Île-de-la-Cité,

---

3 For the establishment of this alliance see Paul Bonenfant, *Du meurtre de Montereau au traité de Troyes* (Brussels: Académie Royale de Belgique, 1958). Recent work has assessed the dual monarchy through the lens of imperialism. Peter Crooks, 'State of the Union: Perspectives on English Imperialism in the Late Middle Ages', *Past & Present*, 212 (2011), pp. 3-42.

4 On Paris' place in the Lancastrian dual monarchy, see Guy Thompson, *Paris and its People under English Rule: The Anglo-Burgundian Regime, 1420-36* (Oxford: Oxford University Press, 1991).

the duke appealed directly to Parisians, proclaiming his intention to reform the royal domain's administration, combat corrupt and tyrannical tendencies in the kingdom, and bring an end to the overwhelming taxes assailing the commons.[5] The duke reminded his audience – a combination of royal princes, urban dignitaries and the University of Paris – that he had come to Paris not for war, but to protect the royal house, the kingdom and the capital. In doing so, Jean sans Peur established an ideological dichotomy that would persevere throughout the civil conflict, juxtaposing a Burgundian emphasis upon anti-fiscal collaborative politics, predicated upon the defence of urban privileges and administrative reform, with the bureaucratically-centralizing, financially exploitative tendencies of the Orléanist princes.[6] Co-opting Parisian agencies and ambitions, Jean sans Peur endeavoured to ally the city's interests with his own by restoring urban rights. For example, the duke ordered that Paris' chains, which had been confiscated in the wake of the Maillotins revolt in 1382, be reforged immediately – partly as a defensive measure, but also in a move that signalled a renewal of Parisian political power.[7] Later, in 1412, the municipal administration or *prévôté des marchands* that had been abolished in 1382 was restored under Burgundian auspices, underscoring Paris' independent stake in politics only to be followed by the Cabochien revolt in 1413, spurred by Jean sans Peur's reformist rhetoric.[8]

This privileging of Parisian opinion and agency is also clear in the political literature that emerged in the immediate aftermath of the 'enlèvement du Dauphin'. Delivering a sermon before Charles VI on 7 November 1405, the theologian and chancellor of the University of Paris Jean Gerson (1363-1429) reiterated Burgundy's reformist programme, highlighting the king's ill-treatment, the dangers of princely tyranny, and the predations of avaricious councillors. As the heir to the *translatio studii* whereby learned insight had descended from Abraham, through Egypt, Athens and Rome to reside in Paris, Gerson envisioned the University as a royal daughter uniquely well-placed to voice France's plight, casting 'par tout le royaulme de France les yeulx de sa consideracion, qui sont plus clers que soleil et plus multiples que ceulx d'Argus'.[9] The following year, a propagandistic Burgundian poem, the *Songe véritable*, depicted Chascun (Everyperson) joining with Commune Renommée (Common Opinion), before proceeding throughout Paris to search for Vérité (Truth), which had been cast out from the city's princely residences and royal institutions. Here, the intersection of Chacun and Commune Renommée summoned the notion of a popular political voice acting as a check upon evil government, though the anonymous poet

---

5 RSD, III, pp. 297-307; Monstrelet, I, pp. 113-19.

6 Françoise Autrand, *Charles VI: La folie du roi* (Paris: Perrin, 1986), pp. 204-13; Claude Gauvard, *De Grâce especial: crime, État et société en France à la fin du Moyen Âge* (Paris: 1991), p. 950; Laurent Tournier, 'Jean sans Peur et l'université de Paris', *Beihefte der Francia*, 64 (2007), pp. 305-06.

7 *Journal*, p. 3; Monstrelet, I, p. 113; RSD, III, pp. 308-09.

8 Jean Favier, *Paris au XVᵉ siècle, 1380-1500* (Paris: Hachette, 1974), pp. 147-51. See also Boris Bove, 'Alliance ou défiance? Les ambiguïtés de la politique des Capétiens envers leur capitale entre le XIIᵉ et le XVIIᵉ siècle' in *Les villes capitales au Moyen Âge* (Paris: Éditions de la Sorbonne, 2006), pp. 131-54.

9 Through the kingdom of France its considerate eyes, which are clearer than the sun and more numerous than those of Argus. Jean Gerson, 'Pour la réforme du royaume: Vivat Rex, Vivat Rex, Vivat Rex' in *Œuvres complètes*, ed. by Palémon Glorieux, vol. 7, pt. 2 (Paris: Desclée, 1960), p. 1138.

warned when describing the latter 'Qu'aucuns dient que la voix d'elle, doit estre creue telle quelle'.[10]

In this anxious climate marked by the claims of Paris' institutions, an emphasis upon urban privilege and the opinion of its inhabitants, an anonymous Parisian also began to write an account of events within the city. The resulting text, the so-called *Journal d'un bourgeois de Paris*, is the only surviving narrative to consistently recount the city's experiences during the turbulent period between 1405 and 1450.[11] It is one of the most extraordinary texts to survive from the Middle Ages, providing insights into the daily lives of Parisians during this violent era, with records of processions, civic ceremonies and warfare, but also food prices, the weather, taxation and rumour. As such, the *Journal* presents an important window onto Parisian experiences for both the Armagnac-Burgundian civil conflict and the Lancastrian occupation of Paris that followed, and the record of the anonymous 'Bourgeois' was fundamentally tied to these circumstances. Although the *Journal*'s first pages are missing, opening part-way through an account of the escalation of hostilities in September 1405, a reference to events 'environ dix ou doze jours' earlier suggests that the text once included an account of the Dauphin's abduction, and this may even have triggered the Bourgeois' writing.[12] Indeed, in these early surviving passages, the Bourgeois recounted the reforging of the city's chains, the populace's assumption of arms to defend the capital for Burgundy, and the fearful murmurs that Louis d'Orléans was preparing to attack the capital: 'les gens de Paris furent si esmeuz, comme ce tout le monde feust contre eulx et les voulsist destruire'.[13]

Taking as his subject Parisians, their rumours and opinions, the *Bourgeois* echoed the emphasis found in the *Songe véritable* upon the city's active role in defining the common good in these political contests.[14] In doing so, his testimony echoes a broader politicization of society, expanding notions of the commons and the increasing stake of these commons in the politics of late medieval Europe.[15] In France, the assertion of Paris' place

---

10 That some say that her voice, should be believed just as it appears. 'Le songe véritable. Pamphlet politique d'un parisien du XVᵉ siècle', ed. by Henri Moranvillé, *MSHP*, 17 (1890), p. 238, lines 317-18. See also Thelma Fenster and Daniel Lord Smail, 'Introduction' in *Fama. The Politics of Talk and Reputation in Medieval Europe* (London: Cornell University Press, 2003), pp. 7-8.

11 There have been several studies, editions and translations of the *Journal d'un bourgeois de Paris* since the seventeenth century. To date, the best scholarly edition remains that published by Alexandre Tuetey in 1881. *Journal d'un bourgeois de Paris 1405-49, d'après les manuscrits de Rome et de Paris*, ed. by Alexandre Tuetey (Paris: Champion, 1881). Since then, an accurate English translation was published by Janet Shirley, and more recently a modernized French version of the *Journal* has been produced by Colette Beaune. See *A Parisian Journal 1405-49*, translated from the anonymous *Journal d'un bourgeois de Paris*, ed. and trans. by Janet Shirley (Oxford: Clarendon Press, 1968); *Journal d'un bourgeois de Paris de 1405 à 1449*, ed. and trans. by Colette Beaune (Paris: Librairie Générale Française, 1990).

12 Around ten or twelve days. *Journal*, p. 1.

13 The people of Paris were so stirred as if the entire world was against them and wanted to destroy them. *Journal*, p. 3.

14 For considerations of the common good in late medieval Europe, see Matthew Sean Kempshall, *The Common Good in Late Medieval Political Thought* (Oxford: Oxford University Press, 1999); *De bono communi: The Discourse and Practice of the Common Good in the European City (13ᵗʰ-16ᵗʰ c.)*, ed. by Élodie Lecuppre-Desjardin and Anne-Laure Van Bruaene (Turnhout: Brepols, 2010).

15 As has been persuasively demonstrated in John Watts, 'The Pressure of the Public on Later Medieval Politics' in *The Fifteenth Century IV: Political Culture in Late Medieval Britain*, ed. by Linda Clarke and Christine Carpenter (Woodbridge: Boydell, 2004), pp. 159-80. See also the essays collected in *La légitimité implicite*, ed. by Jean-Philippe Genet, 2 vols (Paris: Éditions de la Sorbonne, 2015). On the growing politization of society that characterized the

in Valois political culture had already been signalled during the city's fourteenth-century revolts, first in 1306, when currency re-evaluations saw Parisian renters besiege Philippe IV (r. 1285-1314) in the Temple fortress and sack the residence of the royal *maître des monnaies*, Étienne Barbette.[16] In a second uprising, in 1357-58, the *prévôt des marchands* Étienne Marcel attempted to promulgate a *Grande Ordonnance* to impose fiscal limits upon the French monarchy at a moment of acute crisis following Jean II's capture by the English at the Battle of Poitiers in 1356.[17] Lastly, in 1382 a similar revolt erupted against the re-establishment of taxes abolished upon Charles V's death, emulating uprisings in Rouen (the 'Harelle') and southern France (the 'Tuchinat').[18] In remission letters issued for 1358, the Dauphin Charles (future Charles V) had acknowledged that Étienne Marcel and his followers had acted 'a bonne fin et pour la redemption et deliverance de notredit seigneur et le bien public'.[19] While no such acknowledgement followed the Maillotins revolt in 1382, the rioters' concerns for excessive royal taxation foreshadowed the reformist rhetoric that would represent a key element of the Burgundian arsenal after 1405, and find its clearest expression in the later Cabochien revolt of 1413. The contested character of Paris' control meant that the city, its leadership and commons were engaged in national political struggles and Parisians were increasingly prepared to assert their stake in the fate of the kingdom and the public realm.[20]

As a result, the examination of public opinion and political communication has become integral to histories of late medieval France and Paris in particular.[21] During the fourteenth

---

Armagnac-Burgundian conflict, see Nicolas Offenstadt, 'Guerre civile et espace public à la fin du Moyen Âge. La lutte des Armagnacs et des Bourguignons' in *La politisation. Conflits et construction du politique depuis le Moyen Âge*, ed. by Philippe Hamon and Laurent Bourquin (Rennes: Presses Universitaires de Rennes, 2010), pp. 111-29.

16 Bove, 'Alliance ou defiance?'; Boris Bove, 'Y-a-t-il un patriciat à Paris sous le règne de Philippe Le Bel (1285-1314)' in *Construction, reproduction et représentation des patriciats urbains de l'antiquité au XXᵉ siècle*, ed. by Claude Petitfrère (Tours: Presses universitaires François-Rabelais, 1999), pp. 47-63.

17 Analyses have predominantly addressed the events in Paris in the context of the Jacquerie uprisings. See Justine Firnhaber-Baker, *The Jacquerie of 1358: A French Peasants' Revolt* (Oxford: Oxford University Press, 2021); Justine Firnhaber-Baker, 'The Social Constituency of the Jacquerie Revolt of 1358', *Speculum*, 95 (2020), pp. 689-715; Justine Firnhaber-Baker, 'The Eponymous Jacquerie: Making revolt mean some things' in *The Routledge History Handbook of Medieval Revolt*, ed. by Justine Firnhaber-Baker and Dirk Schoenaers (London: Routledge, 2017), pp. 55-75; Raymond Cazelles, 'La Jacquerie fut-elle un mouvement paysan?', *Comptes rendus des séances de l'Académie des Inscriptions et Belles-Lettres*, 122 (1978), pp. 654-66; Michel Mollat and Philippe Wolff, *Ongles bleus, Jacques et Ciompi: les révolutions populaires en Europe aux XIVᵉ et XVᵉ siècles* (Paris: Calman-Lévy, 1970).

18 Léon Mirot, *Les Insurrections urbaines au début du règne de Charles VI (1380-93)* (Paris: Albert Fontemoing, 1905). See also Claude Gauvard, 'Les révoltes du règne de Charles VI: tentative pour expliquer un échec' in *Révolte et société*, ed. by Fabienne Gambrelle and Michel Trébitsch, 2 vols (Paris: Histoire au présent, 1989), I, pp. 53-61; Guy Lurie, 'French Citizenship and the Uprisings of 1380-1383', *The Medieval Chronicle*, 10 (2015), pp. 119-40. For the Tuchins, see Vincent Challet, 'La révolte des Tuchins: banditisme social ou sociabilité villageoise?', *Médiévales*, 34 (1998), pp. 101-12.

19 For a good purpose, and for the ransom and deliverance of our lord [Jean II] and for the common good. Paris, Archives nationales, JJ 86 fols 79r-80r, no. 240.

20 Similar developments have been noted for England, especially in Eliza Hartrich's recent assessment of the 'urban sector' and its centrality to late medieval political culture. Eliza Hartrich, *Politics and the Urban Sector in Fifteenth-Century England* (Oxford: Oxford University Press, 2019). See also the contributions in *Words and Deeds: Shaping Urban Politics from Below in Late Medieval Europe*, ed. by Ben Eersels and Jelle Haemers (Turnhout: Brepols, 2020).

21 Notable studies include Bernard Guenée, *L'opinion publique à la fin du Moyen Âge d'après la chronique de Charles VI du religieux de Saint-Denis* (Paris: Perrin, 2002); Emily Hutchison, 'Knowing One's Place: Space, Violence and Legitimacy in Early Fifteenth-century Paris', *The Medieval History Journal*, 20 (2017), pp. 38-88; Emily Hutchison, '"Pour le bien du roy et de son royaume": Burgundian Propaganda under John the Fearless, Duke of Burgundy, 1405-19' (unpublished

and fifteenth centuries, the city's increasingly central political, cultural and symbolic status as the *caput regni* paralleled the endeavours of its population – clergy, artisans and leading bourgeois alike – to influence royal policy. The city's pre-eminence coincided with the emergence of stable, geopolitically centralized institutions, exemplified by the monarch's regular residence in the city, the development of institutions such as the Parlement and *Chambre des comptes*, or the University of Paris' increasingly politicized role during the fourteenth-century Papal Schism. For Elizabeth Brown, Philippe IV's investments in Paris at the turn of the fourteenth century, marked by the redevelopment of the Cité's Palais and the performance of magnificent ceremonies, enabled the geographical consolidation of a 'public sphere' previously concentrated upon the king's person.[22] Similarly, almost forty years ago Raymond Cazelles signalled the importance of public opinion during the lifetimes of Jean II (1319-64) and Charles V (1338-80), 'sans doute l'élément le plus important pour l'intelligence de ces règnes'.[23] Against this backdrop, more recent studies have concentrated upon public opinion's role during the Armagnac-Burgundian conflict and later Lancastrian occupation of northern France. Analysing a range of media, historians have emphasized Jean sans Peur's successful employment of propaganda to capitalize upon Parisian resentment towards royal taxation.[24] Moreover, in a close study of English-occupied Paris, Guy Thompson highlighted Lancastrian efforts to inculcate support for Henry VI's dual monarchy through ceremony, gifts and even a campaign of 'bread and circuses'.[25] Less well-examined for Paris than Normandy are reactions to the reassertion of Valois rule after 1436 that present telling insights into the consolidation of the French state's apparatus at the end of the Middle Ages.

Following studies that have recognized a broadening of the political to encapsulate activities beyond central government, its institutions and members, this book employs the *Journal d'un bourgeois de Paris* to examine power in terms of the discursive relations that frame societal interaction. Paris' contested character during this turbulent period and its profound political changes render the city an important and useful case study for the examination of medieval public spheres, the multifarious media of communication in fifteenth-century contexts and, ultimately, the importance of public opinion. Responses

---

doctoral thesis, University of York, 2006); Tracy Adams, *Christine de Pizan and the Fight for France* (University Park, PA: Pennsylvania State University Press, 2014); Claude Gauvard, 'Le roi de France et l'opinion publique à l'époque de Charles VI' in *Culture et idéologie dans la genèse de l'état moderne* (Rome: École française de Rome, 1985), pp. 353-66; Raymond Cazelles, 'Une exigence de l'opinion depuis Saint Louis. La réformation du royaume', *Annuaire-Bulletin de la Société de l'histoire de France* (1962-63), pp. 91-99.

22 Elizabeth A.R. Brown, 'Jürgen Habermas, Philippe le Bel et l'espace public' in *L'espace public au Moyen Âge: débats autour de Jürgen Habermas*, ed. by Patrick Boucheron and Nicolas Offenstadt (Paris: Presses Universitaires de France, 2011), pp. 196-99.

23 Undoubtedly the most important element for understanding these reigns. Raymond Cazelles, *Société politique, noblesse et couronne sous Jean le Bon et Charles V* (Geneva: Droz, 1982), p. 3.

24 A series of recent studies have been dedicated to propaganda during the civil conflict, in particular the work of Emily Hutchison, 'Winning Hearts and Minds in Early Fifteenth-Century France: Burgundian Propaganda in Perspective', *French Historical Studies*, 35 (2012), pp. 3-30; Emily Hutchison, 'Partisan Identity in the French Civil War, 1405-18: Reconsidering the Evidence on Livery Badges', *Journal of Medieval History*, 33 (2007), pp. 265-71. See also Séverine Fargette, 'Rumeurs, propaganda et opinion publique au temps de la guerre civile (1407-20)', *Le Moyen Âge*, 113 (2007), pp. 321-33.

25 Thompson, *Paris and its People*.

to civil conflict, foreign occupation and emerging state centralization are evoked in the popular reactions to news and policies, rumours circulating in the city and public participation in civic ceremonies recorded by the Bourgeois. In turn, by focusing upon these elements this study presents a direct response to the methodology first presented in Bernard Guenée's *L'opinion publique à la fin du Moyen Âge* in 2002. Here, Guenée assessed public opinion during Charles VI's reign through the close examination of a single Latin chronicle produced by a monk at the abbey of Saint-Denis located just north of Paris, Michel Pintoin. For Guenée, the chronicle represented an important break with the abbey's established historiographical traditions, a fact exemplified by Pintoin's concern for surveying public opinion as a means of evaluating royal or aristocratic action. Despite being a Latin text compiled outside Parisian society by a member of the kingdom's learned elite, Guenée asserted that the chronicle was not 'un témoignage naïf', with Pintoin consistently 'conscient du poids de l'opinion publique dans la vie politique du royaume'.[26] It was Pintoin's very distance from urban influences that enabled the monk to historiographically assess opinion as a barometer of political power.

A masterful study of this chronicle, Guenée's reliance upon Pintoin was nevertheless problematic.[27] The emphasis upon Pintoin's distant neutrality obscures the fact that the chronicler – like all writers – compiled his narrative from an inherently engaged perspective that conditioned his vision of social hierarchy, authority and agency. Indeed, Guenée himself noted Pintoin's tendency to distinguish the active, influential opinions of elite clergymen and aristocrats from reactionary or passive popular concerns. When Parisian artisans asserted their stake in royal politics, as in 1382 or 1413, Pintoin emulated the typical strategy employed by medieval monastic chroniclers, characterizing the *communis plebs* as guilty of unreasoned ignorance, diabolic inspiration, or simple drunkenness to delegitimate their opinions and actions.[28] This disavowal was a natural consequence of Saint-Denis' ideological place in France, as a site encapsulating royal *auctoritas* through its possession of the coronation regalia, status as the royal necropolis or production of the royally-sponsored *Grandes Chroniques*. Despite Pintoin's alleged impartiality and his focus upon the Île-de-France, the realities of his intellectual, social and geographical distances from Paris reveal obstacles that prevent the chronicle from truly encapsulating the breadth of opinion within urban society. Rather, Pintoin remained embedded within a system of historical reflection that consistently subordinated popular and urban experiences to the political agency of France's elite.

This repudiation of both the discourse and political engagement of France's urban inhabitants in Pintoin's writing and, consequently, Guenée's work, is indicative of the overarching obstacles facing the study of late medieval public opinion. Where recent scholarship has concentrated upon medieval propaganda, news and political communication, this has largely resulted in a unidirectional conception of information's circulation,

---

26 A naïve testimony; awareness of the significance of public opinion in the political life of the kingdom. Guenée, *L'opinion publique*, pp. 27-8.

27 The methodological weaknesses inherent in Guenée's approach have been highlighted by Jan Dumolyn, 'Political Communication and Political Power in the Middle Ages: A Conceptual Journey', *Edad Media*, 13 (2012), pp. 48-9.

28 For these narrative strategies, see Paul Strohm, *Hochon's Arrow: The Social Imagination of Fourteenth-Century Texts* (Princeton, NJ: Princeton University Press, 1992), pp. 33-56.

engendered in part by the nature of surviving source materials. Research has focused on the rhetoric and modes of Burgundian or Lancastrian propaganda, the management of opinion or official media without examining the ways in which medieval people reacted to these messages. Through a concentrated analysis of the Bourgeois of Paris and his community, this book inverts this model, exploring how Parisians appropriated, contested and disseminated information to reveal their construction of delicate and fluid urban ideologies adjacent to dominant models of civic authority and a nascent national identity that have represented the foundations to histories of Paris, the Armagnac-Burgundian civil conflict and Hundred Years War.

In taking the Bourgeois of Paris as its focus, this book also presents a microhistory of the final phase of the Hundred Years War, an approach particularly well suited for assessing the experiences of communities where the survival of sources is especially uneven, as in Paris' case where parish and municipal records rarely survive for the early fifteenth century.[29] While microhistory may be criticized for the narrow historical narratives that result, there is also tremendous value to the approach.[30] As Tom Hamilton has recently argued in his analysis of the sixteenth-century Parisian diarist, Pierre de l'Estoile (1546-1611), microhistory 'not only focuses on individuals but zooms out to understand how those individuals inhabited their world'.[31] Such an approach is more important because of the extent of the uncritical reliance upon the Bourgeois' testimony in present social and political histories of the final phase of the Hundred Years War. A close scrutiny of the *Journal* reveals that the text should be treated as more than hollow window-dressing, a source consigned to revealing the period's dramatic colour but never employed critically or comparatively alongside more traditional sources such as the chronicles of Michel Pintoin, Enguerrand de Monstrelet, Jean Chartier or that attributed to Jean Juvénal des Ursins. Moreover, repositioning the Bourgeois within his world also invites reflection upon the purpose of his narrative. Much like the fictionality with which Natalie Zemon Davis has considered pardon tales, the constructions and ideologies present in the Bourgeois' work, even if 'fictitious' or biased, reveal something integral about his community and the narratives that they shared, precisely because it had to hold appeal for an audience.[32] Whether the account of events in Paris is true or false, Burgundian or Valois, is less significant than the fact that the *Journal* can tell us something meaningful about the political and social discourses available to fifteenth-century Parisians, the themes that they privileged and the ways in which they were strategically employed to facilitate and frame participation in public politics.

---

29 Vanessa Harding, 'Medieval Documentary Sources for London and Paris: A Comparison' in *London and Europe in the Later Middle Ages*, ed. by Julia Boffey and Pamela King (Turnhout: Brepols, 1995), pp. 35-54.

30 For an account of both criticisms and methodological strategies, see Sigurður G. Magnússon and István Szijártó, *What is microhistory? Theory and Practice* (London: Routledge, 2013), pp. 4-7, 119-31.

31 Tom Hamilton, *Pierre de l'Estoile and his World in the Wars of Religion* (Oxford: Oxford University Press, 2017), pp. 14-15 (15). On this approach to microhistory, see also Jill Lepore, 'Historians Who Love Too Much: Reflections on Microhistory and Biography' *The Journal of American History*, 88 (2001), pp. 129-44.

32 For this deconstructive methodology see Natalie Zemon Davis, *Fiction in the Archives: Pardon Tales and their Tellers in Sixteenth-Century France* (Stanford, CA: Stanford University Press, 1987). This approach, moving beyond the empiricist content of historical texts, has more recently been championed by Tom Johnson, 'The Preconstruction of Witness Testimony: Law and Social Discourse before the Reformation' *Law and History Review*, 12 (2014), pp. 127-47.

This rehabilitation of the *Journal*'s place within the Middle French historiographical corpus is also necessary to appreciate how an increasing generic fluidity in medieval historical writing meant that texts destined for a public beyond the traditional aristocratic and monastic audiences of annals and 'official' chronicles increasingly performed a dual function. As Jean-Philippe Genet has stressed, new histories simultaneously codified 'un ensemble de références qui vont pouvoir entrer dans un discours rationnel de jugement et d'estimation du présent', and participated in the 'processus d'individuation qui permet à l'individu de se reconnaître comme membre [d'une] collectivité'.[33] It is in the context of this generic *éclatement* of historical production – and writing more generally – at the end of the Middle Ages that this book proposes an examination of the intersections of oral, written and symbolic forms of communication. An appreciation of the multifarious media related and surveyed by the Bourgeois of Paris, and the ways in which he shaped and conveyed these in his writing for a specific Parisian audience of likely artisans, highlights the importance of assessing public opinion in terms of communication systems wherein media, more than straightforward tools and sites of discussion, are considered as 'un ensemble de structures socialement élaborées', determined by the shared codes of symbols, signs and language constitutive of conventional discourse.[34] In doing so, this present study builds upon the work of Jan Dumolyn, who has pointed to the importance of grounding studies of rituals, ceremonies, interaction and performance within 'the political power of the spoken and written word' concurrently, to thereby comprehend the production, diffusion and appropriation of ideological discourses by urban historical actors.[35] The *Journal* offers unique insights into the intertwined character of these multivalent forms of communication in late medieval Paris.

Finally, by framing the presence of medieval public spheres in terms of opinion communities, the *Journal* emerges as an intriguing interface that captures the relationship between the Bourgeois' perception of political events, the discourses and discussions of the multiple, interconnected communities and institutions of which he was a member, the political assumptions and expectations of his potential audience(s), and the subtle manner in which the Bourgeois could shape his narrative to channel these assumptions and arrogate a degree of authority over the interpretation of Parisian events. Unlike Michel Pintoin at Saint-Denis, the *Journal* is uniquely placed to shed light upon interaction between an individual and his community, between the inhabitants of Paris and their civic institutions and, more widely, between the civic community, royal government and the factions vying for power in fifteenth-century France. The Bourgeois' narrative was driven by a predominant concern for those interactions between Parisians that underlay the constitution of active

---

33 A series of references which will contribute to a rational facilitating the evaluation and assessment of the present; the process of individuation which enabled the individual to situate themselves as members of a collectivity. Jean-Philippe Genet, 'Histoire et système de communication au Moyen Âge' in *L'histoire et les nouveaux publics dans l'Europe médiévale (XIIIᵉ-XVᵉ siècle)*, ed. by Jean-Philippe Genet (Paris: Éditions de la Sorbonne, 1997), p. 25. On the evolution of Middle French historiography in the late Middle Ages see Jean Dufournet, 'L'épanouissement de l'histoire au quinzième siècle', *Fifteenth Century Studies*, 34 (2009), pp. 64-80.

34 A collection of socially elaborated structures. Genet, 'Histoire et système de communication', p. 13.

35 Jan Dumolyn, 'Urban ideologies in later Medieval Flanders: Towards a Methodological Framework' in *The Languages of Political Society*, ed. by Andrea Gamberini, Jean-Philippe Genet and Andrea Zorzi (Rome: Viella, 2011), p. 71.

and critical publics, contrasting popular reactions and discussions with forms of civic and official communication. The *Journal* maps the conflation and tensions between individual perspectives, that of a specific community and those of wider Parisian society during the first half of the fifteenth century, revealing the dynamism of medieval publics 'as those who contested the public sphere shaped and reshaped their messages'.[36]

The *Journal d'un bourgeois de Paris* and its author

The *Journal d'un bourgeois de Paris* is a curious text. Compiled between at least September 1405 (the date of the text's earliest, fragmentary passage) and October 1449 by a Parisian cleric, the *Journal* is popular among historians of Paris and fifteenth-century France for its direct insights into everyday life in a medieval city. Indeed, the text is noteworthy for its potential to provide readers with a 'little more widely representative insight' concerning the issues at the forefront of public debate and discourse beyond treatises and aristocratic chronicles.[37] Crucially, the *Journal*'s civic focus reveals the engagement of members of Paris' artisanal classes in the socio-political issues that marked the contests of the early fifteenth century, while also underscoring the ways in which these prerogatives were channelled and shaped through the contributions of urban clergymen. Although incomplete, the surviving text comprises over nine hundred separate entries, recounting everything from fluctuating food prices and the changing weather to urban rumours, civic ceremonies and the political events of the wider French kingdom from the capital's perspective. The text is not, however, comprehensive. The Bourgeois' selectivity throws into relief the problems that the author and his immediate audience determined to be most acute for the capital, affording the Bourgeois agency in the condemnation or validation of attitudes and events. This authority was also transmitted to his community, facilitating the evaluation of events largely beyond their control.

Although it has been argued that 'the fragmentary nature of the entries eliminates any apparent hierarchical order in the narrative', there is meaning to be derived from this ostensible miscellaneity.[38] The details reported by the Bourgeois cannot simply be perceived as an amalgamation of *faits divers* 'qui ne renvoient à rien d'implicite', as closed passages or anecdotes that deliver immanent information without contextual implications.[39] Such readings of the Bourgeois' record of food prices or natural phenomena overlook the underlying evaluative systems through which the author interpreted his world and conveyed this vision to his audience. While they may have served a pragmatic function for an artisanal audience subject to market fluctuations conditioned by warfare and weather alike, these details also rhetorically substantiated notions of improvement and decline that exemplified the

---

36 Charles Connell, *Popular Opinion in the Middle Ages: Channelling Public Ideas and Attitudes* (Berlin: De Gruyter, 2016), p. 13.

37 David Green, 'National Identities and the Hundred Years War' in *Fourteenth Century England IV*, ed. by Christopher Given-Wilson (Woodbridge: Boydell, 2010), p. 129.

38 Elisabeth Hodges, *Urban Poetics in the French Renaissance* (Aldershot: Ashgate, 2008), p. 28.

39 Which do not refer to anything implicit. Roland Barthes, 'Structure du fait divers' in *Essais critiques* (Paris: Seuil, 1964), p. 189.

fundamental connections between divine judgement and human action. In short, a scholarly categorization of the *Journal*'s content that distinguishes between precise passages pertaining to processions or food prices and 'de grands récits d'une rhétorique complexe et calculée qui nécessite une écriture soignée et déborde le système habituel rythmé de paragraphes courts' ultimately ignores the careful intersections drawn up between these apparent *fait divers* and the Bourgeois' self-conscious and critical consideration of change in his environment.[40]

Nevertheless, it is the *Journal*'s very heterogeneity, and perceptions of the Bourgeois' naïve readiness to convey political information that his community endorsed, that have led scholars to discount the *Journal* as a viable source for understanding political attitudes in fifteenth-century France. Some of this reticence results from the circumstances in which the source has come down to us today. The original, autograph manuscript has been lost and it was already missing the first page or pages, perhaps including a prologue identifying the author and the text's purpose, when the earliest surviving manuscript copy from which all others derive (Rome, Vatican MS Reg. Lat. 1923) was compiled around 1470.[41] Rather, the most complete extant copies begin with the only known examples of Burgundian propaganda publicizing Jean sans Peur's victory against Liégeois rebels at the Battle of Othée (23 September 1408), namely the poems entitled the *Bataille du Liège* and *Sentences de Liège*, before the disorganized first pages of the *Journal* begin partway through the Bourgeois' own account of this same battle.[42] Apparently this first quire was so incomplete for the text's copyist in the 1470s that fragmentary passages covering 1408, 1409, 1411 and 1405 were reproduced in a muddled sequence before the narrative is followed chronologically from August 1409, with information for 1406 and 1407, as well as much of 1405 and 1408, missing altogether. As such, we have lost the Bourgeois' responses to key events in these years, especially the assassination of Louis, duke of Orléans on 23 November 1407 and the pronouncement of the theologian Jean Petit's *Justification* for the murder on 8 March 1408. As we have seen above, allusions to events taking place in the summer of 1405 certainly suggest that the Bourgeois' narrative included an account of Jean sans Peur's occupation of Paris that year. Other sections once present have disappeared from the Vatican manuscript either due to deliberate excision or the ravages of time. Most notably, these include the Bourgeois' reaction to Jean sans Peur's own murder at

---

40 Long accounts of complex and considered rhetoric which required careful composition and move beyond the usual rhythm of short paragraphs. Beaune (ed.), *Journal*, p. 14. A similar interpretation has been advanced in Dufournet, 'L'épanouissement', pp. 74-5.

41 It was not uncommon for medieval chronicles to feature a prologue identifying the author or, at the very least, providing a mission statement for the text. As Rosalind Brown-Grant has argued for Burgundian historiographical texts, prologues were essential to structuring the relationship between narratorial personage, audience and text. Rosalind Brown-Grant, 'Narrative Style in Burgundian Chronicles of the Later Middle Ages', *Viator*, 42 (2011), pp. 233-35. The dating of the Rome manuscript is determined by watermarks dated by Charles Moïse Briquet to between 1471 and 1479, as well as internal evidence. For a list of the manuscript copies of the *Journal*, see the bibliography. Charles Moïse Briquet, *Les Filigranes: Dictionnaire historique des marques du papier*, 4 vols (Paris: Alphonse Picard, 1907).

42 These poems have been examined in Alain Marchandisse and Bertrand Schnerb, 'La bataille du Liège' in *Écrire la guerre, écrire la paix*, ed. by Simone Mazauric (Paris: Éditions du CTHS, 2013), pp. 34-8; Hubert Carrier, '*Si vera est fama*: Le retentissement de la bataille d'Othée dans la culture historique du XVe siècle', *Revue historique*, 303 (2001), pp. 644-46. Pierre Courroux has recently argued that these texts should be considered verse chronicles. Pierre Courroux, 'History, Verse and *Chanson de Geste* in French Chronicles around 1400', *Nottingham Medieval Studies*, 62 (2018), pp. 116-17.

Montereau-fault-Yonne on 10 September 1419, an account that once occupied three folios in the Vatican manuscript and which were perhaps removed by the same owner – clearly a keen supporter of Louis XI – who erased the Bourgeois' criticisms of the then Dauphin in 1444.[43] At the very least, this section had been removed by the time that the earliest copy of the Vatican manuscript, Aix-en-Provence, Méjanes MS 432 (316), was produced in the sixteenth century.[44]

The so-called 'Bourgeois' of Paris

The text has been considered a 'journal' and its author a 'bourgeois' since this moment when it was reproduced in the sixteenth century, reflecting early antiquaries' impression of its regular compilation by a Parisian inhabitant.[45] With regards to the first term, since Alexandre Tuetey's 1881 critical edition a scholarly consensus has emphasised that the so-called 'Bourgeois' was not, in fact, a bourgeois at all, but a cleric. As Colette Beaune has stressed, 'notre auteur n'est pas un bourgeois, même s'il est bien parisien. C'est un clerc, il l'avoue lui-même'.[46] The choice in terminology at once betrays anachronistic distances in the understandings of urban citizenship between the medieval and early modern periods, while also obscuring the very disputed character of clerical and bourgeois status in late medieval Parisian politics.[47] Although growing literacy rates increasingly blurred the boundaries distinguishing members of the lower orders from laymen, clerical status nevertheless continued to encapsulate specific privileges and restrictions for the clericature, including the prohibition of bearing arms, butchering and tavern-keeping, the enforcement of the tonsure and (for lower orders) limits to marrying once.[48]

The *Journal*'s internal evidence highlights the Bourgeois' clerical status and even offers clues as to his possible identity, pointing to his membership of the University of Paris and the cathedral clergy of Notre-Dame. The former is suggested by references to 'notre mere l'Université', the author's enthusiasm for the University's intervention in royal politics during the Cabochien revolt in 1413 and, perhaps most tellingly, his participation in the

---

43 Rome, Vatican Reg. Lat. 1923, fols 16v, 176r, 178v.

44 Once considered a distinct witness to the original text, Aix-en-Provence, Bibliothèque Méjanes MS 432 (316) features the same omissions as those found in Rome, Vatican Reg. Lat. 1923. The only anomaly is the inclusion of several pages of text for 1438 that are missing in its Vatican counterpart. This would seem to be explained by pages having been removed or lost from the Vatican manuscript after the Méjanes copy was completed, as suggested by the disorder of the relevant quire and the appearance of page stubs without corresponding folios in the relevant section of the Vatican manuscript. That Méjanes MS 432 (316) is a copy of Reg. Lat. 1923 is supported by the fact that sixteenth-century marginal annotations found in the Vatican manuscript were repeated in the later Méjanes copy.

45 As demonstrated by the autograph notes of the French bibliophile Claude Dupuy (1545-94), that describe the *Journal* as a 'chronique ou plustost journal d'un bourgeois de Paris, prebstre, comme j'estime' (chronicle or rather journal of a bourgeois of Paris, a priest, I believe). Paris, BNF MS Dupuy 275, fol. 1r.

46 Our author is not a bourgeois, even if he is Parisian. He is a cleric, as he admits himself. Colette Beaune (ed. and trans.), *Journal d'un bourgeois de Paris de 1405 à 1449* (Paris: Librairie Générale Française, 1990), p. 11.

47 Laurence Croq, 'Droit, société et politique: La confusion des concepts et des identités pendant la période pré-révolutionnaire à Paris' in *Être parisien*, ed. by Claude Gauvard & Jean-Louis Robert, (Paris: Publications de la Sorbonne, 2004), pp. 63-80; Joseph di Corcia, 'Bourg, Bourgeois, Bourgeois de Paris from the Eleventh to the Eighteenth Century', *Journal of Modern History*, 50 (1978), pp. 215-29.

48 Martha Howell, 'Citizen-clerics in Late Medieval Douai' in *Individuals, Corporations and Judicial Status in European Cities* ed. by Marc Boone and Maarten Prak, (Leuven: Garant, 1996), p. 12.

theological examination of the Spanish intellectual Fernand de Cordoue at the Collège de Navarre in 1446.[49] Relating this confrontation, the Bourgeois described how Cordoue 'a disputé *a nous* au college de Navarre, *qui estions* plus de cinquante des plus parfaiz clercs de l'Université de Paris, et plus de iii mil autres clercs'.[50] The Bourgeois' proximity to the event, and the resulting discussions within the University, is underscored by the textual parallels between his own account of Fernand de Cordoue and a letter disseminated by a potential colleague, the University theologian Jean de l'Olive (d. 1472), and transcribed by the Picard chronicler Mathieu d'Escouchy of Péronne (c. 1420-81).[51] Similarly, the Bourgeois' connections to Notre-Dame are suggested by his presence at the cathedral's first rogation procession to Montmartre in May 1427, when he complained that 'nous mismes une heure largement a venir de Montmartre a Saint-Ladre'.[52] This affiliation with the cathedral chapter is also indicated by the Bourgeois' active interest in episcopal politics, condemning the royal contestation of the chapter's election of Jean Courtecuisse (d. 1423) and Nicolas Fraillon (d. 1446) as bishops in 1420 and 1427 respectively, as well as his praise for bishop Guillaume Chartier (d. 1472) after his election in 1447.[53]

Most importantly, this internal evidence provides a clear indication of the Bourgeois' neighbourhood and parish. Throughout the *Journal*, the Bourgeois focused predominantly upon events in Paris' populous and mercantile right-bank, particularly in the Halles region near the eponymous marketplace, as well as along the district's main thoroughfares, the rues Saint-Denis and Saint-Martin.[54] Within this neighbourhood, it is notable that from the middle of 1436 references to the Saints-Innocents church and cemetery increase substantially in the text, such that the church becomes the second most-mentioned after Notre-Dame. The Bourgeois' connection to the parish is evidenced through these numerous and detailed references, including mentions of the church and cemetery's interdiction in 1436 and 1441, the institution of new confraternity celebrations, and the church's dedication by the bishop of Paris Denis du Moulin in 1445.[55] These events would have been of profound importance to the Saints-Innocents clergy and the wider parish.

While limited, these indications provide important insights into the Bourgeois' possible identity, representing the foundation to theories proposed in the nineteenth century. These early hypotheses – identifying the Bourgeois as the theologian Jean de l'Olive, the priest of Saint-Nicolas-des-Champs Jean Beaurigout and the University chancellor Jean Chuffart (d. 1451) – were disproved in turn, while twentieth-century editors turned to

---

49 Our mother the University. *Journal*, pp. 28-9, 35-6, 381-82, 385 (385).

50 Disputed *with us* at the College of Navarre, [and] *we were* fifty of the best doctors of the University of Paris, along with three thousand other clerics. *Journal*, p. 381. Emphasis my own.

51 Mathieu d'Escouchy, *Chronique de Mathieu d'Escouchy*, ed. by Gaston du Fresne de Beaucourt, 3 vols (Paris: Renouard, 1864), I, pp. 69-72. For reactions to Fernand de Cordoue and his life, see Julien Havet, 'Maitre Fernand de Cordoue et l'Université de Paris au XVᵉ siècle', *MSHP*, 9 (1882), pp. 193-222.

52 It took us a whole hour to travel from Montmartre to Saint-Lazare. *Journal*, p. 214.

53 *Journal*, pp. 147, 164, 213, 215, 386, 389.

54 For the history of this Parisian district, see Anne Lombard-Jourdan, *Les Halles de Paris et leur quartier dans l'espace urbain (1137-1969)* (Paris: École nationale des chartes, 2009).

55 *Journal*, pp. 325-26, 333, 357, 380.

summarizing the Bourgeois' key traits without proffering new suggestions.[56] However, recent analyses of the Parisian clergy and members of the University of Paris have made a new evaluation of the Bourgeois' characteristics in conjunction with prosopographical databases possible.[57] Through a cross-examination of the internal evidence with this data, it appears that of those theologians who were licensed between 1400 and 1446 (the year of Fernand de Cordoue's examination), one individual encapsulates the Bourgeois' identifying traits. Nicolas Confrant (d. *c.* January 1453) was a canon of Notre-Dame from 1435 and a theologian of the University of Paris, beginning his cursus at the Collège d'Harcourt in 1423.[58] Perhaps most importantly, Confrant is also identified by the college's obits as the *pastore* of the parish church of the Saints-Innocents, and the centrality of this church to Confrant's identity implies that it was one of his principal occupations before his demise. Through these posts, Nicolas Confrant represents a viable potential candidate for identification as the Bourgeois.[59] Unlike Jean Chuffart, Confrant was not so eminent as to have participated in the highest church councils, nor to have frequently travelled in diplomatic missions. And yet, appearing in Jean Maupoint's journal, he *was* involved in the debates taking place at the University during the 1440s, which would situate him in the examination of Fernand de Cordoue.[60]

Other characteristics associated with the Bourgeois are more doubtful. Colette Beaune and Alexandre Tuetey have argued that the Bourgeois was closely connected to the household of Charles VI's queen consort, Isabeau de Bavière, highlighting the Bourgeois' comment in 1424 that the queen was limited to eight *sétiers* of wine daily.[61] Where Tuetey asserted that this detail was clear evidence of Chuffart's authorship, given the chancellor's post as the queen's counsellor from 1425, the lone comment is far from conclusive proof. Janet Shirley suggested that it might intimate that the Bourgeois simply knew someone affiliated with the queen's household, and in this respect it is worth noting that a prominent inhabitant of the local Saint-Martin *quartier* – and a member of the butchers' corporation with which the Bourgeois sympathized – was Marcelet Testart, who acted as Isabeau de

56 For these theories and responses to them, see Auguste Vallet de Viriville, *Histoire de Charles VI, roi de France, et de son époque, 1403-61,* 3 vols (Paris: Jules Renouard, 1862-65), III (1865), p. 97; Auguste Longnon, 'Conjectures sur l'auteur du journal parisien de 1409 à 1449', *MSHP,* 2 (1876), pp. 318-29; Alexandre Tuetey (ed.), *Journal d'un bourgeois de Paris,* pp. ix-xliv; Heinrich Denifle and Émile Chatelain, *Chartularium Universitatis Parisiensis,* 4 vols (Paris: Delalain, 1889-97), IV (1897), pp. xiv-xx; Shirley (ed. and trans.), *A Parisian Journal,* pp. 12-30; Beaune (ed. and trans.), *Journal,* pp. 11-12.

57 In particular, the *Studium Parisiense* database overseen by Jean-Philippe Genet and Thierry Kouamé, http://studium.univ-paris1.fr/home, and the prosopographical research undertaken by Thomas Sullivan. *Parisian Licentiates in Theology, AD 1373-1500. A Biographical Register. vol. II: The Secular Clergy* (Leiden: Brill, 2011). On the database, see Jean-Philippe Genet, Thierry Kouamé and others, 'General Introduction to the "Studium" Project', *Medieval Prosopography,* 31 (2016), pp. 161-70.

58 I have addressed Confrant's possible identification as the Bourgeois elsewhere. See Luke Giraudet, 'Nicolas Confrant, author of the *Journal d'un bourgeois de Paris*?', *Romania,* 139 (2021), pp. 114-40.

59 Henri Louis Bouquet, *L'ancien collège d'Harcourt et le lycée Saint-Louis* (Paris: Delalain, 1891), pp. 703, 706.

60 Jean Maupoint, 'Journal parisien de Jean Maupoint, prieur de Sainte-Catherine-de-la-Coûture (1437-69)' ed. by Gustave Fagniez, *MSHP,* 4 (1877), p. 33.

61 *Journal,* p. 202; Tuetey (ed.), *Journal,* pp. xxx-xxxii; Colette Beaune, 'La rumeur dans le *Journal* du bourgeois de Paris' in *La circulation des nouvelles au Moyen Âge* (Paris: Publications de la Sorbonne, 1993), p. 191; Françoise Autrand, 'Journal d'un bourgeois de Paris' in *Lexikon des Mittelalters,* vol. 5, ed. by Robert Auty, (Stuttgart: Metzler, 1999), p. 639.

Bavière's treasurer from 4 August 1421.[62] Alternatively, at the University of Paris Nicolas Confrant was a close colleague of the theologian Anselme Apart, who served as the queen's confessor and is found in Confrant's cursus during the 1420s.[63] Given the place of each man in Confrant's networks, they might similarly represent sources for this kind of precise detail.

Far more common is the conclusion that the Bourgeois was a supporter of the Burgundian faction during the fifteenth-century civil conflict, described in recent scholarship as 'un clerc bourguignon de l'entourage d'Isabeau' or, more fervently, as being 'rabidly pro-Burgundian'.[64] The *Journal*'s concerted study has been complicated by enduring, pejorative impressions of the text's historiographical value rooted in the author's partiality and perceived political naivety. Interpretations of the text that simply situate the *Journal* as the unmediated consumption of Burgundian propaganda have downplayed its significance as experimentation with historiographical form or the extent of both the Bourgeois' access to political information and his readiness to communicate this further. For Janet Shirley, the Bourgeois 'can hardly have been very eminent in any field, or at least politically, for he would not have swallowed [...] all of his own side's propaganda'.[65] Forty years earlier, Johan Huizinga employed the *Journal* to demonstrate the 'passionate intensity' (*felheid*) of medieval life, describing the Bourgeois as 'een nuchter man, die zich zelden verlustigt in stijlversiering of gedachtenspel'.[66] Indeed, his simplistic style, omission of learned references and reliance upon rumour have all been summoned as reasons to disregard the text's political or historical significance. Explaining his decision to use the *Chronique du Religieux de Saint-Denis* as the foundation to his analysis of late medieval public opinion, Bernard Guenée was compelled to discredit the *Journal*'s potential value, arguing that:

> Les éclairages qui nous sont ainsi donnés sur l'opinion publique parisienne sont riches et vivants. Mais ils restent ponctuels et terriblement partiaux. Car le "Bourgeois" est un "Bourguignon", partisan convaincu du duc de Bourgogne Jean sans Peur. Son journal n'est que le témoignage sans nuances d'un "homme de parti borné".[67]

62 Shirley (ed. and trans.), *A Parisian Journal*, p. 18. For Testart, see Jean Favier, *Les contribuables parisiens à la fin de la guerre de Cent ans. Les rôles d'impôt de 1421, 1423 et 1438* (Geneva: Droz, 1970), pp. 190, 261. For this earliest date of Testart's appointment as treasurer, see Paris, BNF Clairambault 763, p. 93.

63 For Appart, see Denifle and Chatelain, *Chartularium*, IV, pp. 485, 550; Xavier de la Selle, *Le service des âmes à la cour: confesseurs et aumôniers des rois de France du XIIIᵉ au XVᵉ siècle* (Paris: École nationale des chartes, 1995), p. 314.

64 Beaune, 'La rumeur', p. 191; Tracy Adams and Glenn Rechtschaffen, 'The Reputation of the Queen and Public Opinion: The Case of Isabeau of Bavaria', *Medieval Feminist Forum*, 47 (2011), p. 8, n. 17.

65 Shirley (ed. and trans.), *A Parisian Journal*, p. 16.

66 A prosaic man who rarely endeavours to creatively ornament his style. Johan Huizinga, *Herfsttij der Middeleeuwen*, ed. L. Brummel in *Verzamelde werken*, vol. 3, (Haarlem: H.D. Tjeenk Willink and Zoon, 1949), p. 256. Although far from the most commonly cited of Huizinga's sources (43 times in nine chapters), Graeme Small has recently shown that the Bourgeois of Paris can be counted among the eight main medieval authors that constituted up to 54% of Huizinga's total references in the *Herfsttij*. Graeme Small, 'The Making of the *Autumn of the Middle Ages* I: Narrative Sources and their Treatment in Huizinga's *Herfsttij*' in *Rereading Huizinga: Autumn of the Middle Ages, a Century Later*, ed. by Peter Arnade, Martha Howell and Anton van der Lem (Amsterdam: Amsterdam University Press, 2019), pp. 183, 203.

67 The perspectives that we receive regarding Parisian public opinion are rich and lively, but they are nevertheless terribly ad-hoc and partial. For the 'Bourgeois' is a 'Burgundian'; a dedicated supporter of Jean sans Peur, duke of Burgundy. His journal is nought but the unnuanced testimony of a 'party man'. Guenée, *L'opinion publique*, p. 12.

However, a more nuanced examination of the *Journal*, resituating the text in its contexts, reveals that the Bourgeois identified principally with Paris, and was prepared to discredit any faction – 'de quel costé qu'il soit, Francois ou Anglois, Arminac ou Bourgoignon ou Picquart' –, in response to their policies regarding the capital and innate understandings of good government or fair taxation.[68] In this light, the *Journal*'s political character can be attributed as much to Burgundian propaganda as to the ways in which this propaganda successfully played upon existing Parisian sentiment and a strong sense of the city's agency in royal politics – sentiments that found their expression in the uprisings of 1413 and 1418 that, themselves, quickly veered away from a strictly Burgundian perspective to assume a Parisian character of their own. The interests of the Bourgeois and his community therefore evoke a more carefully calculated reciprocal relationship between Parisians and the Burgundian dukes, whereby the Parisian support necessary for Burgundian access to the capital was conditioned by the elaboration of a reform programme designed to lower taxes and enshrine urban privileges. This Parisian focus, accentuated by Burgundian reformist rhetoric during the 1410s, became more pronounced after 1418 when the Bourgeois eschewed an unconditional endorsement of the Burgundian duke to articulate Parisian agencies in the civil conflict. Assuming the perspective of Paris rather than the aristocratic factions vying for its control, the Bourgeois' political leanings appear fluid, influenced by the context of the Halles region whose artisanal inhabitants were hostile to high taxation and continuing warfare, yet who were equally prepared to voice their frustrations with Burgundian authority.

The Journal *and Parisian historiography*

The text's classification as a 'journal' should also be nuanced. When the title was attributed to the text in the sixteenth century, it held specific connotations for the kind of history that it represented and the regularity of its compilation, with Jean Nicot's *Thresor de la langue francoyse* (1606) stating that a 'journal' 'se prend pour le livre du marchand ou banquier, auquel il enregistre par chacun jour sa negotiation'.[69] While the Bourgeois did not keep a daily record of events, his writing was relatively contemporaneous to the circumstances that he described. Commentators have pointed to the Bourgeois' repeated refusal to believe official reports that Henry VI had crossed the Channel in 1430, subsequently confirmed when the Lancastrian monarch arrived at Saint-Denis in November 1431, as evidence that the Bourgeois was writing very soon after the reports in question, rather than reconciling these memories retrospectively.[70] Similarly, in November 1410 the Bourgeois reflected upon the outbreak of the Armagnac-Burgundian conflict, stating that 'le royaulme de France ne recouvra la perte [...] en vingt ans ensuivant, tant viengne bien', suggesting an attitude that could not foresee the four decades' of warfare that would follow.[71] In

---

68 Whatever side they might be on, French or English, Armagnac or Burgundian or Picard. *Journal*, p. 258.

69 Is used for the book of a merchant or banker, in which he records his daily business. Jean Nicot, *Thresor de la langue francoyse, tant ancienne que moderne* (Paris: David Douceur, 1606), p. 358.

70 *Journal*, pp. 253-55, 274-79. See also Craig Taylor (ed.), *Joan of Arc: La Pucelle* (Manchester: Manchester University Press, 2006), pp. 228-29.

71 The kingdom of France will not recover its losses [...] in twenty years, whatever good may come. *Journal*, p. 10.

contrast, other parts of the *Journal* give the impression that the Bourgeois was summarizing an entire year, with much of the account of 1438 compiled that autumn.

Editors and commentators have been content to maintain the 'Journal' title, even though the author may have conceptualized his text as a chronicle. As Pierre Courroux has argued, from the fourteenth century the Middle French *chronique* 'désigne tout récit historique', with the *Journal* evidencing characteristics common to the increasingly prevalent vernacular models that 'font revivre [l'histoire] par une narration, certes souvent breve, mais qui n'a rien à voir avec les annales monastiques'.[72] However, the prologue to the journal of the Châtelet notary Jean de Roye, compiled between 1460 and 1483, implies a contemporary awareness of generic distinction between chronicles and journals, stating: 'Je ne vueil ne n'entens point les choses cy apres escriptes estre appellées, dictes ou nommées Croniques, pour ce que a moy n'appartient, et que pour ce fayre n'ay pas esté ordonné et ne m'a esté permys'.[73] While certainly playing upon the *humilitas* topos, the prologue suggests that Roye perceived chronicle writing to be tied to notions of historiographical authority that were distinct from the scope, materials and audience of Parisian journals such as the Bourgeois'.

This sense of generic distinction is significant for appreciating the function and reception of journals in fifteenth-century Paris. As Gabrielle Spiegel has argued, shifts in medieval historiographical form evoke concurrent changes to social structuration.[74] For Spiegel, the rise of vernacular, prose genealogical chronicles in thirteenth-century France resulted in narratives that reflected and shared the dynastic prerogatives of the French nobility, situating the noble family as the motor of historical development.[75] In France, it has been argued that a prevailing Jacobin 'centralist perspective' in modern historiography has resulted in the side-lining of civic narratives in favour of the historical writing produced at the Valois court.[76] Nevertheless, it is important to recognize that the sudden and rapid emergence of journals in fifteenth-century Paris betrays a socio-political shift analogous to that detected by Spiegel in the thirteenth century, particularly as 'social groups most affected by changes in status tend to be the most conscious of alternative modes of discursive behaviour [...] more sensitive to the power of language to register

---

72 Designates any historical narrative; relive history through a narrative, often brief, but which has nothing to do with monastic annals. Courroux, *L'Écriture de l'histoire*, p. 83.

73 I do not wish nor intend that what is written hereafter be called, described as or named 'Croniques', because it is not my place to compile such writing and I have not been ordered nor permitted to write as such. Jean de Roye, *Journal de Jean de Roye connu sous le nom de Chronique scandaleuse, 1460-83*, ed. by Bernard de Mandrot, 2 vols (Paris: Renouard, 1894-96), I (1894), p. 2. See also Dufournet, 'L'épanouissement', pp. 74-7; Jean Devaux, 'Le genre médiéval du journal et les chemins de mémoire: l'exemple de Jean de Roye', in *La mémoire à l'œuvre*, ed. by Caroline Cazenave (Besançon: Presses universitaires de Franche-Comté, 2014), pp. 337-50.

74 Gabrielle Spiegel, 'History, Historicism and the Social Logic of the Text', *Speculum*, 65 (1990), pp. 59-86. See also Chris Jones, 'Perspectives from the Periphery: French Kings and their Chroniclers', in *The Medieval Chronicle X*, ed. by Ilya Afanasyev, Juliana Dresvina and Erik Kooper (Leiden: Brill, 2015), pp. 69-94.

75 See Gabrielle Spiegel, *Romancing the Past: The Rise of Vernacular Prose Historiography in Thirteenth-Century France* (Berkeley, CA: University of California Press, 1995).

76 Jan Dumolyn and Anne-Laure Van Bruaene, 'Introduction: Urban Historiography in Late Medieval and Early Modern Europe' in *Urban History Writing in North-Western Europe (15th-16th Centuries)*, ed. by Bram Caers, Lisa Demets and Tineke Van Gassen (Turnhout: Brepols, 2019), pp. 13-14.

social transformations'.[77] Such transformations were, indeed, taking place in Paris in the fourteenth and fifteenth centuries. Rising literacy levels and the increasing use of paper shaped new authors and new audiences, among them growing numbers of an unbeneficed 'clerical proletariat'.[78] Meanwhile, the Black Death and Hundred Years War stimulated sudden fluctuations in Paris' population, with the city's population in 1400 roughly half that which it had been in 1328. Concurrently, however, the progressive centralization of royal institutions and the monarch's increasing residence within the capital underscored Paris' place at the heart of royal government, affording Parisians a potent stake in national decision-making. As a result, the close study of fifteenth-century Parisian urban historiography provides important insights into the conceptual framework that conditioned urban understandings of how the realm should be governed, the discourses to which Parisians contributed and the media through which they were communicated. This conception of the city as political stage and agent was inscribed in the Parisian journals that began to emerge in the first decades of the fifteenth century, taking as their subject neither monarch nor aristocracy, but the city and its inhabitants. These texts betray a shifting sense of the constitutional role Parisians believed performed in the national political culture, coupled with visions of an expanding political community. Just as the thirteenth-century transition to vernacular prose historiography reflected an aristocratic means of contesting royal power, informal Parisian historical narratives captured the development of a 'partisan record' codifying the capital's place in national politics.[79]

The *Journal d'un bourgeois de Paris* is therefore exemplary of an evolving genre, distinct from traditional chronicles in style, format, focus, and purpose. Where over a hundred copies of the vernacular *Grandes Chroniques* survive for the late Middle Ages (with fifty being produced during Charles VI's reign alone), fifteenth-century journals typically survive in a single and often fragmentary manuscript.[80] Indeed, if the *Grandes Chroniques* tradition of which Michel Pintoin formed a part represented a historiographical centre, as Kathleen Daly and Gabrielle Spiegel have argued, then the Parisian journals reveal that the historiographical 'periphery' was not merely geographically distant from Saint-Denis (as with Burgundian, Breton or Dauphinois texts).[81] In their focus upon the city these Parisian texts were similarly 'marginal', but endeavoured to situate the city as a constituent member

77 Spiegel, 'History, Historicism', p. 82.

78 For England, the notion of the 'clerical proletariat' and ensuing experimentation with literary production has been advanced by Kathryn Kerby-Fulton, 'The Clerical Proletariat: The Underemployed Scribe and Vocational Crisis', *Journal of the Early Book Society*, 17 (2014), pp. 1-34. For shifting literacy in France, particularly at the University of Paris, see Daniel Hobbins, *Authorship and Publicity Before Print: Jean Gerson and the Transformation of Late Medieval Learning* (Philadelphia, PA: University of Pennsylvania Press, 2009).

79 Spiegel, 'History, Historicism', p. 83.

80 Frédéric Duval (ed.), *Lectures françaises de la fin du Moyen Âge: Petite anthologie commentée de succès littéraires* (Geneva: Droz, 2007), pp. 316-19. See also Anne D. Hedeman, *The Royal Image: Illustrations of the Grandes chroniques de France, 1274-1422* (Berkeley, CA: University of California Press, 1991).

81 Kathleen Daly, '"Centre", "Power" and "Periphery" in Late Medieval French Historiography: Some Reflections' in *War, Government and Power in Late Medieval France*, ed. by Christopher Allmand (Liverpool: Liverpool University Press, 2000), pp. 124-28; Spiegel, *Romancing the Past*, pp. 316-19; Bernard Guenée, '*Les Grandes Chroniques de France*, le *Roman aux Roys* (1274-1518)' in *Les lieux de mémoire. vol. 2: La nation*, ed. by Pierre Nora (Paris: Gallimard, 1986), pp. 189-213.

of the realm, asserting a defence of urban privilege and a unique, cooperative relationship in royal politics.

Nevertheless, the low number of surviving Parisian examples means that the city's historiographical output is yet to have been treated with the same care and attention as its European counterparts. Anne-Laure Van Bruaene has pointed to the dominance of German, Swiss and Italian models of urban writing in the current treatment of medieval urban historiography, with these texts evidencing efforts to legitimate civic authority while stimulating collective identities in ways rarely seen in England, the Low Countries or France.[82] In these instances, the prevalence of urban historiographical texts have been explained by a high degree of regional urbanization and the strength of civic administrations relative to seigneurial authority, though since the 1990s this narrative has been problematized for the Low Countries and England, especially given the extent of urbanization in the late medieval Southern Low Countries.[83] Considering Paris' own status as the most populous city in medieval western Europe, as a centre for clerical learning and a city with strong royal *and* civic institutions, it stands to reason that the production of urban historiography should be nuanced for the French capital. And yet, Paris' place in historiographical production remains largely unacknowledged in the scholarship, even being omitted from Bernard Guenée's survey of medieval historical literature, and it is only more recently that the Parisian journals have been treated as part of a wider Middle French corpus.[84]

The *Journal* exemplifies this emerging Parisian historiography, and points to its accelerated development in the immediate aftermath of 1405, precisely when Jean sans Peur appealed to a Parisian stake in his evolving struggle with Louis, duke of Orléans. Not only was the Bourgeois' *Journal* apparently triggered by the events of that summer, but other Parisian texts shared in this appeal. A rhymed Parisian chronicle, the *Aventures depuis deux cents ans*, appears to have been compiled in a sympathetically Burgundian orbit, a fact further suggested by its earliest appearance in a manuscript once held within the Burgundian

---

82 Anne-Laure Van Bruaene, 'L'écriture de la mémoire urbaine en Flandre et en Brabant (XIVᵉ-XVIᵉ siècle) in *Villes de Flandre et d'Italie (XIIIᵉ-XVIᵉ siècles): Les enseignements d'une comparaison*, ed. by Élodie Lecuppre-Desjardin and Élisabeth Crouzet-Pavan (Turnhout: Brepols, 2008), pp. 149-51. The disproportionate focus upon these regions is also evidenced in Augusto Vasina, 'Medieval Urban Historiography in Western Europe (1100-1500)' in *Historiography in the Middle Ages*, ed. by Deborah Deliyannis (Leiden: Brill, 2003), pp. 317-52; Elisabeth M.C. Van Houts, *Local and Regional Chronicles* (Turnhout: Brepols, 1995), p. 16.

83 This work is now extensive. See Mary-Rose McLaren, *The London Chronicles of the Fifteenth-Century: A Revolution in English Writing* (Woodbridge: Brewer, 2002); Antonia Gransden, *Historical Writing in England. Volume 2, c. 1307 to the Early Sixteenth Century* (Ithaca, NY: Cornell University Press, 1982), pp. 230-48. For the Low Countries, see Anne-Laure Van Bruaene, 'S'imaginer le passé et le présent: conscience historique et identité urbaine en Flandre à la fin du Moyen Âge', *Beihefte der Francia*, 55 (2003), pp. 167-80; Lisa Demets, *Onvoltooid verleden: De handschriften van de 'Excellente Cronike van Vlaenderen' in de laatmiddeleeuwse Vlaamse steden (1440-1500)* (Hilversum: Verlorem, 2020); Lisa Demets and Jan Dumolyn, 'Urban chronicle writing in late medieval Flanders: the case of Bruges during the Flemish Revolt of 1482-90', *Urban History*, 43 (2016), pp. 28-45; Paul Trio, 'The Chronicle attributed to "Oliver van Diksmuide": A misunderstood town chronicle of Ypres from late medieval Flanders' in *The Medieval Chronicle V*, ed. by Erik Kooper (Amsterdam: Rodopi, 2008), pp. 211-25. Comparing both settings, see the recent thesis by Jenneke De-Vries, '"Nothing but Mayors and Sheriefs, and the deare yeere, and the great frost". A study of written historical culture in late medieval towns in the Low Countries and England' (unpublished doctoral thesis, University of Durham, 2019).

84 Bernard Guenée, *Histoire et culture historique dans l'Occident médiéval* (Paris: Aubier, 1980). For the recent inclusion of journals, see Pierre Courroux, *L'Écriture de l'histoire*, pp. 83-6.

ducal library.[85] Traditionally dated to 1409, a more complete version concluding in 1412 reveals an author sensitive to Paris' political struggles and their intersection with royal authority, with unique stanzas recalling the entries of the Emperor Charles IV (January 1378), Charles VI (November 1380) and Isabeau de Bavière (August 1389) and the uprisings of 1382. Also included is an elaborated account of the infamous *Bal des Ardents* on 28 January 1393, a tragic incident where the costumes of nobles dressed as wild men ignited during wedding festivities at the Parisian royal residence of Saint-Pol, endangering the king and provoking widespread Parisian condemnation of the perceived profane luxuries that characterized the court.[86] Compiled after the escalation in Armagnac-Burgundian hostilities in 1410, this version of the *Aventures* ends with an account of the Burgundian siege of Bourges in July 1412 and the ensuing peace at Auxerre (22 August 1412), concluding with the optimistic plea 'que tenir les y veule, tousjours de mieulx en mieulx'.[87]

The compilation of the *Aventures* and the *Journal d'un bourgeois de Paris* coincides with another journal for which only a fragment survives, recounting events in 1412 and 1413. This anonymous author was similarly sympathetic to the Burgundian cause and described in detail the Parisian processions undertaken to support the Burgundian siege of Bourges, as well as the Cabochien revolt the following year, concluding at its climax with the execution of the former *prévôt*, Pierre des Essarts, on 1 July 1413.[88] Against the backdrop of a relative void in Parisian historical writing for the later fourteenth century, these three texts indicate a surge in Parisian production that coincided with Jean sans Peur's validation of the city's place in national political culture and the intensification of a Burgundian propaganda campaign designed to secure the capital's loyalty. Indeed, this period's significance in motivating Parisian writing can even be detected in the journal compiled by the prior of Sainte-Catherine-du-Val-des-Écoliers, Jean Maupoint. Although ostensibly beginning with Charles VII's return to the capital in November 1437, Maupoint included in his journal several Latin passages recalling the murder of Louis d'Orléans three decades earlier, signalling how this marked the beginning of lasting war and resulting desolation.[89]

---

85 The best study of the *Aventures depuis deux cents ans* (though missing an analysis of the longest, 1412 version of the text) remains Claude Gauvard and Gillette Labory, 'Une chronique rimée parisienne écrite en 1409: les *Aventures depuis deux cents ans*' in *Le métier d'historien au Moyen Âge: études sur l'historiographie médiévale*, ed. by Bernard Guenée (Paris: Publications de la Sorbonne, 1977), pp. 183-231. The manuscript in question is Paris, BNF Fr. 14416, mentioned in the inventory of the ducal library for 1467-69, and once joined with Paris, BNF Fr. 14989 (a copy of the *Danse Macabre* poem) and Besançon BM MS 592 (containing poems pertaining to the Thomas Montagu, earl of Salisbury's death at Orléans in October 1428). See Hanno Wijsman, 'Un manuscrit de Philippe le Bon et la *Danse Macabré* du cimetière des Saints-Innocents', *Le Moyen Âge*, vol. CXXVII, no. 1 (2021), pp. 59-69.

86 This more complete version of the *Aventures* is found in a fifteenth-century manuscript, once owned by the noble poet and bibliophile Anne de Graville (*c*.1490-*c*.1540). Paris, Bibliothèque historique de la ville de Paris, 4-MS-RES-10 (527), fols 140r-147v. The *Bal des Ardents* and its condemnation by Parisians was described in detail by Michel Pintoin. *RSD*, II, pp. 70-1.

87 That they wish to keep it, always better and better. *Journal*, fol. 147v.

88 The fifteenth-century fragment is inserted in a miscellaneous collection of French historical and legal texts. Rome, Vatican MS Reg. Lat. 1502 (Volume 1), fols 103r-108v. The fragment was published in Alexandre Tuetey (ed.), 'Journal parisien des années 1412 et 1413', *MSHP*, 44 (1917), pp. 163-82.

89 Jean Maupoint, 'Journal parisien', pp. 23-4.

The examination of the *Journal* within this context of a broader increase in Parisian writing problematizes the argument that royal power and dominant modes of 'official' historical production in France mediated against urban historiography.[90] While these Parisian examples reveal the heterogeneity of such histories, Van Bruaene has usefully distinguished three forms of civic memory through Flemish examples that can usefully be applied to categorize Parisian writing: 'la mémoire urbaine officielle, la mémoire oppositionnelle et la mémoire individuelle'.[91] The first encapsulates historical writing supported by civic institutions, the second that produced by those excluded from civic power, and the third 'des expressions de conscience historique dans lesquelles le public visé n'est pas immédiatement discernable'.[92] Furthermore, Lisa Demets and Jan Dumolyn have proposed a methodological approach for the examination of urban historiography, 'taking into account the authorship and the thematic emphasis' of texts and considering 'the social environment of their circulation and the ideological strategies at work'.[93] As parameters for the generic distinction of premodern urban historiography, these scholars have stressed the urban centre's predominance in the narrative, the civic identities of the author and audience, and privileged an analysis of a given text's codicological history.

The present study follows these approaches, situating the Bourgeois' *Journal* as a politically engaged example of Van Bruaene's 'mémoire oppositionnelle', evidencing the ideological perspectives of a socially-situated and restricted group of Parisians engaged with the political contests of the fifteenth century. In doing so, this book locates the *Journal* within its political and social contexts, echoing J.G.A. Pocock's argument that historiographical production is rooted within a sense of self and more broadly, community, formed through contestation wherein narrative emerged as a means *of* contestation.[94] Through his account of Parisians – 'nos gens' – the Bourgeois exhibited a sense of collective identity developed and reinforced through a shared political consciousness among the artisans, clergymen and bourgeois on the periphery of municipal politics who asserted their stake in Paris' history. Moreover, the examination of the *Journal* substantiates Van Bruaene's conclusion that 'l'interprétation de l'histoire constitue l'un des enjeux des luttes permanentes entre divers groupes de la société urbaine'.[95] Given that in its very creation, historiography seeks to 'confirm, legitimate and reinforce' the continuous being of the group(s) that it identifies, a consideration of the *Journal* as the articulation of a civic consciousness significantly counters Paris' exclusion from assessments of late medieval urban historiography.[96]

As suggested above, the codification of this urban consciousness was intertwined with changes both in literate practice and the relationship between Parisian clerics and the wider civic community. Daniel Hobbins has effectively shown how, at precisely this moment

---

90 Judith Pollman, 'Archiving the Present and Chronicling for the Future in Early Modern Europe' *Past & Present*, Supplement 11 (2016), p. 238.

91 Official urban memory, oppositional memory and individual memory. Van Bruaene, 'S'imaginer le passé', p. 168.

92 Expressions of historical consciousness for which the intended public is not immediately recognizable. Van Bruaene, 'S'imaginer le passé', p. 168.

93 Demets and Dumolyn, 'Urban chronicle writing', pp. 28-31.

94 J.G.A. Pocock, 'Historiography as a form of political thought', *History of European Ideas*, 37 (2011), pp. 1-6.

95 Historical interpretation represents one of the key issues in the constant struggle between various groups in urban society. Van Bruaene, 'S'imaginer le passé', p. 174.

96 Pocock, 'Historiography', p. 5.

at the turn of the fifteenth century, the University chancellor Jean Gerson assumed 'a conviction that the day's pressing need was for people who were self-conscious about the task of writing and skilled in putting it to good use'.[97] Individuals emanating from clerical and university backgrounds – like the Bourgeois, Jean Maupoint or the anonymous author of the 1412-13 fragment –, adapted established literary models to satisfy an increasing demand for political information in urban society. For Hobbins, this transformation is captured by the University of Paris' turn away from traditional pedagogical genres to tracts that 'permitted an author to treat a current, popular topic in a form that could be easily distributed to non-academic audiences'.[98] Fifteenth-century Parisian journals also appear as an experimentation with existing historical genres, designed to render information simultaneously engaging and digestible for lay audiences.[99] In this respect, it is noteworthy that from the middle of 1413 the Bourgeois consistently signalled new entries through 'Item', a strategy already employed by the anonymous 1412-13 fragment and later adopted by the Parlement *greffier* Nicolas de l'Espoisse when he added an account of the 1418 massacres to the final folios of his copy of the *Chroniques* of Guillaume de Nangis.[100] For Nicole Pons, the use of 'Item' bears the hallmarks of scribal practices associated with the chancery and Parlement, and its employment points to narratives structured inflected towards a more pragmatic, direct and less highly stylized consumption, paralleling the logic identified by Hobbins for Gerson's turn to the sermon-tract during this period.[101] Indeed, like the Bourgeois' text, Pons has argued that l'Espoisse's turn to succinct passages was strategic, ensuring 'le souvenir précis de ce que l'on a vécu' in the face of violence, requiring little rhetorical embellishment.[102]

The significance of this experimentation is amplified by the fact that in contrast to other European centres where lay and mercantile communities participated in historiographical production, the early fifteenth-century Parisian journals were compiled almost exclusively

---

97 Hobbins, *Authorship and Publicity*, p. 1.

98 Daniel Hobbins, 'The Schoolman as Public Intellectual: Jean Gerson and the Late Medieval Tract', *American Historical Review*, 108 (2003), pp. 1308-35 (1310).

99 Mary-Rose McLaren has identified similar processes of generic experimentation occurring in the evolution of the fifteenth-century London Chronicles. Mary-Rose McLaren, 'Reading, Writing and Recording: Literacy and the London Chronicles in the Fifteenth Century' in *London and the Kingdom: Essays in Honour of Caroline M. Barron. Proceedings of the 2004 Harlaxton Symposium*, ed. by Matthew Davies and Andrew Prescott (Donnington: Shaun Tyas, 2008), pp. 346-65.

100 Paris, BNF Fr. 23138, fols 232r-233v. On l'Espoisse's historical notes, see Isabelle Guyot-Bachy, 'Culture historique et lecture de l'histoire: Nicolas de Lespoisse et son exemplaire des chroniques de Guillaume de Nangis (BnF fr. 23138)' in *Humanisme et politique en France à la fin du Moyen Âge*, ed. by Carla Bozzolo, Claude Gauvard and Hélène Millet (Paris: Éditions de la Sorbonne, 2018), pp. 39-56; Nicole Pons, 'Information et rumeurs: quelques points de vue sur des événements de la Guerre civile en France (1407-20)', *Revue historique*, 297 (1997), pp. 413-16.

101 Nicole Pons, 'Un exemple de l'utilisation des écrits de Jean de Montreuil: Un memorandum diplomatique rédigé sous Charles VII' in *Préludes à la Renaissance: Actes de la vie intellectuelle en France au XVᵉ siècle*, ed. by Carla Bozzolo and Ezio Ornato (Paris: CNRS, 1992), p. 248. A similarly staccato style characterizes the Parisian historical notes covering 1270 to 1356, copied by a likely member of the *Chambre des comptes* in the early fifteenth century, found in Paris, BNF Latin 4641B, fols 131v-137v. See Nicole Pons, 'Honneur et profit. Le recueil d'un juriste parisien au milieu du XVᵉ siècle', *Revue historique*, 645 (2008), pp. 3-32.

102 The precise memory of lived experience. Pons, 'Information et rumeurs', p. 416. Pierre Courroux has suggested a similar mnemonic function characterizes rhymed Parisian chronicles, including the *Aventures depuis deux cents ans* and the *Dit des roys*. 'History, Verse', p. 120, n. 39.

by clerics. This predominance is unsurprising when we account for the University of Paris' preeminent place in royal and civic politics, as well as the high number of students inhabiting the city because of this prestige. Hobbins has highlighted how the Papal Schism from 1378 compelled the University and its members to assume a 'new public dimension', exemplified by the corporation's shifting attentions from an internal, learned audience to external urban and courtly publics.[103] A similar perception of the University's public role in found in the writings of contemporary commentators. As Tracy Adams has shown through a close examination of Christine de Pizan's (1364-1430) *Livre du corps de policie* (c. 1406-07), Christine adapted traditional models of the body politic to situate the University of Paris in the third estate, alongside the bourgeois, merchants and commons of Paris.[104] In doing so, Adams has argued that Christine de Pizan acknowledged the central role performed by the University of Paris in the management and formation of the opinions of Paris' urban classes, particularly after 1405 and just as the Bourgeois himself started writing.

This impression of clerical influence in civic politics and dissent is further demonstrated by the royal ordinances repeatedly issued throughout the early months of 1408, decrying 'aucuns suppostz de nostre amée fille l'Université de Paris et autres meuz de leur voulenté' who had disseminated bills calling for assemblies 'en intencion et propos [...] de dire et proposer entre autres choses audit peuple plusieurs parolles grandement prejudiciables et dommaigeables a Nous, a nostredit royaulme et a noz subjects et bien publique d'icelluy'.[105] Here, the University's influential public role evokes Jean sans Peur's ability to co-opt the corporation in broader disputes regarding clerical and urban privilege or University status that marked disputes such as the disputed execution of two students by the royal *prévôt* Guillaume de Tignonville in 1408.[106] Fundamentally, Jean sans Peur's appeal to political reform and the preservation of privileges, echoing calls already expressed within the University, provided the institution's members with a firm means of opposing the centralizing tendencies that had come to the fore since the politics of Charles VI's earlier advisors, the so-called Marmousets, and accentuated by Louis d'Orléans' increasing assumption of political control.[107]

Of course, the University of Paris cannot be considered a homogenous entity. From 1410 the University represented a key audience for Armagnac letters in a concentrated epistolary campaign, whereas from 1411 Jean sans Peur sought to secure the loyalties of key members with gifts of wine, both seeking to render the University an extension of their

---

103 Hobbins, 'The Schoolman as Public Intellectual', p. 1311.

104 'En la communité du peuple sont compris trois estas, c'est a savoir par especial en la cité de Paris et aussi es autres citez, le clergié, lez bourgeois et marchans, et puis le commun comme gens de mestier et laboureurs.' (The community of people comprises three estates, as is found especially in the city of Paris and also in other cities: the clergy, the bourgeois and merchants, and then the common artisans and labourers.) Christine de Pizan, *Le livre du corps de policie*, ed. by Angus Kennedy (Paris: Honoré Champion), p. 96; Tracy Adams, 'The political significance of Christine de Pizan's third estate in the *Livre du corps de policie*', *Journal of Medieval History*, 35 (2009), pp. 392-94.

105 Some members of our beloved daughter, the University of Paris, and others moved by ill will [...] with the intention and aim of saying and proposing to the people, among other things, many words that are harmful and detrimental to us, to our kingdom, to our subjects and the common good. *Ordonnances des rois de France*, XII, pp. 224-25.

106 Tournier, 'Jean sans Peur et l'Université de Paris', pp. 299-318.

107 Bertrand Schnerb, *Les Armagnacs et les Bourguignons. La maudite guerre* (Paris: Perrin, 1988), pp. 49-62.

own propaganda enterprises.[108] As a result, the civil conflict provoked significant divisions within the corporation itself, most notably regarding the condemnation of Jean Petit's *Justification* for the murder of Louis d'Orléans and debates on tyrannicide, elaborated through a Parisian council in 1413 and at Constance from 1414.[109] However, compiled by clerics but addressed to lay artisanal audiences, journals emerged exactly as the intersections between the University members, leading bourgeois, the *menu peuple* and the Burgundian faction became more concrete. Where Christine de Pizan's reaction to the Cabochien revolt of 1413 saw her conflate the artisanal classes with the *menu peuple* to undermine the political agency of the former, as groups incapable of speaking 'ordeneement par raisons belle et evidens', texts like the Bourgeois' *Journal* resituated Paris' urban classes as key agents in royal politics and reveal their views being voiced through a clerical mouthpiece.[110]

This communicative purpose is signalled by the internal evidence that reveals the Bourgeois' vision of an audience interacting with his work, contrary to notions of introspective writing implicit in modern definitions of 'journal'. Rather than treating the *Journal* as a passive text situated *outside* Parisian society, a consideration of its potential audience(s) and contexts in Chapter 1 nuances the Bourgeois' intentions and resituates him and his community as political agents. While Janet Shirley suggested that the *Journal* may have been a shorthand for a future chronicle, Colette Beaune has pointed to the prevalence of second-person addresses prior to the Valois reconquest of Paris in 1436, whereafter the Bourgeois 'écrirait pour lui'.[111] Undeniably, these second-person addresses reveal the *Journal*'s communicative character, self-referentially employed as in 'comme vous avez ouy' or 'comme vous orez cy apres', but also to draw the audience's attention to specific information, 'et si sachez que'.[112] There was certainly a clear expectation that others would interact with the text, as demonstrated by the Bourgeois' astonishment by the birth of conjoined twins at Aubervilliers in June 1429, an account which he supported with the inclusion of an illustration of the twins for his readers, 'comme vous voyez'.[113] In other instances, the *Journal* appears as a more immediate point in the relay of information between official channels and local networks, as in August 1428 when, reporting changes to annuities, the Bourgeois remarked that 'plusieurs autres ordonnances furent faictes sur lesdictes rentes, lesquelles on peut savoir ou Chastellet qui veult'.[114] Given the regularity of Châtelet ordinances, the Bourgeois' advice can only have been pertinent in the short-term, indicating a more immediate transmission of information to his audience.[115]

---

108 Tournier, 'Jean sans Peur et l'Université de Paris', pp. 305-10.

109 Alfred Coville, *Jean Petit. La question du tyrannicide au commencement du XV*^e *siècle* (Paris: Picard, 1932).

110 With discipline, through clear and evident reasoning. Christine de Pizan, *The 'Livre de la paix' of Christine de Pizan*, ed. by Charity Cannon Willard (The Hague: Mouton, 1958), p. 131.

111 Was writing for himself. Beaune (ed. and trans.), *Journal*, p. 18; Shirley (ed. and trans.), *A Parisian Journal*, p. 25.

112 As you have heard; as you will hear after this; and you should know that [...] *Journal*, pp. 49, 56, 60, 247, 320.

113 As you can see. *Journal*, p. 238. The illustration was not copied into the Vatican manuscript, though the copyist left space for a later illustrator to add this on the same page. A crude attempt at the drawing, stemming from the textual description provided by the Bourgeois, was attempted by the copyist of the Méjanes manuscript. Rome, Vatican MS Reg. Lat. 1923, fol. 117r; Aix-en-Provence, Bibliothèque Méjanes MS 432 (316), p. 220.

114 Several other ordinances were issued concerning the said *rentes*, about which more can be learned at the Châtelet, for those who wish it. *Journal*, p. 229.

115 For example, different ordinances on the value of these annuities were proclaimed in 1424 and 1441. *Ordonnances des rois de France*, XIII, pp. 47, 339.

This function, and the identity of the Bourgeois' audience, is further demonstrated by the *Journal*'s indisputable Parisian focus. Over half (58%) of entries concern Paris and Parisians specifically and, beyond Paris, the Bourgeois' interests were largely confined to the Île-de-France and Normandy. Urban rumours and popular opinion represent at least a fifth of the *Journal*'s entries, highlighting one of the Bourgeois' chief sources and situating his text as a point of transmission in the local circulation of information. Not only did rumour present the author and his audience with an alternative to material communicated through official channels, but their anonymity and fluidity enabled the Bourgeois to distance himself from compromising perspectives that, instead, were conveyed as common knowledge. More importantly, the repetition of rumour and opinion also accentuated the *Journal*'s projection of the city's inhabitants as the narrative's predominant agents, underscored by the Bourgeois' own eyewitness testimony and the text's very participation in the dissemination of rumours. In contrast, the Bourgeois' rare use of authoritative textual sources is significant in a period when historiographical production was tied to established institutional models and notions of textual *auctoritas*. Such strategies are illustrative of the experimental strategies for conveying narrative authority employed by the Bourgeois.

This Parisian, civic focus is supported by the manuscript evidence. Although editors have hypothesized that the Bourgeois compiled his *Journal* for a University or clerical readership, by the second half of the fifteenth century the text seems to have been patronized by artisans with a stake in Paris' municipal administration. The only positive indication of a fifteenth-century owner of the *Journal* is the signature found on the final folio of the Vatican manuscript, 'Maciot', coupled with the name's appearance (traced faintly with a plummet marker) on the right-hand margin of folio 79 recto.[116] Maciot's hand is distinct from the scribe's, suggesting that he was an owner, and this is underscored by the additions that he made, such as the inclusion of a title alongside the Bourgeois' account of Paris' recapture by Charles VII's on 13 April 1436.[117] Alexandre Tuetey believed that this signature belonged to 'Jean Maciot', a name linked by Colette Beaune to the owners of a contemporary manuscript compilation of the poetry of François Villon and Alain Chartier, Paris, Bibliothèque de l'Arsenal 3523, signed by Jean and Claude Maciot.[118] Although the Arsenal and Vatican Maciots may have been related, it appears unlikely that they were the same individuals. The names in Arsenal 3523 correspond to members of the municipality in the first decades of the sixteenth century – the 1528 *quartenier* Claude Maciot and either his father, Jean, *quartenier* for Saint-Germain between 1507 and 1514, or his brother, also Jean, the 'trésorier du salpètre' for France and Picardie in 1535.[119]

---

116 Rome, Vatican Reg. Lat. 1923, fols 79r, 187r.

117 Rome, Vatican Reg. Lat. 1923, fol. 153r.

118 Tuetey (ed.), *Journal*, p. iii; Beaune (ed. and trans.), *Journal*, p. 8; Paris, Bibliothèque de l'Arsenal, 3523, fol. 409v. For this manuscript, see Emma Cayley, 'Polyphonie et dialogisme: espaces ludiques dans le recueil manuscrit à la fin du Moyen Âge. Le cas de trois recueils poétiques du XVe siècle' in *Le recueil au Moyen Âge: La fin du Moyen Âge*, ed. by Tania Van Hemelryck and Stafania Marzano (Turnhout: Brepols, 2010), pp. 47-53.

119 *Registres des délibérations du bureau de la ville de Paris*, ed. by François Bonnardot and others, 16 vols (Paris: Imprimerie nationale, 1883-1927), I (1883) pp. 87, 91, 93, 104-06, 119-20, 122, 127, 149-50; Alexandre Tuetey (ed.), *Inventaire analytique des livres de couleur et bannières du Châtelet de Paris* (Paris: Imprimerie nationale, 1899), p. 66; Philippe Contamine, 'Les chaînes dans les bonnes villes de France (spécialement Paris), XIVe-XVIe siècle' in *Guerre et société en France, en Angleterre et en Bourgogne XIVe-XVe siècle*, ed. by Maurice Keen, Charles Giry-Deloison and

While the Arsenal 3523 owners likely belong to a generation once removed from the Vatican manuscript's production, the prosopographical evidence provided by these signatures is important, highlighting a Maciot family rising to municipal prominence around 1500. Here we find Jean I Maciot, a *changeur* between 1460 and at least 1484, whose profession brought him into contact with France's elite during a period when the *changeurs* were prevalent in civic politics, regularly fielding *échevins* between 1436 and 1474.[120] Wealthy and of good standing, Jean Maciot loaned money to the crown in 1477 and 1478, while his ties to the city's administration are signalled by his marriage to Catherine Lapite, sister to Jean Lapite, clerk of the *chambre des comptes* and *échevin* in 1499.[121] Through this marriage, Maciot established dynastic connections with the Lapites' maternal Bureau family, whose most notable members included Jean Bureau, *prévôt des marchands* in 1450-54.[122] These dynastic connections were sustained by Maciot's descendants. Germain Maciot, possibly Jean's son, was a Parisian student of canon law whose surviving workbook contains letters to Jean Lapite, 'senatorem egregium'.[123] Another close relative appearing in the workbook is Landéric Maciot, later rector of the University of Paris in 1531. A grandchild, also named Jean Maciot, married Louise Hesselin, granddaughter of Denis Hesselin, municipal *greffier* and once considered the author of the *Journal de Jean de Roye*, while Vincent Maciot, a Parlement *avocat* and *quartenier* from 1525, married Catherine Bardon, daughter of the Parlement *procureur* Jean Bardon.[124]

Revealing a possible group of lay readers closely involved in civic and, increasingly, royal politics, the localized historical knowledge supplied by the *Journal* may have contributed to the Maciot family's ability to consolidate its position on Paris' right bank over ensuing generations. More significantly, this family's status might be indicative of the *Journal*'s intended audience. Like the Bourgeois, the *changeur* Jean I Maciot was based in the Halles district, owning a house at the southern end of the rue Saint-Denis, on the *Petite*

Philippe Contamine (Lille: Publications de l'Institut de recherches historiques du Septentrion, 1991), pp. 299-301; *Les ordonnances royaux sur le faict et jurisdiction de la prevosté des marchands et eschevinage de la ville de Paris* (Paris, 1556), pp. 155-56; Paris, Archives nationales, Inventaire MC ET XXXIII 24, 1543.

120 Paris, Archives nationales Z 1b 286, 'Registre des Changeurs', fols 26r-v, 75r-v; Robert Favreau, 'Les changeurs du royaume sous le règne de Louis XI', *BEC*, 122 (1964), p. 245. See also Boris Bove, *Dominer la ville: prévôts des marchands et échevins parisiens de 1260 à 1350* (Paris: Éditions du Comité des travaux historiques et scientifiques, 2004), p. 73.

121 Paris, BNF Fr. 4487, fol. 27r; BNF Fr. 20685, pp. 672, 693, 728; Jean-François Lassalmonie, *La boîte à l'enchanteur: politique financière de Louis XI* (Paris: Comité pour l'histoire économique et financière, 2002), p. 557; Louis Thuasne (ed.), *Roberti Gaguini, Epistole et Orationes: Texte publié sur les éditons originales de 1498*, 2 vols (Paris: Bouillon, 1903-05), II (1905), p. 506. Catherine Lapite was buried alongside Jean Maciot in the Saints-Innocents cemetery. Paris, Archives nationales LL 434-B, p. 197. Regarding Jean Lapite, see Léon Dorez and Marcel Fournier, *La Faculté de décret de l'Université de Paris au XVᵉ siècle*, vol. 3 (Paris: Imprimerie nationale, 1908), p. 15, n. 1; *Registre des délibérations*, I, pp. 1-2.

122 The precise nature of this relationship is unclear, but in 1497 Jean Lapite was involved in an inheritance dispute with his cousin Merry Bureau, seigneur de la Houssaye (d. 1531), Jean Bureau's nephew. *Minutier central des notaires de Paris. Minutes du XVᵉ siècle de l'étude XIX, inventaire analytique*, ed. by Claire Béchu, Florence Greffe and Isabelle Pebay (Paris: Archives nationales, 1993), p. 458.

123 Jan Pendergrass, 'Lettres, poèmes et débat scolaire de Germain Maciot, étudiant parisien du XVᵉ siècle. MS. Latin 8659 de la Bibliothèque nationale de France', *Bulletin du Cange. Archivum Latinitatis Medii Aevi*, 55 (1997), pp. 187, 241.

124 Ernest Coyecque (ed.), *Recueil d'actes notariés relatifs à l'histoire de Paris et de ses environs au XVIᵉ siècle. vol. 2, 1532-55*, 2 vols (Paris: Imprimerie nationale, 1905-23), II (1923), p. 369, no. 5438; Bernard de Mandrot, 'Quel est le véritable auteur de la chronique anonyme de Louis XI, dite la Scandaleuse?', *BEC*, 52 (1891), pp. 129-30; Camille Trani, 'Les magistrats du grand conseil au XVIᵉ siècle (1547-1610)', *Paris et Île-de-France. Mémoires publiés par la fédération des sociétés archéologiques de Paris et de l'Île-de-France*, 42 (1991), p. 105.

Saunerie adjacent to the Châtelet.[125] Jean was buried in the local Saints-Innocents cemetery alongside his uncle, the merchant Mathurin Saussy and wife Catherine de Lapite, commemorated together by an epitaph that still survived in the seventeenth century.[126] Jean's descendants – Jean II and then Vincent –, served as officers for the local Saint-Germain *quartier* until the mid-sixteenth century. The family's identification as the *Journal*'s potential patrons underscores the didactic function of urban historiography, providing a means of articulating Parisian identities as municipal officers staked their representative vocation in civic society.[127] The alterations that Maciot may have made to the text suggest that these readers employed the *Journal* as a social product, altered through copying, editing and *réécriture*.[128] They were certainly politically conscious and adapted the *Journal* to suit new royal agendas at the end of the fifteenth century, erasing the Bourgeois' criticisms of the Dauphin Louis (Louis XI) and perhaps even deliberately removing his account of Jean sans Peur's assassination at Montereau-fault-Yonne on 10 September 1419 to reflect the Franco-Burgundian tensions that marked the period prior to Duke Charles le Téméraire's death in 1477.[129] At the very least, by the middle of the sixteenth century the *Journal* circulated within new networks of readers among Paris' more elite bourgeois and functionaries. The death of Vincent Maciot in 1554 coincides neatly with the record of the lawyer and later president of the *Cour des monnaies* Claude Fauchet's (1530-1602) ownership of the Vatican manuscript the following year, described in Fauchet's notes as 'un pappier journal ou memoires de quelque personne studieuse'.[130] Through Fauchet, the *Journal* passed into the hands of Parisian bibliophiles and antiquarians, copied and shared among Parlement members, jurists and royal office-holders that included Étienne Pasquier (1529-1615), Claude Dupuy (1545-94) and Pierre de l'Estoile (1546-1611).[131]

---

125 Michel Möring (ed.), *Inventaire sommaire des archives hospitalières antérieures à 1790. vol. 1, L'Hôtel-Dieu* (Paris: Grandremy and Henon, 1882), p. 74.

126 *Épitaphier du vieux Paris: vol. 6, Les Saints-Innocents*, ed. by Hélène Verlet (Paris: Comité des Travaux Historiques de la Ville de Paris, 1997), p. 275, no. 3036.

127 Robert Descimon, 'Le corps de la ville et les élections échevinales à Paris aux XVIe et XVIIe siècles. Codification coutumière et pratiques sociales', *Histoire, Économie et Société*, 13 (1994), pp. 511-14.

128 Paul Zumthor, *Essai de poétique médiéval* (Paris: Seuil, 1972), pp. 65-75; Gérard Genette, *Palimpsestes: La littérature au second degré* (Paris: Seuil, 1982).

129 Rome, Vatican Reg. Lat. 1923, fols 60v-61r, 176r, 178v

130 A paper-journal or the memoires of some studious person. Claude Fauchet, 'Vieilles et observations de plusieurs choses dignes de mémoire en la lecture d'aucuns autheurs francois (1555)', BNF Fr. 24726, fols 44r-v. The year of Vincent Maciot's death is determined by his description as 'feu sire Vincent Maciot' in the Hôtel de Ville's register on 4 January 1555, having been absent since December 1553. Bonnardot, *Registres des délibérations*, IV, (1888), pp. 245, 347.

131 Handwritten notes by Claude Fauchet and Étienne Pasquier are found in the margins of Rome, Vatican Reg. Lat. 1923, with references to 'ceste année 1555' (Fauchet) and 'ceste presente année 1567' (Pasquier). fol. 14v, 25v. Claude Dupuy's and Pierre de l'Estoile's interactions with the manuscript are evidenced by their copies drawn from the text, found respectively in Paris, BNF Dupuy 275 and BNF Fr. 10303. The extent of these bibliophiles' libraries, the nature of their exchanges and their place in the production of local history, are detailed in Hamilton, *Pierre de l'Estoile and his World*, pp. 166-94; Hilary J. Bernstein, *Historical Communities: Cities, Erudition and National Identity in Early Modern France* (Leiden: Brill, 2021), pp. 12-20.

Parisian opinion communities and the medieval public sphere

When Jürgen Habermas presented the idea of *Öffentlichkeit* – the bourgeois public sphere or 'l'espace public' – in his pioneering work, *Strukturwandel der Öffentlichkeit* (1968), he traced the foundations of modern democracy by demarcating a clear shift in political attitudes, access to information and public opinion in the seventeenth and eighteenth centuries.[132] For Habermas, the conflation of rapid technological advancements (the printing press), societal change (intensified urbanization) and economic developments (the emergence of market capitalism) stimulated a commodified demand for news.[133] As a result, news became a product of public interest inflected towards a critique of the state, with themes and interests further discussed in institutionalized public spaces such as urban coffeehouses and salons. These arenas epitomized the public sphere, 'the sphere of private people come together as a public' within discursive spaces where status differences were bracketed to facilitate free, rational conversation as participants mediated between state and society.[134]

As Carol Symes has poignantly argued, Habermas' vision of the public sphere's early modern emergence was predicated upon its juxtaposition with a caricaturized impression of the medieval past, one based in part upon Huizinga's work and therefore, by extension, upon readings of the *Journal*.[135] For Habermas, the public realm was perceived to exist in the medieval (or 'feudal') world not as a space of interaction, discourse and critique, but as the *repräsentativen Öffentlichkeit* – monarchical superiority exhibited *before* the public rather than *in* public.[136] Medieval illiteracy and the lack of an unmediated access to written sources prevented the development of critical rationality and the communicative forms essential to the public sphere's early modern emergence. Equally important, but less well appreciated, is how this impression of feudal interaction shaped Habermas' account of the public sphere's twentieth-century structural transformation. As populations were subjected to unidirectional, showy, mass media communications through radio and television, Habermas contended that they were 'refeudalized'. The result was that private institutions assumed public power, the state entered the private realm, and the public use of critical reason was again reduced to the 'reactions of an uncommitted, friendly disposition', with people repositioned as subjects and spectators to power.[137] Here, Habermas' stereotypical

132 Jürgen Habermas, *The Structural Transformation of the Public Sphere: An Inquiry into a Category of Bourgeois Society*, trans. by Thomas Burger and Frederick Lawrence, (Cambridge, MA: MIT Press, 1991). Originally published as *Strukturwandel der Öffentlichkeit: Untersuchungen zu einer Kategorie der bürgerlichen Gesellschaft* (Berlin: Luchterhand, 1962).

133 More recently, similar processes have been described in Andrew Pettegree, *The Invention of News: How the world came to know about itself* (London: Yale University Press, 2014).

134 Habermas, *Structural Transformation*, p. 27.

135 Carol Symes, *A Common Stage: Theatre and Public Life in Medieval Arras* (London: Cornell University Press, 2007), pp. 127-29. Habermas' dialogue with the ideas of Johan Huizinga and Jacob Burckhardt is rarely acknowledged in studies of the *Structural Transformation*.

136 Translated as 'representative publicness'. Habermas, *Structural Transformation*, pp. 7-11.

137 Habermas, *Structural Transformation*, p. 195. Habermas subsequently revised this model in 1992, acknowledging capacities for resistance within a pluralistic mass public, though he retained his argument that mass media culminated in a 'power-infiltrated public sphere'. Jürgen Habermas, 'Further Reflections on the Public Sphere', trans. Thomas Burger in *Habermas and the Public Sphere*, ed. by Craig Calhoun, (Cambridge, MA: MIT Press, 1992), pp. 436-39.

vision of the medieval world came full circle, emerging as the fundamental backdrop against which his vision of the public sphere's historical transformation could be traced.

Problematizing this vision of medieval communication and demonstrating the public sphere's more complex history – as a sphere of greater and small size, rather than being either present or absent – presents a fundamental corrective to narratives that juxtapose models of interaction in the medieval, early modern or modern worlds. Building upon the recent work by Nicolas Offenstadt and Patrick Boucheron, Carol Symes and Leidulf Melve, who have envisioned new structural paradigms for interrogating medieval public spheres, this book similarly highlights the permanence of political critique and discussion in premodern society.[138] Carol Symes has shown that 'all of the economic conditions to which Habermas ascribes the emergence of the public sphere were present in many medieval communities', demonstrating in her study of thirteenth-century Arras 'how frequently and how cannily people without the power to assert themselves through more conventional means gained other types of power through the use of public media'.[139] Similarly, Christian Liddy has compellingly argued for fifteenth-century England that the potential anachronism of theoretical terminology should not function as a barrier to the analysis of medieval phenomena. Building upon Robert Scribner's studies of Reformation Germany, Liddy has signalled the multiple and interleaving forms that public opinion assumed in late medieval English towns, ranging from an 'official public opinion' (that of the municipality' to the 'public opinion of human interaction' (gossip and rumour), once analysed by Claude Gauvard in terms of *fama*.[140] In yet another paradigm, Leidulf Melve has argued for the concurrent existence of 'elitist', 'semi-elitist', 'semi-plural' and 'plural' public spheres as a model for measuring structuralist changes in Habermasian terms during the investiture controversy of the eleventh and twelfth centuries.[141]

These conceptual approaches have opened up the medieval public sphere, moving beyond understandings rooted in conceptions of state power and monarchical imagery to demonstrate the crucial ways in which townspeople – as those most frequently exposed to public officials – contributed to the discourse of public politics and political culture, sensitive to the unequal distribution of power in late medieval society. Here, the identification of the political community is conceived as intertwined with public opinion and political communication.[142] As Bernard Guenée and John Watts have shown, this was a period when rulers took notice of what people thought and sought to condition this thinking

---

138 Patrick Boucheron and Nicolas Offenstadt, 'Introduction générale: une histoire de l'échange politique au Moyen Âge', in *L'espace public au Moyen Âge: débats autour de Jürgen Habermas*, ed. by Patrick Boucheron and Nicolas Offenstadt, (Paris: Presses Universitaires de France, 2011), pp. 1-21; Symes, *A Common Stage*; Carol Symes, 'Out in the Open in Arras: Sightlines, Soundscapes and the Shaping of a Medieval Public Sphere' in *Cities, Texts and Social Networks, 400-1500*, ed. by Caroline Goodson, Anne E. Lester and Carol Symes, (London: Routledge, 2010), pp. 279-302; Leidulf Melve, *Inventing the Public Sphere: The Public Debate during the Investiture Contest (c. 1030-1122)* (Leiden: Brill, 2007); Leidulf Melve, '"Even the very laymen are chattering about it": The Politicization of Public Opinion, 800-1200', *Viator*, 44 (2013), pp. 25-48. See also Connell, *Public Opinion*.

139 Symes, *A Common Stage*, pp. 127-30.

140 Christian Liddy, *Contesting the City: The Politics of Citizenship in English Towns, 1250-1530* (Oxford: Oxford University Press, 2017), pp. 127-29.

141 Melve, *Inventing the Public Sphere*, pp. 17-22.

142 Dumolyn, 'Political communication and political power'; Aude Mairey, 'Les langages politiques au Moyen Âge (XIIe-XVe siècle)', *Médiévales*, 57 (2009), pp. 5-7.

through propaganda, but in doing so one which also brought into being understandings of a popular stake in the national political stage.[143] The growing circulation of news created more socially diverse, informed publics, while the intensification of interactions between government and local communities framed an increasing popular concern for royal activity, opinion emerged as a force with which authorities increasingly grappled, to varying degrees of success.[144]

In turn, widening conceptions of the medieval public have also translated to a move away from written texts to examining the intersections between writing, speech and action. Scholars have instructively pointed to the political strategies facilitated by political idioms, including 'coercion, resistance, dissimulation, legitimation or de-legitimation'.[145] Here, I address the ways in which Parisians participated in and developed such strategies to define, influence and sometimes challenge the manifestations of power and authority as an expected function of the public sphere. Despite the tentativeness with which public opinion has been considered for late medieval Europe, the point is far from anachronistic. For Aristotle, nature operated determinatively and the power of speech was ordered for the communication essential to facilitating societal harmony, with this human communicative reason evidence of the species' status as a political animal.[146] Medieval authors readily acknowledged that society required a government founded upon the human cooperation ensured by linguistic communication, supported by exchanges through reasoned speech.[147] In the early fourteenth century this view was echoed by Giles of Rome, who argued that the natural end of language was the comprehension of justice, while Oresme's translation of the *Politics* reminded his audience that 'homme a parole par nature, et parole est ordenee a communicacion civile'.[148] As such, medieval scholarship debated the purpose and means of human interaction in terms that anticipated Habermas' own emphasis upon communicative rationality.

This recognition of a medieval stress upon deliberative rationality – particularly in non-written media – is essential to delineating the contours of the medieval public sphere and highlighting the multiplicity of groups that participated in political culture. Already in 1990, Nancy Fraser persuasively critiqued Habermas' idealized paradigm, stressing the historical

---

143 Guenée, *L'opinion publique*, p. 10; Claude Gauvard, 'Le roi de France et l'opinion publique', pp. 353-66; Watts, 'The Pressure of the Public'; Hilde De Weerdt, Catherine Holmes and John Watts, 'Politics, *c.* 1000-1500: Mediation and Communication', *Past & Present*, 238, Supplement 13 (2018), pp. 277-82.

144 Christopher Fletcher, 'News, Noise and the Nature of Politics in Late Medieval English Provincial Towns', *Journal of British Studies*, 56 (2017), pp. 250-72; Xavier Nadrigny, *Information et opinion publique à Toulouse à la fin du Moyen Âge* (Paris: École des Chartes, 2013).

145 Christopher Fletcher, 'What makes a political language? Key terms, profit and damage in the common petition of the English Parliament, 1343-1422' in *The Voices of the People in Late Medieval Europe: Communication and Popular Politics*, ed. by Jan Dumolyn, Jelle Haemers, Hipólito Rafael Oliva Herrer and Vincent Challet (Turnhout: Brepols, 2014), pp. 96-8.

146 *The Politics of Aristotle*, ed. and trans. by Peter L Phillips Simpson (Chapel Hill, NC: University of North Carolina Press, 1997), I, 2, 1252b30-1253b1.

147 See Irène Rosier-Catach, 'Communauté politique et communauté linguistique' in *La légitimité implicite*, ed. by Jean-Philippe Genet, (Paris: Éditions de la Sorbonne, 2015), pp. 225-43.

148 Man speaks by nature, and through speech he is directed towards civil life. *Maistre Nicole Oresme. Le livre de Politiques d'Aristote*, ed. by Albert Douglas Menut (Philadelphia, PA: The American Philosophical Society, 1970), p. 49; *Li livres du gouvernement des rois. A XIIIth Century French Version of Egidio Colonna's Treatise* De Regimine Principum, ed. by Samuel Paul Molenaer (London: Macmillan, 1899), pp. 86-7, 145-50, 269-73.

impossibility of the public sphere's bracketing of social differences, instead pointing to the existing of 'parallel discursive arenas where members of subordinated social groups invent and circulate counterdiscourses to formulate oppositional interpretations of their identities, interests and needs'.[149] Rather than a simple framework for consensus, Fraser's revision reveals the value of the public sphere as a means of understanding ideological contest and negotiation between multiple publics, accounting for both the unequal distribution of power in societies, and the plurality of voices that could find expression in the political arena. While this approach's 'spatialization' was questioned by Harold Mah, given its vision of groups 'entering' the public sphere and claiming a representative function therein, Mah's critique in fact highlights the very ways in which diverse groups construct themselves as 'publics' – imagined communities no less – to buttress participatory claims through the employment of collective singulars, often coupled with assertions of communicative rationality.[150] Consequently, and as Kirk Wetters has argued, the dichotomy advanced by Habermas between a 'rational-discursive apparatus' and representative structures is a false narrative, oversimplifying and colouring oppositions of medieval 'representation' and modern 'reason'.[151] Privileging literary and discursive rationality, Habermas' vision of public opinion overlooks the very ways in which representation functions as an indispensable element of political organization, and nowhere is this clearer than in his own analysis of a circumscribed group of wealthy, white, eighteenth-century men who envisioned themselves as the mouthpieces of opinion in the bourgeois public sphere.

The result of this problematization of Habermas' public-sphere-as-ideal-type is twofold. First, the intersection of communication and representation validates the concentration upon *fama*, reputation and rumour grounded in medieval political and social organization.[152] It also introduces scope to consider what Sandro Landi has termed prediscursive opinion, the often 'nonnegotiable' and 'nonspeakable' ideas of identification or reputation situated within an implicit layer of political communication.[153] Habermas distilled public deliberation to its most regularized aspects, emphasizing formal forums and literate culture at the expense of these more subtle, informal and nondiscursive modes of participation common to the medieval and early modern past.[154] Second, neither

---

149 Nancy Fraser, 'Rethinking the Public Sphere: A Contribution to the Critique of Actually Existing Democracy', *Social Text*, 25/26 (1990), p. 72.

150 Harold Mah, 'Phantasies of the Public Sphere: Rethinking the Habermas of Historians', *The Journal of Modern History*, 72 (2000), pp. 153-68. See also Laura A.M. Stewart, 'Introduction: Publics and Participation in Early Modern Britain', *Journal of British Studies*, 56 (2017), pp. 713-18. Of course, the issue of the public sphere's spatialization is most acute in Francophone research, with 'Öffentlichkeit' translated as 'l'espace public' (public space). See Joseph Morsel, 'Communication et domination sociale en Franconie à la fin du Moyen Âge: l'enjeu de la réponse' in *L'espace public au Moyen Âge: Débats autour de Jürgen Habermas*, ed. by Patrick Boucheron and Nicolas Offenstadt (Paris: Presses Universitaires de France, 2011), pp. 354-55.

151 Kirk Wetters, *The Opinion System: Impasses of the Public Sphere from Hobbes to Habermas* (New York: Fordham University Press, 2008), pp. 95-99.

152 See the collected essays in Thelma Fenster and Daniel Lord Smail (ed), *Fama: The Politics of Talk and Reputation in Medieval Europe* (London: Cornell University Press, 2003); Chris Wickham, 'Gossip and Resistance among the Medieval Peasantry', *Past and Present*, 160 (1998), pp. 3-24.

153 Sandro Landi, 'Beyond the Public Sphere: Habermas, Locke and Tacit Consent', *Revue d'histoire modern et contemporaine*, 59 (2012), pp. 28-30.

154 Symes, *A Common Stage*, pp. 129-30.

rationality nor representative publicness can comfortably be identified as the boundaries of historical change. Rather than seeing an oscillation between the feudal and 'refeudalized', an appreciation of the public sphere's intersections with reputation and representation reveal that opinion is more than the straightforward locus of discussion, but a contested site that maps social hierarchies, simultaneously facilitating modes of social control and the means of resisting that same control. Abandoning the search for a determinable emergence, it becomes possible to ascertain 'des espaces publics occasionels' encapsulating more or less varied groups, with the fifteenth-century French civil conflict already identified as precisely one such moment where the public's role becomes exceptionally clear.[155]

In this light, the Bourgeois' *Journal* reveals that late medieval Parisians were more than capable of engaging in their public sphere, discussing societal and political issues through a wide range of discursive and nondiscursive modes, among which the *Journal* itself should be counted. Methodologically, both Carol Symes and Leidulf Melve have articulated a vision of competing public spheres in the medieval past. Adapting Habermas' theory for medieval contexts, Melve argued that public spheres develop in relation to contentious issues confronted by a given society and are informed by competition. An interpreter (either a public or an individual), presents a controversial problem to a wider audience. This potential public's boundaries are cemented through contact with other publics expressing divergent views, before the public's identity is institutionalized and an imagined community emerges, assuming formal forums for discussion.[156] In both oral and written contexts, this process is underpinned by the relatively restricted networks and spaces within which information is initially discussed. This practice facilitates the formation of a group identity, a 'compositional' process by which the internal identity of a given public sphere engaged externally with others in a relational dynamic. Opinion therefore emerges as the product of tension between multiple spheres involving competing media and groups.[157] Such a model correlates closely with the discussion of opinion formation above, both in respect to the Bourgeois' codification and channelling of news for his lay audiences, but also reflecting Christine de Pizan's own vision of the University of Paris' role in framing urban political attitudes.

While a useful foundation, Melve's methodology is not flawless. As Symes noted in her review for *Inventing the Public Sphere*, Melve's approach reaffirmed Habermas' problematic ideal-type, particularly in its focus both upon ideas of 'emergence' (the twelfth-century Investiture Contest being identified as the only example of a medieval public sphere) and literate, rational communication (only elite ecclesiastical writers participated in this

---

155 Occasional public spheres. Boucheron and Offenstadt, 'Introduction', p. 14; Offenstadt, 'Guerre civile et espace public'; Nicolas Offenstadt, *Faire la paix au Moyen Âge: Discours et gestes de paix pendant la guerre de Cent Ans* (Paris: Odile Jacob, 2007), esp. pp. 216-37; Benoît Léthenet, '"Selon les nouvelles que vous me ferez savoir". Essai sur le renseignement au Moyen Âge', *Revue du Nord*, 402 (2013), pp. 837-57; Hutchison, 'Knowing One's Place', pp. 27-9; Loïc Cazaux, 'Les fonctions politiques de la foule à Paris pendant la guerre civile (1407-20)', *Hypothèses*, 14 (2011), pp. 65-76. See also Pierre Karila-Cohen, 'Introduction. Apologie pour un pluriel: de l'opinion aux opinions' in *S'exprimer en temps de troubles. Conflits, opinion(s) et politisation du Moyen Âge au début du XXᵉ siècle*, ed. by Laurent Bourquin, Philippe Hamon, Pierre Karila-Cohen and Cédric Michon, (Rennes: Presses Universitaires de Rennes, 2012), pp. 15-22 (esp. 18).

156 Melve, *Inventing the Public Sphere*, pp. 12-13.

157 Similar processes have been identified by Jill Maciak Walshaw, *A Show of Hands for the Republic: Opinion, Information and Repression in Eighteenth-Century Rural France* (Rochester, NY: University of Rochester Press, 2014), pp. 14-17.

contest).[158] Where Habermas was critiqued for his omission of plebian public spheres or subaltern counter publics, Symes' research on medieval Arras has demonstrated the importance of moving beyond restrictive definitions of the public sphere marked by reading and writing alone, both by identifying oral and gestural modes of communication, and highlighting the manifold means by which those without formal literate capabilities engaged with the 'social, performative and material media through which texts were negotiated, created and published'.[159] Moreover, public engagement was not limited to the formal, institutionalized confines identified by Habermas and Melve. The medieval public sphere was 'out in the open', in the markets, squares and streets that framed interaction between official and everyday communicative practices.[160] Although a text, the Bourgeois' *Journal* functioned as a mirror of and agent in these diverse communicative processes. Consistently recording the rumours, proclamations, ceremonies and protests to which he bore witness, the author transmuted these into writing and conveyed them further to new audiences in his community, thereby consolidating a repertoire of everyday public engagement integral to political expression. As such, the *Journal* emerges as a textual counterpart to the lived public sphere, a vestige of its operation, and representative of a wider discursive, gestural and sonorous culture intertwined with documentary practices.

The *Journal* was a product of multiple, dialogical processes. Indeed, as Klaus Oschema has already argued, texts like the *Journal* are crucial for assessing the question of the public sphere's control during moments of intense factional contest.[161] An interpreter in Melve's sense, the Bourgeois created and bounded a potential audience through his writing, incorporating individuals from neighbourhood, professional, religious and political settings that blur modern distinctions of public and private. Scholars of the Reformation have emphatically demonstrated the ways in which the dissemination of information through visual and oral media, combined with written texts, enabled communities to 'become part of a supra-local movement', facilitating commentary on wider developments and even asserting claims to representativeness and intentions to alter the public fate.[162] Although medieval authorities attempted to control the tenor of public conversation, the *Journal* testifies to peripheral discussions where rumours and opinions abounded, revealing how Parisians deployed political discourse to secure their stake in civic authority. Through

158 Carol Symes, 'Review: Leidulf Melve, *Inventing the Public Sphere: The Public Debate during the Investiture Contest (c. 1030-1122)*', *American Historical Review*, 114 (2009), pp. 468-69. Already, Hélène Millet has highlighted similar processes taking place in the fourteenth century. 'Un bouillon de culture pour l'opinion publique: le temps du Grand Schisme d'Occident' in *Un Moyen Âge pour aujourd'hui*, ed. by Julie Claustre, Olivier Mattéoni and Nicolas Offenstadt (Paris: Presses Universitaires de France, 2010), pp. 347-55.

159 Carol Symes, 'Popular Literacies and the First Historians of the First Crusade', *Past & Present*, 235 (2017), p. 40; Symes, *A Common Stage*.

160 Symes, 'Out in the Open'. See also Adams, 'The Reputation of the Queen', pp. 12-17; Connell, *Popular Opinion*, pp. 217-36.

161 Klaus Oschema, 'Die Öffentlichkeit des Politischen' in *Politische Öffentlichkeit im Spätmittelalter*, ed. by Martin Kintzinger and Bernd Schneidmüller (Ostfildern: Thorbecke, 2011), pp. 73-8.

162 Jan Bloemendal and Arjan van Dixhoorn, 'Literary Cultures and Public Opinion in the Early Modern Low Countries' in *Literary Cultures and Public Opinion in the Low Countries, 1450-1650*, ed. by Jan Bloemendal & Arjan van Dixhoorn (Leiden: Brill, 2011), p. 12; Robert Scribner, 'Oral Culture and the Diffusion of Reformation Ideas', *History of European Ideas*, 5 (1984), pp. 237-57; Adam Fox, 'Rumour, News and Public Opinion', *The Historical Journal*, 40 (1997), pp. 597-620.

the communication of known idioms and evaluation of key topoi, environments, social relationships and authority structures were (re)conceptualized as mutual contexts for political thought.

If discursive power underpins social relations, examining the ways in which Parisians appropriated and experimented with language presents an important window onto the wider contests taking place in fifteenth-century French society.[163] Sandro Landi's recognition that political conversation was (and is) conditioned by innate assumptions rarely addressed explicitly cyclically underscores Mikhail Bakhtin's own argument that expression is bounded by consensual modes of thinking predicated upon a shared discourse.[164] The Bourgeois' writing captures the conventional discourses employed within his community to discuss socio-political issues. With the public sphere, these discourses delineated and reflected an 'opinion community' within which opinions were discussed and innate assumptions regarding issues shared.[165] Opinion communities like these comprised heterogeneous social networks, with the exposure to shared discourse resulting in collective modes of talking and thinking about issues – idioms understood and used in specific contexts vital to the consideration of collective urban identities. Through ongoing communication, environments, social relationships and authority structures are abstracted as mutual contexts for political thought. As a repository for rumour and opinion, the *Journal* encapsulated the political language of a Parisian subgroup connected to the populous right bank, developed often in dialogue with official channels and underscoring Melve's acknowledgement of *heteroglossia*'s place in opinion formation.[166] A recurring theme in this book is the Bourgeois' ability to derive narrative authority by situating his authorial personage as the mediator between competing views among Parisian subgroups and institutions alike. The *Journal*'s compilation in tandem with events enables the historian to breach these distinctions, reducing the distances between idea, text and reality to reveal writing as an inherently politicized action that exposed relationships between self, group and other. Where Brian Stock argued that literate interaction promoted the development of 'textual communities' within which individual interpreters developed normative ideological practices that reformed a group's thought and action, the *Journal* evidences important parallels in textual function in relation to the opinion community framed by the Bourgeois' writing, revealing the vocabularies employed by Parisians through which political, social and historical events were explained, typically with recourse to a moral framework.[167]

Ultimately, the historiographical tendency to isolate the *Journal* from its context, as a passive reflection of Parisian events, has obfuscated the Bourgeois' real, pervasive

---

163 Michel Foucault, 'Power/Knowledge' in Colin Gordon (ed. and trans.), *Foucault: Selected Interviews and Other Writings, 1972-77*, (London: Harvester, 1980), p. 93.

164 Mikhail Bakhtin, 'Discourse in the Novel' in *The Dialogic Imagination*, ed. and trans. by Caryl Emerson and Michael Holquist (Austin, TX: University of Texas Press, 1981), pp. 262-75.

165 For theoretical approaches to opinion communities, see Claudia Strauss, *Making Sense of Public Opinion: American Discourses about Immigration and Social Programs* (Cambridge: Cambridge University Press, 2012).

166 Melve, *Inventing the Public Sphere*, p. 11.

167 Brian Stock, *Listening for the Text: On the Uses of the Past* (London: John Hopkins University Press, 1990). Similar approaches to premodern texts have been used by urban historians. See Brigitte Bedos-Rezak, 'Civic Liturgies and Urban Records in Northern France, 1100-1400' in *City and Spectacle in Medieval Europe*, ed. by Barbara Hanawalt and Kathryn Reyerson (Minneapolis, MN: University of Minnesota Press, 1994), pp. 34-55.

engagement with contemporary political discussion. As an interface between official media, rumour and the Bourgeois' own perspectives, the *Journal* traced dialogical relationships through oral, written and symbolic forms, negotiating between event and audience. By changing our interpretation to appreciate that the *Journal* was produced for an intended, immediate audience, it becomes impossible to treat the narrative as simply an unmediated insight into the Bourgeois' views. Rather, the text reveals collaborative processes whereby author and audience moulded information to suit their shared perspectives. At first glance, these qualities appear emblematic of a 'hidden transcript' in the sense proposed by James C. Scott.[168] And yet, upon reflection, it is more apparent that the transmission of news and the codification of political assumptions reveals the place of Parisian subgroups as agents in the city's public transcript, participating in accepted and expected forms of the 'mémoire oppositionnelle' highlighted by Van Bruaene. Opinion communities were an integral part of this public repertoire. Far from offstage, their collective consolidation of key political narratives and participation in civic debate were part of the continuous tensions that marked ideological hegemony and framed public processes of negotiation.

This volume therefore presents an analysis of political communication that reveals the Bourgeois' engagement at two superposed levels. At the first, the *Journal*'s insights into public opinion facilitated the mapping of authority within civic society. By privileging Parisian responses and opinions, regardless of their facticity or subjectivity, the *Journal* structured dissonances between urban experiences and the messages promoted by civic and royal officials. At a second level, the Bourgeois assessed the moral character of this human interaction. Portrayals of popular poverty, societal upheaval and urban complaint evidenced the moral corruption of the highest echelons of French society. In this schema, political communication structured through a dichotomy of ruler and ruled underpinned a parallel consideration of Christian sin and virtue. More generally, the *Journal* offers insights into the function of opinion and the operation of public spheres in one of fifteenth-century Europe's largest cities. The Bourgeois' interpretation of political communication codified elements of a nascent urban ideology comprising a heteroglossia of repertoires, demonstrating an overlap between multiple communities in medieval urban space. Finally, this selective reconstruction of communication consolidated the boundaries of a Parisian subgroup, articulating values fundamental to their identity and interests to participate directly in the broader realm of public life.

---

168 James C. Scott, *Domination and the Arts of Resistance: Hidden Transcripts* (New Haven, CT: Yale University Press, 1990).

CHAPTER 1

The Bourgeois of Paris and his Community

It is only through a careful assessment of the *Journal*'s internal evidence that information about the author's contexts, his sources, his envisioned audience and the text's potential fifteenth-century readership can be deduced. Typically, editors of the *Journal* have viewed the Bourgeois' audience as being directly related to his institutional identity. As Colette Beaune has argued, prior to 1436 (after which the Bourgeois stopped using second-person addresses in his writing), the *Journal* was destined for an audience that 'ne pouvait guère être nombreux: ses collègues du chapitre ou de l'Université, aptes à apprécier de beaux morceaux d'éloquence'.[1] When these institutions rallied to Charles VII in 1436, the Bourgeois was left without an audience: 'il écrirait alors pour lui, sans modifier pourtant son écriture'.[2] In contrast, Janet Shirley commented that the *Journal*'s style is 'so terse [...] that one wonders whether what we have here is nothing more than notes for a future work, perhaps even to be written by someone else'.[3] This chapter will assess these hypotheses through an examination of the Bourgeois' institutional *milieux* and the correlation between his account and their own records.

Building upon the codicological evidence examined in the introduction, this review of the *Journal*'s topographical and institutional references points to very different conclusions than those reached by earlier editors and scholars. Primarily, it soon becomes apparent that the *Journal*'s content was defined predominantly not by the Bourgeois' ties to Notre-Dame or the University, but his connections to Paris' right bank, especially the inhabitants of the sympathetically Burgundian Halles district, with this relationship ultimately shaping the *Journal*'s political content. The Bourgeois' writing imparts this district's shared memory, accentuated by detailed topographical references, the identification of inhabitants, a concentration upon their institutions' history, conversations with its members and an encapsulation of their political attitudes, each a component of Pierre Nora's *lieux de mémoire* that buttress collective identities.[4] By concentrating upon the Bourgeois' environment, it becomes possible to resituate the *Journal* within wider Parisian political attitudes and discourses, thereby demonstrating the extent to which the text mirrored but also framed the perspectives of localized Parisian communities. As such, this careful consideration of the Bourgeois' contexts significantly counters earlier impressions of the author's reflexive

---

1 Was unlikely to be numerous: his colleagues at the chapter [of Notre-Dame] or the university, those capable of appreciating well-written and eloquent passages. Colette Beaune (ed. and trans.), *Journal d'un bourgeois de Paris de 1405 à 1449* (Paris: Librairie générale française, 1990), p. 18.
2 He then wrote for himself, yet without changing his style. Beaune (ed.), *Journal*, p. 18.
3 Janet Shirley (ed. and trans.), *A Parisian Journal, 1405-49* (Oxford: Clarendon Press, 1968), pp. 24-5.
4 Pierre Nora, 'Between Memory and History: Les Lieux de Mémoire', *Representations*, 26 (1989), p. 12; Paul Ricoeur, *La mémoire, l'histoire, l'oubli* (Paris: Seuil, 2000), pp. 152-63.

bias, and instead demonstrates the importance of using this understudied source for understanding everyday political concerns within the city, contrary to the perspectives and reflections of those writing from a distance beyond its walls, as in the case of Bernard Guenée's study of public opinion through Michel Pintoin's own chronicle produced at the abbey of Saint-Denis.

The Bourgeois' connections to the Halles are highlighted by comparisons with references to the cathedral and chapter of Notre-Dame as well as the University of Paris. Contrary to earlier analyses that have suggested that the Bourgeois was producing his text for a clerical audience affiliated with these latter institutions, the *Journal* actually presents substantially less information regarding these bodies, with some details inaccurate or even contradicting their official records. Though the Bourgeois was a likely member of both, these discrepancies suggest that the *Journal* was not intended for an audience that could have readily referred to these institutional records or the experiences and perspectives of their members. Rather, the Bourgeois synthesized information regarding these leading Parisian institutions for interpretation and consumption by an audience distanced from their internal workings. This is, in turn, supported by the very fact that the manuscript evidence points to the *Journal*'s patronage, not by clerics, but by the Maciot family on the fringes of Paris' municipal elite that rose to prominence in the latter half of the fifteenth century.

Consequently, this chapter challenges conclusions that have interpreted the *Journal* in an isolated manner, resituating the Bourgeois and his writing within its Parisian contexts.[5] It becomes evident that the Bourgeois reinforced the institutional and collective memories of the communities to which he belonged, articulating their political perspectives, their physical contexts and their symbolic place, delineating the right bank as a distinct entity in relation to Parisian factions and institutions. In doing so, the *Journal* emerges as more than an individual's particular and politicized interpretation of their environment, revealing how the Bourgeois actively attempted to influence the political views, morals and social values of his audience while concurrently giving shape to this very community through his writing, demonstrating his function as an interpreter in the public sphere.

The Halles District

Janet Shirley first emphasized the importance of the Bourgeois' connection to Paris' Halles district, with the jurisdictional *quartiers* of Saint-Martin and the Halles the only two mentioned explicitly in the *Journal*.[6] These were two of the sixteen fiscal and municipal districts into which Paris was divided, comprising administratively distinct neighbourhoods and commanded by agents, the *quarteniers*, who carried out the duties of everyday localised policing and tax collection with the support of their delegates, the *cinquanteniers* and *dizainiers*. Together, these were officers of the Hôtel de Ville who relied upon their

---

5 Shirley (ed. and trans.), *A Parisian Journal*, pp. 12-24; Beaune (ed. and trans.), *Journal d'un bourgeois de Paris*, pp. 18-26.

6 *Journal*, pp. 100, 209, 316; Shirley (ed. and trans.), *A Parisian Journal*, pp. 18-20. For the history of this district see Anne Lombard-Jourdan, *Les Halles de Paris et leur quartier (1137-1969)* (Paris: École des Chartes, 2009), pp. 113-32; Jean Favier, *Nouvelle historie de Paris au XVᵉ siècle, 1380-1500* (Paris: Hachette, 1974), pp. 34-6.

localized, informal and often oral knowledge to pursue their daily affairs, with the *quarte-niers* elected at a district level. The *quarteniers* also claimed a higher stake in the city's municipal administration as part of the *corps municipal* and as more permanent officers who participated in the election of the city's four *échevins* and *prévôt des marchands*.

This was not an entirely static or stable system, for two reasons. First, the establishment of the *quartiers* as a military and policing foundation to the *prévôté des marchands* had a chequered history. The *quarteniers* are first mentioned as militia leaders in the context of Étienne Marcel's uprising in 1357, although Michel Pintoin perceived the establishment of *quarteniers*, *dizainiers* and *cinquateniers*, as well as the use of the city chains, as part and parcel of the Maillotins revolt in 1382.[7] Pintoin's association of their creation with the events of 1382 is nevertheless telling. As Charles VI reasserted his authority over the capital, the *prévôté des marchands* and the militia system that had enabled an urban challenge to royal authority were abolished in January 1383, with the city returning to royal control before the system was replaced by a royally appointed and directed *Garde de la prévôté des marchands*, Jean Jouvenel des Ursins, appointed on 27 January 1389. According to Pintoin, this first concession represented a royal effort to regain urban favour, a move emulated in 1412 when Jean sans Peur appealed to Parisian agency and support with the complete restoration of the municipality's privileges, such that the *quarteniers* returned to their duties in neighbourhood administration and political organization.[8] As such, the history of the Parisian *quartiers* is closely intertwined with the city's role in royal and ducal politics just as the Bourgeois began writing in the first decade of the fifteenth century.

Second, what we know of the *quartiers'* organization and membership has come down to us through tax records headed by the name of the *quartenier* responsible, rather than the location of the district, prompting confusion regarding their precise boundaries.[9] At the very least, the Bourgeois' references to the *quartiers* of Saint-Martin and the Halles as geographical spaces – rather than identifying the names of their *quarteniers* – implies he had a clearer vision of the extent and membership of these districts. These two areas stood on either side of the intervening major thoroughfare, the rue Saint-Denis that was central to the Bourgeois' writing. To the west of the street, the Halles *quartier* encompassed its eponymous marketplace, square and possibly the Saints-Innocents church and cemetery as well as the streets to the market's north. Meanwhile, to the east of the rue Saint-Denis, the Saint-Martin *quartier* stretched north from the central place de Grève to the porte Saint-Martin, newly built at the end of the fourteenth century as part of the urban redevel-opment that had seen the city's suburbs subsumed into the district. The Bourgeois' mental landscape certainly encompassed the evolving character of the Saint-Martin *quartier* in the early years of his writing, prompting Auguste Longnon to suggest that the Bourgeois was Jean Beaurigout, the priest of Saint-Nicolas-des-Champs adjacent to the abbey of

7 RSD, I, p. 132. On this history see Robert Descimon and Jean Nagle, 'Les quartiers de Paris du Moyen Âge au XVIIIe siècle. Évolution d'un espace plurifonctionnel', *Annales ESC*, 34 (1979), pp. 958-63; Georges Picot, 'Recherches sur les quartiniers, cinquanteniers et dixainiers de la ville de Paris', *MSHP*, vol. 1 (1875), pp. 132-66.

8 RSD, I, p. 570. For the ordinance regarding the restoration of the *Prévôté des marchands* in 1412, see *Ordonnances des rois de France*, IX, pp. 668-69.

9 See Jean Favier (ed.), *Les contribuables parisiens à la fin de la guerre de Cent Ans: les rôles d'impôt de 1421, 1423 et 1438* (Geneva: Droz, 1970).

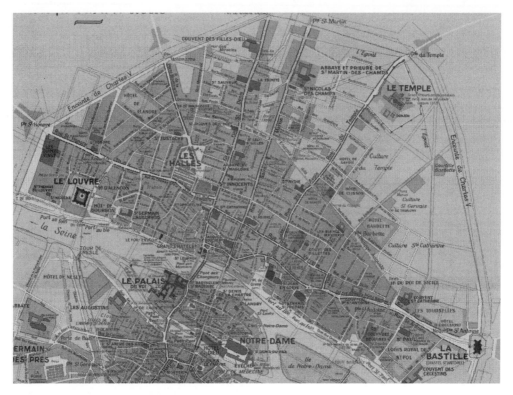

Figure 1. Paris' right bank, as shown on the *Carte de Paris vers la fin du XIVᵉ siècle*. CNRS Éditions. CCØ Paris Musées / Petit Palais, musée des Beaux-Arts de la Ville de Paris.

Saint-Martin-des-Champs on the northernmost point of the rue Saint-Martin.[10] In 1413, the Bourgeois complained that the Cabochien revolt was undone 'en mains de heure que on ne seroit allé de Sainct-Nicolas a Sainct-Laurens', referring to the short distance that separated the church within the walls from the parish just beyond the porte Saint-Martin; in February 1415, a tournament between Spanish and French knights at Saint-Ouen was over in less time 'que on mectroit a aller de la porte Sainct-Martin a celle de Sainct-Anthoine, a cheval'.[11] At the very least, these allusions highlight an individual whose sense of the city was grounded in the geography of the right bank and the commonplaces of the rue Saint-Martin.

The topographical and prosopographical references examined below clearly demonstrate this correlation between the Bourgeois' writing and the political experiences of the Halles.[12] Through these, it can be tentatively suggested that the Bourgeois compiled his

---

10 Auguste Longnon, 'Conjectures sur l'auteur du journal parisien de 1409 à 1449', *MSHP*, 2 (1876), pp. 319-20.

11 In less time that it would take to go from Saint-Nicolas to Saint-Laurent; than it would take to go from the porte Saint-Martin to that of Saint-Antoine by horse. *Journal*, pp. 39, 60.

12 Shirley (ed. and trans.), *A Parisian Journal*, pp. 18-19. For an assessment of Parisian topography, see Bronisław Geremek, *The Margins of Society in Late Medieval Paris*, trans. by Jean Birrel (Cambridge: Cambridge University Press, 1976), pp. 66-78.

Figure 2. Detail, the Halles and the Saints-Innocents (centre). *Carte de Paris vers la fin du XIVe siècle*. CNRS Éditions. CCØ Paris Musées / Petit Palais, musée des Beaux-Arts de la Ville de Paris.

narrative with an audience of the district's inhabitants in mind – most likely the artisans and families occupying the liminal space between an artisanal middling sort of 'mesnaigers' and the 'greigneurs bourgeois' - the urban aristocracy centred on the Hôtel de Ville, the Parlement and the Châtelet.[13] With only one substantial manuscript copy surviving for the fifteenth century, it is difficult to determine how this artisanal audience would have accessed the *Journal*. Stylistically, the sequential presentation of information through *item* means that the Bourgeois plausibly designed his text to be read aloud piecemeal, performing a didactic function as a reference point conflating political news, food prices and the proclamation of ordinances. As such, the text corresponded neatly with the daily functions associated with clerics in Paris for their parochial or institutional audiences, as points of contact that channelled news and information alongside moral teachings. This conclusion is underscored by the Bourgeois' predominant focus upon the Halles area and particularly the Saints-Innocents church, his likely status as a local priest, but also the fact that at least one other cleric produced a narrative with a profoundly similar focus upon events at the

---

13 The late medieval Parisian elite has been studied extensively, see Jean Favier, *Le bourgeois de Paris au Moyen Âge* (Paris: Tallandier, 2012), pp. 415-39; Boris Bove, *Dominer la ville. Prévôts des marchands et échevins parisiens de 1260 à 1350* (Paris: Comité des Travaux Historiques et Scientifiques, 2004); Jean Favier, 'L'élite bourgeoise de Paris et l'expression de sa notabilité entre 1200 et 1400' in *Marquer la prééminence sociale*, ed. by Jean-Philippe Genet and E. Igor Mineo (Paris: Éditions de la Sorbonne, 2014), pp. 95-114; Yvonne-Hélène le Maresquier-Kesteloot, *Les officiers municipaux de la ville de Paris au XVe siècle* (Paris: Commission des travaux historiques de la ville de Paris, 1997), pp. 88-116; Barbara Diefendorf, *Paris City Councillors in the Sixteenth Century: The Politics of Patrimony* (Princeton, NJ: Princeton University Press, 1983); Françoise Autrand, *Naissance d'un grand corps de l'État. Les gens du Parlement de Paris, 1345-1454* (Paris: Publications de la Sorbonne, 1981).

parish level, the 1412-13 journal fragment.[14] Likewise, the prior of Sainte-Catherine-du-Val-des-Écoliers, Jean Maupoint, developed his own journal as a repository for civic ordinances, referring to the official letters to which he had access and placing their content side-by-side with passages assessing contemporary events in the city. In the Bourgeois' case, by privileging the perspectives of the Halles' inhabitants, their participation in political events and their relationship with overarching civic institutions, the *Journal* may also have functioned as an important resource for artisanal families and communities rising to prominence during the political contests of the early fifteenth century, as indicated by the evidence of the text's subsequent ownership. Indeed, benefiting from ongoing political instability and connections to the Burgundian dukes, during the Lancastrian occupation of Paris several families based in the Halles, and who increasingly codified their dynastic memories through contributions to the fabric of Saints-Innocents, rose to prominence in the municipal administration.[15]

The Bourgeois' experiences in this district shaped his writing. A proximity to the Halles marketplace underpinned the *Journal*'s record concerning food supplies and prices as demonstrated by his eyewitness testimony, such as in June 1419 when, following a truce between the Armagnacs and Burgundians, cheeses 'estoient es Halles entassez aussi haults que ung homme' or in 1446 when there were piles of pears 'es Halles de Paris comme je vy oncques de charbon a la Croix de Greve [...] vj ou vij tas sans garde'.[16] It was also in these spaces that the Bourgeois would have encountered the publication of official information, with ten executions reported as taking place in the square north of the Halles market, accompanied by 'le cry que on fist es Halles quant on les decolla'.[17] In September 1413, the Bourgeois noted the publication at the Halles of the peace instated by the Armagnac government as a mark of their newly won control over the rebellious district.[18]

The density of living and working conditions within medieval cities resulted in inhabitants being involved in near-constant interaction, and this was especially true of the Halles, complementing the circulation of information and presenting a challenge to official media as information spread through the informal networks that shaped and enabled political action. For instance, at the Halles marketplace, the acute food shortages experienced in 1420 were underscored by the testimony of the Halle de Beauvais' butchers who

> juroient et affermoient, par la foy de leurs corps, qu'ilz avoient veu par maintes années devant passées que en l'ostel d'un seul boucher de Paris, a ung tel jour, on avoit tué plus de char que on ne fist en toutes les boucheries de Paris.[19]

---

14 Rome, Vatican Library, Reg. Lat. 1502 (vol. 1), fols 103r-108v.

15 Guy Thompson, *Paris and its People under English Rule: The Anglo-Burgundian Regime, 1420-36* (Oxford: Clarendon Press, 1991), pp. 55-61, 153-58, 165-72.

16 Were in piles as tall as a man in the Halles; In Paris' Halles, just as I have seen coal at the Croix de Grève in the past [...] six or seven piles, all unguarded. *Journal*, pp. 125, 384.

17 The cry pronounced at the Halles when they were beheaded. *Journal*, p. 297. On the Halles' jurisdictions see Anne Lombard-Jourdan, 'La ville étudiée dans ses quartiers: autour des Halles de Paris au moyen âge', *Annales d'histoire économique et sociale*, 7 (May 1935), pp. 292-93.

18 *Journal*, p. 46.

19 Swore and confirmed, upon their faith, that in many of the years past they had seen at the stall of a single Parisian butcher, on any day, more meat slaughtered than was now done at all of the butchers' stalls of Paris. *Journal*, p. 138.

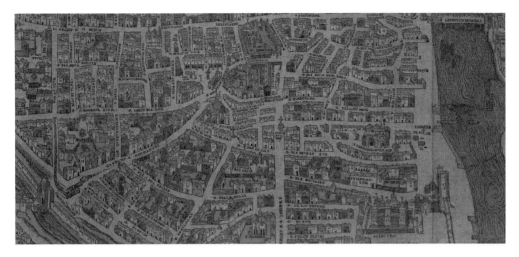

Figure 3. Detail, the Halles District. Saints-Innocents, Sainte-Opportune and the Halles market (top-centre), Saint-Eustache (centre), Saint-Germain-l'Auxerrois (centre-right), the Louvre (bottom-right). Truschet and Hoyau map (c.1553). University Library Basel Kartenslg AA 124.

Such testimony evidences the contact between local clergymen, such as the Bourgeois, and merchants. The Saints-Innocents clergy were subject to the authority of the nearby Sainte-Opportune church, which asserted historic links to the neighbouring markets.[20] On 25 April 1419 parishioners including Hugues Rapiout and Jean Vaillant lamented Sainte-Opportune's poverty, rendering services at the Notre-Dame-du-Bois chapel impossible, despite the fact that it was there that Mass was first sung 'de toutes les marchés et eglises voisines'.[21]

During the first decades of his writing, the Bourgeois concentrated upon the contested character of municipal authority, recording the vicissitudes of the Halles' experiences, while with the reassertion of Valois authority in 1436 the *Journal*'s tenor shifted, focusing increasingly upon the Saints-Innocents as an important Parisian centre while juxtaposing the experiences of the civic community with processes of royal centralization. In doing so, the *Journal* evoked the practices through which inhabitants of the right bank had secured increasing participation in municipal politics during the 1410s and 1420s, before this authority was threatened by the reassertion of direct royal authority. Their rise was conditioned by the reconfiguration of the relationship between the capital and royal centre developed through revolt, the municipality's suppression in 1383 and its reinstatement by

20 Anne Lombard-Jourdan, *Paris, genèse de la ville: La Rive Droite de la Seine des origines à 1223* (Paris: Éditions du CNRS, 1978), pp. 72, 74-5; Hélène Verlet, *Épitaphier du Vieux Paris: vol. 6, Les Saints-Innocents* (Paris: Comité des Travaux Historiques de la Ville de Paris, 1997), p. lii.
21 Of all the markets and neighbouring churches. Paris, Archives nationales, JJ 170, fols 248r-v, no. 304. Hugues Rapiout was *prévôt des marchands* between 1431 and 1434, succeeding Guillaume Sanguin (see below), a detail reported by the Bourgeois, *Journal*, p. 300. Jean Vaillant was a taverner who inhabited the Sainte-Opportune cloister. Le Maresquier-Kesteloot, *Les officiers municipaux*, p. 147, no. 44.

Jean sans Peur in January 1412 as a means of securing his influence over the city.[22] The *Journal*'s concentration upon this district therefore elucidates how these men asserted a newly acquired political status.

The Halles had a reputation for subversive tendencies and Burgundian sympathies during the 1410s.[23] The evocation of these same attitudes in the *Journal* reveals a clear coincidence between the Bourgeois' own political stance and the perspectives of this community. In August 1413, the *quarteniers* of Saint-Eustache north of the Halles marketplace refused to endorse the Treaty of Pontoise that would bring an end to the Cabochien revolt, and which required the assent of the Parisian municipality. When the *quarteniers* were summoned on 3 August by the Cabochien leader, Jean de Troyes, to dispute the peace proposed by the princes, only those of the 'deux quartiers de devers les Halles, et l'hostel d'Artois ou estoit logé le duc de Bourgongne' continued to side with the movement.[24] Following the treaty, the anonymous Cordelier recorded how 'ce non obstant, ceulx du quartier des Halles demourerent tousjours bourguignon couvertement'.[25] Jean sans Peur maintained contact with the Halles' inhabitants and in February 1414 royal edicts revealed that the duke had sent 'certaines lectres patentes scellées de son séel secret […] et icelles fist affichier de nuyt et secretement aux porteaulx de plusieurs eglises'.[26] On 11 December 1415, a *pâtissier* from the Saint-Jacques-de-la-Boucherie parish south of the Halles was executed for sending letters to the duke claiming that five thousand Parisians were ready 'a le recevoir et ly ouvrir la porte de Montmartre ou de Saint-Honoré' (the two gates closest to the Halles).[27] His execution provoked 'grant murmure de sedition', compelling the Armagnac governors to take measures to prevent an uprising.[28] A conspiracy discovered at Easter 1416 had planned to rally the district's population at Saints-Innocents before assaulting the Louvre to detain dukes Jean of Berry and Louis of Anjou.[29] A later chronicle compiled in or around 1429, the *Geste des nobles francoys*, reported that the conspirators proposed 'de faire eslever par nuit, au son de la cloiche de Saint-Eustace, le commun peuple des Halles, et a celle heure courir sus a touz ceulx qui du duc de Bourgoigne estoient contraires'.[30]

---

22 Paris, Archives nationales, K 950 A, no. 10 'Rétablissement de la prévôté des marchands, (Paris, 20 January 1412)'; Jean Favier, *Paris au XVe siècle, 1380-1500* (Paris: Hachette, 1974), pp. 140-52; Thompson, *Paris and its People*, pp. 54-66; Louis Battifol, 'La prévôté des marchands de Paris à la fin du XIVe siècle', *BEC*, 52 (1891), p. 274; *Ordonnances des rois de France*, IX, pp. 668-70.

23 Werner Paravicini, 'Paris, capitale des ducs de Bourgogne?', *Beihefte der Francia*, 64 (2007), pp. 473-76.

24 The two *quartiers* near the Halles, and the Hôtel d'Artois where the duke of Burgundy resided. *Histoire de Charles VI*, p. 484; RSD, V, p. 86. These *quartiers* were, most likely, those of the Halles, Sainte-Opportune and Saint-Eustache.

25 Despite this, those of the Halles *quartier* remained Burgundians in secret. Paris BNF Fr. 23018, fol. 347r.

26 Certain letters patent sealed with his seal […] and at night had these affixed secretly to the doorways of several churches. 'Lettres patentes des 17 et 20 février 1413, contre le duc de Bourgogne', ed. by Louis Douët-d'Arcq in Monstrelet, VI, pp. 152-61. See also. Monstrelet, II, pp. 433-37.

27 To receive him and open the porte de Montmartre or the porte Saint-Honoré. Baye, II, p. 228.

28 Baye, II, p. 229; *Histoire de Charles VI*, pp. 524-25.

29 Léon Mirot, 'Le procès du Boiteux d'Orgemont. Épisode des troubles parisiens pendant la lutte des Armagnacs et des Bourguignons (Suite et fin). Quatrième partie: La vie politique et le procès du Boiteux d'Orgemont', *Le Moyen Âge*, 25 (1912), pp. 368-75; *Histoire de Charles VI*, pp. 531-32; Monstrelet, III, pp. 139-41. For the Bourgeois' account of the sentencing of the conspirators, *Journal*, pp. 70-2.

30 To rally the commons of the Halles at night by the sound of the Saint-Eustache bell, and at that hour ambush all of those opposed to the duke of Burgundy. 'Geste des nobles Francoys' ed. by Vallet de Viriville in *Chronique de la Pucelle*

Throughout the first decades of the fifteenth century, the *Journal* concentrated upon the conversations and reputations of those who were prevalent on the city's right bank, tracing these in relation to major upheavals and political shifts. When the Burgundians captured the capital on 29 May 1418 the Halles emerged as a centre of Burgundian support, with the Saint-Eustache church becoming the site of a confraternity dedicated to St. Andrew, Burgundy's patron saint. The *Journal* emphasises that the more than 720 rose garlands produced for the confraternity were taken up before the end of the morning.[31] The Bourgeois' own ties to the district are signalled through his account of the massacres that summer. On 20 June, he reported how a Châtelet *sergent*, Pierre Boudaut, had been commissioned to massacre the inhabitants of the Halles days before the Burgundian entry to subjugate the duke's supporters. The passage's stress upon Boudaut's residence, 'demourant en la grant rue Sainct-Denis', suggests that he was known locally and perhaps represented a figure of vilification, not least because of his complicity in the disbanding of the prominent butchers' corporation in 1416.[32] The Bourgeois' emphatic denunciation of a municipal officer bent on annihilating the Halles certainly evidences the author's own awareness of the district's Burgundian reputation, and a perception of Armagnac efforts to eradicate support for Jean sans Peur in the city. Indeed, Guy Thompson has shown that the Burgundian duke relied upon 'a substantial sector of society, including many clerics, the well-organized municipal hierarchy and the inhabitants of the Halles to support him against the threat of an Armagnac resurgence'.[33] Of 222 known beneficed clerics who swore the oath of fealty to Jean sans Peur in 1418, 35% were clergymen of Notre-Dame cathedral and 32% belonged to churches in the Halles region, contrasting with just fifteen (7%) for the Grève and twenty-one (9%) for the left bank.[34]

The *Journal*'s focus upon this Burgundian-leaning, artisanal district parallels a broader, growing merchant interest in historical writing during the late Middle Ages. This is best demonstrated by the London Chronicles, which Mary-Rose McLaren has argued satisfied 'broad-based interest' in civic affairs and attempt to develop 'a documentary or perhaps an official history' inherently based upon the lived experiences of middle-class citizens,

---

ou *Chronique de Cousinot suivie de la Chronique normande de P. Cochon* (Paris: Adolphe Delahays, 1859), pp. 153-54. For the dating of this chronicle, see Philippe Contamine, 'Une chronique pour un prince? Le "Geste des nobles Francois"', *Pariser Historische Studien*, 47 (1998), pp. 239-34.

31 *Journal*, p. 95. See also Charlotte Denoël, *Saint André: Culte and iconographie en France (V^e-XVe siècles)* (Paris: École des Chartes, 2004), p. 93; Catherine Vincent, *Les confréries médiévales dans le royaume de France, XIIIe-XVe siècles* (Paris: Albin Michel, 1994), p.107.

32 Residing in the grand-rue Saint-Denis. *Journal*, pp. 99-100. The 1416-17 city accounts reveal that the *prévôt* Tanneguy du Chastel dispatched Pierre Boudaut to Paris' suburbs to announce the sale of the newly created butchers' stalls around Paris to the highest bidder in an effort to fragment the butcher families' monopoly on the industry. Henri Sauval, *Histoire et recherches des antiquités de la ville de Paris*, 3 vols (Paris: Moette and Chardon, 1724), III, p. 274.

33 Thompson, *Paris and its People*, p. 158.

34 The remainder belonged to churches on the Île-de-la-Cité, with 13% at the Sainte-Chapelle. Thompson, *Paris and its People*, pp. 152-55. To collate this data Thompson used the list of those who swore fealty to Jean sans Peur, 'État des bourgeois de Paris qui prêtèrent serment entre les mains de Jean sans Peur, duc de Bourgogne' in *Paris et ses historiens aux XIVe et XVe siècles. Documents et écrits originaux*, ed. by Antoine le Roux de Lincy and Lazare-Maurice Tisserand (Paris: Imprimerie impériale, 1867), pp. 371-89.

preserved for posterity.[35] Through writing, the Bourgeois elaborated processes whereby the Parisians of the Halles endeavoured to record and make sense of the events that they witnessed, participated in, and considered important. Asserting control over the city's history and its narratives during an era of political turbulence enabled the inhabitants of the Halles rising in civic politics to negotiate their place in the broader hierarchies constituting Parisian civic society. This focus upon the Halles persisted even as the animosities between the Burgundians and Armagnacs dissipated in the later years of the Bourgeois' writing, with the author drawing information from the locality and documenting its inhabitants' memories, moulding the Halles' population into a cohesive group through the references to the district's community and topography.[36] In 1430, the Bourgeois related how 'une jeune fille née des Halles' rescued a brigand from execution by proposing to marry him; in the winter of 1438, wolves devoured a child 'en la place aux Chatz derriere les Innocens'.[37] When the Lancastrian *prévôt* Simon Morhier and the remainder of Paris' English garrison attacked the Halles during the Valois reconquest in April 1436, the Bourgeois reported the deaths of 'ung tres bon marchant nommé le Vavasseur' as well as 'Jehan le Prebstre et ung autre nommé Jehan des Croustez [...] tres bons mesnaigers et hommes de honneur' outside the parish church of Saint-Merry on the rue Saint-Martin.[38] Although Elisabeth Hodges has argued that the Bourgeois' inclusion of named individuals represented material for the elaboration of a totalizing urban history, many of those named can be identified as simply having a specific relevance for the Halles and its surrounding quartier.[39] Like the sergeant Boudaut, in 1418 the Bourgeois criticized an obscure Armagnac, Pierre le Gayant, described as a 'personne sismatique, herite contre la foy'.[40] However, the distribution of properties confiscated by the Lancastrian regime reveals that Gayant owned a house situated on the rue des Arcis opposite Saint-Merry, suggesting that he, too, was known locally.[41] An apparently miscellaneous passage in June 1418 describes Vincent Lormoy's appointment as a Châtelet *procureur du roi*, but evidence from the available tax records

35 Mary-Rose McLaren, 'The Aims and Interests of the London Chroniclers of the Fifteenth Century', in *Trade, Devotion and Governance: Papers in Later Medieval History*, ed. by Dorothy J. Clayton, Richard G. Davies and Peter McNiven (Stroud: Sutton, 1994), pp. 162-63, 170-71.

36 Similar roles for urban historiography have been demonstrated by Lisa Demets and Jan Dumolyn, 'Urban chronicle writing in late medieval Flanders: the case of Bruges during the Flemish Revolt of 1482-90', *Urban History*, 43 (2016), pp. 44-5; Jan Dumolyn, Johann Oosterman, Tjamke Snijders and Stijn Villerius, 'Rewriting Chronicles in an Urban Environment. The Dutch "Excellent Chronicle of Flanders" Tradition', *Lias*, 41 (2014), p. 95.

37 A young girl born in the Halles; in the place aux Chats behind Saints-Innocents. *Journal*, p. 250. A similar case whereby a woman saved a prisoner from the English garrison of Pontoise, held in the abbey of Saint-Martin-des-Champs north of the Halles, was reported by the Bourgeois in 1442.

38 A very good merchant named [...] le Vavasseur; Jehan le Prebstre and another named Jehan des Croustez, good householders and men of honour. *Journal*, pp. 316-17.

39 Elisabeth Hodges, *Urban Poetics in the Renaissance* (Aldershot: Ashgate, 2008), pp. 28-9.

40 A schismatic person, a heretic against the faith. *Journal*, p. 94. Pierre le Gayant is found serving as the *greffier criminel du Châtelet* from at least 1393. Already in 1406-08, le Gayant had been the subject of an inquest regarding his abuse of authority. See Henri Duplès-Agier (ed.), *Registre criminel du Châtelet de Paris du 6 septembre 1389 au 18 mai 1392*, 2 vols, (Paris: Lahure, 1861-64), I (1861), p. xiv; Gustave Fagniez, 'Fragment d'un répertoire de jurisprudence parisienne au XVe siècle'. *MSHP*, 17 (1890), pp. 43-44.

41 'Compte des confiscations de Paris, depuis le 20 décembre 1423' in Sauval, *Histoire et recherches*, III, p. 308.

indicates that Lormoy is recorded in 1421 as living in the Saint-Martin *quartier*.[42] Likewise, in 1433, the Bourgeois briefly noted how Philippe de Morvilliers was dismissed as the *premier président* in the Parlement, being replaced by Robert Piédefer, 'demourant pour lors empres la porte Sainct-Martin'.[43]

The right bank's importance to the Bourgeois' sense of community is underscored by the passages dedicated to activities in the Halles region. After Easter 1425, the *Journal* described the efforts of the Saint-Martin *quartier*'s inhabitants to repair the porte Saint-Martin, which had been walled up, 'a leurs coustz et despens'.[44] The Bourgeois proudly stated that 'les habitans de la grant rue Saint-Martin y firent si grant diligence et si bonne de leur peine et de leur argent, que on povait bien dire que ilz avoient le cueur a l'euvre'.[45] The attention paid to the clergy's involvement again points to the ties between lay and religious members of the district, with the labour fostering community bonds. Once the gate was open, the Saint-Martin inhabitants 'firent bonne chere ce jour de Sainct Laurens', now able to process beyond the city walls to the church of Saint-Laurent to celebrate the feast as a testament to the inhabitants' devotion and the importance of local traditions, with the Bourgeois reporting that 'dist on que passé avoit xxx ans on n'y avoit veu passer autant de gens comme ce jour y passa'.[46] Indeed, this passage alone situates the Bourgeois in conversation with other members of the *quartier*, drawing upon their memories to underscore the significance of the gate's reopening in their own lifetimes. When the gate was closed again on 14 September the following year, the Bourgeois similarly portrayed this event as concerning the entire community of the *quartier*. Here, the *dizainiers* and other honourable bourgeois in the neighbourhood joined to successfully petition the *prévôt des marchands* and *échevins* to reopen the gate. In relating the *prévôt des marchands*' response to the petition, that 'Entre vous bourgeois et mesnaigers ceste porte soit ouverte et gardée a voz perilz', the Bourgeois further underscored the community endeavour that focused upon the preservation of local infrastructure.[47]

These specific allusions to the Saint-Martin *quartier* and its inhabitants can also help us to determine the socio-professional character of the Bourgeois' neighbourhood, with reference to the surviving tax rolls for 1421 and 1438.[48] In 1421, 188 individuals representing

---

42 *Journal*, p. 99. Favier, *Les contribuables*, p. 197, no. A1048. See also Olivier Martin (ed.), 'Sentences civils du Châtelet de Paris (1395-1505), publiées d'après les registres originaux. (Suite)', *Nouvelle revue historique de droit français et étranger*, 38 (1914), pp. 67-8, no. 69.

43 At that time residing near the porte Saint-Martin. Robert Piédefer is found inhabiting the *quartier* in the tax roll of 1421. Favier, *Les contribuables*, p. 198.

44 At their cost and expense. *Journal*, p. 203.

45 The inhabitants of the grande rue Saint-Martin worked with such great diligence and so well through their efforts and their money, that it can truly be said that they had their hearts in the work. *Journal*, p. 204.

46 Held great celebrations this St. Laurent's day; it was said that so many people had not been seen passing through the gate in thirty years, as passed through that day. *Journal*, p. 204.

47 May this gate be opened and guarded by you, the bourgeois and householders, at your peril. *Journal*, p. 209.

48 This data is presented in 'Quartier Jehan de Vaynes' in *Les contribuables*, pp. 194-208. For the identification of this *quartier* see Jean Guerout, 'Fiscalité, topographie et démographie à Paris au Moyen Âge', *BEC*, 130 (1972), pp. 99-100. It is important to note that the precise boundaries of the *quartiers* are unknown, and that even the association of specific geographical districts with individual *quarteniers* was debated by Jean Favier and Jean Guérout in the 1970s. See Jean-Philippe Genet, 'Compte rendu. Jean Guérout, Fiscalité, topographie et démographie à Paris au Moyen Âge', *Annales ESC*, 31 (1976), pp. 1162-63; Jean Favier, 'Les rôles d'impôt parisiens du XVe siècle (à propos d'un article récent)', *BEC*, 130 (1972), pp. 467-91.

forty-seven professions were sufficiently wealthy to be taxed, including bakers, leatherwork-ers, taverners and metalworkers.[49] The prevalence of the latter may explain the Bourgeois' isolated comment regarding the low price of metals in January 1419, and it is in the rue Saint-Martin that the Guillebert De Mets identified the 'ouvriers d'arein' residing in his 1434 *Description* of the city.[50] Moreover, although Saint-Martin featured the highest num-ber of people taxed in the Grève region, it was also the poorest in terms of contributions to the 1421 tax. Here, the average individual contribution for Saint-Martin was 3 ounces, 11 sterling silver, half the Grève region's average of 7 ounces, 7 sterling.[51] While the tax excluded day-labourers and 'frappe dans leur ensemble quelques gros métiers', the data suggests that Saint-Martin was densely populated and home to a high proportion of a 'middling sort' of artisans susceptible to the increasing taxation that rendered them natural supporters of Burgundian antifiscal rhetoric.[52] Revealing the professional heterogeneity and artisanal dominance of the *quartier*, the tax data implies that the Bourgeois may have resided in one of Paris' poorer neighbourhoods on the right bank, while his profession was focused upon the wealthier area surrounding the Halles market.[53]

The Bourgeois' connection to these *quartiers* is further highlighted by the description of festivities organized by the Saint-Leu-Saint-Giles parish in 1425, when 'proposerent aucuns de la parroisse faire ung esbatement', with a goose and money placed upon a greased pole as a prize for whoever could reach the top.[54] Where historians have attributed such events to the Lancastrian regime's policy of 'bread and circuses', the Bourgeois again exhibited a localized pride through his emphasis upon the parishioners' agency in organizing the entertainment that left little room for an acknowledgement of Lancastrian influences.[55] A similar event was the 'jeu des aveugles et du cochon' held at the Hôtel d'Armagnac on the rue Saint-Honoré west of the Saints-Innocents in August that same year, whereupon blind men armed with clubs entered an enclosure to attempt to kill a pig, the entertainment derived from the amusement of seeing the blind men strike one another in their efforts.[56] Olivier Richard has suggested that the game was introduced to Paris through Burgundian influences, with its organization communicating implicit political messages: 'le choix du lieu et du spectacle revêt un caractère politique évident. Il vise à ridiculiser les Armagnacs,

---

49 Many of those taxed were not identified by profession. Favier, *Les contribuables*, pp. 16-17.

50 *Journal*, p. 121; Guillebert De Mets, 'Description de la ville de Paris' in *Paris et ses historiens aux XIVe et XVe siècles*, ed. by Antoine le Roux de Lincy and Maurice-Lazare Tisserand (Paris: Imprimerie impériale, 1867), p. 209.

51 That is, the average for the six *quartiers* constituting the Grève region. This evaluation is based on the data presented in Favier, *Les contribuables*, p. 62.

52 Largely concerned several key industries. Favier, *Les contribuables*, p. 41.

53 Geremek, *The Margins of Society*, pp. 72, 74. The disparity in wealth between the Halles and Saint-Martin *quartiers* is substantiated by the more complete tax records for 1438, where the average contribution in the Halles was 33% higher than that of Saint-Martin. Favier, *Les contribuables*, p. 62.

54 Some of the parishioners proposed an amusement. *Journal*, pp. 204-05.

55 Auguste Vallet de Viriville, *Histoire de Charles VII, roi de France, et de son époque, 1403-61*, 3 vols (Paris: Jules Renouard, 1862-65), II (1863), p. 325; Thompson, *Paris and its People*, p. 192.

56 *Journal*, p. 204. Rightly, this example has recently come to the fore in studies of medieval attitudes towards disability. See Irina Metzler, *A Social History of Disability in the Middle Ages: Cultural Considerations of Physical Impairment* (London: Routledge, 2013), p. 163.

assimilés à ces pauvres combattants'.[57] However, although the Bourgeois named the loca-tion the 'Hôtel d'Armagnac', in 1418 it had passed to Philippe le Bon, duke of Burgundy and was formally named the 'Hôtel de Charolais' in official documentation, making it more likely that the duke was using his property to accentuate his personal ties to the Halles region.[58] In 1412 and August 1418, Jean sans Peur had similarly opened his Hôtel d'Artois in the Saint-Eustache parish to the commons, inviting Parisians to banquets to strengthen these same bonds.[59]

The management and development of the Halles' parish churches also represented an important means of consolidating this Burgundian affiliation and shaping community net-works.[60] As already seen above, the church of Saint-Eustache had become a key centre for Burgundian sympathisers following the 1418 coup, when the confraternity of St. Andrew held its celebrations. Deep ties in the history of the locality bound the confraternity, its members and the parish community to the Burgundian household. Not only was Jean sans Peur's Parisian residence located within the Saint-Eustache parish, but the chaplains of the Saint-André chapel in the parish church were also the *seigneurs* of the fief de Gif upon which the Burgundian Hôtel d'Artois had been built, meaning that the close connections between the Burgundian duke and his Halles followers was rooted in the jurisdictional makeup of the district.[61] As a result of this interconnection, Saint-Eustache 'en tant que paroissiale des ducs [...] était l'un des lieux de dévotion qu'ils fréquentaient et aussi un sanctuaire qui attirait leurs bienfaits'.[62]

The importance of other churches to the maintenance of Burgundian networks can also be deciphered in the Bourgeois' writing. For instance, an apparently miscellaneous reference to the singing of the canonical hours at Saint-Jacques-de-la-Boucherie on 16 January 1429, 'comme a Notre-Dame', assumes new meaning in light of the donation made in 1426 by Jean Fortier, counsellor to the dukes of Burgundy and parish churchwar-den, to support precisely these prayers.[63] As such, the record of their singing evokes the Bourgeois' interest in Burgundian investments that underscored the common and spiritual good of his district. The Halles region was also a centre for the butchers' corporation, whose experiences the Bourgeois closely followed between 1416 and 1418 and whose

57 The choice of spectacle and location exhibits a clear political character. It sought to ridicule the Armagnacs, who were compared to the poor [blind] combatants. Olivier Richard, 'Le jeu des aveugles et du cochon. Rite, handicap et société urbaine à la fin du Moyen Âge', *Revue historique*, 675 (2015), p. 547.

58 Archives départementales du Nord B 1923, fols 203v-204r, cited in Florence Berland, 'La Cour de Bourgogne à Paris (1363-1422)' (unpublished doctoral thesis, Université de Lille 3, 2011), p. 92.

59 Ernest Petit, *Itinéraires de Philippe le Hardi et de Jean sans Peur, ducs de Bourgogne (1363-1419)* (Paris: Imprimerie nationale, 1888), pp. 443-44; Florence Berland, 'Access to the Prince's Court in Late Medieval Paris' in *The Key to Power? The Culture of Access in Princely Courts, 1400-1750* ed. by Dries Raeymaekers and Sebastiaan Derks (Leiden: Brill, 2016), p. 36.

60 Paravicini, 'Paris, capitale', pp. 473-74; Paravicini and Schnerb, 'Les "investissements" religieux', pp. 197-209.

61 Anne Lombard-Jourdan, 'Fiefs et justices parisiens au quartier des Halles', *BEC*, 134 (1976), pp. 340-47.

62 As the parish church of the dukes [...] was one of the devotional places that they frequented as well as a sanctuary that attracted their sponsorship. Paravicini and Schnerb, 'Les "investissements" religieux', p. 197.

63 As at Notre-Dame. *Journal*, p. 233. For Fortier and his donation, see Étienne Villain, *Essai d'une histoire de la paroisse de Saint-Jacques-de-la-Boucherie* (Paris: Praolt, 1758), pp. 108-09; Pierre Cockshaw, *Prosopographie des secrétaires de la cour de Bourgogne (1384-1477)* (Ostfildern: Jan Thorbecke Verlag, 2006), p. 40, no. 30. The best study of Saint-Jacques-de-la-Boucherie is Laurence Fritsch-Pinaud, 'La vie paroissiale à Saint-Jacques-de-la-Boucherie au XVe siècle', *MSHP*, 33 (1982), esp. pp. 52-61.

fortunes were intimately tied to those of the dukes of Burgundy. When the corporation was reinstated in 1418, the Saint-Louis chapel in Saint-Jacques-de-la-Boucherie became the site for its confraternity.[64] Like Fortier, the butchers played a crucial role in Burgundian politics, with its members leading the Cabochien revolt and later rising to prominence in the Anglo-Burgundian administration.[65] The Bourgeois' attention to the corporation's experience after 1416 may have been driven by local concerns, especially since several participants in the 1416 conspiracy owned houses along the rues Saint-Martin and Saint-Denis.[66] Examples like Saint-Jacques-de-la-Boucherie reveal the extent to which political connections and factional affiliation underscored the patronage of and investment in the city's spiritual and monumentary landscape, signalling the contributions of these families to the city's common good. As we shall see in the following section, the leading members of the Halles concentrated these energies in the cemetery and church of Saints-Innocents, with the memories enshrined in this institution permeating the Bourgeois' own record.

The church and cemetery of the Saints-Innocents

The relationships between geographical, professional, dynastic and political elements are encapsulated by the Bourgeois' specific attention to the Saints-Innocents, a parish church and urban cemetery that represented a heterogenous space of competing jurisdictions and influences. Indeed, the cemetery was a prominent site for meetings and festivities, processions, sermons and economic exchanges as well as criminal activities.[67] For this very reason, the communicative endeavours of artisans and bourgeois, dukes and monarchs within the cemetery's space reveals its potent character as a microcosm of the public sphere in late medieval Paris, a space whose symbolic centrality to the identity of the Halles neighbourhood and the city itself was codified through the *Journal*. The Bourgeois' proximity to this particular church was exhibited in his writing from 1436, whereupon the church emerges as the second most-mentioned by the author after Notre-Dame cathedral. This includes the report of a fight between beggars in the church's nave in June 1436; the attention paid to the church's professional confraternities, with the *pelletiers* celebrating their first Mass for Mary's Assumption in the Saint-François chapel in August 1437; the impact of the cemetery's closure by the bishop Denis du Moulin for four months in 1441;

---

64 Sylvain Leteux, 'Liberalisme et corporatisme chez les bouchers parisiens (1776-1944)' (unpublished doctoral thesis, Université Charles de Gaulle – Lille 3, 2005), p. 65; Fritsch-Pinaud, 'La vie paroissiale', pp. 11-13.

65 Thompson, *Paris and its People*, p. 160; Benoît Descamps, 'La toile [sociale] et la trame [urbaine]: la place des bouchers parisiens au Moyen Âge', *Anthropology of Food*, 13 (2019), https//journals.openedition.org/aof/9814; Alfred Coville, *Les Cabochiens et l'ordonnance de 1413* (Paris: Hachette, 1888), pp. 101-05, 148-52, 185-91.

66 These include individuals such as Guillaume Sanguin, who inhabited a house on the rue des Bourdonnais, Augustin Ysbarre who owned houses on the rue de la Chanvrerie and rue des Lombards, and Jean le Courtillier, who owned a house on the rue de la Mortellerie near the place de Grève. Guillebert De Mets, 'Description de la ville de Paris', p. 200. Those implicated in the conspiracy are identified in Léon Mirot, *Les d'Orgemont. Leur origine, leur fortune – le Boiteux d'Orgemont* (Paris: Champion, 1913), p. 185.

67 Paris, Archives nationales Y 2, fol. 217r. Examples of criminal behaviour and trade practices, ranging from pickpocketing and the fencing of stolen goods to the fabrication of poisons, can be found in Duplès-Agier (ed.), *Registre criminel du Châtelet de Paris*; II (1864), pp. 386, 422-25. See also Geremek, *The Margins of Society*, p. 86; Vanessa Harding, *The Dead and the Living in Paris and London* (Cambridge: Cambridge University Press, 2002), pp. 104-06.

the construction of a new cottage for the anchorite Jeanne la Verrière in 1442; and, lastly, the church's dedication by Denis du Moulin in 1445.[68]

Established in the twelfth century, the Saints-Innocents parish was miniscule. Hemmed in between the much larger parishes of Saint-Eustache, Saint-Merry, Sainte-Opportune and Saint-Germain-l'Auxerrois, the parish comprised the streets that ran the length of its cemetery's boundaries.[69] Nevertheless, despite its small size, the cemetery and church occupied a central place in the contemporary vision of the city, its history closely intertwined with the development of the adjoining Halles marketplace. As early as 1186, the Dionysian monk Rigord recorded that 'cimeterium enim illud antiquitus fuerat platea grandis, omnibus transeuntibus pervia et vendendis mercibus exposita'.[70] By the end of the fourteenth century, Raoul de Presles remarked in his translation of St. Augustine's *City of God* that the cemetery had been established outside the city 'si comme l'en le faisoit anciennement', only to be reabsorbed as the city expanded: 'Pres de ce cimetiere l'en commenca a faire le marchié [...] Et puis petit a petit y ediffierent maisons; et y fist l'en hales pour vendre toutes manieres de denrées'.[71] This perception of the space's heterogeneity – part market, part place of worship – endured in the fifteenth century. While the largest cemetery framed a dense array of religious activities encompassing funerals, obits, processions and sermons, it had to struggle against the market activities from the crowded Halles that spilled into the cemetery's space. As a place of passage, the majority of the goods unloaded by barge at the place de Grève or travelling from the left bank cut across the cemetery for direct access to the market halls.[72] Meanwhile, the Parisian chapter, the *prévôté* and the churchwardens of Saints-Innocents pursued a continual struggle to regulate and restrict the economic activities taking place in the cemetery, where sellers of books, clothes and metals displayed their wares on the tombstones.[73] The cemetery and church also represented a confluence of distinct Parisian jurisdictions: the priest of Saints-Innocents was appointed by the canons of Sainte-Opportune, themselves subject to the chapter of Saint-Germain-l'Auxerrois.[74] The cemetery was divided between the administrators of the Hôtel-Dieu, the rue Saint-

---

68 *Journal*, pp. 325-26, 333, 357, 366-67, 380.

69 At the end of the thirteenth century, the Saints-Innocents parish was the smallest on the populous right bank. The tax rolls for 1296 and 1299 indicate 46 and 51 taxable individuals respectively. Guy-Michel Leproux, 'L'église des Saints-Innocents' in *Les Saints-Innocents*, ed. by Michel Fleury and Guy-Michel Leproux, (Paris: Délégation à l'action artistique de la ville de Paris, 1990), p. 75.

70 This cemetery had in ancient times been a wide open space open to all who came and destined for the sale of goods. Rigord, 'Gesta Philippi Augusti' in *Œuvres de Rigord et de Guillaume le Breton, historiens de France*, ed. by H. François Delaborde, 2 vols (Paris: Renouard, 1882-85), I (1882), p. 70.

71 As was done in ancient times; Near the cemetery a market was begun [...] and then little by little houses were built there; and then the Halles were constructed to sell all manner of goods. Raoul de Presles, 'Commentaire ajouté par Raoul de Presles a sa traduction de la *Cité de Dieu*' in *Paris et ses historiens aux XIV*ᵉ *et XV*ᵉ *siècles*, ed. by Le Roux de Lincy and Tisserand (Paris: Imprimerie Impériale, 1867), p. 110.

72 Lombard-Jourdan, *Les Halles de Paris*, p. 37.

73 For example, the bishop of Paris' ordinance forbidding the sale of books upon the cemetery's tombs on 20 February 1402. Paris, Archives nationales, Y 2, fol. 217r.

74 Anne Massoni, 'Les collégiales parisiennes, "filles de l'évêque" et "filles du chapitre" de Notre-Dame' in *Notre-Dame de Paris 1163-2013*, ed. by Cédric Giraud (Turnhout: Brepols, 2013), pp. 257-61; Anne Massoni, *La collégiale Saint-Germain l'Auxerrois de Paris (1380-1510)* (Limoges: Presses Universitaires de Limoges, 2009), p. 51.

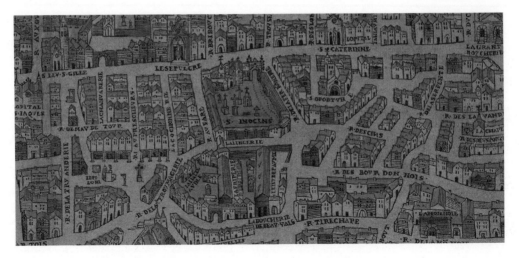

Figure 4. Detail. The Saints-Innocents and the Halles markets. Truschet and Hoyau map (c.1553). University Library Basel, Kartenslg AA 124.

Denis' Sainte-Catherine hospital, the churchwardens of Saints-Innocents and the chapter of Saint-Germain-l'Auxerrois.[75]

From the late fourteenth century, the Saints-Innocents underwent a significant phase of architectural and artistic development that evidences the Halles' inhabitants negotiation of and investment in this sacred space. Both cemetery and church became replete with murals, sculptures, epitaphs, tombs and charnel houses that evoked their vision of the neighbour-hood community, but that also jostled for space with royally and ducally sponsored artworks designed to shape popular understandings of the city and its hierarchy. With regards to understanding the composition and character of the Bourgeois' community, these sources enable social network analysis by evidencing the symbolic manifestation of communities through dynastic connections and social capital. Most monuments were intended to morally instruct passers-by, reminding Parisians of their predecessors' contri-butions to the parish fabric while encouraging prayers for their memory. In doing so, they created a normative framework for an idealized parish and civic community. For instance, of fifty-four known epitaphs from this period, thirty were funded by individuals identified as merchants or bourgeois (or their wives); eight belonged to members of the Paris Parlement and seven were royal or Châtelet notaries.[76]

Professional and dynastic characteristics were combined through the epitaphs and their relative location in the cemetery and exhibited through arms painted or engraved upon the

---

75 Massoni, *La collégiale Saint-Germain l'Auxerrois*, pp. 151, 288. On 17 September 1457 Charles VII confirmed the chapter of Saint-Germain-l'Auxerrois' rights in a dispute uniting the parish churches of Saint-Eustache, Saint-Jacques-de-la-Boucherie, Saint-Sauveur and Saint-Germain-l'Auxerrois, the Hôtel-Dieu and the Sainte-Catherine hospital in response to transgressions by the churchwardens of Saints-Innocents. Paris, Archives nationales, L 570, 'Cimetière des Saints-Innocents. 1218-1786', no. 4.
76 Paris, BNF Fr. 8220, pp. 239-63; Paris, Archives nationales, LL 434-B; L 656, no. 1. See also Verlet, *Épitaphier de Paris*, VI.

monuments. As Helen Swift has suggested, the increasing wordiness of French epitaphs in the fifteenth century evidenced a concurrent growth in anxieties about oblivion, as the deceased (and their living relatives) attempted to inscribe individual deeds and dynasties upon the built fabric of the neighbourhood.[77] Many of the families who funded epitaphs during the first half of the fifteenth century belonged to the class of merchants who rose to prominence under the Anglo-Burgundian regime. By establishing a monument, they cemented their status as leading bourgeois despite political vicissitudes and articulated their socio-political connections and civic ties.[78] Tellingly, a quarter of the known Parisians implicated in the 1416 conspiracy to betray Paris to Jean sans Peur funded epitaphs in the cemetery, with several of these men going on to serve as *prévôts* or *échevins* during the period of Anglo-Burgundian rule between 1418 and 1436.

The above suggests that Parisians connected to the Burgundian regime marked their political ascendancy through these commemorative strategies. Anne-Marie Sankovitch considered these as processes through which the parish church became an 'archive' that supplemented the fragility of human memory.[79] At the Saints-Innocents, a prime example is that of the grocer Jean de l'Olive (d. 1434), an *échevin* in 1412-15 and 1420-22 who endorsed the Cabochien revolt of 1413 and participated in the 1416 conspiracy.[80] L'Olive was survived by his wife Marguerite Orlant and their combined epitaph denotes the importance of their marriage, explicitly identifying Marguerite as the daughter of the wealthy Florentine 'changeur et bourgeois de Paris', Henri Orlant (Enrico Orlandini), a dependable financier of the Burgundian dukes and Philippe le Hardi's *valet de chambre*.[81] One of Orlant's sons, Philippot, had joined the Cabochien revolt, whereas another, Thomassin, was implicated in the 1416 conspiracy alongside l'Olive.[82] L'Olive's (or his wife Marguerite's) decision to draw the attention of passers-by to this connection to the Orlants consolidated those ties developed through their dynasties' shared support for the dukes of Burgundy. The adjoining charnel house displayed the epitaph of Henri's fourth daughter Anne (d. 1475) and her husband André Marcel (d. 1475), implying the development of a focused

---

77 Helen Swift, *Representing the Dead: Epitaph Fictions in Late-Medieval France* (Brewer: Cambridge, 2016), p. 14.

78 This approach to studying civic relationships through epitaphs follows the methodology developed in David Harry, *Constructing a Civic Community in Late Medieval London: The Common Profit, Charity and Commemoration* (Woodbridge: Boydell, 2019), pp. 97-102, 108-17. For Paris, it has persuasively been employed by Julie Claustre, 'La prééminence du notaire (Paris, XIVᵉ et XVᵉ siècles)' in *Marquer la prééminence sociale*, ed. by Jean-Philippe Genet and E. Igor Mineo (Paris: Éditions de la Sorbonne, 2014), pp. 75-91.

79 Anne-Marie Sankovitch, 'Intercession, Commemoration, and Display: The Parish Church as Archive in Late Medieval Paris' in *Demeures d'éternité: Églises et chapelles funéraires aux XVᵉ et XVIᵉ siècles*, ed. by Jean Guillaume (Paris: Picard, 2005), pp. 250-51.

80 Thompson, *Paris and its People*, pp. 55, 58; Emily Hutchison, 'Knowing One's Place: Space, Violence and Legitimacy in Early Fifteenth-century Paris', *The Medieval History Journal*, 20 (2017), p. 64, n. 88, 90; Coville, *Les Cabochiens*, pp. 214, 361, 401.

81 Paris, Archives nationales, LL 434-B, p. 61; Mirot, *Les d'Orgemont*, pp. 169-72; Berland, 'La cour de Bourgogne à Paris', pp. 224-28, 399. See also Marc Boone and Jan Dumolyn, 'Les officiers-créditeurs des ducs de Bourgogne dans l'ancien comté de Flandre: aspects financiers, politiques et sociaux', *Publications du Centre Européen d'Études Bourguignonnes*, 39 (1999), pp. 225-41.

82 Mirot, *Les d'Orgemont*, pp. 169-70. Thomas Orlant would go on to serve as *échevin* in 1436. Jean Favier, 'Une ville entre deux vocations: la place d'affaires de Paris au XVᵉ siècle', *Annales ESC*, 28 (1973), p. 1250.

family necropolis.[83] Together, the epitaphs' relative location demonstrates their strategic use by Parisian bourgeois rising to prominence during the first decades of the fifteenth century, who advertised and archived their dynastic relationships in the cemetery's space. A further seven families connected to the Burgundian dukes are similarly represented among the cemetery's known early fifteenth-century epitaphs, including household suppliers, *échevins* appointed by the Anglo-Burgundian regime, participants in the Cabochien revolt or 1416 conspiracy, and ducal councillors.[84] Visitors to the cemetery perusing the epitaphs engaged with the symbolic and mnemonic manifestations – invitations to prayer, monuments and heraldry – that exhibited this class's political factionalism, familial bonds and professional connections.

The ties between the Halles' residents and the Burgundian faction are further demonstrated by substantial alterations made to the church's fabric. The *changeur* Guillaume Sanguin (d. 14 February 1442), a 1416 conspirator and *prévôt des marchands* for the Anglo-Burgundian regime in 1429-31, had enjoyed Philippe le Hardi's favour before being appointed Jean sans Peur's *premier maître d'hôtel*.[85] So significant were Sanguin's financial contributions to the ducal court that Bertrand Schnerb has concluded that, following the merchant's death, 'l'apurement des créances et des dettes […] fut une opération complexe' for the Burgundian administration.[86] Guillaume's investments in the Saints-Innocents culminated in the foundation of the Saint-Michel chapel, in which he was buried in 1442.[87] The chapel was decorated with tiles depicting the Sanguin arms, while Guillaume's epitaph reminded readers of his patronage and connections to the Burgundian administration, as the 'M^e d'hostel de monsig^r le Duc de Bourgogne'.[88] Sanguin's links were complemented and echoed by others connected to the Anglo-Burgundian administration buried within the church. Imbert Deschamps (d. 1464), a mercer involved in the 1416 plot and *échevin* in 1419-20 and 1429-30 was buried near Saints-Innocents' Saint-Sébastien chapel, while Jean Fortier (d. 6 February 1434) was buried in the Notre-Dame chapel with an epitaph reminding observers of his post as 'conseiller de monseigneur le duc de Bourgogne'.[89]

The prosopographical overview of those with links to the Saints-Innocents reveals the importance of patronage on the part of bourgeois affiliated with the Burgundian dukes during the first half of the fifteenth century, in turn helping us to contextualize princely investment in the church and cemetery. Most famously, in 1408 Jean, duke of Berry financed sculptures added to the Saints-Innocents church depicting the moral legend of the

---

83 Paris, Archives nationales LL 434-B, p. 52. André Marcel was a merchant and municipal official. Le Maresquier-Kesteloot, *Les officiers municipaux*, pp. 132, 244, no. 1519.

84 The list of those buried at the Saints-Innocents who belonged to families loyal to the Burgundian dukes or connected to their household is extensive, including the Guérin, Neufville, Louviers, Ysbarre, Tireverge, Dourdin and Piédefer families.

85 Mirot, *Les d'Orgemont*, pp. 144, 173; Léon Mirot, 'Jean sans Peur de 1398 à 1405, d'après les comptes de sa Chambre aux deniers', *Annuaire-Bulletin de la Société de l'histoire de France*, 74 (1938), pp. 133-34, n. 7.

86 The auditing of the debts and monies outstanding […] was a complex operation. Bertrand Schnerb, 'Jean sans Peur, Paris et l'argent', *Beihefte der Francia*, 64 (2007), p. 272.

87 Paris, Archives nationales, L 656, no. 1, p. 4.

88 Paris, Archives nationales, L 656, no. 1, p. 4. Fragments of these tiles were recovered during the archaeological excavations of the cemetery in the 1970s. Leproux, 'L'église des Saints-Innocents', p. 81.

89 Paris, Archives nationales, L 656, no. 1, pp. 10, 12.

Trois Morts et Trois Vifs, a moralizing encounter between three young aristocrats and three animated corpses while hunting, to mark Louis d'Orléans' assassination in Paris the previous year.[90] Where Ashby Kinch has argued that the sculpture exemplifies Berry's endeavour to use 'public art patronage ostentatiously to display his humility',[91] the dedicatory poem reveals the eschatological message that Berry imparted to the Halles' inhabitants:

> Touts humains corps,
> Tant aye biens ou grand cité,
> Ne peut eviter les discords
> De la mortelle adversité.
> Doncq pour avoir felicité,
> Ayons de la mort souvenir,
> Afin qu'apres perplexité
> Puissent aux saints cieux parvenir.[92]

Berry's interest in the Saints-Innocents fed into a wider array of ducal interests in Parisian churches. For instance, the Burgundian dukes 'ont réellement "investi" le champ religieux parisien' consolidating their ties to the city's communities; Berry similarly offered substantial donations to the Augustins Convent and his Parisian parish of Saint-André-des-Arts.[93] Anticipating the *Danse Macabre* and instituted in the tense political context of 1408, as the circumstances of Louis d'Orléans' life and death were debated at court, Berry's sponsorship of the *Trois Morts* possibly represented a thinly veiled form of political commentary, reminding the Halles' Burgundian sympathizers that Jean sans Peur was not immune to the vicissitudes of fortune, echoing the legal and theological discussions concerning tyrannicide then predominant at court exemplified by Jean Petit's *Justification* for Louis d'Orléans' murder.[94] Christine Kralik has argued that by the mid-fourteenth century, the *Trois Morts* was sufficiently popular 'that an image of the story could function on its own without an intended textual exposition', with the image being 'more successful the more striking

---

90 Paris, Archives nationales, L 656, no. 1, pp. 1-2. Sophie Oosterwijk, 'Of Dead Kings, Dukes and Constables: The Historical Context of the *Danse Macabre* in Late Medieval Paris', *Journal of the British Archaeological Association*, 161 (2008), pp. 133-35. Berry's close interest in the moral is underscored by the illuminations depicting the encounter in his manuscripts, most notably his *Petites Heures* (c. 1375) and *Très Riches Heures* (c. 1416). Paris, BNF Latin 18014, fols 282r-286r; Chantilly, Bibliothèque Condé, MS 65, fol. 86.

91 Ashby Kinch, *Imago Mortis: Mediating Images of Death in the Medieval Culture* (Leiden: Brill, 2013), p. 137.

92 All human bodies regardless of their wealth and lands cannot avoid the discord of mortal adversity. So, to achieve happiness remember Death such that after suffering the heavens can be reached. Paris, Archives nationales L 656, no. 1, p. 2.

93 Schnerb and Paravicini, 'Les "investissements" religieux', pp. 216-18; Françoise Lehoux, 'Mort et funérailles du duc de Berri (juin 1416)', *BEC*, 114 (1956), p. 83.

94 On the relationship between these poems, and their differences, see Christine Kralik, '"A Matter of Life of Death": Forms, Functions and Audiences for "The Three Living and the Three Dead" in Late Medieval Manuscripts' (unpublished doctoral thesis, University of Toronto, 2013), pp. 12-16. For the debates that followed Louis d'Orléans' assassination, see Bernard Guenée, *Un meurtre, une société. L'assassinat du duc d'Orléans, 23 novembre 1407* (Paris: Gallimard, 1992), pp. 180-221; Alfred Coville, *Jean Petit. La question du tyrannicide au commencement du XVᵉ siècle* (Paris: Picard, 1932), pp. 403-38.

and persuasive it was', underscoring its propagandistic potential.[95] Indeed, visiting the church before 1434, Guillebert De Mets felt compelled to comment upon the sculpture's appearance, 'engigneusement entailliés de pierre'.[96] The combined poem and sculpture therefore recalled to the Halles' inhabitants that Jean sans Peur was subject to the same logic employed to legitimate Orléans' assassination, while perhaps eliciting prayers for the murdered duke that counteracted the influence of Jean Petit's *Justification* pronounced that year, reminding its audience 'qu'il convint a toutes creature [...] mourir et tendre a pourriture'.[97] Where Jean sans Peur endeavoured to argue, through Petit's *Justification*, that princes who held themselves above the law as tyrants could not morally escape sanction, Berry's sculpture retorted that no prince, whatever his power, could escape death. The *Trois Morts'* location on the redeveloped southern entrance leading to the Sanguin chapel was poignant, representing a decidedly Orléanist stamp on the contributions of Burgundy's Parisian allies to the Saints-Innocents fabric.[98]

The famous *Danse Macabre* mural, the first historical mention of which occurs in the Bourgeois' *Journal* for 1425, informed and was informed by this framework of political contest and social stratification within the cemetery.[99] While Amy Appleford has argued that the *Danse* was 'an ecclesiastical, not a civic production', Sophie Oosterwijk suggested that the mural 'is unlikely to have been paid for by the impoverished parish' of the Saints-Innocents.[100] It must have been an expensive undertaking, and Oosterwijk has insightfully noted the circumstantial and internal evidence pointing to the mural's potential commissioning by Philippe le Bon, most notably references to the infamous 'Bal des Ardents' weaponized in Jean Petit's 1408 *Justification* to denigrate Louis d'Orléans, a theme that also resurfaced in the sympathetically Burgundian verse history of Paris, the *Aventures depuis deux cents ans*.[101] Philippe le Bon's possession of one of the earliest copies of the *Danse* in a Parisian manuscript dated to the 1420s is also telling, and the character of bourgeois investment at Saints-Innocents all point to Burgundian influences, either ducal or more

95 Christine Kralik, 'Dialogue and Violence in Medieval Illuminations of the Three Living and the Three Dead' in *Mixed Metaphors: The* Danse Macabre *in Medieval and Early Modern Europe*, ed. by Sophie Oosterwijk and Stefanie Knöll (Newcastle-upon-Tyne: Cambridge Scholars Publishing, 2011), pp. 133-36, 154.
96 Ingeniously sculpted in stone. Guillebert De Mets, 'Description de la ville de Paris', p. 192. Guillebert De Mets was operating in Paris from roughly 1405. Possibly a clerk in the Burgundian ducal household, Mets had close connections to Paris' book trade and the University of Paris (he was even excommunicated following a dispute with the University of Paris regarding the sale of books in 1424). In the colophon to his manuscript copy of *Sidrac et Lucidaire*, Mets described himself as a "libraire du duc de Bourgogne", signalling his role in the supply of manuscripts to the duke. For Mets' career in Paris, see Dominique Vanwihnsberghe and Erik Verroken, *'A l'Escu de France': Guillebert de Mets et la peinture de livres à Gand à l'époque de Jan van Eyck (1410-50)* (Brussels: Institut royal du Patrimoine artistique, 2017), pp. 38-43; Nicole Grévy-Pons, 'Jean de Montreuil et Guillebert de Mets', *Revue belge de philologie et d'histoire*, vol. 58, no. 3 (1980), pp. 565-87.
97 It is the nature of all creation [...] to die and tend to rot. Paris, Archives nationales, L 656, no. 1, p. 1.
98 Leproux, 'L'église des Saints-Innocents', pp. 80-1.
99 *Journal*, p. 203.
100 Amy Appleford, *Learning to Die in London, 1380-1540* (Philadelphia, PA: Pennsylvania University Press, 2015), p. 88; Oosterwijk, 'Of Dead Kings, Dukes and Constables', p. 135.
101 Sophie Oosterwijk, 'Of Dead Kings, Dukes and Constables: The Historical Context of the *Danse Macabre* in Late Medieval Paris', *Journal of the British Archaeological Association*, 161 (2008), p. 152; Clifford Davidson and Sophie Oosterwijk (eds), *John Lydgate, The Dance of Death, and its model, the French* Danse Macabre (Leiden: Brill, 2021), pp. 53-4.

indirect, in this conceptualization of civic hierarchy and urban relationships, a notion that underscores Laurent Ungeheuer's recent suggestion that the Burgundian sympathiser Guillaume Sanguin may plausibly have been the *Danse*'s patron.[102] The depiction of French society found in the *Danse* also presented a distorted image of stability when contrasted with the realities of the French kingdom's fractured character. The absence of a duke from the *Danse*'s schema, in particular, reflects tensions surrounding the place and status of dukes in France's political hierarchy following Jean sans Peur's assassination in 1419 and Philippe le Bon's endorsement of the Treaty of Troyes.[103] Conspicuous by its omission, Oosterwijck has suggested that the duke's absence suggests a ducal patron's desire to avert satire and criticism, but there may be something deeper here. If the *Trois Morts* functioned as a subtle warning that the Burgundian dukes would receive due retribution in death for their actions in life while prompting prayers to secure the reputations and salvific destinies of both Berry and Orléans, the omission of the duke from the *Danse macabre* served to invert this messaging and entirely erase the notion of fortune's reversal and ensuing damnation for the Burgundian duke.

Consequently, through the *Danse macabre* the Saints-Innocents cemetery emerges as an arena where anxieties about France's socio-political order were played out by and before Parisian audiences, echoing debates expounded in other situations and texts. As Kinch has argued, the *Danse* 'mediated social relations in subtle and sophisticated ways by re-presenting to the Parisian community an image of itself at a time when that image was under threat of radical realignment'.[104] It was exactly this realignment that the Bourgeois traced in his own writing, but it was also a process in which Parisian families participated and endeavoured to stabilize through their mnemonic and monumental investments in the cemetery and church fabric. Tensions regarding the place of the king, the duke and officers in society captured the overarching political debates that had surrounded Louis d'Orléans assassination, bringing to the fore the moral and theological issues that framed contemporary interpretations of the French civil conflict. In particular, the *Journal* echoed Jean Petit's own assertion that cupidity was the root of sin, developing a perception of immorality tied to the aristocracy's failure to fulfil their obligation as integral components of the body politic and, in doing so, threatening Paris' fragile social and religious harmony. Comments regarding the interplay of fortune and societal fracture underpinned the Bourgeois' record of political upheaval, conveying this disconnect following the Cabochien revolt in August 1413:

---

102 Hanno Wijsmann, 'Un Manuscrit de Philippe le Bon et la *Danse macabré* du cimetière des Saints-Innocents', *Le Moyen Age*, 127, 1 (2021), pp. 59-80; Laurent Ungeheuer, 'La Danse macabre du cimetière des Saints-Innocents et celle de deux livres d'heures contemporains: propositions de liens, de sources et de commanditaires', *Annales de Bourgogne*, 92, 3-4 (2020), pp. 37-8.

103 Sophie Oosterwijk, 'Death, Memory and Commemoration: John Lydgate and "Macabrees Daunce" at Old St Paul's Cathedral, London' in *Memory and Commemoration in Medieval England. Proceedings of the 2008 Harlaxton Symposium*, ed. by Caroline M. Barron and Clive Burgess (Donington: Shaun Tyas, 2010), pp. 186-89.

104 Kinch, *Imago Mortis*, p. 228.

Ainsi ouvroit fortune a la vollée en ce royaulme, et qu'il n'y avoit ne gentil, ne autre qui sceust quel estat estoit le meilleur: les grans s'entre-hayoient, les moyens estoient grevez par sussides, les tres pouvres ne trouvoient ou gaigner.[105]

Diverging from the real tensions between societal groups, the *Danse macabre* may have functioned like the epitaphs that surrounded it, establishing and codifying an ideal of ordered Parisian society precisely as institutions and individuals alike were compelled to reorient themselves towards Anglo-Burgundian rule following the Treaty of Troyes in 1420. As we have already seen, Burgundian allies residing upon Paris' right bank had a vested interest in popularizing and consolidating a vision of order under a Lancastrian regime that simultaneously counted upon these same individuals for administrative and political support. The list of those who funded epitaphs in the Saints-Innocents cemetery who belonged to families affiliated with the Anglo-Burgundian regime is long and several are especially worthy of mention. Nicolas de Neufville (d. 1474), a fishmonger, served as *échevin* during the Lancastrian occupation in 1429-30 and later in 1442-44, with his epitaph proudly stating his office as a 'maitre d'hotel du duc Philippes de Bourgogne'.[106] The butcher and queen's treasurer, Marcelet Testart, also *échevin* in 1418-20 and 1430-32, was commemorated with his wife Catherine Huvé.[107] Other epitaphs marked dynasties close to the Burgundian regime in a similar fashion to the Orlants. For example, Jacques Dourdin (d. 1432) was a *tapissier* and known supplier to the ducal household whose son Raoul Dourdin served as *échevin* in 1422 and 1425 alongside Raoul's son-in-law, Jean de La Poterne.[108] In this light, the dynastic stability and political role asserted by the Halles' leading merchant families paralleled the societal order envisioned by the *Danse macabre* around which their epitaphs clustered and emphasized their role in securing the city's common good.

Writing for his patron, Philippe le Bon, Guillaume De Mets' own description of the *Danse*, as art 'pour esmouvoir les gens a devotion', certainly implies its success in provoking emotional responses among those who would come to the Halles not only to commemorate and remember, but to trade, commune and exchange news.[109] In the disturbed context of the 1430s when De Mets finished his *Description* of the city, the moralizing rhetoric that echoed the *Trois Morts* must have served to reinforce social and political bonds that took the leading dynasties of the Halles as their focus. Indeed, this overlap between propaganda and moral instruction is further demonstrated by Isabeau de Bavière's own donation of a copy of the *Somme le Roi* to the Saints-Innocents parish 'afin que ceste matiere fust sceue

---

105 So Fortune worked at will in this kingdom, and no one, neither noble nor otherwise, knew which estate had it best: the great all hated each other, the middling sort were burdened by taxes, and the very poor people found no means of earning their living. *Journal*, p. 43.

106 Paris, Archives nationales LL 434-B, p. 30.

107 Until now, the 'Martelet' referred to by this epitaph has been unidentified, but the accompanying description of the epitaph's arms matches that known to belong to the Testart family. Verlet, *Épitaphier du vieux Paris*, VI, p. 296.

108 *Épitaphier du vieux Paris*, VI, p. 230.

109 To move people to devotion. Guillebert De Mets, 'Description de Paris sous Charles VI', p. 193. The autograph manuscript of Mets' *Description* was also found in Philippe le Bon's library in 1467-69. Evelyn Mullally, *Guillebert De Mets: Description de la ville de Paris 1434: Medieval French text with English Translation* (Turnhout: Brepols, 2015), pp. 25-31.

comme souveraine de tous ceulx qui la le vouldroient lire. Et le fist exprimer par un maistre en theologie'.[110] Like the *Trois Morts* and *Danse Macabre*, the *Somme le Roi* served a clear moral and didactic function, inculcating an understanding of the Ten Commandments, the twelve articles of faith, vices, virtues and the Pater Noster – the ways of leading a good life prior to inevitable death, ensuring the maintenance of community cohesion.[111] Fundamentally, this moral discourse was integral to the ways in which theologians tied to the royal court were also conceptualizing the issues surrounding the French civil conflict in the first decades of the fifteenth century.

The Saints-Innocents' relevance was not, therefore, confined to those local families who asserted their status and influence through epitaphs, instead emerging as an arena where princes and civic officials competed to inculcate moral values and political attitudes and where their agendas intersected directly with the political endeavours of the district's inhabitants. The churchyard assumed an 'important role in the mythology of Parisian identity', functioning as a site of '*visuality* and *textuality*', through sermons, processions and the public reading and interpretation of images.[112] The cemetery's moral significance was consistently evoked in fifteenth-century poetry. Contemplating the charnel-houses' skulls and glossing the *Danse Macabre*, François Villon remarked in his *Testament* (1461): 'Or sont-ilz morts! […] Aient été seigneurs ou dames, Souef et tendrement nourris […] Les os déclinent en poudre, auxquels ne chaut d'ébats ne ris'.[113] Likewise, Jean Meschinot's *Lunettes des Princes* (*c.* 1461-65) portrayed the epitaphs of Saints-Innocents as 'a remedy for readerly vanity'.[114] These reactions, combined with the Bourgeois' own attention to the cemetery's importance, reveal the cultural impact of such investments, their didactic influence and propagandistic potential.

In the context of these investments the apparently miscellaneous incidents reported by the Bourgeois, such as the beggars' shedding of blood within the Saints-Innocents church in June 1436 resulting in its de-consecration, assume new significance. When the bishop Denis du Moulin was unwilling to re-consecrate the church, the Bourgeois expressed frustration at the inability to perform 'messe, matines, ne vespres, ne corps en terre ou cymetiere ne fut, ne le sainct service de nulle heure' for twenty-two days, particularly because the interdict compromised the church's ability to fulfil its obligations

---

110 So that this subject can become known as the most important of all for those who wish to read it there. And [she] had it preached there by a master in theology. The donation is recorded in the colophon to Isabeau de Bavière's personal copy of the *Somme le Roi*, BNF Fr. 22935, fol. 2r. The manuscript is dated *c.* 1415-20.

111 The *Somme le Roi* formed an integral part of an effort to accentuate common moral edification by Philip III, who originally commissioned the text in 1279-80. Throughout the fourteenth century, the text was favoured by royal women. See Anne-Françoise Leurquin-Labie, 'La Somme le roi: de la commande royale de Philippe III à la diffusion sous Philippe IV et au-delà' in *La moisson des lettres: L'invention littéraire autour de 1300*, ed. by Hélène Bellon-Méguelle, Olivier Collet, Yasmina Foehr-Janssens, and Ludivine Jaquiéry (Turnhout: Brepols, 2011), pp. 195-212.

112 Emphases in the original. Julie Singer, 'Eyeglasses for the Blind: Redundant Therapies in Meschinot and Villon', *Fifteenth Century Studies*, 35 (2010), pp. 118-19.

113 So they are dead! They were lords and ladies, gentle and tenderly raised. Now their bones turn to dust, they no longer enjoy games nor laughter. François Villon, 'Le Testament Villon' in *François Villon: Lais, Testament, poésies diverses*, ed. by Jean-Claude Mühlethaler (Paris: Champion, 2004), pp. 258-60, Lines 1734-35, 1760-67.

114 Singer, 'Eyeglasses for the Blind', pp. 113-14.

towards its wealthy patrons.[115] This also explains the Bourgeois' exasperation in 1441, when du Moulin again placed an interdict upon Saints-Innocents that lasted four months, prompting the Bourgeois to highlight the danger that this posed to the duties towards the dead since 'on n'y enterra oncques personne *petit ne grant*, ne on n'y fist procession, ne recommandacion pour quelque personne'.[116] The timing of the interdict coincides with known high-profile deaths and burials in the church, including the Parlement president Robert Piédefer (d. 1438), Simon Bureau (d. 1438) and his wife Hélène (d. 1442) who were mother and father of Jean Bureau (*prévôt des marchands* for 1450-52), and Guillaume Sanguin (d. 1442).[117] Consequently, the Bourgeois emphasized the importance of memory, commemoration and concentrated piety within Saints-Innocents, exhibiting its purpose for the wider community in the face of challenges posed by an avaricious bishop.

This attitude was substantially altered from 1442 when, on 11 October, the bishop blessed the immuration of the recluse Jeanne la Verrière, 'et fist on ung bel sermon devant elle et devant moult grant foison de peuple'.[118] On 22 February 1445, the Bourgeois reported how du Moulin re-dedicated the church in a move that Hélène Couzy has identified as confirming the series of building projects financed by patrons such as Guillaume Sanguin over the preceding decades, as suggested by the dedication's specific reference to the newly constructed Notre-Dame chapel.[119] This section of the church included the St. Francis chapel funded by the *pelletiers* corporation, and the Bourgeois had already related that their confraternity sang its first Mass there in August 1437.[120] As such, Denis du Moulin's dedication consolidated a series of architectural developments organized through the patronage of families tied to the Anglo-Burgundian administration.

The Bourgeois' account of the church in the late 1440s therefore demonstrates its rise as a Parisian spiritual centre, at the culmination of decades of investment. Testamentary data supports this impression. Surveying 136 wills registered in the Paris Parlement in the late fourteenth and early fifteenth centuries whose testators left bequests to Parisian institutions, the highest proportion of known burials (19.1%) and bequests (26.5%) went to the Saints-Innocents.[121] Reflecting the culture and piety of a burgeoning upper-middle class of bureaucrats paralleling the wealthier artisans of the Halles region, half of those interred were Parlement *procureurs*, *huissiers* or *avocats* who elected to be buried in the 'fosses aux pauvres' as a sign of their humility. Other plans for burial reflected the dynastic strategies evoked by the cemetery's epitaphs. In 1412, the widow of the *changeur* Guillaume

---

115 Neither masses nor matins or vespers, nor could bodies be buried in the ground of the cemetery, nor the holy services be performed at any time, nor any holy water acquired. *Journal*, pp. 325-26.

116 no one was buried there, *great or small*, nor were processions performed, nor funeral prayers for anyone whomsoever. Emphasis my own. *Journal*, p. 357.

117 Verlet, *Épitaphier de Paris*, VI, pp. 38, 88, 242.

118 And a good sermon was pronounced before her and before a great many people. *Journal*, p. 367.

119 *Journal*, p. 380; Paris, Archives nationales, L 656, no. 1, pp. 2-3. Hélène Couzy, 'L'église des Saints-Innocents à Paris', *Bulletin Monumental*, 130 (1972), p. 291.

120 *Journal*, p. 333.

121 This data is derived from the register of wills found published by Alexandre Tuetey (ed.), *Testaments enregistrés au Parlement de Paris sous le règne de Charles VI* (Paris: Imprimerie nationale 1880), supplemented by the registers found in Paris, BNF Moreau 1161 and 1162. On these wills, see Danielle Courtemanche, *Œuvrer pour la postérité: les testaments parisiens des gens du roi au début du XVᵉ siècle* (Paris: Le Harmattan, 1997).

Marcel, Perrenelle, chose to be buried 'prope locum in quo mater sua et Martinus des Essars, frater suus, sunt sepulti', demonstrating the close ties between the family of the disgraced *prévôt* of 1358 (Guillaume's cousin) and the family of the individual then serving in the same office, Pierre des Essarts.[122] The Bourgeois signalled Saints-Innocents' growing status by stressing bishop Guillaume Chartier's interest in the church, delivering a sermon there in April 1448 and again focusing on commemorative elements, according 'absolucion a tous les trespassés qui [...] estoient excommeniez par negligence ou autrement apres leur trespassement'.[123] Finally, in 1449 and 1450 the church's ascendancy in Parisian devotional practice was signalled by the performance of two novel processions wherein Parisian children travelled to hear Mass at Saints-Innocents before proceeding to Notre-Dame in the company of the church's relic, the head of Richard, a child allegedly murdered by Jews in Pontoise in 1179.[124] In 1449 the procession was a crucial marker of the church's devotional centrality. The subsequent procession in April 1450 marked Charles VII's victory at Formigny and confirmed the site's sacred potential, emblematic of the district's ties to episcopal and royal authority.[125]

Investment in the Saints-Innocents during the first half of the fifteenth century encapsulated the methods and media available to Parisian merchants who secured their status in the municipal government in part through their ties to the Anglo-Burgundian regime. The Bourgeois' writing, by focusing upon this site not only as his workplace but also as a rapidly developing cultural centre, offered these dynastically intertwined families a means for immortalizing their contributions to the spiritual and temporal wellbeing of their parish community and to the governance of Paris. The Bourgeois' record of the increasingly close ties between the bishopric and the local church validated their patronage.

The examination of the Bourgeois' neighbourhood demonstrates a close relationship between the *Journal*'s content and the political attitudes of those who inhabited the Halles district. The Halles consisted of a community of artisans and wealthier bourgeois connected to the Burgundian dukes who collectively and consistently exhibited support for the Burgundian regime during the first decades of the fifteenth century. The *Journal*'s narrative fundamentally evidences this influence, suggesting that the Bourgeois was writing with this community in mind, sharing and reinforcing its views. Written records such as the *Journal* were 'replete with social meaning' and were essential testaments to social status rooted in the past.[126] In this light, the text complemented the architectural and mnemonic strategies employed at Saints-Innocents, binding the parish community through the memory of its political experiences as well as through a record of devotional elements

---

122 Near the place where her mother and her brother, Martin des Essarts, are buried. Paris, BNF Moreau 1162, fol. 228v. For Guillaume Marcel, see Henri Fremaux, 'La famille d'Étienne Marcel, 1250-1397', *MSHP*, 30 (1903), pp. 184-86. The ties between the Marcel and des Essarts families in the fourteenth century have also been noted by Boris Bove, both directly and as part of the broader *échevinal* network. *Dominer la ville*, pp. 277-78, 342.

123 Absolution to all those deceased who had been excommunicated by negligence or otherwise after their death. *Journal*, p. 389.

124 *Journal*, p. 392.

125 Jean Chartier, *Chronique de Charles VII, roi de France*, ed. by Auguste Vallet de Viriville, 3 vols (Paris: Jannet, 1858), II, pp. 200-01.

126 Frederik Buylaert and Jelle Haemers, 'Record-Keeping and Status Performance in the Early Modern Low Countries', *Past & Present*, Supplement 11 (2016), pp. 131-33.

including the establishment of confraternities and the history of the parish church. More-over, through its account of political contests framed according to the perspectives of the Halles' inhabitants, the *Journal* may have provided a means for these Parisians to reflect upon political action and discourse, restate their cohesion and articulate their ideological goals. With the decline of Burgundian influence from the 1420s, these prerogatives shifted, with Saints-Innocents increasingly portrayed as being in dialogue with other Parisian institutions such as the cathedral as a testament to its civic importance and that of its patrons.

The clergy and chapter of Notre-Dame cathedral

While the Bourgeois' likely connections to Notre-Dame suggest that the cathedral chapter and clergy influenced his writing, the paucity of details regarding the chapter's struggles with royal authority during this period are stark in contrast to the wealth of information supplied for Paris' right bank communities. Although earlier editors have argued that the Bourgeois was writing for a clerical audience comprising members of the cathedral clergy or University of Paris, the resulting dissonance suggests that the text was compiled for audiences less familiar with these contexts. The *Journal* rarely overlaps with information found in the chapter's registers, instead tracing the cathedral's interaction with other civic institutions or Valois and Lancastrian authority. As such, the Bourgeois synthesized the cathedral's political and pastoral roles for an audience external to the clergy community itself. In particular, the *Journal* evidences a profound interest in the question of episcopal and, implicitly, canonical authority during the 1420s and 1430s when this was challenged by the Lancastrian regime. In contrast, from the 1440s episcopal agency was perceived pre-dominantly in relation to Saints-Innocents. The *Journal*'s representation of Notre-Dame therefore supports the conclusions elucidated above, suggesting that the Bourgeois was primarily interested in understanding the representative role performed by the cathedral for the wider civic community, especially in its contests with royal government. Funda-mentally, the Bourgeois endorsed the constitutional powers of the chapter over royal imposition, evoking underlying concerns about the political turbulence that the latter posed to Parisian institutions more generally.

The Bourgeois did not describe these challenges in detail, summarizing the problematic elections of Jean Courtecuisse and Nicole Fraillon as Paris' bishops in 1420 and 1427 respectively. A theologian, Courtecuisse was elected by the thirteen canons remaining in Paris in December 1420 following the death of the Armagnac sympathiser bishop Gérard de Montaigu. The election provided the Bourgeois with a means of mapping the relationship between the capital and the Lancastrian regime in the immediate aftermath of the Treaty of Troyes' conclusion, with the chapter rejecting Henry V's candidate, the canon of Amiens Philibert de Montjeu.[127] The Bourgeois' subsequent endorsement of the

---

127 Georges Grassoreille, 'Histoire politique du chapitre de Notre-Dame de Paris pendant la domination anglaise, 1420-37', *MSHP*, 9 (1882), pp. 127-30.

'proudomme' Courtecuisse is understandable.[128] A prominent University theologian, dean of the faculty and nominated as chancellor in Jean Gerson's absence in 1419, Courtecuisse had been an active proponent of the Cabochien reforms in 1413 and in 1414 refused to condemn Jean Petit's *Justification* of Jean sans Peur's murder of Louis, duke of Orléans.[129] Although the *Journal* does not provide details regarding Courtecuisse's election as bishop, the attention paid to the cathedral chapter's privileges suggests that the Bourgeois perceived the community as performing a representative role in the city's interactions with Henry V, especially given the assertion that Courtecuisse had been elected 'par l'Université et par le clergé et par le Parlement'.[130] The University was complicit in securing papal confirmation of Courtecuisse's election, received on 16 October 1421, while the Parlement had addressed letters to Henry V imploring the Lancastrian monarch to accept Courtecuisse's candidature.[131] Such institutional resistance threatened to jeopardize the Lancastrians' fragile hold over Paris, especially when coupled with Henry V's attempt to tax the urban clergy in January 1422, whereupon priests subordinate to Notre-Dame retorted that they had not consented to any taxes at the Estates General, declaring that they were entirely incapable of contributing funds at present.[132] This was a fact emphasized by the Bourgeois himself when he reported in the winter of 1420 that 'avoient [...] pouvres prebstres mal temps, que on ne leur donnoit que ij solz parisis pour leur messe'.[133] Consequently, when the Bourgeois reported Courtecuisse's inability to abandon the safety of the abbey of Saint-Germain-des-Prés in May 1422 'pour ce qu'il n'estoit en la grace du roy d'Angleterre', he evoked a struggle that encapsulated wider Parisian resistance to Lancastrian authority.[134]

Although Henry V succeeded in securing Courtecuisse's transferal to Geneva in 1422, this event was tellingly omitted by the Bourgeois, with the *Journal* simply relating an oblique reference to an unnamed 'evesque de Paris nouvel' officiating at Charles VI's funeral in November that year.[135] In September 1423 the Bourgeois glossed a vociferous dispute between this diocesan administrator Jean de la Rochetaillée and the Lancastrian government, when the former was appointed archbishop of Rouen. According to the *Journal*, 'fist tant l'evesque de Paris qui estoit patriarche, qu'il fut arcevesque de Rouen par faulte de souffisance'.[136] Again, the case demonstrates the Bourgeois' *distance* from the chapter in the 1420s. Rochetaillée had actually initially refused the nomination to Rouen, arguing that he was unaware of the pope's order of transferral and eliciting the support

---

128 *Journal*, p. 147.
129 Alfred Coville, 'Recherches sur Jean Courtecuisse et ses œuvres oratoires', BEC, 65 (1904), pp. 471-85.
130 By the University and by the clergy and by [the] Parlement. *Journal*, p. 164.
131 Similarly, it was only through the influence of the University that the Parlement 'octroia a Jehan Courtecuisse, esleu confermé evesque de Paris, lettres recommendatoires adrecans au roy d'Angleterre'. (Accorded letters of recommendation addressed to the king of England to Jean Courtecuisse, the elected [and] confirmed bishop of Paris). Fauquembergue, II, p. 24.
132 Objected that they had not consented to anything at the Estates General, alleging their almost complete lack of resources. Grassoreille, 'Histoire politique du chapitre', p. 145.
133 The poor priests had a very hard time since they were only paid two *sols parisis* for their masses. *Journal*, p. 145.
134 Because he did not enjoy the king of England's favour. *Journal*, p. 164.
135 The new bishop of Paris. *Journal*, p. 179. In fact, Courtecuisse's temporary successor, Jean de la Rochetaillée, was never explicitly identified by the Bourgeois.
136 Not having had enough, the bishop of Paris, who was [also] a patriarch, did such that he managed to become archbishop of Rouen. *Journal*, p. 190.

of Notre-Dame's canons to remain in his Parisian office.[137] The situation was such that Rochetaillée's successor, Jean de Nant, was waiting at the abbey of Saint-Victor to make his first entry into the city precisely as Rochetaillée contested his transferral. The Bourgeois' unawareness of the chapter's endorsement of Rochetaillée, his approbation of his successor Jean de Nant and the absence of any reference to the series of disputes between the chapter and bishop during the latter's tenure, supports Shirley's argument that if the author was associated with the cathedral during the early 1420s, this cannot have been as a canon.[138]

Jean de Nant's death in October 1426 triggered a third contest, and this time the Bourgeois reported concerns regarding the failed election of Notre-Dame's archdeacon, Nicolas Fraillon, in opposition to the Anglo-Burgundian candidate, the treasurer of Reims Jacques du Chastelier.[139] The contention again crystallized relations between Paris and the Lancastrian regime. In January 1427, the Bourgeois reported that Fraillon had been elected the previous December and 'receu a Notre-Dame', with the passage's timing coinciding with Fraillon's actual withdrawal from the chapter for fear of his life on 27 January.[140] The Bourgeois' record therefore contradicted the chapter's actual circumstances, presenting Fraillon's election as a *fait accompli* that stressed the chapter's authority relative to the regent John, duke of Bedford's. It was only six months later, in June, that the Bourgeois expressed consternation at Chastelier's appointment:

> ne fut plus parlé de l'election qui davant avoit esté faicte, c'est assavoir, de messire Nicolle Frallon, lequel avoit esté esleu de tout le chappitre de Notre-Dame, mais nonobstant l'ellection [...] ledit Nicollas Frollon en fut debouté, et l'autre dedens bouté, car ainsi le plaisoit aux gouverneurs.[141]

Chastelier's nomination had, however, been confirmed in April 1427, indicating the Bourgeois' refusal to acknowledge the *status quo* until it became incontestable. While the emphasis upon the chapter's agency reveals the Bourgeois' attachment to the cathedral's privileges, the narrative confusion suggests that he was not privy to the chapter's internal discussions.

This juxtaposition of the cathedral with Paris' governors was elaborated on 25 May 1427, when the Bourgeois described his participation in Notre-Dame's first rogation procession to Montmartre. Having stressed the devotion of those processing in the pouring rain, the Bourgeois was offended when John, duke of Bedford and his wife, Anne of Burgundy, rode past the clergymen

> dont ilz tindrent moult peu de compte, car ilz chevaulchoient moult fort, et ceulx de la procession ne porent reculler, si furent moult toulliez de la boue que les piez des

---

137 Grassoreille, 'Histoire politique du chapitre', pp. 155-59.

138 Shirley (ed. and trans.), *A Parisian Journal*, p. 17.

139 Grassoreille, 'Histoire politique du chapitre', pp. 164-69; Véronique Julerot, *"Y a ung grant desordre". Élections épiscopales et schismes diocésains en France sous Charles VII* (Paris: Publications de la Sorbonne, 2006), pp. 79-80.

140 Received at Notre-Dame. *Journal*, p. 213.

141 No one spoke any more of the election that had taken place beforehand, that is of my lord Nicole Fraillon, who had been elected by the entirety of the chapter of Notre-Dame; but despite the election [...] the said Fraillon was dismissed and the other admitted, for that is what pleased the governors. *Journal*, p. 215.

chevaulx gectoient par devant et darriere, mais oncques n'y ot nul si gentil qui, pour chasse ne pour procession, se daingnast ung pou arrester.[142]

Coinciding with the disputes surrounding Fraillon's election, the Bourgeois signalled the tensions between the clergy and Bedford, dramatizing the regent's lack of respect for the cathedral, its liturgical and saintly traditions, as well as its authority within Parisian space. The mention of Anne of Burgundy is significant, since she too had attempted to influence the episcopal election through 'litteras domini regentis et domine ejus uxoris' in November 1426.[143] The account of this confrontation was, in the *Journal*, immediately followed by news of Chastelier's reception as bishop. Read together, the passages demonstrate the Bourgeois' increasing engagement with the challenges facing the chapter, evidencing displeasure at Bedford's subversion of Notre-Dame's privileges and Paris' wider independence.

In turn, increasing textual parallels between the *Journal* and the Parisian chapter's register of acts suggest that, by the 1430s at least, the institution had also become a source of information for the Bourgeois' record. This is evidenced by the description of the sermon delivered at the Augustins convent on 25 May 1431 by a master theologian, relating the indulgences accorded by Martin V for those who participated in Corpus Christi celebrations. The Bourgeois clearly presented the indulgences' pronouncement as an oral and aural experience: 'la fut faicte une predicacion, en laquelle predicacion fut monstré et decleré le tres hault bien espirituel que pappe Martin V[e] de ce nom avoit donné'.[144] And yet, the *Journal*'s account was evidently drawn from a copy of the bull itself, a Latin version of which is found with a French translation on the last folios of the chapter's register, dated 1432 and signed by Notre-Dame's notary, Guillaume de Rivery.[145] In this respect, the Bourgeois' decision to reproduce the vernacular copy of the sermon circulating among the cathedral clergy underscores the likelihood that his audience comprised lay members rather than clerics, a fact further suggested by the sermon's very inclusion, as information pertinent to the salvific redemption of lay Christians.

Elsewhere in his narrative the Bourgeois selectively and carefully glossed events pertaining to the cathedral's administration or even overlooked them altogether, instead prioritizing those of significance for the wider Parisian community. Processions organized to support English military campaigns were omitted, as were the disputes in the Paris Parlement between the chapter and bishops Jean de Nant or Jacques du Chastelier.[146] It was only in 1441, when the Bourgeois may well have been a canon, that he described bishop Denis du Moulin as facing 'plus de cinquante proces en Parlement', an allusion to

---

142 For whom they had little regard because they were riding so hard, and those participating in the procession could not step back so that they were dirtied by the mud that the horses' feet kicked up before and behind them, but among them there were none kind enough to stop for [the sake of] the reliquaries or the procession. *Journal*, p. 214.

143 Letters from my lord the regent and my lady his wife. Paris, Archives nationales, LL 113, 'Registres capitulaires (1425-32)', p. 72.

144 There took place a sermon, during which the very spiritual good granted by pope Martin V (of this name) had granted was shown and declared. *Journal*, p. 264.

145 Paris, BNF Latin 17740, fols 398r-v.

146 Pierre-Clément Timbal and Josette Metman, 'Evêque de Paris et chapitre de Notre-Dame: la juridiction dans la cathédrale au Moyen Âge', *Revue d'histoire de l'Église de France*, 50 (1964), pp. 67-72.

the numerous suits that saw the cathedral clergy confront their bishop between 1440 and 1443.[147] In turn, while identifying Chastelier as a Lancastrian governor who maintained 'toute ceste mallefice et dyabolicque guerre' in 1436, the Bourgeois deliberately obfuscated connections between the chapter and the Lancastrian regime.[148] When Henry VI of England was crowned king of France in Paris in December 1431, the Bourgeois avoided any reference to the cathedral clergy's participation in the organization and performance of the accompanying ceremonies. A key moment at which Notre-Dame could assert its spiritual and traditional centrality by appropriating the ritual repertoires associated with traditional sites such as Reims and Saint-Denis, even adapting the Reims *ordo* to Parisian space, the *Journal* was silent about the close collaboration between the cathedral clergy and the Lancastrian regime that the event represented.[149] Nor did the Bourgeois mention the dispute between the chapter and Lancastrian governors that ensued regarding the coronation's administration. In contrast, Monstrelet claimed that Jacques du Chastelier was disgruntled when the English cardinal and bishop of Winchester Henry Beaufort sang the Mass in Notre-Dame, while the royal officers' reprisal of the chalice used by Henry VI to ceremoniously offer wine to the cathedral 'grandement despleut aux chanoines d'ycelle église, pour tant qu'ilz disoient ce appartenir a eulx de droit'.[150] In the *Journal*, Notre-Dame appears as a passive stage for a predominantly English ceremony, disguising the chapter's active complicity.

The last two bishops appearing in the *Journal*, Denis du Moulin (1439-47) and Guillaume Chartier (1447-72), encapsulate the Bourgeois' perception of Notre-Dame's authority. First, Denis du Moulin was presented as an imposition upon the cathedral by royal power, 'pour ce qu'il estoit du conseil du roy'.[151] The Bourgeois repeatedly stressed that it was through this connection to the royal centre that Moulin simultaneously possessed the bishopric of Paris and archbishopric of Toulouse, where Moulin had served since 1422, reporting upon his reception on 9 October 1440 that 'ainsi fut-il arcevesque et evesque de Paris'.[152] In contrast, the canons' successful election of Guillaume Chartier, 'homme de tres bonne renommée' was endorsed by the Bourgeois, demonstrating the chapter's constitutional authority.[153] It is perhaps for this reason that the *Journal* described in detail the constitutional elements of Chartier's reception, with the canon 'sacré et beney [...] en l'abbaie de Sainct-Victor-lez-Paris' before processing to Notre-Dame, where he was received 'a tres grant honneur'.[154] The enthusiasm parallels that of the chapter's clerks who also included a description of Chartier's coronation, procession and reception in

---

147 Had more than fifty cases in the Paris Parlement. *Journal*, p. 357. See also Longnon, 'Conjectures sur l'auteur du journal parisien', pp. 325-29.

148 All of this evil and diabolical warfare. *Journal*, p. 312.

149 See Jean-Baptiste Lebigue, 'L'ordo du sacre d'Henri VI à Notre-Dame de Paris (16 décembre 1431)' in *Notre-Dame de Paris, 1163-2013*, ed. by Cédric Giraud (Turnhout: Brepols, 2013), pp. 319-63.

150 Greatly displeased the canons of this church because they claimed that this belonged to them by right. Monstrelet, V, p. 5.

151 Because he was a member of the royal council. *Journal*, p. 344.

152 So he was an archbishop and bishop of Paris. *Journal*, p. 355. Timbal and Metman, 'Evêque de Paris', pp. 48, 65

153 A man of very good renown. *Journal*, p. 386. Chartier was the first Parisian canon to be elected bishop successfully since Aimery de Maignac in 1373.

154 Crowned and blessed [...] in the abbey of Saint-Victor-lez-Paris; with great honour. *Journal*, p. 388.

their registers, unlike for previous bishops.[155] The Bourgeois praised Chartier's preaching, contrasted with Denis du Moulin who had delegated the Lendit sermon in 1444 to the theologian Jean de l'Olive.[156] Likewise, where Moulin had threatened those possessing letters of absolution with excommunication, Chartier examined the archdeacon's registers of excommunications, 'et y mist tres bonne ordonnance contre ceulx de la court de l'Eglise' such that none would be excommunicated upon their death.[157]

The Bourgeois viewed Notre-Dame as an institution attuned to and representative of Parisian concerns, capable of challenging royal authority. The *Journal*'s adaptation of and deviation from narratives that were more fully developed in the chapter's registers strongly suggests that the text was not destined for an audience of canons, though the Bourgeois may well have drawn on some of these records himself. Despite concerns for the cathedral's political role, no evidence suggests that the narrative was destined for those intimately involved with its administration, especially in those instances where the *Journal* directly contradicts the chapter's own political stances. It is also unlikely that the canons themselves, wealthy men who exhibited close ties to Paris' civic and royal institutions, would have required a text like the *Journal* for information compared to that derived from the cathedral's registers, those of the officiality or the Paris Parlement.[158] Instead, it appears more plausible that the Bourgeois summarized the cathedral's political role for an audience less concerned by the intricacies of chapter politics and invested in the clergy's representative role for the city. Consequently, the cathedral community's portrayal was partisan, and from 1420 the Bourgeois consistently stressed the threat posed by royal authority to the cathedral's privileges and jurisdiction. Elaborating these issues, the *Journal* concentrated upon two distinct themes: an idalization of the Parisian bishop and the constitutional processes underpinning his authority. Predominantly, the Bourgeois favoured the chapter's authority relative to the royal imposition of bishops, presenting the canons as representatives of the city's independence threatened by royal encroachment. Due to this perspective, the ties between the cathedral and Lancastrian regime were deliberately obfuscated. As such, the behaviour of those bishops imposed by royal authority, such as Jacques du Chastelier and Denis du Moulin, were earmarked for particular criticism that redounded upon Lancastrian or Valois legitimacy, with these two prelates presented as tyrants.

---

155 Paris, Archives nationales LL 116, p. 482.

156 *Journal*, pp. 373-74, 389.

157 Put them in very good order against those of the Church court. *Journal*, pp. 376-77, 389.

158 See Véronique Julerot, 'Les chanoines cathédraux au parlement de Paris: Entre service de l'État et intérêts personnels' in *Église et état, église ou état? Les clercs et la genèse de l'État moderne*, ed. by Christine Barralis, Jean-Patrice Boudet, Fabrice Delivré and Jean-Philippe Genet (Paris: Éditions de la Sorbonne, 2014), pp. 88-95; Vincent Tabbagh, 'Les chanoines de la fin du Moyen Âge étaient-ils au service de l'État?' in *Église et État, Église ou État? Les clercs et la genèse de l'État moderne*, ed. by Christine Barralis, Jean-Patrice Boudet, Fabrice Delivré and Jean-Philippe Genet (Paris: Éditions de la Sorbonne, 2014), pp. 149-51.

The University of Paris

This representative function can also be perceived in the Bourgeois' account of the University of Paris. Although Colette Beaune argued that the *Journal* was compiled for fellow University members, the relative scarcity of references to the University renders this hypothesis difficult to substantiate.[159] Key moments include concern for the arrest of the University rector in 1418 and a similar assault upon the rector in 1444, but between these dates passages referring to the University are intermittent.[160] To become a doctor in theology the Bourgeois would have studied a lengthy cursus that, altogether, lasted up to twenty years.[161] Even brilliant theologians required a significant amount of time to become licensed: Jean Gerson spent eleven years studying and Gérard Machet, Charles VII's confessor, took thirteen years to complete the cursus.[162] If the Bourgeois can be identified as the theologian Nicolas Confrant, it also becomes possible to examine the parallels between the Bourgeois and the Norman theologian, who spent eleven years studying theology following his reception at the Collège d'Harcourt in 1423.[163] With regards to the size of the community of theologians, at least seventy-six doctors achieved the licentiate between 1421-30, reflecting the higher number of individuals who began their studies during the relative stability of the first decade of the fifteenth century. In contrast, during 1431-40 the number of graduates dropped to fifty.[164] As such, when combined with deaths and migration, the community of licensed theologians in Paris was especially small – a tiny fraction of the city's population that, even at its lowest point, numbered 80,000 people between 1421 and 1438.[165]

As a corporation, the University of Paris represented a 'fictional entity' encapsulating a consortium of different groups.[166] By the fourteenth century students spent the majority of their time within the framework of one of the four nations (French, Norman, Picard and Anglo-German), institutions that generated intense loyalties. The same might be said for the forty-five colleges that had been founded by the end of the fourteenth century,

---

159 Beaune (ed. and trans.), *Journal d'un bourgeois de Paris*, p. 18.
160 *Journal*, pp. 84-5, 375-76. On these incidents see *Chartularium Universitatis Parisiensis*, ed. by Heinrich Denifle, 4 vols (Paris: Delalain, 1889-97), IV (1897), pp. 336-38, 642-43; Pearl Kirbe, *Scholarly Privileges in the Middle Ages: The Rights, Privileges and Immunities of Scholars and Universities at Bologna, Padua, Paris and Oxford* (London: Medieval Academy of America, 1961), pp. 212-16.
161 On the cursus see Bernard Guenée, '"*Scandalum inter antiquos et juvenes theologos*". Un conflit de générations à la Faculté de théologie de Paris au début du XVᵉ siècle' in *Un roi et son historien: Vingt études sur le règne de Charles VI et la Chronique du religieux de Saint-Denis* (Paris: Boccard, 1999), p. 359.
162 Guenée, '*Scandalum inter antiquos et juvenes theologos*', p. 360. See also Cécile Fabris, *Étudier et vivre à Paris au Moyen Âge: Le Collège de Laon (XIVᵉ-XVᵉ siècles)* (Paris: Ecole des Chartes, 2005); Jacques Verger, 'Prosopographie et cursus universitaire' in *Medieval Lives and the Historian: Studies in Medieval Prosopography*, ed. by Neithard Bulst and Jean-Philippe Genet (Kalamazoo: Medieval Institute Publications, 1986), pp. 316-18.
163 On this possible identification, see the Introduction. For Confrant's University cursus and membership, see Luke Giraudet, 'Nicolas Confrant, author of the *Journal d'un bourgeois de Paris*?', *Romania*, 139 (2021) pp. 126-34.
164 These statistics are sourced from the *Studium Parisiense* database, containing upwards of 15,000 files for students in medieval Paris. http://studium.univ-paris1.fr/index.php.
165 J. Jacquart, 'Le poids démographique de Paris et de l'Ile-de-France au XVIᵉ siècle', *Annales de démographie historique* (1980), pp. 90-1; Favier, *Le bourgeois de Paris*, pp. 116-17.
166 William J. Courtenay, *Rituals for the Dead: Religion and Community in the Medieval University of Paris* (Notre Dame, IN: University of Notre-Dame Press, 2019), p. 2.

representing the essential context to everyday student life, though Alan Cobban has warned that before 1400 they housed only a small proportion of the overall University population.[167] These colleges were established to support students with shared regional origins during their studies. Indeed, for the late fourteenth and early fifteenth centuries, Jacques Verger has demonstrated an increasing correlation between locality and university membership throughout France, with recruitment stemming from each university's respective 'aire naturelle' and 92% of Paris' students arriving from northern France.[168] A significant proportion of these came from Normandy, with the University *rotulus* for 1403 revealing as many as 41% of members with Norman origins.[169]

Paris' colleges were governed by the varying statutes instituted by their founders, invariably stipulating the students' wealth, moral character and geographical origin. Those accorded bursaries had to demonstrate their relative poverty, with Nicolas Confrant's Collège d'Harcourt fixing a maximum annual revenue of twelve *livres parisis* for artists.[170] Student life was stringently regulated, with rules controlling clothing and appearance, movement outside the college and profane discussion monitored, the frequentation of taverns or 'lieux de plaisir' forbidden, while attendance at communal meals or masses and the recitation of prayers were carefully supervised.[171] Acceptance of a bursary involved an oath sworn to respect these statutes. Moreover, corporate sentiment was fostered through concern for the memory of deceased masters and students. The thirteenth century saw 'une certaine dispersion de la mémoire individuelle des morts entre plusieurs lieux parisiens', with one central *lieu de mémoire* favoured by University masters being the convent of Sainte-Catherine-du-Val-des-Écoliers, where Nicolas Confrant was buried.[172]

Regarding language, eight colleges founded in the fourteenth and fifteenth centuries specified that their students communicate solely in Latin, with the Collège de Plessis only allowing conversation in the vernacular with outsiders and 'illiterati'.[173] While the repetition of these statutes implies that the vernacular was becoming prevalent, they also demonstrate that young students entering colleges found themselves immersed in tightly-knit communities where Latin was the expected, if not the dominant, language of conversation. University records do present the institution as being characterized by a

167 Alan B. Cobban, 'The Role of Colleges in the Medieval Universities of Northern Europe, with special reference to England and France', *Bulletin of the John Rylands Library*, 71 (1989), pp. 50-53. See also Simone Roux, *La rive gauche des escholiers (XVᵉ siècle)* (Paris: Éditions chrétiennes, 1992); Fabris, *Étudier et vivre à Paris*.

168 Jacques Verger, 'La mobilité étudiante au Moyen Âge', *Histoire de l'éducation*, 50 (1991), pp. 77-81. See also Nathalie Gorochov, 'L'université recrute-t-elle dans la ville? Le cas de Paris au XIIIᵉ siècle' in *Les universités et la ville au Moyen Âge: cohabitation et tension*, ed. by Patrick Gilli, Jacques Verger and Daniel Le Blévec (Leiden: Brill, 2007), pp. 275-76.

169 Lyse Roy, 'Histoire d'une université régionale: l'Université de Caen au XVᵉ siècle', *Paedagogica Historica*, 34 (1998), p. 406. For the rotulus, see *Chartularium*, IV, pp. 61-125.

170 Henri Bouquet, *L'ancien collège d'Harcourt et le Lycée Saint-Louis* (Paris: Delalain, 1891), p. 581, no. 8.

171 Bouquet, *L'ancien collège*, pp. 579-90. See also Fabris, *Étudier and vivre à Paris*, pp. 55-60; Nathalie Gorochov, *Le collège de Navarre de sa fondation (1305) au début du XVᵉ siècle (1418): histoire de l'institution, de sa vie intellectuelle et de son recrutement* (Paris: Champion, 1997), pp. 159-69; Courtenay, *Rituals for the Dead*, pp. 46-50.

172 A certain dispersal of the individual memory of the dead between several Parisian places. Nathalie Gorochov, 'La mémoire des morts dans l'Université de Paris au XIIIᵉ siècle', *Beihefte der Francia*, 55 (2003), pp. 119, 123-25; Courtenay, *Rituals for the Dead*, pp. 13-16; Giraudet, 'Nicolas Confrant', p. 138.

173 Serge Lusignan, 'L'enseignement des arts dans les collèges parisiens au Moyen Âge' in *L'enseignement des disciplines à la Faculté des Arts (Paris et Oxford, XIIIᵉ-XVᵉ siècles)*, ed. by O. Weijers and L. Hortz (Turnhout: Brepols, 1997), p. 46.

'monopole du latin'.[174] In this context, the Bourgeois' decision to write in the vernacular is significant, again implying the *Journal*'s appeal to an audience outside the University. While University sermons were delivered in Latin, contemporary theologians would often switch to French for lay audiences to effectively communicate moral teachings.[175] To this end, a growing proportion of fifteenth-century sermons survive in French, including those pronounced by Jean Courtecuisse and Jean Gerson, evoking the aggrandizement of the vernacular found in tandem with the translation movement that gained pace at the court of Charles V in the second half of the fourteenth century.[176] The *diglossia* common to Paris' theologians therefore encapsulated ideological as much as straightforward linguistic choices.[177] While Latinity was integral to a clerical identity founded upon a close interpretation of the Bible and Church Fathers, the Collège de Cluny's 1308 statute requiring its pupils to practice French for preaching suggests that the vernacular had emerged as the most effective channel for lay spiritual education.[178] Margriet Hoogvliet has similarly pointed to the growing use of French vernacular Bible translations in the fifteenth century 'in an urban context [...] [for] retail merchants, shopkeepers, artisans, servants and their close relatives'.[179] Such widespread recognition that the vernacular assumed a didactic purpose before lay audiences substantiates the view that the Bourgeois did not envision a clerical audience for his writing, particularly one based at the University whose members would have expected the eloquence that they would have found in Latin texts, as Colette Beaune has suggested.[180]

Inversely, the Bourgeois' likely affiliation with a University college as a student underscores the importance of the political role performed by the corporation in the opening decades of the fifteenth century, a role that exhibits significant parallels with the stances of the Halles' inhabitants and even the cathedral chapter of Notre-Dame. Ultimately, the cohesion of the college and nation format also meant that these bodies developed clear political stances. The Collège de Navarre supplied the Armagnac government and Dauphin Charles with numerous bureaucrats, with ten serving the administration in 1418.[181] Similarly, the Collège d'Harcourt was closely connected to the Cabochien revolt. In February 1413, the college pursued a dispute with the *prévôt* Pierre des Essarts when a dead horse was left before its gate by a Châtelet *sergent*, culminating in a University petition decrying the infringement of its privileges that served as a prelude to the uprising.[182] The theology

174 Philippe Riché and Jacques Verger, *Des nains sur des épaules de géants: maîtres et élèves au Moyen Âge* (Paris: Taillandier, 2006), p. 206.
175 Serge Lusignan, 'Le français et le latin aux XIIIᵉ-XIVᵉ siècles: pratique des langues et pensée linguistique', *Annales ESC*, 42 (1987), pp. 962-63.
176 Serge Lusignan, *Parler vulgairement: Les intellectuels et la langue française aux XIIIᵉ et XIVᵉ siècles*, pp. 154-68.
177 Serge Lusignan, *Essai d'histoire sociolinguistique: le français picard au Moyen Âge* (Paris: Classiques Garnier, 2012), pp. 35-9; Brian Stock, 'Medieval Literacy, Linguistic Theory and Social Organization', *New Literary History*, 16 (1984), 17.
178 Michel Félibien et Guy-Alexis Lobineau, *Histoire de la ville de Paris*, 5 vols (Paris: Guillaume Despréz et Jean Desessarts, 1725), III, p. 281; Lusignan, *Parler vulgairement*, pp. 41-59, 141-49.
179 Margriet Hoogvliet, 'Encouraging Lay People to Read the Bible in the French Vernaculars: New Groups of Readers and Textual Communities', *Church History and Religious Culture*, 93 (2013), pp. 240, 266-74.
180 Able to appreciate fine pieces of eloquent rhetoric. Beaune (ed. and trans.), *Journal*, p. 18.
181 Gorochov, *Le collège de Navarre*, p. 567.
182 'La geste des nobles Francoys', pp. 145-46; Coville, *Les Cabochiens*, p. 183.

master and college bursar, Ursin de Talevande, spoke before the assembled estates in February 1413 to promote royal reform and again on 4 August, this time in the *volte face* undermining the revolt that vexed the Bourgeois.[183] In 1414, Talevande emerged at the centre of a contest between the Norman and French nations when he opposed an Armagnac-favoured candidate, Jean de Marle, for the bishopric of Coutances. The dispute culminated in Talevande's Norman supporters attacking the University rector, Jean Campan, demonstrating how profoundly the civil conflict altered relations within the University.[184] Regional allegiances should not be underestimated. Jean Petit employed Norman scholars to produce copies of the *Justification*, while Norman delegates to the Council of Constance were divided regarding the treatise's condemnation in 1415 and 1416.[185] The attitudes of Norman scholars and the Collège d'Harcourt's members alike may explain, in part, the Bourgeois' antipathy towards the Armagnacs if his identification as Confrant is accepted.

The Bourgeois' own engagement with the theology faculty is evidenced by his consistent identification of and praise for theologians. In 1420, Jean Courtecuisse was described as a 'maistre en theologie et proudhomme'; the 1419 rector was identified as the theologian Jean l'Archer (licensed 1424), and Jean de l'Olive (licensed 1442) was similarly named upon his appointment by bishop Denis du Moulin to preach the Lendit sermon in 1444.[186] Likewise, the theologian and Mathurins minister Étienne du Mesnil, who pronounced a sermon before Charles VI in 1410, was described by the Bourgeois as a 'tres bonne personne'.[187] In contrast, the unnamed rector assaulted by tax officials in 1444, Albertus Scriptoris, was an Arts master from the German Nation, and this might explain the Bourgeois' failure to identify him.[188] Like the inhabitants of the Halles, these theologians were known for their sympathies towards the Burgundian dukes. Courtecuisse had attempted to maintain neutrality during the civil conflict, but had also played a role in the condemnation of the *prévôt* Guillaume de Tignonville in 1408 and is known to have frustrated Jean Gerson's attempts to condemn the *Justification* for Louis d'Orléans' murder in 1414.[189] The *Journal* presents Jean l'Archer as delivering a 'moult piteux' sermon in Jean sans Peur's memory on 29 September 1419, and l'Archer was also commissioned by Philippe le Bon to draft the sermon advocating the Dauphin Charles' condemnation for *lèse-majesté*

183 Serge Lusignan, '*Vérité garde le roy*': *La construction d'une identité universitaire en France (XIIIᵉ-XVᵉ siècle)* (Paris: Éditions de la Sorbonne, 1999), p. 196.
184 *Chartularium*, IV, pp. 289-92; Coville, *Jean Petit*, p. 452.
185 Coville, *Jean Petit*, pp. 135-40, 228; Alfred Coville, 'Le véritable texte de la Justification du duc de Bourgogne par Jean Petit (8 mars 1408)', *BEC*, 72 (1911), pp. 64-69. These tensions have recently been analysed in Annick Brabant, 'Un pont entre les obédiences: expériences normandes du Grand Schisme d'Occident (1378-1417)' (unpublished doctoral thesis, Université de Caen Basse-Normandie, 2013), pp. 363-65.
186 Master in theology and a wise man. *Journal*, pp. 132, 147, 373-74 (147). Regarding these theologians see Thomas Sullivan, *Parisian Licentiates in Theology, AD 1373-1500: A Bibliographical Register, vol. 2. The Secular Clergy* (Leiden: Brill, 2011), pp. 45, 179-84, 397.
187 Very good person. *Journal*, p. 9.
188 *Journal*, p. 376; *Chartularium*, IV, pp. 642-44.
189 *Chartularium*, IV, pp. 148-49; Fauquembergue, I, p. 183; *Histoire de Charles VI*, pp. 528-29; Coville, 'Récherches sur Jean Courtecuisse', pp. 476-79.

in December 1420.[190] Consequently, the Bourgeois' identification of University members implied a focus upon 'Burgundian' members whose sympathies mirrored those of the Halles.

Indeed, early in his writing the Bourgeois envisioned the University as being politically sympathetic to the Parisians who endorsed Jean sans Peur, assuming a representative role for the civic community. Mesnil's 1410 sermon warned the king of the dangers posed by treachery and corruption.[191] When the theologian was insulted by the Orléanist cardinal, Louis I of Bar, the Bourgeois related how the University rallied to his defence, a fact echoed in Michel Pintoin's own chronicle, which portrayed Jean, duke of Berry as conceding that the 'Universitas Parisiensis, cives quoque et communitas' collectively supported Burgundy.[192] In June 1412 University members were compelled to join the processions eliciting divine support for the Burgundian siege of Bourges 'sur peine de privacion', thereby publicly demonstrating their endorsement of Jean sans Peur.[193] In 1413, the Bourgeois valued the University's involvement in the Cabochien revolt when, 'par grant diligence et grant sens', members drew up a petition accusing officials of treachery that legitimated the revolt.[194] When the University subsequently performed a political *volte face* in August, abandoning the Cabochien leaders vying for reforms perceived to be favourable to Paris' commons, the Bourgeois was infuriated: the University had been advised by the devil and 'proposerent tout au contraire de ce qu'ilz avoient devant conseillé par plusieurs foys'.[195]

This confusion regarding the University's political stance again indicates that the Bourgeois was distant from its administration. As with Notre-Dame, the Bourgeois surveyed the University's political engagement for an external audience, obfuscating compromising details. For example, describing a feast held at the Palais on 21 June 1428 attended by John, duke of Bedford, the Bourgeois omitted the reason for this celebration, namely the appointment of four new doctors in canon law, two of whom, Guillaume Bonnel and Alan Kirkton, had been nominated by Bedford.[196] Thus, the Bourgeois disguised the extent of Lancastrian influence over Paris' institutions. He was also unwilling, or unable, to divulge details regarding the theological and political discussions taking place at the University regarding the Great Schism or war. Only definitive conclusions were reported while specific events, such as the 'Concile de la Foi' organized by Jean Gerson at Paris in 1413-14 that involved attempts to discredit Jean Petit's *Justification*, may have been omitted

---

190 *Journal*, p. 132; Monstrelet, IV, p. 19; Paul Bonenfant, *Du meurtre de Montereau au traité de Troyes* (Brussels: Académie royale de Belgique, 1958), p. 177.

191 *Journal*, pp. 9-10.

192 University of Paris, citizens and community. RSD, IV, p. 342.

193 Upon pain of privation. *Journal*, p. 12.

194 With great diligence and great sense. *Journal*, p. 28. On the compilation of this dossier see Monstrelet, II, pp. 307-32; Coville, *Les Cabochiens*, pp. 167-74.

195 They proposed completely the opposite of what they had previously advised upon several occasions. *Journal*, p. 35.

196 *Journal*, p. 227; *Chartularium*, IV, p. 476; Christopher Allmand, 'Alan Kirketon: a clerical royal councillor in Normandy during the English occupation in the fifteenth century', *The Journal of Ecclesiastical History*, 15, 1 (1964), p. 36.

precisely because of their anti-Burgundian character.[197] When compared with the extensive transcription of sermons found in Pintoin's chronicle, the *Journal*'s brevity reinforces the impression that the text was destined for an audience that was perhaps not as heavily invested in either ecclesiastical or University matters.

Deviations from the official record support this impression, as in 1426 when the Bourgeois alluded to the inquisitorial examination of five Parisians who had used cabalistic formulae in an endeavour to uncover treasure.[198] Alexandre Tuetey believed the reference evidenced the 'main d'un prêtre de Notre-Dame mêlé aux incidents de la vie capitulaire'.[199] However, the account contrasts with that of the chapter's own *greffier*, Nicolas Sellier.[200] Firstly, the accused were not 'd'obscurs hérétiques', as Tuetey implied in his own analysis.[201] At least one of these was in fact a Burgundian officer, namely the ducal secretary Guillaume Vignier, appointed *trésorier des guerres* in 1418 and serving as a royal secretary in the mid-1420s.[202] Second, the trial provoked a jurisdictional debate between the bishop Jean de Nant, the University and the French Grand Inquisitor Jean Graverent, requiring resolution by papal decree.[203] Although the Bourgeois' relation of the procession to Saint-Magloire in September 1426 'encontre aucuns hereses qui avoient herré contre notre foy' suggests a limited awareness of these tensions, the diminution of the event's importance may reflect a deliberate attempt to obfuscate the examination of prominent Burgundians, a point underscored by the absence of an earlier passage alluded to by the Bourgeois, 'comme devant est dit, ou moys de may mil iiij^c xxiiij', regarding the trial.[204] The inquisition began in June 1425 but the Vatican manuscript shows no signs of text missing at this time, suggesting that the Bourgeois may have carefully revised the *Journal* to disguise the condemnation of key figures in the Anglo-Burgundian administration.

Other records sourced from within the University were readily incorporated into the *Journal*, indicating that participation in the corporation enabled the Bourgeois to communicate political information to local Parisian audiences. One such example is the transcription of the Treaty of Troyes found in surviving copies of the *Journal*, situated immediately after the Bourgeois' account of Henry V's marriage to Catherine of Valois in his narrative.[205] Although it is possible that the treaty's text was a later addition to the *Journal*, it seems unlikely that this would have occurred after 1436, with Jean-Marie Moeglin

---

197 Charles Vulliez, 'Les maîtres orléanais (*doctores*) au service de l'Université, de l'Église et des pouvoirs séculiers au temps de Charles VI' in *Saint-Denis et la royauté. Études offertes à Bernard Guenée* (Paris: Publications de la Sorbonne, 1999), p. 86. For the Concile de la Foi see Coville, *Jean Petit*, pp. 439-501; Guenée, *Un meurtre, une société*, pp. 239-56.

198 *Journal*, pp. 209-10.

199 The hand of a Notre-Dame priest involved in instances of the chapter's life. Tuetey (ed.), *Journal*, p. xx.

200 Paris, Archives nationales, LL 113, pp. 134-38.

201 Obscure heretics. Tuetey (ed.), *Journal*, xx.

202 For Guillaume Vignier see Richard Vaughan, *John the Fearless: The Growth of Burgundian Power*, Second Edition (Woodbridge: Boydell, 2002), pp. 130-31.

203 *Chartularium*, IV, pp. 446-48, 453, 461-62. Zénon Kaluza has examined this case through the *Propositio* regarding the jurisdiction dispute pronounced by Gilles Charlier, found in Bordeaux, Bibliothèque municipale MS 117-18, fols 37r-50v in 'Nouvelles remarques sur les oeuvres de Gilles Charlier', *Archives d'histoire doctrinale et littéraire du Moyen Âge*, 47 (1973), pp. 161-62.

204 Against some heretics who had erred against the faith; as stated earlier in May 1424. *Journal*, pp. 209-10.

205 The treaty has been omitted in editions of the *Journal* since the nineteenth century. It is found between folios 66v and 72v of the Vatican manuscript.

persuasively demonstrating the hesitancy with which French authors evoked the alliance in the wake of the Valois resurgence and reconquest of northern France.[206] Not only was the version of the treaty copied into the *Journal* analogous to that circulated among Charles VI's secretaries, as demonstrated by a reference to its scribe, Jean de Rinel, but both signature and text are also identical to the copies found in the archives of the *Trésor des Chartes* and Paris Parlement. The copy in the *Trésor des Chartes* provides important indications as to the treaty's publication in Paris, with a codicil noting its pronouncement before the members of the University's three faculties on 3 June 1420 and, again, before the entirety of the four nations the following day at Saint-Julien-le-Pauvre.[207] As a student, it is likely that the Bourgeois would have encountered the treaty's text in these circumstances and possibly incorporated a version into his writing.

Similarly, the *Journal*'s account of Jeanne d'Arc's condemnation trial suggests that the Bourgeois interacted with documents circulating at the University of Paris and drew upon these sources. For the former, the Bourgeois' presentation of the accusations against Jeanne closely mirrored the content of the Twelve Articles of Accusation developed by Jean d'Estivet, promotor and procurator general for the trial.[208] Their incorporation into the *Journal* also appears to have followed a rhetorical, argumentative logic: instead of restating the accusations point-for-point, the Bourgeois reworked their order to present a careful case for Jeanne d'Arc's condemnation. By beginning with those localised crimes committed by Jeanne d'Arc with which Parisians would have been acutely familiar, namely her assault upon Paris in 1429 and her inspiration of idolatry in Senlis, followed by her perpetration of violence throughout Christendom 'comme chacun scet', the Bourgeois geographically situated the *mala fama* required as the fundamental basis to the condemnation trial.[209] With this established, the Bourgeois presented the accusations against Jeanne d'Arc by moving from her voices and claims to divine inspiration through to her mission and clothing, examining her signs before finally commenting upon her military role. At the core of this presentation is a single sentence, 'Item, dist que elle est certaine de estre en paradis en la fin de ses jours'.[210] Like a sermon's emphasis upon a single Biblical citation, the isolation of this phrase in contrast to the surrounding entries implies that the Bourgeois recognized the controversial significance of this assertion. In particular, it tellingly parallels the Rouen judges' response to Jeanne's claim that she believed she would be saved 'as firmly as if she was already there', with the implicit consequence that she had committed no mortal sin, such that her interrogators warned that this was a reply 'of great weight'.[211]

If the Bourgeois was a member of the theology faculty by 1429, then this analysis suggests that he participated in the discussion of the articles by the faculty that took place

---

206 Jean-Marie Moeglin, 'Réécrire l'histoire de la Guerre de Cent Ans. Une relecture historique et historiographique du traité de Troyes (21 mai 1420)', *Revue historique*, 664 (2012), pp. 907-16.

207 Paris, Archives nationales, JJ 171, fols 74r-76r (76r); X 1ᵃ 8603, fol. 61r; Paris, BNF Fr. 10468, fols 296v-300r. Published in *Ordonnances des rois de France*, XI, pp. 86-90.

208 Pierre Tisset and Yvonne Lanhers (ed.), *Procès de condamnation de Jeanne d'Arc*, 3 vols (Paris: Klincksieck, 1960-71), I (1960), pp. 289-97.

209 *Journal*, pp. 266-67. The accusations are elaborated over pages 266-69.

210 *Journal*, p. 268.

211 Tisset and Lanhers, *Procès de condamnation*, I, pp. 148-49.

on 29 April and 14 May 1431.[212] Similarly, Vincent Tabbagh has argued that members of the University who did not attend the Rouen trial or the Paris assemblies may have received 'des écrits simplifiant ses [Jeanne's] positions ou des témoignages indirects de ses réponses aux interrogatoirs'.[213] Indeed, while Confrant is not identified among those doctors present at Rouen, he was certainly closely connected to some who did attend the proceedings: having studied theology alongside the inquisitor Jean Graverent, Confrant is found teaching in the faculty in 1434 with known judges including Jean Beaupère, Denis Sabrevois and Thomas de Courcelles.[214]

Consequently, as with the struggles experienced by the chapter of Notre-Dame, the Bourgeois' references to the University and its involvement in Parisian politics invariably synthesized more complex developments for an external audience, as demonstrated by the *Journal*'s deviation in the record of University contestation. At the height of Armagnac authority in February 1418, the Bourgeois reported how celebrations of Pope Martin V's election were suppressed. When the rector Raoul de la Porte organized small-scale masses in Martin's name, 'pour tant fut mis en prinson et x ou xij maistres avecques lui'.[215] Read straightforwardly, the account evidenced Armagnac investment in the outcome of the Council of Constance, especially given Bernard, count of Armagnac's continued endorsement of Antipope Benedict XIII.[216] Tuetey argued that the Bourgeois deliberately altered the circumstances of la Porte's imprisonment, which actually resulted from an ongoing debate regarding the collation of benefices whereupon la Porte asserted that this power belonged to the recently elected pope.[217] However, the Bourgeois' manipulation of the dispute to underscore an Armagnac defiance of the Council of Constance is clear, indicating an alteration of University events to suit an anti-Armagnac perspective. Similarly, the assault upon the rector Albertus Scriptoris by tax officials in 1444 was related to wider challenges to University privileges by royal power. Having criticized royal management of the *écorcheurs* in the previous passage, the Bourgeois described how Scriptoris had intended to 'deffendre et garder les libertés et franchises de ladite Université' when students were targeted by fresh taxes.[218] The statement that the officials 'mirent la main au recteur' hints that the Bourgeois was manipulating an official account, with the text in the *CUP* reporting that 'contra rectorem et procuratores Franciae et Picardiae *manus levaverunt* rectoremque vulneraverunt "usque ad effusionem sanguinis".'[219] Through his account the Bourgeois

---

212 Tisset and Lanhers, *Procès de condamnation*, I, pp. 356-62.
213 Writings simplifying her responses or indirect testimony to her answers to the questioning. Vincent Tabbagh, 'Les assesseurs du procès de condamnation de Jeanne d'Arc' in *De l'hérétique à la sainte. Les procès de Jeanne d'Arc revisités*, ed. by François Neveux (Caen: Presses universitaires de Caen, 2012), pp. 115-16.
214 *Chartularium*, IV, pp. 563, 574.
215 For this he was put in prison, and ten or twelve masters along with him. *Journal*, p. 85.
216 Klaus Oschema, 'Nouvelles de Perpignan en France et Bourgogne (1415) – un non-lieu historique?' in *Perpignan 1415. Un sommet européen à l'époque du Grand Schisme en Occident*, ed. by Aymat Catafau, Nikolas Jaspert and Thomas Wetzstein (Zurich: Lit Verlag, 2019), pp. 48-9; Noël Valois, *La France et le Grand Schisme d'Occident*, 4 vols (Paris: Alphonse Picard, 1896-1902), IV (1902), pp. 153-56.
217 Tuetey (ed.), *Journal*, p. 85, n. 3; Fauquembergue, I, pp. 61-3, 76; Kirbe, *Scholarly Privileges*, pp. 236-38.
218 Protect and keep the liberties and exemptions of the said University. *Journal*, p. 375; Kirbe, *Scholarly Privileges*, p. 212.
219 Laid hands upon the rector; they raised their hands against the rector and procurators of the French and Picard [nations] and wounded the rector to the extent that blood was shed. *Chartularium*, IV, p. 643; *Journal* pp. 375-76.

rhetorically situated the University within overarching Parisian contentions regarding the increasingly regular direct taxation imposed by the Valois administration.

The examination of the University context through the lens of Nicolas Confrant's cursus indicates the problems inherent in assuming that the *Journal* was compiled for a University audience. College statutes encouraged members to converse in Latin and refrain from discussing profane topics, undermining the *Journal*'s suitability for this context. Instead, the vernacular was primarily reserved for interaction with Paris' laity, especially regarding moral and political issues. As with Notre-Dame, it therefore seems likely that the Bourgeois drew upon his University experiences to supplement the *Journal*'s narrative, but that ultimately this record was directed beyond the confines of the University itself, situating the institution within an overarching panoply of civic institutions.

Conclusion

This analysis of the Bourgeois' neighbourhood and ties to the church and parish of Saints-Innocents, the cathedral and chapter of Notre-Dame as well as the University of Paris provides crucial indications regarding the *Journal*'s contexts, its envisioned audience(s) and some of the author's sources. Together, these elements demonstrate the problems inherent in assuming an identity between the Bourgeois' characteristics and those of the *Journal*'s readers. Fundamentally, the internal evidence reveals that the Bourgeois was an active member of multiple groups simultaneously, with overlapping interests in several distinct contexts. The *Journal*'s passages relating to the University of Paris and the cathedral of Notre-Dame are, however, substantially briefer and less frequent than those concerning the right bank of Paris and specifically the Halles district. At times there are clear contradictions between the information supplied by the Bourgeois and that recorded in 'official' records, such as the cathedral chapter's registers. The resulting impression is that the *Journal* was not destined, at least primarily, for an audience of members of either of these institutions, who would have probably already had a similar understanding of the relevant issues as described by the Bourgeois and would have had access to alternative sources.

Rather, the Bourgeois' presentation of the University of Paris and the cathedral of Notre-Dame situates these institutions that claimed a representative role for the city in relation to other civic institutions, underscoring those moments where their interests and political prerogatives intersected with the goals and perspectives of the artisanal inhabitants of the Halles district and the rue Saint-Martin. In particular, the *Journal* addressed and encapsulated the perspectives of leading inhabitants of the Halles, members of some of the city's most influential corporations, such as the butchers, or those who rose to prominence in the urban administration due to their ties to the dukes of Burgundy. In doing so, the text consolidated their political perspectives, codified their experiences and repeatedly presented these in relation to the spaces and topography of the right bank. The *Journal* therefore encapsulated the memory of a community defined by its opposition to the Armagnac faction and its ties to the Burgundian dukes during the 1410s. During the political shifts of the 1420s and 1430s, however, the Bourgeois' writing evidences increasing interest in the role of Parisian institutions as representative of the wider civic community when confronted by the challenges to the city's independence posed by English rule or, later, Valois centralization. Having risen to positions of municipal responsibility, this community no longer consistently viewed itself through an Armagnac-Burgundian dichotomy, but through a lens that juxtaposed civic identities with external authorities.

As we have already seen in the Introduction, this impression of the Bourgeois' political engagement and his likely artisanal and bourgeois Halles audience is underscored by the available evidence of the text's readership and patronage in the latter half of the fifteenth century. The association of the Maciot family with the Vatican manuscript of the *Journal* suggests that the *Journal* continued to hold meaning for individuals rising in municipal politics and endeavouring to join a civic elite, as suggested by the near-hereditary office-holding performed by Jean, Claude and Vincent Maciot in their posts as *quarteniers* of the Saint-Germain-l'Auxerrois *quartier* over successive generations, and whose memories were similarly inscribed in the architectural and monumentary fabric of the Halles. Accounting for the agency of the Halles' inhabitants in municipal and royal politics, the *Journal* may have provided an important textual resource for these relative newcomers in civic politics as they strove to secure their status as members of the *corps municipal*.

CHAPTER 2

Official Communication and Popular Reactions

Throughout the *Journal*, official communication – the information disseminated by royal and civic bodies –, was considered in tandem with popular Parisian perspectives.[1] Here, the Bourgeois assumed the role of interpreter discerned by Leidulf Melve, arrogating an important agency in the framing of a public sphere through his authorial selectivity by privileging certain narratives over others to inculcate, reflect and express specific attitudes. The present chapter evaluates the *Journal* as the determined agglomeration of material that the Bourgeois wanted his audiences to consider, and an illustration of the ways in which he expected them to react. This manipulation is evidenced by the narrative strategies that the Bourgeois employed to represent instances of official communication. Elements contrary to the Bourgeois' socio-political beliefs and those of his envisioned audience were deliberately obfuscated, altered or omitted, while the author developed heightened emotional rhetoric to evaluate the morality of political decisions, aristocratic behaviour, and structure desired reactions. The close examination of popular interactions with official communication, as presented by the *Journal*, suggests that the Bourgeois' organization of information was performed as part of his active contribution to his public sphere. It was precisely in relation to official communication and civic or institutional prerogatives that these subaltern Parisian spheres were made manifest and, in turn, the Bourgeois' channelling of information and response through his text further delineated the boundaries of his opinion community. Ultimately, an appropriation of official information reveals how Parisians could participate in the public transcript of civic governance, while developing alternative political and historiographical narratives to critique official perspectives.

An assessment of official communication also reveals the function and the limits of propaganda in late medieval Paris. Providing an early framework founded upon the study of the modern phenomenon, Jacques Ellul identified propaganda as the psychological manipulation of opinion of which the subject is not conscious. For Ellul, propaganda was either agitative (encouraging specific behaviours) or integrative (determining specific ideological beliefs to elicit conformity).[2] Such processes consistently condition societal interaction, though more recently Scott-Morgan Straker has adapted Cambridge School approaches

---

1 For approaches to official communication in late-medieval contexts, see Veronika Novák, 'Places of Power: The Spreading of Official Information and the Social Uses of Space in Fifteenth-Century Paris', in *Towns and Communication*, 1, ed. by Neven Budak, Finn-Einar Eliassen and Katalin Szende (Akron, OH: University of Akron Press, 2011), pp. 49-51; Veronika Novák, 'La source du savoir: Publication officielle et communication informelle à Paris au début du XVᵉ siècle', in *Information et société à la fin du Moyen Âge* ed. by Claude Boudreau, Kouky Fianu, Claude Gauvard and Michel Hébert (Paris: Publications de la Sorbonne, 2004), pp. 151-53; Christian Liddy, *Contesting the City: The Politics of Citizenship in English Towns, 1250-1530* (Oxford: Oxford University Press, 2017), pp. 142-50.

2 Jacques Ellul, *Propaganda*, trans. by Konrad Kellen and Jean Lerner (New York: Vintage, 1973), esp. pp. 70-9.

to argue that medieval propagandists were simultaneously constative and performative, deliberately obscuring the distances between 'motive and intention'.[3] In turn, Vian Bakir and her colleagues have developed a new conceptual framework for propaganda's operation concentrating upon Organized Persuasive Communication comprising the 'deception, incentivization and coercion' through which powerful actors influence behaviour.[4] Their approach supports an important conceptual leap, from considering propaganda as straightforwardly symbolic communication of positive or negative forms, in a Bourdieuan sense, to recognizing that propaganda involves *concrete* action incorporating symbolic elements. In this light, propaganda is never simply the discursive, but a tangible practice involving the communication of ideas, their media of expression, the spaces in which they take place and underlying, more innate systems of persuasion.

The model highlights a conceptual overreliance upon a white-black dichotomy that distinguishes examples where the original source of information is concealed (black) from those where the source is evident (white), with the latter often perceived as being more accurate and truthful when compared to the former and leaving no space for 'half-truths or omissions'.[5] The epistemological difference inherently stems from the ways in which would-be propagandists either acknowledge or obfuscate their informational sources to achieve their objectives. Frequently, the identification of a factual, authoritative basis is required for successful persuasion, meaning that propaganda typically appeals to an established, rationalized framework designed to elicit emotional responses. As such, credibility is sustained through an audience's recognition that the presented information conforms to and sustains an existing logic.

Sophia Menache argued that medieval urban centres represented 'the most fruitful arena for legitimizing a new order which encouraged the use of propaganda and the manipulation of popular opinion in a modern sense, though by more primitive means'.[6] Each of the modes of non-consensual persuasive communication identified by Bakir were certainly commonplace in fifteenth-century France, including deception, distortion, misdirection, incentivization and coercion. However, it is also vital to recognize that the Bourgeois himself was invested in the dissemination of persuasive information that was deliberately designed to rhetorically shape his audiences' views – selecting, interpreting, transmitting and omitting the propaganda that he encountered in Paris. Indeed, for every instance where the Bourgeois refuted official discourse through recourse to public opinion, there is an occasion where he willingly transmitted tenuous information that coincided with his audience's expectations.

3 Scott-Morgan Straker, 'Propaganda, Intentionality and Lancastrian Lydgate' in *John Lydgate: Poetry, Culture and Lancastrian England*, ed. by Larry Scanlon and James Simpson (Notre Dame, IN: University of Notre Dame Press, 2006), pp. 101-04.

4 Vian Bakir, Eric Herring, David Miller and Piers Robinson, 'Organised Persuasive Communication: A new conceptual framework for research on public relations, propaganda and promotional culture', *Critical Sociology*, 45 (2018), pp. 311-28.

5 Garth Jowett and Victoria O'Donnell, *Propaganda and Persuasion*, Seventh Edition, (Thousand Oaks, CA: SAGE, 2018), p. 18; Bertrand Taithe and Tim Thornton, 'Propaganda: A Misnomer of Rhetoric and Persuasion?' in *Propaganda: Political Rhetoric and Identity, 1300-2000*, ed. by Bertrand Taithe and Tim Thornton (Sutton: Stroud, 1999), p. 2.

6 Sophia Menache, *The Vox Dei: Communication in the Middle Ages* (Oxford: Oxford University Press, 1990), p. 7.

Testifying to propaganda's growing role in fifteenth-century society and the potential for its manipulation by its audiences, the *Journal* presents Parisians as constantly striving to evaluate the authority and veracity of the political messages that they encountered through direct comparisons with their own beliefs and expectations. Often, the result was a recognition of the dissonance between civic or royal discourse and the horizon of expectations shared among popular Parisian audiences. Immediately recognisable instances of propaganda were portrayed by the Bourgeois as being openly decried and rejected by Parisians, with rumour frequently being privileged as a reliable alternative to official narratives that juxtaposed urban expectations with governing prerogatives. When the Bourgeois' *Journal* revealed these acts of condemnation, critique and open resistance, the passages were designed to question the political legitimacy of those institutions, factions or individuals responsible for disseminating the messages. Alternatively, the Bourgeois himself could be invested in the repetition of propaganda either to deliberately shape his own audience's views, or because this propaganda effectively concorded with the community's and his own horizon of expectations. In short, the *Journal* evidences the multivalent ways in which propaganda was consistently questioned, debated, accepted, rejected and even unrecognized, in a manner that complicates the established perspective that the Bourgeois simply repeated the propaganda that he encountered without considering its impact, sources and purpose.

Underscoring this interaction, emotional displays performed an inherently communicative function and their deployment actively altered the meaning of socio-political interaction in medieval society. While studies of modern Britain have emphasized the growing importance of emotional rhetoric used by political leaders and news media alike, texts like the *Journal* reveal that this is far from a recent phenomenon, with the Bourgeois similarly juxtaposing the emotional agencies of aristocratic and popular groups. Reacting to the rationalist emphasis in Habermas' paradigm, Barry Richards has proposed the existence of emotional public spheres resulting from the 'highly complex field of emotional forces' integral to determining political choice, opinion and participation.[7] Crucially, these contributions have begun to acknowledge the fundamental role emotions perform in news, communication and the public sphere's establishment, situating emotional rhetoric as part and parcel of individuals' rational actions in public space. Following this work, the Bourgeois' writing evinces the centrality of emotion to political interaction in fifteenth-century Paris, with emotional rhetoric often escaping official control, instead being employed to buttress a moralized critique of authority. Reciprocally, public feeling was managed and channelled to determine political legitimacy and contest authority. Here, the social dynamic to emotional rhetoric is significant: conformity to behavioural norms facilitated collective social action against identified outsiders whose emotional isolation vindicated a collectively negative moral judgement, with accounts of emotional experiences predicated upon the 'political economies in which they arise'.[8] By developing an evaluative system of emotional rhetoric throughout the *Journal* to nuance political commentary, rationalize

7 Barry Richards, *Emotional Governance: Politics, Media and Terror* (Basingstoke: Palgrave MacMillan, 2007), pp. 57-8.
8 Lila Abu-Lughod and Catherine A. Lutz, *Language and the Politics of Emotion* (Cambridge: Cambridge University Press, 1990), p. 13.

events and map authority, the Bourgeois asserted his own agency in condemning the wrongs of aristocratic action and appraised the nobility according to an understanding of emotionally-inspired divine justice ingrained in his community and institutional stances. Through emotion, the Bourgeois and his audience participated in the discursive contests that shaped the political culture of late medieval France.

This chapter will examine the multifarious rhetorical and narrative strategies available to the Bourgeois in his consideration of official communication in relation to Parisian royal, civic and ecclesiastical institutions. Through an artificial juxtaposition of official and popular realms of communication that the Bourgeois deliberately structured through his writing, the author arrogated an important authority in the determination of the news, propaganda and responses that he chose to privilege for his audience. Consequently, this chapter sheds light on the importance of propaganda and emotion in this very interplay between institutional communication and popular response in late medieval Paris.

Official communication and its limits

The Bourgeois consistently identified several of the means by which he accrued information to supplement his narrative and these media were central to framing the constant dialogue between official messages and Parisian responses. Examining communication in fifteenth-century Paris, Veronika Novák has defined official information as 'tout message distribué dans la société, dont les émetteurs explicites sont des institutions ou des autorités qui s'expriment comme telles'.[9] Concentrating upon the cry, written media, public executions and sermons, Novák has followed Claude Gauvard and Colette Beaune in demonstrating the extent of communication's ritualization, distinct from the rumours and subversive opinions believed to proliferate in relation to the availability of news.[10] In contrast, Jan Bloemendal and Arjan Van Dixhoorn have presented a collaborative paradigm for the circulation of information, arguing that in the fifteenth century 'the public provision of news and the formation of public opinion were collective projects'.[11] Here, beyond official channels, the *Journal* bears witness to the 'informal web of individual conversations [...] perpetual guesswork and deductions based on available facts, personal experiences and frameworks of interpretation' necessary for the development of coherent understandings of current events and narratives that accounted for them.[12] Within this

---

9 Any message disseminated in society for which the explicit transmitters are institutions or authorities that express themselves as such. Veronika Novák, 'La source du savoir', p. 151.
10 See Veronika Novák, 'L'espace du cri à Paris aux XIVᵉ-XVIᵉ siècles: recherches sur les 'lieux accoutumés', *Revue historique*, 696 (2020), pp. 61-86; Claude Gauvard, 'La *Fama*: une parole fondatrice', *Médiévales*, 24 (1993), pp. 5-9; Claude Gauvard, 'Rumeur et gens de guerre dans le royaume de France au milieu du XVᵉ siècle', *Hypothèses*, 4 (2001), pp. 287-89; Colette Beaune, 'La rumeur dans le Journal du Bourgeois de Paris' in *La circulation des nouvelles au Moyen Âge* (Paris: Publications de la Sorbonne, 1994), pp. 191-96. See also Séverine Fargette, 'Rumeurs, propagande et opinion publique au temps de la guerre civile (1407-20)', *Le Moyen Âge*, 113 (2007), pp. 311-13.
11 Jan Bloemendal and Arjan Van Dixhoorn, 'Literary Cultures and Public Opinion in the Early Modern Low Countries', in *Literary Cultures and Public Opinion in the Low Countries, 1450-1650*, ed. by Jan Bloemendal and Arjan Van Dixhoorn (Leiden: Brill, 2011), p. 26.
12 Bloemendal and Van Dixhoorn, 'Literary Cultures', p. 26.

process, the Bourgeois could assume messages disseminated and incorporate them into his narrative without acknowledging the real circumstances of their diffusion, reception, or his own interaction with the source. Once in public, officially disseminated messages quickly escaped the control of authorities. An assessment of the Bourgeois' engagement with the official channels of communication in fifteenth-century Paris reveals the author's own narrative goals, his community's consideration of the reliability and credibility of such sources, and even the value that they presented for himself and his audience as they asserted their stake in civic politics.

The town cry was the quintessential channel of medieval urban communication. In Paris, the municipality and Châtelet respectively assumed responsibilities for the dissemination of messages arriving at the Hôtel de Ville and royal ordinances. Dedicated criers performed duties in the publication of food and wine prices or royal proclamations, though this dissemination of information could also be assured through the city's neighbourhood officials, the *quarteniers* and *dizainiers*. The Bourgeois referred to such instances of communication at least eighty-two times, or in almost 10% of the *Journal*'s entries, demonstrating the extent to which the text functioned as an extension of the public sphere created by criers themselves.[13] Here, cries pertained to four broad categories: the pronouncement of peace; the relation of information relating to currency fluctuations and taxes; interdictions or defensive policies; and, finally, orders concerning the price and availability of supplies. Their prevalence underscores the Bourgeois' concern for civic government, with the period of Armagnac dominance between 1413 and 1418 in particular being portrayed predominantly through the consistent relation of proclaimed ordinances, often without commentary. In turn, the *Journal*'s criers were anonymous and the Bourgeois never distinguished between the kinds of cry that he heard, though food prices or security measures would have been the responsibility of different officials such as the *crieur de vin* or the Châtelet's *crieur public*.

Albeit unidentified, these proclamations inherently represented the official communication by Paris' royal, civic and municipal rulers, with the Bourgeois' selectivity in their relation exhibiting his own narrative authority. The messages' incorporation in the *Journal* integrated the Bourgeois into broader processes of informational diffusion. For instance, reporting a cry concerning the value of rents proclaimed in August 1428, the Bourgeois encouraged his audience to seek further details, 'lesquelles on peut savoir ou Chastellet qui veut'.[14] In this particular case, through the present tense the *Journal* functioned as an extension of the official channels of communication that it described. This information's authority was also framed by impressions of its omnipresence engendered in the Bourgeois' writing. Although Novák has shown that Parisian criers adopted heterogenous routes through the city, selecting different sites of publication to reach specific audiences, a quarter of the Bourgeois' references to ordinances simply stressed their proclamation 'parmy Paris'.[15] In doing so, the *Journal* asserted their universal pertinence, invoked as the pillars of a common knowledge that bound the civic community. Linked to this universality was the

---

13 As noted in Novák, 'L'espace du cri', p. 62.
14 Which can be found at the Châtelet, for those who wish [to know more]. *Journal*, p. 229.
15 Novák, 'L'espace du cri', pp. 70-7.

ritual performance of proclamation, tied to its visual and sonorous qualities. Trumpets and minstrels conveyed pronouncements of peace, sometimes at odds with Parisian reactions. On 16 September 1418, the Bourgeois ruefully related the proclamation of the Treaty of Saint-Maur concluded between Jean sans Peur, Isabeau de Bavière and Jean V of Brittany: 'qui que en fust courcé ou joyeulx, et fut criée parmy Paris à quatre trompes et à six menestriers'.[16] Moreover, while the record of ordinances enabled the Bourgeois to trace developments during the phase of Armagnac rule in the 1410s without explicitly condemning their promulgation, indicative of the proclamation's role as 'un lien politique entre gouvernants et gouverné', it is telling that the Bourgeois never described Lancastrian edicts as being proclaimed 'à son de trompe', suggesting that their description and recognition was inherently tied to notions of authority and, here, a refusal to acknowledge Lancastrian legitimacy.[17]

The Bourgeois' reference to the Châtelet in 1428 reveals an awareness of the textual supports upon which official communication relied and which the Bourgeois himself may even have regularly accessed to supplement his record, indicated by comments like that referring to the 'lettres' published informing Parisians of Antipope Felix V's abdication in 1449.[18] However, with the exception of the Treaty of Troyes in 1420 and, implicitly, the indulgences for Corpus Christi in 1431, the Bourgeois did not choose to transcribe or even explicitly refer to more authoritative documentation.[19] His sparing use of official material therefore contrasts with the tentativeness of other fifteenth-century Parisian journal authors who referred their audiences directly to texts independent of their narrative. For instance, when Jean Maupoint related currency changes in 1444, he cited the signature of the royal edict that he had before him to authenticate his source; that same year, Maupoint informed his audience that he had 'la copie céans' of the ordinance reinstating the Lendit fair, as well as 'le double du traicté' between France and England concluded at Tours on 28 May.[20] Likewise, the anonymous journal fragment for 1412-13 transcribed the truce concluded at the culmination of the Burgundian siege of Armagnac-held Bourges on 12 July 1412.[21] These Parisian journal authors emulated the established strategies commonly found in the works produced by chroniclers connected to court settings, such as Enguerrand de Monstrelet, Michel Pintoin and even the so-called Chronique des Cordeliers. In contrast, the Bourgeois reduced his sources to an interpretative gloss that obfuscated their textual origin, suggesting that the Journal went beyond simply transmitting news to commenting upon this official information, synthesizing news and directing its reception for his Halles audience. This process can readily be deciphered in the Bourgeois' decision to default to a straightforward list of ordinances during the Armagnac governance of Paris

---

16 Whoever was angered or joyful, and [the peace] was cried at Paris with four trumpets and six minstrels. *Journal*, p. 114.

17 A political link between governors and governed. Didier Lett and Nicolas Offenstadt, 'Les pratiques du cri au Moyen Âge' in *Haro! Noël! Oyé! Pratiques du cri au Moyen Âge*, ed. by Didier Lett and Nicolas Offenstadt (Paris: Publications de la Sorbonne, 2003), p. 32.

18 *Journal*, p. 390.

19 On these materials, see above, Chapter 1.

20 The copy here; a copy of the treaty. Jean Maupoint, 'Journal parisien de Jean Maupoint, prieur de Sainte-Catherine-de-la-Couture (1437-69)', ed. by Gustave Fagniez, *MSHP*, 4 (1877), pp. 30-32.

21 Rome, Vatican Reg. Lat. 1502 (vol. 1), fols 106v-107r.

between 1413 and 1418, when the risks of subversive political commentary compelled the author to adopt a more neutral stance to avoid possible censure.

Alongside proclamations, civic celebrations were crucial to publicizing political developments, exhibiting official strategies designed to elicit urban support. Moreover, their public nature resulted in their emergence as a forum for widened participation in political discourse, framing criticism and moral reflection regarding France's state and the nature of good government during the Hundred Years War. When Paris' Lancastrian governors marked the English victory at Cravant (31 July 1423) with bonfires and dances, the Bourgeois complained that 'mieulx on deust avoir plouré; car, comme on disoit que III^m ou plus furent mors des Arminalx'.[22] Instead of perceiving the victory as God-given, the news of such violence provoked reflection upon the moral dangers posed by continued Christian infighting. Juxtaposing Parisian celebrations with the realities of conflict's brutality, the Bourgeois supplemented his reflections with the *exemplum* of Calchas, the Argive seer who (following the *Journal*) was deceived by the Devil and defected from Troy to join the Greeks.[23] Here, the celebrations engendered a thinly veiled criticism of the political *status quo* following Charles VI's death and the assertion of Lancastrian rule under John, duke of Bedford in November 1422. Implying Paris' status as Troy's historical successor through the *translatio imperii*, the Bourgeois developed an analogy between the Parisian collaborators who celebrated Lancastrian victories and Calchas, persuaded by the Devil to side with their ancient English enemy and risking damnation as a result.[24] Through these clear allusions to the 'anti-English function of the Trojan myth', the Bourgeois neutralized the impact of Lancastrian propaganda and envisioned the Parisian support that it elicited as morally compromising, all the while excluding the city's Lancastrian governors from understandings of the Christian community to counter their claims to a divine mandate.[25] The account tempered the real extent of Lancastrian influence over the religious ceremonies marking the victory, deliberately omitting the Parisian processions described by Clément de Fauquembergue and thereby disguising the religious ties that bound the capital to the Lancastrian administration.

The passage from 1423 reveals the manner in which celebrations marking political and military developments not only channelled public feeling, but served as a litmus test for urban enthusiasm. These ceremonies elicited reactions ranging from begrudging compliance to an outright refusal to participate. For instance, the Bourgeois emphasized Parisian scepticism in reaction to the celebrations marking Henry VI's arrival in Calais on 23 April 1430, the first leg of a 'coronation campaign' designed to energize the Lancastrian claim to France following Charles VII's own coronation at Reims on 17 July 1429 and his concurrent military successes with the assistance of Jeanne d'Arc, which had witnessed

---

22 It would have been better to cry because, as it was said, three thousand Armagnacs or more had been killed. *Journal*, p. 187.

23 *Journal*, pp. 188-89.

24 For France's status as a new Troy and the *translatio imperii* in Parisian literature, see Chapter 4.

25 Colette Beaune, *The Birth of an Ideology: Myths and Symbols of Nation in Late-Medieval France*, trans. Susan Ross Huston, ed. Fredric L. Cheyette (Oxford : University of California Press, 1991), p. 233. See also Colette Beaune, 'L'utilisation politique du mythe des origines troyennes en France à la fin du Moyen Âge' in *Lectures médiévales de Virgile. Actes du colloque de Rome (25-28 octobre 1982)* (Rome: École française de Rome, 1985), pp. 341-42.

Paris' return to the status of a frontier city encircled by Valois forces.[26] Although 'certaines nouvelles' of Henry's arrival in Calais reached the capital, as demonstrated by the record of the Parlement *greffier* Clément de Fauquembergue, the Bourgeois noted a Parisian refusal to believe the news, again omitting the religious processions prompted by the king's coming.[27] The omission was indicative of Parisian attitudes towards the Lancastrian regime, twinned with a desire to minimize the city's ties to the dual monarchy, just as in 1423. Critiquing Lancastrian priorities, the Bourgeois presented the celebrations as vain in light of recent French successes following Charles VII's resurgence the previous year:

> le peuple s'esbahissoit de ce que les Arminalx avoient partout le meilleur [...] Si estoit le monde aussi comme au desespoir de ce que on ne gaingnoit rien, et que les gouverneurs leur faisoient ainsi entendant que brief ilz auroient secours.[28]

Moreover, Lancastrian discourse, symbolism and ceremony were effectively challenged by popular incredulity. In April 1430 none believed the announcement of Henry VI's crossing, 'dont il n'estoit rien'.[29] This cynicism resurfaced in June, when the Bourgeois again contradicted celebrations by arguing that 'n'estoit encore aucune nouvelle du roy Henry d'Angleterre qu'il fut point passé la mer'.[30] The refusal to believe official reports was framed by a reliance on alternative, popular hearsay, with opinion framed as paralleling the Bourgeois' own record, given that 'bien savoient les aucuns qu'il n'estoit point passé deca la mer'.[31] Sharing in this outright refusal to accept the news disseminated by Paris' English governors, the Bourgeois gave voice to a profound distrust of the Lancastrian administration in the wake of 1429, a sense of Paris' own disconnection from the regime, all the while evidencing an ability on the part of popular commentators to discern, evaluate and ultimately reject the propaganda designed to assuage urban anxieties and stabilize the Lancastrian dual monarchy in the face of a mounting political crisis.

While less common, the refusal to participate in celebrations or, alternatively, the decision to conduct spontaneous celebrations beyond the remit of official control, represented an essential means of challenging official agendas. Indeed, where celebrations ostensibly tied the city to the outcome of military events, rendering Parisians agents in factional conflict through intercessory prayer, the refusal to participate implied a straightforward condemnation of royal policy. After Paris' return to French rule in 1436, the Bourgeois decried the 'doloreuse' taxation and voracious targeting of Paris' churches, stripped of their material wealth to support French operations against the English.[32] In this context, the news that the Valois had captured Montereau-fault-Yonne on 10 October 1437 but

---

26 On this campaign, see Anne Curry, 'The coronation expedition and Henry VI's court in France, 1430-32' in *The Lancastrian Court: Proceedings of the 2001 Harlaxton Symposium*, ed. by Jenny Stratford (Donnington: Shaun Tyas, 2003), pp. 29-52.

27 Fauquembergue, II, pp. 105-06.

28 The people were astonished because the Armagnacs had the upper hand everywhere [...]. Likewise, everyone despaired because there was nothing to be earned and the governors made out that soon they would have aid. *Journal*, p. 254.

29 Nothing came about of it. *Journal*, p. 254.

30 There was still no news of the king Henry of England's crossing of the sea. *Journal*, p. 255.

31 Some people knew very well that he had not crossed the sea. *Journal*, p. 255.

32 The Bourgeois was scathing about the scale of taxation in 1437, described as 'une trop grosse taille', 'la plus estrange taille', 'celle doloreuse taille', 'une autre deshonneste'; 'Brief, ilz prindrent tant de finance a Paris que a peine en seroit

permitted the English garrison to leave freely provoked Parisian condemnation, expressed through the refusal to perform celebrations to mark Charles VII's victory: 'ceulx de Paris s'en tindrent bien mal comptents, et ne firent point pour la prinse du chastel ne joie, ne feuz allumerent, ne n'en tindrent compte, [...] et tout ce fut delaissé par ce que on avoit delivré les Anglois'.[33] The Bourgeois' reaction contrasts sharply with the impression of the Berry Herald, who envisioned the delivery of the English garrison as an act of royal mercy resulting from the intercession of the Dauphin Louis.[34] These contested visions centred on impressions of royal power. Besides decrying persistent and far-reaching taxation, the Bourgeois also carefully related this refusal to Charles VII's upcoming *jocundus adventus*, described in the same passage, illustrating the Parisians' ability to signal their condemnation of royal policy precisely as the Valois monarch sought to assert his new-found authority over the capital. Complaints regarding taxation such as these were inherently designed to test the boundaries of royal power, question the viability of Valois military campaigns (a common theme for the Bourgeois throughout the 1440s) and echoed the longer history of royal taxation that had framed Parisian political agency during the Armagnac-Burgundian conflict two decades earlier. Refusal to participate may have represented the only effective means of voicing dissatisfaction with the regime, since Parisians 'de nulle rien ilz n'osoient parler qui touchast le bien publique, car ilz avoient tant d'oppressions, tant des tailles'.[35] The leniency shown towards the English called into question the appropriate use of the taxes ostensibly exacted for the *bien public*, with Parisians inherently challenging Charles VII's legitimacy immediately prior to his entry, underscoring the celebrations' function as a medium for dialogue between ruler and ruled.

Celebrations for victories like those for Cravant or Montereau-fault-Yonne were therefore interrelated with the elaboration of commentary regarding warfare, administration, taxation and the state of the kingdom. Acknowledging the role played by Parisians in eliciting divine favour for factional endeavours, they also reveal the extent to which this Parisian support for these enterprises was both conditional and contested. Similar processes were at work in the 1410s. When Armagnac forces captured Burgundian-held Soissons by force on 21 May 1414, processions to Notre-Dame were held, followed by festivities and bonfires in the streets.[36] And yet, as with Cravant almost a decade later, the Bourgeois deplored celebrations for the city's sacking, especially since 'dit on que on n'ouyt oncques parler que les Sarazins feissent pis que firent ceulx de l'ost en ladicte ville par le mauvais conseil qui pour lors estoit entour le bon roy, dont homme n'osoit parler'.[37] Acknowledging that

---

homme creu'. (Too great a tax; the strangest tax; this painful tax; another dishonest [tax]; In short, they took so much money from Paris that it could scarcely be believed). *Journal*, pp. 333-34.

33 The people of Paris were very displeased, and for the capture of the castle did not organize celebrations nor light fires, nor did they care about it at all, [...] all of this was abandoned because the English had been allowed to go free. *Journal*, p. 335.

34 *Les chroniques du roi Charles VII par Gilles le Bouvier, dit le Héraut Berry*, ed. by Henri Courtault and Léonce Celier (Paris: Klincksieck, 1979), pp. 185-86.

35 Did not dare to speak out about anything concerning the common good, because they experienced such oppression and such taxes. *Journal*, p. 335.

36 For the processions, see Baye, I, pp. 185-86.

37 It is said that it had never been heard that the Saracens acted worse than did those of the army in the town, because of the evil counsel that then surrounded the good king, concerning which none dared speak. *Journal*, p. 53. There was a

none criticized the celebrations openly, the Bourgeois' own comments positioned his opinion community as subaltern and distanced from Armagnac agendas, decrying those who celebrated 'comme ce eussent esté Sarazins ou mescreans que on eust destruis'.[38] As in 1423, the hypocrisy of Armagnac joy positioned the faction's members as Saracen emulators, excluding them from a sympathetically Burgundian conception of the Christian community and inviting doubt regarding the king's counsel in Jean sans Peur's absence.

Similar commentaries on government and warfare even marked traditional, established celebrations. In June 1438, the constable Arthur de Richemont joined Charles VII's sister Marie, prioress of Poissy, to light the bonfire on the place de Grève that represented the climax of the St John Baptist celebrations. The festivities again provided an important opportunity to reflect upon the state of France's administration, in the wake of heavy taxation and a military stalemate between the English and French. Richemont's presence enabled the Bourgeois to relay rumours that the constable was 'favorable aux Anglois plus qu'au roy ne que aux Francois, et disoient les Anglois qu'ilz n'avoient point paour de guerre, ne de perdre, tant comme il seroit connestable de France'.[39] Whether or not the rumours of a covert alliance were true, the Bourgeois was assured that Richemont 'se monstroit tres mauvais ou tres couart en toutes ses besongnes', subsequently abandoning the siege of Pontoise in 1438.[40] Richemont's own biographical chronicle, compiled by his squire Guillaume Gruel, similarly suggests that the constable was undergoing a reputational crisis in 1438, at least among Parisians. Almost no space is dedicated to the events of 1438, in the aftermath of Pontoise's sudden recapture by the English in February 1437. However, the little content that is found for this period concentrates upon Richemont's relations with the capital's inhabitants. Upon his arrival in the city in 1438, Gruel insisted that Richemont 'reconforta ceulx de Paris qui murmuroient fort, et mist bonne garnison a Saint Denis, tant que tous furent très contens'.[41] The stark contrast between the *Journal* and Richemont's biography implies that Gruel worked hard to reshape these events, emphasizing and inverting the reality of feeling on the ground, and the dangers this posed to Richemont's reputation as an effective commander.

The fact that celebrations offered a framework for political commentary is further demonstrated by those moments when Parisians took it upon themselves to celebrate events beyond official purview. In 1441, the Bourgeois condemned the actions of Parisian sergeants who waited outside churches on Ascension Day, looking out for labourers leaving the churches whom they then conscripted for Charles VII's army before Creil. An example of the Châtelet's heavy-handedness, since 'qui en parloit tant fust pou, il estoit mis en

---

broad consensus in the condemnation of the excessive violence following Soissons' capture in the surviving chronicles. RSD, V, 324-31; *Histoire de Charles VI*, p. 496; Monstrelet, III, pp. 8-10; Jean le Fèvre, *Chronique de Jean le Fèvre, seigneur de Saint-Remy*, ed. by François Morand, 2 vols (Paris: Renouard, 1876-81), I (1876), pp. 165-67; Gilles le Bouvier, *Les chroniques*, p. 62.

38 As if it had been Saracens or heretics that had been destroyed. *Journal*, p. 54.

39 More loyal to the English than either the king or the French, and the English said that they had no fear of fighting or defeat so long as he was constable of France. *Journal*, p. 340.

40 Proved himself to be very incompetent or very cowardly in all of his deeds. *Journal*, p. 341.

41 Reassured those of Paris who murmured loudly, and placed a strong garrison at Saint-Denis such that all were most contented. Guillaume Gruel, *Chronique d'Arthur de Richemont, connétable de France, duc de Bretagne (1393-1458)*, ed. by Achille le Vavasseur (Paris: Renouard, 1890), p. 143.

prinson villainement et lui coustoit moult', the sudden news that Creil had surrendered provoked widespread feasting among the labourers: 'et sonna on par toutes les eglises de Paris moult haultement, et apres souper on fist grans feus comme a la Sainct Jehan ou plus, et dansoit on parmy Paris, et les enfens crioient "Nouel" moult haultement'.[42] More than simply favouring Valois success, the Bourgeois portrayed Creil's capitulation as a moment of divine intercession for the city's labourers, with the result that these celebrations also represented a statement of urban privilege in the face of royal encroachment. In another instance, Charles VI's return to Paris on 13 October 1414 following Soissons' conquest by Armagnac forces was met with unsolicited popular celebrations: 'soudainement, environ huit heures de nuyt, commencerent les bonnes gens de Paris *sans commandement* a faire feus et a baciner le plus grandement que on eust veu passé C ans devant'.[43] The sudden festivities counterbalanced the Armagnac-oriented ceremonies that had marked Soissons' capture earlier in the year. As Stephen Mileson has argued for medieval England, 'creating and controlling noise was a significant expression of social authority [...] people sometimes actively resisted by making noise'.[44] In 1414, this 'rough music' proved an effective means by which Paris' Burgundian sympathizers could limit Armagnac authority in the wake of the failed Cabochien uprising, reminding the city's governors of their disruptive potential.[45] These unofficial celebrations exhibited independent organization, with Parisians seizing the opportunity to demonstrate their loyalty to Charles VI as an alternative to the realities of Armagnac rule. Their seditious character may be implied by their occurrence at night and the Parisians' ability to dramatically occupy the city's space, with 'les tables en my les rues drecées a tous venans'.[46] That these celebrations represented a medium for subversive discourse is subsequently demonstrated by Armagnac ordinances, issued in May 1416, forbidding unsupervised celebratory gatherings for weddings for fear of their role in the consolidation of conspiratorial networks. Their description, in 1414 and 1441 alike, permitted the Bourgeois and his audience to reflect upon an enduring popular agency at moments marked by heavy-handed government, evaluating but also questioning the ties that bound Parisians to their king.

---

42 Whomever spoke out about it, even if a little, was wickedly imprisoned and it cost him significantly; and the bells were loudly rung from all the churches in Paris, et after supper great fires were lit like those for the feast of St John, and people danced throughout Paris while the children loudly exclaimed 'Noel!'. *Journal*, pp. 359-60.

43 Suddenly, around the eighth hour at night, the good people of Paris began *without instruction* to light fires and drum more greatly than had been seen in a hundred years previously. *Journal*, p. 57. Emphasis my own.

44 Stephen Mileson, 'Sound and Landscape' in *The Oxford Handbook of Later Medieval Archaeology in Britain*, ed. by Christopher Gerrard and Alejandra Gutiérrez (Oxford: Oxford University Press, 2018), p. 714. Niall Atkinson has similarly demonstrated the importance of bells in coordinating the Ciompi revolt in fourteenth-century Florence. 'The Republic of Sound: Listening to Florence at the Threshold of the Renaissance', *I Tatti Studies in the Italian Renaissance*, 16 (September 2013), pp. 77-82.

45 On the potential of rough music, see Andy Wood, 'Collective Violence, Social Drama and Rituals of Rebellion in Late Medieval and Early Modern England' in *Cultures of Violence: Interpersonal Violence in Historical Perspective*, ed. by Stuart Carroll (London: Palgrave Macmillan, 2007), p. 99; Michael Sizer, 'Murmur, Clamor and Tumult: The Soundscape of Revolt and Oral Culture in the Middle Ages', *Radical History Review*, 121 (2015), pp. 9-10.

46 Tables erected in the middle of the streets for all comers. *Journal*, p. 57.

Public sentences

Public executions were an essential source of political information, conveyed through highly ritualized and propagandistic frameworks designed to appeal to commonly held understandings of justice, predicated upon the true/false dichotomy associated with criminal guilt.[47] With the sentence pronounced upon the scaffold in the presence of the convicted, the Bourgeois rarely questioned the validity of those executions that he chose to report. In fact, these often served as a conduit for further rumours while unpredictable, disturbed performances provoked an evaluation of the authority of civic governors. The "spectacular language" of violent punishment was integral to the effectiveness of the sentence as a form of communication, while their exemplarity was underscored by their rarity.[48] Robert Mills has argued that observers, including the Bourgeois, focused upon the 'exceptional torments meted out to traitors, not the penalties administered to the vast majority of offenders', distorting impressions of fifteenth-century justice.[49] While true, this reading fails to address precisely why these executions occupied the Bourgeois' attention, and how they facilitated ideological communication within the Parisian public sphere. In communicative terms, Foucault long ago argued that graphic descriptions of violence were integral to the symbolic discourse surrounding the 'triomphe de la loi'.[50] Interpreting executions in this moral and political manner, the Bourgeois brought to the fore of his narrative crowd expectations, political stereotypes and rumours, with such reactions challenging assumptions that medieval audiences were passive when confronted with exemplary punishment.

The power of public sentences as a medium of political communication is first demonstrated by the significance attributed to appearance, as revealed by two detailed examples related by the Bourgeois: the execution of the Burgundian captain Colinet de Puiseux in November 1411, and the sentencing of the canon of Notre-Dame Nicolas d'Orgemont in April 1416. Each sentence struck at the heart of several prominent themes of contest in late medieval Paris regarding treason, deceptive appearances and, perhaps most importantly, clerical status.[51] Charged with defending the suburban fortress of Saint-Cloud, Puiseux had endangered Paris when he betrayed his post to the Armagnac forces besieging the capital

---

47 Esther Cohen, 'Symbols of Culpability and the Universal Language of Justice: The Ritual of Public Executions in Late Medieval Europe', *History of European Ideas*, 11 (1989), pp. 407-10; Claude Gauvard, *Condamner à mort au Moyen Âge* (Paris: Presses universitaires de France, 2018), pp. 107-16; Claude Gauvard, *'De Grâce Especial': Crime, État et société en France à la fin du Moyen Âge*, 2 vols (Paris: Publications de la Sorbonne, 1991), pp. 896-904. Several studies have closely analysed executions in late medieval Paris, see Esther Cohen, *The Crossroads of Justice: Law and Culture in Late Medieval France* (Leiden: Brill, 1993), esp. pp. 181-201; Veronika Novák, 'Le corps du condamné et le tissu urbain. Exécution, pouvoir et usages de l'espace à Paris aux XVe-XVIe siècles', *Histoire urbaine*, 47 (2016), pp. 149-66.

48 See Claude Gauvard, *Violence et ordre public au Moyen Âge* (Paris: Picard, 2005), pp. 53-60. The centrality of the notion of 'exemplarity' to the punishment of political crimes has been explored in detail in Gauvard, *Condamner à mort*, pp. 121-25.

49 Robert Mills, *Suspended Animation: Pain, Pleasure and Punishment in Medieval Culture* (London: Reaktion, 2005), pp. 15-16; Gauvard, *Condamner à mort*, pp. 216-22.

50 Michel Foucault, *Surveiller et punir: Naissance de la prison* (Paris: Gallimard, 1975), pp. 36-72. For a problematization of Foucault's vision of medieval punishment, see Claude Gauvard, 'Justification and Theory of the Death Penalty at the Parlement of Paris in the Late Middle Ages' in *War, Government and Power in Late Medieval France*, ed. by Christopher Allmand (Liverpool: Liverpool University Pres, 2000), pp. 190-91.

51 Disputes surrounding the punishment of clerics were a consistent feature of Parisian executions during the late fourteenth and fifteenth cenutries. See Gauvard, *Condamner à mort*, pp. 167-72. 258-61.

on 13 October 1411. According to the Bourgeois, when Jean sans Peur recaptured the fortress a month later, Puiseux had attempted to hide in the spire of the walled town's Saint-Clodoald chapel, 'vestu en habit d'un prestre'.[52] Consequently, upon his execution at the Halles marketplace for treason on 12 November, Puiseux appeared 'vestu comme il fut prins, comme ung prestre' before being stripped, beheaded and quartered.[53] The emphasis upon Puiseux's clothing functioned as an effective means of rendering palpable his cowardice, his betrayal and his underhanded attempt to evoke clerical immunity. The captain's transformation from false cleric to nakedness ritualistically conveyed his societal worthlessness as a traitor, a process underscored by rumours of the extensive damage his betrayal had provoked that circulated upon his execution: 'on disoit tout certainement que ledit Colinet, par sa faulce et desloyaute traison, fist dommaige de plus de II^m lyons en France'.[54] This symbolic use of clothing contrasts with Nicolas d'Orgemont's own sentencing on 24 April 1416, following his participation in a conspiracy to betray Paris to Jean sans Peur.[55] Despite being a latecomer to the plot, Paris' Armagnac governors recognized the political value of the conviction of a high-profile Burgundian, elevating d'Orgemont to the status of ringleader.[56] This leading status was conveyed through d'Orgemont's place in the conspirators' procession to the Halles scaffold, with the canon seated in a cart 'vestu d'un grant mantel de violet et chapperons de mesmes', flanked by two accomplices riding donkeys, Robert de Belloy and Regnault Maillet.[57] Although d'Orgemont's clerical status spared him from execution, his inclusion among those processing to the scaffold dramatized Armagnac authority, symbolically inverting the conspirators' own (alleged) plans to capture the dukes of Berry and Anjou, shave their heads and have *them* process through Paris.[58]

The Bourgeois' opposition to Armagnac rule resulted in a careful reconstruction of these events, demonstrating his ability to mediate and neutralize their propagandistic potential in a manner that anticipated his distortion of later Lancastrian celebrations. Emphasizing the good reputation of the accused, the Bourgeois implied a profound dissonance between the visions of the civic community conceived by the Armagnacs and the perspectives of those Burgundian sympathizers residing in the Halles, all the more so given the Bourgeois' omission of any reference to the imprisonment of Armagnac sympathizers by Burgundian administrators in 1411.[59] Crucially, the Bourgeois' description

---

52 Dressed in a priest's habit. *Journal*, p. 15.

53 Dressed as he was when he was captured, as a priest. *Journal*, p. 17.

54 It was said with certainty that the said Colinet, through his false and disloyal treason, had caused more than 2,000 *lyons'* worth of damage in France. *Journal*, p. 17. As Simon Cuttler noted, 1411 marked a considerable shift in the Parisian *prévôt*'s powers to prosecute treason with respect to the Armagnac faction. S.H. Cuttler, *The Law of Treason and Treason Trials in Later Medieval France* (Cambridge: Cambridge University Press, 1981), p. 60.

55 On the 1416 conspiracy, see Léon Mirot, 'Le procès du Boiteux d'Orgemont. Épisode des troubles parisiens pendant la lutte des Armagnacs et des Bourguignons (Suite et fin). Quatrième partie: La vie politique et le procès du Boiteux d'Orgemont', *Le Moyen Âge*, 25 (1912), pp. 353-410; Léon Mirot, *Les d'Orgemont. Leur origine, leur fortune – le Boiteux d'Orgemont* (Paris: Champion, 1913), pp. 167-226.

56 According to his confession before the Paris chapter, d'Orgemont had only learned about the plot in the week before Easter, when it was supposed to take place. Mirot, *Les d'Orgemont*, p. 267.

57 Dressed in a great purple cloak and hood of the same colour. *Journal*, pp. 70-1.

58 Monstrelet, III, p. 140.

59 This inversion of the repression seen in 1416 was noted by the Ursins Compiler. *Histoire de Charles VI*, pp. 466-67.

of d'Orgemont's sentencing framed competing notions of citizenship, factional identity and the boundaries of the civic community. Where Paris' Armagnac governors endeavoured to demonstrate the conspirators' exclusion from this community, the Bourgeois resorted to a careful delineation of their *fama publica* to assert that, in contrast, those convicted were representative of the community. To do so, the Bourgeois omitted the public declaration of d'Orgemont's crimes and his humiliating ceremony of destitution at the Bastille where, 'present moult grant pueple, il a esté rez en estat de diacre'.[60] Indeed, the record compiled by the Parlement *greffier* and Notre-Dame canon Nicolas de Baye reveals how, in a move analogous to Puiseux's execution, public transitions in d'Orgemont's appearance communicated shifts in status paralleling culpability. For Baye, a fellow Parisian canon involved in the sentencing, d'Orgemont's appearance in a violet cloak exhibited his worldly pride, having been 'l'un des plus riches clers de France', an attribute redressed by his tonsuring. Where the *Journal* had accentuated Puiseux's pride in his assumption of clerical clothing, the Bourgeois tellingly avoided any such references when describing d'Orgemont's sentencing for a crime that he and his community tacitly endorsed.

The Bourgeois' account of this condemnation deliberately counterbalanced its function as a symbolic statement of Armagnac authority, omitting details such as the conspirators' plans to arrest or even assassinate the dukes of Berry and Anjou, and instead stating more ambiguously that they had planned 'de prendre ceulx qui ainsi tenoient Paris en subgection'.[61] In doing so, the Bourgeois inverted the sentencing's rhetoric, situating the conspirators as defenders of the city's common good and emphasizing Armagnac oppression, as opposed to Burgundian betrayal. By comparison, the well-informed Ursins chronicler recorded how the former *échevin* Robert de Belloy, '*confessa* [...] qu'ilz avoient intention de tuer le roy de Sicile, le duc de Berry et ceux qu'on soupconnoit estre [...] du party du duc d'Orléans'.[62] Baye similarly insisted that d'Orgemont had been sentenced 'considerée la confession simplement, franchement et voluntairement faicte'.[63] Where these authors highlighted the formality of d'Orgemont's condemnation to underscore his culpability, the Bourgeois endeavoured to restore the reputation of the conspirators even upon the scaffold, described as 'moult honnestes hommes et de moult bonne renommée'.[64] Securing the memory of these men as representatives of the wider Halles community and Burgundian faction within the city, the Bourgeois simultaneously countered suggestions of a popular endorsement of their conviction by omitting the crowd's reaction to the executions, contrasting with the opinions shared upon Colinet de Puiseux's death five years earlier. The omission again tellingly diverges from Baye's account, which remarked that at d'Orgemont's ecclesiastical sentences, 'les rues d'environ Nostre-Dame, et le parvis

---

60 Before a great crowd of people, he was shaved according to his status as a deacon. Baye, II, p. 249.
61 To arrest those who held Paris in subjection. *Journal*, p. 70.
62 *Confessed* that they had intended to kill the king of Sicily [Louis II, duke of Anjou], the duke of Berry and those who they suspected of supporting the Orléanist party. *Histoire de Charles VI*, p. 532. Emphasis my own.
63 Considering the confession was made simply, frankly and voluntarily. Baye, II, p. 249. As a member of the Notre-Dame chapter, Nicolas de Baye would have had access to the records of d'Orgemont's interrogation, which similarly emphasized his confession by 'pure et liberalle volunté sans aucune force ou contrainte'. Mirot, *Les d'Orgemont*, p. 267.
64 Very honest men and of very good reputation. *Journal*, p. 71.

et grant partie de l'Eglise [estoient] toutes pleinnes du peuple'.[65] Fundamentally, these divergences suggest deeper contentions regarding the perception and memory of the 1416 plot in its immediate aftermath. Where institutions such as the Châtelet and cathedral chapter were prepared to condemn the conspirators, the *Journal* signals wider sympathies within the Halles and a total rejection of the political narrative conveyed through the series of executions and sentences that characterized the Armagnac governors' response. Consequently, d'Orgemont's conviction underscores the historical and political potential of the Bourgeois' selectivity, restructuring events and shaping the memories of his immediate community to contest official communication.

Observers' reactions were integral to the Bourgeois' consideration of the messages communicated through executions.[66] As Margaret Owens has argued, spectators' horizons of expectations when witnessing executions were essential to their ritual-judicial character and their validation, albeit with a risk of inciting "counter-discourses".[67] The Bourgeois summoned popular responses either to reinforce the guilt of the convicted, as illustrated by Pierre des Essarts' execution in July 1413, or question the sentence's validity, as with Jeanne d'Arc in May 1431. The description of Essarts' death was distinguished by a profound disconnect between the behaviour of the convicted and the assembled Parisians, a disconnect that – much like d'Orgemont's execution – was moulded by factional tensions within the city at the height of the Cabochien revolt. The incongruity underscores how emotional elements performed an inherently communicative function determined by context and normative interpretations of appropriateness that were socially constructed.[68] The Bourgeois deliberately stressed inappropriate emotional responses as a fundamental demonstration of immoral character. Upon the scaffold Essarts

> ne faisoit touzjours que rire comme il faisoit en sa grant majesté, dont le plus de gens le tenoient pour vray foul; car tous ceulx qui le veoient plouroient si piteusement que vous ne ouystez oncques parler de plus grans pleurs pour mort de homme, et lui tout seul rioit, et estoit sa pencée que le commun le gardast de mourir. Mais il avoit en sa voulenté, s'il eust plus vesqu, de trahir la ville [...] et de faire lui-mesmes tres grans et cruelles occisions, et piller et rober les bons habitans de la bonne ville de Paris qui tant l'aymoient loyaulment [...] comme il apparoit qu'il avoit prins si grant orgueil en soy.[69]

---

65 The streets around Notre-Dame, and the parvis and a great part of the cathedral were all filled with people. Baye, II, pp. 248-49.

66 On the power of this spectating community, see Marla Carlson's study based on the *Journal d'un bourgeois de Paris*. 'Painful Processions in Late Medieval Paris', *European Medieval Drama*, 6 (2003), pp. 65-81.

67 Margaret E. Owens, *Stages of Dismemberment: The Fragmented Body in Late Medieval and Early Modern Drama* (Newark, DE: University of Delaware Press, 2005), pp. 116-26.

68 A similar interpretation of the execution of Pierre des Essarts has been advanced by Claude Gauvard, who notes the juxtaposition of the enormity of Essarts' crimes with his laughter. *Condamner à mort*, p. 90.

69 Did nothing but laugh as he had done at the time of his greatest majesty, for which reason most people considered him to be truly mad. For all those that saw him wept so piteously that you have never heard speak of greater tears for a man's death. And he alone laughed, for he believed that the commons would save him from dying. But it was his intention, should he have lived, to betray the city and deliver it into the hands of its enemies, and he himself would commit very great and cruel killings, and pillage and rob the good inhabitants of the good city of Paris who had loved him so loyally [...] as it appears that his pride had become so great. *Journal*, p. 33.

Essarts' lack of emotional conformity, demonstrated by his mad laughter juxtaposed with the commons' pious tears, exhibited the cupidity and pride that had exemplified his 'majesty' and ultimately driven him to conspire against the Parisians who supported him. With the emotional comparison underscoring Essarts' immorality, the Bourgeois resituated the former *prévôt* beyond the boundaries of the Christian community and in opposition to the Parisian body politic, prepared to sacrifice the common good, that 'finalité de la vie politique', for personal gain as an embodiment of tyranny.[70] Nor was he alone in doing so. The anonymous author of the journal fragment for 1412-13 likewise asserted that Essarts was beheaded 'comme traitre et desloyal a la coronne' but that, 'nonobstant qu'il avoit bien deservy, le peuple le pleignoit moult et ot pitié de luy'.[71] This moralization was predicated upon an innate awareness of the 'feeling rules' or normative behaviour that should govern public executions, while underscoring the performative role accorded to the crowd in the legitimation of violence. Moreover, this distinction inherently justified the overarching Cabochien seizure of power while asserting widespread support for the reformist movement, demonstrating the community's endorsement of the overthrow of tyrannical government.[72]

Where Essarts' guilt was illustrated through an emotional disparity between criminal and crowd, reactions to Jeanne d'Arc's death were more complicated. Like Essarts, Jeanne's execution was structured around a juxtaposition that conveyed societal order, rationality and morality. The declaration of Jeanne's crimes was portrayed by the Bourgeois as having an immediate impact upon observers who 'orent moult grant orreur quant ilz ouirent raconter les grans erreurs qu'elle avoit eues contre notre foy'.[73] Jeanne's disruptive character was similarly emphasized by Clément de Fauquembergue's concentration upon the written paraphernalia included in her execution, including her mitre that read 'heretique, relapse, apostate, ydolatre' and the placard before the scaffold that described Jeanne as a 'blasphemeresse de Dieu [...] malcreant de la foy de Jhesu-Crist, invocaterresse de deables, apostate, scismatique et heretique'.[74] Both descriptions excluded Jeanne from conceptions of the Christian community, with the Bourgeois stressing the popular shock contrasted with her obstinacy, since Jeanne 'ne s'en effroioyt ne esbahissoit [...] comme celle qui estoit toute plaine de l'Ennemy d'enfer'.[75] Assuming the role that the commons had performed at Essarts' execution, the University of Paris 'si humblement la prioient qu'elle se repentist et revocast de celle malle erreur [...] ou ce non elle seroit davant tout

70 Ultimate end of political life. Bénédicte Sère, 'Aristote et le bien commun au Moyen Âge: Une histoire, une historiographie', *Revue française d'histoire des idées politiques*, 32 (2010), pp. 281-82.

71 As a traitor and disloyal to the crown; despite the fact that he truly deserved it, the people lamented his death and had pity for him. Rome, Vatican MS Reg. Lat. 1502, fol. 108v.

72 This point is stressed in an account compiled by Nicolas de Baye in the Paris Parlement's *Registre des matines*, where he stated that Essarts was executed 'par l'auctorité du roy ou des commissaires ordonnez a cognoistre des prisonniers prins puiz ii ou iii moiz a Paris' (upon the authority of the king or the commissioners ordered to examine prisoners captured in the last two or three months in Paris). Baye, II, pp. 116-17. More explicitly, the Ursins Compiler attributed Essarts' execution to 'les bouchers et leurs alliés' (the butchers and their allies), *Histoire de Charles VI*, p. 481.

73 Were especially horrified when they heard the report of the great errors that she had committed with respect to our faith. *Journal*, p. 269.

74 Heretic, relapsed, apostate, idolater; Blasphemer of God, an unbeliever in the faith of Jesus Christ, an invoker of devils, apostate, schismatic and heretic. Fauquembergue, II, pp. 13-14.

75 She was neither afraid nor shocked [...] like one who was entirely dedicated to the Enemy of hell. *Journal*, p. 269.

le peuple arse et son ame dampnée'.[76] Nevertheless, each narrative also betrays a substantial shift in opinion following Jeanne's death. Where Essarts' execution had been integral to the legitimation of the Cabochien revolt, the Bourgeois related discussions surrounding Jeanne's execution as indicative of divided opinion regarding Valois legitimacy: 'Assez avoit la et ailleurs qui disoient qu'elle estoit martire et pour son droit signeur, autres disoient que non, et que mal avoit fait qui tant l'avoit gardée; ainsi disoit le peuple'.[77] Fauquembergue similarly wrote a postscript in Latin that explained that Jeanne had recanted for her sins before death, 'Deus sue anime sit propicius et misericors'.[78] Jeanne d'Arc's execution reveals both the persuasive mechanisms employed in public and their limitations. Analyses of later reactions to public executions for heresy reveal that observers rarely identified with fierce prosecution and, where persuasion depends upon the audience's inherent receptiveness to the communicated message, persistent doubts were reinforced by the crime's publicity.[79] Given these entrenched perspectives, the Bourgeois himself appeared unwilling to commit to a coherent narrative of Jeanne's guilt, instead objectively concluding that 'quelle mauvestie ou bonté qu'elle eust faicte, elle fut arse cellui jour'.[80]

Disputed ideals of civic belonging, political right and culpability were more acute when executions were disturbed or disturbing, when the execution's meaning was disputed or its performance disrupted. These challenges reveal the ways in which executions approximated the civic community to the intertwined notions of royal and divine justice and, in rare cases, even miraculous intervention, as in 1443 when a woman stepped forth from the crowd to plead for the life of an English soldier captured at Pontoise two years earlier, 'et pour ce nul ne se doit deffier de Notre Seigneur, ne soy desesperer pour nulle paine'.[81] These incidents reveal that contrary to the smooth process envisioned by authorities whereby the condemned died penitent and recognized the truth of their crimes before passive audiences, disturbances inherent in the practice of exemplary punishment provoked doubt regarding its very nature.[82] One such disturbed 'execution' that framed contested political stances was that of Jacques de la Rivière, chamberlain first to Louis d'Orléans and then to the Dauphin Louis, duke of Guyenne, who was imprisoned at the beginning of the Cabochien revolt on 28 April 1413. La Rivière's subsequent death took place under strange circumstances and the surviving narratives parallel the distinction between Parisian journals and more established, elite chroniclers. For the Bourgeois and the anonymous author of the 1412-13 journal fragment, both sympathetic to the Cabochien

---

76 So humbly begged her to repent and recant this evil error […] otherwise she would be burned before the people and her soul damned. *Journal*, p. 269.

77 There were many people there and elsewhere who said that she had been a martyr and for her true lord; others said that this was not the case, and that he who had so supported her had done wrong. So spoke the people. *Journal*, p. 269.

78 God be kind and merciful to her soul. Fauquembergue, II, p. 14.

79 Juliaan Woltjer, 'Public Opinion and the Persecution of Heretics in the Netherlands, 1550-59' in *Public Opinion and Changing Identities in the Early Modern Netherlands. Essays in Honour of Alastair Duke*, ed. by Judith Pollmann and Andrew Spicer (Leiden: Brill, 2006), pp. 103-06.

80 Whatever evil or good thing that she had done, she was burned this day. *Journal*, 270.

81 And because of this none should doubt Our Lord, nor let suffering drive us to despair. *Journal*, p. 368.

82 Similar circumstances have been studied in detailed for sixteenth-century Parisian executions. See Tom Hamilton, 'Contesting public executions in Paris towards the end of the Wars of Religion' in *Cultures of Conflict Resolution in Early Modern Europe*, ed. by Stephen Cummins and Laura Kounine (London: Routledge, 2017), pp. 179-202.

movement, when confronted with proof of his treason by the Cabochien commissioners appointed to investigate his crimes, the chamberlain had committed suicide by striking himself repeatedly on the head with a tin jug.[83] Conversely, the chroniclers Enguerrand de Monstrelet, Michel Pintoin and the Ursins Compiler dismissed this notion of suicide as a popular Parisian rumour. According to their accounts, La Rivière had been murdered in jail by the Cabochien captain, Elyon de Jacqueville.[84]

In either case, after his death Jacques de La Rivière's corpse was processed through Paris to the Halles' scaffold, where it was decapitated. Despite the rumoured circumstances of La Rivière's demise, the ceremony provided the Bourgeois with the opportunity to codify the Cabochien account of events within his own narrative, 'car il estoit mort et c'estoit tué d'une pinte plaine de vin, dont il s'estoit feru sur la teste si grant cop qu'il ce cassa le test et la cervelle'.[85] Rather than denouncing La Rivière's suicide, the mutilation of his body during the execution of his accomplice, the squire Simonnet Petit-Mesnil, was conveyed as redounding upon the Cabochien reformist movement and its role as the defender of the common good, since 'de eulx deux ce avoit esté la plus belle prinse qui eust esté faicte pour le royaulme passé avoit xx ans'.[86] These tensions among Burgundian supporters regarding the extrajudicial murder of a royal chamberlain, Cabochien claims to represent the common good, and the very place of the scaffold are revealed through the competing accounts of La Rivière's death, decried by the Ursins chronicler as 'un bien merveilleux cas, de tuer un homme es mains de justice'.[87] In contrast, the contemporary journal fragment for 1413 took its audience within the prison to heighten La Rivière's culpability:

> Il confessa que luy et plusieurs aultrez qu'il nomma avoient emprins a mettre la bonne ville de Paris en tel estat que on eust dit 'Yci fust Paris', et plusieurs moult horribles traysons contre la couronne il confessa sans gehinne.[88]

The parallels between the 1413 fragment and the Journal certainly suggest that among Parisians the execution served to fortify the conviction that La Rivière's death was proof not of extrajudicial murder, but an example of the gravity of the crimes that the chamberlain and his Armagnac allies had conspired to commit against the city and crown. Michel Pintoin was far more circumspect, and even appears to have recognized how the Cabochien

83 Journal, p. 32; Rome, Vatican Reg. Lat. 1502, fol. 108v.
84 Monstrelet, II, p. 370; RSD, V, pp. 54-9; Histoire de Charles VI, pp. 479-80. See also, Alfred Coville, Les Cabochiens et l'ordonnance de 1413 (Paris: Hachette, 1888), pp. 327-29. Monstrelet and Pintoin repeated the rumour only to discredit it as the 'vulgarem oppinionem', while the Ursins Compiler ignored the rumour altogether to emphasise Jacqueville's perpetration of the murder. It is, of course, impossible to know the truth of the matter, though it is worth noting that Claude Gauvard has recently based her assessment of the disgrace of public executions in medieval society by focusing on La Rivière's decision to commit suicide and evade the scaffold, without acknowledging the possibility that this was a Parisian rumour designed to disguise La Rivière's murder. Claude Gauvard, Condamnner à mort, p. 103.
85 For he had died, and he had killed himself with a jug filled with wine, with which he hit himself over the head so forcefully that he damaged his skull and brain. Journal, pp. 31-2.
86 These two had represented the best capture to take place for the kingdom in twenty years. Journal, p. 32.
87 An astonishing event, to kill a man in the hands of justice. Histoire de Charles VI, p. 480.
88 He confessed that he and others that he identified had conspired to render Paris in such a state that people would have said, 'Paris was once here'; and he confessed many other horrible treasons against the crown without torture. Emphasis my own. Rome, Vatican MS Reg. Lat. 1502, fol. 108v.

narrative that followed La Rivière's death explicitly anticipated contested perspectives at his execution. Here, when confronted by proof of his treason La Rivière had exclaimed 'Non videbo quod villani Parisienses gaudeant super ignominiosa morte mea!' before killing himself.[89] Although Pintoin was quick to assert the falsity of the Cabochien narrative and the reality of La Rivière's murder in jail, his account demonstrates the degree to which Parisians bearing witness to the execution played an active role in validating precisely that execution. Robbed of this opportunity, sympathizers such as the fragment author and Bourgeois were compelled to draw their audiences into the prison itself.

Transforming extrajudicial murder into formal execution to legitimate Cabochien actions, disturbed executions could also be employed strategically to question the civic right of Paris' governors. On 15 December 1427, the Bourgeois described the hanging of Sauvage de Frémainville, a noble found among the Burgundians in 1419 who, in December 1425, had attempted to ambush the Lancastrian regent John, duke of Bedford before being captured by Parisian forces led by the city's *prévôt*, Simon Morhier.[90] The execution, undertaken immediately upon Bedford's orders, was overseen by the former sergeant and cobbler turned Parisian *receveur* and Bedford's treasurer for Maine, Pierre Baillé. When Frémainville asked to be confessed Baillé refused, instead forcing the brigand up the ladder with insults and striking him with his staff, before turning his anger upon the executioner 'pour ce qu'il l'interrogoit du sauvement de son ame'.[91] Intimidated by Baillé's aggression, the executioner rushed the ordeal: the rope snapped and Frémainville fell, breaking his ribs and a leg, in which condition he was forced by Baillé to climb the ladder again to be hanged. As in the cases of Jeanne d'Arc and Pierre des Essarts, the Bourgeois' description of Frémainville's execution ends with rumour and ambiguity. Bedford 'lui pourtoit une tres malle grace', even if some Parisians murmured that Frémainville had killed a bishop in Flanders or Hainaut, highlighting the more legendary aspects of his villainy. And yet, despite Frémainville's reputation, it was the action of Pierre Baillé that occupied the Bourgeois' attention, resurfacing in the *Journal* when Frémainville's body was taken down in September 1428, whereupon the Bourgeois recalled how 'Pierre Baillé fist tant de desplaisir quant on le pendoit', all the while reminding his audience that Baillé had been Paris' *receveur*.[92]

This last element indicates how the botched execution could be deciphered as a measure of good government, complicating Elisabeth Hodges' view that each account of Frémainville's execution 'furnishes the information without commentary'.[93] Overseen by the *prévôt* and acting under Bedford's direct orders as a representative of Paris' Lancastrian administration, Baillé's cruelty enabled the Bourgeois to imply a broader abandonment of due royal justice under the English, a fact emphasized both by the immediacy of Bedford's

---

89 I will not [live to] see the villeins of Paris rejoice in my own ignominious death! *RSD*, V, p. 36.

90 See Germain Lefevre-Pontalis, 'Épisodes de l'invasion anglaise. La guerre des partisans dans la Haute Normandie, 1424-29 (suite et fin), *BEC*, 97 (1936), pp. 108-09. For a close analysis of the Bourgeois' description as evidence of medieval attitudes to capital punishment, see Elisabeth Hodges, *Urban Poetics in the French Renaissance* (Farnham: Ashgate, 2008), pp. 36-7.

91 Because he asked him [Frémainville] about the salvation of his soul. For this and what follows, *Journal*, pp. 223-24.

92 Pierre Baillé had treated him so brutally when he was hanged. *Journal*, p. 229.

93 Hodges, *Urban Poetics*, p. 37.

sentence 'sans estre ouy en ses deffenses' and Baillé's refusal, in confronting both the executioner and Frémainville himself, to permit the brigand's confession.[94] Indeed, the Bourgeois' observations and the disdain expressed at this misconduct upon Frémainville's execution underscores the pivotal function that the public performed as a check upon the sentence's procedure, as the custodians of the memory of executions and, consequently, the authority to perform these executions.[95] In recording the disruption and cruelty that accompanied Frémainville's demise – reported twice in the *Journal* – the Bourgeois redirected this same memory to call into question the validity of his execution and the nature of Lancastrian authority.

This disorder can be juxtaposed with the accounts of far more ordered and penitent executions found in the *Journal*. For instance, the Bourgeois marvelled at the death of Paris' own executioner, Capeluche, condemned for the murder of a pregnant woman during the 1418 massacres. Stepping up to the scaffold, Capeluche instructed his replacement how to perform the office, trimming and preparing the block for his own neck 'tout ainsi comme s'il voulsist faire ladite office a ung autre', before pleading for divine mercy.[96] Five years earlier, Essarts had kneeled before Capeluche and kissed the executioner's silver figure before forgiving him for his death. In contrast, through the disturbed process of Frémainville's own execution the Bourgeois signalled a readiness throughout the Lancastrian regime to defy the due, formal processes affiliated with criminal trial and public execution.

Public sentences represented a crucial medium through which civic and royal authorities sought to control political narratives, with the judgements proclaimed representing a key informational source for the *Journal*. In the text, executions emerged as an interface that juxtaposed the crowd and criminal in public space, allowing the Bourgeois to define the parameters of moral and political right. Parisian authorities were adept at employing clothing, symbolism and processional order to convey information to audiences without resorting to proclamations, and the importance of these elements is demonstrated by the detail with which the Bourgeois incorporated these events into his narrative. Nevertheless, the rhetorical manipulation of these executions also reveals how the Bourgeois exerted his own authority to determine their meaning once disseminated in the public sphere. The detail with which these events were described was relative to their perceived political value. Consequently, an analysis of the executions recorded within the *Journal* not only reveals their importance as a medium of official communication, but also the ways in which Parisians could appropriate or mitigate official meaning for their own ends. Executions were far from straightforward, direct and unilateral instances of communication between rulers and ruled. Instead, in the *Journal* they emerge as moments that *tested* public opinion and determined support for the governing regimes.

---

94 Without his defence being heard. *Journal*, p. 223.
95 Claude Gauvard, *Condamner à mort*, p. 220.
96 Just as if he wished to perform the office for another. *Journal*, p. 111.

Sermons and preaching

Jeanne d'Arc's execution highlights a final key medium of communication that reached a wide audience: sermons and preaching.[97] The parish clergy were invested with a crucial role in preaching, prayer and processions that inculcated values and communicated socio-political information at a grassroots level, and David d'Avray has even argued that the standardization and dissemination of mendicant sermons during the thirteenth century neared a system of 'mass communication'.[98] While the diversity of preachers and sermons means that the medium could be exploited to assert, influence or resist civic and royal authority, as best demonstrated by Jean Gerson's sermons at court during the first decade of the French civil conflict, this section will examine the official impetus behind the sermons recorded by the Bourgeois, how their messages were received and the circumstances integral to authoritative communication.[99] Here, the didactic function traditionally accorded to the sermon was conflated with political messages. Emotionally encouraging audiences to assume virtuous behaviours, these same rhetorical strategies inculcated political loyalty and legitimated societal hierarchies. Indeed, Gerson advocated preaching as a means of reiterating a divinely mandated hierarchy, as the "natural means" through which the public heard the word of God and maintained their spiritual life.[100]

In his own writing, the Bourgeois typically noted the combination of procession and sermon, as demonstrated by his descriptions of ritual at the Saints-Innocents. Since the fourteenth century, religious sermons had increasingly overlapped with the dissemination of political messages and emerged as integral pillars of an emerging public sphere characterised by a growing appetite for information, with Hervé Martin suggesting that 'les sources françaises mentionnent surtout des énoncés mixtes, des hybrides de sermons et de harangues, dus à des clercs ou à des laïcs, engagés dans les luttes politiques'.[101] Like other media, the record of sermons reveals a direct relationship with written materials circulating in Paris. In the case of the sermon explaining the indulgences for Corpus Christi announced by Pope Martin V delivered by a theology master on 25 May 1431, the Bourgeois evidently conflated a written text with the record of a sermon he attended. Although the *Journal* stressed the sermon's oral character – 'la fut *faicte une predicacion*',

---

97 Preaching's place in official communication has been highlighted by Novák, 'La source du savoir', pp. 152-58; Sophia Menache, *The Vox Dei*, pp. 238-41. See also Filippo de Vivo, *Information and Communication in Venice: Rethinking Early Modern Politics* (Oxford: Oxford University Press, 2007), pp. 187-89.

98 David d'Avray, *Medieval Marriage Sermons: Mass Communication in a Culture without Print* (Oxford: Oxford University Press, 2005), pp. 16-17; Julien Briand, 'Foi, politique et information en Champagne au XVᵉ siècle', *Revue historique*, 653 (2010), pp. 81-9.

99 On Jean Gerson's adaptation of his sermon rhetoric to advocate the University of Paris' role in royal politics, see Nancy McLoughlin, *Jean Gerson and Gender: Rhetoric and Politics in Fifteenth-Century France* (Basingstoke: Palgrave Macmillan, 2015), pp. 97-127.

100 Jean Gerson, 'Pour la réforme du royaume: Vivat Rex, Vivat Rex, Vivat Rex' in *Œuvres complètes*, ed. by Palémon Glorieux, vol. 7, pt. 2 (Paris: Desclée, 1960), p. 1145; Catherine Brown, *Pastor and Laity in the Theology of Jean Gerson* (Cambridge: Cambridge University Press, 1987), p. 19.

101 French sources typically cite mixed utterances, hybrids of sermons and exhortations resulting from clerics or laymen engaged in political contests. Hervé Martin, 'Les sermons du bas Moyen Âge. Un réexamen en cours', *Revue d'histoire de l'Église de France*, 86 (2000), pp. 454-55. See also Daniel Hobbins, *Authorship and Publicity before Print: Jean Gerson and the Transformation of Late Medieval Learning* (Philadelphia, PA: University of Pennsylvania Press, 2009), p. 10.

'ainsi furent les dessudits pardons *publiez*' –, the Bourgeois had transcribed a vernacular copy of the papal edict.[102] The passage suggests that the Bourgeois supplemented his account with relevant written materials to provide authoritative information, though his refusal to acknowledge this textual support suggests that he was more concerned with the act of publication itself. Publicity functioned as a means of authorization, with the sermon integrated into a verbal paradigm that ascribed the text's authority to the speaker, a process familiar to late medieval clerics aware that the preacher's authority stemmed not from the individual, but from the textual authorities that supported him, such as the *verbum Dei*.[103]

This relationship between public preaching and official text is further demonstrated by the Bourgeois' description of the Dominican inquisitor Jean Graverent's sermon in Paris following Jeanne d'Arc's execution. The widespread publication of Jeanne's crimes was essential to consolidating her conviction for heresy and formed part of a concerted Lancastrian propaganda campaign, as indicated by the letter issued in Henry VI's name to the prelates of France on 28 June 1431.[104] When Graverent preached in Paris on 4 July, therefore, he was fulfilling the royal prescription that the letter's content be delivered publicly 'pour le bien et exaltacion de nostre dicte foy'.[105] The Bourgeois' decision to supplement his already detailed account of Jeanne's crimes with Graverent's sermon highlights his own perception of Graverent's preaching as the 'official' stance regarding Jeanne's beliefs, intended to allay the public doubts that the Bourgeois had evoked earlier upon her execution. Craig Taylor has suggested that Parisian theologians may have even directly influenced the composition of Henry VI's letter, meaning that as a University member the Bourgeois might also have been acutely aware of the underlying tensions surrounding Jeanne d'Arc's execution.[106] The parallels between the Bourgeois' account of Graverent's sermon and Henry VI's letter are revealed by the introduction of the notion that Jeanne recognized the falsity of her visions immediately prior to her death, an element that diverged from the Bourgeois' initial account.[107] Henry's letter insisted that Jeanne

> véant approuchier son finement, elle congnut plainnement et confessa que les esperilz qu'elle disoit estre apparus a elle souventes fois, estoient mauvais et mensongiers, et que la promesse que iceulz esperilz lui avoient plusieurs fois faicte de la delivrer estoit faulse ; et ainsi se confessa par lesditz esperilz avoir esté moquée et deceue.[108]

---

102 There a sermon was pronounced; and in that manner the aforesaid pardons were published. *Journal*, pp. 264-66. On this copy, see Chapter 1.

103 Carolyn Muessig, 'Sermon, Preacher and Society in the Middle Ages', *Journal of Medieval History*, 28 (2002), p. 86; Carlo Delcorno, 'Medieval Preaching in Italy (1200-1500)' in *The Sermon*, ed. by Beverley Mayne Kienzle (Turnhout: Brepols, 2000), pp. 486-87.

104 'Licterarum quas dominus noster rex scripsit prelatis ecclesie, ducibus, comitibus et aliis nobilibus et civitatibus regni sui Francie' in *Procès de condamnation de Jeanne d'Arc*, ed. by Pierre Tisset and Yvonne Lanhers, 3 vols (Paris: Klincksieck, 1960-71), I (1960), pp. 426-30. The broader propaganda campaign has been considered by Philippe Contamine, 'Naissance d'une historiographie. Le souvenir de Jeanne d'Arc, en France et hors de France, depuis le 'procès de son innocence' (1455-56) jusqu'au début du XVIe siècle', *Francia*, 15 (1987), pp. 233-36.

105 For the good and exaltation of our said faith. 'Licterarum quas dominus noster rex', p. 430.

106 Craig Taylor (ed.), *Joan of Arc: La Pucelle* (Manchester: Manchester University Press, 2006), p. 23.

107 An official view echoed by Fauquembergue's Latin postscript, perhaps amended following the letter's dissemination. See above, n. 75.

108 Seeing that her end was nearing[...] admitted and confessed fully that the spirits that she claimed often appeared to her were evil and dishonest, and that the promises that these spirits had proffered to her several times to free her [from

As related by the Bourgeois, Graverent's sermon rendered this deception vivid, describing the Devil, 'qui moult avoit grant paour qui ne la perdist', appearing before Jeanne following her abjuration in the guise of her saintly protectors, reassuring Jeanne that '"nous te garderons moult bien de tous"'.[109] However, when Jeanne was again brought to the scaffold, 'elle appela les ennemys [...] en guise de sains, mais oncques puis qu'elle fut jugée nul ne s'apparut a elle pour invocacion qu'elle sceust faire. *Adong s'avisa, mais ce fut trop tart*'.[110]

The differences between this account and the Bourgeois' earlier description of Jeanne d'Arc's trial, drawn from the Twelve Articles of Accusation examined at the University of Paris, may explain why the Bourgeois decided to repeat an account of Jeanne's execution.[111] Their juxtaposition also reveals the Bourgeois' participation in ongoing discussions regarding the trial's significance, and what it meant for Lancastrian and Valois royal legitimacy, particularly given Jeanne's role in securing Charles VII's Reims coronation in 1429. Ultimately, instead of simply revising his original account with reference to the information supplied by Graverent, the Bourgeois bracketed the sermon as a distinct, Lancastrian perspective. Whether forced or voluntary, Jeanne's resumption of her beliefs following her initial condemnation in 1431 complicated the trial's propagandistic and symbolic value, risked rendering Jeanne a martyr, and compelled Lancastrian apologists to emphasize her demonic inspiration before Parisian audiences to deter the doubts, echoed by the *Journal* upon her death, that Charles VII enjoyed divine favour. Jeanne's persistence in her views underscored her dedication to her 'droit seigneur', with her execution setting precisely the kind of dangerous example that might provoke a reconsideration of political allegiances. Here, the links between the *Journal*, its record of Graverent's sermon and the underlying influence of Henry VI's letter demonstrate how sermons functioned as an effective means of propaganda, but also how the Bourgeois' organization of information could temper and channel the interpretation of this propaganda and the identification of its purpose to facilitate Parisian engagement with broader political and societal debates. Moreover, as with the earlier Corpus Christi sermon, the Bourgeois eschewed references to the textual underpinnings of Graverent's sermon in Henry VI's letter, demonstrating that it was the confirmatory publication of this information that the Bourgeois considered as evidence of an official stance, with the sermon directly addressing undercurrents of debate in the Parisian public sphere.

These debates about both female agency and the discernment of spirits were amplified by the related sermons recorded by the Bourgeois regarding Jeanne's case. Prior to Jeanne's trial, two of her accomplices were denounced through sermons preached on Paris' *parvis* on 3 September 1430 before being condemned by the episcopal officiality – Piéronne

---

captivity] were false. And so she confessed to having been deceived and misled by the said spirits. 'Licterarum quas dominus noster rex', p. 430.

109 That greatly feared that they would lose her; 'we will protect you well from everyone'. *Journal*, p. 271.

110 She called the devils [...] [who were] disguised as saints, but ever since she had been condemned none appeared to her, regardless of the invocations that she knew. *Hence she realized [her error], but it was too late. Journal*, p. 271. Emphasis my own.

111 On the possible connection to the trial documents, see Chapter 1.

'la Bretonne' and an unnamed female companion.[112] Anticipating Graverent's sermon the following year, the Bourgeois ordered his account of this condemnation according to the list of Piéronne's crimes as declared by the preacher, noting her habit of receiving the Eucharist twice daily, her claims that God appeared to her in human form dressed in a white robe, and her faith in Jeanne's own divine inspiration.[113] Underlying this synthesis of the information preached regarding Piéronne and Jeanne was an essential condensation of the broader discussions concerning spiritual inspiration taking place at the University of Paris and, later, the Council of Basel, for lay Parisian audiences. These debates had their origins in the climate of theological disputation that had met Jeanne's appearance in April 1429, as demonstrated by the circulation of the treatise, *De mirabili victoria*, in Paris, Italy and the Low Countries, followed by its condemnation in a response compiled by a Parisian canon lawyer in September 1429 that prefigured both the Twelve Articles of Accusation and the Bourgeois' own critique of Jeanne in 1431.[114] Both texts subsequently appeared at the Council of Basel in the company of Jeanne's judges, including Nicolas Lamy, who certainly discussed the cases of Jeanne and Piéronne with the Dominican theologian Johannes Nider since they were reproduced, upon Lamy's authority, in Nider's *Formicarius*.[115]

In short, through the record of sermons condemning female visionaries, the Bourgeois connected his Parisian audience to the public sphere of debate and commentary regarding these issues framed by the University of Paris and the Council of Basel, rendering these discussions key components of Parisian discourse and identity-formation. The ways in which these sermons brought together Parisian institutional, political and spiritual identities is further demonstrated by the Bourgeois' similarly detailed account of Jeanne d'Arc's imposter, Claude des Armoises, examined by the University of Paris while being 'monstrée au peuple au Pallays sur la pierre de marbre en la grant court, et la fut preschée et toute sa vie et tout son estat'.[116] Like Piéronne, Claude also appeared in Nider's *Formicarius*, whereupon the inquisitor described the examination and excommunication of an armed woman in Cologne in 1436.[117] As such, the Bourgeois' record of the sermons regarding Piéronne, Jeanne and Claude prefigures the widely debated theological issues taking place

---

112 This unknown companion was possibly Catherine de La Rochelle, another female visionary whom Jeanne d'Arc encountered at Jargeau, and who claimed that her divine inspiration instructed her to rally French towns to Charles VII and encourage them to donate funds to the French monarch. Catherine's testimony 'by confession made before the officiality of Paris' was directly referenced in the promotor Jean d'Estivet's Articles of Accusation. *Procès de condamnation*, I, pp. 264-66.

113 *Journal*, pp. 259-60.

114 The Parisian response to *De Mirabili Victoria* is simply known as 'La réponse d'un clerc parisien'. For these two treatises, see Deborah Fraioli, *Joan of Arc: The Early Debate* (Woodbridge: Boydell, 2000), pp. 143-49, 159-72; Noël Valois, 'Un nouveau témoignage sur Jeanne d'Arc: Réponse d'un clerc parisien à l'apologie de la Pucelle par Gerson (1429)', *Annuaire-Bulletin de la Société de l'histoire de France*, 43, 2 (1906), pp. 161-79.

115 *Procès de condamnation et de réhabilitation de Jeanne d'Arc*, ed. by Jules Quicherat, 5 vols (Paris: Renouard, 1841-49), IV (1847), pp. 387-88; Michael D. Bailey and Edward Peters, 'A Sabbat of Demonologists: Basel, 1431-40', *The Historian*, 65 (2003), pp. 1381-82.

116 Shown to the people upon the marble table in the great court of the Palais, and there her entire life and her status were preached. *Journal*, pp. 354-55.

117 *Procès de condamnation*, V (1849), pp. 324-25. See also Pierre-Gilles Girault, 'Les procès de Jeanne-Claude des Armoises' in *De l'hérétique à la sainte. Les procès de Jeanne d'Arc revisités*, ed. by François Neveux (Caen: Presses universitaires de Caen, 2012), pp. 197-210.

at Basel and elaborated in Nider's own writing, and the *Journal* suggests a Parisian sensitivity to the debates taking place within this international public sphere, not least given his regular complaint, from 1433, that 'n'estoit nouvelle du conseil de Balle, ne en sermon, ne autre part'.[118] Combining this information as it was received through sermons, the *Journal* concentrates the more complicated textual combinations of theological material circulating among ecclesiastical officials, conveying this information for lay Parisian audiences.

The Bourgeois' description of these sermons also highlights the Parisian University's and clergy's ties to political developments and their integration within wider communicational networks that sustained an awareness of French political shifts. For instance, during the negotiations between England and France overseen by the papal legate Niccolò Albergati in 1432 and 1433, Albergati frequently visited Paris, preaching sermons promoting peace and informing urban audiences of the negotiations' progress.[119] The cardinal's first visit to Notre-Dame, on 20 February 1432, tellingly coincided with the Bourgeois' own synthesis of the contending diplomatic arguments:

> l'un estoit nommé Charles de Valoys, et se disoit par droicte ligne estre roy de France, et l'autre estoit nommé Henry, lequel se disoit roy d'Angleterre par succession de ligne, et de France par le conquest de son feu pere.[120]

Again, these sermons enabled the Bourgeois to connect his community to the wider disputes framing the kingdom's politics. Albergati's own interest in keeping Parisian institutions informed of the negotiations is demonstrated both by the letters received and published by the Parlement on 15 March 1432 and the unnamed bishop that the Bourgeois described as being sent by Albergati to preach a sermon at Notre-Dame in March 1433, when English and French delegates were due to meet at Corbeil.[121] For the Bourgeois, the sermon was directly linked to the negotiations at this 'concile', and although the bishop performed the office 'si matin que tres grant partie de toutes orders a ce jour faillirent', the regular presence of those involved with the Anglo-French negotiations reveals the communicational ties connecting the city to overarching political developments and the potential for news to spread through these sermons.[122] Parisians certainly engaged with this news, as suggested by the vocal criticism that followed the failure of talks at Auxerre in November 1432.[123] When the Lancastrian ambassadors returned to Paris, the administration 'fist entendent au peuple que tres bien besongné avoient', whereupon the Bourgeois explained that

---

118 There was no news of the Council of Basel, either through sermons or other means. *Journal*, p. 302.

119 Margaret Harvey, *England, Rome and the Papacy, 1417-64: The Study of a Relationship* (Manchester: Manchester University Press, 1993), pp. 150-57.

120 One was named Charles of Valois, and he asserted that by direct descent he was the king of France, and the other was named Henry, who styled himself king of England by direct succession, and of France through the conquest achieved by his late father. *Journal*, pp. 280-81.

121 Fauquembergue, III, pp. 38, 41-44; Jocelyne Dickinson, *The Congress of Arras 1435: A Study in Medieval Diplomacy* (Reprint. New York: Biblo and Tannen, 1972), p. 82.

122 So early in the morning that the majority of the members of every order failed to appear that day. *Journal*, p. 293.

123 For these negotiations, see Urbain Plancher, *Histoire générale et particulière de Bourgogne avec les preuves justificatives*, 4 vols (Dijon: Frantin, 1739-81), IV (1781), pp. 166-67; Harvey, *England, Rome and the Papacy*, pp. 154-55.

le contraire estoit. Et quant le peuple le sceut au vray, si commencerent a murmurer moult fort contre ceulx qui y avoient esté, dont plusieurs furent mis en prinson, dissimulant que c'estoit a fin celle que le peuple ne s'esmeust.[124]

Clearly, the presence of Albergati and his associates in Paris, as well as the sermons that they preached, integrated Parisians into the broader political contestations in France, revealing a recognition of the importance of keeping urban populations informed, not least to maintain morale and signal the representation of popular interests in these negotiations.

The power of these sermons was accentuated by the heightened emotional states produced during the processions that frequently preceded them, with the result that beyond the communication of political news, preaching was naturally integral to the reinforcement and delineation of moral values and understandings of Christian community precisely when these values became contested elements in the rhetoric of civil and national conflict. Such preaching inculcated a perception of Paris' and France's enemies as amoral Others, a fact keenly demonstrated by Graverent's portrayal of Jeanne d'Arc in the context of a general procession to Saint-Martin-des-Champs. This moralization of political issues was, of course, nothing new. In 1405 Jean Gerson's *Vivat Rex* had targeted the corruption resulting from lordly cupidity and Charles VI's diminished authority, themes that were subsequently reprised by Jean Petit's 1408 *Justification* for Louis d'Orléans assassination.[125] The *Journal* illustrates this politico-moral boundary making through the sermon preached before Charles VI by Étienne du Mesnil, minister of the Mathurins convent, in the summer of 1410. Echoing *Vivat Rex*, Mesnil identified evil counsel and treachery as compromising royal authority, exacerbated by the growing trends of civil disorder provoked by the Armagnac faction, 'disant qu'il failloit qu'il y eut traitres en ce royaulme'.[126] Although the sermon was delivered at court, just like Jean Petit's *Justification* and *Vivat Rex* before it, the Bourgeois' ability to condense and comment upon Mesnil's message highlights the dynamics by which court politics were translated in the public sphere, with the *Journal* suggesting an implicit awareness of the key themes that had comprised courtly political debates throughout the first decade of the fifteenth century. Additional ceremonies and sermons formalized the exclusion envisioned in Mesnil's preaching, most notably the sentences of excommunication pronounced against the Armagnac leadership at Notre-Dame the following year. As a result, sermons not only communicated essential news but inherently shaped political attitudes, framing political identities through the erection of moral frontiers that, in the *Journal*, distinguished Armagnac sinners from devoted Parisians.

The moral tangent proposed through sermons also points to their inherently subversive potential, a fact exemplified by official reactions to the preaching of the itinerant Dominican, Brother Richard, who appeared in Paris in the spring of 1429. Richard's charisma was such that his sermons, building upon St. Vincent Ferrer's own visions of Antichrist's coming and the preaching of Bernardino of Sienna in northern Italy, quickly

---

124 Made out to the people that they had worked very hard [...] [but] it was in fact the opposite. When the people knew the truth, they began to murmur very loudly about those who had been there [at the negotiations]; several were imprisoned under the pretence of preventing a popular uprising. *Journal*, p. 290.

125 Jean Gerson, 'Vivat Rex', pp. 1150-51; Jean Petit, 'Justification' as recorded in Monstrelet, I, pp. 184-89.

126 Saying that there must be traitors in the kingdom. *Journal*, p. 9.

drew large numbers, inspired emotional reactions, and provoked substantial changes in Parisian behaviour. Richard's sermons continued for a week straight, beginning at the abbey of Sainte-Geneviève on the left bank and taking place at different points throughout the city before reaching their climax at the Saints-Innocents cemetery, where Richard delivered a sermon with his back to the *Danse Macabre* before an audience of five or six thousand people.[127] Like the condemnations of Jeanne d'Arc and Piéronne la Brétonne – and as Andrew Brown has shown – Richard's sermons fed into a growing climate of prophetic anxiety in Paris, with the Bourgeois reporting a blood-red spring erupting in 1421, an epidemic 'air corrupu' descending upon the capital in September 1427, flooding throughout 1426 and 1427, plagues of maybugs in the spring of 1428 and the birth of conjoined twins and animals during the summer of 1429.[128] In this highly charged atmosphere, where worldly order seemed unstable and insecure, Richard warned his audiences that Antichrist was accruing followers in the Middle East and that over the next year 'on verroit les plus grandes merveilles que on eust oncques veues'.[129] Encouraging bonfires of the vanities and summoning great crowds to religious sites in Paris' suburbs, Richard's preaching was met with a more ambivalent response by the city's authorities. In May 1429 Richard declared that he would preach his final sermon at Montmartre, in response to which six thousand people assembled at the site, only for the preacher to be compelled to leave the city by the authorities without delivering his sermon. The Bourgeois refused to comment upon the circumstances of the preacher's expulsion, but remarked that 'les bonnes gens furent moult troublez' upon his forced departure.[130] Richard's position as an eschatological herald may have become untenable and compromising in the Lancastrian city when news of Jeanne d'Arc reached Paris that year. Indeed, while Monstrelet reported that Richard was expelled because his preaching 'se moustroit trop favourable et estre de la partie des Francois', Thomas Basin later suggested that it had resulted from a move by the theology faculty to silence the preacher because 'habuit tantum populorum favorem'.[131] The chroniclers' allusions demonstrate the extent to which civic institutions may have made a concerted effort to silence subversive and challenging voices in the city, a fact underscored by Richard's imprisonment in Poitiers in March 1431 when the French inquisitor, Valois Parlement and bishop of Poitiers forbade the friar's preaching.[132]

Finally, the Bourgeois' description of Brother Richard illustrates the importance of a preacher's identity and authority to the successful transmission of his message. The

---

127 *Journal*, pp. 233-34.

128 Corrupted air. *Journal*, pp. 153-54, 208, 216-17, 222, 225, 238-39. See Andrew Brown, 'Charisma and Routine: Shaping the Memory of Brother Richard and Joan of Arc', *Religions* 3 (2012), pp. 1165-66; David A. Fein, 'Acts of Nature and Preternatural Acts in the *Journal d'un bourgeois de Paris (1405-49)*', *Fifteenth Century Studies*, 20 (1993), pp. 65-75; Hodges, *Urban Poetics*, pp. 30-4.

129 People would see the greatest marvels that had ever been seen. *Journal*, p. 235.

130 The good people were greatly troubled. *Journal*, p. 237.

131 Showed itself to be too favourable towards the party of the French. Monstrelet, IV, p. 335. Enjoyed so much of the people's favour. Thomas Basin, *Histoire des règnes de Charles VII et de Louis XI*, ed. by Jules Quicherat, 4 vols (Paris: Renouard, 1855-59), IV (1859), p. 104.

132 Siméon Luce, *La France pendant la guerre de Cent Ans: épisodes historiques et vie privée aux XIVᵉ et XVᵉ siècles*, 2 vols (Paris: Hachette, 1890-93), II (1893), p. 198; Jules de La Martinière, 'Frère Richard et Jeanne d'Arc à Orléans, mars-juillet 1430', *Le Moyen Âge*, 44 (1934), p. 190.

effectiveness of the anti-Armagnac sermon preached by Étienne du Mesnil was accorded, in part, to the fact that Mesnil was a reliable, trustworthy and 'tres bonne personne'.[133] Wandering preachers such as Brother Richard and Jean Creté relied upon their charisma, holding an ephemeral power to incite radical alterations in their audiences. When Creté, a Franciscan preacher, arrived in Paris in the summer of 1445, the Bourgeois described him as a 'petit homme de tres doulx regart [...] lequel fu tenu à ung des meilleurs prescheurs qui oncques eust esté a Paris depuis cent ans'.[134] Creté's popularity was complemented by his skill. He knew the Bible and *Légende dorée* by heart, 'et tous les anciens livres de toutes nacions du monde, et oncques on le vit faillir de revenir a son propos, et partout ou il preschoit le moustier estoit tout plan de gens'.[135] Brother Richard was an 'homme de tres grant prudence, scevant a oraison, semeur de bonne doctrine pour ediffier son prosime', combining the qualities of spiritual judgement and intellect.[136] Naturally, such effects were underscored by Richard's emotional impact upon his audiences, instilling devotional frenzies and turning crowds to tears. These abilities were inherently essential to the persuasiveness of the preachers' moral instruction, and the Bourgeois explicitly pointed to Richard's emulation of better-known preachers like Vincent Ferrer and Bernardino of Siena, the latter converting more people in Italy 'que tous les prescheurs qui depuis II^C ans devant y avoient presché'.[137] As with public executions, these sermons depended upon an interplay between message, medium and audience response. When Richard was compelled to leave Paris by the episcopal authorities, the Bourgeois related this news' immediate effect: 'les gens grans et petiz plouroient piteusement [...] comme s'ilz veissent porter en terre leurs meilleurs amis', a description that paralleled onlookers' responses to Charles VI's funeral, with the emotional bonds that had motivated devotional behaviour encouraging a wider condemnation of the civic authorities' expulsion of the preacher.[138]

The Bourgeois was highly attuned to the multitudinous media employed by Parisian civic and royal officials to communicate news, and frequently integrated these into his narrative to map the extent of official influence. When these messages were incorporated into the *Journal*, the author arrogated and deployed his own narrative authority to channel or even contest their purpose. Predominantly, this was achieved through a focus upon symbolic elements and a stress upon the constitutive function of audience responses that invariably characterized official media designed to mould public opinion and, inversely, traced the extent to which openly expressed reactions could neutralize officially disseminated messages. Another phenomenon highlighted by this assessment of official communication is the Bourgeois' reluctance to explicitly refer to written texts, despite an evident awareness of their wider distribution and even their direct use as sources for the *Journal*.

---

133 A very good person. *Journal*, p. 9.
134 A small man with a gentle expression [...] who was reputed as being one of the best preachers who had been heard in Paris for a hundred years. *Journal*, pp. 379-80.
135 And all the ancient books of all of the world's nations, and never was he seen to fail to return to his subject, and every church in which he preached was completely filled with people. *Journal*, p. 380.
136 A man of great prudence, skilled in rhetoric, the sower of good doctrine to edify his neighbour. *Journal*, pp. 233-34.
137 Than all of the preachers who had preached beforehand for two hundred years. *Journal*, p. 236.
138 The people great and small wept so piteously [...] as if they were witnessing the burial of their best friends. *Journal*, p. 236.

What mattered was not a single authorial document and its content, but the means by which this content was made public, with the act of publicity rendering information authoritative. Ultimately, the Bourgeois' concentration upon the public effects of information in conjunction with the report describing the messages disseminated enabled him to redirect their influence, articulating an awareness of propaganda's potential and a willingness to contest official discourse by concentrating upon popular responses.

Emotion and communication

These instances of official communication – celebrations and proclamations, executions and sermons – each reveal the central role that emotion played in the transmission and reception of political messages. Fundamentally, emotion's place strikes at the heart of the loftier Habermasian ideal of rational and informed public debate as something distinct from emotionally conditioned responses, undermining hegemonic models that differentiate the emotional and the rational, or the subjective from the objective. This last section will examine the manner in which emotional rhetoric was part and parcel of the experience of public discussion and was ultimately intertwined with the mechanisms required to rationalize political experiences and attitudes. In doing so, it confronts the long-standing grand narrative of affective change developed by Norbert Elias, who argued that the consolidation of state power in early modernity paralleled a societal 'rationalization' through the control of emotional expression.[139] Reading the work of Johan Huizinga and, in doing so, inherently building upon Huizinga's vision of the 'passionate intensity' of medieval life drawn in part from the *Journal*, Elias concentrated upon the emergence of socio-political strategies of emotional moderation that mitigated against the 'authentic' display of feeling in the early modern court, underscoring a vision of 'rationality' linked to Weberian ideals that favoured the consideration of the long-term consequences of human action over shorter-term emotional expression.[140] Stemming from these early twentieth-century theorists, the result has been a vision of medieval emotional behaviour as uninhibited, irrational and child-like as distinct from the calculated, internalized mores of the present – degrees of modern discipline and self-restraint that Foucault argued distorted human nature.[141] Habermas' development of the public sphere is inherently tied to this emergent rationalization and the decline of violent behaviour in early modernity, as rational discussion emerges as a force for instilling order, regulating social interaction and facilitating conflict resolution in early modern salons and coffeehouses.

---

[139] Norbert Elias, *The Civilizing Process: Sociogenetic and Psychogenetic Investigations*, Revised Edition, trans. by Edmund Jephott, ed. by Eric Dunning, Johan Goudsblom and Stephen Mennell (Oxford: Blackwell, 2000), pp. 374-414; Damien Boquet and Piroska Nagy, 'L'historien et les émotions en politique: entre science et citoyenneté' in *Politique des émotions au Moyen Âge*, ed. by Damien Boquet and Piroska Nagy (Florence: Edizioni des Galluzzo, 2010), pp. 8-9.

[140] This relationship between the work of Huizinga and Elias has recently been addressed in Damien Boquet and Laurent Smagghe, 'L'émotion comme désir de vie' in *L'Odeur du sang et des roses: Relire Johan Huizinga aujourd'hui*, ed. Élodie Lecuppre-Desjardin (Villeneuve d'Acq: Presses Universitaires du Septentrion, 2019), pp. 195-214.

[141] Stuart Carroll, 'Thinking with Violence', *History and Theory*, 55 (2017), pp. 25-6.

Huizinga turned to the Bourgeois of Paris to give credence to Sigmund Freud's contrasting of the childlike tendencies of medieval man and the internalization of desire that distinguished modern civilization alongside the emergence of modern forms of communication. Highlighting the Bourgeois' account of Brother Richard, Huizinga argued that 'wij krantenlezers kunnen ons nauwelijks meer de geweldige werking van het word op een onverzadigde en onwetende geest voorstellen'; factional partisanship was evidence of 'Hoe hevig de gemoedsbeweging van vorstentrouw werken kon'.[142] The result was the impression that the 'Tusschen leed en vreugde… scheen de afstand grooter dans voor ons; al wat men beleefde had nog dien graad van onmiddellijkheid en absoluutheid, dien… [zij] hebben in den kindergeest'.[143] Such emotional sensitivity could be read in the 'expressive violence' of an era that would only gradually be canalized by a rationalized 'instrumental violence' tied to modernity.[144] Although the Bourgeois himself could situate overwhelming emotion as the opposite of a rational 'memoyre de Dieu', a close examination of the *Journal* complicates the rigid distinction between the modern and premodern advanced by earlier studies.[145] An alternate reading of the Bourgeois' emotional discourse can situate this within a broader strategic repertoire employed by the author to delineate relations of power between groups and individuals in fifteenth-century Parisian society. Primarily, emotional discourse represented a rhetorical tool that rationalized and moralized human behaviours. Emotions were (and are) inherently communicative, with their interpretation bounded by cultural norms, and as such are apt to such rhetorical instrumentalization. Instead of considering the *Journal* as an unmediated window onto the Bourgeois' inner emotional experiences, a more nuanced approach should appreciate how his writing of emotion was intrinsically tied to fluctuating conceptions of authority, a fact exemplified by the Bourgeois' regular juxtaposition of collective and individual expression to articulate both popular reactions and aristocratic power. Such an approach exposes emotional rhetoric's place within a public transcript where commons and rulers alike elaborated visions of power. While Elias perceived the internalization of emotion as a form of power, the *Journal* reveals how its expression and record facilitated commentaries on authority and legitimacy integral to the public sphere.

This relationship between emotional expression and the public sphere, only recently underscored in modern sociological studies, has long been recognized by historians. Gerd Althoff has proposed an epistemological distinction between irretrievable, lived, 'authentic' emotions and their discursive function within rhetorical systems.[146] This discursive function can be linked to the performative quality of emotional discourse, its function

---

142 We, readers of newspapers, can hardly imagine anymore the tremendous impact of the spoken word on naive and ignorant minds; how violent the emotions caused by the attachment to the prince could become. Johan Huizinga, *Herfsttij der Middeleeuwen*, ed. L. Brummel in *Verzamelde werken*, vol. 3, (Haarlem: H.D. Tjeenk Willink & Zoon, 1949), pp. 9, 22.

143 The distance between sorrow and joy… seemed greater than for us [today]; everything experienced had that degree of immediacy and absoluteness that… they still have in the minds of children. Huizinga, *Herfsttij der Middeleeuwen*, p. 1.

144 Carrol, 'Thinking with violence', p. 28.

145 *Journal*, p. 96.

146 Gerd Althoff, 'Du rire et des larmes. Pourquoi les émotions intéressent-elles les médiévistes?', *Écrire l'histoire*, 2 (2008), pp. 27-39.

as 'un acte de langage *réel*, qui agit sur soi et sur l'interlocuteur'.[147] William Reddy in particular has conceptualized emotions as both bodily experiences and social habits, such that within social groupings this expression constitutes 'emotional regimes', with emotional speech acts underscoring truth-claims.[148] Influencing actor and audience, Reddy asserted that the institution and management of emotional regimes reflects power relationships, whereby 'emotives are modelled through ceremony or official art forms; individuals are required to utter emotives in appropriate circumstances, in the expectation that normative emotives will be enhanced and habituated'.[149] These approaches interpret emotion as being conditioned by cultural norms that distinguish social status and frame authority, ultimately revealing the extent to which historically specific cultures determine the freedom and navigation of emotional expression. They are not, however, unidirectional. Public emotional expression is negotiated and, echoing James Scott's hidden transcripts, Reddy points to the presence of 'emotional refuges' in strict regimes that establish different spheres of emotional consensus where norms are relaxed or reversed, and otherwise illicit affective connections established.[150]

Recent work has increasingly emphasized emotions' role in the ordering of urban socio-political relations. These approaches reveal the complementarity of Reddy's emotional regimes, functioning as a bridge between, first, the idea of opinion communities consolidated around texts and, second, Barbara Rosenwein's own theory of simultaneously coexisting 'emotional communities'.[151] For Rosenwein, emotional communities encapsulate 'different groups that have their own mode of interaction, form of emotional expression and valuation of particular emotions' and, as such, reveals the place of emotional discourse in the consolidation of opinion communities bound by shared attitudes.[152] All three approaches validate the place of emotions' communicative role for the structuring of social-political relations and the shaping of the public sphere.[153] Emotional discourse therefore played a crucial role in the historiographical narratives that traced this interaction, a fact best demonstrated by Bernard Guenée's decision to dedicate a substantial part of his analysis of late medieval public opinion to an examination of the emotional registers employed by Michel Pintoin to articulate his view of the world.[154] Indeed, emotional display and expression were crucial to medieval governance, and while chroniclers drew

---

147 A real speech act is still produced which acts upon both the self and audience. Boquet and Piroska, 'L'historien et les émotions en politique', p. 22.

148 William Reddy, *The Navigation of Feeling: A Framework for the History of Emotions* (Cambridge: Cambridge University Press, 2001).

149 William Reddy, 'Emotional Liberty: Politics and History in the Anthropology of Emotions', *Cultural Anthropology* 14 (1999), p. 273.

150 Reddy, *The Navigation of Feeling*, p. 129; James C. Scott, *Domination and the Arts of Resistance: Hidden Transcripts* (New Haven, CT: Yale University Press, 1990). See also Damien Boquet and Piroska Nagy, 'Pour une histoire des émotions. L'historien face aux questions contemporaines' in *Le sujet des émotions au Moyen Âge*, ed. by Piroska Nagy and Damien Bouqet (Paris: Beauchesne, 2008), p. 38.

151 This complementarity has in particular been signalled by Laurent Smagghe, *Les émotions du prince. Émotion et discours politique dans l'espace bourguignon* (Paris: Classiques Garnier, 2012), p. 17.

152 Barbara Rosenwein, *Emotional Communities in the Early Middle Ages* (London: Cornell University Press, 2007), p. 2.

153 As Reddy noted for the late eighteenth century. *Navigation of Feeling*, p. 311.

154 Bernard Guenée, *L'opinion publique à la fin du Moyen Âge d'après la chronique de Charles VI du religieux de Saint-Denis* (Paris: Perrin, 2002), pp. 51-75.

clear distinctions between the agency of aristocrats and masses, it is also apparent that there was 'a highly developed emotional voice available for popular use, cultivated by the masses into a political tool'.[155] Through its own presentation of emotions witnessed, felt and envisioned, the *Journal* simultaneously reflected and shaped the experiences of its audience within a self-referential form, designed to evoke responses that validated the author's outlook. The intricacy of key emotional passages, most notably the allegorical description of the 1418 massacres, reveals the care underlying these narratives. Far from immediate, irrational and even infantile responses, these moments exhibited the Bourgeois' cautious introspection, rhetorically reconstructing emotional experiences to provide his audience with an 'exemplary' moral reaction to political circumstances.

While shaping this audience's perspectives, much like the preachers that he described, the Bourgeois' own emotional rhetoric was a product of his culturally determined understandings of morality, influenced by the common affective culture that characterized clerical learning and University status. It is therefore unsurprising that the *Journal* elaborated a paradigm juxtaposing emotion and reason. The connection of emotion to virtue by Aristotle had important implications for its moralization by medieval thinkers. For Thomas Aquinas, emotions were unruly elements that reason strove to govern: if directed to the moral good, they could be determined as rational.[156] Concerns for the power of emotions and rhetoric continued to be debated at the University of Paris at the end of the fourteenth century. In his *Tractatus de Anima* (1380), Pierre d'Ailly contended that 'no amount of cognition could ever have extrinsic motivational force, as emotions do', while his pupil Jean Gerson was certainly aware of rhetoric's potential 'to stir the passions'.[157] For Gerson, there were clear ties between human rationality and emotion – as humans had free will, they should be governed by 'spiritual passions' rather than those of the body.[158] Similarly, members of the faculty of medicine at the University of Paris in the fifteenth century would have been familiar with the physiognomical idea of the soul's governance of the body, but also the ways in which the emotions could cause a disproportionality in this same body that was conducive to sickness. Emotions therefore had to be mastered to preserve the body's state, with these same medical ideas applied conceptually to the notion of the body politic and its decline in early fifteenth century France by authors including Jean Gerson

---

155 Vincent Challet and Ian Forrest, 'The Masses' in *Government and Political Life in England and France, c.1300–c.1500*, ed. by Christopher Fletcher, Jean-Philippe Genet and John Watts (Cambridge: Cambridge University Press, 2015), p. 294. On the place of emotional expression in communication and government, see Laurent Smagghe, *Les émotions du prince*.

156 See Peter King, 'Aquinas on the Emotions' in *The Oxford Handbook of Aquinas*, ed. by Brian Davies and Eleonore Stump (Oxford: Oxford University Press, 2012), pp. 212, 218-23; Barbara Rosenwein, 'Emotion Words' in *Le sujet des émotions au Moyen Âge*, ed. by Piroska Nagy and Damien Boquet (Paris: Beauchesne, 2008), pp. 194-96.

157 Peter King, 'Emotions in Medieval Thought' in *The Oxford Handbook of Philosophy of Emotion* (Oxford: Oxford University Press, 2012), p. 182; Laura Ackerman Smoller, *History, Prophecy and the Stars: The Christian Astrology of Pierre d'Ailly, 1350-1420* (Princeton: Princeton University Press, 1994), p. 43; Barbara Rosenwein, *Generations of Feeling: A History of Emotions, 600-1700* (Cambridge: Cambridge University Press, 2016), pp. 229-47. In *c.* 1408-09 Gerson compiled *De passionibus anime* and later a second pamphlet with the same title (*c.* 1410-15). See Palémon Glorieux, 'La vie et les œuvres de Gerson: Essai chronologique', *Archives d'histoire doctrinale et littéraire du Moyen Âge*, 18 (1950-51), p. 173; Jean Gerson, *De passionibus animae* in Jean Gerson, *Œuvres complètes*, ed. by Palémon Glorieux, 10 vols (Paris: Desclée, 1959-73), IX (1973), no. 423, 437.

158 Rosenwein, *Generations of Feeling*, p. 234.

and Christine de Pizan, as Laurent Smagghe has shown.[159] Going further, Rosenwein has argued that direct parallels can be seen between Gerson's emotional vocabulary and Burgundian emphases upon pity, with the result that Monstrelet – much like the Bourgeois – endeavoured 'to record the piteous events of his day, and so evidently wanted his readers to know that the right response to those events was pity'.[160] Gerson's relation of rhetoric to the passions is particularly instructive, not least in its reinforcement of the perception that University theologians had a role to play in moving public audiences in a 'moral sphere', precisely as rational logic 'leaves the heart cold'.[161] In doing so, Gerson's reflections upon rhetoric take us back to the place that Christine de Pizan accorded to University members in her vision of the body politic, as those who held disproportionate affective influence over the people and were summoned to transform wisdom into virtue for the wider populace.[162]

The Bourgeois' treatment of emotion was influenced by this same stress upon human agency, morality and instruction, best demonstrated in those instances where he accentuated emotional rhetoric to substantiate moral assessments, as in his description of the Parisian massacre of suspected Armagnacs that occurred on 12 June 1418, two weeks after the Burgundian takeover of the capital. Here, the Bourgeois joined Michel Pintoin in structuring the massacres through the juxtaposition of rational institutional authorities with popular emotional experiences, elaborating the same dichotomies that had earlier framed records of official communication. For Pintoin, the Parisian commons were 'temulenti forurem dyabolicum', motivated by a drunken fury that enabled them to transgress hierarchical boundaries.[163] Where this rhetoric signalled disdain for a momentary popular seizure of power, the Bourgeois used the same dichotomy to rationalize the rioters' behaviours:

> Lors se leva la deesse de Discorde, qui estoit en la tour de Mau-Conseil, et esveilla Ire la forcenée et Convoitise et Enragerie et Vengence, et prindrent armes de toutes manieres, et bouterent hors d'avec eulx Raison, Justice, Memoyre de Dieu et Atrempance, moult honteusement.[164]

Huizinga suggested that this allegory revealed the Bourgeois' efforts to 'verheffen wil op een gedachtenniveau boven dat van de alledaagsche gebeurtenissen', that constituted the majority of his *Journal*, providing a means 'uitdrukkingsmiddel van het tragisch besef'.[165] Indeed, while Florence Bouchet and Colette Beaune have similarly argued that this stylistic shift evoked profound moral uncertainty in the face of the ongoing massacres, the paradigm

---

159 Laurent Smagghe, *Les émotions du prince*, pp. 37-59, 83-6.
160 Rosenwein, *Generations of Feeling*, p. 246.
161 Hobbins, *Authorship and Publicity*, p. 116.
162 Tracy Adams, 'The political significance of Christine de Pizan's Third Estate in the *Livre du corps de policie*', *Journal of Medieval History* 35 (2009), p. 394.
163 Intoxicated by diabolical fury. RSD, VI, p. 244. For Pintoin's account of the events of 1418 see pp. 228-67.
164 Then arose the goddess of Discord who resided in the tower of Mau-Conseil, and she awoke mad Anger, and Lust and Rage and Vengeance, and they took up arms of all kinds and very shamefully expelled Reason, Justice, the Memory of God and Temperance. *Journal*, p. 96.
165 Rise to an intellectual level beyond that of the description of everyday events; of expressing his sense of tragedy. Huizinga, *Herfsttij der Middeleeuwen*, p. 245.

also made sense of these complicated events.[166] Reason, Justice and the Memory of God, the qualities envisioned as safeguarding the common good, were here forgotten due to overwhelming emotion. The portrayal of Ire echoed Aristotle's own presentation of anger, as an emotion that 'mishears' reason, being quick to redress wrongs perceived by the individual, with the late fourteenth-century translator Nicole Oresme glossing: 'le courroucié ot le commencement de raison mais ne actent pas la fin'.[167] Anger therefore emerges here as a cognitive, evaluative belief tied to understandings of justice and grounded in an early sense of reason, overtaken by the perceived immediacy of the issues confronted by the individual.

In this evaluation, the *Journal* presented a paradigm for the socio-political interpretation of human feeling, political action and communication according to the moral binaries between virtuous direction and intent found in theological discussion. The binary provided medieval commentators with an emotional disposition system that eased their interpretation of the world and crucially hints at the kinds of prediscursive or innate predispositions underlying opinion communities, as pre-existing expectations about types of people summed up in stereotyped roles, identities and situations. Operating heuristically, disposition systems enable individuals to effectively navigate and make sense of their political contexts – particularly at times of crisis –, forming attitudes based upon past experiences. In this sense emotions are not culturally constructed, but their interpretation was determined by the culture enveloping the Bourgeois and his community – read in the Bible and devotional literature, heard in preaching and physically experienced in architecture, mystery plays and the liturgy. For instance, when Henry V and Charles VI entered Paris side-by-side in December 1420, the Bourgeois could remark that the mystery of Christ's Passion performed at their welcome was so compelling that 'n'estoit homme qui veist le mistere à qui le cueur n'apiteast'.[168] The imagery appears to have represented part of the Bourgeois' everyday backdrop, with the Passion performed 'selon que elle est figurée autour du cueur de Notre-Dame de Paris'.[169] This envelopment determined the Bourgeois' predisposition to moral judgement through the emotional evaluations that peppered his narrative. Prediscursive, they were employed almost as unconscious assumptions, following the symbioses of morality and emotion that framed his emotional disposition and provided a backdrop to the interpretation of ongoing urban conflicts.[170] In doing so, they provided ready models for intuitive responses to political events, but – like Rosenwein's interpretation of Monstrelet – could also be consciously deployed and imbued with moral overtones to direct the reactions of the *Journal*'s audience. Highlighting the role played by emotional

---

166 Florence Bouchet, 'Dire l'horreur: les relations du massacre des Armagnacs à Paris (juin 1418)' in *L'horreur au Moyen Âge*, ed. by Jean-Claude Faucon (Toulouse: Éditions universitaires du Sud, 2000), pp. 7-13; Colette Beaune (ed. and trans.), *Journal d'un bourgeois de Paris de 1405 à 1449* (Paris: Librairie de Poche, 1990), p. 200, n. 14.

167 The angered person has the beginnings of reason but does not await the ends. Nicole Oresme, *Le livre de Ethiques d'Aristote*, ed. by Albert Douglas Menut (New York: Stechert, 1940), p. 383

168 The hearts of all those who saw the mystery were moved to pity. *Journal*, p. 144.

169 As it is depicted around the choir of Notre-Dame of Paris. *Journal*, p. 144.

170 As suggested by Sandro Landi in his examination of prediscursive opinion. Sandro Landi, 'Opinions et conflits. Une relecture des *Histoires de Florence* (Istorie fiorentine) de Machiavel' in *S'exprimer en temps de troubles. Conflits, opinion(s) et politization du Moyen Âge au début du XXᵉ siècle*, ed. by Laurent Bourquin, Philippe Hamon, Pierre Karila-Cohen and Cédric Michon (Rennes: Presses universitaires de Rennes, 2012), pp. 25-49.

responses in political evaluations, this symbiosis fundamentally reveals the central place of emotional discourse and experience to the rationalization of debate and action in the medieval public sphere.

Read in this light, the emotional descriptions found in the *Journal* do not simply provide a window onto the Bourgeois' personal experiences. Rather, they represent the result of narrative strategies employed by the author to craft an emotional narrator that facilitated interpretive shortcuts, bringing the audience closer to the truths of human behaviour that qualified moral legitimacy in the public sphere. These emotional descriptions both inspired a moral assessment of behaviour and evoked emotional responses on the part of the audience. In doing so, the emotional accounts that pervaded descriptions of public events and instances of official communication provided a textual means of questioning aristocratic authority, establishing a script by which the Bourgeois and his audience 'read' power.

One such strategy was the use of second-person addresses that approximated the audience to the phenomena described. For example, remarking upon the numbers of homeless and starving children in the winter of 1421 that the Bourgeois linked to food shortages and high taxation caused by the continual presence of Armagnacs in the city's hinterland, the audience is warned that 'ne vous eussiez esté en quelque compaignie que vous ne veissiez les ungs lamenter ou plourer à grosses lermes, maudisant leur nativité, les autres fortune, les autres les signeurs, les autres les gouverneurs'.[171] Proximity engendered sympathy on the audience's part, but this sympathy also performed a political function. As Lydwine Scordia has demonstrated, in late medieval France the rhetoric of 'malédiction' – of the commons cursing their lords – represented a means of contesting the political authority of tyrants by eliciting divine intervention.[172] The victims' poverty accentuated their proximity to God and, coupled with their curse, the *Journal* accorded the city's poor a potent political agency. The Bourgeois effectively channelled this emotion through the use of direct speech, envisioning a direct appeal to God: 'En disant maintes foys, "Vray Dieu, *vindica sanguinem sanctorum!* Venge le sang des bonnes creatures qui meurent sans deserte par ces faulx traistres Arminalx!"'[173]

Malediction's effectiveness in the *Journal* was predicated upon both this envisioned, physical proximity and the interconnection of moral and emotional discourse. Scordia has highlighted the importance of the appeal's expression directly from the commons to God, without (explicitly) passing through the ecclesiastical structures that typically canalized this communication.[174] Nevertheless, the *Journal* reveals that clerics harnessed this vision of the poor's plight to buttress their political condemnation. Another example can be found in *Loquar in tribulacione* (*c.* 1439), when Jean Juvénal des Ursins reflected upon the impact of continued fighting in France and the dangers posed by an aristocratic reluctance to

---

171 Regardless of the company that you were in, you would have seen some lamenting or crying with great tears, cursing their birth, other cursing Fortune, others the lords, others the governors. *Journal*, pp. 162-63.

172 Lydwine Scordia, *'Le roi doit vivre du sien': La théorie de l'impôt en France (XIIIᵉ-XVᵉ siècles)* (Paris: Institut d'Études Augustiniennes, 2005), pp. 290-301.

173 Stating many times, 'True God, *vindica sanguinem sanctorum!* Avenge the blood of the good creatures who die unjustly because of these false Armagnac traitors!' *Journal*, p. 163.

174 Scordia, *'Le roi doit vivre du sien'*, p. 296.

resolve the ongoing conflict. Ursins warned Charles VII that God paid heed to the clamour of the suffering, 'les larmes des pauvres, les lamentations des veuves, les soupirs des orphelins', that jeopardized royal legitimacy and potentially compromised divine favour for the regime.[175]

A second narrative strategy directly counterbalanced these aristocratic and popular emotional experiences, demonstrating the extent to which political stereotypes married emotional agency with power.[176] Gerd Althoff has argued that a prince's ability to freely express emotion was indicative of authority, as a communicative practice engendering socio-political effects.[177] The description of princely emotion in chronicles, as well as responses to this agency, enabled writers such as the Bourgeois to frame the public dimension to their authority, derived from their status within a divinely ordained, hierarchical social order. Aristocratic anger, as an active and other-directed emotion that provoked action, was typically presented in juxtaposition with popular suffering that signalled the populace's powerlessness. Those rarer moments where popular anger was evoked, in contrast, tested the normative limits of aristocratic authority. The Bourgeois derived authorial agency from his situation between these two poles, manipulating popular experiences as a barometer that indicated the morality of aristocratic behaviour. The marked emotional distance from the commons also underscored the Bourgeois' own social standing: while the plight of 'povres gens et pouvres prebstres' was rhetorically significant, sympathy simultaneously marked social distinction as an other-oriented emotional marker.[178]

The contrast of ruler and ruled in the *Journal* also demonstrates the unequal distribution of emotional capital in fifteenth-century Parisian society. Related to other forms of Bourdieuian capital, emotional capital comprises the means of linking individual resources and processes to 'macro-structural' forces of social hierarchy, inequality and cohesion. As an interpersonal resource, the ability to manage emotional expression in public and convey it effectively, for instance through rhetoric, become skills that underpin a social advantage and are integral to the maintenance of power as a form of 'embodied' cultural capital.[179] While sociologists have reserved interpretations of emotional capital for the domestic sphere, the *Journal* reveals the fundamental importance of emotional expression in public as a means of exhibiting and testing authority. Consequently, the *Journal*'s emphasis upon emotional expression and the Bourgeois' development of an emotional personage as narrator enabled the author to arrogate social and political authority for himself and his audience.

---

175 The tears of the poor, the lamentations of the widows, the sighs of the orphans. Jean Juvénal des Ursins, 'Loquar in tribulacione' in *Écrits politiques de Jean Juvénal des Ursins*, ed. by Peter S. Lewis, 3 vols (Paris: Klincksieck, 1978-92), I (1978), pp. 416-17.

176 Laurent Smagghe, 'Discours princiers de l'émotion dans les Pays-Bas bourguignons à la fin du Moyen Âge' in *The Languages of Political Society: Western Europe, 14th-17th Centuries*, ed. by Andrea Gamberini, Jean-Philippe Genet and Andrea Zorzi (Rome: Viella, 2011), pp. 326-30; Tracy Adams, 'The Armagnac-Burgundian Feud and the Languages of Anger' in *Writing War in Britain and France, 1370-1854*, ed. by Stephanie Downes, Andrew Lynch and Katrina O'Loughlin (London: Routledge, 2018), pp. 66-7.

177 Gerd Althoff, 'Demonstration und Inszenierung. Spielregeln der Kommunikation in mittelalterlicher Öffentlichkeit', *Frühmittelalterliche Studien*, 27 (1993), pp. 27-50; Lutz and Abu-Lughod, *Language and the Politics of Emotion*, p. 11.

178 Poor people and poor priests. *Journal*, p. 145.

179 Marci Cottingham, 'Theorizing Emotional Capital', *Theory and Society*, 45 (2016), p. 452.

The dichotomy between individual aristocratic expression and popular response was essential to the Bourgeois' rationalization of power, bringing to light Rosenwein's emotional communities. Delineating the varied modes of emotional expression, norms and moral appraisals available to distinct communities in public space, emotional communities overlapped with professional and social contexts.[180] Returning to the entry of Charles VI and Henry V in December 1420, we find the Bourgeois reporting that:

> Ilz encontroient par toutes les rues processions de prebstres revestuz de chappes et de seurpeliz, portans saintuaires, chantans *Te deum laudamus, Benedictus qui venit*, et fut entre v et vj heures apres medi, et toute nuyt quant ilz revenoient en leurs eglises. Et ce faisoient si liement et de si joyeux cueur, et le commun *par cas pareil*.[181]

The Bourgeois accentuated the symbolic features that rendered the Parisian clergy distinct from the commons, despite their *shared* emotion, suggesting the conventional elements that framed collective interaction with royalty within a "multidimensional" procession fusing "narrative, sound and image".[182] The emotions shared by the commons and clergy undermines Rosenwein's argument that social boundaries promote different emotional experiences, instead revealing that socio-professional markers influenced means of expression and communication.[183] In 1420, sentimental fluidity resulted in a collective expression of joy that tied the civic community to the Treaty of Troyes. Groups were defined not by distinct emotion, but by its expression according to pre-established norms that defined socio-political status.

Conclusion

As Andy Wood has argued for early modern England, 'domination, subordination and resistance did more than maintain a fluid, contradictory, conflictual system of social relations; they also generated feelings: repression, anger, frustration and humiliation'.[184] Through his account of these feelings, the Bourgeois appropriated and developed a particular kind of moral authority, and experimented with especially potent forms of rhetoric, to evaluate and condemn aristocratic behaviours or legitimate the actions of the Parisian commons. For himself and his immediate community, the *Journal* emerges as an example of Reddy's 'emotional refuges', a 'safe release from prevailing social norms

---

180 Barbara Rosenwein, 'The Political Uses of an Emotional Community: Cluny and its Neighbours, 833-965' in *Politique des émotions au Moyen Âge*, ed. by Damien Boquet and Piroska Nagy (Florence: SISMEL, 2010), p. 205.

181 In every street they encountered processions of priests dressed in copes and surplices, carrying reliquaries, singing *Te deum laudamus, Benedictus qui venit*, and this between the fifth and sixth hour of the afternoon, and all night as they returned to their churches. And they did this so happily and with such joyful heart, and the commons in a similar manner. *Journal*, pp. 144-45.

182 Thomas A. Boogaart, 'Our Saviour's Blood: Procession and Community in Late Medieval Bruges' in *Moving Subjects: Processional Performance in the Middle Ages and the Renaissance*, ed. by Kathleen Ashely and Wim Hüsken (Amsterdam: Rodopi, 2001), 69. See also Lawrence Bryant, *Ritual, Ceremony and the Changing Monarchy in France, 1350-1789* (Farnham: Ashgate, 2010), pp. 33-37.

183 Plamper, 'The History of Emotions: An Interview', pp. 253-54; Rosenwein, *Emotional Communities*, pp. 192-96.

184 Andy Wood, 'Fear, Hatred and the Hidden Injuries of Class in Early Modern England', *Journal of Social History*, 39 (2006), p. 807.

which may shore up or threaten the existing regime', distinguishing the ways in which the Bourgeois and his audience could consider emotion within their restricted opinion community when compared to the culturally- and politically determined (and restricted) modes of emotional expression that framed the public transcript.[185] Revolts and riots were precisely the stages upon which conflicting emotional repertoires were confronted, and this is how the Bourgeois envisioned them. Where authorities implicitly expected their subjects to repress their negative emotions to ensure conformity and cohesion – a fact underscored when the Bourgeois portrayed the dialogue between the Parisian *prévôt* and the commons – emotional refuges presented avenues for experimentation with political repertoires resulting from this dissonance between different realms of behavioural expectation. Crucially, the *Journal* reveals that Parisian actors knew how to make careful and calculated use of emotion to buttress their claims to political participation and, in doing so, determining ideas of justice and good government. In these collective social and political movements, participants actively searched for reasons 'to recover and legitimate' emotions, and through his writing the Bourgeois directly contributed to this discursive process.[186] In short, the *Journal* indicates how those peripheral to power in fifteenth-century Paris appropriated emotional discourse to assert their own perspectives and interpret authority within the wider public sphere. The community that used and was defined by this textual refuge cut across pre-existing political and social boundaries, as evidenced by the fact that the Bourgeois, a cleric, wrote for a lay, artisanal audience. Emotional regimes, therefore, do not operate in a vacuum, with the *Journal* portraying shifting emotional styles that changed power relations through expression that means that the success of any single regime is never total and always contested.

The *Journal* highlights the predominance of emotions in medieval public life and political discourse. Interaction between rulers and ruled was inherently determined by notions of appropriate and inappropriate emotional response that defined the political and social agency of actors. An assessment of the ways in which the Bourgeois employed emotional rhetoric, even in the most extreme of cases, to rationalize political events betrays the fact that, rather than being unthinking and childlike, emotional discourse was integral to a coherent and effective discursive logic. This logic framed the Bourgeois' interpretation of political communication in the public sphere, with emotion functioning as an essential means of communicating princely and popular perspectives while mapping relative authority and political agency. Unlike the conclusions of modern sociologists, therefore, the *Journal* demonstrates particularly clearly the enduring emotional character of the public sphere and counters a grander narrative of 'rationalization' beginning with Norbert Elias' 'civilizing process' in the early modern period and accelerating with increased literacy rates and bourgeois social spaces in the eighteenth century. Consonant with the conclusions of cognitive psychologists, the *Journal* reveals an implicit conception of emotional behaviour that presented a means of rationalizing and moralizing human behaviour and explaining political developments. Although the Bourgeois certainly subscribed to a conception of

185 Reddy, *The Navigation of Feeling*, p. 129
186 Helena Flam, 'Anger in Repressive Regimes. A Footnote to *Domination and the Arts of Resistance* by James Scott', *European Journal of Social Theory*, 7 (2004), p. 173.

negative emotionality that contrasted with principles such as divine wisdom and justice, even the description of overwhelming emotion served an important function in explaining how and why the commons behaved during the 1418 Parisian massacres.

In turn, the Bourgeois' perception of official communication and its incorporation into the *Journal* enabled him to exert authority through the reconstruction of interactions between civic or royal authorities and Parisian audiences. The *Journal* portrayed Parisian reactions in relation to the messages disseminated through official media, thereby demonstrating the extent to which these could be questioned, accepted and rejected, reverting the processes whereby information acquired authority by accentuating the audience's role in recognizing their effectiveness, granting greater agency to Parisians contrasted with overarching bodies. This chapter has sought to highlight the means by which the *Journal* gave voice to public opinion and framed the dimensions of the public sphere, a forum that was invariably determined by spatial and rhetorical considerations that the Bourgeois integrated into his narrative. Communication was about power and legitimacy, and the *Journal*'s stress upon the elements that coalesced in the processes of official communication simultaneously expressed the legitimacy of contest and codified the strategies employed by Parisians excluded from typical institutions of authority to exert their agency over political developments. In this light, the *Journal* traced a public transcript that was constantly being produced through repeated interactions between official bodies and public opinion, framed by specific Parisian spaces, symbols and discourses.

CHAPTER 3

Rumour and Resistance

Rumour represented an integral part of medieval urban life and its prevalence within the *Journal* – first acknowledged by Colette Beaune – was a consequence of the period's turbulence and a wider distrust of official sources.[1] Rumour also evokes the sources to which the Bourgeois had most direct access in the form of the discussions taking place in his local and professional communities.[2] On the one hand, the incorporation of rumour into the *Journal* had a stylistic function, emphasizing the Bourgeois' proximity to events and conversations while enhancing the text's mimetic qualities, conveying the 'reality' of Parisian opinion. On the other, the record and transmission of rumour also assumed a significant political role. As we have already seen, medieval historiography typically portrayed popular rumour in relation to royal or aristocratic authority.[3] This same dichotomy characterized the writing of elite chroniclers, who could present popular rumour as troublesome and disruptive though, in doing so, they simultaneously acknowledged its significance within the public transcript as a medium of public expression and political commentary. More pragmatically, official discourse endeavoured to mitigate against the potency of public opinion, speech and rumour through counter rumours, propaganda and often coercive measures. This chapter proposes that through the *Journal*, rumour can be resituated as the expression of ingrained and often archetypal narratives that formed part of the emotional regimes discussed in Chapter 2 – eliciting response and engendering political participation. In turn, it becomes clear that the behaviours that were frequently dismissed by chroniclers as murmuring or grumbling were evocative of far more considered political and discursive practices entrenched in the public transcript.

As a basic definition, rumours represent unverified instances of information whose transmission depends upon their emotional appeal and relevance to the socio-political interests of those who participate in their dissemination. They consistently appear anonymous and ephemeral, lacking an authoritative source and remaining ambiguous, apparently spontaneous (or atemporal) and freely circulating in public space.[4] Rumours also occupy an ambivalent place in relation to truth. As Jean-Noël Kapferer has argued, 'Rumours do

---

1 Colette Beaune, 'La rumeur dans le *Journal du Bourgeois de Paris*' in *La circulation des nouvelles au Moyen Âge* (Paris: Publications de la Sorbonne, 1994), pp. 191-203.

2 Beaune, 'La rumeur', p. 192; Séverine Fargette, 'Rumeurs, propagande et opinion publique au temps de la guerre civile (1407-20)', *Le Moyen Âge*, 113 (2007), pp. 313-16, 326; Boris Bove, 'Deconstructing the Chronicles: Rumours and Extreme Violence during the Siege of Meaux (1421-22)', *French History*, 24 (2010), pp. 502-05; Loïc Cazaux, 'Les fonctions politiques de la foule à Paris pendant la guerre civile (1407-20)', *Hypothèses*, 14 (2011), pp. 68-70.

3 Bernard Guenée, *L'opinion publique à la fin du moyen âge d'après la chronique de Charles VI du religieux de Saint-Denis* (Paris: Perrin, 2002), p. 126.

4 Fargette, 'Rumeurs, propagande', p. 313; Françoise Reumaux, 'Traits invariants de la rumeur', *Communications*, 52 (1990), pp. 141-42.

not precede persuasion, they are rather its visible manifestation. The labels "information" and "rumour" are not attributed before believing or disbelieving; they are consequences of belief and disbelief'.[5] Rumour's objective veracity, therefore, is less consequential than its interpretation by those who engage with it and its correspondence to an audience's horizon of expectations. These individual interpretations of rumour are influenced by collectively shared social and political conventions. Since the wartime research of Robert Knapp or Gordon Allport and Leo Postman, theorists have recognized rumour's character as a form of wish-fulfilment, with information satisfying an emotional need, including a desire to explain events and allay societal anxieties: 'rumour rationalizes what it relieves'.[6] Rather than substituting for an absence of 'official' news, as scholars of medieval France have argued, rumours fulfil intrinsic emotional and social demands that underpin community cohesion.

The circulation of rumour and its dependence upon emotional investment reveal the ways in which it contributes to disposition systems that enable individuals to make sense of their shared environments. Allport and Postman pointed to simultaneous processes of 'levelling', 'sharpening' and 'association' that culminate in the coalescence of the details forming a rumour's core and producing a foundation for common knowledge and, therefore, public opinion.[7] As rumours circulate, extraneous details are stripped from the message (levelling), with those that remain accentuated (sharpening) according to socio-political contexts (association), reflecting 'the powerful attractive force exerted upon rumour by habits, interests and sentiments existing in the listener's mind'.[8] This model has subsequently been adapted by Lindsay Porter to analyse historical contexts, concentrating upon rumour during the French Revolution. Nuancing the role performed by expectation and context, Porter's model demonstrates rumour's importance for the reinforcement of social bonds that underpinned opinion communities, facilitating the development of core political narratives framed by a 'repertoire of common references [...] a body of "knowledge" that [rumours] simultaneously bring into existence'.[9] Negative stereotypes and rumours attributed to group outsiders (such as the Bourgeois' 'Armagnacs') therefore perform a role in reinforcing a sense of self and community, dialectically substantiating the marginalization of groups within Parisian society by identifying an 'Othered' subject.[10] As rumours rise to the status of common knowledge their collective resonance eventually serves as their own proof.

---

5 Jean-Noël Kapferer, *Rumors: Uses, Interpretations and Images*, trans. by Bruce Fink (New Brunswick, NJ: Transaction Publishers, 1990), p. 12.

6 Gordon Allport and Leo Postman, 'An Analysis of Rumor', *The Public Opinion Quarterly*, 10 (1946-47), p. 503. See also Robert H. Knapp, 'A Psychology of Rumor', *The Public Opinion Quarterly*, 8 (1944), p. 23; Elena Martinescu, Onne Janssen and Bernard A. Nijstad, 'Gossip and Emotion' in *The Oxford Handbook of Gossip and Reputation*, ed. by Francesca Giardini and Rafael Wittek (New York, NY: Oxford University Press, 2019), pp. 156-60.

7 Allport and Postman, 'An Analysis of Rumor', pp. 504-06. On the relationship between rumour, gossip and common knowledge see Chris Wickham, 'Gossip and Resistance among the Medieval Peasantry', *Past and Present*, 160 (1998), pp. 4-6, 18; Megan Cassidy-Welch, 'Testimonies from a Fourteenth-Century Prison: Rumour, Evidence and Truth in the Midi', *French History*, 16 (2002), pp. 20-1.

8 Lindsay Porter, *Popular Rumour in Revolutionary Paris, 1792-94* (Basingstoke: Routledge, 2017), p. 215.

9 Porter, *Popular Rumour*, p. 8.

10 Claude Gauvard, 'Rumeur et gens de guerre dans le royaume de France au milieu du XVᵉ siècle', *Hypothèses*, 4 (2001), p. 281.

As such, rumours reinforce a subjective worldview while structuring a collective memory and conventional discourse, those common ways of discussing and thinking about a topic that influence and frame political perspectives. Rumour's role in the consolidation of community ideals highlights its overlap with understandings of the public sphere, as group boundaries are reinforced through an active participation in information's oral transmission. Rumours in circulation are exemplary as elements of the idioms and assumptions that bind opinion communities, embodying collectively shared beliefs but also performing an overt political function. For Eni Orlandi, rumour's interdiscursivity decentralizes the subject and enables the individual to participate in political processes as an interface between historical events and the machinations of an underlying collective memory that reinforces group identity.[11] This results from the absence of a clear 'author function' for rumour.[12] Without a fixed source, rumours are subject to appropriation, manipulation and (re)interpretation by those involved in their circulation, assuming fixity only when they emerge in text or official discourse and are attributed an identifiable basis. Rumour's ability to assume the status of widely shared beliefs is especially significant when these common assumptions conflict with official communication, when rumours emerge as alternative narratives that reinforce community identity *in opposition to* institutions that are perceived as disingenuous, as has already been seen above in Chapter 2. As Porter has concluded, occasionally rumour 'so resonates with the current climate that it reflects a collective desire to believe' contrary to official sources.[13]

Rumour, therefore, serves a relatively unacknowledged role in socio-political relationships, enabling individuals to grasp the connections between personal feeling and more widely held reactions, consolidating the community's emotional regimes in the process. It is precisely this emotional investment that explains why rumour's official contradiction frequently fails to counter its continued diffusion. Evocative of enduring socio-political anxieties, their expression functions as a form of social catharsis through which communities develop narratives in response to perceived insecurities, reinforcing a sense of belonging. In medieval communities, political rumour occupied a place close to gossip and *publica fama* – the intersection of common knowledge and personal reputation – that was determined by informal conversations between community members: 'the group is actually constituted by who has the right to gossip about outsiders, and moral values are constantly reinforced by gossip'.[14] For Chris Wickham, rumour and gossip therefore function as a means of defining 'the hugely complex network of social relationships which construct our social world, hierarchically and hegemonically', providing a 'direct guide to the lines of power'.[15]

---

11 Eni Orlandi, 'Rumeurs et silences: Les trajets des sens, le parcours du dire', *Hypothèses*, 4 (2001), pp. 258-60.

12 This follows the idea of the 'fonction auteur' described in Michel Foucault, 'Qu'est-ce qu'un auteur?' in *Dits et écrits*, vol. 1 (Paris: Gallimard, 1994), pp. 803-06.

13 Porter, *Popular Rumour*, p. 143.

14 Chris Wickham, 'Gossip and Resistance', p. 11. On *fama* see Claude Gauvard, 'La fama, une parole fondatrice', *Médiévales*, 12 (1993), pp. 5-13; Thelma Fenster and Daniel Lord Smail, 'Introduction' in *Fama: The Politics of Talk and Reputation in Medieval Europe*, ed. by Thelma Fenster and Daniel Lord Smail, (London: Cornell University Press, 2003), pp. 1-11.

15 Wickham, 'Gossip and Resistance', p. 18. *Fama* and rumour therefore play a role similar to Bourdieu's social capital, wherein groups or individuals accrue actual or virtual resources through social relationships as a mark of an individual's integration. Pierre Bourdieu and Loïc J. D. Wacquant, *An Invitation to Reflexive Sociology* (Cambridge: Polity Press,

In this light, a close examination of the rumours reported in the *Journal* enables the reader to ascertain the ideological dynamics at stake in fifteenth-century Parisian political communication, the means by which opinion communities determined their boundaries, and the ways in which Parisians employed rumour to participate in urban political life.

Methodologically, Porter has distinguished three important categories of rumour. First, those that are structured by archetypal beliefs found in common knowledge and collective memories, expressing 'a common bond [and] shared language' while 'representing time-less, universal fears'.[16] The prevalence of such archetypes in late medieval discourse are evident, in the rumours of sacrilegious crimes committed by Jews, perceived Muslim traits or the stereotypical portrayal of men-at-arms and brigands. Second, the contemporaneous rumours that impart the 'anxieties of the day' while drawing upon these archetypes and, finally, rumours through which the community brings 'the narrative of the "other" within its own circle, stigmatizing specific classes or indeed individuals'.[17] Both of these categories are exemplified by the Bourgeois' account of rumours circulating in Paris during the 1418 massacres that exaggerated Armagnac hostility and otherness. Moreover, they demonstrate that rumours, despite their apparent ephemerality and spontaneity as stressed by present-day historians of late medieval France, are in fact structured by extant narratives and a social imaginary that concurrently reinforce group identity and collective memory.

This chapter follows this typology to reveal how the Bourgeois' record of rumour, its confirmation and its rejection, enabled him to arrogate authority and determine perspectives within his opinion community. Viewing the *Journal*'s relation of rumour as strategic problematizes current interpretations that argue, first, that the Bourgeois unquestioningly reported rumours that echoed his own political perspectives and, second, that rumour was (and is) antonymic of official communication, accentuated in periods when news was scarce.[18] By writing rumours, the Bourgeois codified their expression, mnemonically fixing them within the community's history of political engagement. This had implications for the perception of their historical veracity. Even when proven false, the *Journal* evidenced an interest in rumour as a social fact – a testimony to popular responses that reflected the political agendas of his local community. After assessing the techniques used by the Bourgeois to convey rumour and codify its impact, this chapter will consider rumour's socio-political function in two distinct ways. Firstly, an analysis of the development of a stereotypical trope through the repeated use of rumour in the *Journal* that underpinned the elaboration of perceived 'Armagnac' characteristics, permits the reader to trace the way rumour consolidated political identifications through juxtaposition with imagined Others,

---

1992), p. 119. See also Claude Gauvard, 'Introduction' in *La rumeur au Moyen Âge: du mépris à la manipulation, Vᵉ-XVᵉ siècle*, ed. by Maité Billoré and Myriam Soria (Rennes: Presses Universitaires de Rennes, 2011), p. 27.

16 Porter, *Popular Rumour*, p. 138. More recently, Jill Maciak Walshaw has nuanced the approach to early modern rumour in works such as Robert Darnton's *The Great Cat Massacre*, arguing that archetypes were used strategically by people distant from elite politics. *A Show of Hands for the Republic: Opinion, Information and Repression in Eighteenth-Century Rural France* (Woodbridge: University of Rochester Press, 2014), pp. 23-4

17 Porter, *Popular Rumour*, pp. 112, 139-40.

18 These views are widely held among scholars who have studied the *Journal*. Janet Shirley (ed. and trans.), *A Parisian Journal, 1405-49* (Oxford: Clarendon Press, 1968), 16; Colette Beaune, 'La rumeur', pp. 191-95; Claude Gauvard, 'Aux origines de la chronique judiciaire: l'exemple du royaume de France aux derniers siècles du Moyen Âge', *Histoire de la justice*, 20 (2010), pp. 16-17; Claude Gauvard, 'La "fama"', pp. 5-8.

building upon and manipulating existing archetypal narratives and the use of emotional rhetoric. Through the repetition of anti-Armagnac rumours the Bourgeois effectively articulated a system of political commentary that rationalized continued Parisian opposition to the Orléanist faction.

Secondly, this chapter will explore the conjunction between the circulation of rumour and popular participation in civic and royal politics, focusing upon the uprisings of 1413 and 1418. Armagnac authorities employed a series of measures recorded by the Bourgeois that were intended to limit the potential for political discussion among Parisians, ranging from the surveillance of public gatherings and spaces to the disruption of corporations and the employment of spies in neighbourhoods. An examination of the Bourgeois' rationalization of these uprisings similarly evidences the political importance of popular rumour, employed within the *Journal* to explain violent behaviours and a popular assumption of power. Where, in 1413, rumours of the aristocratic exploitation of royal government were designed to legitimate the Parisian assumption of power and execution of civic officials, by 1418 the archetypal rumours concerning dangerous Others had been brought within the community, provoking a series of massacres following a heightened paranoia regarding the presence of Armagnacs within the city after the Burgundian coup in May that year. At that moment, the Bourgeois' decision to privilege rumour at moments of political tension reveals its fundamental role in validating Parisian political agency while concurrently delineating the boundaries of a Parisian community defined through opposition to the Armagnac faction.

Writing rumour

The circulation of rumour has typically been considered a counterpoint to official channels of communication. It has long been argued that rumours fill a void engendered by a lack of official and reliable information and that, in medieval contexts, their prevalence reveals the existence of an 'infrapolitics', that 'broad area of discussion, complaint and dissent that fell somewhere between wholehearted consent and open rebellion'.[19] In this scholarship, rumour emerges as subversive discourse due to its omnipresence and ambiguity, its elasticity and potential to contradict 'hegemonic ideology'.[20] As Jan Dumolyn and Jelle Haemers have acknowledged, it is difficult for historians to trace the circulation and content of rumour or subversive speech directly. Subsisting 'in the form of fragments and indirect quotations in hostile chroniclers, fictional texts, as well as political, legal and repressive documents', they can only be accessed in an archaeological manner.[21] Likewise, Vincent Challet has noted that it is rare for remission letters issued after revolts to detail popular rumours and speech. Instead, 'les expressions du type *vociferando et clamando* abondent

19 Simon Walker, 'Rumour, Sedition and Popular Protest in the Reign of Henry IV', *Past and Present*, 166 (2000), p. 33
20 Mary C. Flannery, *John Lydgate and the Poetics of Fame* (York: Boydell and Brewer, 2012), pp. 38-9; Peter McNiven, 'Rebellion, Sedition and the Legend of Richard II's Survival in the Reigns of Henry IV and Henry V', *Bulletin of the John Rylands University Library of Manchester*, 76 (1994), pp. 114-16.
21 Jan Dumolyn and Jelle Haemers, '"A Bad Chicken was Brooding": Subversive Speech in Late Medieval Flanders', *Past & Present*, 214 (2012), p. 51.

dans les sources judiciaires sans qu'aucune précision ne nous soit apportée'.[22] Nevertheless, even ambiguous murmurs assumed central political functions, and Pierre Prétou has suggested that by the fifteenth century, popular shouting was integral to manifestations of civic, regional and national identity.[23]

Sociologists have been hesitant to identify the phenomenon as occurring in premodern societies. For Pascal Froissart, 'la rumeur, au sens actuel du terme, n'a pas une place claire dans le champ sémantique du Moyen Âge français', calling upon the Bourgeois *Journal* to emphasize how 'la rumeur n'est pas la 'catégorie abstraite' qu'elle est devenue'.[24] Indeed, there was no one word for 'rumour' in Middle French. As recent studies of the late Middle Ages have shown, *rumor* had close epistemological connections to more ambiguous ideas of noise, murmur and clamour.[25] These associations are exemplified by Alain Chartier's *Quadrilogue invectif* (1424), where the character of 'Le Peuple' (People) gave voice to popular concerns at the aristocracy's failure to defend France:

> Si estoit la voix du peuple comme les mouetes qui par leur cry denoncent les floz de la mer, car noz parolles, que tu appelles murmure, signifioient des lors le meschief qui pour ces causes estoit a advenir. Or, est ainsi que d'oultraige et de desordonnance vient murmure, de murmure rumeur, et de rumeur division, et de division desolation et esclandre.[26]

In Alain Chartier's view, the murmuring of People emerges here as integral to effective political commentary. Complaint was not simply nor straightforwardly a form of outright sedition, but also protest designed to counter political disorder and evil government. The logic echoed that articulated by Nicole Oresme in his translation of Aristotle's *Politics*, and underscored rumour's accepted place in political culture. As Oresme reckoned, the exclusion of elements of the body politic and the pursuit of excess risked sedition and, as Chartier warned, by ignoring popular grievances France's ruler risked precisely this seditious *rumeur*.[27] No common vocabulary existed for this complaint, with authors variably employing *bruit*, *noise*, *clameur* and *murmure*, with these last three invoking pejorative notions of subversive speech. *Nouvelles* was used in substantially different ways. For

---

22 Phrases such as 'vociferando et clamando' abound in the judicial sources without any precision. Vincent Challet, '"Morayn, los traidors, morayn": Cris de haine et sentiment d'abandon dans les villes languedociennes à la fin du XIVᵉ siècle' in *Emotions in the Heart of the City (14th-16th century)*, ed. by Anne-Laure Van Bruaene and Élodie Lecuppre-Desjardin (Turnhout: Brepols, 2005), p. 87.

23 Pierre Prétou, 'Clameur contre fureur: Cris et tyrannie à la fin du Moyen Âge' in *Violences souveraines au Moyen Âge*, ed. by François Foronda, Christine Barralis and Bénédicte Sère (Paris: Presses Universitaires de France, 2010), pp. 271-80.

24 Rumour, in the modern sense, does not have a clear place in the semantic fields of the French Middle Ages; rumour was not the abstract category that it has since become. Pascal Froissart, 'Historicité de la rumeur', *Hypothèses*, 4 (2001), p. 318.

25 Christopher Fletcher, 'Rumour, Clamour, Murmur and Rebellion: Public Opinion and its Uses before and after the Peasants' Revolt (1381)' in *La Communidad medieval como esfera publica*, ed. by Hipólito Rafael Oliva Herrer, Vincent Challet, Jan Dumolyn and Mariá Antonia Carmona Ruiz (Sevilla: Universidad de Sevilla, 2014), p. 197.

26 The voice of the people was like that of the gulls who by their cries condemn the sea's waves, because our words, which you call murmurs, signalled the evils that would result from these problems. So it is that from excess and disorder follows murmur, from murmur rumour, from rumour division, and from division, desolation and misfortune. Alain Chartier, *Le Quadrilogue invectif*, ed. by E. Droz (Paris: Champion, 1923), p. 35.

27 Nicole Oresme, *Maistre Nicole Oresme: Le Livre de Politiques d'Aristote*, ed. by Albert Douglas Menut (Philadelphia, PA: American Philosophical Society, 1970), pp. 203-06.

Monstrelet and the *Chronique des Cordeliers*, news circulated in aristocratic and courtly spheres and was pre-emptively verified, representing an important motivation for political action. In contrast, the overwhelming majority (69%) of the Bourgeois' references to *nouvelles* signalled their absence, with references to a lack of news promoting a distrust of an unreliable official communication and justifying the author's reliance upon rumour. More systematically, Jean Maupoint's *Journal* reveals a two-step reception of news: first its arrival and reporting, followed by a comment on whether it had been verified: 'lesquelles nouvelles furent trouvées vraies'.[28] Maupoint's perception of news in the middle of the fifteenth century therefore complicates the distinctions proposed by Claude Gauvard, who has argued that during this period 'les mécanismes de la rumeur se séparent rapidement de ceux de la nouvelle'.[29] Rather, news – like rumour – could circulate long before its verification.

Contrasted with *nouvelles*, Gauvard concluded that 'la rumeur/bruit est du domaine du peuple'.[30] And yet, Parisian authors used *bruit* and *nouvelles* interchangeably to denote the circulation of information, a terminological ambiguity accentuated by Monstrelet's own use of *bruit* to refer to renown. More common, *murmure* was far from the preserve of Paris' social substrata. As just one example, in a letter following the exacerbation of princely tensions in 1405, Jean sans Peur drew attention to the problems caused by taxation, 'considéré la murmuracion du clergié, des nobles et du peuple'.[31] Rather than highlighting wholly subversive means of discourse, therefore, murmuring and rumour were crucial forms of political participation that allowed Parisians of all backgrounds to voice critique of government. They were integral to a more coherent system of political communication, and the Bourgeois' *Journal* suggests that murmuring may even have been a desired response to propaganda, as when Philippe III le Bon, duke of Burgundy and John, duke of Bedford presented a manifesto before Parisians in July 1429, met with a 'grant murmure […] et telz avoit grant aliance aux Arminalx qu'ilz les prindrent en tres grant haine'.[32] Through the provocation of murmur, the proclamation had the desired effect of accentuating popular emotional responses and redirecting them towards an Armagnac other.

Beyond this terminology, it is perhaps possible to detect approaches to rumour through its record. The Bourgeois signalled the subjectivity of rumour through indirect speech that captured its oral circulation, typically employing expressions such as 'on disoit' and 'on affermoit'. This framework reinforced an impression of ephemerality and anonymity, and earlier scholars may have seen in this the muffled and indirect subversive speech integral to infrapolitical discourse.[33] However, the Bourgeois' very ability to integrate these rumours into his writing – as a priest and possibly a canon – reveals how accessible these narratives were to multiple social classes in Parisian society, underscoring John Watts' argument that

---

28 Which news was found to be true. Jean Maupoint. 'Journal parisien de Jean Maupoint, prieur de Sainte-Catherine-du-Val-des-Écoliers (1437-69)', ed. by Gustave Fagniez, *MSHP*, 4 (1877), pp. 80, 82-3.
29 The mechanisms of rumour are quickly separated from those of news. Gauvard, 'Rumeur et stéréotypes', p. 167.
30 Rumour/noise is of the popular domain. Gauvard, 'Rumeur et stéréotypes', p. 162.
31 Transcribed in Monstrelet, I, p. 118.
32 A great murmur […] and those who had supported the Armagnacs then viewed them with great hatred. *Journal*, p. 241.
33 See, for instance, Walker, 'Rumour, Sedition'; James C. Scott, 'Infrapolitics and Mobilizations: A Response by James C. Scott', *Revue française d'études américaines*, 131 (2012), p. 114.

it is difficult to associate discourses with any single medieval group.[34] Rather, rumour fed into existing public transcripts that political elites monitored and responded to, ultimately facilitating dialogue between ruler and ruled. Indeed, Jan Dumolyn and Jelle Haemers have concluded that while this popular speech 'formed an essential part of a rebellious repertoire of symbolic violence', speech acts themselves 'remained within a dominant ideological framework' wherein the expressions 'could be understood by all social states in the town'.[35] Rumours were far from the preserve of the politically excluded. Offering a means of broad participation, fifteenth-century rulers strategically stimulated rumours to discredit their rivals, measure popular support and satisfy local agendas.[36]

Rumour's potency as a field for evoking communitarian criticism is framed by the rhetorical strategies that mitigated against the identification of a specific origin, eliciting a vision of rumour's ubiquity and status as common knowledge. Where sources were identified by the Bourgeois, these typically took the form of ambiguous references to the 'peuple'. When John, duke of Bedford returned from Saint-Denis with the royal sword borne before him, as regent following Charles VI's funeral in November 1422, 'le peuple murmuroit fort', indicating their questioning of Bedford's character and Lancastrian legitimacy.[37] When Charles VI had left Paris due to fears of a Burgundian assault in October 1408, 'le peuple fut moult troublé; et disoient bien que, ce le duc de Bourgogne eusté icy, qu'ilz ne l'eussent pas fait'.[38] These references imply the class-character of rumour, a feature highlighted by Claude Gauvard and Séverine Fargette who have insisted upon its unofficial nature when juxtaposed with the official cry, as 'modes d'expression populaire [...] qui nous révèlent des pans de l'opinion publique'.[39] However, while the Bourgeois' selection and record of rumour was certainly conditioned by his membership of a homogenous socio-political group in Parisian society, this privileging of rumour simultaneously underscored its ubiquitous character, its place in collective commentary and status as a regular feature of civic politics. Such features are encapsulated by the 'on dit' that furthered impressions of common knowledge, assumed an 'omniscient authority' and otherwise legitimated unverified information.[40] Indeed, the 'on dit' comprises a process of attribution whereby rumours are

---

34 John Watts, 'Popular Voices in England's Wars of the Roses, c. 1445-85' in *Voices of the People in Late Medieval Europe*, ed. by Jan Dumolyn, Jelle Haemers, Hipólito Rafael Oliva Herrer and Vincent Challet (Turnhout: Brepols, 2014), pp. 115-16.

35 Dumolyn and Haemers, '"A Bad Chicken"', pp. 80-1. See also Andy Wood, 'Collective Violence, Social Drama and Rituals of Rebellion in Late Medieval and Early Modern England' in *Cultures of Violence: Interpersonal Violence in Historical Perspective*, ed. by Stuart Carroll (London: Palgrave Macmillan, 2007), p. 107.

36 Gilles Lecuppre and Élodie Lecuppre-Desjardin, 'La rumeur: un instrument de la compétition politique au service des princes de la fin du Moyen Âge' in *La Rumeur au Moyen Âge du mépris à la manipulation, Vᵉ-XVᵉ siècle*, ed. by Maité Billoré and Myriam Soria (Rennes: Presses Universitaires de Rennes, 2011), pp. 149-75; Xavier Nadrigny, 'Rumeur et opinion publique à Toulouse à la fin du Moyen Âge', *Annales du Midi*, 121 (2009), p. 26.

37 The people murmured loudly. *Journal*, p. 180.

38 The people were greatly troubled, and they claimed that if the duke of Burgundy had been there, they [the Orléanist lords] would not have done it. *Journal*, p. 4. On Parisian reactions to the assertion of Lancastrian authority in 1422, see below, Chapter 5.

39 Modes of popular expression [...] that reveal parts of public opinion to us. Séverine Fargette, 'Rumeurs, propagande', p. 311. See also Claude Gauvard, 'Introduction', pp. 29-31; 'Rumeur et stéréotypes', pp. 161-64.

40 Lindsay Porter has similarly examined the use of the phrase 'On dit' in records of rumour during the first years of the French Revolution. *Popular Rumour*, p. 141.

expressed in terms that underscore their ubiquity and status as common knowledge.[41] By presenting rumours through 'on disoit', the Bourgeois envisioned them in a fixed form, not least through the past tense, as captured instances of more public talk.

Claude Gauvard recently identified the manner in which rumour's circulation engendered 'la construction d'un espace public où se sont confrontés les points de vue' in the context of the Armagnac-Burgundian conflict.[42] This notion of confrontation supports an appreciation of the ways in which the circulation of news was strongly influenced by, and in turn influenced, the content of rumour in a dialogical relationship. As modern studies of propaganda have shown, 'the public may receive information from the media and carry it back to opinion leaders for explanation or confirmation', with the result that publications represent just one step in a broader circulatory system and often have to adapt their content to satisfy public demand and respond to popular concerns.[43] Consequently, instead of perceiving the Bourgeois' record of rumour as simply 'le reflet exact de tel ou tel texte de propagande', the *Journal* is a telling demonstration of the ways in which narratives produced by governors were designed to respond to and anticipate the concerns voiced by the populace.[44]

The 'on dit', a singular form, created a liminal space between the collective and the individual, at once the speech of all and none. 'On disoit', 'ilz disoient' or even 'le peuple disoit' distanced the Bourgeois from any culpability for the rumours he reported as an eyewitness engaged in an historical phenomenon. This ambiguity meant that rumour could be effectively deployed within the narrative to evidence popular feeling as a form of political commentary and critique while instilling a sense of collective political consciousness. Of course, not all rumours were integrated into the *Journal* with the implicit awareness of their subjective character that indirect speech suggested. Many rumours rooted in propaganda or with which the Bourgeois closely identified were portrayed as historical facts. For example, although the repeated descriptions of atrocities committed by soldiers were influenced by propaganda employed by factions to denigrate their adversaries, the Bourgeois often repeated accusations without questioning their rumoured character. Accordingly, the *Journal* blurs the lines between official and unofficial information, fact and fiction, or propaganda and news. Where rumours represented a medium that could sustain and diffuse widely accepted aspects of propaganda, officials also drew elements from extant rumours to render their communication acceptable to their publics. In this sense, rumour and propaganda held a mutually validating status which rendered both credible. They did not, therefore, constitute discrete categories, nor were they expressed in consistent forms. Rather, their subjectivity was deliberately manipulated for political effect.

While often denoting rumour's spoken subjectivity, the Bourgeois also attested to the certainty of these speech acts. Rather than confirming the content of the rumour itself, these affirmations reinforced the veracity of its *having been said*, and the author's place

---

41 Michel-Louis Rouquette, 'Le syndrome de rumeur', *Communications*, 52 (1990), 120.

42 The construction of a public sphere where distinct perspectives were confronted. Gauvard, 'Introduction' in *La rumeur*, p. 29.

43 Garth Jowett and Victoria O'Donnell, *Propaganda and Persuasion*, Seventh Edition (Thousand Oaks, CA: SAGE, 2018), p. 326.

44 The exact reflection of this or that propaganda text. Beaune, 'La rumeur dans le *Journal*', p. 202.

as a witness relating information heard to his audience. For instance, regarding a rumour concerning Denis du Moulin, bishop of Paris, in 1441, the Bourgeois wrote how '*pour vray*, on disoit qu'il avoit plus de cinquante proces en Parlement, car de lui n'avoit-on rien sans proces'.[45] Ephemeral, speech acts themselves were substantiated by the Bourgeois' narrative voice, emphasizing his own status as witness. At stake was not the rumour's content, itself inherently subjective, but a stress upon the veracity that this was what Parisians were saying and thinking, and how they could critique the French kingdom's elite. In turn, this function accorded the Bourgeois authority as an arbiter of rumour's veracity. A stress upon the act of witnessing underscored the Bourgeois' confirmation of the least believable (or most mystical) elements of his narrative, but he also deployed first-person interventions to confirm or deny those rumours circulating in Paris more generally. There is a clear connection between these first-person statements and assertions of veracity, and we might conclude that expressions of plausibility implied the Bourgeois' own experiences. Declarations including 'pour vray', 'pour certain', 'vray est que' and 'vraiment' appear in 121 instances (over 10% of passages). Most intriguingly, the recourse to this veridical vocabulary occurred precisely when doubt was most prevalent: when concerns about the character of a 'true' Christian or French person, or the veracity of information, were most acute.

Following Brian Stock, strategies of truth and witnessing highlight the 'routinization' of the Bourgeois' narrative authority within the text.[46] The Bourgeois' narrative voice performed this function through first-person interventions, evoking the author's eyewitness status and establishing authority through a spatial and temporal proximity to the information related. In the *Journal*, first-person interventions evoked sermon-like discourse designed to convey moral commentary, with Elizabeth Lapina arguing that theological understanding of 'witness' were crucial to medieval historiography, particularly regarding the testimony of those disciples who saw Christ's resurrection.[47] This tension between seeing, believing and ultimately understanding God's will was similarly at work in the Bourgeois' interpretation of events as he reported the incidents that he had seen.

This relationship is underscored by the Bourgeois' reinforcement of his personal experiences through a vocabulary of truth as a form of historical verification that determined the veracity of rumour. This process is demonstrated by his account of Romani people arriving at Saint-Denis in August 1427. When Parisians flocked to see the Romani, rumours began to circulate regarding their activities as soothsayers or thieves in communion with the devil:

---

45 Truly, people said that he had fifty cases in Parlement, because no one could have anything from him without a case. *Journal*, p. 357. Emphasis my own.

46 Brian Stock, 'The Self and Literary Experience in Late Antiquity and the Middle Ages', *New Literary History*, 25 (1994), pp. 848-49. See also Larry Scanlon, *Narrative, Authority and Power: The Medieval Exemplum and the Chaucerian Tradition* (Cambridge: Cambridge University Press, 1994), pp. 39-53.

47 Elizabeth Lapina, '"Nec signis nec testibus creditur...": The Problem of Eyewitnesses in the Chronicles of the First Crusade', *Viator*, 38 (2007), p. 119; Jean-Marie Moeglin, 'La vérité de l'histoire et le moi du chroniqueur' in *La vérité: Vérité et crédibilité: construire la vérité dans le système de communication de l'Occident (XIIIᵉ-XVIIᵉ siècle)*, ed. by Jean-Philippe Genet (Paris: Éditions de la Sorbonne, 2015), pp. 523-30.

Et vrayement, je y fu iii ou iiij foys pour parler a eulx, mais oncques ne m'aperceu d'un denier de perte, ne les vy regarder en main, mais ainsi le disoit le peuple partout, tant que la nouvelle en vint a l'evesque de Paris.[48]

The Bourgeois situated himself in dialogue with popular rumour, emphasizing his role as an eyewitness in determining the truth of the Romani's behaviour by stressing his personal interaction with them. The narrative voice mediated Parisian experiences for a future audience. By juxtaposing popular reports with his own impression of the Romani, the Bourgeois brought to light the potency of rumour and even its monitoring by institutions, here represented by Paris' bishop. The passage highlights the Bourgeois' determination of rumour as a historical source, while the description of his role as a witness illustrates the responsibility that he accorded to himself, as author, in the verification of these rumours.

The substantiation of rumour and sensational events is further highlighted by the Bourgeois' relation of the birth of conjoined twins at Aubervilliers in June 1429. Perhaps anticipating scepticism on his audience's part, the Bourgeois included an illustration of the children alongside the account.[49] Stressing his own interaction with the children, the Bourgeois conveyed through the conjunction of image and text a visual aspect that rendered the audience eyewitnesses as well. 'Pour vray, je les vy et les tins entre mes mains […] et avoient, comme vous voyez, deux testes, quatre bras, deux coulz, iiij jambes, quatre piez'.[50] The language used by the Bourgeois countered this expected incredulity by asserting a proximity between textual and visual experiences that rendered the *Journal*'s audience witnesses *through* the author's account and his illustration. The text, in this sense, codified the Bourgeois' physical proximity to the event to substantiate his account.

Silence could also signal the political sensitivity of rumour. When articulated in the first person, this silence was presented as a decision that exhibited the Bourgeois' authorial control over the presentation of information. For instance, when envoys were sent to Paris by the dukes of Berry and Burgundy to conclude a treaty prepared at Pontoise in August 1413, designed to bring the Cabochien revolt to an end, the Bourgeois stressed that:

Quant est des demandes et des responces, je me tays, car trop longue chose seroit, mais bien scay que ilz demandoient touzjours a leur povoir la destrucion de la bonne ville de Paris et des habitans.[51]

Through this rhetorical silence, the Bourgeois wielded narrative authority to convey what he believed to be the most important element in the negotiations for his audience, namely the Armagnacs' lasting intent to destroy the capital. This is similarly demonstrated by

---

48 And truly, I went there three or four times to speak to them but never did I perceive that a single penny [of mine] was lost, nor did I see them looking in hands, but so said the people everywhere, such that the news reached the bishop of Paris. *Journal*, p. 220.

49 The illustration was not reproduced by the copyist of the Vatican manuscript, though a space was left on the relevant folio for its inclusion. Rome, Vatican MS Reg. Lat. 1923, fol. 117r. The scribe of the Méjanes manuscript did, on the other hand, attempt a crude sketch, apparently based on the description provided by the text. Aix-en-Provence, Bibliothèque Méjanes, MS 432 (0316), p. 220.

50 Truly, I saw them and held them in my hands […] and as you can see, they had two heads, four arms, two necks, four legs, four feet, and they had only one stomach as well as one navel; two heads, two backs. *Journal*, p. 238.

51 I will not speak of their demands and the responses they received because it would be too long, but I know very well that they continued to request the power to destroy the good city of Paris and its inhabitants. *Journal*, p. 35.

his identification of events that could *not* be discussed as a form of political criticism. In the autumn of 1436, the Bourgeois argued that French captains 'ne fist quelque bien dont on doye aucunement parler, senon rober et pillier par nuyt et par jour'.[52] The lack of detail was deliberate. If the diffusion of news supported political authority, then the rejection of official narratives undermined the governors' power to influence Parisian audiences. Consequently, the Bourgeois emphasized the significance of the rumours he selected by stressing his complete access to information, with silence probably disguising real limitations. Such criticism encouraged further, extratextual political criticism on the part of the audience without directly compromising the narrator, yet with the Bourgeois retaining control over the direction of such censure. In doing so, the Bourgeois influenced political perspectives beyond the text through a paradoxical emphasis upon the unsayable.

The Bourgeois actively compensated for the uncertainty surrounding news and rumour, drawing authority from his role as an arbiter of information's veracity. Popular and official discourses were portrayed as juxtaposed spheres that intersected through the *Journal*'s narrative. Through such juxtaposition, realms of socio-political authority were articulated which corresponded to the Bourgeois' own political perspectives, as he privileged those narratives he believed, or at least valued. The contending voices in the public sphere concurrently mapped official perspectives and underlying societal observations on noble behaviour, popular suffering and political agency, often expressed through murmuring in response to official failures and excesses. It was through this dichotomy that the Bourgeois could privilege and validate popular as an alternative to official discourse.

Writing rumour also changed it. Most scholars have concentrated upon premodern rumour's oral nature, as the most natural medium for its circulation within urban centres characterized by high levels of illiteracy and close proximity in workplace and domestic settings. However, the Bourgeois' *Journal* reveals that rumour was not confined to 'le cadre du bouche à oreille, propulsé par des canaux non-officiels et populaires'.[53] The *Journal* itself could serve as a medium for rumour's transmission, anticipating the sixteenth-century Dutch chroniclers shown by Henk van Nierop to have noted rumours on scraps of paper before incorporating them into their narratives, such that their reading is 'like being plunged into an oral world'.[54] Where Nierop argued that rumours, due to their oral character, 'ceased to exist' when recorded in historical narratives, their repetition in the *Journal* may have facilitated their diffusion, conveying information to further audiences. Mary-Rose McLaren has argued that the compilers of the London Chronicles were similarly engaged in processes of transforming 'what is essentially visual and oral into a literary network' in ways distinct from the processes associated with royally-appointed historiographers or

---

52 The French captains did no good of which we should speak at all, but robbed and pillaged night and day; He did nothing there that should be spoken of except wasting money and oppressing the poor people. *Journal*, p. 327.

53 The oral framework, propelled by non-official and popular channels. Gauvard, 'Rumeur et stéréotypes', p. 163.

54 Henk Van Nierop, '"And ye shall hear of wars and rumours of wars". Rumour and the Revolt of the Netherlands' in *Public Opinion and Changing Identities in the Early Modern Netherlands*, ed. by Judith Pollman and Andrew Spicer (Leiden: Brill, 2006), pp. 69-73. Janet Shirley suggested a similar purpose for the *Journal d'un bourgeois de Paris*. Shirley (ed. and trans.), *A Parisian Journal*, p. 25.

monks.[55] Following the typology suggested by Kathleen Daly, through this employment of rumour Parisian journals emerge as peripheral narratives, subliminal to hegemonic 'official' histories such as the *Grandes Chroniques* by privileging urban experiences through the validation of rumour as an historical source.[56] The focus of authors like the Bourgeois and Jean Maupoint upon rumours, even when these were false, evidences a perception of their status as 'social facts' worthy of remembering and constitutive of an urban experience through their capacity to sustain collective action.[57] In short, the inclusion of rumour suggests careful strategies linked to socio-political concerns, with their positive or negative valence asserted to legitimate or discredit political perspectives.

By relating rumour *as rumour*, the Bourgeois developed the 'plausible likeness, rather than objective truth' recognized by Janet Coleman as being necessary for a mimetic account.[58] Specifically, rumour underscores the development of an *effet de réel* encapsulating the 'convincing, plausible representation of objects, characters, actions and emotions'.[59] For Roland Barthes, the effect produces 'l'illusion référentielle' that induces a reader's belief and comprehension as they relate the text to their own experiences, while obfuscating the fact that the text is not, in this instance, a direct transmission of rumour.[60] This focus also enabled the Bourgeois to forego the traditionally authoritative sources used by other chroniclers, such as letters or edicts, instead relying upon subjective rumours circulating in Paris. Rumours therefore assumed a rhetorical function, whereby their repetition enhanced a descriptive mimesis that portrayed the 'reality' of Parisian thought, discussion and reaction. Such transformations certainly could and did distort the real course of events for rhetorical and political effect. But through writing, the Bourgeois translated this 'unofficial' discourse into the political experience, memory and identity of the city, with rumours playing a crucial role in the consolidation of the civic community.

Rumour and *Fama* in fifteenth-century Paris

The rumours reported by the Bourgeois were closely connected to the evolution of political issues and the circulation of news, reflecting the increasingly diverse political culture found in late medieval towns. Colette Beaune believed that the Bourgeois' concentration upon stereotypes promoted 'une lecture réductrice des événements', though it is clear that these stereotypes represented an important shorthand for the assessment of political

55 Mary-Rose McLaren, *The London Chronicles of the Fifteenth Century: A Revolution in English Writing* (Woodbridge: D.S. Brewer, 2002), pp. 50-1.
56 Kathleen Daly, '"Centre", "Power" and "Periphery" in Late Medieval French Historiography: Some Reflections' in *War, Government and Power in Late Medieval France*, ed. by Christopher Allmand (Liverpool: Liverpool University Press, 2000), pp. 124-28.
57 Van Nierop, '"And ye shall hear of wars and rumours of wars"', pp. 82-3.
58 Janet Coleman, *Ancient and Medieval Memories: Studies in the Reconstruction of the Past* (Cambridge: Cambridge University Press, 1992), p. 315. See also Pierre Courroux, *L'Écriture de l'histoire dans les chroniques françaises (XIIᵉ-XVᵉ siècle)* (Paris: Classiques Garnier, 2016), pp. 810-33.
59 Nancy Freeman Regalado, '*Effet de réel, effet du réel*: Representation and Reference in Villon's *Testament*', *Yale French Studies*, 70 (1986), 64.
60 Roland Barthes, 'L'effet de réel', *Communications*, 11 (1968), p. 88.

behaviour that signalled appropriate reactions to the Bourgeois' audience, much like his emotional rhetoric.[61] Influenced by archetypes and wider socio-political conversations, it is doubtful that the rumours incorporated into the *Journal* were the product of spontaneous discussion, instead being modified by levelling, sharpening and the Bourgeois' selective reporting. Having analysed the rhetorical means available to the Bourgeois to signal rumour and approximate audience and subject, the *Journal* emerges as more than a straightforward window onto Burgundian propaganda or popular discourse. The Bourgeois' readiness to relay rumours criticizing the leaders of every faction suggests that he selected material from a wider body of competing narratives in the public sphere, choosing those which suited political contexts, and articulated his community's concerns. The audience's role was crucial, with the Bourgeois' strategies inherently moulded by their horizon of expectations, as communities attempt to plausibly interpret events through their combined intellectual resources.

As a cleric, the Bourgeois was likely familiar with the correlation between rumour, widespread opinion and individual reputation expressed as *fama publica*.[62] *Fama* was integral to conceptions of societal belonging, with Sandy Bardsley arguing that in late medieval England, a focus upon 'sins of the tongue' enabled authors 'to reinscribe traditional social hierarchies and discourage disruptive and inflammatory speech'.[63] By recording incidences of subversive speech or rumour, the Bourgeois evoked *fama*'s essentially juridical framework to question aristocratic authority, mirroring the efforts of civic authorities to monitor popular criticism.[64] Where Sarah Rees Jones has argued, for York, that 'turning "chatter" into a record also gave it a status in the political process', with the 'very act of recording dissidence eventually [increasing] its impact on the public government of the city', the Bourgeois similarly codified rumour and reputation within his public sphere.[65] Lori J. Walters has noted that elite authors such as Christine de Pizan were acutely aware of *fama*'s political function, communicating 'theological insights on government to a public no longer restricted to clerics'.[66] Moralized readings of aristocratic reputation

61 A reductive reading of events. Beaune. 'La rumeur', p. 197. See also Gauvard, 'Rumeur et stéréotypes', p. 158.

62 Claude Gauvard, 'Fama explicite et fama implicite: Les difficultés de l'historien face à l'honneur des petites gens aux derniers siècles du Moyen Âge' in *La légitimité implicite*, ed. by Jean-Philippe Genet (Paris: Éditions de la Sorbonne, 2015), pp. 39-41; Elisabeth Lusset, 'La *fama* et l'*infamia* des clercs réguliers d'après les suppliques adressées à la pénitencerie apostolique au XVᵉ siècle' in *Faire jeunesses, rendre justice*, ed. by Antoine Destemberg, Yann Potin et Émile Rosenblieh (Paris: Publications de la Sorbonne, 2015), pp. 25-7. See also Ruth Mazo Karras, 'The Regulation of Sexuality in the Late Middle Ages: England and France', *Speculum*, 86 (2011), pp. 1019-20.

63 Sandy Bardsley, 'Sin, Speech and Scolding in Late Medieval England' in *Fama: The Politics of Talk and Reputation in Medieval Europe*, ed. by Thelma Fenster and Daniel Lord Smail (London: Cornell University Press, 2003), p. 146. See also Sandy Bardsley, *Venomous Tongues: Speech and Gender in Late Medieval England* (Philadelphia, PA: University of Pennsylvania Press, 2006).

64 Paul Strohm, *England's Empty Throne: Usurpation and the Language of Legitimation, 1399-1422* (London: Yale University Press, 1998), p. 23; Jamie K. Taylor, *Fictions of Evidence: Witnessing, Literature and Community in the Late Middle Ages* (Columbus, OH: Ohio State University Press, 2013), pp. 17-20. Wendy Scase similarly assesses the role of public clamour in *Literature and Complaint in England, 1272-1553* (Oxford: Oxford University Press, 2007), pp. 56-72.

65 Sarah Rees Jones, 'Emotions, Speech and the Art of Politics in Fifteenth-Century York: House Books, Mystery Plays and Richard, Duke of Gloucester', *Urban History*, 44 (2017), p. 602.

66 Lori J. Walters, 'Constructing Reputations, Fama and Memory in Christine de Pizan's *Charles V* and *L'Advision Cristine*' in *Fama: The Politics of Talk and Reputaton in Medieval Europe*, ed. by Thelma Fenster and Daniel Lord Smail (London: Cornell University Press, 2003), p. 119.

framed by popular perspectives assumed a similar function in the *Journal*, synthesizing theological teachings and conveying these as political commentary that, in the Bourgeois' case, reinforced understandings of evil government. Defamatory language had typically been presented as a threat to societal cohesion and the common good, but the Bourgeois used subversive talk to structure boundaries between Parisian in-groups, representative of the common good, and those governors who threatened its stability.

Reputation played a crucial role in the factional contests that enveloped French towns in the 1410s.[67] Where Chapter 4 will explore how clothing was used to control public presence and identify allegiances, these considerations also extended to language. From its inception, the Bourgeois used the term 'Armagnac' pejoratively to designate those who 'avoit autant de pitié de tuer ces gens comme de chiens', implying amoral cruelty and tyranny.[68] Inversely, 'Bourguignon' was employed as an insult by Armagnacs. Examples of such exchanges can be found throughout northern France. In 1420, Pierre Guiasse of Margny (County of Nevers) killed Martin Labuse for calling him an 'Arminac et coupaut'.[69] That same year, Thomas Philippe of Le Mesnil-Aubry (twenty-four kilometres north of Paris) was accosted by Armagnac soldiers who called him a '"faulx traictre et Bourguignon"'.[70] Designating immoral enemies, these insults drew upon the principal fears and obsessions of society to define community boundaries, castigating members and legitimating violence. Integral to this process was an insult's publicity, typically occurring in the neighbourhood inhabited by both offender and offended.[71] In this context, the Bourgeois' description of the rioters shouting '"Ses faulx traistres arminaz angloys!"' prior to perpetrating massacres in 1418 illustrates the means by which those perceived to pose a threat to the common good were identified and violence against envisioned enemies legitimated.[72] As a result, preserving oneself from identification with the enemy became essential to survival. In the summer of 1419, a Parisian *jardinier*, Jean Chevalier, accused the tailor Christophe Martin of supporting the Armagnacs, hoping that through Martin's imprisonment he could sell on for profit the cows that Martin had previously loaned to him. To this effect, Chevalier reported to the Châtelet authorities that he had heard Martin exclaim:

> "Maugré on ait Dieu! Quant monseigneur de Bourgongne entra oncques en ceste ville et que puis ne gaigna croix", et quant les Armignacs estoient a Paris il gaignoit

67 Emily Hutchison, 'Winning Hearts and Minds in Early Fifteenth-Century France: Burgundian Propaganda in Perspective', *French Historical Studies*, 35 (2012), 4, 19; Guy Lurie, 'Citizenship in Late Medieval Champagne: The Towns of Châlons, Reims, and Troyes, 1417-c. 1435', *French Historical Studies*, 38 (2015) pp. 370, 375-80.

68 Killed people pitilessly like dogs. *Journal*, p. 10.

69 An Armagnac and a cuckold. Paris, Archives nationales, JJ 171, fol. 231r.

70 A false traitor and Burgundian. Paris, Archives nationales, JJ 172, fol. 99v.

71 A feature also noted in Daniel Lord Smail, 'Hatred as a Social Institution in Late-Medieval Society', *Speculum*, 76 (2001), pp. 94-6; Jelle Haemers, 'Filthy and Indecent Words: Insults, Defamation and Urban Politics in the Southern Low Countries, 1350-1550' in *The Voices of the People in Late Medieval Europe: Communication and Popular Politics*, ed. by Jan Dumolyn, Jelle Haemers, Hipólito Rafael Oliva Herrer and Vincent Challet (Turnhout: Brepols, 2014), pp. 252-54.

72 These false English Armagnac traitors! *Journal*, p. 97.

beaucoup. Et oultre qu'il avoit dit que avant qu'il feust demi an, il y auroit du sang respendu et en feroit lui-mesmes respendre.[73]

Unfortunately for Jean Chevalier, Martin was known to be loyal to Jean sans Peur, at least officially if not publicly, as demonstrated by his appearance in the register of those who swore fealty to the duke in August 1418.[74] Chevalier was arrested when he reported his claims to the 'commissaire' and subsequently confessed to making false accusations. To restore Martin's reputation, Chevalier was subjected to several public and ritualized punishments. He was first 'condempné a estre tourné au pillory es Halles de Paris, mittré d'une mitre ou avoit escript en grosses lettres "faulx accuseur"', before being led 'nue teste, sans chapperon et sans saincture' to Martin's house in the rue de la Vieille-Monnaie, where he publicly declared that '"je vous ay accusé faulsement et maulvaisement a tort et sans cause en vous imposant, contre verité, que vous tenez le party d'Armignac et de cellui qui se dit daulphin"'.[75] Rehabilitating Martin in the public spaces where he had been defamed, the case nevertheless reveals the issues inherent in identifying political allegiances. Chroniclers relating the Parisian massacres were intensely aware of the pretext's exploitation to settle personal scores, with some killed 'soubz umbre de ce que on disoit yceulz avoir esté et estre favorisans au conte d'Armignac contre le duc de Bourgoigne'.[76] Clément de Fauquembergue noted the Parlement's release of one 'Boquet' from the Châtelet, wrongfully imprisoned upon suspicion of being an Armagnac, while the loyal counsellor Robert Houel was murdered by 'aucuns ses hayneux ou malveillans [...] pour souspecon d'avoir tenu ou favorisé [...] d'Armaignac'.[77] As Monstrelet concluded: 'il ne faloit que dire, "Véla ung armignach!", tantost il estoit mis a mort sans en faire aucune informacion'.[78]

Remission letters and the chroniclers' testimony provide insights into how language and rumour were being regulated in urban centres during the first decades of the fifteenth century. The formal and informal controls imposed by *fama* and political authorities alike underscore the dangers of considering public spaces as 'le point de convergence de tout ce qui n'était pas officiel', exhibiting an 'exterritorialité' of speech.[79] While Chevalier's case in

---

73 'God damn it! We haven't earned anything since my lord of Burgundy entered this town', and that when the Armagnacs had been in Paris, he had earned a lot. And besides this, he had said that within six months there would be blood spilled and that he himself would participate in the spilling of blood. For this and what follows, Paris, Archives nationales, JJ 171, fol. 52r-53v.

74 Antoine Le Roux de Lincy and Lazare-Maurice Tisserand (ed.), 'État des bourgeois de Paris qui prêtèrent serment entre les mains de Jean sans Peur, duc de Bourgogne au mois d'aout 1418' in *Paris et ses historiens aux XIV*e *et XV*e *siècles* (Paris: Imprimerie impériale, 1867), p. 379.

75 Condemned to being turned on the pillory at the Halles of Paris, mitred with a mitre upon which was written in bold letters 'false accuser'; head bare, without a hood or belt; 'I have accused you falsely and unjustly, wrongfully and without cause in asserting, contrary to the truth, that you supported the party of the Armagnacs and he who calls himself the Dauphin'.

76 Under the pretext that people said they had been and are supporters of the count of Armagnac against the duke of Burgundy. Fauquembergue, I, p. 131.

77 Some of his rivals and evildoers [...] upon suspicion of having supported and favoured the Armagnacs. Fauquembergue, I, p. 129; Paris, Archives nationales, JJ 170, fol. 191v.

78 All that had to be said was, 'There's an Armagnac', and he was immediately put to death without [due] investigation. Monstrelet, III, p. 271.

79 Mikhail Bakhtin, *L'œuvre de François Rabelais et la culture populaire au Moyen Âge et sous la Renaissance*, trans. by Andrée Robel (Paris: Gallimard, 1970), p. 156. See also Nicolas Offenstadt, *Faire la paix au Moyen Âge* (Paris: Odile Jacob, 2007), pp. 231-32.

1419 reveals the judicial measures employed to reverse reputational damage, a similar case in January 1418 indicates how rumour was policed. A labourer, Jean Jourdain, was reported to have proffered 'aucunes injurieuses paroles de notre personne et du gouvernement' that were recorded by 'les commissaires ordonnez nagaires sur le fait des rebellions et desobeissans'.[80] Both letters point to the role of 'commissaires', Châtelet officers employed to counteract the effects of subversive speech within Paris, perhaps occupying a role similar to that of the 'commission' established in December 1418 to prevent outbreaks of violence.[81] Moreover, these documents illuminate the Bourgeois' own report that in 1417 'par toutes les rues de Paris avoit espies qui estoient residans et demourans a Paris, qui leurs propres voisins faisoient prendre et emprinsonner', while also providing a possible explanation for the brevity of the Bourgeois' entries between April 1416 and the beginning of 1418 at the height of Armagnac surveillance when expressions of Burgundian support were especially compromising.[82] Christian Liddy has similarly pointed to the status of fifteenth-century English towns as 'surveillance societies' in the context of the Wars of the Roses, in which inhabitants monitored one another's behaviour and reported abuses to the government.[83] While 'medieval ideals of neighbourliness and neighbourly behaviour are inextricably linked to the act of witnessing' and testimony, what appears to have been of greater concern for the Bourgeois was the increasing institutionalization of this *fama* to survey language and control public space.[84]

The political potential of *mala fama* framed by rumour and propaganda is evidenced in the *Journal* through the Bourgeois' criticism of the Treaty of Saint-Maur, provisionally concluded between Jean sans Peur, Isabeau de Bavière and Jean V, duke of Brittany on 16 September 1418, to be ratified by the Dauphin Charles.[85] Here, the Bourgeois reported rumours that the Armagnac leaders had been responsible for poisoning the Dauphins Louis de Guyenne (d. 1415) and Jean de Touraine (d. 1417), and were prepared to betray France to the English, 'et savoit-on bien que ce avoit esté et fait faire'.[86] The Bourgeois related these rumours – inspired by Burgundian propaganda – despite earlier attempts by Paris' Armagnac administration to dismiss them. On 16 July 1417, Clément de Fauquembergue described an inquest where Burgundian letters were read to the Parlement, reportedly containing a 'libelle diffamatoire [...] en tant qu'elles font mencion de l'empoisonnement de feu monseigneur de Guyenne et de feu monseigneur le Daulphin'.[87]

---

80 Some injurious statements regarding ourselves and the government; the officers recently instructed to examine issues of rebellion and disobedience. Paris, Archives nationales, JJ 170, fol. 122r-122v.

81 *Ordonnances des rois de France*, X, pp. 500-01.

82 In all of Paris' streets there were spies who resided and lived in Paris, who had their own neighbours arrested and imprisoned. *Journal*, p. 79. On urban spies see Benoît Léthenet, '"Selon les nouvelles que vous me ferez savoir". Essai sur le renseignement au Moyen Âge', *Revue du Nord*, 402 (2013), pp. 839-40, 847-49; Pierre-Henri Guittonneau, 'Entre pratique et discours: les villes de la région parisienne face au secret au début du XVe siècle', *Questes*, 16 (2009), pp. 12-24.

83 Christian D. Liddy, 'Cultures of Surveillance in late Medieval English Towns: The Monitoring of Speech and the Fear of Revolt' in *The Routledge Handbook of Medieval Revolt*, ed. by Justine Firnhaber-Baker and Dirk Schoenaers (London: Routledge, 2017), pp. 312-13.

84 Taylor, *Fictions of Evidence*, pp. 90-114 (91).

85 For the Treaty of Saint-Maur see RSD, VI, pp. 278-83; Monstrelet, III, pp. 287-89.

86 And people knew well that this had happened and been orchestrated. *Journal*, p. 114.

87 A defamatory libel [...] since they mention the poisoning of the late lord of Guyenne and the late Dauphin. Fauquembergue, I, p. 32.

In response, Fauquembergue's record emphasized how the two princes' bodies 'furent ouvers en presence de medicins et autres, et n'y avoit quelque signe d'empoisonnement'.[88] The letters, which also contained an incitement to rebel and a Burgundian promise to lower taxes for the common good, were declared 'mauvaises, sedicieuses et scandaleuses' before being torn apart and burned.[89] On this occasion, Burgundian propaganda evidently drew upon prevalent repertoires that expressed wider societal anxieties and engendered further rumours. Poisoning occupied a particular place in the fifteenth-century political psyche, a fact demonstrated by Jean Petit's accusation in 1408 that Louis d'Orléans had attempted to poison Charles VI, as well as the rumours of the poisoning of Charles VII's mistress, Agnès Sorel, that resulted in the highly politicized trial of the royal officer Jacques Cœur in 1451.[90]

The record of executions and sentences discussed in Chapter 2 reveals that the Bourgeois and his audience were sensitive to the interplay of rumour, *fama*, perceived truth and its political effects. For example, throughout his account of Jeanne d'Arc's 1431 trial, the Bourgeois was careful to establish Jeanne's *mala fama* as the essential pretext to her treatment. This assesment began by establishing Jeanne's known reputation, stressing her culpability for crimes that had become common knowledge, 'comme chacun scet', before pointing to localized cases and rumours that would have been familiar to Parisian audiences, such as Jeanne's assault upon Paris in September 1429, or how she had compelled her followers to idolatry in Senlis.[91] When Jeanne appeared upon the scaffold in Rouen, the *Journal* underscored how 'chacun la povait veoir bien clerement vestue en habit de homme', alluding to the essential fact that her appearance and presence substantiated ideas of her transvestitism that represented an integral element in her condemnation.[92] This establishment of Jeanne's identity – and her condemnation for wearing men's clothes – was paralleled during her execution, when the fire was raked back so that she 'fue veue de tout le peuple toute nue, et tous ls secrez qui povent estre ou doyvent estre en femme, pour oster les doubtes du peuple'.[93] Through this emphasis upon Jeanne's identity and reports of her crimes, the *Journal* actively worked to underpin the juridical basis that framed the University of Paris involvement in her trial, and even demonstrating the prevalence of her crimes in the archdiocese of Sens.

The impact that Jeanne d'Arc's trial was designed to have upon Charles VII's own authority, presenting the French monarch as deceived and undermining the legitimacy of his 1429 coronation at Reims, performed with Jeanne d'Arc's assistance, underscores the

---

88 Were opened up in the presence of doctors and others, and there was found no sign of poisoning. Fauquembergue, I, p. 32.

89 Evil, seditious and scandalous. Fauquembergue, I, p. 33.

90 Alfred Coville, *Jean Petit. La question du tyrannicide au commencement du XVᵉ siècle* (Paris: Picard, 1932), pp. 325-32; Kathryn Reyerson, 'Le procès de Jacques Cœur' in *Les procès politiques, XIVᵉ-XVIIᵉ siècle*, ed. by Yves-Marie Bercé (Rome: École française de Rome, 2007), pp. 123-29; Franck Collard, 'Meurtres en famille. Les liens familiaux à l'épreuve du poison chez les Valois (1328-1498)' in *Familles royales: Vie publique, vie privée aux XIVᵉ et XVᵉ siècles*, ed. by Christine Raynaud (Aix-en-Provence: Presses Universitaires de Provence, 2010), p. 188.

91 As everyone knows. *Journal*, pp. 266-67.

92 Each could see her very clearly dressed in men's clothing. *Journal*, p. 269.

93 Was seen naked by all of the people, and all of the secrets that can and should belong to a woman, to allay the people's doubts. *Journal*, p. 269.

manner in which the record of *mala fama* served a political purpose, enabling Parisians to engage with questions of aristocratic reputation and situate these within a moral framework. Through the Bourgeois' account of these incidents, it emerges that the establishment of *fama*, in part through the circulation, repetition and refutation of rumour, enabled Parisians to situate themselves within the political contests of their time, determine their allegiances and consolidate their political stances. During the Armagnac-Burgundian conflict, where few external, ethnic or cultural features could determine friend from foe within Paris, the establishment of *fama* became key to identifying the social fault lines of partisanship within the city. It is rumour's role in this process of political identification and that will be analysed in the next section, examining the Bourgeois' active employment of *fama* to establish the stereotypical identity of the 'Armagnac' as a means of rationalizing collective Parisian action throughout the early fifteenth century.

The Armagnac stereotype

Rumours concerning the atrocities committed by men-at-arms in the Île-de-France are among the most striking reported by the Bourgeois. Claude Gauvard argued that these depictions drew upon archetypal notions of violent behaviour, the result of a longer tradition associated with the eleventh-century Peace of God movement.[94] Here, rumours appear to engender 'des figures simplifiants et facilite focalisations, sans souci de la vérité' while dividing society between 'bons et méchants'.[95] Gauvard's quantitative analysis of the remission letters issued during Charles VI's reign revealed a disparity between the prevalence of pejorative descriptions of men-at-arms in contemporary literature and the proportion of pardoned crimes that 'restent minoritaires par rapport aux rançonnements et aux *patis* qui par ailleurs ne sont pas retenus dans le stéréotype'.[96] Pointing to a mythification of military behaviour in fifteenth-century discourse, Gauvard's work highlighted rumour's othering function, indicating that the depredations related in the *Journal* represent that repertoire of common references through which contemporaries defined community boundaries and actively participated in political critique.[97] Like the emotional disposition system explored in Chapter 2, stereotypes provided a shortcut for evaluating factionalism and condemning abuses associated with the civil conflict. Indeed, the Bourgeois appropriated and developed a common discourse of pillage, rape, murder and theft, enhancing these stereotypical notions through their conflation with the 'Armagnac' faction. Recent studies have indicated that medieval urban communities were not as cohesive as previously thought, but that cohesion was 'cultivated in the face of external and internal threats' given expression

94 Claude Gauvard, *'De Grâce especial': Crime, état et société en France à la fin du Moyen Âge*, 2 vols (Paris: Publications de la Sorbonne, 1991), II, pp. 566-68.
95 Simplifying figures and facilitated focalizations, without concern for the truth. Gauvard, 'Rumeur et gens de guerre', p. 281.
96 Which remain in the minority compared to the ransoms and *patis* which, besides, are not included in the stereotype. Gauvard, 'Rumeur et stéréotypes', p. 160.
97 Porter, *Popular Rumour*, pp. 135-40.

through rumour.[98] The evolution of an Armagnac rumour represents precisely one means of understanding how the Bourgeois and his Halles audience understood the conflict that enveloped them, reinforcing a feeling of unity in the face of a palpable sense of difference, distinguishing Parisians within the city from an ambiguous, threatening group without.[99]

By tracing stereotypical rumours in the *Journal* it becomes possible to identify how these correspond to Porter's typology, ranging from almost folkloric narratives to troubling rumours that triggered communitarian introspection.[100] As Beaune and Gauvard have argued, these rumours were essentially a revival of older beliefs, part and parcel of a wider historiographical, religious and political discourse.[101] Their emotional impact was key to shocking audiences and voicing fears of an omnipresent Armagnac threat that in turn reinforced community cohesion beneficial to the Burgundian and, later, the Lancastrian regime. Through the processes of levelling, sharpening and assimilation, these rumours enabled Parisians to mould commonly acknowledged narratives into a specific critique of their Armagnac rivals, conflating the identities of Orléanist supporters with the imagined character of violent soldiers. While this conflation became more firmly established, it also provoked re-examinations of Parisian identity. As we have already seen, suspicions of partisanship were prevalent in Paris during the 1410s, restated through notions of treachery or tyranny that were increasingly adapted to perceived class and neighbourhood boundaries. When the political pendulum swung towards the Burgundians after their occupation of the capital in May 1418, the overthrow of Paris' Armagnac governors elicited an explosion of anti-Armagnac rhetoric in the *Journal*, motivated by the repressive measures instituted by the faction, and which conditioned the Bourgeois' impression of French politics throughout the ensuing decade. With the reassertion of Valois authority over the city in 1436, these pejorative qualities evolved in the Bourgeois' writing, but did not entirely disappear. Characteristically 'Armagnac' qualities of cruelty and barbarism were reframed in terms of the excesses of rampant mercenaries – the *écorcheurs* – and employed to signal the failures of Valois military policy, functioning as an effective means of political criticism in the last decade of the Hundred Years War.

The overlap between propaganda, opinion and rumours regarding the soldiery was signalled by the Bourgeois in his first use of the term 'Armagnac' following the sermon pronounced before Charles VI by the Mathurins minister Étienne du Mesnil in 1410. At this moment, tensions between the Orléanist and Burgundian camps were growing rapidly. In April 1410, the dukes of Berry, Orléans and Brittany along with the counts of Armagnac, Clermont, Alençon and Charles d'Albret had concluded an alliance at Gien to

---

98 Justin Colson and Arie van Steensel, 'Cities and Solidarities: Urban Communities in Medieval and Early Modern Europe' in *Cities and Solidarities: Urban Communities in Pre-Modern Europe*, ed. by Justin Colson and Arie van Steensel (London: Routledge, 2017), 5. See also Lorraine Attreed, 'Urban Identity in Medieval English Towns', *The Journal of Interdisciplinary History*, 32 (2002), pp. 571-73.

99 On the 'otherness' of Armagnacs in fifteenth-century French chronicles see Tracy Adams, 'Feuding, Factionalism and Fictions of National Identity: Reconsidering Charles VII's Armagnacs', *Digital Philology*, 1 (2012), pp. 16-18; Tim Pollack-Lagushenko, 'Le parti Armagnac: nouveaux modèles de violence politique dans la France du bas Moyen Âge', *Annales du Midi*, 118 (2006), pp. 441-46; Michael Sizer, 'The Calamity of Violence: Reading the Paris Massacres of 1418', *Journal of the Western Society for French History*, 35 (2007), p. 23.

100 Porter, *Popular Rumour*, p. 105.

101 Gauvard, 'Rumeur et stéréotypes', p. 161; Beaune, 'La rumeur', p. 198.

oppose Jean sans Peur before marching upon Paris in August, with Armagnac supplying the largest contingent of forces.[102] The assault was accompanied by an outpouring of Orléanist propaganda in the form of letters and manifestos exposing the ills of the kingdom and Burgundy's jeopardizing of the *bien public*.[103] It was in this context that, according to the Bourgeois, Mesnil's sermon responded by describing the dangers posed by the Orléanist leadership, emphasizing 'la crualité que ilz faisoient par deffaulte de bon conseil'.[104] The Bourgeois tied this cruelty to the personal reputation of Bernard, count of Armagnac: 'pour certain [...] quelconques estoit tué de dela, on disoit, "c'est ung Armignac", car ledit conte estoit tenu pour tres cruel homme et tirant et sans pitié'.[105]

The remarks indicate the levelling and sharpening taking place among Paris' Burgundian sympathizers, confusing Bernard d'Armagnac's personal reputation with the envisioned behaviour of his soldiers. This close association anticipated attempts to conflate the faction's qualities with the count's standing, as demonstrated by royal letters following the Burgundian coup in 1418 that identified Orléanist supporters as those 'tenans le party de Bernart d'Amignac' or as the count's 'aliés, satellices, complices'.[106] The *Journal* indicates that this conflation cyclically reinforced the count's reputation as responsible for Armagnac military cruelty, with multivalent discourses concerning violence condensed within the figure of the count. The Bourgeois recast the 'Armagnacs' as an illegitimate political movement embodying cruelty and tyranny, introducing a series of conceptions that were reiterated during the civil conflict. Underscoring this point, where rumours were typically conveyed through indirect speech that highlighted their subjective character, the Bourgeois reported news regarding Armagnac atrocities as factual events. Building upon existing archetypes integral to common knowledge, these rumours required little substantiation, with the effects of Armagnac extraneity reinforcing their plausibility.

The importance of rumours relating military depredations is underscored by their frequency. Eighty-six descriptions of military behaviour are present in the *Journal*, being unsurprisingly abundant at times of acute political tension, as demonstrated by their substantial increase in 1418-19 after the Parisian massacres and Jean sans Peur's murder at Montereau-fault-Yonne, and in 1429-30 following the Valois resurgence led by Jeanne d'Arc. In the first case, the number of reports rose from two in 1416-17 to nine in 1418 and eleven in 1419.[107] In the second, there was a single account of violence in the years 1425-28, compared to eight in 1429 and ten in 1430.[108] Rumours of military atrocities were conveyed through formulaic means that evidence their archetypal structure, especially through verb-lists. Soldiers performed a combination of actions including: *piller, rober,*

---

102 Bertrand Schnerb, *Les Armagnacs et les Bourguignons: la maudite guerre* (Paris: Perrin, 1988), pp. 103-09.

103 Monstrelet, II, pp. 82-6.

104 The cruelty that they committed due to a lack of good counsel. *Journal*, p. 9.

105 Certainly [...] whoever was killed in that manner, people said 'That's an Armagnac', because the said count was reputed to be a very cruel man, a tyrant and without pity. *Journal*, p. 10.

106 Supporting the party of Bernard d'Armagnac; allies, satellites and accomplices. For example, Paris, Archives nationales, JJ 170, fols 151r-v, 152v-153r.

107 That is, from an average of 4.5% of the total number of passages per year in 1416 and 1417, to 14% of passages in 1418 and 39% of all passages in 1419.

108 In terms of proportionality, this also shifted from being only one of the 72 passages for the years 1425-28 to 22% of the total passages for 1429 and 38% of those in 1430.

gaster, tuer, bouter feux, efforcer and *prendre gens a rancon* that became integral components of Armagnac behaviour.[109] These lists were increasingly common following Jean sans Peur's assassination in 1419 and, by 1423, they were so customary that the Bourgeois no longer repeated them fully. When Armagnacs sacked the region surrounding Mantes-la-Jolie, they often rode to 'piller et rober [...] comme acoustumé l'avoient'.[110] This repetition and its vision of generic behaviours reveal an accepted, credible perception of Armagnac behaviours that framed more specific rumours regarding the faction's depravity. As the Anglo-Burgundian alliance neared its ratification in the spring of 1420, the *Journal* reported that the Armagnacs had burned Champigny-sur-Marne, south-east of Paris:

> et quant aucuns des hommes sailloient pour la destresse du feu, ilz mectoient leurs lances a l'androit et ains qu'ilz fussent a terre, ilz estoient percez de iij ou iiij lances, ou de leurs haches. Celle cruelle felonnie firent la et ailleurs cedit jour.[111]

These rumours fed into a broader effort to rationalize the Anglo-Burgundian alliance taking shape in 1420. On the following page in the Vatican manuscript, the Bourgeois recounted how the Armagnacs had entirely succumbed to cruelty, and

> faisoient tous les maulx en tyrannie et en cruaulté qui pussent estre faiz par deable ne par homme, par quoy il convint que on traictast au roy d'Engleterre, qui estoit l'ancien ennemy de France, maugré que on eust, pour la cruaulté des Arminalz.[112]

Here, visions of tyrannical Armagnac behaviour and military abuses effectively excused the rapprochement between the two ancient enemies. Armagnac cruelty rendered the Lancastrian party the lesser of two evils, compelling submission to the English 'maugré que on eust'. Blurring the lines between reality, rumour and propaganda while capitalizing upon Parisian anxieties, this moralized dynamic rendered resistance to the Armagnacs imperative to maintaining an ordered Christian society ruled for the common good.

These processes are best illustrated by the Bourgeois' account of Meaux's capitulation to Henry V on 10 May 1422, having been besieged for seven months in the 'longest period of resistance experienced by Henry V in France'.[113] As Rémy Ambühl has shown, the terms of the town's surrender were especially severe, and the Bourgeois concentrated upon the fates of two of Meaux's captains, namely the Bâtard de Vauru and his cousin Denis de Vauru.[114] These captains and their execution occupied significant attention in English and French accounts of the siege alike. Where the Ursins Compiler stressed Vauru's

---

109 Pillaging, robing, laying waste, killing, burning, raping and capturing people for ransom. For example, *Journal*, pp. 128-30, 136-37, 176, 182, 194, 225, 251, 294, 308.

110 Pillage and rob, as they were accustomed to doing. *Journal*, p. 182.

111 And when some of the men sought to jump from the dangers of the fire, the Armagnacs placed their lances at the escape so that, when the men reached the ground, they were pierced by three or four lances or cut down with their axes. It was this cruel violence that they committed there and elsewhere on that day. *Journal*, p. 137.

112 Performed all of the tyrannical and cruel evils that could be done by either devils or men, such that it was necessary to negotiate with the king of England, who was the ancient enemy of France, whatever reluctance there may be, because of the Armagnacs' cruelty. *Journal*, p. 139. These descriptions occur on folios 65r-v of Rome, Vatican MS Reg. Lat. 1923.

113 Rémy Ambühl, 'Henry V and the Administration of Justice: The Surrender of Meaux (May 1422)', *Journal of Medieval History*, 43 (2017) p. 75.

114 Ambühl, 'Henry V and the Administration of Justice', p. 76.

loyalty to the Dauphin Charles, Boris Bove has argued that the execution of the Vauru cousins for resisting Henry V was legitimated by the violent and tyrannical characteristics attributed to these figures, as revealed by sympathetically Burgundian chroniclers including the Bourgeois and the anonymous *Chronique des Cordeliers*.[115]

These narratives demonized the Armagnacs, deflecting attention from Meaux's dedi-cation to the Dauphin Charles and Henry V's failure to quickly take the town. In the *Journal*, the Bâtard's death was exemplary of rigorous justice, with the noble exempted from Henry V's grace in the treaty of surrender.[116] Instead, the captain was 'trainé parmy toute la ville de Meaulx, et puis la teste coppée et son corps pendu a ung arbre [...] et dessus lui fut mise sa teste en une lance au plus haulte de l'arbre, et son estendart dessus son corps'.[117] This particular tree was central to all accounts of the execution, as the same site where Vauru had tyrannically hanged peasants and prisoners who could not afford their ransoms. The Bourgeois' detailed description of the circumstances of the Bâtard's execution was designed to parallel the brutal acts the captain had committed during his life, with similar attitudes to retributive justice signalled by the short chronicle produced for the English knight, Sir John Fastolf. This related that Vauru's death was commanded by Thomas Beaufort, duke of Exeter who, upon hearing that the captain had hanged peasants at the elm tree, 'ot tresgrant pitié et les fist descendre et ensepulturer, et jura que s'il povoit avoir ledit bastart, que il le feroit mourir de pareille mort'.[118] Indeed, by hanging his victims at an elm tree Vauru parodied cultural conceptions of good rule, with the elm an archaic symbol of justice, as the Bourgeois himself noted in 1440 when he envisioned foreign rulers sarcastically describing Charles VII as 'le droit ourme aux larrons de chrestienté' because of his continued support for the *écorcheurs*.[119] However, while the *Journal* conforms to other accounts in this respect, it also intriguingly deviates in its estab-lishment of significant differences between the Bâtard's character and that of his cousin Denis, who embodied stereotypical Armagnac qualities. The text makes no reference to the Bâtard's involvement in the peasant murders at the elm tree, instead associating these with Denis. This distinction is significant given their conflation in other sources, suggesting the Bourgeois' discrepancy between legitimate resistance to the English, as represented by

---

115 *Histoire de Charles VI*, p. 566; RSD, VI, p. 451; Cordeliers, p. 315. Boris Bove has tabulated the various chronicle descriptions of the siege of Meaux. 'Deconstructing the Chronicles', pp. 520-21.

116 Ambühl, 'Henry V and the Administration of Justice', pp. 84-7.

117 Dragged throughout the town of Meaux, and then he was decapitated and his body hanged from a tree [...] and above him his head was stuck upon a pike at the top of the tree, and his standard above his body. *Journal*, p. 170.

118 He was filled with pity and had the bodies taken down and buried, and he swore that if he could take the said bastard, he would put him to death in a similar manner. London, College of Arms, MS 9, fol. 45v. This chronicle was composed in 1459 by Peter Basset, Luke Nantron and Christopher Hanson, a German who had served Thomas Beaufort, duke of Exeter and whose contribution may explain the focus upon the duke in this passage. For the manuscript, see Anne Curry and Rémy Ambühl (ed.), *A Soldiers' Chronicle of the Hundred Years War: College of Arms Manuscript M 9* (Woodbridge: Boydell and Brewer, 2022); Benedicta J.H. Rowe, 'A Contemporary Account of the Hundred Years War from 1415 to 1429', *The English Historical Review*, 41 (1926), pp. 504-13; Anne Curry, 'Representing War and Conquest, 1415-29: The Evidence of College of Arms Manuscript M9' in *Representing War and Violence, 1250-1600*, ed. by Joanna Bellis and Laura Slater (Woodbridge: Boydell, 2016), pp. 139-58.

119 A complete elm tree [i.e. a judge] for the brigands in Christendom. *Journal*, p. 355. See also Bove, 'Deconstructing the Chronicles', p. 507, n. 25.

the Bâtard, and the tyrannical abuses committed by Armagnac troops evidenced by Denis' actions.[120]

In the town's treaty of surrender, Denis de Vauru is identified as one of Meaux's four captains who capitulated to Henry V in order to be judged, but for the Bourgeois his figure came to encapsulate the anti-Armagnac stereotypes developed through Parisian rumour.[121] In the *Journal*, Denis' character was illustrated through a single detailed anecdote describing how a young, pregnant peasant woman had failed to secure the ransom for her labourer husband, one of Denis de Vauru's prisoners. When the woman learned of her husband's ensuing death she insulted Denis in her grief, provoking the captain to tie her to his 'Arbre de Vauru', before leaving her and her unborn child to be devoured by wolves.[122] Boris Bove and Colette Beaune have argued that the anecdote echoes explicit Lancastrian attempts to mould French opinion following the siege.[123] However, the description is unique to the *Journal* and is not repeated by Burgundian chroniclers who would have presumably seized the chance to denigrate their Armagnac enemies.[124] Rather, Ambühl has persuasively shown that the rumour reflects local anxieties, pointing to the threat posed by the garrison at Meaux to Paris' security and linked to the fact that Parisians had earlier petitioned Henry V to capture the town.[125] In this context, the Bourgeois' account demonstrates rumour's cathartic function, not only giving voice to the fears resulting from the dangers posed by the Armagnacs in the Île-de-France, but also presenting a figure of vilification that united the Parisian community and legitimated support for Henry V's French conquest. For Bove, the Bourgeois presented an *exemplum horribilis* that 'gives a rhetorical sketch perfectly in line with the most sinister rumours going about the city'.[126] The pregnant woman's murder represented a powerful statement of the inversion of social values resulting from warfare, while the account's vivid detail, focusing upon her wails and the wolves' tearing apart of her unborn child, would have provoked disgusted responses that conditioned moral reflection upon war's conduct.

The Bourgeois' portrayal of Denis de Vauru as an antithesis to Christian values therefore illustrates a Parisian contribution to anti-Armagnac discourse and the means by which the city's inhabitants rationalized their support for the Lancastrian regime in opposition to these 'tyrannical' figures, with Denis de Vauru described as acting 'pour la grant cruaulté

---

120 The distinction is similarly evidenced by an abridged chronicle for the years 1403-42 compiled in Paris, Bibliothèque de l'Arsenal 4655, which states (for 1420) that 'la fust prins le bastard de Vauru, capitaine des gens d'armes, qui fust décapité, et Denis de Vauru, aussy grant capitaine, fust pendu a ung ourme près de Meaulx et son estandart dessus sa teste'. (There the bastard of Vauru, captain of the men-at-arms was captured, who was beheaded, and Denis de Vauru, a similarly important captain, was hanged at an elm near Meaux with his standard above his head). Nicole Pons, 'Mémoire nobiliaire et clivages politiques: le témoignage d'une courte chronique chevaleresque (1403-22)', *Journal des Savants* (2002), p. 334.

121 'Traité de la reddition de Meaux (2nd May 1422)' in Paris, BNF Fr. 1278, fols 87v-90r.

122 *Journal*, pp. 171-72.

123 Beaune, 'La rumeur' pp. 198-200; Bove, 'Deconstructing the Chronicles', pp. 532-36.

124 For instance, the accounts of Monstrelet, IV, pp. 91-6; Cordeliers, pp. 314-15; Jean le Fèvre de Saint-Rémy, *Chronique de Jean le Fèvre, seigneur de Saint-Rémy*, ed. by François Morand, 2 vols (Paris: Renouard, 1876-81), II (1881), pp. 54-5.

125 Ambühl, 'Henry V and the Administration of Justice', p. 86.

126 Bove, 'Deconstructing the Chronicles', p. 514.

dont il estoit plain, car on n'ouy oncques parler de plus cruel chrestien en tirannie'.[127] In particular, the rumoured anecdote of Denis de Vauru's tyranny could be effectively contrasted with the Bourgeois' account of Henry V's marriage to Catherine of Valois in June 1420. Here, Henry V was depicted as giving a speech to his forces, declaring that instead of superfluous jousting each English knight should march upon Sens "'et monstra sa proesse et son hardement, car plus belle proesse n'est ou monde que de faire justice des mauvays affin que le pouvre peuple se puisse vivre".'[128] Effective combat was a better mark of prowess than the tournament, and Meaux's capture represented the pursuit of this ambition to preserve justice and defend the poor that the Bourgeois attributed to Henry V.[129] This was underscored by the clemency that the monarch was envisioned as showing to Meaux's inhabitants, proclaiming upon his entry that 'chascun revenist a son propre hostel, et que chascun feist son labour, comme devant faisoient'.[130] In this light, not only did Denis de Vauru emerge as the embodiment of Parisian fears, he also represented a vision of the political disorder that could be juxtaposed with Henry V's military and political efficacy, rhetorically substantiating the faith placed in the Lancastrian monarch's claim to uphold good order in France. As the Bourgeois' description of Henry V's protection of the poor and labourers suggests, the Vauru narrative also captured specific fears about the protected status of non-combatants and the maintenance of societal norms by focusing upon the woman's treatment and the death of her unborn child, a fundamental transgression conveying anxieties surrounding productivity and the stability of Christian society. These were stereotypes remembered long after Paris' reconquest in 1436. Writing from the city to Charles VII in 1444 to plead for the realm's remedy, Jean du Bois reminded the monarch how troops of all colours – Burgundian, English and Valois – had been responsible for 'tant violences d'eglises, comme en vierges defleurer, en femmes veufves et mariées efforcier, en femmes grosses arrachier le fruict de leur ventre du conduit de nature'.[131]

The rhetorical accentuation of details to engender disgust represents a significant element in accounts such as the Bourgeois' description of Vauru. When the pregnant woman was tied to Vauru's tree, 'dessus luy avoit iiij^{xx} ou cent hommes panduz […] les bas aucunes foiz, quant le vent les faisoit brandeler, touchoient a sa teste, qui tant lui faisoient de freour que elle ne se povait soustenir sur piez'; the wolves 'lui ouvrirent a leurs cruelles dens, et

127 Because of the great cruelty with which he was filled, since none had heard of a more tyrannical and crueller Christian. *Journal*, p. 170.

128 Demonstrate your prowess and courage, because there is no greater prowess in the world than exacting justice upon evildoers so that the poor people can live. *Journal*, p. 140.

129 Craig Taylor, *Chivalry and the Ideals of Knighthood during the Hundred Years War* (Cambridge: Cambridge University Press, 2013), p. 95.

130 That everyone returned to their own home, and that each performed their labour just as they had done before. *Journal*, p. 168.

131 So much violence towards the church, such as the deflowering of virgins, the rape of widows and married women and the tearing of the fruit from pregnant women's stomachs through their natural conduct. Jean du Bois, 'Conseils et prédictions adressés à Charles VII en 1445 par un certain Jean du Bois', ed. by Noël Valois, *Annuaire-Bulletin de la Société de l'histoire de France*, 46 (1909), p. 220.

tirerent l'enffent hors par pieces, et le remenant de son corps despecerent tout'.[132] Rumours regarding the roasting of men and children, the cutting of throats or the burning of merchants must also have elicited a similar sense of horror.[133] The interplay of horror and disgust was central to defining the boundaries between Christian and other, as Alexandra Cuffel has demonstrated in her examination of impurity and filth in Crusading rhetoric, distinguishing human from unhuman and informing moral responses.[134] The Bourgeois conflated disgust and aversion at the treatment of Christians, stressing these elements that disturbed 'identity, system, order'.[135] Fundamentally, the emotional reactions provoked by these rumours reinforced a sense of community solidarity based on this aversion and established clear moral boundaries that distinguished the Parisian community from their Armagnac opponents. Disgust's role in shaping community relations is possible due to its contagious character, as a 'signalling mechanism advantageous to spread uniform aversive tendencies throughout a population'.[136] It is also made possible by the 'sympathetic magic' underpinning disgust's function, relying upon an understanding of contagion ('once in contact, always in contact') and similarity ('shared properties indicate shared identity') that reinforce boundaries between the (morally) pure ingroup and the outgroup, permanently tainted by association.[137] Ultimately, disgust maintains cultural orders and social hierarchies, equating unfamiliarity and harm potential with wrongness. It also encourages distance from the polluting other, inculcating an alterity that underpins group identity. It can therefore reinforce xenophobia by determining reactions both to moral violations and a perceived outgroup, focusing on a stereotypical vision of their behaviours that, for the Bourgeois, tied the Armagnacs to violent and sacrilegious predispositions that rendered them amoral and inhuman.

Typified Armagnac behaviours gave voice to these socio-political concerns, juxtaposing the Parisian community with an ambiguous and ubiquitous Other infesting the *plat pays* beyond the city walls. Excluding his descriptions of the 1418 massacres, the Bourgeois employed 'Armagnac' exclusively to designate the armed forces serving Charles VII *outside* Paris. This spatial dynamic was crucial, and Paul Zumthor has stressed the importance of distance in structuring otherness 'qualitativement, comme étrangeté [...] [et] quantitativement, comme continuation spatiale'.[138] Following the massacres of 1418, the Parisians were portrayed as being isolated by the Armagnac forces surrounding the city, with the inhabitants fearing reprisals for their endorsement of the Burgundian coup. In October,

---

132 Above her there were eighty or a hundred men hanging [...] sometimes when the wind made the lower ones move the bodies touched her head, which frightened her so much that she could not keep herself upon her feet; eviscerated her with their cruel teeth and tore out the child in pieces, before tearing apart the remainder of her body. *Journal*, p. 172.

133 *Journal*, pp. 87, 129, 137, 297, 306, 352.

134 Alexandra Cuffel, *Gendering Disgust in Medieval Religious Polemic* (Notre-Dame, IN: University of Notre-Dame Press, 2007), pp. 3-7, 87-106.

135 Julia Kristeva, *Powers of Horror. An Essays on Abjection* (New York, NY: University of Columbia Press, 1982), pp. 4-17; Willian Ian Miller, *The Anatomy of Disgust* (Cambridge: Harvard University Press, 1997), p. 154.

136 Joshua Gert, 'Disgust, Moral Disgust and Morality', *Journal of Moral Philosophy*, 12 (2015), p. 37.

137 Mary Douglas, *Purity and Danger: An Analysis of Concepts of Pollution and Taboo* (Reprint. New York: Routledge, 2001), pp. 18-25, 59-71, 115-25.

138 Qualitatively, like strangeness [...] and quantitatively, as a spatial continuation. Paul Zumthor, *La Mesure du monde. Représentation de l'espace au Moyen Âge* (Paris: Éditions du Seuil, 1993), p. 146.

'les Arminax […] venoient souvent empres Paris prendre proies et hommes et femmes', and by March 1419 the Armagnacs appeared 'jusques aux portes de Paris sans cesser, et nul homme n'osoit yssir'.[139] Armagnac proximity framed an insider-outsider contrast while also stoking fears regarding Paris' autarky. Rumours of foodstuffs being destroyed, the ambushing of merchants and murder of labourers assume meaning as expressions of concerns about the city's provision. The Bourgeois, in particular, was sensitive to the dangers posed by warfare, economic fluctuations, adverse weather and epidemics to the availability of foodstuffs in an already overpopulated city.[140]

In turn, the perceived existential threat posed to the civic community that motivated the internal hunt for Armagnacs in 1418 was exacerbated by the reports of other towns' experiences. When Armagnac forces captured Soissons in May 1414, the town was sacked as an example to Burgundian supporters.[141] The Bourgeois countered the praise exhibited in the ensuing Parisian celebrations by expressing horror at the Armagnac treatment of Soissons' inhabitants:

> plusieurs en furent penduz, et les femmes de religion et autres prudes femmes et bonnes pucelles efforcées, et tous les hommes ranconnez, et les petiz enffans, et les eglises et reliques pillées et livrées et vestemens. Et avant qu'il fut dix jours apres la prinse de la ville, elle fut si pillée au net qu'i n'y demoura chose que on peut emporter. Et dit-on que on n'ouyt oncques parler que les Sarazins feissent pis que firent ceulx de l'ost en ladite ville.[142]

Soissons presented a model for later descriptions of Armagnac reprisals that performed an important rhetorical function after the Burgundian coup in 1418, legitimating Parisian support for Jean sans Peur. Primarily, rumours of the massacres perpetrated by Armagnacs throughout northern France justified those that occurred within Paris' walls, structuring an "us-or-them" mentality, rendering the elimination of Armagnac sympathizers crucial to neutralizing internal threats. This danger was demonstrated by news of incidents such as the massacre of Sens' inhabitants in March 1419 by its captain, Guillaume de Chaumont, seigneur de Guitry, 'pour ce que ceulx de la cité voulaient mectre les Bourguignons dedens sans son seu'.[143] This possibility of annihilation found its most vivid expression in Jeanne d'Arc's assault upon the city on 8 September 1429, with the Bourgeois portraying the Pucelle as shouting to Paris' defenders: '"Ce vous ne vous rendez avant qu'il soit la nuyt,

---

139 The Armagnacs […] often came up to Paris' walls to take prey, and men and women; ceaselessly up to the gates of Paris, and no man dared leave. *Journal*, pp. 116, 123.

140 Regarding Paris' provisioning, see Laurent Vissière, 'La bouche et le ventre de Paris', *Histoire urbaine*, 16 (2006), pp. 85-9.

141 Monstrelet, III, pp. 8-11; Cordeliers, p. 222; RSD, V, pp. 324-31.

142 Several were hanged, and nuns, other worthy women and maidens raped, and all of the men ransomed as well as the small children, and the churches pillaged of their relics, books and vestments. Before ten days had passed following the capture of the town, it had been ransacked so thoroughly that nothing remained that could be taken away; people said that they had never even heard of Saracens behaving worse than the actions of those of the army towards the said town. *Journal*, p. 53.

143 Because the inhabitants of the town wanted to let the Burgundians enter without his knowing. *Journal*, p. 123.

nous y entrerons par force [...] et tous serez mis à mort sans mercy!'"[144] Underpinning this
threat was the rumour that Jeanne d'Arc had promised her soldiers that

> sans nulle faulte ilz gaignerent a cellui assault la ville de Paris [...] et qu'ilz seroient tous
> enrichiz des biens de la cité, et que tous seroient mis qui y mectroient aucune deffence a
> l'espée, ou ars en sa maison.[145]

These rumours impart the Bourgeois' sustained rhetorical efforts to rationalize Paris'
political stance, justifying continued resistance to Charles VII through the repeated fears
of potential reprisals. This juxtaposition was reinforced through the Armagnacs' direct
contrast with non-combatants. Throughout the *Journal*, Armagnacs were portrayed as
avoiding open military engagements and preying upon defenceless civilians, subverting
understandings of honourable combat and the exemption of specific sections of society
from violence. These rumours also performed an essential political role. For example,
in 1420, the brutality of such crimes were destined to explicate Charles VI's submission
to Henry V's demands in the conclusion of the Treaty of Troyes, culminating in the
agreement that his daughter Catherine would marry the English monarch:

> Brief, ilz faisoient tous les maulx en tyrannie et en cruaulté qui pussent estre faiz par
> deable ne par homme, par quoy il convint que on traictast au roy d'Engleterre, qui estoit
> l'ancien ennemy de France, maugré que on eust, pour la cruaulté des Arminalz, et lui fut
> donnée une des filles de France, nommée Katherine.[146]

Here, the threat of destruction conjured by the Bourgeois' vision of the Armagnac faction,
by their diabolical and violent character, compelled the inhabitants of Paris to reconceptualize their historical and political place. With Jean sans Peur assassinated by Armagnac
leaders in September 1419, the Bourgeois' depiction of Burgundian sympathizers being
caught between two evils echoed the discussions taking place at the Burgundian court
itself, who concluded 'que de deulx maulx le moins pire est a eslire'.[147] For the Bourgeois
and his community, the enumeration of rumours describing Armagnac violence facilitated
precisely this rationalization of Paris' political realignment and, ultimately, explained the
necessity of a Burgundian alliance with France's 'ancient enemies'.

As the assessment of Denis de Vauru and Henry V has shown, the Armagnac stereotype's othering function was tied to its moralizing effect, excluding Armagnacs from the
Bourgeois' conception of the Christian community. Given the absence of immediately per-
ceptible markers of Armagnac difference, the Bourgeois constructed a rhetorical paradigm

---

144 'If you do not surrender before nightfall, we will enter the city by force [...] and all will be put to death without mercy!'
   Journal, p. 245.
145 Without any difficulty they would capture the city of Paris through this assault [...] and that they would all be enriched
   by the city's goods, and that all of those people who attempted to put up any defence would be put to the sword or
   burned in their houses. *Journal*, p. 246.
146 In short, they accomplished all of the tyrannical evils that could be done by devil or man, and because of which it was
   necessary to negotiate with the king of England, who was the ancient enemy of France, because of the cruelty of the
   Armagnacs; and one of the daughters of France was given to him, called Catherine. *Journal*, p. 139.
147 Between two evils, the lesser is the one to choose. 'Mémoire consignant, à l'intention du conseil du duc de Bourgogne,
   les arguments pour ou contre l'acceptation des conditions de paix du roi d'Angleterre' in Paul Bonenfant, *Du meurtre de
   Montereau au traité de Troyes* (Brussels: Académie royale de Belgique, 1958), p. 218.

that situated the faction as an amoral Christian antithesis. First, the Bourgeois conflated the archetype of military violence with an equally archetypal vision of Saracen behaviour, drawing from the common repertoire established by crusading rhetoric and religious litera-ture that at once situated the Armagnacs beyond the boundaries of Christian society and reinforced Paris' status as a most-Christian city, described by Jean Gerson as 'la lumiere de nostre foy'; le beau cler soleil de France, voir de toute crestienté'.[148] This moral otherness was reinforced by a profound conviction that the Armagnacs represented earthly manifesta-tions of Christian sin that framed the civic conflict in absolutes, presenting audiences with a clear distinction of good and evil. Bernard d'Armagnac and his followers were described as devils, a move that capitalized upon Louis d'Orléans' association with diabolical practices in texts such as Jean Petit's *Justification* and later accentuated by Charles VII's association with controversial visionaries like Piéronne, Jeanne d'Arc and Guillaume le Berger between 1429 and 1431, each mentioned by the Bourgeois.[149] Coupled with the record of Armagnac violence, these rumours sustained a paradigm that rationalized Lancastrian successes as a form of divine punishment for French sin, while rumours of diabolical behaviour legiti-mated Parisian resistance.

Comparing the Armagnacs to Saracens, pagans and Roman tyrants, the Bourgeois evoked deeper notions of cultural alterity prevalent in the Middle Ages. Fuelled by crusad-ing rhetoric, these same Christian reactions coupled notions of the 'Saracen' with apocalyp-tic evil, drawing upon tropes prevalent in crusading propaganda and perhaps echoing the increase in this rhetoric that followed the Franco-Burgundian disaster at Nicopolis in 1396, the notion of Saracen or Turk becoming enmeshed with that of divine punishment.[150] By comparing the Armagnacs to Saracens, the Bourgeois introduced tropes of indiscriminate violence and spiritual irreverence that rendered the comparison an effective form of politi-cal commentary. The association was immediate. Relating rumours of brutality in August 1411, the Bourgeois stated that the Armagnacs

> firent tant de maulx comme eussent fait Sarrazins, car ilz pendoient les gens, les uns par les poulces, autres par les piez, les autres tuoient, et ranconnoient, et efforcoient femmes, et boutoient feuz. Et quiconques ce feist, on disoit "ce font les Arminalx".[151]

---

48 Cited in Bernard Guenée, *Un meurtre, une société. L'assassinat du duc d'Orléans, 23 novembre 1407* (Paris: Gallimard, 1992), p. 122. On Paris' centrality see below, Chapter 4.

49 *Journal*, pp. 259-60, 266-72, 274-75.

50 Charles-Louis Morand Métivier, 'Narrating a Massacre: The Writing of History and Emotions as Response to the Battle of Nicopolis (1396)' in *Affective and Emotional Economies in Medieval and Early Modern Europe*, ed. by Andreea Marculescu and Charles-Louis Morand Métivier (London: Palgrave Macmillan, 2018), pp. 196-202. This attitude ran counter to changing views among Burgundian courtiers, whom Hilmi Kaçar and Jan Dumolyn have argued as embracing a new vision of Ottoman power that could even be exemplary for failing Christian princes. 'The Battle of Nicopolis (1396), Burgundian Catastrophe and Ottoman Fait Divers', *Revue belge de philologie et d'histoire*, 91 (2013), p. 932.

51 They committed such evils as Saracens would have done, because they hanged people, some by their thumbs, others by their feet; others they killed, others they ransomed, and raped women and started fires. And whoever did this, people said 'that is what Armagnacs do'. *Journal*, p. 11.

With the faction's leaders excommunicated three months later, the characterization of Armagnac violence as Saracen became a common trope.[152] Armagnacs undertaking *courses* before Paris in 1422 'faisoient des maulx tant que oncques firent tyrans Sarazins'; later that year they evaded Burgundy's forces, 'et firent [...] tous les maulx que on peust pencer, comme eussent fait Sarazins'.[153] Such language exhibited a snowballing phenomenon as rumours gained additional detail.[154] Moreover, the comparison presented the Bourgeois with a rhetorical shorthand that facilitated the moral condemnation of Armagnac violence, summoning common knowledge of crusading discourse that enabled audiences to readily configure the Armagnac stereotype according to religious features that excluded those identified from popular (Burgundian) understandings of the French and Christian communities, stressed by the portrayal of Armagnacs' opposition to traditional order, inherent sinfulness and willingness, even their delight, in the shedding of Christian blood.

The situation of the Armagnac faction beyond the boundaries of the Christian community enabled the Bourgeois to call attention to demonic features, as demonstrated by his diatribe following Jean sans Peur's assassination.

> Cuide en ma conscience que ledit conte d'Arminac estoit ung ennemy en fourme de homme, car je ne voy nul qui ait esté a lui ou qui de lui ce renomme [...] qui tienne point la loy ne foy chrestienne. Ains ce maintiennent envers tous ceulx dont ilz ont la maistrise, comme gens qui auroient renyé leur Creatour.[155]

The correlation of the Armagnacs with the diabolic was achieved through the repetition of rumoured anti-Christian violence, sacrilegious behaviours and heretical beliefs reinforced by official efforts including the faction's excommunication in November 1411 that eased these rumours' acceptance. For instance, when Bernard d'Armagnac was appointed French constable on 30 December 1415, the Bourgeois reminded his audience of the count's illegitimacy as a 'personne escommeniée comme devant est dit'.[156] Cyclically, the rumours of Armagnac depredations reinforced the sentence's validity. For example, the Bourgeois retrospectively justified the murders perpetrated by Parisians in 1418 by focusing upon the amoral characteristics of the Armagnac leaders. Remonnet de La Guerre was described as the commander of 'larrons' who 'faisoient pis que Sarazins'; Philippe de Villette, abbot of Saint-Denis, was a 'tres faulx papelart'; and, finally, Pierre le Gayant was a 'personne sismatique, herite contre la foy' whose beliefs had already been condemned in public sermons, with the Bourgeois concluding that the cleric was 'digne d'ardoir'.[157]

---

152 *Journal*, pp. 16-17; *Histoire de Charles VI*, p. 462; Hutchison, 'Winning Hearts and Minds', pp. 21-22. On the excommunication of Armagnac leaders in Paris, see below, Chapter 5.

153 And committed evils as bad as those once committed by Saracen tyrants; and committed all of the evils that can be thought of, as Saracens would have done. *Journal*, p. 163.

154 Porter, *Popular Rumour*, p. 112.

155 I believe in my conscience that the said count of Armagnac is a devil in human form, because I cannot see anyone who followed him or who claims to support him [...] who follows either the Christian law or faith. In fact, they behave towards those over whom they have authority like men who have forgotten their Creator. *Journal*, p. 134.

156 An excommunicated person, as stated above. *Journal*, p. 68.

157 Committed worse deeds than Saracens; a very false hypocrite; a schismatic person and heretic against the faith [...] worthy of being burned. *Journal*, p. 94.

Rumours surrounding the visionaries associated with the Armagnacs reinforced this perception of heretical, even diabolical, inspiration. The Bourgeois' account of Jeanne d'Arc's conviction focused upon her desire to destroy Paris 'a feu et a sang' on the feast of the Virgin's Nativity, and how 'elle avoit fait ydolatrer le simple peuple'.[158] These accusations were compounded by Jean Graverent's later sermon, whereupon the inquisitor described Jeanne as 'accompaignée de l'Ennemy d'enfer, et depuis vesqui homicide de chrestienté plaine de feu et de sanc'.[159] Jeanne's spiritual experiences emulated Bernard d'Armagnac's perceived diabolical inspiration, undermining the moral and political legitimacy Charles VII had accrued through her aid. This was underscored by the presence of other dubious visionaries. In 1431, Guillaume le Berger 'faisoit les gens ydolatres en luy', whereas Piéronne la Bretonne was executed in Paris in September 1430 for asserting that 'Dieu [...] parloit a elle comme amy fait a autre' in terms that anticipated Graverent's description of demonic interaction.[160] Ultimately, rumours of demonic inspiration reinforced the distinction between the Bourgeois' conception of a pious, Christian community and an antithetical, Armagnac Other.

Indicative of his clerical perspective, the Bourgeois highlighted a strong connection between Armagnac desecrations and their diabolical character. In turn, these descriptions reiterated the sense of an overwhelming crisis facing Christian society, with attacks upon churches endangering a framework of social provision.[161] The rhetoric can be compared with those rumours associated with Denis de Vauru, contributing to an impression of the violation of fundamental societal norms by Armagnacs, with Vauru's murder of the pregnant woman a microcosmic example of wider societal discord. Consequently, as the Bourgeois warned, unless the Armagnacs returned to the fold of the Christian community, 'tout le royaume est a perdicion ce Dieu n'en a pitié, qu'on y veuille de sa grace ouvrer', again situating the Armagnacs as an Other external to French, Christian society.[162] Conflating amoral characteristics with accusations of tyrannical cruelty, such rumours therefore emerged as a fundamental means of asserting Armagnac illegitimacy as an iteration of the threat posed by the faction both to the common good and to Christendom itself.

The development of stereotypes that reinforced the boundaries between friend and foe or insider and outsider were integral to rationalizing a civic conflict during which it was impossible to identify the enemy according to evident ethnic, cultural or linguistic factors. The othering of Armagnacs sustained animosity and legitimated resistance in a war where both sides simultaneously espoused an identification as being 'French'. Through the coalescence of long-standing archetypal rumours and stereotypes, the Bourgeois buttressed sympathetically Burgundian narratives, codifying an ideal of 'Armagnac' alterity. First among these was the assimilation of the term Armagnac with understandings of cruelty and violence associated with the uncontrolled soldiery since the High Medieval Peace of

---

158 She had rendered the simple people idolaters. *Journal*, p. 267.

159 Accompanied by the Enemy of hell, and since then lived according to Christian killing replete with fire and blood. *Journal*, p. 270.

160 Rendered people idolatrous; God [...] spoke to her as a friend does to another. *Journal*, pp. 272, 260.

161 As noted by Bronisław Geremek. *The Margins of Society in Late Medieval Paris*, trans. by Jean Birrell (Cambridge: Cambridge University Press, 1987), pp. 167-92.

162 The entire kingdom will be damned if God does not take pity and if we wish to elicit his grace. *Journal*, p. 129.

God movement that had distinguished the status of combatants and non-combatants, but that in France had been exacerbated by the 'Grandes Compagnies' who terrorized France in the years following the Treaty of Brétigny in 1360.[163] Burgundian propagandists had drawn upon this memory when they orchestrated the ritual excommunication of Armagnac leaders at Paris on 13 November 1411, taking as their basis for this move the papal bull issued by Pope Urban V on 9 May 1367 stating that groups who took up arms against the French sovereign warranted excommunication.[164] Building upon this context, the Bourgeois portrayed sedition and violence towards non-combatants as essential Armagnac characteristics by repeating rumours of atrocities, from typical notions of burning, pillaging and rape to more detailed accounts of murder designed to provoke horror and disgust. The dynamic suggested by the sentence of excommunication in 1411 was crucial to this de-humanization of the Armagnac faction, further accomplished by the Bourgeois association of the faction both with commonly held assumptions regarding Saracen behaviour towards Christians and notions of diabolical inspiration. Through these stereotypical attributions, the *Journal* reveals the processes whereby Parisians justified their continued resistance to Charles VII, despite his claim to be the rightful king of France, by situating the Armagnac faction as an antonym to Christian society.

Although Paris' political status shifted dramatically with its reabsorption into the Valois polity in April 1436, the Armagnac stereotype had an afterlife, evolving well into the 1440s. This enduring appeal underscores its origins in perceptions of the soldiery and, more importantly, the malleability of these archetypal ideals to suit fast-changing political contexts. In his later writing, the Bourgeois continued to repeat the tropes that had defined Armagnac behaviour, this time as a means of questioning Valois legitimacy. Much of this critique was centred upon the activities of the *écorcheurs*, those soldiers left unemployed by the cessation of hostilities between Philippe III le Bon, duke of Burgundy and Charles VII after the 1435 Arras Congress and whose activities were amplified between 1438 and 1440.[165] When Bernard d'Armagnac's son, Bernard, count of Pardiac entered Paris in June 1439, the Bourgeois evoked memories of his father to criticize Valois military efforts. Pardiac was 'ung autre aussi mauvais ou pire [...] filz du conte d'Arminal qui fut tué pour ses demerites, et admena une autre grant compaignie de larrons et de meurdriers qui pour leur mauvaise vie et detestable gouvernement furent nommez les escorcheurs'.[166]

---

163 Philippe Contamine, 'Les compagnies d'aventure en France pendant la guerre de Cent ans', *Mélanges de l'École française de Rome*, 87 (1975), pp. 369-76; Taylor, *Chivalry*, pp. 223-24.

164 *Ordonnances des rois de France*, IX, pp. 652-53; RSD, V, pp. 532-34; Monstrelet, II, p. 210.

165 In doing so, the *Journal* echoes other contemporary conflations of 'Armagnac', 'French' and 'écorcheur', as in Monstrelet, V, p. 340. For the *écorcheurs*, see Philippe Contamine, *Guerre, État et société à la fin du Moyen Âge: Études sur les armées des rois de France, 1337-1494*, 2 vols (Paris: Mouton, 1973), I, pp. 265-67; Alexandre Tuetey, *Les Écorcheurs sous Charles VII. Épisodes de l'histoire militaire de France au XVᵉ siècle d'après des documents inédits* (Montbéliard: Barbier, 1874); Valérie Toureille, 'Pillage ou droit de prise. La question de la qualification des écorcheurs pendant la guerre de Cent Ans' in *La politique par les armes. Conflits internationaux et politisation (XVᵉ-XIXᵉ siècle)*, ed. by Laurent Bourquin, Philippe Hamon, Alain Hugon and Yann Lagadec (Rennes: Presses universitaires de Rennes, 2013), pp. 169-82.

166 Another evil man [...] the son of the count of Armagnac who was killed for his dishonourable behaviour, and he brought with him a great company of brigands and murdered who because of their evil lifestyle and odious government were named the *écorcheurs*. *Journal*, p. 346.

With the *écorcheurs*, the Armagnac stereotype continued to play a role in the ratio-nalization of conflict and the evaluation of good rule. As in the earlier decades of the fifteenth century, rumours of the *écorcheurs'* depredations increased during the noble revolt against Charles VII known as the Praguerie in 1440.[167] The Bourgeois traced news of the *écorcheurs* in Burgundy, where they captured livestock and penned them in to starve when peasants failed to pay their ransom, and their direct role in the rebellion whereupon the *écorcheurs* 'faisoient guerre au pouvre peuple'.[168] In 1443, the *larrons'* behaviour was perceived as an extension of royal disorder and exploitation. It is at this moment that the Bourgeois sarcastically remarked that foreign kings called Charles VII 'le droit ourme aux larrons' because of his favour for the *écorcheurs*.[169] When the Dauphin Louis appeared at Meaux that year, the Bourgeois' criticized his proclivity for dancing and hunting, all the while paying *écorcheurs* for every horse and cow that they stole, such that the Bourgeois exclaimed that: 'toute ceste douloureuse tempeste que ainsi se souffroit [******] Dalphin et des gouverneurs faulx et traistres au roy'.[170] Indeed, even when the Swiss campaign of 1444-45 was undertaken to remove the *écorcheurs* from the kingdom, the Bourgeois complained that both the campaign and the attention paid to these 'larrons et murdriers, boutefeux, efforceux de toutes femmes' distracted Charles VII and the Dauphin from their duty to combat the English, 'et ilz alloient lui et son filx en estranges terres ou ilz n'avoient rien, despendre et gaster ses gens et la finance de son royaume'.[171] Fundamentally, rumours of the *écorcheurs'* barbarity undermined Charles VII's already unstable authority. In doing so, the *Journal* reveals the function of rumour as a means of expressing societal fears prompted by widespread violence and the threat of retribution, enabling Parisians to justify their political stance on an emotional, moral, and political basis.

Rumour and revolt: The Parisian uprisings of 1413 and 1418

Two major Parisian uprisings were described in detail by the Bourgeois. The first, the Cabochien Revolt in 1413, occurred in the context of the meeting of the Estates General in January that year to discuss fresh taxes and general reform, and saw the Parisian populace – led by butchers and skinners – rise up to demand reform when the Estates were dismissed, occupying the city throughout the summer.[172] The suppression of the revolt led to five

---

167 Élodie Lecuppre-Desjardin and Valérie Toureille, 'Servir ou trahir. La réaction des grands féodaux face aux innovations étatiques, au temps de la Praguerie', *Publications du Centre européen d'études bourguignonnes*, 60 (2020), pp. 7-14.

168 Made war upon the poor people. *Journal*, pp. 350-52 (351).

169 *Journal*, p. 355.

170 All of this dreadful storm was caused [erased words] Dauphin and the king's false and treacherous governors. *Journal*, p. 369. The words – and others condemning the Dauphin Louis – were erased by a conscious reader of the Vatican manuscript, presumably during Louis XI's reign. Rome, Vatican Reg. Lat. 1923, fol. 176r. On these readers see the Introduction.

171 Brigands and murderers, fire-starters, ravishers of all women; and he and his son went into foreign lands where they had no business to spend and waste their men and the kingdom's wealth. *Journal*, p. 375.

172 The best history of the Cabochien Revolt remains Alfred Coville, *Les Cabochiens et l'ordonnance de 1413* (Paris: Hachette, 1888). More recently, Emily Hutchison has undertaken a series of studies analysing distinct aspects of the revolt. Emily Hutchison, 'Knowing One's Place: Space, Violence and Legitimacy in Early Fifteenth-Century Paris', *The Medieval History Journal*, 20 (2017), pp. 1-51.

years of Armagnac governance in Paris, before a small group of Burgundian sympathizers led by the iron-seller Perrinet le Clerc betrayed the city to Burgundian forces on 29 May 1418.[173] While the Dauphin Charles fled the city, the days and months after the Burgundian coup were marked by riots as Parisians attempted to root out suspected Armagnac sympathizers within the city, culminating in massacres on 12 June and 21 August.

Although Vincent Challet has rightly emphasized important distinctions between the two major Parisian uprisings of the 1410s, their interrelation in fifteenth-century Parisian understandings of political participation through revolt are underscored by the similarities in the Bourgeois' employment of rumour to consider these popular movements.[174] Boris Bove has interpreted these uprisings as part and parcel of a royal 'crise dynastique et politique' rather than predominantly urban concerns.[175] However, their examination reveals the means by which Parisians participated in revolt to communicate their grievances to royal, ducal and civic authorities, following Xavier Nadrigny's recognition that 'révolte et sujétion sont les deux facettes de la meme relation a-critique nouée entre gouvernants et gouvernés'.[176] In each revolt, rumour fed into broader communicative processes, focalizing Parisian anxieties and enabling Burgundian supporters to rally themselves through the production of cohesive political narratives. Just as they were essential to the commons' political participation, these rumours were also central to commentators' efforts to rationalize revolt. In both 1413 and 1418, the Bourgeois employed rumours of an Armagnac threat to Charles VI and the broader common good to retrospectively legitimate Parisian violence. As Paolo Viola has argued for the French Revolution, this rationalization by observers strips violence of its cultural significance, enabling the crowd to assert its representative status and sovereignty in its power to punish enemies, evoking a symbolic *bricolage* to assert their perspective.[177] Conjuring this popular agency in urban politics, the Bourgeois' record of rumour was presented as counterbalancing official communication, while rebel claims reveal the third element of Porter's typology, whereupon snowballing

---

173 For the history of the 1418 coup, see Sizer, 'The Calamity of Violence', pp. 19-39.

174 Vincent Challet, 'Violence as a Political Language: The Uses and Misuses of Violence in late Medieval French and English Popular Rebellions' in *The Routledge Handbook of Medieval Revolt*, ed. by Justine Firnhaber-Baker and Dirk Schoenaers (London: Routledge, 2017), pp. 279-80. Challet argues that a major difference is the 1418 massacres' relative 'radicalization' when compared to 1413, escaping the control and influence of Jean sans Peur. However, recent scholarship has demonstrated that the Cabochien rebels also expressed urban grievances that differed substantially from those of the Burgundian regime. See Hutchison, 'Knowing One's Place', pp. 1-51.

175 Dynastic and political crisis. Boris Bove, 'Alliance ou défiance? Les ambiguïtés de la politique des Capétiens envers leur capitale entre le XIIᵉ et le XVIIᵉ siècle' in *Les villes capitales au Moyen Âge* (Paris: Publications de la Sorbonne, 2006), p. 142.

176 Revolt and constraint are two sides of the same acritical relation developed between governors and subjects. Xavier Nadrigny, 'Espace public et révolte à Toulouse à la fin du Moyen Âge (v. 1330-1444)' in *L'espace public au Moyen Âge: débats autour de Jürgen Habermas*, ed. by Patrick Boucheron and Nicolas Offenstadt (Paris: Presses Universitaires de France, 2011), p. 322. Revolt's place as a channel of political communication has become far better established in recent scholarship. Patrick Lantschner, 'Revolts and the Political Order of Cities in the Late Middle Ages', *Past and Present*, 225 (2014), pp. 4-11.

177 Paolo Viola, 'Violence révolutionnaire ou violence du peuple en révolution?' in *Recherches sur la Révolution*, ed. by M. Vovelle and A. de Baecque (Paris: La Découverte, 1991), 96; David Andress, 'Popular Violence in the French Revolution: Revolt, Retribution and the Slide to State Terror' in *Cultures of Violence: Interpersonal Violence in Historical Perspective*, ed. by Stuart Carroll (Basingstoke: Palgrave Macmillan, 2007), p. 177.

narratives became destructive forces within the community.[178] It is this phenomenon that underscores Challet's impression of radicalization: the competing accounts circulating in 1418 conjure an increasingly paranoid climate, with Parisians turning on their neighbours as they attempted to identify an ambiguous and elusive Armagnac threat to the common good.

In 1413 and 1418 the Bourgeois reported rumours that the Armagnac faction intended to destroy Paris and its inhabitants to explain the immediacy of collective action. When Charles VI returned to Paris in October 1412 in the company of Armagnac lords, the Bourgeois juxtaposed popular feeling with the faction. These lords were 'moult amez du roy et du commun qui avoit grant joie de la paix', but rumours of the Armagnacs' darker intentions had begun to circulate: 'ilz ne tendoient que a la destrucion du roy et especialment de la bonne ville de Paris et des bons habitans'.[179] The rumours employed to justify the 1418 massacres assumed a similar dynamic: 'Tant hayoient ceulx qui gouvernoient ceulx qui n'estoit de leur bande qu'ilz proposerent que par toutes les rues ilz les prendroient et tueroient sans mercy'.[180] The narratives served to divide Parisians along clear factional lines that overlapped with envisioned class dynamics, reducing Parisian political tensions to a black-and-white mentality: resist the Armagnac governors or face destruction.[181] Resurfacing notions of a threat to the common good, and to the commons themselves, enabled largely artisanal, Burgundian supporters to unite in opposition to dangers that the Armagnac faction were perceived to pose. As a result, these rumours reveal the profundity of civic divisions that characterized Parisian experiences of the civil conflict, accentuated by rhetoric that consolidated existing group divisions.

In each uprising, the Bourgeois portrayed popular action as being primarily motivated by a single rumour, enhanced by the Armagnac stereotype. The Cabochien revolt was triggered by murmurs that the upcoming marriage of Catherine d'Alençon and Louis VII, duke of Bavaria (Isabeau de Bavière's brother) would present the Armagnacs, led by Paris' *prévôt* Pierre des Essarts, with an opportunity to remove Charles VI from the capital, rendering them 'maistres de Paris, de en faire leur voulenté, qui moult estoit malvaise'.[182] In the context of Paris' resistance to Armagnac sieges in 1410 and 1411 and an outpouring of support for the Burgundian siege of Bourges in 1412, Parisian fears focused upon the possible reprisals that could result from continued Armagnac animosity, highlighting deeper concerns that the rapprochement between Charles VI and the Orléanists jeopardized Paris' own political place.[183] One of the rumour's strengths was its conflation of royal

---

178 Porter, *Popular Rumour*, p. 135.

179 Beloved of the king and the people who were overjoyed by the peace; they desired nothing more than the destruction of the king and the good city of Paris and its good inhabitants. *Journal*, p. 27.

180 Those who governed hated so much those who were not of their faction that they plotted to mercilessly capture and kill them on every street. *Journal*, fol. 43v.

181 Nicole Gonthier, *Cris de haine et rites d'unité: La violence dans les villes, XIIIeme-XVIeme siècle* (Turnhout: Brepols, 1992), pp. 22-3; Nicolas Offenstadt, 'Guerre civile et espace public à la fin du Moyen Âge. La lutte des Armagnacs et des Bourguignons' in *La politisation. Conflits et construction du politique depuis le Moyen Âge*, ed. by Philippe Hamon and Laurent Bourquin (Rennes: Presses universitaires de Rennes, 2010), pp. 111-29.

182 Masters of Paris so that they could act according to their will, which was very evil. *Journal*, p. 28.

183 Coville, *Les Cabochiens*, pp. 179-84. On the perceived relationship between Paris and Charles VI, particularly in 1413, see below, Chapter 4; on support for the siege of Bourges, see Chapter 5.

and civic political perspectives, developing a sense of mutual dependence in opposition to the Armagnacs: if the king and capital were separated, the Armagnacs would exert their authority all the more easily. The Bourgeois presented the response to these rumours as a moment that brought Parisian institutions together in the defence of the common good and Burgundian politics. The University of Paris was depicted as taking the lead, producing written lists of those implicated in the Armagnac plot that it 'fist savoir au duc de Bourgongne et au prevost des marchans', prompting the taking up of arms in the city.[184]

Where, in 1413, Charles VI was envisioned as the target of Armagnac machinations, in 1418 the Bourgeois portrayed Armagnac governors as plotting the annihilation of the city's Burgundian partisans. Before Burgundian forces could enter the city, these governors planned to go through the streets, murdering suspected Burgundian adherents and drowning their wives in sacks made from cloth requisitioned from the city's merchants under the pretence of creating royal pavilions; those who were meant to be spared from the massacre were to be identified by black tokens with a red cross disseminated throughout the city. Once the Burgundian elements within Paris had been suppressed, the capital would then be delivered to Henry V of England, with whom the Armagnacs had secretly concluded an alliance.[185]

In 1418, rumours like these performed two functions. First, as in 1413, they reinforced the boundaries between Armagnac and Burgundian communities within the capital, compelling Parisians to declare their loyalties when faced with the threat of destruction. Second, detailed descriptions of the violent acts proposed by the Armagnacs retrospectively legitimated the violent Parisian behaviours that followed the Burgundian entry, which the Bourgeois described in the same passage. This latter aspect was accentuated by the rumour's snowballing, accompanied by the levelling and sharpening of key details. These included the Armagnac-English agreement to deliver Paris, as well as the belief that tokens had been secretly circulated among Armagnac supporters. Most importantly, just as the rumoured Armagnac violence retrospectively rationalized the realities of anti-Armagnac massacres in 1418, the news that Armagnac governors intended to betray Paris to the English justified the city's *actual* betrayal to Jean sans Peur. In recording and transmitting these notions, the Bourgeois inverted a narrative that had a longer history. Already in 1417, the *Journal* reveals that Armagnac propagandists had used sermons to accuse Jean sans Peur of concluding an alliance with the English, asserting that 'il voulloit estre roy de France, et que par lui [...] estoient les Engloys en Normendie'.[186] The Burgundian entry witnessed the reversal of these ideas of betrayal. Demonstrating His favour for the Burgundian faction, God had awakened Fortune, 'et donna hardement a aucuns de Paris de faire assavoir aux Bourguignons que ilz, tout hardiement, venissent [...] et ilz les mettroient dedens Paris par la porte Sainct-Germain'.[187] Explaining a sudden Parisian intervention in royal politics, the Bourgeois' enumeration of these rumours highlights efforts to rationalize dramatic shifts in

---

184 *Journal*, pp. 28-9.
185 *Journal*, p. 87.
186 He wanted to be king of France, and that because of him [...] the English were in Normandy. *Journal*, p. 79.
187 And gave such confidence to some Parisians that they informed the Burgundians that they should come boldly [...] and they would let them into Paris through the porte Saint-Germain. *Journal*, pp. 87-88.

the political *status quo*, emphasizing the immediate threat posed by the Armagnac faction and demonstrating a strategic exploitation of predominant anxieties.

Once the Burgundians were inside the city, these rumours fuelled persecution as Burgundian soldiers and their Parisian supporters searched for evidence that confirmed suspicions of Armagnac treachery. It is here that the idea of Armagnac tokens became potent, with the Bourgeois reporting that they had produced sixteen thousand, 'qui depuis furent trouvées en leurs maisons'.[188] Again, these tokens satisfied two rhetorical demands. First and foremost, they satisfied an immediate identificatory need, reflecting the real difficulties inherent in detecting Armagnac supporters due to a lack of distinctive physical, linguistic or cultural traits. Evidencing pervasive paranoia following the years during which Parisians had been compelled to publicly identify themselves as Armagnacs by wearing their sash, the tokens substantiated the 'Armagnac' character of those imprisoned or murdered. Second, the drive to find these tokens and uncover the secret associations that they denoted justified the transgressive ransacking of Armagnac houses, unveiling their hidden 'tresors' and legitimating their pillage in the process.[189] Such searches were vital in a context where many Armagnac governors had been driven into hiding immediately after the Burgundian entry. These included Bernard, count of Armagnac himself, who – according to Burgundian reports – was later found in a cellar disguised 'en tres petit et pauvre habit, portant la croix saint Andry', the symbol of the Burgundians, to disguise his real status.[190] The alleged discovery of these tokens – and their detailed description – simultaneously justified popular transgressions and stimulated belief in the Armagnac threat to Paris.

The tokens illustrate the increasingly detailed character of anti-Armagnac rumours, conflated with English symbolism through levelling and sharpening. The Bourgeois first described the tokens as 'ung escu noir a une croix rouge', with this imagery perhaps sufficient to conjure impressions of an Armagnac adoption of St. George's cross.[191] However, when they were described again in July, the tokens' appearance clearly underscored the conflation of Armagnac and English identities.

---

188 Which were subsequently found in their houses. *Journal*, p. 88.

189 *Journal*, p. 89.

190 In very poor clothing, wearing the St. Andrew saltire. 'Les journées parisiennes de mai-juin 1418: d'après des documents des archives de la couronne d'Aragon', ed. by J. Vielliard and Aznar Pardo de la Casta, *Bulletin de la Société de l'histoire de France*, 76 (1940), p. 132; Cordeliers, pp. 255-56.

191 A black coat of arms with a red cross. *Journal*, p. 87. Henry V's early ventures into Normandy had emphasized the symbolism associated with St. George without reference to his French throne; contemporary military ordinances demanded that English soldiers bear St George's arms. Neil Murphy, 'Ceremony and Conflict in Fifteenth-Century France: Lancastrian Ceremonial Entries into French Towns, 1415-31', *Explorations in Renaissance Culture*, 39 (2013), p. 116; Anne Curry, 'The Military Ordinances of Henry V: Texts and Contexts', in *War, Government and Aristocracy in the British Isles, c. 1150-1500*, ed. by Christopher Given-Wilson, Ann Kettle and Len Scales (Woodbridge: Boydell and Brewer, 2008), p. 244.

> Estoit la monnoye telle: ung pou plus grant que ung blanc de iiij deniers parisis, en la
> pille ung escu a deux lieppars, l'un sur l'autre, et une estoille sur l'escu; en la croix, a ung
> des quingnez, une estoille, a chacun bout de la croix, une couronne.[192]

The descriptions spoke to numerous symbols at play in the context of the English invasion
of Normandy in 1417. While the leopard may have appeared intuitively 'English', the two
superposed heraldic examples might have evoked Henry V's claims to the Norman duchy,
having adopted the title as early as December 1417 upon the surrender of Falaise, a move
consistent with his appeals to Norman separatism.[193] Moreover, the plausibility of such
tokens' existence underscored the rumour's effectiveness, especially given the circulation of
similar Burgundian and French badges, discovered in the Seine in the nineteenth century,
that designated supporters of Charles VI, Isabeau de Bavière and Jean sans Peur.[194] The
token envisioned by the Bourgeois certainly bears some resemblance to the English gold
noble (a model for later tokens found in the Seine), which depicted a cross on the reverse
divided by four crowns.[195] These coins were circulating in Paris in 1418, as demonstrated
by the pardon issued to Colin de Sales, who had robbed the *changeur* Pierre Marade in
the Hôtel de Ville, 'ou il avoit prist [...] xviij nobles d'Engleterre et des demis-nobles ne
scet point le nombre'.[196] The more detailed account in July, therefore, suggests that the
Bourgeois' vision had accrued specific characteristics tying Armagnac tokens with possible
symbols of English conquest, thereby presenting an almost tangible proof of Armagnac
treachery.

The snowballing effects of rumour could also be applied to formerly neutral symbols
that emerged as catalysts for commentary regarding good government and political action.
The idea that banners had been prepared to welcome the English occupied a central place
in this rhetoric. During the massacres on 12 June, the Bourgeois depicted the rioting
Parisians as exclaiming that the Armagnacs '"ont fait faire estandars pour le roy d'Engleterre
[...] pour mettre sur les portes de Paris, quant ilz l'auront livré aux Englois"'.[197] Like the
Armagnac tokens, such claims were portrayed as being substantiated through the discovery
of hidden evidence. When the Hôtel de Bourbon was sacked during the riots in August,
the commons found within 'une grant baniere comme estandart, ou il avoit ung dragon
figuré qui par la gueule gectoit geu et sang'.[198] Both the Bourgeois and the anonymous
author of the *Chronique des Cordeliers* depicted the commons interpretating the banner as

---

192 And the money was like this: a little larger than a *blanc* of four *deniers parisis*; on the obverse was a shield with two
leopards, one superposed upon the other and a star upon the shield; on the reverse in one of the corners was a star, and a
crown at every point of the cross. *Journal*, p. 103.

193 Christopher Allmand, *Henry V* (London: Methuen, 1992), pp. 186-87; Christopher Allmand, *Lancastrian Normandy,
1415-50: The History of a Medieval Occupation* (Oxford: Clarendon Press, 1983), pp. 122-26.

194 Emily Hutchison, 'Partisan identity in the French civil war, 1405-18: reconsidering the evidence on livery badges',
Journal of Medieval History, 33 (2007), pp. 269-70; Denis Bruna, *Enseignes de pèlerinage et enseignes profanes* (Paris:
Réunion des musées nationaux, 1996), pp. 279-86.

195 Arthur Forgeais, *Collection de plombs historiés trouves dans la Seine*, vol. 3 (Paris: Aubry, 1864), pp. 190-94.

196 Where he had taken [...] eighteen English nobles and he does not know how many half-nobles. Paris, Archives
nationales, JJ 170, fols 93v-94r.

197 'they have made banners for the king of England [...] to place upon Paris' gates when they will have delivered it to the
English!' *Journal*, p. 97.

198 A large banner like a standard, upon which there was a dragon spewing fire and blood from its mouth. *Journal*, p. 110.

further evidence of an Armagnac-English alliance. Each account described how the banner was brandished as proof of the continued presence of subversive Armagnac forces within Paris. First, the rioters processed through the streets with the banner, crying "'Veez-cy la baniere que le roy d'Angleterre avoit envoiée aux faulx Arminalx, en signifiance de la mort dont ilz nous devoient faire mourir".'[199] After the banner had been 'partout monstré', it was brought before Jean sans Peur, 'en lui disant, "encores y avoit-il des Armignas a Paris" before the rioters tore it before them and affixed fragments to their weapons'.[200] The symbolism attributed to the banner redefined the boundaries between Parisian-Burgundian ingroup and Armagnac-English outsider, but also reinforced Parisian agency in urban politics precisely as these 'radicalized' elements defied Jean sans Peur's efforts to restore order. Once the duke had seen the banner from his window, the chroniclers implied that the rumours had been confirmed and, in doing so, accorded the rioters important degrees of agency and legitimacy in their perpetration of massacres that escaped ducal control.

This symbolic confrontation encapsulated the growing tensions between Burgundian prerogatives and Parisian anxieties that framed the second series of massacres on 21 August 1418, giving voice to the deeper problems of falling living standards due to continuous conflict. In this instance, the combination of rumour and violent action reveals the multivalent ways in which the riots facilitated a popular condemnation of the Armagnac faction alongside a more nuanced critique of Burgundian justice – or the lack thereof. When the Parisian commons assaulted the Châtelet, the Bourgeois rationalized the ensuing violence by recounting popular frustrations:

> Car trop souffroit le peuple de griefz par eulx [the Armagnacs], car riens ne povoit venir à Paris qui ne fust ranconné deux foys plus qu'il ne valloit, et toutes nuys guet de feu, de lanternes en my les rues, aux portes, faire gens d'armes et riens gaigner, et tout cher plus que de raison.[201]

Indeed, a royal edict issued on 4 September 1418 regarding the watch indicates the scale of popular discontent with measures introduced for Paris' security: 'nous avons entendu plusieurs bourgois, manans et habitans […] ont esté et sont contredisans, reffusans et se veulent exempter de aller aux guez', with the letter reminding the municipality that 'toutes manieres de gens', officers and clergymen included, were required to participate.[202] Popular experiences of poverty were contrasted with an enduring impression of aristocratic wealth and bureaucratic corruption, and the Bourgeois' narrative reveals the power of the medieval moral economy as a source of criticism, underscoring the ways in which market grievances were tied to understandings of community harmony and the function of govern-

---

199 Look, here is the banner that the king of England had sent to the false Armagnacs as a sign of the death that they would exact upon us. *Journal*, p. 110.

200 Telling him that 'there were still Armagnacs in Paris'. *Cordeliers*, p. 262.

201 The people suffered greatly because of them, because nothing could reach Paris without being ransomed for twice its value, and every night watches had to be kept with fires, lanterns in the streets, at the gates, providing for soldiers and earning nothing, and everything excessively expensive. *Journal*, p. 107.

202 We have heard that several bourgeois, residents and inhabitants […] have been and are objecting, refusing and wish to exempt themselves from the watch. Paris, Archives nationales, KK 950A, no. 25.

ment in preserving norms and obligations.[203] In the account of the 21 August massacres, Parisian complaints regarding provisions and defensive obligations were intertwined with the perceived injustices upheld by Jean sans Peur. Gathering before the Bastille, the commons refused to be abated until they were shown the prisoners within, spurred by rumours that 'ceulx que on mectoit oudit chasteau estoient tousjours delivrez par argent, et les boutoit on par les champs, et faisoient plus de maulx que devant', asserting that aristocratic complicity enabled Armagnacs to continue posing a threat to Paris' security and, by extension, demanding the devolution of justice.[204]

Judging by its emergence in the pardon granted to Pierre Denis of Senlis in March 1420, this logic connecting the Armagnac threat to prevalent injustices was widespread in Burgundian-occupied towns. In his remission letter, Denis confessed to having participated in the murder of Armagnac prisoners because 'tous autres prisonniers Armignacs que l'en prenoit et amenoit l'en en ladite ville de Senliz estoient delivrés en paiant finance aux gens d'armes [...] et que tant feussent mauvais nul n'en recevoit mort'.[205] In Paris, this same moral economy conditioned tensions between Jean sans Peur and the commons. While the duke attempted to appease the crowd 'par doulces parolles', the Bourgeois signalled the crowd's tenacity as evidence of the injustice's truth; when Jean sans Peur 'bien veoit qu'ilz disoient verité', he assented to deliver the prisoners to the crowd under the condition that they be imprisoned – under their own guard – in the Grand Châtelet.[206] In the event, the Parisians murdered the prisoners once they had been escorted from the Bastille. With this passage immediately followed by the account of the 'English' banner's discovery, the *Journal* reveals how the rhetoric of rumour was contrived to substantiate the common's authority to exact justice upon Paris' enemies, even in the face of Burgundian power. It was for this reason that both the Bourgeois and Cordelier indulged the banner's ritualistic demonstration as proof, reinforcing popular legitimacy in direct contrast to Jean sans Peur's power and enabling the rioters to go 'de rue en rue parfaire leur journée, tuant et dépéchant tous ceulx que on disoit estre Armignas, eussent la croix Saint Andrieu ou non'.[207]

E.P. Thompson's notion of the crowd's moral economy and rumour's role in rationalizing revolt illustrates the ways in which crowd action was instilled with purpose, according its members extensive degrees of agency. In this process, rumours performed an emotional and cohesive function, bringing to the fore shared fears and providing a medium for the

---

203 E.P. Thompson, 'The Moral Economy of the English Crowd in the Eighteenth Century', *Past and Present*, 50 (1971), pp. 78-9. In addressing ducal failures to protect the city and common good, the Bourgeois echoed earlier chronicle accounts of popular revolt, particularly those tracing the Jacquerie. Justine Firnhaber-Baker, 'The eponymous Jacquerie: making revolt mean some things' in *The Routledge Handbook of Medieval Revolt*, ed. by Justine Firnhaber-Baker and Dirk Schoenaers (London: Routledge, 2017), p. 67; Justine Firnhaber-Baker, 'Two Kinds of Freedom: Language and Practice in Late Medieval Rural Revolts', *Edad Media. Revista de Historia*, 21 (2020), p. 132.

204 Those incarcerated within the castle were always freed with money, and were released into the country and then performed more evils than before. *Journal*, p. 108.

205 All of the other Armagnac prisoners that were captured and brought to the town of Senlis were freed by paying a ransom to the men-at-arms [...] and no matter how evil they were, none received death. Paris, Archives nationales JJ 171, fols 57r-v.

206 With gentle words; saw well that they spoke the truth. *Journal*, p. 108.

207 From street to street to complete their day's work, killing and butchering all of those who were said to be Armagnacs, whether they had the St. Andrew's cross or not. Cordeliers, p. 263.

expression of collective anger throughout opinion communities. This was a Durkheimian 'collective effervescence', resulting from physical assembly in space and a shared focus for diverse and multivalent attentions. This focus became mutual precisely as Parisians shared in the circulation of rumour, the performance of gestures or chanting, thereby defining the moral terms of collective action and consolidating their solidarity.[208] The familiarity of the narratives in which Parisians shared political anxieties, their repetition and their increasing specificity over time also point to rumours place in the broader complex of rites that endowed violence with legitimacy and meaning.[209] Rumours accentuate the moral component of crowd behaviour, underpinning collective action in the crucible of a normative crisis. Emotionally bounded collective action accords participants an agency in political events that becomes the foundation for further action, determined by collective loyalties enhanced by participation in the circulation of rumours and conspiracy theories.[210] These groups are strengthened by the 'reciprocal emotions' that rumour evokes, while experiences of fear and anxiety 'can be a strong force in creating a sense of collectivity and an attractive force in collective actions'.[211]

Historical interpretations of crowd behaviour are conditioned by the character and number of the surviving sources, their function and their authors' inherent socio-political goals. By relating rumour, the Bourgeois delineated distinct emotional communities within Paris, captured by the juxtaposition of the emotional crowd with calm, reasoned civic officials on 12 June or Jean sans Peur on 21 August.[212] In particular, rumour's emotional character enabled the Bourgeois to ground the commons' motivations in familiar, quasi-ritualized tropes, evoking and evolving into the slogans and programmes that captured Parisian assertions of political agency.[213] In his allegorical description of the massacres, Ire and Forcenerie were portrayed as speaking 'par la bouche du peuple', listing anti-Armagnac rumours:

> "'Aussi ont-ilz fait sacs pour nous noyer et noz femmes et noz enffens, et ont fait faire estandars pour le roy d'Engleterre [...] Item, ilz ont fait escussons a une rouge croix

---

208 Émile Durkheim, *The Elementary Forms of Religious Life*, trans. by Carol Colman (Oxford: Oxford University Press, 2001), pp. 157-59, 283-85; Randall Collins, 'Social Movements and the Focus of Emotional Attention' in *Passionate Politics: Emotions and Social Movements*, ed. by Jeff Goodwin, James M. Jaspers and Francesca Polletta (London: University of Chicago Press, 2001), pp. 27-32.

209 Following Natalie Zemon Davis, 'The Rites of Violence: Religious Riot in Sixteenth-Century France', *Past and Present*, 59 (1973), pp. 51-91.

210 James M. Jasper, 'Emotions and Social Movements: Twenty Years of Theory and Research', *Annual Review of Sociology*, 37 (2011), p. 292.

211 James M. Jasper, 'The Emotions of Protest: Affective and Reactive Emotions in and around Social Movements', *Sociological Forum*, 13 (1998), pp. 417-21; Jan Dumolyn and Élodie Lecuppre-Desjardin, 'Propagande et sensibilité: la fibre émotionnelle au cœur des luttes politiques et sociales dans les villes des anciens Pays-Bas bourguignons. L'exemple de la révolte brugeoise de 1436-38' in *Emotions in the Heart of the City (14th-16th century)*, ed. by Elodie Lecuppre-Desjardin and Anne-Laure Van Bruaene (Turnhout: Brepols, 2005), p. 51; Ron Eyerman, 'How Social Movements Move: Emotions and Social Movements' in *Emotions and Social Movements*, ed. by Helena Flam and Debra King (London: Routledge, 2005), p. 43.

212 On the intersection of emotional and opinion communities see Chapter 2.

213 Cazaux, 'Les fonctions politiques de la foule', pp. 66-9. For an early modern comparison see William Beik, 'The Violence of the French Crowd from Charivari to Revolution', *Past and Present*, 197 (November 2007), p. 77; Suzanne Desan, 'Crowds, Community and Ritual in the Work of E.P. Thompson and Natalie Davis' in *The New Cultural History*, ed. by Lynn Hunt (Los Angeles, CA: University of California Press, 1989), pp. 56-70.

plus de xxx milliers, dont ilz avoient proposé de seigner les huys de ceulx qui devoient estre tuez ou non. Si ne nous en parler plus de par le diable!'"[214]

A force for popular critique, these rumours enabled the crowd to challenge the 'Pitié, Justice et Raison' stressed by the *prévôt* Guy de Bar in his attempts to appease the crowd.[215] Through his emphasis upon the rumours underpinning the rioters' violence, the Bourgeois established the crowd's logic, implying an aggregation of individuals with their own reasons for action, rather than some disembodied abstraction endeavouring to perform meaning-less destruction.[216] Moreover, the recourse to allegory evidences the heightened discursive means employed by the Bourgeois to explain and describe the events that took place evoking his own strength of feeling – as Bernard Rimé has argued, traumatic or catastrophic experiences provoke an important sense of disharmony between the individual and his (ideological) conception of the world, where existing paradigms 'ne suffit plus à absorber l'expérience'.[217] In this destabilization, the Bourgeois resorted to new and more abstract paradigms to account for Parisian behaviour.

The Bourgeois' treatment of rumour in 1413 and 1418 also sheds light on the prevalent role assumed by conspiracy theories and the ways in which they underpinned collective emotional experiences, justifying the popular seizure of authority.[218] Michael Barkun has suggested that conspiracy theories represent 'des modes de penser, voire des modèles imposés au monde pour donner à des événements un semblant de logique', encapsulating 'des visions alternatives ou déviantes' often incompatible with official narratives.[219] This is partly due to the collective formulation of conspiracy theories themselves, structuring boundaries between in-group and perceived external threat, with these theories taking root within groups that feel inherently powerless and insecure. Once assumed, conspiracy theo-ries become integral to identification and difficult to counter through other informational sources, reinforcing related beliefs, as demonstrated by rumour's capacity to snowball.[220] Rumours of plots to remove the king from Paris or massacre Burgundian sympathisers promoted negative integration through which fear engendered solidarity and collective

---

214 By the mouth of the people; 'Also they have made sacks to drown us and our wives and children, and they have made standards for the king of England [...] Item, they have made more than thirty thousand badges with a red cross, which they plotted to affix to the doorways of those who should be killed or spared. So, for the devil's sake do not speak to us any more of it!' *Journal*, p. 97.

215 *Journal*, p. 97.

216 K.J. Kesselring, 'Deference and Dissent in Tudor England: Reflections on Sixteenth-Century Protest', *History Compass*, 3 (2005), p. 2.

217 Bernard Rimé, 'Les émotions médiévales. Réflexions psychologiques' in *Politique des émotions au Moyen Âge*, ed. by Damien Bouquet and Piroska Nagy (Florence: SISMEL, 2010), p. 327.

218 An epistemological framework for the analysis of medieval conspiracy theories is currently lacking, with only recent research beginning to examine these issues. See Cornel Zwierlein, 'Conspiracy theories in the Middle Ages and the Early Modern Period' in *The Routledge Handbook of Conspiracy Theories*, ed. by Michael Butter and Peter Knight (London: Routledge, 2020), pp. 542-54.

219 Ways of thinking, even models imposed upon the world to give elements a sense of logic; alternative and deviant visions. Michael Barkun, 'Les théories du complot comme connaissance stigmatisée', trans. by Brigitte Rollet, *Diogène*, 249-50 (2015), p. 168.

220 Michael Butter and Peter Knight, 'Combler le fossé. L'avenir des recherches sur les théories du complot', trans. Nicole G. Albert, *Diogène*, 249-50 (2015), 25.

action, heightening the notion of a normative threat posed by the 'bandez' that generated solidarity among Jean sans Peur's Parisian supporters.

These conspiracy theories, simultaneously eliciting and underpinned by rumour, made the normative threat to morality, societal stability and Parisian security appear real. Moreover, rumour's ability to permeate ordinary discursive interactions promoted an increasing sense of the threat's ubiquity, with the idea that the enemy was 'either circling without or drawing ever closer or, more worryingly still, hidden within', inducing a sense of constant, other-directed anxiety.[221] As a result, the discovery of the banner in the Hôtel de Bourbon, an anodyne symbol in normal circumstances, was accorded meaning consonant with underlying conspiracies, presented by the rioters as evidence of an envisioned alliance between the Armagnacs and the English.[222] Likewise, the rumoured discovery of hidden tokens similar to badges known to have existed reinforced the impression that unidentified conspirators were ubiquitous throughout the civic community. This sense of a hidden threat subsequently found its expression in the repeated proofs provided by the Bourgeois through the increasingly detailed descriptions of tokens and symbols found in Armagnac houses.

These same conspiracies were deployed by the Bourgeois to question the legitimacy of the Armagnac governance of Paris, pointing simultaneously to the exploitation of finance by officials and plots organized through municipal government. Retrospectively justifying the Burgundian coup, the *Journal* elaborated a plot whereby the Armagnac authorities had requisitioned cloth from merchants ostensibly to manufacture pavilions for the king, 'et c'estoit pour faire les sacs pour noyer lesdites femmes'.[223] When the rioters took to the streets and demanded the Armagnac prisoners, the Bourgeois portrayed them as shouting fears of this same plot.[224] Similarly, the *Journal* presented public executions as a vital means of confirming these conspiracies by reporting the testimony and confessions of the condemned, channelling popular feeling and publicly codifying widespread rumours. Pierre Boudaut, a Châtelet sergeant executed on 20 June, confessed that he had been 'a l'estroit conseil des bandez, et avoit eu commission de par le prevost et les autres […] de faire tuer tout le quartier des Halles', stressing the immediate danger that the Armagnac regime had posed to the Bourgeois' own neighbourhood and audience.[225] A week later, the wealthy draper and former *échevin* for 1415-16, Guillaume d'Auxerre, 'congnut tant de traisons contre le roy et son royaulme que lui et ceulx de ladite bande avoient machinées, et fait aliance aux Englois que fort seroit a croire'.[226] The Bourgeois emphasized the municipal status and political connections to the Armagnacs of each of the accused to legitimate their intimate knowledge of the alleged plots threatening Paris, and this knowledge was

---

221 Porter, *Popular Rumour*, p. 19.

222 Colette Beaune suggested that the banner 'peut s'agir d'une ancienne devise de la maison de Bourbon utilisée pour une fête' (Might have been an older symbol for the Bourbon house used for festivities). Colette Beaune (ed. and trans.), *Journal d'un bourgeois de Paris* (Paris: Librairie Générale Française, 1990), p. 128, n. 181.

223 And it was to make sacks with which to drown the said women. *Journal*, p. 87.

224 Also they have made sacks to drown us and our wives and children. *Journal.*, p. 97.

225 In the close counsel of the *bandez*, and had received orders from the *prévôt* and others […] to have the entirety of the Halles *quartier* killed. *Journal.* pp. 99-100. On the Halles, see above, Chapter 1.

226 Admitted such treasons against the king and kingdom that he and those of the said *bande* and planned, and had concluded an alliance with the English, that it would be hard to believe. *Journal*, pp. 100-01.

substantiated by their implication of other officers, namely the *échevin* Simonnet Taranne and a *sergent*, 'Monmelian'. These accusations pointed to the ubiquitous character of the threat posed by the Armagnacs by evoking past crimes – Monmelian had been responsible for beheading 'le sieur de l'Ours de la porte Baudet', the royal *sergent d'armes* Jean Roche who had been identified as a ringleader of the 1416 conspiracy – while incriminating those who had escaped the city with the Dauphin Charles, such as Taranne, undermining the Dauphin's own legitimacy by pointing to his continued association with traitors.[227] As in the execution of the former *prévôt* Pierre des Essarts at the height of the Cabochien revolt in July 1413, the detailed account of these exactions was designed to legitimate the popular unrest taking place in 1418, retrospectively justifying the popular seizure of power stemming from Burgundian factions within the city.

Rumours defining the boundaries between Armagnac and Parisian by presenting the former as an existential threat to the latter were integral to the Bourgeois' explanation of and justification for Parisian uprisings. In the *Journal*, manifestations of public resistance coincided with the retrospective enumeration of rumours that concurrently shed light upon the Parisian anxieties that the Bourgeois considered to legitimately motivate the revolt, be they fears of Charles VI's abduction in 1413 or the threat of annihilation by the Armagnacs in 1418, and functioned as an essential medium for rallying Burgundian partisans. Since those participating in these revolts were typically described by chroniclers as belonging to the lower orders of Parisian society, the 'populares', 'menu peuple', 'commun' or 'gens de petit estat', the rumours they shared were manipulated by the Bourgeois to provide an essential basis to their seizure of authority in a manner that inverted the discourse of elite chroniclers such as Pintoin who stressed their madness, fury and disorganization.[228] Moreover, in 1418, there is clear evidence that the anti-Armagnac stereotype that had been gradually developing since 1410 snowballed, evidencing much more serious fears. In part, the gravity of the rumours reported by the Bourgeois in 1418 matched the altered circumstances of the revolt when compared with 1413. Five years earlier, the commons had risen within the context of grievances and reforms proposed by the University of Paris and generally endorsed by the Estates General; in 1418, the Burgundian entry provoked violence that required more immediate justification. From an originally vague description in the Bourgeois' first entry, this rumour accrued greater detail before emerging as a clear symbol based upon real examples of coins that not only symbolized Armagnac duplicity, but demonstrated a conflation of Armagnac and English identities. Consequently, the Bourgeois' description of rumours during 1413 and 1418 demonstrates their importance for the consideration and manipulation of popular movements within a fifteenth-century historical narrative. Crucially, the legitimating aspect of these rumours demonstrated that

---

227 Monmelian has not been identified. The 'sieur de l'Ours de la Porte Baudet' executed in 1416 was a royal *sergent d'armes* dedicated to Jean sans Peur, Jean Roche. Paris, Archives nationales, JJ 172, fols 246v-248r. Simon Taranne's escape from Paris is demonstrated by the letters ordering the confiscation of his property. Paris, Archives nationales, JJ 173, fols 102v-103r, 270r-270v.

228 On this juxtaposition, see Chapter 2. For depictions of the 1418 rioters, see RSD, VI, pp. 230, 244; Cordeliers, p. 263; Fauquembergue, I, p. 148.

Parisian anger was not unthinking but, on the contrary, as the killings were repeated, they came to the fore in the *Journal* as clear evidence of the commons' right to seize power in Paris.

Conclusion

Describing the prevalence of rumour in the *Journal*, Colette Beaune remarked that the 'Bourgeois est le seul de sa génération à s'être intéressé au témoignage oral. Il est sans cesse en quête des rumeurs et murmures. La rumeur est omniprésente dans son œuvre'.[229] Rumour's predominance in the *Journal* was a direct consequence of the character of fifteenth-century urban interaction, particularly during the Armagnac-Burgundian conflict, with its relation enabling the Bourgeois to trace political contest. His writing sheds light upon two distinct elements of rumour's function in late medieval urban society. Participation in the expression and development of rumour accorded Parisians agency in political events, developing their own narratives that contested official records and reinforced their own political views. Rumour also played a vital cathartic role. Through its circulation, Parisians shared emotional experiences that bound members of the civic community in contrast to perceived and real threats without and, sometimes, within their groups. As a consequence of rumour's function as an implicit medium of political participation and its exclusionary character, reinforcing group and community boundaries, the Bourgeois drew upon existing, archetypal narratives to rationalize Parisian political stances, blurring previously neat historiographical and conceptual boundaries that have distinguished official information, propaganda and rumour. In this light, popular speech, rumours and propaganda were fluid and intersecting, used by commentators and officials alike to define the parameters during the political turbulence of the fifteenth century. The Bourgeois was especially invested in the development and accentuation of an Armagnac stereotype that conflated the political faction with violent, anti-Christian and amoral tendencies as a means of justifying continued Parisian opposition. Similarly, the centrality of rumour and conspiracy to the popular uprisings of 1413 and 1418 indicate how rumours were incorporated into the *Journal* and employed by Parisians themselves as a means of contesting official authority, redefining the community's boundaries and legitimating the popular arrogation of power.

Finally, the prevalence of rumour and the reporting of popular speech in the *Journal* parallels the absence of explicit references to written texts or official documentation assessed in the previous chapter. Primarily, the Bourgeois was not concerned by the factual content of speech itself, but rather the nature of what was said and who said it. Through this focus, the Bourgeois fundamentally accorded agency and power to public opinion in an era that had seen the leaders of competing factions become increasingly sensitive to the importance of securing Parisian support to maintain their political advantages. The focus upon more popular agencies also represented an important historiographical shift, with attention turning from the actions of society's elite to examining more closely

---

229 Is the only person of his generation to have been interested in oral testimony. He was forever in search of rumours and murmurs. Rumour is omnipresent in his writing. Beaune (ed. and trans.), *Journal*, pp. 14-15.

how Parisians considered elite behaviour. This consideration undermines the neat scholarly boundaries that have been established between official news and unofficial rumour, between the confirmed/unverified and the true/false. By according rumour a pivotal role in the *Journal*, the Bourgeois consolidated opinion's significance in the evaluation of official action or information. These processes were also important for the manifestation of a collective Parisian identity. Ultimately, it was through writing that the Bourgeois codified and translated a seemingly 'unofficial' and disruptive discourse into the very 'official' fabric, social memory and identity of the city and its inhabitants.

CHAPTER 4

Public Space and Political Contest

Places and contexts were crucial to effective communication in late medieval cities and Paris was exemplary in this regard, as a site for the intense circulation of information. Urban space had a heterogeneous character, 'imbued with quantities and qualities marking the presence of bodies, signs and thoughts'.[1] Control over the direction of bodies, symbols and ideas in space represented a potent expression of power, but spaces had historical and cultural connotations that meant that communities could also use them – and organize themselves within them – in diverse and politically meaningful ways.[2] Historiographical approaches to space typically take Henri Lefebvre's ideas as their foundation, adapting his tripartite interpretation of space comprising *spatial practice*, *representations of space* and *representational spaces* encapsulating social, physical and mental dimensions.[3] Beyond a straightforward physical dimension, Lefebvre's conceptual triad envisions space as socially produced, culturally lived and subjectively imagined. It is precisely this representational aspect that the present chapter will explore through the *Journal*, revealing how spaces emerged as realms of contest that 'the imagination seeks to change and appropriate', enacted through a 'more-or-less coherent system of non-verbal symbols and signs' that found their expression in the Bourgeois' writing.[4] Here, we find that while the ritualized and prescribed character of official communication – through clothing, sound and spatial distinction – substantially altered space, the Bourgeois also regularly pointed to ways in which Parisians appropriated these means to articulate their own conception of the civic community.[5] The approach complements recent scholarship that has stressed the dangers

---

1 Barbara Hanawalt and Michal Kobialka, 'Introduction' in *Medieval Practices of Space*, ed. by Barbara Hanawalt and Michal Kobialka (University of Minnesota Press, 2000) p. xi.

2 This has been demonstrated recently by Emily Hutchison, 'Knowing One's Place: Space, Violence and Legitimacy in Early Fifteenth-Century Paris', *The Medieval History Journal*, 20 (2017), pp. 1-51. The scholarship on the relationship between authority and space in the Middle Ages is extensive. For examples, see Peter Arnade, Martha Howell and Walter Simons, 'Fertile Spaces: The Productivity of Urban Space in Northern Europe', *The Journal of Interdisciplinary History*, 35 (2002), pp. 515-48; Christian Liddy, *Contesting the City: The Politics of Citizenship in English Towns, 1250-1530* (Oxford: Oxford University Press, 2017), pp. 57-66; Tom Johnson, *Law in Common: Legal Cultures in Late-Medieval England* (Oxford: Oxford University Press, 2020), pp. 55-85.

3 Henri Lefebvre, *The Production of Space*, trans. by Donald Nicholson-Smith (Oxford: Blackwell, 1991). The triad has been addressed in recent medieval studies, including Liddy, *Contesting the City*; Megan Cassidy-Welch, 'Space and Place in Medieval Contexts', *Parergon* 27 (2010), pp. 1-12; Meredith Cohen, Fanny Madeline and Dominique Iogna-Prat, 'Introduction', *Space in the Medieval West: Places, Territories and Imagined Geographies*, ed. by Meredith Cohen and Fanny Madeleine (Farnham: Ashgate, 2014), pp. 6-9.

4 Lefebvre, *The Production of Space*, p. 39.

5 See Veronika Novák, 'Places of Power: The Spreading of Official Information and the Social Uses of Space in Fifteenth-Century Paris' in *Towns and Communication*, vol. 1, ed. by Neven Budak, Finn-Einar Eliassen and Katalin Szende (Akron, OH: University of Akron Press, 2011), pp. 47-66; Veronika Novák, 'L'espace du cri à Paris aux XIVᵉ-XVIᵉ siècles: recherches sur les 'lieux accoutumés', *Revue historique*, 696 (2020), pp. 61-86.

of conflating notions of the 'public sphere' with physical spaces, inviting an awareness of the relationship between the abstract 'space' of opinion and the places in which this is structured and developed. Societies concurrently delineate mental, physical and social spaces imbued with symbolic significance, underscoring their representational meaning at specific moments, especially in instances of official communication.

As Veronika Novák and Emily Hutchison have shown, official communication and the authority upon which its acceptance relied were bound to understandings of public space used in a formalized manner by officials.[6] The *Journal* evidences how these public spaces were multiform, encapsulated heterogeneous functions and were rather more porous than authorities may have wished.[7] While assemblies in public spaces such as marketplaces or squares maximized the public reception of official messages, they also substantially increased the dangers of dissent and subversive behaviour.[8] In this respect, the *Journal* indicates the extent to which public spaces were perceived as the arenas of contest and negotiation, rather than simply forums for the unilateral communication of political information.[9] Building upon this interconnection, Carole Symes has demonstrated how medieval actors appropriated public space to assert their authority.[10] Likewise, Peter Arnade, Martha Howell and Walter Simons have argued that medieval urban representations of space were mapped through physical structures encompassing jurisdictions.[11] Moving beyond anachronistic interpretations of space that have modelled a strict public-private divide, an examination of the *Journal* suggests that the 'public' was defined primarily by the authority to communicate ideological and political information in given spaces as a process underscoring authority. In short, publicity was an – if not the – fundamental element for the assertion of power in the late medieval city.

Fifteenth-century Parisians certainly had an awareness of specifically *public* or official spaces. In one of the key moments of the city's reorganization during the Armagnac-Burgundian conflict, the royal edict ordering the destruction of the Grande Boucherie in 1416 (inherently motivated by the corporation's pro-Burgundian stance) was framed in these terms, with the accusation that the butchers' insalubrities 'ne sont a tolérer ne a souffrir es lieux si publics, comme de ladite place en laquelle afflue communément grand

---

6 Novák, 'Places of Power', p. 52; Hutchison, 'Knowing One's Place', pp. 43-5, 49-54, 60-74.

7 A phenomenon similarly demonstrated in Carol Symes, 'Out in the Open in Arras: Sightlines, Soundscapes and the Shaping of a Medieval Public Sphere' in *Cities, Texts and Social Networks, 400-1500: Experiences and Perceptions of Medieval Urban Space*, ed. by Caroline Goodson, Anne Elisabeth Lester and Carol Symes (Farnham: Ashgate, 2010), pp. 279-81.

8 Hutchison, 'Knowing One's Place', pp. 50-1; James Masschaele, 'The Public Space of the Marketplace in Medieval England', *Speculum*, 77 (2002), pp. 390-91; Symes, 'Out in the Open', pp. 279-85.

9 Jelle Haemers, 'Social Memory and Rebellion in Fifteenth-Century Ghent', *Social History*, 36 (2011), p. 448; Marc Boone, 'Urban Space and Political Conflict in Late Medieval Flanders', *The Journal of Interdisciplinary History*, 32 (2002), p. 640; Élodie Lecuppre-Desjardin, *La ville des cérémonies: Essai sur la communication politique dans les anciens Pays-Bas bourguignons* (Turnhout: Brepols, 2004), pp. 235-39.

10 Carol Symes, *A Common Stage: Theatre and Public Life in Medieval Arras* (London: Cornell University Press, 2007), pp. 3-4.

11 Arnade, Howell and Simons, 'Fertile Spaces', p. 535. See also Martha Howell The Spaces of Late Medieval Urbanity' in *Shaping Identity in Late Medieval Europe*, ed. by Marc Boone and Peter Stabel (Leuven: Garant, 2000), p. 11.

peuple'.[12] The ordinance underscored the Grande Boucherie's proximity to the Grand Châtelet, seat of Paris' royal *prévôt*, revealing how the control of potentially subversive spaces was tied to the maintenance of civic and institutional authority. More generally, this public power was manifested through the distinction of speaker and audience in space, and the Bourgeois' identification of specifically public places can be discerned through the socio-political functions that they assumed with respect to jurisdictionally-aligned institutional communication. This politico-legal framework meant that spaces used for official communication also emerged as forums within which Parisians challenged authority by appropriating their semiotic function.[13] Indeed, what arises here is the phenomenon insightfully identified by Shannon McSheffrey, whereby *uses* of space conditioned the 'public' character of action, with publicity rendered 'situational as well as spatial'.[14] By describing how these spaces were used, the Bourgeois mapped respective political authorities within Paris, playing upon the relationship between the representational appropriateness of space and message. The relativity evokes Michel de Certeau's distinction of space and place: where the latter represented elements 'distributed in relationships of coexistence', these were transformed through their practice as space – the operations that 'orient it, temporalize it and make it function'.[15]

The *Journal*'s focus upon public space as defined by experience, practice and ideology is brought into greater focus by the relative absence of references to areas operating ostensibly beyond the realm of direct institutional authority, such as taverns or domestic settings.[16] None of the four thousand taverns that his contemporary Guillebert De Mets envisioned as being found in Paris were mentioned by the Bourgeois, and this despite the fact that we can identify at least twenty-three of the taverns found on the Bourgeois' local rues Saint-Denis and Saint-Martin in 1457 alone.[17] The practices of the city's *taverniers* were alluded to only implicitly through the Bourgeois' regular summary of retail prices for wine cried by the *crieurs de corps et de vins*, municipal officials that acted as the 'auxiliaires

---

12 Are not to be tolerated nor suffered in such public places, like at the said square in which a great number of people come together. *Ordonnances des rois de France*, X, p. 361.

13 The multivalent character of Parisian space is addressed by Michelle Camille, but in terms of signs and symbols rather than speech. 'Signs of the City: Place, Power and Public Fantasy in Medieval Paris', in *Medieval Practices of Space* ed. by Barbara A. Hanawalt and Michael Kobialka (Minneapolis, MN: University of Minnesota Press, 2000), pp. 11-14

14 Shannon McSheffrey, 'Place, Space and Situation: Public and Private in the Making of Marriage in Late-Medieval London', *Speculum*, 79 (2004), pp. 960-90.

15 Michel de Certeau, *The Practice of Everyday Life*, trans. by Steven Randall (Los Angeles, CA: University of California Press, 1988), 117; Barbara A. Hanawalt and Michael Kobialka, 'Introduction', pp. x-xii.

16 On the tavern's importance for notions of crime, revolt and the delineation of public spaces see Susan Dudash, 'Christinian Politics, the Tavern and Urban Revolt in Late Medieval France' in *Healing the Body Politic: The Political Thought of Christine de Pizan*, ed. by Karen Green and Constant J. Mews (Turnhout: Brepols, 2005), pp. 35-59; Barbara A. Hanawalt, 'The Host, the Law and the Ambiguous Space of Medieval London Taverns' in *Medieval Crime and Social Control*, ed. by Barbara A. Hanawalt and David Wallace (Minneapolis, MN: University of Minnesota Press, 1999), pp. 205-14.

17 Guillebert De Mets, 'La description de la ville de Paris' in *Paris et ses historiens aux XIVe et XVe siècles*, ed. by Antoine Le Roux de Lincy and Lazare-Maurice Tisserand (Paris: Imprimerie impériale, 1867), p. 232. The taverns found on the rues Saint-Denis and Saint-Martin are listed in Pierre Champion, 'Liste des tavernes de Paris d'après des documents du XVe siècle', *BSHP*, 39 (1912), pp. 259-67.

des taverniers'.[18] The *Journal* therefore obfuscates the central place that taverns occupied in the city's political life, especially as sites that provided the backdrop to subversive political encounters, arguments and even scheming.[19] Nevertheless, the omission of taverns is also significant for our understanding of the Bourgeois' vision of the Parisian public sphere. Their absence implies the disdain for taverns as sites of impious speech, depravity and temptation contrary to the city's common good found in the writings of Jean Gerson and Christine de Pizan. As Susan Dudash has argued, for Christine de Pizan the tavern represented 'the locus of social turmoil *par excellence*', especially in the context of rising factional tensions in 1405, whereby 'la lecherie des tavernes et des friandises dont ilz usent a Paris peut conduire a mains maulz et inconveniens'.[20] If Aristotelian thinking determined rational conversation as the defining characteristic of man-as-political-animal, then the tavern's influences depoliticized the *menu peuple*. It was precisely the rhetoric of drunkenness that chroniclers such as Michel Pintoin employed to discredit popular uprisings, decrying the Armagnac massacres in 1418 as being perpetrated by those whose diabolical fury was inspired, in part, by overindulging in wine.[21] The Bourgeois' own exclusion of taverns encapsulated a similar sense of their place 'outside' a formal public sphere, delineating the contours of legitimate political interaction.

A similar lack of information regarding domestic experiences reinforces this sense of a bounded publicness, capturing the Bourgeois' predominant concern for events out in the open. In the *Journal*, the penetration of domestic spaces presented a means of evaluating civic authority and giving voice to its author's vision of oppressive policies, particularly in relation to taxation.[22] In this light, internal spaces emerged as pivotal sites of contest between Parisians and the royal agendas embodied by the Châtelet, underscored by concerns about governmental tyranny and the city's common good that elaborated a traditional vision of taxation's limitations – that the king 'doit vivre du sien' rather than upon the goods of his subjects.[23] If instances of indirect taxation such as currency debasements provoked significant reflection regarding the 'communal functionalist' character of medieval society, as a harmful practice damaging the body politic, this disruption was mirrored in the transgression of domestic boundaries by royal officers that traced the dichotomy of ruler

18 The taverners' assistants. Yvonne-Hélène Le Maresquier-Kesteloot, *Les officiers municipaux de la ville de Paris au XVe siècle* (Paris: Commission des travaux historiques de la ville de Paris, 1997), p. 64.

19 Several conspiracies to betray Paris between 1410 and 1436 were elaborated within tavern settings, as demonstrated by surviving pardons. For examples, see Paris, Archives nationales JJ 170, fol. 96r; Auguste Longnon, *Paris pendant la domination anglaise (1420-36)* (Paris: Champion, 1878), pp. 302-08, 348-53.

20 Dudash, 'Christinian Politics', p. 39. The taverns' licentiousness and the appetites that they satisfy in Paris can lead to many evils and harms. Christine de Pizan, *Le livre du corps de policie*, ed. by Angus J. Kennedy (Paris: Honoré Champion, 1998), pp. 106-07.

21 RSD, VI, p. 244.

22 For late medieval England, Tom Johnson has argued that the monitoring of domestic spaces by authorities culminated in a system of 'domestic scrutiny' underpinning the law courts' routine searching of houses and shops. Johnson, *Law in Common*, pp. 71-3.

23 Lydwine Scordia, *'Le roi doit vivre du sien': La théorie de l'impôt en France (XIIIe-XVe siècles)* (Paris: Institut d'Études Augustiniennes, 2005), pp. 49-57, 335-40; Maurice Rey, *Le domaine du roi et les finances extraordinaires sous Charles VI (1388-1413)* (Paris: SEPVEN, 1965), pp. 41-3. The reform and autarky of the royal domain represented a predominant focus for the Cabochien rebels in 1413. Alfred Coville, *Les Cabochiens et l'ordonnance de 1413* (Paris: Hachette, 1888), pp. 225-35.

and ruled.[24] In an early example, the so-called 'tax of silver marks' in 1421 was accompanied by an account of the consequences for those who refused to contribute: 'tantost avoit sergens en sa maison et estoit mené en prinsons diverses, et ne povait parler a lui'.[25] The vision became a leitmotif for the Bourgeois' critique of royal taxation, appearing when taxes were raised in 1439 to support the Valois siege of Meaux 'qui moult grevoient le povre commun, car quant ilz estoient dedens les maisons, ilz les convenoit gouverner de grans despens, car c'estoient les varletz au deable'.[26] In each of these instances, taxation for warfare and the penetration of domestic spaces underpinned a perception of aristocratic cupidity and royal oppression conveyed through spatial transgressions to the detriment of the wider body politic and Paris' *menu peuple* in particular.[27]

The recognition that domestic spaces represented a potent boundary to the realm of public authority seemingly validates much of the earlier scholarship highlighting the intersections of gender and space that suggested rigid divides between male-public and female-private.[28] And yet, while strict distinctions between the household and the street may be perceived in the Bourgeois' writing, these were not inherently gendered. Women, like men, moved through realms of spatial experience and emerge, too, as actors in the public and political realms imagined through the *Journal*.[29] Here, women's public place deviates substantially from the instructions conveyed by the anonymous *Ménagier de Paris* writing in the final decade of the fourteenth century for his young wife, warning her to keep her gaze lowered in the street, to keep reputable company, 'ne rire, ne arrester a parler a aucun sur les rues'.[30] Rather, the *Journal* depicts women as assuming an important, representative role for the city, a vision distinct from Michael Camille's own argument that Paris' streets were masculinized spaces, 'not only because it was where public men went out to do business leaving wives and daughters at home, but because its very signs were a network of phallic significations'.[31] Contradicting these impressions of restricted behaviour, the Bourgeois depicted women as actively circulating in Parisian space and witnessed reputable women participating in public politics. At moments of political tension and crisis, women emerged as expressive agents.[32] When white hoods were distributed during the Cabochien revolt, 'en prindrent hommes d'eglise et femmes d'onneur marchandes',[33] as the corpses of

---

24 Cary J. Nederman, 'Tolerance and Community: A Medieval Communal Functionalist Argument for Toleration', *Journal of Politics*, 56 (1994), pp. 912-18.

25 They immediately had sergeants in their houses and were led to various prisons, and they could not be spoken to. *Journal*, p. 161.

26 Which greatly burdened the poor commons, because when they [the sergeants] entered their houses, they were compelled to maintain them at great expense, for they were the servants of the devil. *Journal*, p. 349.

27 These tensions have been highlighted by Vanessa Harding, 'Space, Property and Propriety in Urban England', *The Journal of Interdisciplinary History*, 32 (2002), pp. 549-69.

28 For instance, Martha Howell, *The Marriage Exchange: Property, Social Place, and Gender in the Cities of the Low Countries, 1300-1550* (Chicago: University of Chicago Press, 1998).

29 Sarah Rees Jones, 'Public and Private Space and Gender in Medieval Europe' in *The Oxford Handbook of Women and Gender in Medieval Europe*, ed. by Judith Bennett and Ruth Karras (Oxford: Oxford University Press, 2013), pp. 246-59.

30 [And] neither laugh nor stop to speak to anyone in the streets. *Le Ménagier de Paris*, ed. by Georgine Brereton and Janet Ferrier (Oxford: Oxford University Press, 1981), p. 11.

31 Camille, 'Signs of the City', p. 27.

32 As demonstrated by Anne Curry, 'Soldiers' Wives in the Hundred Years War' in *Soldiers, Nobles and Gentlemen: Essays in Honour of Maurice Keen*, ed. by Peter Coss and Christopher Tyerman (Woodbridge: Boydell, 2009), pp. 200-02.

33 Clergymen and honourable tradeswomen took them up. *Journal*, p. 31.

murdered Armagnacs lay strewn in the streets following the 1418 massacres, the Bourgeois reported how even the

> femmes, et enfens, et gens sans puissance qui ne leur povaient pis faire, les maudisoient en pasant par empres, disans "Chiens traistres, vous estes mieulx que a vous n'appartient. Encore en y a il, que pleust Dieu que tous feussent en tel estat!"[34]

Assuming a representative function, the women seen in public could evoke the city's grandeur and even act on its behalf. For instance, when the Holy Roman Emperor Sigismund visited Paris in March 1416, the Bourgeois overlooked his visit to the Parlement to instead relate how the 'damoiselles de Paris, et des bourgeoises les plus honnestes' were assembled to feast with the emperor.[35] More than superfluous frivolity, these women may also have had a symbolic part to play in ongoing negotiations between France and England, overseen by Sigismund.[36] For Parisian commentators, Sigismund's visit and subsequent departure for England were intertwined with diplomatic efforts to secure a truce in the wake of the French defeat at Agincourt almost six months earlier.[37] Reactions to this defeat by leading writers such as Christine de Pizan and Alain Chartier were characterized by an emphasis upon the suffering of those women who had lost their lovers.[38] In this context, the Bourgeois' account of the women dining with Sigismund assumes a double meaning, at once revealing women as representatives of the city but also implying their place as intercessors in contemporary politics. An analogous role can be seen in April 1435, when in the prelude to the Congress of Arras the *damoiselles* and *bourgeoises* of Paris processed to visit Isabella, duchess of Burgundy in the Hôtel d'Artois, before beseeching 'moult piteusement a la duchesse qu'elle eust la paix du royaulme pour recommandée'.[39]

Intriguingly, the Bourgeois' emphasis upon the public appearance of women captures a sliding scale of female status that could be evoked to convey impressions of the common good and its decline. Female intercessors or the wives of Burgundian adherents were 'femmes d'honneur', and their embodiment of public appropriateness was juxtaposed with the presence of those women who openly celebrated Armagnac successes in 1414, 'toutes d'estat, non pas d'onneur, toutes bandées'.[40] Their description moves past the dichotomies associated with women's public presence, whereby 'le privé protège les femmes et les

---

34 Women, children and powerless people who could not do worse to them, cursed the bodies when they passed near them in the street, saying 'Treacherous dogs, you are better off than you deserve. Some still remain, and if only it pleased God that all of you were in such a state!' *Journal*, p. 91.

35 The maidens of Paris, and the most honest bourgeoises. *Journal*, p. 69.

36 For Sigismund's visit, see Veronika Novák, 'Cérémonies problématiques: Les pratiques des rencontres au sommet à la fin du Moyen Âge et la visite de Sigismond de Luxembourg à Paris en 1416' in *'M'en anai en Ongria'. Relations Franco-Hongroises au Moyen Âge*, vol. 2, ed. by Attila Györkös and Gergely Kiss (Debrecen: Kapitális, 2017), pp. 105-25.

37 RSD, V, p. 746; *Histoire de Charles VI*, pp. 530-31; Cordeliers, p. 232.

38 Craig Taylor, '"La maleureuse bataille": Fifteenth-Century French Reactions to Agincourt', *French History*, 33 (2019), pp. 360-61; Marianne Ailes, 'Literary Responses to Agincourt: The Allegories of *Le Pastoralet* and the *Quadrilogue invective*', *Reading Medieval Studies*, 41 (2015), pp. 1-26; Renate Blumenfeld-Kosinski, 'Two Responses to Agincourt: Alain Chartier's *Livre des quatre dames* and Christine de Pizan's *Épistre de la prison de vie humaine*' in *Contexts and Continuities*, vol. 1, ed. by Angus Kennedy (Glasgow: University of Glasgow Press, 2002), pp. 75-85.

39 The duchess very piteously that she keep the kingdom's peace under her consideration. *Journal*, p. 305.

40 All of estate but not of honour, all Armagnacs. *Journal*, p. 54.

valorise; le public les expose et les marginalise'.[41] Rather, the Bourgeois' portrayal of women accorded them a vital, active role to play in securing the civic community. The rhetorical power of women's public portrayal is further underscored by their depiction in relation to visions of the common good. In 1448 the arrival in Paris of Charles VII's mistress, Agnès Sorel, was criticized as the manifestation of the monarch's 'grant pechié et sa grant honte' through recourse to the explicit language of publicity.[42] Sorel's public ostentation undermined the kingdom's common good 'car quant ung grant signeur ou dame fait publicquement grant pechez, ses chevaliers et son peuple en est plus hardy a pecher'.[43] This criticism may have echoed more widespread, politicized commentary. Sorel's visit occurred at a politically fraught moment, precisely as her affiliates at court – the *grand sénéchal* Pierre de Brézé and the Dauphin Louis' secretary, Guillaume Mariette – were being tried for conspiring to provoke discord between the Dauphin and Charles VII.[44] Although unmentioned by the Bourgeois, this context may have driven his condemnation of Sorel's appearance, not only because of her sexual relationship with the king – 'sans foy et sans loy et sans verité a la bonne royne qu'il avoit espousée' – but also betraying deeper concerns surrounding Sorel's influence at court.[45]

The political inflection of female publicity is further underscored by the Bourgeois' comments, in 1446, upon the clothing regulations for Paris' prostitutes, juxtaposed with the promiscuity of the late *prévôt* Ambroise de Loré to critique the city's administration upon his death. Like Charles VII, it was because Loré spurned his honourable wife to maintain 'partout les femmes folieuses, dont trop avoit a Paris' that the Bourgeois could portray Loré as having done less for the common good than any other *prévôt* for forty years.[46] The preceding ordinance determining the clothing to be worn by prostitutes exemplifies the extent to which the city's common good was intertwined with the public regulation of women's bodies.[47] Indeed, the Bourgeois may have been particularly sensitive to such issues. The local church of Saint-Merry on the rue Saint-Martin had long been involved in disputes with the prostitutes inhabiting the adjacent rue Baillehoe. In 1424, the churchwardens asserted their status as members of one of the city's most notable parishes to decry the prostitutes' presence 'qui est chose tresmal seant et non convenable a l'onneur qui doit estre defferee a l'eglise et a bien chacun catholique, de mauvais exemple

---

41 Privacy protects women and validates them; the public exposes and marginalizes them. Claude Gauvard, *'De Grâce especial': Crime, état et société en France à la fin du Moyen Âge*, 2 vols (Paris: Publications de la Sorbonne, 1991), I, p. 346.

42 Great sin and great shame. *Journal*, p. 388.

43 For when a great lord or lady performs great sins publicly, their knights and their people are more brazen in sinning themselves. *Journal*, p. 388.

44 Mathieu d'Escouchy, *Chronique de Mathieu d'Escouchy*, ed. by Gaston du Fresne de Beaucourt, 3 vols (Paris: Jules Renouard, 1863-64), I (1863), pp. 135-38; Franck Collard, '*Rex abhorret a sanguine?* De l'effusion à l'abstinence, Charles VII et le sang versé', *Revue historique*, 693 (2020), pp. 124-25.

45 Without faith, without loyalty and without truth for the good queen that he had married. *Journal*, p. 388.

46 Loose women everywhere, of which there were too many in Paris. *Journal*, p. 383.

47 Controls on appearance, circulation and spaces were common in late medieval cities, evoking notions of urban health, public cleanliness and the common good. Bronisław Geremek, *The Margins of Society in Late Medieval Paris*, trans. by Jean Birrell (Cambridge: Cambridge University Press, 1987), pp. 211-41; Carole Rawcliffe, *Urban Bodies: Communal Health in Late Medieval English Towns and Cities* (Woodbridge: Boydell and Brewer, 2013), pp. 104-06.

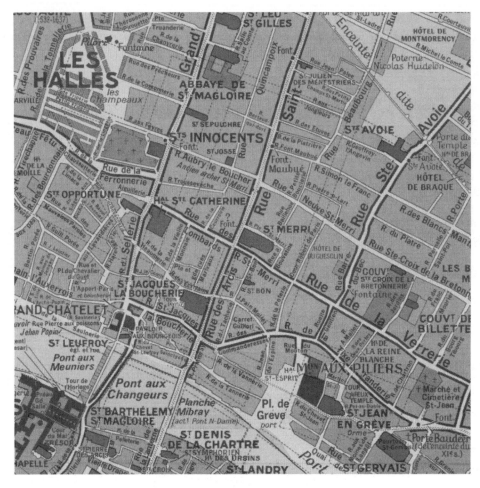

Figure 5. Detail, Saint-Merry and the Saints-Innocents (centre). *Carte de Paris vers la fin du XIVᵉ siècle*. CNRS Éditions. CCØ Paris Musées/Petit Palais, Musées des Beaux-Arts de la ville de Paris.

vil et abhominable, mesmement a gens notables, honnoriables et de bonne vie'.[48] Without doubt, visions of female status and public conduct fed into broader contentions about the administration of Parisian space and the conditions of good government.

In turn, the *Journal* demonstrates that precise forms of communication were expected in specific spaces that reflected institutional jurisdictions, mirroring the experiences of other late medieval cities, such as Venice, where subversive conversations and the circulation

---

48 Which is very unseemly thing and not befitting the honour that should be due to the church and each Catholic person; of evil, vile and abominable example, even for people of worthy, honourable and good life. Paris, Archives nationales, JJ 173, fols 65r-v, no. 130. On the Bourgeois' possible connections to Saint-Merry, see Luke Giraudet, 'Nicolas Confrant, author of the *Journal d'un bourgeois de Paris*?', *Romania*, 139 (2021), p. 137. Several other ordinances and petitions had already been issued regarding prostitution near Saint-Merry. See Jill Harsin, *Policing Prostitution in Nineteenth-Century Paris* (Princeton, NJ: Princeton University Press. 1985), pp. 59-60.

of rumour were equally site-specific and related to institutional centres of authority.[49] Medieval Paris was overlaid by a complex patchwork of distinct jurisdictions. Besides the judicial territories of individuals and institutions, such as the bishop of Paris, cathedral chapter or Parlement, up to sixty *seigneuries* claimed jurisdictional authority within the city, including seventeen religious bodies with *haute justice*.[50] Every institution with this authority jealously guarded its rights to proclaim and enforce law, with the result that beyond the royal domain, royal law still encountered challenges in its application at the beginning of the fifteenth century.[51] As the previous chapters have shown, the Bourgeois' predominant focus upon the right bank meant that the *Journal* privileged informational exchanges and public events that took place in the region of the Halles marketplace, including executions in the Halles square, sermons at nearby religious institutions and the proclamations declared at major crossroads.[52] Each of these emerged as focal points for the community's public expression, underscoring the market's centrality to circulation and informational exchanges, as a microcosm 'of the institutional density characteristic of the late medieval city'.[53] Public celebrations took place in Paris' main thoroughfares, though those organized officially, such as the bonfires for the feast of St. John Baptist, were located at the place de Grève. Likewise, community cohesion was reinforced through the celebratory and devotional atmospheres associated with these spaces, as demonstrated when the Bourgeois pointed to the context of Jean sans Peur's funerary service at Notre-Dame on 8 November 1419, emphasizing the cumulative effects of light, collective mourning and sermon:

> y avoit ou moustier iij mil livres de cire toutes en cierges et en torches, et ot ung moult piteux sermon [...] Et apres ce le firent toutes les parroisses de Paris et toutes les confraries de Paris, l'un apres l'autre, et partout faisoit-on la presentacion de grans cierges et de grans torches, et estoient les moustiers encourtinez de noyres sarges.[54]

Through collective mourning, Parisians affirmed their loyalty to the duke down to the parish level. Local churches were similarly decorated, not simply with black sheets, but with

---

49 See Claire Judde de Larivière, 'Du Broglio a Rialto: cris et chuchotements dans l'espace public à Venise (XVIᵉ siècle)' in *L'espace public au Moyen Âge. Débats autour de Jürgen Habermas*, ed. by Patrick Boucheron and Nicolas Offenstadt (Paris: Presses Universitaires de France, 2011), pp. 119-30.

50 Guy Thompson, *Paris and its People: The Anglo-Burgundian Regime 1420-36* (Oxford: Clarendon Press, 1991), pp. 49-50; Simone Roux, 'Modèles et pratiques en histoire urbaine médiévale: L'espace parisien à la fin du Moyen Âge', *Histoire, économie et société*, 13 (1994), p. 420; Georges Huisman, *La juridiction de la municipalité parisienne de Saint Louis à Charles VII* (Paris: Ernest Leroux, 1912), pp. 199-206; Jean-Georges Vondrus-Reissner, 'Présence réelle et juridiction ecclésiastique dans le diocèse de Paris (fin XVème-1530)', *Histoire, économie et société*, 7 (1988), pp. 45-8; Joseph Petit (ed.), *Registre des causes civiles de l'officialité épiscopale de Paris, 1384-87* (Paris: Imprimerie nationale, 1919), pp. xix-xxix.

51 See Katia Weidenfeld, 'Le contentieux de la voirie parisienne à la fin du Moyen Âge', *Revue historique*, 301 (1999), pp. 211-36.

52 On the ritual character and location of Parisian proclamations, see Novák, 'L'espace du cri'.

53 Johnson, *Law in Common*, p. 63. The marketplace's centrality to communication and exchange has been highlighted by numerous studies, most notably Mikhail Bakhtin's *Rabelais and His World*, trans. by Helene Iswolsky (Bloomington, IN: Indiana University Press, 1984), pp. 153-95. See also James Masschaele 'The Public Space of the Marketplace', pp. 383-421; Peter Stabel, 'The Market Place and Civic Identity in Late Medieval Flanders' in *Shaping Identity in Late Medieval Europe*, ed. by Marc Boone and Peter Stabel (Leuven: Garant, 2000), p. 52.

54 In the church there were three thousand pounds of wax all as candles and torches, and there was pronounced a piteous sermon [...] And after this each of Paris' parishes and all of the confraternities, one after another, did the same, and everywhere people offered great candles and torches, and the churches were decorated with black serge. *Journal*, p. 132.

Burgundian arms – 'les escus qui ont esté mis au piliers de l'esglise en faisant le service de mons. de Bourgogne', as demonstrated by the accounts for the confraternity of the St. James Pilgrims based at Saint-Jacques-l'Hôpital on the rue Saint-Denis.[55] Moreover, architectural grandeur framed speakers' authority. By excommunicating factional leaders or condemning heretics on the Notre-Dame parvis, the bishop of Paris drew power from the intricately awe-inspiring cathedral façade that signified the city's centre. It was there that the Armagnac leaders were excommunicated in 1411, where Nicolas d'Orgemont's crimes and condemnation were publicized in 1416 and, finally, where the heretical behaviours ascribed to the female visionary Piéronne la Bretonne were preached prior to her execution.[56] It was for good reason that Jean Graverent chose the prestigious abbey of Saint-Martin-des-Champs, which claimed jurisdiction over as many as 30,000 Parisians and was one of the city's wealthiest institutions, to pronounce his sermon denouncing Jeanne d'Arc's crimes in 1431.[57]

Fifteenth-century manuscript illuminators focused upon these same sites when they endeavoured to depict Paris in their works. Where Notre-Dame is ubiquitous in Jean Fouquet's paintings, the calendrical cityscapes of Jean, duke of Berry's *Très Riches Heures* (*c.* 1412-16) or the Froissarts of Commynes (*c.* 1472) and Louis de Gruuthuse (*c.* 1470-75) privileged sites of royal power and prestige: the Palais, the Louvre, the Sainte-Chapelle and the Bastille.[58] In contrast, the Bourgeois' narrative focus upon Paris' populous right bank, the Saints-Innocents cemetery and Halles markets framed interaction in spaces distant from the square, town hall, Palais or Châtelet. Streets themselves appear as the quintessential form of public space. Liminal, these were at once between places but also an essential site of interaction themselves, and the *Journal* highlights the degrees to which stepping out into the street involved competing pressures that fashioned identities. Through clothing, gesture and the very act of looking, entering the street brought the individual into contact with the collective, and demanded that Parisians situate themselves as compositional parts of the broader civic entity: they cannot be reduced to discrete forums of economic exchange or political display alone. Rather, streets represented ambiguous public arenas for the negotiation of social and political relationships where competing visions of the common good were elaborated and resistance to authority articulated.[59] Organic metaphors describing the city accounted for the streets' fundamentally communicative and circulatory character, as the arteries of movement and encounter that secured the health of the urban

---

55 The arms that were affixed to the pillars of the church for the service in the duke of Burgundy's memory. Henri Léonard Bordier, 'La confrérie des Pèlerins de Saint-Jacques et ses archives', *MSHP*, 2 (1876), p. 394.

56 *Journal*, pp. 16-17, 259-60; Baye, II, pp. 249-50.

57 *Journal*, pp. 270-72. See Siméon Luce, 'Les menus du prieur de Saint-Martin-des-Champs en 1438 et 1439', *Comptes rendus des séances de l'Académie des Inscriptions et Belles-Lettres*, 26 (1882), p. 112.

58 On Notre-Dame in the paintings of Jean Fouquet, see Raphaëlle Skupien, 'La cathédrale transfigurée: Notre-Dame de Paris dans les image de la fin du Moyen Âge (XVᵉ-XVIᵉ siècle)', *Livraisons de l'histoire et de l'architecture*, 38 (2019), pp. 23-37.

59 Riitta Laitinen and Thomas Cohen, 'Cultural History of Early Modern Streets – An Introduction' in *Cultural History of Early Modern European Streets*, ed. by Riitta Laitinen and Thomas Cohen (Leiden: Brill, 2009), pp. 1-10. On competing uses of street space see Liddy, *Contesting the City*, pp. 57-66.

body.[60] In turn, these were everyday spaces that complicate rigid distinctions of public and private: locations where neighbourhood communities congregated to discuss the welfare of their *quartier*, often challenging municipal discourses laying claim to superior jurisdiction. Beyond a strict Habermasian privileging of public discussion in formal environments, such as the coffeehouses and salons of early modernity, competing visions of action and presence in the medieval street underscored the potential for communities to produce their own definitions of public fate.

Rendering the street an arena of encounter and political engagement, the Bourgeois shared in a vision that had already become integral to the laudatory urban descriptions produced a century earlier. Around 1300, Guillot de Paris' *Dit des rues de Paris* took the capital's streets as the subject of a celebration of Paris' grandeur, portraying these environments as a hub of social interaction where women gossiped and friends met, traders cried their wares and neighbours argued.[61] The fifteenth century witnessed a renewed interest in these themes. The city's streets emerged as the principal focus of Guillebert De Mets' *Description de Paris* (1434).[62] Around the same time, an anonymous Parisian poet parodied Guillot de Paris' earlier *Dit* to recount the plight of a suburban villager who lost his wife in the busy capital, forced to travel throughout the city's streets to find her. In his quest, the protagonist encounters characters including 'Dame Baudas' of the rue Saint-Hilaire, as well as communities of clerics, labourers, merchants, lawyers, students, and chambermaids.[63] These texts, and the other lists and descriptions that became increasingly common from the middle of the fifteenth century, envisioned the streets as the city's fundamental fabric, enumerated as a rhetorical means of communicating Paris' wealth and grandeur.[64]

The Bourgeois' own conception of the street and its publicness played on this ideal of constant, collective interaction. As shown in Chapter 2, these were spaces invested for popular celebrations, framing participation in the city's political life. When Charles VI returned to Paris on 17 March 1409 following the fragile reconciliation between Charles, duke of Orléans and Jean sans Peur at Chartres, the Bourgeois portrayed ordinary inhabitants occupying the city space and soundscape to celebrate the reunion of king and capital. Neighbours feasted 'en my les rues par hèr joyeuse hère, et firent feus tous partout Paris, et bassynoient de bassins tout parmy Paris'.[65] Five years later, the king's arrival following

---

60 Hannah Skoda, *Medieval Violence: Physical Brutality in Northern France, 1270-1330* (Oxford: Oxford University Press, 2013), pp. 53-5.

61 Paris, BNF Fr. 24432, fols 257v-261v. The poem survives in a single manuscript and it has been published in a nineteenth-century edition. Edgar Mareuse (ed.), *Le dit des rues de Paris (1300) par Guillot (de Paris)* (Paris: Librairie Générale, 1875).

62 Brussels, Bibliothèque royale de Belgique, MS 9559-64, fols 118r-142v. Published in Antoine Le Roux de Lincy and Lazare-Maurice Tisserand (ed.), *Paris et ses historiens aux XIVᵉ et XVᵉ siècles* (Paris: Imprimerie royale, 1867), pp. 131-236.

63 London, British Library, Cotton Vitellius E. X., fols 62r-72v. Published in Hercule Géraud (ed.), *Paris sous Philippe-le-Bel, d'après des documents originaux* (Paris: Crapelet, 1837), pp. 567-79. On this text see Laurent Vissière, 'Goûter la ville. Réflexions sur la poésie ambulatoire de Paris au Moyen Âge' in *Les œuvres littéraires du Moyen Âge aux yeux de l'historien et du philologue*, ed. by Ludmilla Evdokimova and Victoria Smirnova (Paris: Classiques Garnier, 2014), pp. 277-92.

64 Several examples of these lists – in manuscript and print – survive. For instance, Paris, BNF Fr. 4437, fols 242r-246v; Paris, Bibliothèque Sainte-Geneviève, MS 2521, fol. 122r; Rome, Vatican MS Reg. Lat. 1389, fols 211r-220r.

65 In the middle of the streets with very joyous fare, and bonfires were lit everywhere in Paris, and people banged pots throughout Paris. *Journal*, p. 5.

the Armagnac siege of Arras was again marked by spontaneous feasts, with tables 'en my les rues drecees a tous venans par toutes les rues de Paris qui poin aient de renon'.[66] Here, precisely those 'rues de non' that had represented the focus of the earlier *Dits* emerged as the stage for interactions framed by significant political developments, as places of communion and celebration or dispute and commiseration. During the plague epidemic of the autumn of 1418, so many died that 'touzjours jour et nuyt on n'estoit en rue que on ne recontrast Nostre Seigneur que on portoit aux maladez', whereas the next year currency fluctuations provoked shortages such as that 'si eussiez veu a Paris ou marchandise couroit touzjours debat, fust a pain ou a vin ou autre chose'.[67]

While the record of interaction in Paris' streets represented a potent means of tracing the city's shifting fortunes, tensions regarding good government were also played out through public space. Throughout the fifteenth century, the management of urban infra-structure including the maintenance of Paris' streets, the administration of its gates or the performance of the night-watch encapsulated tensions between local neighbourhoods and the overarching authority of the royal *prévôté* that were captured by the *Journal*. On 30 May 1417, the Bourgeois noted an Armagnac levy imposed upon Parisians 'de quelque estat qu'ilz fussent, prebstres ou clercs, ou autres, à curer les voiries ou à faire curer à leur argent'.[68] Inherently, the clearing of Paris' public ways juxtaposed competing visions of the city's good administration, with the regular recurrence of ordinances regarding the streets' clearing revealing the extent to which this management was a source of everyday conflict between Parisians and the *prévôté*.[69] Although such concerns translated a desire to avoid Paris' descent into an *urbs deformata* at moments of crisis, the act of accruing funds was conveyed by the Bourgeois as a careful critique of Armagnac government. Rather than putting the taxed funds to their intended purpose, 'quand on poyoit pour cent, on n'y mectoit mie xl, et avoient les gouverneurs le remenant', with Paris' administration undermined for factional profit.[70] The account was central to the Bourgeois' establishment of contrasting visions of good government. Just as the Armagnacs exploited civic revenues, the *Journal* related Jean sans Peur's own march upon Paris, proclaiming 'de par le roy et le Dalphin, et de par luy, que on n'y paiast nulle subsides'.[71] Clearly, the vision of legitimate royal authority encapsulated by the Burgundian repeal of extraordinary taxation was juxtaposed with impressions of an Armagnac exploitation of civic wealth framed by tensions surrounding the *voirie*.

These frictions regarding the administration of public space extended to the defensive measures that became a common feature of Parisian life during the political contests that marked the fifteenth century. Unsurprisingly, surveillance measures imposed greater

---

66 Tables put up in the streets for all comers in all of the streets of Paris worthy of a name. *Journal*, p. 57.

67 Day and night there was no streets where Our Lord was not encountered, as it was brought to the sick; you would have seen throughout Paris where trade took place arguments, be it regarding bread or wine or other things. *Journal*, pp. 115, 126.

68 Whatever their status, be they priests or clerics, or others, to clean the streets or have them cleaned at their expense. *Journal*, p. 77.

69 Weidenfeld, 'Le contentieux de la voirie'. See also Hutchison, 'Knowing One's Place', pp. 8-17.

70 For every hundred paid, the governors only allocated forty and they kept the remainder for themselves. *Journal*, p. 78.

71 In the name of the king and the Dauphin, and himself, that none should pay any subsides. *Journal*, pp. 78-9.

obligations upon the Parisian populace. Inhabitants were compelled to keep fires at their expense in winter when wood was expensive, surrender their time to participate in the watch or, at the very least, contribute resources to support it. Nevertheless, the diligent administration of such duties at times of political uncertainty was symptomatic of the city's good government. During the Armagnac siege of Paris in 1410, the Parisians loved the *prévôt* Pierre des Essarts

> pour ce qu'il gardoit si bien la ville de Paris. Car toute nuyt et toute jour il alloit tout parmy la ville de Paris, tout armé lui et grant foison de gens d'armes, et faisoit faire aux gens de Paris toutes les nuys le plus bel guet qu'ilz povaient, et ceulx qui n'y povaient aller faisoient veiller davant leur maison, et faire grans feuz par toutes les rues jusques au jour, et y avoit quarteniers, cinquanteniers, diseniers qui ce ordonnoient.[72]

Essential for the city's defence in 1410, such praise quickly turned to critique when Paris was confronted with acute shortages in 1418. As we have already seen, although the Burgundian coup on 29 May 1418 was met with a popular readiness to contribute to the watch, by the summer the continual state of siege in which Paris found itself following the expulsion of its Armagnac governors led to the imposition of duties emerging as one of the major grievances for Parisian rioters. When the commons assembled on 21 August, the Bourgeois rationalized their sedition by referring to the burdens imposed by the demands of civic defence and consequent shortages of wood and increased taxation.[73] Consequently, while the pressures associated with keeping watch in Paris' streets could signal the good administration of the city, these same pressures, experienced at times of acute hardship and political turmoil, were deployed by the Bourgeois as a means of evoking the everyday challenges confronting Parisian neighbourhoods, demands that resurfaced throughout the crisis years following the Burgundian coup.

More importantly, the maintenance of this defensive infrastructure was intimately connected to control of public space and the consequent preservation of urban privileges, a fact enshrined by the disputed use of the city's chains which had become the symbolic tools of Parisian revolt during Étienne Marcel's uprising in 1358 and the Maillotins rebellion in 1382.[74] Rising factional tensions that took Parisian civic independence as their focus meant that, from 1405, the issue of Paris' chains returned to the city's political agenda. Upon entering Paris in August that year, Jean sans Peur ordered the chains' restoration as part of his broader endeavour to inculcate urban support and co-opt Parisian military energies against his Orléanist rivals.[75] As in 1358 and 1382, the chains once again became integral symbols in the contest between the factions competing for control of the capital.

---

72 Because he protected Paris so well. For every night and every day he went throughout the city of Paris, fully armed and with a great number of men-at-arms, and he instructed the people of Paris to keep the best watch that they could every night, and those who could not join the watch kept vigil in front of their houses, and [Essarts] had big fires lit in all of the streets until daybreak. This was all organized by the *quarteniers*, *cinquanteniers* [and] *dizainiers*. *Journal*, p. 8.

73 *Journal*, p. 107.

74 Philippe Contamine, 'Les chaînes dans les bonnes villes de France (spécialement Paris), XIVᵉ-XVIᵉ siècle' in *Guerre et société en France, en Angleterre et en Bourgogne, XIVᵉ-XVᵉ siècle*, ed. by Maurice Keen, Charles Giry-Deloison and Philippe Contamine (Lille: Septentrion, 1991), p. 294; *The Chronicle of Jean de Venette*, ed. and trans. by Jean Birdsall and Richard Newhall (New York: Columbia University Press, 1953), pp. 66-7; RSD, I, pp. 130-31.

75 *Journal*, p. 3; RSD, III, p. 309; Hutchison, 'Knowing One's Place', p. 15.

Where the Bourgeois celebrated their return in 1405, with iron workers labouring day and night to produce new chains, the subsequent threat of their confiscation by hostile governors preoccupied Parisian commentators. In 1408, Michel Pintoin reported rumours that Isabeau de Bavière was plotting to remove the city's chains, prompting the circulation of a subversive pamphlet warning the *prévôt des marchands* that should this occur, he would face the same fate as his predecessor Étienne Marcel, murdered by the Parisian mob in 1358.[76] Central to the control and administration of Parisian space, the presence of these chains' paralleled shifts in authority within the city. In 1416, the Bourgeois reported that the chains were confiscated as part of the repressive Armagnac measures designed to mitigate against the threat of revolt following the discovery of the d'Orgemont's conspiracy to betray the city.[77] Restored in the wake of the Burgundian coup two years later, the Bourgeois complained that 'cuida on tout trouver, mais il s'en faillit III^C que les bandez en leur vivant avoient degasté en leur prouffit, on ne scet en quel lieu'.[78] This anxiety regarding the chains' preservation as a symptom of Paris' own security and defence of its privileges finds echoes in surviving civic records. As late as 1430, an inquest heard that in 1418 the murdered merchant Pierre Emery had been commissioned by the city's Armagnac governors to collect Paris' chains, with 29,346 pounds of iron rods subsequently discovered in his house.[79] Similarly, in 1420 a dispute had broken out in the Arbour tavern on the rue des Gravilliers adjoining the rue Saint-Martin, whereupon Thomas Pasquier accused the saltpeterer Guillaume Lucas of purchasing the city's chains, adding 'que c'estoit mal fait de acheter les chaynes de Paris'.[80] As with the *voirie* in 1417, the rhetoric surrounding the city's chains enabled the Bourgeois to situate the Armagnac faction as tyrannically exploiting urban infrastructure, undermining the city's privileges and common good for factional advantage and signalling the faction's illegitimacy in Parisian space.

Controlling the city

Controlling the public sphere was 'au cœur de la concurrence entre les pouvoirs' in the fifteenth century, and it is therefore unsurprising that measures to regulate Parisian behaviour and speech are consistently highlighted by the *Journal*.[81] Through prescriptions regarding clothing, celebrations, gatherings and even with the penetration of domestic spaces, successive Parisian regimes were identified as developing strict surveillance measures that

---

76 RSD, IV, pp. 136-38; *Histoire de Charles VI*, pp. 441-42.

77 *Journal*, p. 72.

78 It was thought that all could be found, but three hundred were missing that the *bandez* had destroyed for their own profit, who knows where. *Journal*, p. 101.

79 Tuetey (ed.), *Journal*, p. 101, n. 1.

80 That it was a bad thing to buy Paris' chains. Paris, Archives nationales, JJ 171, fols 121v-122v, no. 214.

81 Nicolas Offenstadt, *Faire la paix au Moyen Âge: discours et gestes de paix pendant la guerre de Cent Ans* (Paris: Odile Jacob, 2007), p. 234. See also Nicolas Offenstadt, 'Guerre civile et espace public à la fin du Moyen Âge. La lutte des Armagnacs et des Bourguignons' in *La Politisation. Conflits et construction du politique depuis le Moyen Âge*, ed. by Philippe Hamon and Laurent Bourquin (Rennes: Presses Universitaires de Rennes, 2010), pp. 111-29; Klaus Oschema, 'Espaces publics autour d'une société de cour: l'exemple de la Bourgogne des ducs de Valois' in *L'espace public au Moyen Âge: débats autour de Jürgen Habermas*, ed. by Patrick Boucheron and Nicolas Offenstadt (Paris: Presses Universitaires de France, 2011), p. 166.

channelled and restricted political activity and communication within the city. The *Journal* presents a record of exactly how these surveillance practices were tied to the control of key Parisian spaces and public identities, practices that facilitated the monitoring of speech and seditious rumour denoted in the preceding chapter. The development and accentuation of these practices was closely related to the undulation of Paris' political fortunes, but their perception by the Bourgeois and his community was evidently conditioned by his own status as a victim of the measures introduced by Paris' governors. As such, while defensive measures designed to protect the city from external threats come to the fore of the narrative during periods of Burgundian and Anglo-Burgundian government before 1413 and after 1418, moments marked by internal dissent and an Armagnac ascendancy were configured as an oppressive environment wherein sympathetically Burgundian expression was curtailed. In turn, these measures were heightened in response to the sudden discovery of internal plots that threatened to destabilize Parisian regimes, most notably in 1416, but also following a spate of conspiracies beginning in 1430 that marked the final years of Lancastrian rule. In short, tracing the measures identified by the Bourgeois for the monitoring and control of Parisian space also supports Christian Liddy's recent move to reconceptualize revolt in the light of the measures consistently enacted by urban authorities. Rather than extraordinary events, examining surveillance measures leads to a contextualization of revolt against a more extensive backdrop of sustained political resistance, activated through symbolism, presence and speech, that characterized political contexts in the late medieval city.[82]

Among the most important of these contested sites was clothing and its control, an element that itself constituted a medium of communication signalling adherence to the ruling regime through semiotic forms that captured collectively recognized relationships.[83] Such recognition was crucial in the context of a civil conflict where few features distinguished partisans. Rather, as stereotypical perceptions of 'Burgundians' and 'Armagnacs' became entrenched and repeated ordinances legitimated violence towards members of the opposing faction, open identification with the governing regime became paramount for Parisians' survival but also integral to factions that sought to inculcate support and repress subversive speech.[84] Where in 1410 the Bourgeois identified Armagnacs by their sash, 'car le duc de Berry portoit celle bende, et tous iceulx de par luy',[85] in 1411 the Ursins Compiler reported how supporters of Jean sans Peur 'laisserent la croix droite blanche, qui est la vraye enseigne du roy, et prirent la croix de Sainct-André, et la devise du duc

82 Christian Liddy, 'Cultures of Surveillance in Late Medieval English Towns: The Monitoring of Speech and the Fear of Revolt' in *The Routledge Handbook of Medieval Revolt*, ed. by Justine Firnhaber Baker and Dirk Schoenaers (London: Routledge, 2017), pp. 311-29.

83 See Colette Beaune, 'Costume et pouvoir en France à la fin du Moyen Âge: les devises royales vers 1400', *Revue des sciences humaines*, 55 (1981), pp. 125-26; Simona Slanicka, 'Male Markings: Uniforms in the Parisian Civil War as a Blurring of the Gender Order (AD 1410-20)', *The Medieval History Journal*, 2 (1999), pp. 226-40; Susan Crane, *The Performance of Self: Ritual, Clothing, and Identity During the Hundred Years War* (Philadelphia, PA: University of Pennsylvania Press, 2002), pp. 10-11.

84 Such ordinances include that issued on 3 October 1411, legitimating violence against suspected Armagnacs and their identification as enemies. See *Ordonnances des rois de France*, IX, pp. 635-37; X, p. 34. Their effects are described by the Bourgeois, *Journal*, pp. 11-12; RSD, IV, pp. 454-58.

85 Because the duke of Berry wore this sash, and all those who followed him. *Journal*, p. 9.

de Bourgone, le sautouer'.[86] During the vicissitudes of the ensuing decades, the Bourgeois signalled clothing's increasing importance as a means of publicly identifying the factions' respective supporters.

Through clothing, Parisians actively subscribed to the policies and stereotypes the factions were perceived to comprise. For instance, the Armagnac sash or 'bande' was easily conflated with the homonym 'bande' – an illegal association or armed group – used by contemporaries such as the Bourgeois to assert the faction's illegitimacy, referring to the group as the 'bandez' as soon as these symbols appeared in 1410.[87] As Clifford Geertz has argued, symbols are inherently *public* elements of communication that 'synthesize a people's ethos; their most comprehensive ideas of order'.[88] This symbolism was especially important in late medieval society, where signs represented a potent means of transmitting immediate information, securing loyalties and inculcating political views, especially since 'communication was primarily orally-based and belief in appearances strong'.[89] Consequently, prescriptions by civic governors to wear specific kinds of clothing in public compelled Parisians to make conscious choices regarding their political allegiances. Considering these issues, the Bourgeois reveals how competing factions employed an identificatory system that embodied political claims that are 'produced socially and enter into the realm of assertion, contestation and negation'.[90] With regards to space, clothing enabled governors to manage Parisians' public presence by compelling those who would oppose them to identify with the reigning faction to circulate freely, or accept relegation to private spheres. In doing so, Paris' governors implicitly employed understandings of *fama publica* to alter their adversaries' public allegiances. These strategies were prominent in the wake of the Cabochien revolt, when the Parisians had compelled the king and leading nobles to don white hoods that demonstrated sympathy for the reform movement and echoed the clothing worn by the rebels of Ghent in 1382.[91] Indeed, at this moment in May 1413 an official delegation arrived in Paris from Ghent, appearing before Jean sans Peur before banqueting at the Hôtel de Ville. As Marc Boone has noted, the distribution of the Ghent hoods might be seen at once as a symbol of Cabochien autonomy and the widespread perception of Jean sans Peur's stance as a champion of urban liberties in Paris.[92] In the revolt's immediate aftermath, Paris' Armagnac governors responded by distributing purple hoods 'ou il avoit

---

86 Abandoned the upright white cross which is the true sign of the king and assumed the St. Andrew cross and the emblem of the duke of Burgundy, the saltire. *Histoire de Charles VI*, pp. 468-69.

87 *Journal*, pp. 9-10. The term 'bande' was used to describe Burgundy's opponents as early as 1406 in the *Songe véritable*. 'Le Songe véritable, pamphlet politique d'un parisien du XVe siècle', ed. by Henri Moranvillé, *MSHP*, 17 (1890), p. 251, lines 775-82.

88 Clifford Geertz, *The Interpretation of Cultures* (New York: Basic Books, 1973), p. 89; *Available Light: Anthropological Reflection on Philosophical Topics* (Princeton, NJ: Princeton University Press, 2000), p. 15.

89 Colette Beaune, *The Birth of an Ideology. Myths and Symbols of Nation in Late Medieval France*, trans. by Susan Ross Hueston (Berkeley, CA: University of California Press, 1991), p. 197. See also Laurent Hablot, 'Les signes de l'entente. Le rôle des devises et des ordres dans les relations diplomatiques entre les ducs de Bourgogne et les princes étrangers de 1380 à 1477', *Revue du Nord*, 84 (2002), pp. 320-30.

90 Floya Anthias, 'The material and the symbolic in theorising social stratification', *The British Journal of Sociology*, 52 (2001), p. 376.

91 *Journal*, p. 31; Hutchison, 'Knowing One's Place', pp. 33-4.

92 Marc Boone, *Gent en de Bourgondische hertogen ca. 1384 – ca. 1453: Een sociaal-politieke studie van een staatsvormingsproces* (Brussels: Paleis der Academïen, 1990), p. 213; Coville, *Les Cabochiens*, p. 193.

foison feulles d'argent, et en escript d'argent, "le droit chemin"',[93] the motto representing 'an overtly anti-Burgundian message', configuring the Armagnacs as the representatives of the only 'true' route forward, their supporters who assumed the cloaks becoming true servants of the crown.[94] In May 1414, criers proclaimed that it was obligatory for Parisians to wear the Armagnac sash in a move that, inversely, identified those who harboured Cabochien sentiments.[95] When the Armagnac governors instituted their own St. Laurent confraternity at the Blancs-Manteaux in August that year, the Bourgeois related the dangers of appearing in public without the sash:

> N'osoit homme ne femme estre ou moustier ne à leur feste, s'il n'avoit la bande, et aucunes personnes d'onneur qui y estoient alés [...] en furent en tres grant danger de leur bien, pour ce qu'ilz n'avoient point de bande.[96]

Consequently, the Bourgeois perceived prescriptions regarding clothing as a means of restricting movement or participation in public events that, ostensibly, also neutralized opportunities for subversive speech. There was certainly an official belief that unregulated confraternities could represent forums for resistance. A confraternity dedicated to the Eucharist established in Saint-Eustache in May 1421 was permitted 'pourveu toutesvoies que en ladite confrarie ne soit faite aucune assemblée ne monopole ou prejudice de nous, de nostre royaume et de noz successeurs rois de France', implying a risk that the confraternity would be employed to question Lancastrian authority following the Treaty of Troyes.[97] When the congregation of Saint-Laurent in Paris' suburbs north of the porte Saint-Martin requested permission from the Lancastrian authorities to institute a confraternity in May 1428, the *prévôté* decreed that at the confraternity's meetings 'leur sera deputé aucun nostre officier qu'ilz auront tousjours present avec eulx' to counter subversive talk.[98]

These strategies were pursued throughout the period, with the attention paid to public identification and appearance at its most acute when civic authority was weakest. On 17 March 1436, a month before Paris' reconquest by the Valois, the city's Lancastrian governors ordered that 'chacun portast la croix rouge, sur peine de la vie et de perdre le sien'.[99] Clothing's importance to resistance was, finally, demonstrated by the Bourgeois' description of the Valois entry on 13 April that year. When 'le peuple en sceut parmy Paris la nouvelle, si prinrent tantost la croix blanche droicte, ou la croix Sainct Andry' with their adoption signalling collective submission to the Valois forces.[100] Paris' capture in 1436

---

93 Where there were many silver leaves, and written in silver was 'le droit chemin' [The Right Way]'. *Journal*, p. 44.

94 Emily Hutchison, 'Partisan Identity in the French Civil War, 1405-18: Reconsidering the Evidence of Livery Badges', *Journal of Medieval History*, 33 (2007), p. 272.

95 *Journal*, p. 50. Monstrelet also reports that wearing the sash became mandatory. Monstrelet, III, p. 21.

96 Neither men nor women dared to go to church nor to their feast if they were not wearing the sash, and some honourable people who did go [...] were in great danger of having their property confiscated because they were not wearing the sash. *Journal*, p. 55.

97 As long as in the said confraternity no assemblies, conspiracies, or prejudices occur against us, our kingdom or our successors, the kings of France. Paris, Archives nationales, JJ 172, fol. 34v, no. 70.

98 One of our officers will be delegated to them whom they will always have present with them. Paris, Archives nationales, JJ 174, fol. 65r, no. 154. See also Thompson, *Paris and its People*, p. 177.

99 Everyone wear the red cross, upon the pain of death and confiscation of belongings. *Journal*, p. 313.

100 The people throughout Paris learned of this news, they immediately took up the upright white cross or the St. Andrew's cross. *Journal*, p. 315.

reveals that while clothing enabled the city's governors to manage presence in public space, it also offered Parisians a crucial means of voicing their own perspectives as a result of the political choices that clothing engendered. Lasting sentiments of Burgundian partisanship appeared here through the adoption of the St. Andrew's saltire, the symbol employed by Jean sans Peur's followers in the 1410s.[101] Furthermore, the ease with which the Parisians of 1418 and 1436 adopted new symbols according to political context suggests that the city's inhabitants often had access to multiple symbols simultaneously. This is supported by surviving examples of badges that feature pins enabling them to be hidden within sleeves.[102] Other badges were deliberately neutral, perhaps designed to communicate allegiances in compromising contexts. Parisian tokens dated to Hugues Rapiout's tenure as *prévôt des marchands* (1431-34) displayed the city's arms with the motto 'Vive le roy et ses amis', ambiguously evoking the capital's ties to the royal centre without assuming any specifically factional symbolism.[103] As such, although historians have often considered the adoption of specific signs as a means of directly communicating statements of political ideology and identification, it is important to view them as fluid and alterable means of negotiation, with conformity essential for Parisians who simply sought to survive the consequences of shifting regimes.[104] Parisians may have engaged far less with the ideological meaning inherent in badges and clothing than those aristocrats who manipulated them.[105]

In this light, these same symbols were integral to contests within public space, as demonstrated by the struggle within the Halles' Saint-Eustache parish in the 1410s. One reason for the early success of Jean sans Peur's adoption of the saltire was its potential to fuse religious imagery with the Burgundian stance, blurring the boundaries between the moral and political.[106] The Ursins Compiler remarked that

> mettoit-on aux images des saincts la devise de la croix Sainct André ; plusieurs prestres en faisant leur signacles a la messe, ou en baptisant les enfans, ne daignoient faire la croix droite en la forme que Dieu fut crucifié, mais en la forme comme Sainct André fut crucifié.[107]

---

101 See Bertrand Schnerb, 'La croix de Saint-André, *ensaigne congnoissable* des Bourguignons' in *Signes et couleurs des identités politiques du Moyen Âge à nos jours*, ed. by Denis Turrel, Martin Aurell and Laurent Hablot (Rennes: Presses Universitaires de Rennes, 2008), pp. 45-55.

102 Auguste Vallet de Viriville, 'Notes sur deux médailles de plomb relatives à Jeanne d'Arc et sur quelques autres enseignes politiques ou religieuses, tirées de la collection Forgeais (Suite)', *Revue Archéologique*, 3 (1861), pp. 426-27; Hutchison, 'Partisan Identity', pp. 268-74.

103 Jules Rouyer, 'Jetons municipaux de la ville de Paris au XVe siècle', *Mémoires de la Société impériale des Antiquaires de France*, 4 (1869), p. 124.

104 Emily Hutchison, 'Winning Hearts and Minds in Early Fifteenth-Century France: Burgundian Propaganda in Perspective', *French Historical Studies*, 35 (2012) p. 22; Denis Bruna, 'De l'agréable à l'utile: le bijou emblématique à la fin du Moyen Âge', *Revue historique*, 301 (1999), pp. 3-5.

105 Hutchison, 'Partisan Identity', pp. 253-65; Michel Pastoureau, 'Emblèmes et symboles de la Toison d'Or' in *L'ordre de la Toison d'Or de Philippe le Bon à Philippe le Beau (1430-1505). Idéal ou reflet de la société?*, ed. by C. Van den Bergen-Pantens (Turnhout: Brepols, 1996), p. 101.

106 Charlotte Denoël, *Saint André: Culte & iconographie en France (Ve-XVe siècles)* (Paris: École des Chartes, 2004), pp. 91-4.

107 Upon the images of the saints were placed the symbol of the St. Andrew's cross; many priests, in making the sign of the cross during the mass, or when baptising children, did not deign to make the sign of the cross in the form of Christ's crucifixion, but in the form of St. Andrew's martyrdom. *Histoire de Charles VI*, 466.

While certainly exaggerated, the account demonstrates the extent to which religious and political rhetoric were conflated in church space. For one significant case, several sources report that on 13 September 1414, 'ung jeune homme osta la bande à l'ymage de Sainct Huistace que on lui avoit baillée, et la deschira en despit de ceulx qui lui avoient baillée'.[108] The incident at Saint-Eustache highlights how Paris' Armagnac governors attempted to symbolically alter the church fabric and assert their authority over a district known for its Burgundian sympathies and how, in turn, inhabitants of the Halles resisted this imposition. The removal of the sash was perceived as an act of open defiance and the Armagnac response reveals an explicit attempt to reassert control over the divided district. The culprit was 'tantost prins, fust tort ou droit, [et] lui fut le poing coppé sur le pont Allaiz, devant Sainct-Huistace, et fut banny a touzjours mais'.[109] The punishment was exemplary, with its performance moved from the customary Halles square to the church, while the culprit's banishment signalled the exclusion of those who symbolically or actively resisted Armagnac authority from civic society. The control of these religious spaces was essential for the maintenance of civic authority, as demonstrated by the 1416 conspiracy, which included a plan to provoke an uprising among the 'commun peuple des Halles' by ringing Saint-Eustache's bell and assembling at Saint-Germain-l'Auxerrois or the Saints-Innocents.[110]

As both the above and Chapter 3's consideration of rumour have demonstrated, the factional conflicts within Paris triggered the development of increasingly pervasive surveillance techniques by the city's authorities to control subversive speech, circulation and the interaction that underscored networks of conspirators and factional opponents within the city. Restrictions controlling public pronouncements and circulation within and without Paris often framed the imposition of the *prévôté*'s authority over Parisian spaces, and evoked the ways in which these could be contested by local populations. In response to the murder of Louis d'Orléans in November 1407, the *prévôt* Guillaume de Tignonville ordered that it be cried 'hastivement' that *hôteliers* provide the identity of their guests to the Châtelet, as were those inhabitants who had rented their houses or rooms to 'aucuns estrangiers'.[111] The ordinance coincided with new restrictions regarding university preaching and assemblies, the public carrying of weapons and instructions to keep streets lit at night.[112] While Armagnac and Burgundian elements alike were banished from the city during the 1410s, in the 1420s Lancastrian remission letters highlight the imprisonment of those who communicated with individuals in Valois territory.[113] In 1422, Jeannette Bonfils was imprisoned for having corresponded – through relayed oral messages and a letter that she shredded on her way to the Châtelet upon her arrest – with Jean Rontier, master of

---

108 A young man removed the sash that had been placed upon the statue of St. Eustace, and tore it up in spite of those that had placed it there. *Journal*, p. 56. This is also related in RSD, V, p. 446.
109 Immediately captured, whether it was right or wrong, and had his hand cut off on the pont Allaiz, in front of Saint-Eustache, and was banished forever. *Journal*, p. 56.
110 Guillaume Cousinot, 'Geste des nobles' in *Chronique de la Pucelle ou Chronique de Cousinot suivie de la Chronique normande de P. Cochon*, ed. by Vallet de Viriville (Paris: Adolphe Delahays, 1859), pp. 153-54.
111 Any strangers. *Ordonnances des rois de France*, IX, p. 261.
112 *Journal*, pp. 293-94, 311, 369-71.
113 The banishment of significant subsections of the population for factional affiliation during the 1410s was recorded by several chroniclers. *Journal*, pp. 57-8; Baye, II, pp. 268-69; Fauquembergue, I, pp. 39-41.

the mint in Valois-held Puy-en-Velay (Auvergne).[114] Three years later, the butcher Jean Michault was imprisoned for allowing a visitor from Tours to spend the night in his house without reporting his presence to the authorities; in February 1427 the baker Jean du Pré was similarly imprisoned for failing to disclose the arrival of his brother, Guillaume, arguing that he had feared that Guillaume's ill condition would have been worsened by imprisonment.[115] The Bourgeois' also condemned the limitations to circulation experienced under the Lancastrian regime following the expulsion of the English in 1436, lamenting how 'nulle personne n'osoit yssir hors de Paris sans congé, ne riens porté, sans *passe porte*, tant fust pou de chose, et disoit on "vous allez en tel lieu, revenez à telle heure, ou ne revenez plus".'[116]

The *prévôté*'s involvement in practices of surveillance was explicitly addressed in the *Journal* following the discovery of the d'Orgemont conspiracy in April 1416, when Paris' Armagnac governors redoubled their efforts to control public space and counter opportunities for subversive behaviour.[117] Reflecting the dangers associated with expressing Burgundian sympathies following the plot's discovery, the Bourgeois' own style shifted from loose and varied political commentary to a far more circumspect and restrained list of the policies and ordinances introduced by the Armagnac authorities to combat Burgundian influences and subversive Parisian tendencies. This narrative shift implies that the Bourgeois and his community were also subjected to these strictures and the risk of denunciation that accompanied them. As such, we learn that on the day after the conspiracy's discovery, the 20 April 1416, the *prévôt* Tanneguy du Châtel forbade all assemblies, directly targeting 'assemblées, confrairies et autres grans assemblées et nopces'.[118] The Bourgeois noted that those weddings that did take place were monitored by Châtelet sergeants 'aux despens de l'espouse, pour garder que homme ne murmurast de rien'.[119] On 15 May 1416 proclamations instructed those safeguarding the belongings of thirty-three banished conspirators, including some of Paris' wealthiest bourgeois such as Imbert Deschamps and Augustin Ysbarre, be delivered to the Châtelet 'sans aucuns en retenir ou receler sur peine de perdre corps et biens'.[120] Those discovered to be harbouring fugitives would themselves be considered culpable of *lèse-majesté*. Further measures sought to obviate the potential dangers of a Parisian revolt. Weapons were declared forfeit and 'tout homme, prestre, clerc

---

114 Auguste Longnon (ed.), *Paris pendant la domination anglaise (1420-36)* (Paris: Champion, 1878), pp. 81-3.

115 Longnon (ed.), *Paris pendant la domination anglaise*, pp. 227, 238. In total, some twenty-six remission letters from this period treat Parisians communicating with individuals in Valois territories, or requests from those who left Paris in 1418 or 1419 to be permitted to return to the capital.

116 No one dared to leave Paris without permission, nor have anything taken there without a passport, no matter how little it was, and people were told 'you are going to this place; return by this time, or do not return at all'. *Journal*, p. 319.

117 For this plot, see Chapters 1 and 2.

118 Assemblies, confraternities and other great assemblies and weddings. 'Archives de la Préfecture de Police, livre vert vieil du Châtelet', fol. 71r cited in Léon Mirot, 'Le procès du Boiteux d'Orgemont. Épisode des troubles parisiens pendant la lutte des Armagnacs et des Bourguignons (Suite et fin)', *Le Moyen Âge*, 25 (1912), p. 387. See also Alexandre Tuetey (ed.), *Inventaire analytique des livres de couleur et bannières du Châtelet de Paris*, 2 vols (Paris: Imprimerie nationale, 1899-1907), I (1899), p. 113, no. 1959.

119 At the bride's expense to ensure that no man murmured about anything. *Journal*, p. 72.

120 Without keeping or hiding any upon pain of death and the confiscation of belongings. 'Archives de la Préfecture de Police, livre vert vieil du Châtelet', fol. 89r, cited in Mirot, 'Le procès du Boiteux d'Orgemont', p. 384, n. 1.

ou lay' was instructed to deposit his arms in the Bastille; the city's chains were confiscated, while the main gates were walled up to prevent enemy entries.[121]

These last measures reveal how Armagnac repression could be inscribed upon the built environment, an aspect of the factional conflict that is especially clear with regards to both the destruction of the Grande Boucherie and the treatment of the bodies of the condemned as sites of struggle. Tensions surrounding the management and appropriation of urban spaces would have been familiar to a member of the University of Paris like the Bourgeois. Throughout the first decades of the fifteenth century, the University's efforts to secure its influence in royal politics were mirrored by contests over Parisian spaces with the city's lay authorities. In 1404, the baron Charles de Savoisy was condemned by the Paris Parlement for the dispute that had erupted between members of his household and University students processing to Sainte-Catherine-du-Val-des-Écoliers.[122] The incident enabled the University – led by Jean Gerson – to stake its claim to privileged precedence as a royal 'daughter', and redress for Savoisy's slight against its prestige was configured spatially: it was ordered that Savoisy's Parisian manor be destroyed and its materials attributed to Sainte-Catherine-du-Val-des-Écoliers' fabric, a new chapel commemorating the assault be built, and the site of Savoisy's manor be left bare as a potent *lieu de mémoire* attesting to the University's triumph.[123] As Nancy McLoughlin has demonstrated, the creation of the public square and expiatory chapel 'cemented the inviolable nature of clerical privileges' and the University's authority in Parisian space, precisely as the University's role in royal politics was contested by the duke of Orléans and his allies (among whom Savoisy could be counted in 1404).[124]

Other disputes juxtaposed the University and Parisian *prévôté* directly. In May 1408, the *prévôt* Guillaume de Tignonville was condemned by Gerson for the hanging of two University students for theft, who prior to their execution had plead the benefit of clergy and therefore (ostensibly) fell under the University's jurisdiction.[125] As in 1404, the 1408 condemnation connected the University to broader political debates in the immediate aftermath of Louis d'Orléans assassination in November 1407. Tignonville had led the initial investigation to determine culpability for the murder, and in siding with the University to secure the *prévôt*'s destitution, Jean sans Peur obtained an important ally in his struggle for control over the capital and the means to justify his actions.[126] As a result

---

121 *Journal*, pp. 72-3. The Bourgeois' relation of this ordinance closely follows the wording of the Châtelet proclamation, demonstrating how little he embellished his text as this repression unfolded. See Mirot, 'Le procès du Boiteux d'Orgemont', p. 389; *Ordonnances des rois de France*, X, p. 360.

122 RSD, III, pp. 184-95; Laurent Tournier, 'L'Université de Paris et Charles de Savoisy: Une affaire d'honneur et d'état', *BSHP*, 122-24 (1995-97), pp. 71-88.

123 Baye, I, pp. 100-14. On the University's claims to privileged status in the dispute, see Nancy McLoughlin, *Jean Gerson and Gender: Rhetoric and Politics in Fifteenth-Century France* (Basingstoke: Palgrave Macmillan, 2015), Chapter 3.

124 McLoughlin, *Jean Gerson and Gender*, pp. 76, 80-4 (81).

125 RSD, III, pp. 722-29; Baye, I, p. 231; *Histoire de Charles VI*, pp. 439-40; Antoine Destemberg, 'Morts violentes et lieux de mémoire. Les réparations faites à l'Université de Paris à la fin du Moyen Âge', *Traverse. Zeitschrift für Geschichte*, 2 (2008), p. 40; Antoine Destemberg, *L'honneur des universitaires au Moyen Âge. Étude d'imaginaire social* (Paris: Presses Universitaires de France, 2015).

126 See P. Raymond, 'Enquête du prévôt de Paris sur l'assassinat de Louis, duc d'Orléans (1407)', *BEC*, 26 (1865), pp. 215-49; Bernard Guenée, *Un meurtre, une société. L'assassinat du duc d'Orléans, 23 novembre 1407* (Paris: Gallimard, 1992), pp. 182-83.

of the University dispute, Tignonville was replaced as *prévôt* on 30 April 1408 by a Burgundian sympathiser, Pierre des Essarts, before being compelled to perform a public apology, ritually processing to return the bodies to the Mathurins college in the heart of the University district on 16 May.[127] Similar contests resurfaced throughout the fifteenth century. In 1413, a Châtelet sergeant left a dead horse outside the gate of the University's Collège d'Harcourt, prompting a University protest and conflict between the sergeants and students on the eve of the Cabochien revolt.[128] In 1440, another dispute between University members and Châtelet sergeants resulted in the death of the theology master Pierre Gougis, an event that was also marked by Gougis' ritual reburial, the performance of a public *amende honourable* by the sergeant responsible for his murder, and the erection of an epitaph commemorating the conflict at the Mathurins convent.[129] As each of these cases suggests, records of contest inscribed upon Parisian space mapped the fluctuations in broader political and jurisdictional issues throughout the French kingdom, with Paris' representing a concentrated microcosmic stage where these debates, discussions and issues were played out.

This same logic can be seen in the alterations to Parisian space that followed the discovery of the 1416 conspiracy. Given the butchers' ties to Jean sans Peur and their earlier involvement in the Cabochien revolt, on 15 May the Grande Boucherie's destruction was ordered and the butchers' corporation dispersed, with new stalls established in separate areas throughout Paris.[130] Just like the friction regarding the use of Paris' chains, in the late fourteenth century tensions had arisen between the royal *prévôté* and the corporation, a fact demonstrated by the *prévôt* Hugues Aubriot's destruction of butchers' stalls in 1375 as a reprisal for the corporation's role in Marcel's 1358 revolt, followed by the abolition of privileges in 1382 for the butchers' participation in the Maillotins' uprising (restored in 1388).[131] According to the royal ordinance, the Grande Boucherie's dismantlement in 1416 was officially undertaken for reasons of insalubrity, with pollution a common problem for the butchers' trade in most late medieval cities.[132] Ideas of contamination and bloodiness associated with the trade meant that the corporation was perceived as peripheral in medieval society; butchery frequently inspired anxieties regarding disease, uncleanness and foulness associated with epidemics that inspired attempts to distance the trade from residential areas and circumscribe activities in public spaces.[133] Paralleling this cultural aversion, Jean Favier has argued that the butchers assumed an outside position in civic politics, being portrayed as aggressive and vulgar, and of a status below that of

---

127 Riccardo Famiglietti, *Royal Intrigue: Crisis at the Court of Charles VI, 1392-1420* (New York: AMS Press, 1986), p. 68.

128 'Geste des nobles', pp. 145-46; Coville, *Les Cabochiens*, pp. 182-83. On the Collège d'Harcourt see Chapter 1 and Giraudet, 'Nicolas Confrant', pp. 133-34.

129 Destemberg, 'Morts violentes', pp. 41, 45.

130 *Journal*, p. 73. For instance, before the Saint-Leufroy church. Paris, Archives nationales, JJ 170, no. 8. See Benoît Descamps, 'La destruction de la grande boucherie de Paris en mai 1416', *Hypothèses*, 7 (2004), pp. 109-18.

131 Benoît Descamps, 'La toile [sociale] et la trame [urbaine]: la place des bouchers parisiens au Moyen Âge', *Anthropology of Food*, 13 (2019), http://journals.openedition.org/aof/9814.

132 *Ordonnances des rois de France*, X, p. 361.

133 See Rawcliffe, *Urban Bodies*, pp. 147-50; Bernard Chevalier, 'Les boucheries, les bouchers et le commerce de la viande à Tours au XVᵉ siècle' in *Commerce, finances et société, XIᵉ-XVIᵉ siècles*, ed. by Bertrand Schnerb, Philippe Contamine and Thierry Dutour (Paris: Presses de l'université de Paris-Sorbonne, 1993), pp. 157-69.

the six elite *corps des marchands* who typically had a stake in municipal politics.[134] The butchers' role in revolts nevertheless signals their place as central players in urban politics. The guild jealously guarded rights to hereditary monopolies, control over their stalls and the trade within Paris, while its wealthiest members were able to finance the reconstruction of the Grande Boucherie between 1419 and 1421 themselves.[135] The 1416 ordinance was, therefore, a political condemnation as much as it was a move for sanitary improvement. In configuring the intertwined nature of these political and social struggles, the ordinance juxtaposed the image of an ordered and spacious Châtelet with the threatening, unhygienic and cramped butchers stalls that lay before it. As the ordinance stressed, the butchers' stalls would be dismantled so that Paris 'peust estre tenue et gardee belle, spacieuse, plaisante et nette de toutes ordures, infections et immondices nuisables a corps humain'.[136] The dangers posed by the stalls, both to the city's 'decoracion' and to the health of its inhabitants, were neither to be tolerated nor suffered in public spaces where the city's inhabitants congregated, especially 'de gens notables, tant nos officiers comme autres reparans et frequentans en nostredit Chastellet'.[137]

Here, debates about cleanliness and pollution in the city paralleled notions of political order and disruption, as well the social hierarchies that underscored the common good of the city. Butchery was synonymous not simply with physically pollutive practices, but also with the politically corruptive tendencies harboured by the Burgundian sympathisers constituting the corporation identified as threatening Paris' common good. This conflation of political order with the absence of pollution, a feature of Armagnac politics already evoked in the cleansing of the *voirie* described by the Bourgeois, is further underscored by the butchers' petition for the reinstatement of the Grande Boucherie two years later, in August 1418. The corporation decried how Bernard, count of Armagnac and his allies, in hatred and contempt for the butchers 'qui ont aidé ou favorisé [...] le duc de Bourgogne [...] firent abatre et demolir ladite boucherie disans *et faignans* que ce estoit pour la coracion de notredite ville de Paris'.[138] As the 1418 petition demonstrates, contemporaries were well aware of how the alterations to Parisian space in 1416 encapsulated shifts in authority, with the butchers' corporation having previously asserted the right to determine the creation of

---

134 Jean Favier, *Paris au XVe siècle, 1380-1500* (Paris: Hachette, 1974), pp. 37-8; Coville, *Les Cabochiens*, pp. 101-04.

135 This power and these rights were not unique to Paris' butchers. In the towns of the Low Countries, such as Brussels, Ghent and Liege, the butchers also represented key political players, participating in revolts throughout the fourteenth and fifteenth centuries. Chloé Deligne, Claire Billen and David Kusman, 'Les bouchers bruxellois au bas Moyen Âge. Profils d'entrepreneurs' in *Patrons, gens d'affaires et banquiers: Hommages à Ginette Kurgan-van Hentenryk*, ed. by Serge Jaumain and Kenneth Bertrams (Brussels: Timperman, 2004), pp. 69-92.

136 Can be maintained and kept beautiful, spacious, pleasant and clear of all detritus, contamination and filth harmful to the human body. *Ordonnances des rois de France*, X, p. 361.

137 Notable individuals such as our officers and others who travel to and frequent our said Châtelet. *Ordonnances des rois de France*, X, p. 361.

138 Who have helped and supported the duke of Burgundy, Paris [...] had the said butchers' stalls torn down and demolished, stating *and feigning* that this was for the improvement of our said city of Paris. Emphasis my own. Archives nationales, JJ 170, fols 224v-225v, no. 263. See also Gisela Naegle, 'Armes à double tranchant? *Bien commun* et *chose publique* dans les villes françaises du Moyen Âge' in *De Bono Communi. The Discourse and Practice of the Common Good in the European City (13th-16th c)*, ed. by Élodie Lecuppre-Desjardin and Anne-Laure Van Bruaene (Turnhout: Brepols, 2010), p. 65.

Figure 6. Detail, the Châtelet and the Grande Boucherie (bottom, centre). *Carte de Paris vers la fin du XIV*e *siècle*. CNRS Éditions. CCØ Paris Musées / Petit Palais, musée des Beaux-Arts de la Ville de Paris.

Figure 7. The Grande Boucherie and Châtelet as depicted on the Truschet and Hoyau map (c.1553). University Library Basel, Kartenslg AA 124.

new stalls in Paris.[139] In light of these acknowledged political motives, the Bourgeois' own monitoring of additional restrictions upon the butchers' rights, including their exclusion from selling wares upon the pont Notre-Dame in the first week of September 1416, suggests a 'punitive strategy' designed to neutralize the butchers' political cohesion and centrality.[140]

The subsequent redistribution of the butchers' stalls, the suppression of the corporation and confraternity, and the disruption of the family ties binding the butchers represented strategies employed by Paris' Armagnac governors to neutralize this perceived threat to civic authority and undermine the butchers' connections to the potentially disruptive population of the Halles. It also mirrored the enduring tensions between the maintenance of civic privilege and the imposition of royal authority, with the new stalls established at four separate Parisian sites surrendered 'au prouffit du roy au plus offrant'.[141] Nevertheless, the Bourgeois' account of the corporation's vicissitudes is indicative of narrative efforts to consolidate the corporation's identity when confronted with its fragmentation. The attention paid to the erection of new stalls throughout 1416 and 1417 meant that the *Journal* itself worked to produce and structure the cohesiveness of the corporation while in a state of flux, inherently delineating the boundaries of the Halles' corporate and political identities as Burgundian sympathisers in Paris struggled with their Armagnac rivals. By the spring of 1417, the Bourgeois even described the relocation of the Saint-Germain-des-Prés stalls, being transferred to a new site within the city on the left bank near the Cordeliers convent, 'en ung lieu en maniere de celier, ou on descendoit a degrez qui avoient dix marches'.[142] Moving literally underground, the reference infers the practical implications of the continued repressive policies that targeted the trade. Lighting was a contentious issue in the sale of raw meat, with traders manipulating lighting to render their wares more appealing and, as Carole Rawcliffe has shown, anxieties about the relationship between the concealment of unsanitary meat and the spread of disease were common in the fifteenth century.[143] The *Journal* therefore testifies as much to the fragmentation of the butchers' corporation, given its leading role in Burgundian politics within the city, as to the increasing pressures the corporation faced in its daily practice. The community's memory was anchored in these experiences of political contest. Restored upon the Burgundian takeover of Paris in 1418, the butchers' petition for the rebuilding of the Grande Boucherie inverted the rhetoric of *nuisance* employed by the Armagnac government in 1416, insisting

---

139 Simone Roux, 'Les bouchers et les juges à Paris à la fin du Moyen Âge' in *Un Moyen Âge pour aujourd'hui: Mélanges offerts à Claude Gauvard*, ed. by Julie Claustre, Olivier Mattéoni et Nicolas Offenstadt (Paris: Presses Universitaires de France, 2010), p. 271.

140 Marc Boone has explored how manipulations of urban space constituted a means of mitigating urban resistance in 'Urban Space', pp. 639-40

141 To the highest bidder for the king's profit. *Journal*, p. 75.

142 In a place akin to a cellar where people descended a staircase with ten steps. *Journal*, p. 82.

143 Rawcliffe, *Urban Bodies*, pp. 127-28, 147-48, 243. On 7 August 1399, the *prévôté* of Paris had forbidden the butchers of the Grande Boucherie from keeping lit candles on their stalls to deceive customers: 'En ce que pres tout au long du jour ilz avoient et tenoient grant foison de chandelles alumees en et sur leurs estaulx par quoy souventesfois leurs chars qui estoient moins loyales et marchandes, jaunes, corrompues et flestries sembloient aux achetteurs d'icelle tresblanches et fresches soubz la lueur d'icelles chandelles'. (Because for almost all of the day they have numerous candles lit on their stalls, by which those meats that are less trustworthy and worthy of sale, yellowed, corrupted and withered, seemed to their buyers to be most white and fresh in the light of these candles). Paris, Archives nationales, Y/2, fol. 219v.

upon the corporation's efforts to serve the 'bien public' of the city, the ancient nature of its customs, and the manner in which the creation of new stalls had endangered these privileges.[144] Indeed, the damages suffered between 1416 and 1418 continued to frame the corporation's political interventions long after this date. For instance, when the Lancastrian *prévôt* Simon Morhier commanded the butchers to provide supplies for the English army at Montargis in 1427, the corporation declared its inability to comply, 'recalling their sufferings at the hands of the Armagnacs'.[145] In doing so, the corporation deliberately pointed to the lasting effects of oppression, intimating that the Lancastrian requests could be perceived as equally oppressive and detrimental to the corporation's good. By tracing the corporation's experience in time and space, the *Journal* codified memories of political contest essential to the identity of the Halles, revealing efforts to establish an 'imaginary urban landscape' emphasizing the simultaneously real, imagined and symbolic practices integral to Burgundian partisanship in Paris.[146]

These same parallels between pollution, morality, spatial practice and factional contest during the 1410s were brought into relief through executions.[147] Just as the record of the confiscation of chains, the surveillance of assemblies and the destruction of butchers' stalls enabled the Bourgeois to trace shifts in civic authority, so too did the displacement and burial of condemned bodies. Naturally, by hanging bodies at the gibbet of Montfaucon or displaying quartered parts upon Paris' 'mestresses portes', the capital's authorities communicated their sense of royal justice precisely when Charles VI's agency was weakest, during the 1410s. Much like the destruction and reconstruction of buildings, the hanging and removal of bodies signalled debated impressions of moral sanctity and political right throughout the early decades of the fifteenth century.[148] Gates and scaffolds were integral fixtures of community identity, and the movement of bodies upon them reveals how visions of the community could be challenged and reshaped.[149]

While the performance of justice represented a fundamental means of (re)asserting authority over subversive Parisian spaces, as demonstrated by the case of Saint-Eustache in 1414 seen above, it was nevertheless a single part of an extensive panoply of formal procedures designed to communicate law, process disputes and signal factional power.[150] As Paris fluctuated between Burgundian and Armagnac control, revolts erupted or conspiracies were discovered, the city emerged as the site of executions that heralded the corruption of royal officers or the pecuniary, moral and spiritual threat posed by treachery

---

144 See above, note 142.

145 Thompson, *Paris and its People*, p. 167.

146 Steve Pile, *The Body and the City: Psychoanalysis, Space and Subjectivity* (London: Routledge, 1996), p. 236.

147 On reactions to executions and public sentences see above, Chapter 2.

148 Henrietta Benveniste, 'Dead Body, Public Body: Notes on Death by Execution in the Middle Ages', *Law and Critique*, 4 (1993), pp. 21-42.

149 Claude Gauvard, 'Mémoire du crime, mémoire des peines. Justice et acculturation pénale en France à la fin du Moyen Âge' in *Saint-Denis et la royauté*, ed. by Françoise Autrand, Claude Gauvard and Jean-Marie Moeglin (Paris: Éditions de la Sorbonne, 1999), pp. 691-710; Veronika Novák, 'Le corps du condamné et le tissue urbain. Exécution, pouvoir et usages de l'espace à Paris aux XVe-XVIe siècles', *Histoire urbain*, 47 (2016), pp. 151-53.

150 Tom Hamilton, 'Contesting Public Executions in Paris towards the end of the Wars of Religion' in *Cultures of Conflict Resolution in Early Modern Europe*, ed. by Stephen Cummins and Laura Kounine (London: Routledge, 2017), p. 179. This follows the close association between capital punishment and power advocated by Michel Foucault, *Surveiller et punir. Naissance de la prison* (Paris: Gallimard, 1975).

within the civic community. Beheadings at the Halles conveyed understandings of treason, enabled onlookers to read sudden shifts in political power, and signalled the purification of the civic body. This was extended to the treatment of the bodies themselves. Although heads were displayed at the Halles, bodies were expelled from the city and hanged from the gibbet of Montfaucon, as was the case for Jean de Montaigu in 1409, Colinet de Puiseux in 1411 and Pierre des Essarts in 1413. The demands of this process were such that, immediately preceding the discovery of the 1416 conspiracy, in March that year the *prévôt* Tanneguy du Châtel ordered the erection of a second Montigny gibbet adjoining that at Montfaucon.[151]

Formal, ritualized expulsions of harmful entities were, however, troubled when these bodies were brought back within the city, either as a gesture of reconciliation or to convey dramatic alterations in the political *status quo*. The Bourgeois and his contemporaries traced the politics of reburial carefully, rhetorically signalling changes to civic authority while evaluating past injustices and determining those in the present. Despite the provocative risks associated with the sanctified reburial of the condemned, the accounts also reveal that Parisian authorities frequently felt strongly enough about rehabilitation to proceed with this strategy as a means of asserting their authority and rewriting the memories of Parisian contest. For instance, having been left at Montfaucon for three years after his execution in 1409, the body of the controversial royal *maitre d'hôtel*, Jean de Montaigu, was removed upon the instruction of the Dauphin Louis de Guyenne on 27 September 1412.[152] Convicted under the trumped-up charge of conspiring with Louis d'Orléans to murder Charles VI, the rehabilitation of Montaigu's body exhibited the shifting tides of Parisian politics following the factional reconciliation at Auxerre in August 1412.[153] However, unlike the two clerics executed by Guillaume de Tignonville in 1408, whose bodies were ceremonially removed before an audience of 40,000 people before being accompanied through the city with processions, Montaigu's repatriation occurred under cover of darkness, with only twelve torch bearers witnessing the removal of his head from the spike at the Halles.[154] This secrecy underscores the potential for these movements to provoke popular responses, a fact addressed directly by the Bourgeois when the Armagnac authorities redressed the memory of two years of Burgundian dominance and the bloodshed of the Cabochien revolt the following year. Two weeks after the revolt's collapse, on 23 August 1413, the Bourgeois reported that the bodies of two leading figures executed by the Cabochiens, the *prévôt* Pierre des Essarts and the royal chamberlain Jacques de La Rivière were reinterred, 'et n'y avoit que deux torches, que on le fist tres celéement pour le commun'.[155]

151 Henri Sauval (ed.), *Histoire et recherches des antiquités de la ville de Paris*, vol. 3 (Paris: Moette and Chardon, 1724), III, p. 269. See also Pascal Bastine, *Une histoire de la peine de mort. Bourreaux et supplices, 1500-1800* (Paris: Seuil, 2011), pp. 60-1; Claude Gauvard, *Condamner à mort au Moyen Âge: Pratiques de la peine capitale en France, XIIIᵉ-XVᵉ siècle* (Paris: Presses Universitaires de France, 2018), p. 230.
152 Monstrelet, II, pp. 300-01; RSD, IV, pp. 722-27; *Histoire de Charles VI*, p. 474.
153 *Journal*, p. 6; Monstrelet, II, pp. 50-9; RSD, IV, pp. 272-76; Famiglietti, *Royal Intrigue*, pp. 78-81; Hutchison, 'Partisan Identity', p. 263.
154 *Journal*, p. 27; Monstrelet, II, p. 301.
155 And there were only two torches, because it was done secretly for [fear of] the commons. *Journal*, p. 44.

On each occcasion, the act of reburying those expelled from the civic community and branded traitors by Burgundian actors represented a means of undoing a Burgundian appropriation of royal justice within Parisian space and challenging the *mala fama* attributed to those executed. These processes of Armagnac rehabilitation required the careful manipulation of urban space and the employment of potent religious sites. Brought within Paris to be reunited with its head 'en ung sarcus', Montaigu's body was subsequently brought from the capital to the Célestins monastery that Montaigu had founded at Marcoussis in 1406.[156] The movement not only reiterated Montaigu's spiritual and political integrity, it also fundamentally inverted his damnation that, at least initially, had been founded upon accusations of the embezzlement of royal funds, to which foundations such as that at Marcoussis allegedly bore witness. The hostile Parisian political poem, the *Songe véritable*, had condemned these very investments, identifying a corrupt Montaigu as

> cellui qui a despendu
> tant que devroit estre pendu.
> Et que soit vray, avisés-cy
> le bel chastel de Marcoussy.[157]

Consequently, the movement of bodies reflected contested visions of justice in a turbulent period. While the Bourgeois had been circumspect regarding Montaigu's execution in 1409, his reburial in 1412 only served to affirm his perception of Montaigu's criminality, 'lequel avoit eu la teste couppée pour ses demerites'.[158] Similar comments met the reinterment of Colinet de Puiseux in September 1413, beheaded and quartered for betraying the fortress of Saint-Cloud during the Armagnac siege of Paris in 1411. Having jeopardized the capital's security, the moment of reburial provided the Bourgeois with an opportunity to criticize Armagnac justice. Puiseux 'estoit mieulx digne d'estre ars ou baillé aux chiens que d'estre mis en terre benoiste, sauf la chrestienté, mais ainsi faisoit a leur voulenté les faulx bandez'.[159] Similar tensions regarding the memory of the condemned can be seen in the reburial of those convicted for participating in the 1416 conspiracy. As has already been demonstrated in Chapter 2, the Bourgeois strove to preserve the reputation of these Burgundian partisans upon their execution, and this process was continued upon the Burgundian occupation of the capital in 1418. With the restoration of Burgundian power, the bodies of those executed in 1416 were taken down from the gibbet, 'et furent mis en terre saincte, et fait leur service honnestement'.[160] Their treatment was directly juxtaposed with the execution of Armagnac governors taking place in 1418. First, just as the former *échevin* Robert de Belloy had been beheaded for his role in the attempt to overthrow the Armagnac government, Guillaume d'Auxerre – also a former *échevin* – was accused of an analogous crime in conspiring to betray Paris to the English. Second, the Bourgeois

---

156 In a coffin. Monstrelet, II, p. 301.
157 He who has spent so much that he should be hanged. To prove this, simply consider the beautiful castle at Marcoussis. 'Le songe véritable', p. 259, lines 1073-76.
158 Who had been beheaded for his faults. *Journal*, p. 27.
159 Was more worthy of being burned or fed to the dogs that being buried in hallowed ground, saving his Christianity, but the false *bandez* did everything as they willed. *Journal*, p. 44.
160 And were placed in hallowed ground, and their service performed solemnly. *Journal*, p. 101.

underscored the Armagnac sergeant Monmelian's culpability directly through an account of his role in the demise of the Burgundian conspirators two years earlier, having 'fait par son prourchaz decapiter le sieur de l'Ours de la Porte Baudet', one of the 'moult honnestes hommes et de moult bonne renommée' beheaded in May 1416.[161] Consequently, just as Armagnac authorities elaborated the strategies used by the University of Paris to redress complicated memories, these contested visions of the past – and of the provision of justice in the present – were codified in the Bourgeois' writing as a means of challenging Armagnac power.

The manipulation of space therefore framed contests between ruler and ruled. The removal of chains, destruction of buildings and displacement of bodies were reported by the Bourgeois to effectively trace these contests. In this respect, the portrayal of oppressive and tyrannical government was also focused upon the disintegration of the boundaries distinguishing street space from domestic interiors, with Armagnac authority condemned through a record of official interventions in enclosed spaces. On 9 May 1416, the butchers' weapons were seized *en leurs maisons*, in August Parisians were ordered to reorganize their homes, removing chests, pots, baskets and kindling from windowsills that could pose a threat to Armagnac officers and, as we have already seen, from 1421 the Bourgeois expressed increasing discontent with fiscal impositions by stressing Châtelet transgressions of private spaces and the arrests that ensued.[162]

The revolts of 1413 and 1418 inverted this relationship, complicating the boundaries that distinguished aristocratic spaces from the public spaces that were consistently subjected to challenges in late medieval cities.[163] When the commons transgressed the boundaries of these spaces in 1413 and 1418, secretive aristocratic lifestyles were rendered public, revealing the heightened anxieties regarding wasteful, luxurious and sinful customs enjoyed by the nobility. Such concerns were especially pronounced following the catastrophe of the *Bal des Ardents* in 1393, when costumed dancers at a royal ball were accidentally set alight by Louis, duke of Orléans, endangering Charles VI and prompting aggressive Parisian responses to news of sinful courtly frivolity.[164] The commons' confrontation with closed, elite spaces was integrated into the critique of Orléanist authority presented by the *Songe véritable*, which depicted the challenges facing Paris' populace through allegory. The *Songe* depicted 'Everyperson' (Chascun) searching throughout Paris for Vérité and

---

161 Having had the owner of the Bear Inn at the porte Baudet decapitated upon his instigation; very honest men of great renown. *Journal*, pp. 100-01, 71-2.

162 In their houses; and whoever refused immediately had sergeants in their house and were led to various prisons. *Journal*, pp. 72-3.

163 Harding, 'Space, Property and Propriety', pp. 549-69; Johnson, *Law in Common*, pp. 70-2, 76-81.

164 The *Bal des Ardents* particularly marked the imaginary of those hostile to Louis, duke of Orléans. The immediate reaction is reported by Jean Froissart, 'Chroniques' in *Œuvres de Froissart*, ed. by Joseph Kervyn de Lettenhove, 28 vols (Brussels: Devaux, 1867-77), XV (1872), pp. 90-2; RSD, II, p. 71. The accident was conveyed as an attempt upon Charles VI's life by Jean Petit in his *Justification* for the duke of Orléans' murder. Monstrelet, I, p. 233. Parisian versions of the *Aventures depuis deux cents ans* noted that at the ball 'joua l'ennemi de ses enchantemens' (the Devil worked with his enchantments), and it may even have been referenced in the *Danse Macabre* mural painted at the Saints-Innocents in 1425. Paris, Bibliotheque historique de la Ville de Paris MS 527, fol. 146r; Sophie Oosterwijk, 'Of Dead Kings, Dukes and Constables: The Historical Context of the *Danse Macabre* in Late Medieval Paris', *Journal of the British Archaeological Association*, 161 (2008), pp. 152-54. See also Jan Veenstra, *Magic and Divination at the Courts of Burgundy and France: Text and Context of Laurens Pignon's* Contre les divineurs *(1411)* (Leiden: Brill, 1998), pp. 89-95.

Everyperson's daughter, Pecune, ravaged annually before 'prinse a esté en ma maison, maugré moy et contre raison'.[165] Reiterating the everyday penetration of domestic spaces by royal officers and the boundaries that distinguished aristocratic spaces, Everyperson is portrayed as knocking on the doors of the mansions belonging to the dukes of Berry, Bourbon and Orléans (among others) as well and the bishop of Paris and the Châtelet, asking where Truth is hidden.[166] The occupants block Everyperson's access and even deny Truth's worth, with the poem signalling innate tensions regarding separate, elusive and exclusive spaces that evaded the purview and openness of public politics.

For the Bourgeois, the Cabochien revolt was predicated upon a logic that blurred the boundaries between private and public, aristocratic and common. In May 1413, rumours that the queen-consort's brother Louis VII of Bavaria and Pierre des Essarts had plotted to abduct the king under the pretence of the former's wedding outside the city culminated in the commons' penetration of queen Isabeau de Bavière's bedchamber at the Hôtel Saint-Pol to arrest her brother 'et prindrent avecques lui XIII ou XIIII, que dames que damoiselles, qui bien savoient la malvaistié'.[167] Michel Pintoin also related the tensions surrounding hidden actions within royal residences. The following month, at the height of the revolt, the Cabochien captain of the night-watch, Hélion de Jacqueville, overheard sounds of merriment emanating from the Dauphin's residence. Storming the building, Jacqueville openly condemned the Dauphin's behaviour before the prince, provoked, attacked and stabbed the captain. False reports of Jacqueville's murder spread quickly throughout Paris; the Parisians surrounded the mansion, with the Dauphin only being spared by Jean sans Peur's timely intervention.[168] Five years later, the massacres of suspected Armagnacs were similarly predicated upon a search for hidden evidence within their houses, where the Bourgeois alleged that tokens were found demonstrating the inhabitants' complicity in plots to betray Paris to the English or to have the Burgundian supporters of the city massacred, as well as revealing the wealth that suspected Armagnacs had illicitly amassed.[169] Together, Burgundian soldiers and the Parisian commons assaulted Armagnac houses 'et leur fist rompre leurs portes et effundrer leurs tresors'.[170] These scenes reveal the contested character of Parisian space and the resulting blurring of boundaries between public and private. Popular movements were predicated upon rumours of hidden behaviours within bourgeois or princely mansions that threatened the common good and motivated their transgression, revealing a constant contest over spatial boundaries consonant with expressions of civic authority.[171]

Revolts similarly evoked contests regarding the jurisdiction of public spaces, and reveal a common awareness of how open space could be utilised to achieve political ends. In 1418, upon the cry of 'Alarm', Parisian rioters rallied simultaneously in the city's main squares of

---

165 Has been taken in my house, in spite of myself and against reason. 'Le songe véritable', p. 232, lines 107-08.

166 'Le songe véritable', pp. 234-38, lines 169-292.

167 And captured with him thirteen or fourteen [people], ladies and young women, who knew all about their evil plans. *Journal*, p. 30.

168 RSD, V, pp. 78-80; Coville, *Les Cabochiens*, pp. 331-32.

169 *Journal*, pp. 87-8. On the significance of these rumoured tokens, see above, Chapter 3.

170 And had their doors broken down and their treasures poured out. *Journal*, p. 89.

171 Hutchison, 'Knowing One's Place', pp. 43-4, 69-74.

the Grève, Maubert and Halles.[172] Although the Bourgeois portrayed these gatherings as the consequence of sudden panic, their perceived simultaneity suggests that these spaces framed popular organization, just as Saint-Eustache's bell had been proposed as a signal for the commons to rally at Saints-Innocents in 1416. In 1413, the Cabochien leaders' use of space was certainly more formalized. When the Dauphin Louis, duke of Guyenne re-asserted his authority over the capital, the Cabochiens assembled with the commons before the Hôtel de Ville in the place de Grève, to encourage the commons to resist the counter to the rebellion and highlighting the infrastructure that underpinned their authority.[173] By investing this space the Cabochien leadership endeavoured to appropriate the tangible manifestations of authority and legitimacy that embodied the civic community. Attempting to maintain control, the revolt's leaders told the assembled commons 'comment la paix qui estoit traictée n'estoit point a l'onneur du roy, ne du duc de Bourgongne, ne au prouffit de la bonne ville ne des habitans'.[174] Through the record of the Parisians' response, the *Journal* further demonstrates how the commons could employed public space to negotiate their political stance. 'Le menu commun qui ja estoit assemblé [...] qui moult desiroient la paix, ne vouldrent oncques recevoir leurs parolles, mais ilz commencerent touz a une voix a crier, "La paix! La paix!"'.[175] Those who supported peace with the princes unanimously gathered on the right-hand side of the square, communicating through the space itself the evaporation of the Cabochiens' political foundations. Marc Boone has described the town hall as encapsulating a 'need to tie the locus of power within the city to the power to exercise organized violence', and it is clear in the cases of 1413 and 1418 that the commons opposed to civic government recognized the importance of assembly and the symbolic use of space to legitimate and express their ideological stance as a 'central spot of contestation and rebellion'.[176] The Hôtel de Ville's potency as a site for contesting royal authority was affirmed in 1421, when the commons emulated the Cabochiens of 1413 and assembled at the site to context currency fluctuations imposed by the Lancastrian regime: 'Sy se coursa le commun et firent parlement en la maison de ville'.[177] The move was effective. Seeing the Parisians rallying, Paris' governors 'si orent paour' and were compelled to backtrack on the tax, offering an alteration of the terms for the payment of rents 'dont le peuple se deporta et

---

172 *Journal*, p. 96. According to the Ursins compiler, those who assembled at the place de Grève were led by a potter called Lambert. *Histoire de Charles VI*, p. 542. For the role of the alarm as a summoning cry, see Michael Sizer, 'Murmur, Clamor and Tumult. The Soundscape of Revolt and Oral Culture in the Middle Ages', *Radical History Review*, 121 (January 2015), p. 16.

173 *Journal*, p. 38; RSD, V, p. 121; *Histoire de Charles VI*, p. 483; Coville, *Les Cabochiens*, pp. 350-60. On the importance of town halls to urban revolts see Marc Boone, 'The Dutch Revolt and the Medieval Tradition of Urban Dissent', *Journal of Early Modern History*, 11 (2007), p. 370; Robert Descimon, 'Le corps de ville et le système cérémoniel parisien au début de l'âge moderne' in *Statuts individuels, statuts corporatifs et statuts judiciaires dans les villes européennes (Moyen Âge et temps modernes)*, ed. by Marc Boone and Maarten Prak (Leuven: Garant, 1996), p. 79; Samuel Cohn Jr., 'The Topography of Medieval Popular Protest', *Social History*, 44 (2019), pp. 408-09.

174 And showed them how the peace that had been negotiated was not to the king's honour, nor that of the duke of Burgundy, the good city or its inhabitants. *Journal*, p. 38.

175 The commons who were already assembled there [...] who greatly desired peace did not wish to listen to their words, but instead began shouting in one voice: 'Peace! Peace!'. *Journal*, p. 38.

176 Boone, 'Urban Space', p. 630; Liddy, *Contesting the City*, pp. 129, 144-57.

177 The commons became angered and held an assembly in the city hall. *Journal*, p. 155.

fut apaisie'.[178] Consequently, against the backdrop of earlier revolts, the Parisian complaint of 1421 reveals that the Bourgeois and his community were profoundly aware of the almost formulaic modes through which policies could be contested.

Besides the Hôtel de Ville, Paris' fortresses and prisons also became key targets for rebels who sought to appropriate official spaces to assert their control over judicial processes and determine the common good. Where acts of transgression and imprisonment emerged as the contested boundaries of the public sphere during periods of repressive rule, in 1413 and 1418 the commons endeavoured to identify criminals, determine their imprisonment and ensure that they were brought to justice. In 1413, those aristocrats taken from the royal residence were detained in the Louvre and the Conciergerie – eminent sites of royal authority – by the Cabochiens.[179] Chroniclers were sensitive to the written supports that underpinned this right to imprison suspected traitors. At the outbreak of the revolt, the Bourgeois reported that the University of Paris had prepared a list of those 'de la maldite et faulce traison'.[180] In each encounter where the Cabochien leaders confronted the royal court, they presented these lists of criminals, beginning with sixty people on 11 May and culminating in a second roll naming aristocrats on 22 May.[181] In the revolt's aftermath, the Ursins compiler deliberately tied the existence of documents like these to the rebels' sedition, stating that rolls had been found listing those to be banished, murdered, imprisoned and ransomed.[182] In turn, the Bourgeois' denunciation of the University's *volte-face* at the revolt's climax in August was grounded in this control over the city's prisons. Acting 'comme ce le dyable les eust conseillez', the University suggested that those currently imprisoned in the Louvre, Conciergerie and Petit Châtelet be released, 'et ne proposerent point pour la paix de ceulx qui avoient gardé a leur povair la ville de Paris et qui avoient esté consentans d'emprisonner les devantdits prisonniers pour leurs demerites'.[183] Here, the identity of the Cabochien rebels was fundamentally intertwined with control of prisons and the power to exact justice, and it was through the ritualized reversal of this power that the *Journal* portrayed the rebellion as being undone. Processing through the city with trumpets, the Dauphin demanded the release of aristocratic prisoners from the Louvre and the Palais, the latter in direct contestation of the authority secured by the Cabochien leader Jean de Troyes as the Palais' *concierge*. With the prisoners in his company, the Dauphin continued to the royal residence of Saint-Pol 'comme s'il venissent de faire le plus bel fait c'om puist faire en ce monde de sarazinesme ou d'autre part'.[184]

Parisian rebels also appropriated official spaces for their own ends, underscoring their claims to represent the common good. Contest regarding the jurisdictions of the Châtelet

---

178 They were frightened; as a result of this the people were calmed and dispersed. *Journal*, p. 155.
179 *Journal*, p. 30.
180 Of the cursed and false treason. *Journal*, p. 28.
181 RSD, V, pp. 28-40; Monstrelet, II, pp. 350-53.
182 *Histoire de Charles VI*, p. 486.
183 As if the devil had advised them; they proposed nothing for the peace of those who had safeguarded Paris and those who had supported the imprisonment of the aforesaid prisoners for their crimes. *Journal*, pp. 35-6.
184 As if they had returned from performing the greatest deeds that could be done in Saracen lands or elsewhere. *Journal*, p. 39.

and Palais again characterized the 1418 riots.[185] Appropriating the public right to perform justice through the occupation of official spaces, after his murder on 12 June 1418, Bernard, count of Armagnac's mutilated body was processed through the streets before being displayed for 'deux jours entiers au pié du degré du Palays, sur la pierre de marbre'.[186] The marble table within the Palais' hall represented 'un lieu de mémoire du pouvoir judiciare' where the constable exercised authority, oaths of loyalty were received and judicial ceremonies performed.[187] The Palais and its hall had originally been designed as public spaces that encapsulated different aspects of the royal government. Consequently, this violence could be interpreted as a text in itself, with Vincent Challet describing violence as a 'language of dominance and submission' that developed dialogue between ruler and ruled.[188] Given its ties to the constabulary, the display concurrently symbolized the Parisians' appropriation of justice within the site of royal authority and the complete subversion of Bernard d'Armagnac's power.

This right to appropriate spaces for the performance of justice was inverted upon Paris' reconquest by the Valois in 1436, where once again the movement of bodies signalled shifts in authority and efforts at reconciliation. Once displayed at the Palais, the bodies of Bernard d'Armagnac and his affiliated leaders were buried in the cultivated land adjoining Saint-Martin-des-Champs, 'en ung grant fumier qui est la'.[189] Yet, the reburial of these bodies in 1436 suggests a palpable awareness within the civic community that the memory of the 1418 massacres had to be addressed and rewritten to accommodate a return to Valois rule. For the Bourgeois, efforts to reconcile memories of Charles VII's flight from the city and the Parisian performance of justice in 1418 with the realities of a Valois return almost two decades later were centred upon the physical presence of Bernard, count of Armagnac. Among passages recording the processional celebrations undertaken to mark the Valois return and the appointment of new municipal officers, the Bourgeois included the fact that Parisians hurried to reinter the remains of the count and his allies within the abbey proper, 'c'est assavoir, le conte d'Arminac dedens le cueur, a dextre du grant autel'.[190] The move was significant not least because it implied a reversal of the Bourgeois' relentless rhetorical attempt to situate the Armagnacs beyond the boundaries of the French,

---

185 See Michael Sizer, 'The Calamity of Violence: Reading the Paris Massacres of 1418', *Proceedings of the Western Society for French History*, 35 (2007), pp. 29-30.

186 For two entire days at the foot of the Palais' steps, upon the marble table. *Journal*, p. 98. See also Cordeliers, p. 259.

187 Yann Potin, 'Les rois en leur Palais de la Cité' in *Le Paris du Moyen Âge*, ed. by Boris Bove and Claude Gauvard (Paris: Belin, 2018), p. 85. Michael Sizer ambiguously describes the marble table as the site 'where court cases and petitions would be heard', but since the fourteenth century the table also served a specific jurisdictional function, distinct from the powers of the wider Paris Parlement. Sizer, 'The Calamity of Violence', p. 25. See Loïc Cazaux, 'Le connétable de France et le Parlement: la justice de guerre au royaume de France dans la première moitié du XVᵉ siècle' in *Justice et guerre de l'Antiquité a la première guerre mondiale*, ed. by Marie Houllemare and Philippe Nevet (Amiens: Encrage, 2011), pp. 54, 60.

188 Vincent Challet, 'Violence as a Political Language: The Uses and Misuses of Violence in late Medieval French and English Popular Rebellions' in *The Routledge Handbook of Medieval Revolt*, ed. by Justine Firnhaber-Baker and Dirk Schoenaers (London: Routledge, 2017), p. 280 *et passim*; Sizer, 'The Calamity of Violence', pp. 31-2.

189 In a great rubbish pit found there. *Journal*, p. 323.

190 [That is, the count of Armagnac beneath the choir, to the right before the great altar. *Journal*, p. 323 For the celebrations marking the Valois reconquest in 1436, see pp. 320-23.

Christian community.[191] Their damnation had been sealed through their burial in profane ground, but their reinterment reflected shifting understandings of French identity. Where this appears to have been a Parisian move deliberately intended to appease Charles VII, the next step resulted from royal agency. Two weeks after Charles VII' entry in 1437, a service was organized for the Bernard d'Armagnac's remains in Saint-Martin-des-Champs, in the presence of Armagnac's youngest son, Bernard, count of Pardiac, the king and the clergy from all of Paris' churches.[192] Following the service, the remains were removed in a funerary procession across the city to Notre-Dame-des-Champs. The decision to transport the remains across the diameter of the right and left banks of the city impressed upon the entire Parisian populace the count's rehabilitation, while the instruction that all present wear black imposed not only mourning for his demise, but rendered evident the extent of Parisian guilt and complicity in his death. Through Armagnac's restoration in the presence of the king, there was no escaping the fact that the Parisians were being collectively identified as responsible for his murder. Nevertheless, the *Journal* reveals that the memory of Armagnac excesses was hard to overcome. When no alms were given at the funeral, as the assembled Parisians expected, the Bourgeois reported that 'telz iiij[M] personnes y allerent qui n'y fussent ja entrez s'ilz n'eussent cuidé que on y eust fait donnée, et les maudirent qui avant prierent pour luy'.[193]

The events of 1413 and 1418 emerged against the backdrop of a panoply of surveillance measures designed to constrain political resistance that, in and of themselves, simultaneously engendered new opportunities for the Parisian commons to challenge the city's administration. Not only did public spaces form the basis to the organization and performance of resistance, but these revolts depended upon notions of the common good and public profit, and sought to make public the hidden aristocratic machinations that threatened the wellbeing of the town and its inhabitants. By rendering this evidence, as they perceived it, visible to all – both townspeople and aristocrats – the commons asserted their claim to the right to perform and exact justice, a notion further demonstrated by the actual executions that their leaders organized in those places habitually used by Parisian institutions in order to secure their authority. Through these processes, the city's streets and squares became fluid arenas for trials that juxtaposed popular conceptions of justice with aristocratic might, questioning (and even inverting) established societal hierarchies. It was through action in public space that the Parisian commons manifested their right to participate in the politics of the realm and to secure their own perception of the common good.

Envisioning the city

Through purification and control, the city was rendered a microcosm of the wider French body politic, the site where struggles regarding competing visions of the common

---

191 On this identification of the Armagnacs, see Chapter 3.

192 *Journal*, p. 337.

193 Such that 4,000 people were there who would never have entered there if they had known that there would be no alms, and so they cursed the man whom they had earlier been praying for. *Journal*, p. 337.

good, political right and justice were enacted. Redounding upon the reputation of the condemned in an era of ever-shifting politics, the movement of bodies within and without Paris also brought to the fore competing visions of the city itself as sanctified centre. Over the course of the fourteenth century Paris had emerged as the realm's indisputable capital, the first in a hierarchy of the *bonnes villes* characterized by institutional centralization in the form of the Paris Parlement and the monarch's increasing residing in the Île-de-France during the reigns of Charles V and Charles VI. This concentration of royal energies upon the capital was accompanied by the elaboration of historical narratives, first begun during the reign of Philippe Auguste in the twelfth century, that situated Paris as the core of the realm, the foundation of French identity and the origin of the Frankish settlement of Gaul. However, the political turbulence of the early fifteenth century fundamentally altered this perception of Paris' pre-eminence in French politics. In an increasingly divided France, Paris' status and its very existence became the *topoi* of ideological debates between Lancastrian, Burgundian and Valois sympathisers. Where the threat of Paris' eventual destruction was evoked by its enemies as the natural consequence of its continued loyalty to the Anglo-Burgundian regime, within the city Parisians themselves also turned the vision of the city's gradual decline against its rulers. Economic hardship, isolation and emigration were noted as evidence of political mismanagement and exploitation that called into question the commitment of the city's governors to the common good and, as a result, their right to rule.

Indeed, the city's sanctity and its central place within a burgeoning French royal ideology were bounded with its built fabric. An acrostic poem attributed to a Norman clerk in 1418, *Paris étymologisé*, captures this impression of the capital at the beginning of the fifteenth century. For the poet, Paris' 'P' signalled 'Parfaicte paix, proesce preferee' while its inhabitants were a 'Peuple piteux pres paradis posé'.[194] Conjuring Paris' status as the *caput regni*, the city emerged as a *locus amoenus* as the poem emphasized its physical attributes – its 'Ponts precieux' and 'pleine place paree', its 'Palais prisié' and 'Pays plaisant, plantureuse pasture'.[195] Other poets echoed this emphasis upon Paris' infrastructure. Eustache Deschamps bid farewell to the Grand Pont, the Halles and the 'moustiers ou l'on voit les doulz sains',[196] while also elaborating the notion of Paris as a city 'sans pair' and 'la cité sur toutes couronnée, Fonteines et puis de sens et de clergie'.[197]

Heralding the city's beauty, late medieval Parisian literature also stressed the city's interconnection with the Valois monarchy, the urban counterpart to France's historical and

---

194 Perfect peace, preferred prowess; A piteous people placed close to Paradise. The poem is found in the only manuscript copy of Guillebert De Mets' *Description de Paris*, Brussels, Royal Library, MS 9559-64, fols 116r-117r. It was published in Le Roux de Lincy and Tisserand (ed.), *Paris et ses historiens*, pp. 506-11.

195 Precious bridges; decorated open squares; glorious Palace; Pleasant country, with plentiful pasture. Brussels, Royal Library, MS 9559-64, fol. 116r.

196 Churches where the gentle saints are seen; Eustache Deschamps, 'Adieux à Paris' in *Œuvres complètes d'Eustache Deschamps*, ed. by Queux de Saint-Hilaire, 11 vols (Paris: Firmin Didot, 1887), V (1887) pp. 51-2.

197 The city crowned above all others, the fountain and well of knowledge and clergy. Eustache Deschamps, 'Balade sur Paris (1394)' in *Œuvres complètes*, I (1878), pp. 301-02. See also Paul Meyer, 'Paris sans pair', *Romania*, 11 (1882), pp. 579-81.

spiritual exceptionalism.[198] Royal investment in the city's construction was mirrored by royally sponsored literature that equated the capital's development with the French monarchy's own foundation.[199] When Philippe Auguste ordered the construction of new defences and the paving of streets at the close of the twelfth century, the Dionysian abbot Rigord depicted the monarch as emulating his mythical Trojan ancestors who had made Paris the foundation of their Frankish kingdom.[200] Almost two centuries later, when Charles V similarly oversaw the construction of the Louvre, castle of Vincennes and new walls on Paris' right bank, Raoul de Presles' translation of *The City of God* reiterated Rigord's vision, tracing Paris' ancient vestiges to explain the city's historical interconnection with the French realm.[201] Similarly, in the *Livre des fais et bonnes meurs de Charles V* (1404) and *L'Avision Christine* (1405), Christine de Pizan nostalgically configured Paris as a 'second Athens', the site of great Fame, the *translatio imperii* and the heart of learning.[202] The result is that while Paris' built splendour, its envisioned paradisical quality and its status as the pinnacle of the *translatio studii* were intertwined with visions of the French monarchy's 'most-Christian' status, the contested and evolving ideal of the city also represented a potent means of mapping shifts in political authority and the kingdom's very decline during the turbulence that marked the early decades of the fifteenth century.

Given how entrenched this conception of Paris' place in the French kingdom was at the royal court, it is little wonder that Paris remained geopolitically central to visions of France, despite the Armagnac-Burgundian conflict and ensuing English occupation of the city. Begun at the culmination of several decades of regular royal residence and urban development, the Bourgeois' *Journal* is emblematic of the attitude, expressed by Jean Gerson in 1415, that Paris remained the city 'in qua majestas regia consistebat et erat solita residere'.[203] From this perspective, the city emerged as an agent in royal politics. In part, this impression of the close ties between monarchy and capital was accentuated by the political vacuum resulting from Charles VI's mental illness. As the dukes of Burgundy and Orléans jostled for control of the city, its royal institutions and the king's person, the Bourgeois portrayed Paris as yet another entity vying for royal attention. Fundamentally, access to the monarch enabled Parisians to voice complaint and elicit reform, underpinning the kingdom's good government. Inversely, the threat of Charles VI's separation from the capital was conveyed as a manifestation of the noxious consequences of Armagnac

198 Guenée, *Un meurtre*, pp. 121-31; Bernard Guenée, 'Paris et la cour du roi de France au XIVᵉ siècle' in *Villes, bonnes villes, cités et capitales. Études d'histoire urbaine (XIIᵉ-XVIIIᵉ siècle) offertes à Bernard Chevalier*, ed. by Monique Bourin (Tours: Publications de l'Université de Tours, 1989), pp. 259-65.

199 See Boris Bove, 'Aux origines du complexe de supériorité des parisiens: les louanges de Paris au Moyen Âge' in *Être Parisien*, ed. by Claude Gauvard and Jean-Louis Robert (Paris: Éditions de la Sorbonne, 2004), pp. 423-43.

200 See Colette Beaune, 'Raoul de Presles et les origines de Paris' in *Penser le pouvoir au Moyen Âge (VIIIᵉ-XVᵉ siècle)*, ed. by Dominique Boutet and Jacques Verger (Paris: Presses de l'École normale supérieure, 2000), pp. 17-32.

201 'Commentaire ajouté par Raoul de Presles à sa traduction de *La Cité de Dieu* (Livre V, Chapitre XXV)' in Le Roux de Lincy and Tisserand (ed.), *Paris et ses historiens*, pp. 99-115.

202 See *Le livre de l'Avision Christine*, ed. by Christine Reno and Liliane Dulac (Paris: Champion, 2001), p. 15. See also Lori J. Walters, 'Constructing Reputations: *Fama* and Memory in Christine de Pizan's *Charles V* and *L'Avision Christine*' in *Fama. The Politics of Talk and Reputation in Medieval Europe*, ed. by Thelma Fenster and Daniel Lord Smail (London: Cornell University Press, 2003), pp. 122-23, 136-37.

203 Where the royal majesty was maintained and was accustomed to reside. Jean Gerson, *Joannis Gersonii Opera Omnia*, vol. 5, ed. by Louis Ellies Dupin (Antwerp: Peter de Hondt, 1728), c. 893.

interference in royal politics. As early as 1411, the Bourgeois integrated Burgundian propaganda into his narrative to this effect, reporting Jean sans Peur's declaration that the Armagnacs 'n'avoient guerre que au roy et a la bonne ville de Paris'.[204] This close relationship accorded Parisian institutions a direct role in royal counsel. In 1410, the University theologian Étienne de Mesnil could warn the royal court that the Armagnac faction committed cruelty 'par deffaulte de bon conseil, disant qu'il failloit qu'il y eust des traistres en ce royaume',[205] whereas in 1413 the Cabochien Revolt was portrayed by the Bourgeois as directly emanating from the University's intervention to counter an Armagnac conspiracy to extract Charles VI from the capital 'pour estre maistres de Paris, de en faire toute leur voulenté, qui moult estoit maulvaise'.[206] Far from transgressive, in this light the revolt emerged as a means of reinforcing royal authority while defending 'le roy et le prouffit commun'.[207]

Prior to Charles VI's death in 1422, the Bourgeois mapped power and envisioned the state of the kingdom in terms of this Parisian access to the king. However, from this date, the disputed character of France's political centre meant that issues of access abated, replaced by implicit concerns regarding Paris' own place within a kingdom divided between the English, Burgundian and Valois parties. During the late 1420s and throughout the 1430s, Paris was transformed into a frontier town located at the epicentre of the embittered conflict between these forces.[208] The resulting sense of claustrophobia, exposure to danger and predation were already present in the Bourgeois' writing as early as 1420, when he lamented that 'tous ungs et autres n'avoient envie que sur la ville de Paris seullement, et seullement pour la richesse qu'ilz cuidoient a eulx usuper'.[209] Paris' subordination to regional or factional centres, such as Rouen or the towns of the Loire valley, also became pronounced during these decades, not least when the Bourgeois complained upon Bedford's departure from Paris in 1427 that 'le regent [...] touzjours enrichissoit son pais d'aucune chose de ce royaulme, et si n'y rapportoit riens que une taille'.[210] By contrast, Philippe III le Bon, duke of Burgundy's own lengthy absence from the capital, particularly after his elevation to the regency of the Parisian *vicomté* in October 1429, enabled the Bourgeois to contrast English and Burgundian administrative failings.[211] Bedford's successful reprovisioning of the capital in January 1431 prompted the conclusion that Burgundy had reneged upon the implicit reciprocity owed between capital and ruler, 'car ceulx de

---

204 Were only at war with the king and the good city of Paris. *Journal*, p. 11.

205 Due to a lack of good counsel, saying that it must be that there were traitors in the realm. *Journal*, p. 9.

206 To be the masters of Paris and do with it whatever they intended, which was most evil. *Journal*, p. 28.

207 The king and the common profit. *Journal*, p. 27.

208 See Léonard Dauphant, '"Si grant charté a Paris [...] par defaulte du roy": Governmental Practice and the Customary Geography of the Absence and Presence of the King in France (1364-1525)' in *Absentee Authority across Medieval Europe*, ed. by Frédérique Lachaud and Michael Penman (Woodbridge: Boydell and Brewer, 2017), pp. 153-70.

209 Each and every one had designs on the city of Paris alone, and this only for the wealth that they thought they could usurp for themselves. *Journal*, p. 137.

210 The regent always enriched his country with something from this kingdom, and never brought anything back except taxes. *Journal*, p. 218.

211 Philippe III le Bon, duke of Burgundy's naming as regent was a direct consequence of the Valois successes in 1429. *Journal*, p. 247; Monstrelet, IV, pp. 361-62. The decree ceding the governance of the territory to Burgundy was transcribed into the "Chronique dite 'des Cordeliers'", Paris, BNF Fr. 23018, fols 493r-494v.

Paris especialment l'amoient tant comme on povait amer prince et, en verité, il n'en tenoit compte s'ilz avoient faing ou soif, car tout ce perdoit par sa negligence'.[212]

Concurrent themes of royal absence and economic exploitation similarly marked the reassertion of Valois authority after 1436. While the ceremonies marking Paris' submission, including the reburial of Bernard d'Armagnac's remains, augured the capital's reunification with its Valois monarchical counterpart and the reconciliation of past enmities, Charles VII's persistent avoidance of the city compromised visions of the constitutional dynamic that had predominated during his father's reign, when Paris had been the kingdom's 'mestresse cité'.[213] This absence was regularly decried. In September 1436, 'n'estoit nouvelle du roy nullement, ne que se il fust a Romme ou en Jherusalem'.[214] Even in the aftermath of Charles VII's 1437 joyous entry, by 1439 the Bourgeois could still assert that 'il n'y avoit ne roy, n'evesque qui tenist compte de la cité de Paris, et ce tenoit le roy tousjours en Berry, ne il ne tenoit compte de l'Isle de France, ne de la guerre, ne de son peuple'.[215] When Charles VII visited Paris in 1442, he arrived 'comme ung homme estrange', emulating the Bourgeois' earlier impression of Bedford by raising taxes before departing 'derechief en son pais de Berry a celle fin que on ne lui demandast quelque relache de malles tostes'.[216] This sense of distance was perceived to compromise Parisian involvement in the processes of political administration while exacerbating anxieties regarding the influence of evil counsellors, who consolidated their power over the king's person 'comme on fait ung enfent en tutelle'.[217] In a similar vein, Jean Juvénal des Ursins admonished Charles VII, identifying his absence as the cause of his inability to hear popular complaint: 'Vous voulez estre mussé et caché en chasteaulx, meschans places et manieres de petites chambretes, sans vous monstrer et ouir les plaintes de vostre peuple ainsi tourmenté'.[218] The king's persistent absence, the pervasive character of taxation and its challenge to the privileges of Paris' churches and University revealed a new dynamic to the relations between king and capital. As Charles VII's authority had grown during the 1420s, Paris' exclusion from and opposition to Valois authority had undone its role as an ideological pillar of Valois power, ultimately demonstrated by Charles VII's and later Louis XI's lukewarm attitude towards the capital.

As the above demonstrates, the constant warfare that marked the first half of the fifteenth century provoked substantial alterations to the ideological connections binding the monarchy and Paris. If the union of these two entities was conducive to good, ordered government, then their separation was perceived to engender mutual decline. As the

---

212 For those of Paris loved him especially as much as a prince could be loved and, in truth, he did not care whether they were hungry or thirsty, and everything was lost by his negligence. *Journal*, p. 262.

213 *Journal*, p. 317.

214 There was no news whatsoever of the king, as if he was at Rome or Jerusalem. *Journal*, p. 327.

215 There was no king nor bishop who cared for the city of Paris, and the king still remained in Berry, and he did not care for the Île-de-France, the war or his people. *Journal*, p. 344.

216 As a stranger; immediately for his country of Berry so that no one could ask him to relieve the *maltôtes* [indirect taxes on goods]. *Journal*, 364.

217 Just as children kept in tutelage. *Journal*, p. 362.

218 You wish to remain hidden in castles, evil places and kinds of small chambers, without showing yourself or listening to the complaints of your tortured people. Jean Juvénal des Ursins, 'Loquar in tribulacione' in *Écrits politiques de Jean Juvénal des Ursins*, ed. by P.S. Lewis, 3 vols (Paris: Klincksieck, 1978-93), I (1978), p. 323.

contrast of Charles VI and Charles VII suggests, the former's death marked a watershed moment for the Bourgeois' consideration not only of Paris' enduring place in the French kingdom, but its very existence. When the monarch's effigy was borne through the city in November 1422, Parisians cried: 'Nous sommes bien taillez que nous ne soions en la maniere de la chetyvoison des enffans de Israel, quant ilz furent menez en Babiloine'.[219] Charles VI's death captured anxieties surrounding the prospects of Paris' own destruction at a moment of internecine conflict, acute epidemic, famine and poverty. If the late king represented the *rex christianissimus* brought to his knees by the English, then the Bourgeois envisioned Paris experiencing analogous suffering as an earthly manifestation of God's New Israel.[220]

After 1422, this impression of the very erasure of Paris' built fabric became a commonplace in the Bourgeois' writing that channelled and challenged the visions of the city found in courtly and university literature. At every turn, continuing warfare and English domination signalled the city's subjection, its decline and, ultimately, the very spectre of Paris' destruction. As noted in Chapter 2, the celebrations marking the English victory at Cravant in July 1423 compelled the Bourgeois to draw comparisons between the experiences of Paris' Trojan ancestors and the city's present circumstances.[221] Such analogies between Paris and Troy were common, not only drawing upon urban panegyric but also fourteenth-century pageants including the depiction of Troy's conquest performed for Isabeau de Bavière's 1389 coronation entry, or the Parisian round table of 1330 that opposed thirty-six Parisian 'Trojans' against 'Greeks' arriving from other French towns.[222] The account of Calchas' defection to the Greeks upon foreseeing Troy's eventual destruction exemplified the relation between Paris and the English and voiced condemnation of those who betrayed France by collaborating with the city's new governors.

Through passages like this, the Bourgeois participated in the broader discourse regarding the possibility of Paris' decline and destruction that shaped competing visions of the capital during the Anglo-Burgundian occupation. For the Norman Robert Blondel, Parisian participation in the Burgundian coup of 1418 heralded the inhabitants' perpetration of their own self-destruction. Echoing the Bourgeois' parallels between Paris, Jerusalem and Troy, Blondel warned that where Jerusalem's priests had been murdered, 'Parisiusque vide ne fias altera Troja!'[223] Comparably, as Valois forces led by Jeanne d'Arc approached Paris

---

219 We are in such a state that we are like the children of Israel, when they were led into captivity in Babylon. *Journal*, p. 178.

220 On this theme, see Jacques Krynen, *L'Empire du roi: Idées et croyances politiques en France XIIIe-XVe siècle* (Paris: Éditions Gallimard, 1993), pp. 345-83; Jacques Krynen, *Idéal du prince et pouvoir royal en France à la fin du Moyen Âge, 1380-1440* (Paris: Picard, 1981), pp. 274-75; Jacques Krynen, '"Rex Christianissimus": A Medieval Theme at the Roots of French Absolutism', *History and Anthropology*, 4 (1989), pp. 79-96; Beaune, *Birth of an Ideology*, pp. 172-93; Joseph Strayer, 'France: The Holy Land, the Chosen People and the Most Christian King' in *Medieval Statecraft and the Perspective of History* (Princeton, NJ: Princeton University Press, 1971), pp. 300-14.

221 *Journal*, p. pp. 188-89.

222 On the 1389 entry see Froissart, 'Chroniques' in *Oeuvres complètes*, XIV, pp. 5-25; RSD, I, pp. 610-17. For the jousts of 1330 see Boris Bove, 'Les joutes bourgeoises à Paris, entre rêve et réalité (XIIIe-XIVe s.)' in *Le tournoi au Moyen Âge*, ed. by Nicole Gonthier (Lyon: Centre d'histoire médiévale, 2003), pp. 142-44.

223 Paris, beware that you do not become another Troy! Robert Blondel, 'Desolatio regni francie' in Nicole Pons and Monique Goullet, 'Robert Blondel, *Desolatio regni francie*, un poème politique de soutien au futur Charles VII en 1420', *Archives d'histoire doctrinale et littéraire du Moyen Âge*, 68 (2001), p. 332, line 282.

a decade later, Christine de Pizan cautioned the city against continued disloyalty to its rightful monarch, Charles VII:

> O Paris tresmal conseillié!
> Folz habitans sans confiance!
> Ayme[s]-tu mieulz estre essillié
> Qu'a ton prince faire accordance?
> Certes, ta grant contrariance,
> Te destruira, se ne t'avises![224]

The Bourgeois, too, could invert these tropes to signal Paris' uniquely divine status in the face of existential threats. When Jeanne d'Arc assaulted the city on 8 September 1429, the Bourgeois depicted the Pucelle as echoing Christine de Pizan's own warning, exclaiming that if the Parisians failed to surrender '"nous y entrerons par force, veuillez ou non, et tous serez mis a mort sans mercy!"'[225] Jeanne's failure was conveyed as a testament to the city's sanctity, since 'Dieu qui mua la grant entreprise d'Olofernes par une femme nommée Judihe ordonna par sa pitié autrement qu'ilz ne pensoient'.[226] Tellingly, it was through the legend of Judith, previously employed by Christine de Pizan to validate Jeanne's claims to spiritual inspiration, that the Bourgeois signalled the potential for divine retribution upon those who endangered his chosen people, reiterating the subtle interrelation envisaged by the Bourgeois between Paris and its Israelite antecedents.[227]

These visions of Paris' impending destruction – expressed by enemies and inhabitants alike – found their elaboration in the Bourgeois' perception of the French kingdom's changing state. Through narratives of destruction, desolation and eventual renewal, the Bourgeois enshrined the physical state of the world as a means of articulating the character of factional government. Particularly striking was the image of societal disruption and the transgression of cultural codes that could be inscribed upon a built environment marred by conflict. In 1419, the English invasion of Normandy had disrupted livelihoods and forced non-combatants from their homes, such that:

> La plus grant partie qui soulloit labourer et estre en son lieu, lui, sa femme, sa mesnie, et estre sans danger marchans, marchandises, gens d'eglise, moynes, nonnains, gens de touz estaz ont esté boutez hors de leurs lieux, estrangers comme eussent esté bestes sauvaiges, dont il convient que les uns truandent qui soulloient donner, les autres servent qui soulloient estre serviz [...] tant d'eglises arses et bruies, et chappelles,

---

224 Oh Paris, so ill-advised! Foolish inhabitants without trust! Would you prefer to be destroyed, rather than reconcile with your prince? Certainly, your great hostility will destroy you, if you are not careful. Christine de Pizan, 'Ditié de Jehanne d'Arc' in Angus Kennedy and Kenneth Varty, 'Christine de Pisan's 'Ditié de Jehanne d'Arc' (Part I)', *Nottingham Medieval Studies*, 18 (1874), p. 48, lines 433-38.

225 We will enter by force, whether you like it or not, and all will be put to death without mercy. *Journal*, p. 245.

226 God who thwarted the great enterprise of Holofernes through a woman called Judith, in his Mercy ordained something other than they had expected. *Journal*, p. 246.

227 Christine de Pizan, 'Ditié de Jehanne d'Arc', p. 43, lines 217-24. See Deborah Fraioli, 'Why Joan of Arc never became an Amazon' in *Fresh Verdicts on Joan of Arc*, ed. by Bonnie Wheeler and Charles Wood (London: Garland, 1996), pp. 189-204.

maisons dieu, malladeries ou on soulloit faire le sainct service Notre Seigneur et les oeuvres de miséricorde, ou il n'a mais *que les places*.[228]

The collapse of societal order evidenced by the destruction of the kingdom's built environment threatened France's moral probity, inculcating a situation that endangered individual salvation and compelled the destitute to pursue violence themselves. This threat was heightened by the unravelling of a network of religious infrastructure satisfying spiritual need and, forgetting God, the French were transformed into wild beasts, such that 'on povait mieulx dire la Terre Deserte que la terre de France'.[229]

The same transformation perceived as taking place throughout France also shaped Paris in particular, as the microcosm and head of the kingdom. By tracing the decline of Paris' urban fabric in tandem with its depopulation, the Bourgeois gave voice to fears of the capital's fading centrality and its transformation from the *locus amoenus* once described in the city's panegyric literature into a debilitated wasteland.[230] Nor was the Bourgeois alone in reflecting upon the effects that warfare, economic crisis and depopulation had suddenly wrought upon the city within three decades. Completed at the peak of Paris' demographic and economic decline under the Lancastrian regime in 1434, Guillebert De Mets' *Description de la ville de Paris* presented an idealized, nostalgic vision of Paris at the beginning of the century 'en l'an quatorze cent, et quant la ville estoit en sa fleur'.[231] A time when Paris was replete with aristocratic patrons, worthy preachers, clerics and writers, for De Mets this golden era was also marked by the development of the built environment to support a growing population and ensure charitable support, exemplified by Nicolas Flamel's construction of houses for artisans whose rents, in turn, supported the poor labourers who lived above them.[232]

Three complaint poems produced during the Anglo-Burgundian era similarly underscored the state of Paris' decline, juxtaposing images of an idealized historical city with the capital's present state, summarized within the idea that the city 'Jadis fu riche, or est en friche'.[233] An appeal to Bedford in 1434 that at least reached the members of London's Guildhall assumed Paris' voice, lamenting that:

---

228 The majority of men who used to labour the land and reside in their dwellings, him, his wife and his household without danger, merchants and goods, clergymen, monks, nuns, people of all estates, all have been driven out from their places, becoming strangers as if they were wild animals, such that those who were used to giving now beg, others serve who used to be served [...] so many churches burned down, and chapels, hospitals and infirmaries where the Our Lord's holy service used to be performed as well as works of charity; now only the sites remain. *Journal*, pp. 133-34.

229 It would be better to say the desert land than the 'land of France'. *Journal*, p. 113.

230 On celebrations of Paris, see above, note 193. See also Anne-Hélène Miller, 'Revisiting Urban Encomia in Fourteenth-Century Paris: Poetics of Translation, Universalism, and the Pilgrim City', *Viator*, 45 (2014), pp. 193-210.

231 In the year 1400, when the city was in its flower. Guillebert De Mets, 'La description de la ville de Paris', p. 160. This period coincided with the time spent at Paris by Guillebert De Mets early in his career, between roughly 1405 and 1419. See Evelyn Mullally (ed. and trans.), *Description de la ville de Paris, 1434* (Turnhout: Brepols, 2015), pp. 10-23; Dominique Vanwihnsberghe and Erik Verroken, *'A l'Escu de France': Guillebert de Mets et la peinture de livres à Gand à l'époque de Jan van Eyck (1410-50)* (Brussels: Institut royal du Patrimoine artistique, 2017), pp. 38-43.

232 Guillebert De Mets, 'La description de la ville de Paris', pp. 232-36.

233 Once was rich, now it is desolate. Paris, BNF NAF 6221, fol. 6r. This complaint poem has been published by Gaston Raynaud (ed.), 'La complainte de Paris en 1436', *BSHP*, 27 (1900), pp. 36-41 (41).

Roys, ducs, princes de France et de l'Empire
Jadiz firent avec moi leur deport,
De tous pays me revenoit l'apport,
Marchandise m'anvoioit toute terre.
J'avoye argent autant que j'ay de fuerre
Mais, Fortune m'a virer ma chance,
Mettez moy hors de celle dure serre
Ou vous perdrez Paris et toute France.[234]

The stanza played upon the trope of centrality that formed a pillar of Parisian panegyric. The rightful home to the kingdom's aristocracy – upon which the city's artisans depended for patronage and financial security – the city's abandonment by the Lancastrian regime had provoked an economic crisis. Despite this, the anonymous poet persisted in asserting a vision of the city's integral place in the Anglo-Burgundian regime. Should it be lost, English power in France would be lost with it. A year later, the author of a second *complainte* traced Paris' economic transformation as a realm of 'perdicion' onto its built environment:

Regard bien les rues
Abatues
Les maisons dedans la ville
Qui sont toutes effondues
Et perdues,
C'est une chose bien vile.
Plus en y a de deux mille
Par Sainct Gilles,
Vuides, vagues, ruyneuses.[235]

The Bourgeois joined this wider Parisian evaluation of Lancastrian governance, summoning alterations to urban space in his reflections upon Bedford's administration following the city's reconquest in April 1436

Je cuide en ma conscience que oncques nul [Anglais] ne fist semer blé ne advoyne, ne faire une cheminée en hostel qui y fust, ce ne fut le regent de Bedfort, lequel faisoit touzjours maconner en quelque pais qu'il fust, et estoit sa nature toute contraire aux Anglois, car il ne vouloit avoir guerre a quelque personne.[236]

---

234 Kings, dukes, princes of France and the Empire once enjoyed their pleasures with me. From all countries riches came to me, all lands sent goods my way. I had as much money as fodder but Fortune has turned my luck. Release me from this hard vice, or you will lose Paris and all France. London, London Metropolitan Archives, Archives of the Corporation of London, MS Letter Book K, fol. 103r.

235 Look at the streets, neglected, the houses in the city which have all collapsed and been lost. It is a most unworthy thing. There are more than two thousand, by St. Giles! Empty, vacant, ruined. Paris, BNF Fr. 5332, fols 82r-v. Published in A. Auvray (ed.), 'Complainte sur les misères de Paris composée en 1435', *BSHP*, 18 (1891), pp. 84-7.

236 I believe in my conscience that no Englishman ever sowed wheat nor oats, nor built a chimney in any house, except for the regent, the duke of Bedford, who was always building in whatever country he found himself in; his nature was entirely unlike the English, for he never wanted to make war on anyone. *Journal*, p. 320.

While Bedford's heavy investment in his Parisian residence of the Tournelles may have approximated the English regent to the Valois monarchs that preceded him, the Bourgeois was nevertheless highly sensitive to the ways in which the city's depopulation and economic decline had altered Paris' state.[237] Bringing together records of fluctuating food prices, emigration and (de)construction, the *Journal* effectively conjured an evaluation of the city's changing state, with this approach to the text challenging readings that have viewed the *Journal* as a work of jarring contrasts.[238]

The dangers posed to the urban fabric by evil government could be traced through financial disparities to its effects upon the broader civic population. When currencies were devalued by a factor of four in July 1421, the royal ordinance prefaced this measure by underscoring the responsibility 'en telle maniere que le fait et gouvernement de la chose publicque puisse estre conduicte et maintenu en habondance de biens, communicacion de peuple, et accroissement de subgetz'.[239] By December, the Bourgeois criticized Paris' landlords for continuing to demand the payment of rents in 'forte monnoie', such that 'estoit chacun si grevé de paier sa maison que plusieurs renoncerent en ce temps a leurs propres heritaiges [...] et s'en alloient par desconfort vendre leurs biens sur les carreaux, et ce partoient de Paris comme gens desesperez'.[240] In this manner, the internal economic crisis facing Paris in 1421, traced back to administrative ordinances, mirrored the decline that the Bourgeois had witnessed in wider French society only years earlier. As Parisians were compelled to abandon their livelihoods 'par le faulx gouvernement des loups ravissans', the city itself confronted both physical and moral ruin.[241] Two years later, those landlords who insisted that their rents be paid in hard cash 'amoient mieulx tout perdre que faire humanité [...] et par celle deffaulte de foy on eust trouvé a Paris de maison vuydes et croisées, saines et entieres, plus de xxiiij milliers ou nulli habitoit'.[242] As in Normandy during 1419, those who left Paris during the 1420s were portrayed as abandoning civic society, their families and their faith, despairing of their poverty 'et commencerent par l'ennortement de l'ennemi à faire tous les maulx que pevent faire chrestiens'.[243]

Through these passages, the Bourgeois captured the ways in which the Parisian rental market crisis of the 1420s fractured the city's societal bonds, emulating the fragmentation already perceived in broader French society. Mass emigration engendered multiple problems for local neighbourhoods, not least because buildings made of timber and plaster required regular upkeep. The ruin of abandoned buildings held important implications

---

237 Jenny Stratford, *The Bedford Inventories. The worldly goods of John, duke of Bedford, regent of France (1389-1435)* (London: Society of Antiquaries of London, 1993), pp. 109-11.

238 For instance, Elisabeth Hodges, *Urban Poetics in the French Renaissance* (Aldershot: Ashgate, 2008), pp. 27-33.

239 In this manner that the goal and government of the common good can be conducted and maintained in the abundance of goods, the circulation of people, the increase of subjects. *Ordonnances des rois de France*, XI, pp. 122-25 (122).

240 Hard cash; everyone was so burdened by paying for their house that several renounced their own inheritances [...] and were compelled in their despondency to sell their belongings on the street, leaving Paris altogether like people in despair. *Journal*, p. 162.

241 Of these ravenous wolves. *Journal*, p. 162.

242 Preferred to lose everything than act benevolently [...] and by this lack of faith could be found more than twenty-four thousand houses in Paris in solid and complete condition, empty with no one living within them. *Journal*, p. 192.

243 And upon the temptation of the devil began to commit all the evils that Christians can. *Journal*, p. 250.

for entire streets as gutters and dividing walls subsequently went unrepaired.[244] The visible emptiness of Paris' houses was evocative of the punctures in the very networks of mutual aid conducive to the city's common good. It is perhaps for this reason that when the Bourgeois commented upon the fragility of old buildings during a storm in October 1434, he stressed its proximity to his own property and – by implication – its place within his neighbourhood, collapsing 'pres de ma maison'.[245] This fragmentation of the streets' communities was significant because networks of credit and rent paralleled informal, everyday interactions. Where Julie Claustre demonstrated that in 1488-89, 85% of all imprisoned debtors had a single neighbouring creditor, Boris Bove has suggested that equally close, local networks were found in the rental market, shaped by 'des liens d'interconnaissance car […] on emprunte avant tout à son voisin et qu'on ne prête qu'à des gens d'honneur'.[246] Consequently, when the Bourgeois related instances of mass migration from Paris and the ensuing ruin of the city's buildings, he also evoked the fracturing of these fragile, personal networks that sustained the city, coupled with the disruption of more commonly understood notions of honour and cooperation.[247] Contrasting the exploitative character of Paris' governors with the civic good, the Bourgeois could juxtapose the familiar image of the city's impending destruction with the demands for spiritual care. The *Journal* exposed the effects of combined high taxation and famine through the plight of the poor wandering through the city's streets, stressing 'les longs plains, lamentacions, criz piteables, que oncques je croy que Jheremie le prophete ne fist plus doloreux quant la cité de Jherusalem fut toute destruite'.[248] Rather than leaving Paris susceptible to the spiritual and demographic desolation taking place beyond its walls, the Bourgeois underscored the efforts of Paris' bourgeois communities to redress the city's decline in the face of its overbearing governors. Echoing the networks of spiritual support emphasized by Guillebert De Mets and perceived to be integral to the maintenance of society by the Bourgeois in 1419, together the 'bons habitans de la bonne ville de Paris' bought abandoned houses and transformed them into three hospitals for the suffering, distributed equally throughout the city at the place de Grève, Île-de-la-Cité and place Maubert.[249]

This conflation of localized efforts to revitalize the urban fabric with the possibility of decline engendered by civic ordinances is encapsulated by the tensions surrounding the city's gates found in the *Journal*. Here, the binary record of the gates' closure or restoration

---

244 For resulting conflicts in the 1430s, see Yvonne-Hélène le Maresquier-Kesteloot, 'Un conflit de voisinage devant le Parlement de Paris au XVᵉ siècle' in *Un Moyen Âge pour aujourd'hui*, ed. by Julie Claustre, Olivier Mattéoni and Nicolas Offenstadt (Paris: Presses Universitaires de France, 2010), pp. 239-46; Yvonne-Hélène le Maresquier-Kesteloot, 'Le voisinage dans l'espace parisien à la fin du Moyen Âge: bilan d'une enquête', *Revue Historique*, 299 (1998), pp. 47-70; Simone Roux, 'L'habitat urbain au Moyen Âge: le quartier de l'Université à Paris', *Annales ESC*, 2 (1969), pp. 1196-1219.

245 Near my house. *Journal*, pp. 300-01 (301).

246 Links marked by a close mutual acquaintance because […] people borrowed first and foremost from their neighbours and only loaned to those they considered honourable. Boris Bove and others., 'Du proche au lointain: essais de restitution de l'espace vécu à Paris à la fin du Moyen Âge', *BSHP*, 134-35 (2007-08), p. 22; Julie Claustre, *Dans les geôles du roi. L'emprisonnement pour dette à Paris à la fin du Moyen Âge* (Paris: Éditions de la Sorbonne, 2007), pp. 212-19.

247 On this relationship between France's crisis and the disruption of urban networks, see Tyler Lange, *Excommunication for Debt in Late Medieval France: The Business of Salvation* (Cambridge: Cambridge University Press, 2016), pp. 120-37.

248 The long moans, lamentations, pitiful cries, worse than those that ever Jeremiah the prophet made when the city of Jerusalem was entirely destroyed. *Journal*, p. 150.

249 The good inhabitants of the good city of Paris. *Journal*, p. 150.

represented a key rhetorical means of mapping Paris' shifting fortunes. The walling of gates communicated heightening political tensions to the city's inhabitants, as in 1405, when all but the four 'maistres portes' were closed, or in 1418 when only two – those of Saint-Jacques and Saint-Denis – remained open.[250] Inversely, their ceremonial reopening illustrated transitions in Paris' political order. Following the Burgundian coup in 1418, the return of Jean sans Peur and Isabeau de Bavière was celebrated by their passage through the recently un-walled porte Saint-Antoine, whereas on 23 November 1436 the Valois constable Arthur de Richemont passed through the 'porte de Bordelles qui nouvellement avoit esté desmurée'.[251] Gates were also sites integral to civic identities, simultaneously porous and binding, joining neighbourhoods to suburbs and marking the boundaries of civic authority. At the same time, gates acting as surveillance points brought municipal, royal and neighbourhood prerogatives into conflict. In 1424 and 1436, the Bourgeois condemned the sergeants stationed at gates who exacted levies upon regional wine imports 'sans loy et sans droit'; between 1413 and 1418, the garrisoning of Armagnac captains at local gates signalled the faction's oppressive hold upon the capital, particularly when local inhabitants were expelled from their homes such that 'ceste larronnaille couchoit en leurs lictz'.[252] Throughout the *Journal*, therefore, the city gates emerged as a crucial and everyday point of contact between Parisians and their governors, their depiction encapsulating discourses regarding good government, rightful taxation, devotional practice and the ties between Paris, its suburbs and hinterland.

The tensions between renewal and decline, local agencies and civic order, are exemplified by the Bourgeois' consistent account of the porte Saint-Martin, his own local gate. Closed due to the threat posed by Burgundian forces at Saint-Denis in February 1414, the gate was only reopened in August 1425 upon the petition of the Saint-Martin quartier whose members – including priests and clerics – assembled and collected funds to rebuild the gate and drawbridge in time for the feast of St. Laurent, marked by a fair at the eponymous church in the *quartier*'s suburbs.[253] Its guard entrusted to district's municipal officers, the efforts surrounding the porte Saint-Martin's repairs reveal vital negotiations between Paris' civic government and neighbourhoods on the subject of renewal. This interaction was underscored when the gate was again closed in September 1426, only to be reopened upon petition by the 'dizeniers du quartier et plusieurs autres gens d'onneur', with the *prévôt des marchands* conceding that 'Entre vous bourgoys et mesnaigers cest porte soit ouverte et gardée a vos perilz'.[254]

These detailed passages underscore the gate's symbolic place in the Bourgeois vison of the local urban landscape, crucial to ensuring the free circulation essential to devotional and trade practices, especially given that upon its opening 'dist on que passé avoit xxx ans, on n'y avoit veu passer autant de gens'.[255] These memories, evoked and transcribed in the

---

250 *Journal*, pp. 2, 101.
251 The porte de Bordelles which had recently been un-walled. *Journal*, pp. 327-28.
252 Without law and without right; these thieves slept in their beds. *Journal*, pp. 66, 327-28.
253 *Journal*, pp. 47, 203-04.
254 The *dizainiers* of the *quartier* and many other people of honour; 'Among you, bourgeois and inhabitants, may this gate be opened and defended at your risk'. *Journal*, p. 209.
255 It was said that there had not been so many people passing through the gate in thirty years. *Journal*, p. 204.

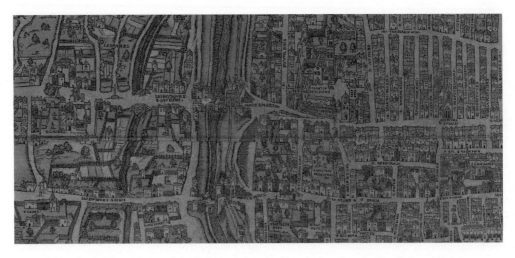

Figure 8. The porte Saint-Martin and the Saint-Laurent suburb as depicted on the Truschet and Hoyau map (*c.*1553). University Library Basel, Kartenslg AA 124.

Journal, highlight the gate's own status as a mnemonic marker that enabled Parisians to trace changes to their city. An impression of temporal change framed the gate's reopening in 1425, with the Bourgeois both depicting the gate as exhibiting forty years' worth of damage before facilitating more traffic than had been seen in thirty years. Likewise, in August 1429 the gate's closure in response to the approaching forces led by Jeanne d'Arc was equated with a shift in the *quartier*'s devotional practices and uses of urban space, representing the first time that the St. Laurent celebrations were held in the courtyard of Saint-Martin-des-Champs within the city's walls rather than in the Saint-Laurent suburbs.[256] When the gate was finally reopened fifteen years later, the ceremony presented the Bourgeois and his community with an opportunity to reflect upon the way that France's political fragmentation had marked their very personal, local experiences. At this point, he recalled how the gate had been closed ever since 'la Pucelle vint devant Paris, le jour de la Notre Dame en septembre ensuivant, que on fist premier la feste de Sainct Laurens en la grant court Sainct-Martin'.[257] Here, just as in 1425, the gate's changing status captured both the *quartier*'s place within the broader civic framework and situated the city within a kingdom whose now past conflict had shaped its spaces. In reflecting upon the distances between 1429 and 1444, the Bourgeois could convey the significance of Valois reconciliation for his own community, and acknowledged the ways in which this community's identity had been shaped and moulded according to the challenges faced in the intervening period.

---

256 *Journal,* p. 243.
257 The Pucelle came before Paris, on the feast of Our Lady that following September, when the feast of St. Lawrence was first celebrated in the great courtyard of Saint-Martin. *Journal,* p. 374.

Conclusion

In a context of continual warfare, famine and epidemics, the Bourgeois' Paris was a site of dramatic flux whose alterations mirrored the challenges faced by the urban community. Throughout the *Journal*, political communication was bounded by spatial parameters tied to implicit understandings of institutional jurisdictions and civic authority. The public evoked Lefebvre's triad, presenting the intersection of subjective, social and physical experiences of space. While spaces framed authority, these semiotic processes could be inverted when the commons, as in 1418, took control of public space for their own expression. Through his concentration upon the spatial contexts of interaction, the Bourgeois mapped fluctuations in official and popular authority, structured through an understanding of how people could act and speak in specific places. The decision to wear forms of clothing or discuss controversial topics of conversation were conveyed by the Bourgeois as challenges to the hegemonic control of Parisian space that could be used to contest authority. Such contests subsequently came to the fore during rebellions that concurrently witnessed blurring of public and private boundaries by Paris' commons, with symbolic inversion challenging a civic government and elite as the transgression of private boundaries brought the enigmatic lives of the aristocracy into the public sphere.

In turn, this approach to the Bourgeois' vision of his city reveals how the very idea of Paris, its history and its future were integral to the public debates that framed Parisian political agencies during the first decades of the fifteenth century. If the presence of the king and his royal institutions in the capital had been integral to Paris' assumption of a geopolitically central status during the fourteenth century, then the *Journal* evidences Parisian anxieties regarding the city's growing isolation after 1422, and the direct result that this had upon the city's ability to influence political decision-making in the wider realm. Fundamentally, the Armagnac-Burgundian conflict and Paris' subsequent occupation by the English provoked a substantial alteration to the ideological bonds that had once conjoined ruler and capital, evoked at an institutional level by figures such as Jean Gerson, who had insisted upon the University of Paris' status as the 'fille du roi', with a unique role in advising on political matters as an extension of the royal entity. Where once the union of king and capital encapsulated good, ordered government, their separation was perceived by Parisians as engendering their mutual decline. Chapter 5 continues this discussion of Paris' eschatological and ideological place by exploring the Bourgeois' reconstruction of civic ceremony and the ways in which such ceremonies mediated between ruler and ruled, God and city. As we shall see, even as Paris' political influence faded during the 1420s and 1430s, the Bourgeois and his community continued to assert the city's central place during the climax of the Armagnac-Burgundian conflict. Where ducal and royal attention turned to alternative centres in France – to Lancastrian Rouen, Burgundian Flanders or the Valois towns of the Loire –, the Bourgeois' vision of the city became introspective. Regardless of these political fluctuations, Paris inherently remained central for its inhabitants and it is in this light that the Bourgeois' narrative exposes an underlying but constant dialogue between the multiple centres and nodes that constituted the political culture of late medieval France, distinct from the earlier vision of Bernard Guenée that emphasized the centrality of the king's person.

Lastly, in 1436, Paris' reconquest by Charles VII reignited hopes of a return to the city's collaborative and cooperative place as an agent in Valois politics. Beginning with the celebrations that marked Arthur de Richemont's entry into the city that were subsequently commemorated annually by the *prévôté des marchands* and cathedral clergy, the *Journal* stressed themes of reconciliation and spiritual centrality, through the multiple reinterments of Bernard d'Armagnac's remains in 1436 and 1437 to the repatriation of the Île-de-France's precious artefacts, culminating in the return of the Passion relics in August 1445, secreted away by a monk of Saint-Denis 'pour le temps que les Anglois gouvernoient le royaulme'.[258] Overshadowing this apparent stability, however, was the spectre of Paris' altered relationship with the Valois monarchy. Charles VII's persistent absence, the pervasive character of taxation and its challenge to the privileges of Paris' churches and University evoked a new dynamic in the ties between king and capital. As Charles VII's authority had grown independently of the capital during the 1420s, Paris' exclusion from and opposition to Valois authority altered its place as an ideological pillar of royal power, as demonstrated by Charles VII's and, later, Louis XI's lukewarm attitude towards the capital.

---

258 During the time that the English governed the kingdom. *Journal*, p. 378.

CHAPTER 5

Civic Ceremony and the Royal Centre

Having explored modes of official communication and the Bourgeois' channelling of popular opinion and rumour, this chapter will assess how civic ceremony represented an important interface between these two spheres in the *Journal*, concurrently framing official communication and providing a forum for wider participation in political discourse. Historians have long recognized the place of late medieval civic, royal and religious ceremonies as a medium for dialogue between ruler and ruled, playing an important role in ideological communication in an era where both literacy and contact with the royal centre were more limited.[1] For France, Bernard Guenée has demonstrated that ceremonies were integral to the elaboration of a 'religion royale', while Lawrence Bryant suggested that, during the king's Parisian *jocundus adventus*, 'la formulation des relations personnelles et associatives entre le roi et ses sujets constitue un excellent exemple de l'équilibre du pouvoir et de l'esprit constitutionnel à l'époque médiévale'.[2] More recently, Élodie Lecuppre-Desjardin has underscored the status arrogated by civic communities as pillars of royal authority, delineating the limits of princely power.[3] These approaches stem from an overarching conviction that urban rituals performed a didactic function, designed to inculcate normative ideals of societal organization that facilitated urban cohesion and recognition of hierarchical order.[4] For instance, Charles Phythian-Adams envisioned ceremonies as integrative phenomena that promoted urban harmony, expressed social tensions and manifested the community through their 'crucial clarifying role'.[5] However, by concentrating predominantly upon the participation of urban elites in civic ceremony, these studies have typically ignored how the political messages conveyed through ritual were subsequently interpreted, appropriated or contested by urban participants as part and

---

1   Most recently, Neil Murphy, *Ceremonial Entries, Municipal Liberties and the Negotiation of Power in Valois France, 1328-1589* (Leiden: Brill, 2016).

2   The composition of personal and voluntary relations between the king and his subjects constituted an excellent example of the balance of power and of the constitutional spirit of the medieval era. Lawrence Bryant, 'La cérémonie de l'entrée à Paris au Moyen Âge', *Annales ESC*, 41 (1986), p. 536; Bernard Guenée and Françoise Lehoux, *Les Entrées royales françaises de 1328 à 1515* (Paris: Éditions du CNRS, 1968), p. 18. See also Ralph Giesey, 'Inaugural Aspects of French Royal Ceremonials' in *Coronations and Early Modern Monarchic Ritual*, ed. by Janos M. Bak (Los Angeles: University of California Press, 1990), p. 39.

3   Elodie Lecuppre-Desjardin, *La ville des cérémonies: Essai sur la communication politique dans les anciens Pays-Bas bourguignons* (Turnhout: Brepols, 2004), pp. 6-10; Robert Descimon, 'Le corps de ville et le système cérémoniel parisien au début de l'âge moderne' in *Statuts individuels, statuts corporatifs et statuts judiciaires dans les villes européennes (moyen âge et temps modernes)*, ed. by Marc Boone and Maarten Prak (Leuven: Garant, 1996), pp. 74-8.

4   Barbara Hanawalt, *Ceremony and Civility: Civic Culture in Late Medieval London* (Oxford: Oxford University Press, 2017), pp. 3-11.

5   Charles Phythian-Adams, 'Ceremony and the Citizen: The Communal Year at Coventry, 1450-1550', in *Crisis and Order in English Towns, 1500-1700*, ed. by Peter Clark and Paul Slack (London: Routledge and Kegan Paul, 1972), p. 69.

parcel of regular participation in the medieval public sphere. Enveloping urban topography, rituals incorporated different social strata and structured political discourse to facilitate negotiation within the civic community as well as between the civic community and external entities, framing a hierarchization of participation in political culture. This chapter therefore proposes an examination of civic ritual from the Bourgeois' perspective, measuring the distances between the performance of these events and their narrative reconstruction to determine how observers engaged with ideological messages.

It is from their very publicity that ceremonies derive their potential as a communicative medium. As Edward Muir has shown, 'the constructed dynamics of processions created ritual-specific ways of seeing', key to which was the 'reciprocity of gazes' – the interaction through which ceremony defined the relative status of participants.[6] Socio-political hierarchies depended upon the public exposure of networks of geographical, institutional and professional communities, 'composant par la même autant de groupes sociaux qu'il existe de critères identitaires'.[7] Ceremonies also established a distinction between public figures asserting their precedence, those *seen*, and a subordinate 'community' of observers. The dynamic is further underscored by the relative place occupied by participants, thereby physically mapping socio-political status.[8] However, this position depended upon a tacit acceptance and concordant interpretation of the ideological messages that ceremonies encapsulated. Indeed, scholars have generally taken it for granted that participants understood the multiple messages and rituals integral to civic ceremonies. Rather, their very publicity rendered it impossible for authorities to control these interpretations in the wider public sphere.

Philippe Buc and Alain Boureau have stressed the ambiguities inherent in medieval ritual.[9] Andrew Brown has similarly noted how 'symbolic meaning tends to evade immediate recognition; symbols and gestures remain ambiguous and obscure', whereas David Harry has recently suggested that medieval civic officials were aware of the limitations of ritual as a communicative medium, incorporating 'competing messages into the ceremonies, deliberately speaking to a range of diverse audiences'.[10] Through ceremonies, multiple and fluid media, narratives, sound and image were 'fused' to establish meaning for the participant, evoking concurrent and profoundly subjective processes of communication

6 Edward Muir, 'The Eye of the Procession: Ritual Ways of Seeing in the Renaissance' in *Ceremonial Culture in Pre-Modern Europe*, ed. by Nicholas Howe (Notre Dame, IN: University of Notre Dame Press, 2007), p. 130.

7 Comprising in that way as many social groups as there were identificatory criteria. Lecuppre-Desjardin, *La ville des cérémonies*, p. 4; Peter Arnade, 'City, State and Public Ritual in the Late Medieval Burgundian Netherlands', *Comparative Studies in Society and History*, 39 (1997), pp. 315-18.

8 Andrew Brown, 'Liturgical Memory and Civic Conflict: The Entry of Emperor Frederick III and Maximillian, King of the Romans, into Bruges on 1 August 1486', *Publications du Centre européen des études bourguignonnes*, 52 (2012), pp. 132-34.

9 Philippe Buc, *The Dangers of Ritual: Between Early Medieval Texts and Social Scientific Theory* (Princeton, NJ: Princeton University Press, 2001), pp. 8-11; Alain Boureau, 'Les cérémonies royales françaises entre performance juridique et compétence liturgique', *Annales. ESC*, 46 (1991), pp. 1253-64. See also Gerd Althoff, 'The Variability of Rituals in the Middle Ages' in *Medieval Concepts of the Past: Ritual, Memory, Historiography*, ed. by Gerd Althoff, Johannes Fried and Patrick J. Geary (Cambridge: Cambridge University Press, 2002), pp. 71-87.

10 Andrew Brown, *Civic Ceremony and Religion in Medieval Bruges, c. 1300-1520* (Cambridge: Cambridge University Press, 2011), p. 25; David Harry, *Constructing a Civic Community in Late Medieval London: The Common Profit, Charity and Commemoration* (Woodbridge: Boydell, 2019), pp. 70-1.

and interpretation. In this respect, Neil Murphy has pointed out that child monarchs, such as Henry VI or Charles VIII, 'lacked the scholarly capacity to interpret the difficult symbolism of their entries'.[11] Given the relational nature of the signs and symbols shared by actors and observers, wherein their ideological meaning is loose and shifting, Umberto Eco long ago argued that symbols themselves are negotiated to produce socially shared – and perhaps multivalently contested – meanings that reinforce, sustain or trouble the collective imagination, defined from distinct, subjective and embodied perspectives.[12] While Buc, Boureau and Gerd Althoff have concluded that ritual cannot be reduced to discrete symbolic parts, but must be viewed as a 'chain of actions' or 'séquences d'actions ou de pensée', they also warn that these are rooted in interpretation, rather than conveying retrievable, empirical meaning.[13] These contributions collectively highlight the polysemy in ritual, and this ambiguity is integral to recognizing the ways in which the 'language of ritual articulates power and power relations between individuals and collectivities': the ways in which it contributes to meaning, its production and reproduction, rather than straightforward consensus.[14] In turn, this emphasis upon negotiated meaning also harbours the very real danger that symbols, rituals and events are misunderstood or misrecognized altogether, assuming new and diverse meanings as observers and participants attempt to make sense of them. Kathleen Ashley has likewise stressed that rituals and processions require interpretation not simply as communicative moments, but also in terms of their effect upon participants, exploring the 'multi-layered conjunction of events' beyond purely linguistic messages.[15] As such, narrative descriptions of ceremony impart what observers subjectively *thought happened* or *wanted* to have happen, with their meaning framed by the contexts and audiences influencing the author.[16]

Rather than any fixed meaning, chronicles reveal the messages that authors expected civic ceremonies to convey, and their interpretation of those messages. The *Journal* evidences these processes of narrative reconstruction, appropriating and manipulating ceremonial messages, while demonstrating how audiences contested ritual meaning. In particular, the Bourgeois articulated perceived distances between ruler and ruled as a form of socio-political commentary that formed part of the very interplay between official, ceremonial communication and Parisian response. As with rumour and propaganda, the Bourgeois-as-narrator situated himself as an interpreter of ritual for his wider community, producing material that reflected ongoing discussions regarding the meaning of the events

---

11 Murphy, *Ceremonial Entries*, p. 10

12 Umberto Eco, *A Theory of Semiotics* (Bloomington, IN: Indiana University Press, 1976), p. 7; Umberto Eco, *The Limits of Interpretation* (Bloomington, IN: Indiana University Press, 1994), p. 41.

13 Althoff, 'The Variability of Rituals', p. 18; Boureau, 'Les cérémonies royales', p. 1258; Buc, *The Dangers of Ritual*, pp. 2-3.

14 Joelle Rollo-Koster, *Raiding Saint Peter: Empty Sees, Violence and the Initiation of the Great Western Schism (1378)* (Leiden: Brill, 2008), p. 87.

15 Kathleen Ashley, 'Introduction: The moving subjects of processional performance', in *Moving Subjects: Processional Performance in the Middle Ages and the Renaissance*, ed. by Kathleen Ashley and Wim Husken (Amsterdam: Rodopi, 2001), p. 12.

16 This argument follows Michel Foucault's stress upon the *fonction auteur* as a subjective control of expression and support of authority. Michel Foucault, 'Qu'est-ce qu'un auteur?' in *Dits et Écrits*, vol. 1 (Paris: Gallimard, 1994), pp. 795-99; Marie Bouhaïk-Gironès, 'À qui profite l'auteur? Théâtre, responsabilité de la parole et fonction-auteur à la fin du Moyen Âge', *Parlement[s], Revue d'histoire politique*, 8 (2012), pp. 27-31.

witnessed and developing a coherent account of these ceremonies to consolidate his opinion community. Given this nuance, greater attention must be paid to the ways in which contemporary authors selectively reconstructed civic ceremonies and what these can tell us about the hermeneutic struggles surrounding medieval ritual.

This chapter approaches issues of conceptual ambiguity surrounding ritual by examining the Bourgeois' interpretation of ceremony. Crucial here is Catherine Bell's model of *ritual practice*, with Bell highlighting how rituals involve a 'redemptive process' whereby participants construe the establishment of social and political relationships in a way 'that affords the actor the sense of a sphere of action'.[17] Following this, it is as a framework for communication between groups juxtaposed in urban space that ritual accorded Parisians agency in the determination of civic ideology, developing a shared public transcript. Where studies of late medieval ceremony have focused upon didactic messages conveyed by a royal or civic elite, the contributions of Buc and Boureau, coupled with ritual practice, highlight the fragility of such assumptions; since rituals comprise a 'heterogeneous repertoire' of symbols, they are inherently open to multiple interpretations that exhibit multiple agencies.[18] Indeed, ceremonies captured the varied 'economy of symbolic exchanges' through which Pierre Bourdieu argued that symbolic power functions as a means of conditioning an individual's awareness of the gestural, linguistic and semiotic codes that structure interaction, alongside their ability to participate in political discourse.[19] Bourdieu contended that these 'symbolic systems' enabled one group to dominate another, but it is also apparent that the ways in which medieval authors selectively reconstructed and manipulated ceremonial events in writing presented a medium for the assertion of their own authority over the community's memory, identity and notions of group interaction.[20]

The *Journal*'s presentation and reconstruction of ceremony will be explored in two ways. First, this chapter surveys the extraordinary processions designed to consolidate civic identity and affirm spiritual ties between capital, king and God. By deploying Paris' spiritual capital to secure political and environmental changes in France, these processions directly accorded every participant agency in ongoing political events. Given the potentially beneficial and influential character of Parisian prayer, it is unsurprising that the Burgundian, Armagnac and Lancastrian regimes competing for control in France attempted to exploit a devotional framework to inculcate Parisian and, consequently, divine support. Addressing the circumstances of these ceremonies, their frequency, structure and messages, this chapter also examines what the *Journal* reveals about the ways in which Parisians interpreted these messages and how they could be channelled, appropriated or excluded through writing. The Bourgeois' attitude towards these occasions in his narrative, as well

---

17 Catherine Bell, *Ritual Theory, Ritual Practice* (Oxford: Oxford University Press, 1992), pp. 81-88 (84).
18 Claude Lévi-Strauss, *The Savage Mind* (London: Weidenfeld and Nicholson, 1968), pp. 16-32; Edward Muir, *Ritual in Early Modern Europe* (Cambridge: Cambridge University Press, 1997), p. 3.
19 That is, the *habitus* by which 'collective practices are produced and the matrix in which objective structures are realized within the (subjective) dispositions that produce practices'. Bell, *Ritual Theory*, p. 79; Pierre Bourdieu, *Practical Reason on the Theory of Action* (Stanford, CA: Stanford University Press, 1998), pp. 96-101. See also Remi Lenoir, 'Pouvoir symbolique et symbolique du pouvoir' in *La légitimité implicite*, vol. 1, ed. by Jean-Philippe Genet (Paris: Éditions de la Sorbonne, 2015), pp. 49-58.
20 Pierre Bourdieu, *Language and Symbolic Power* trans. Gino Raymond and Matthew Adamson (Cambridge: Polity Press, 1991), p. 167.

as his manipulation of their supposed success or failure, enabled him to comment more generally upon the levels of Parisian support that these factions could elicit. In turn, the second part of this chapter explores how ceremonies framed negotiation between ruler and ruled. Through reflections upon underlying Parisian conversations, rumours and complaints taking place during and after these ceremonies, the *Journal* demonstrates how those excluded from power developed their own narratives of identity and, in turn, wielded them to impress understandings of kingship that were subsequently codified within the *Journal*'s text. Contested ideals came to the fore in the Bourgeois' description of Henry VI of England's entry and coronation ceremonies in 1431. A cross-examination of the *Journal* with three other contemporary descriptions of these ceremonies reveals the strategies that the Bourgeois employed to variously stress Paris' centrality or the dissonances between Lancastrian invented tradition and Parisian expectation, thereby articulating significant ideological issues inherent in the Lancastrian dual monarchy of England and France. Here, a detailed examination of the *Journal*'s record of civic and religious ceremony reveals the multifarious methods available to Parisians to engage with power both directly and indirectly, articulating their own ideological understandings and even arrogating for themselves a stake in political issues and the success of royal policy.

Parisian processions and the French monarchy

Paris witnessed a tremendous surge in processions in the late fourteenth and early fifteenth centuries, reflecting the troubled context of Charles VI's reign, marked by the monarch's mental illness, the papal schism and the growing tensions between the Orléanist and Burgundian houses. Where on average the chapter of Notre-Dame organized a single extraordinary procession annually between 1326 and 1380, this number increased to four during Charles VI's reign until 1422.[21] Relating this to more general changes in devotional practices throughout Europe, Jacques Chiffoleau argued that 1412 marked a turning point for Paris, whereupon processions appeared as events 'dignes de mémoire' in historiographical narratives, as evidenced by their detailed description in the *Journal* and contemporary 1412-13 fragment.[22] Historians have also assessed the role of Parisian ceremonial as a framework for social organization and the communication of propaganda, concentrating on the messages communicated, with Guy Thompson arguing that processions effectively moulded the participants' political attitudes.[23] In contrast, this section will demonstrate how civic ceremonies functioned as a medium through which Parisians interacted with authorities and communicated their own perspectives, but also how writers challenged and obfuscated ceremonies' political influence.

---

21 Bernard Guenée, 'Liturgie et politique. Les processions spéciales à Paris sous Charles VI' in *Un roi et son historien: vingt études sur le règne de Charles VI et la Chronique du Religieux de Saint-Denis* (Paris: Boccard, 1999), p. 428.

22 Jacques Chiffoleau, 'Les processions parisiennes de 1412: Analyse d'un rituel flamboyant', *Revue historique*, 284 (1990), p. 46.

23 Guy Thompson, *Paris and its People under English Rule: The Anglo-Burgundian Regime, 1420-36* (Clarendon Press: Oxford, 1991), pp. 179-86.

Methodologically, this approach reprises Thompson's distinction of 'civic' from 'royal' ceremonies.[24] Where the latter framed dialogue between ruler and ruled, the former denote those processions conducted under the auspices of urban institutions.[25] Barbara Hanawalt has argued that ceremonies served a primarily didactic purpose, instilling the values of civic society and intertwined with a reification of urban ideology based upon the 'common good', embodied in 'shared, self-imposed codes of behaviour'.[26] These arguments underpin impressions that ceremonies were pillars of a civic religion, exhibiting the employment of religious ritual by secular authorities.[27] However, differences in chronicler reactions reveal the extent to which ceremonies and processions were composed of interlaced symbolic codes embedded within ritual texts that resulted in the polysemy of messages interpreted and appropriated by participants and observers alike. Andrew Brown has noted that 'the connections between the exercise of authority and the use of ceremony are very indirect', meaning that processions represented 'an insecure means to establish social or political domination'.[28] Parisian processions were open to multiple interpretations by observers, with their purpose appropriated and contested by different socio-political groups during and after their performance.

Thompson also distinguished liturgical 'ceremonial processions' from 'extraordinary processions', those 'held in response to some particular event or need'.[29] The former were rarely mentioned in the *Journal* and other Parisian narratives. Rather, extraordinary processions served an important socio-political function highlighted by these texts, translating unexpected or inexplicable events into a normative discourse. Chroniclers brought extraordinary processions into relief against a backdrop of standardized ritual practice, with ceremonies drawing upon liturgical traditions and saints' cults that had become established elements in Parisian identification.[30] Even strictly 'religious' events described in the *Journal*, such as the bishop's first entry to the city, were loaded with political significance.[31] Interpretations of extraordinary processions offer tentative indications as to how Parisians conveyed ideological messages through these religious elements.

Five different kinds of extraordinary procession can be identified in fifteenth-century sources. These include Guenée's distinction between processions *pro rege* (for the wellbeing of the king), *pro pace* and for the Church, but also processions undertaken *for the city* of Paris and those responding to inclement weather or epidemics.[32] Although ostensibly for peace, processions *pro pace* can also be considered to include those ceremonies undertaken to elicit divine favour for military campaigns that, if successful, were considered to bring

---

24 Thompson, *Paris and its People*, pp. 182-86; Guenée, 'Liturgie et politique', p. 428.

25 Thompson, *Paris and its People*, p. 181; Guenée, 'Liturgie et politique', pp. 431-34.

26 Hanawalt, *Ceremony and Civility*, p. 3; Bernard Chevalier, *Les bonnes villes de France du XIVᵉ au XVIᵉ siècle* (Paris: Aubier Montaigne, 1982), pp. 256-61.

27 Andrew Brown, 'Civic Religion in Late Medieval Europe', *Journal of Medieval History*, 42 (2016), pp. 339-46; Richard Trexler, *Public Life in Renaissance Florence* (London: Cornell University Press, 1980), pp. 45-54.

28 Brown, *Civic Ceremony and Religion*, p. 27.

29 Thompson, *Paris and its People*, p. 181.

30 Descimon, 'Le corps de ville', p. 81.

31 On the bishop's entry see Véronique Julerot, 'La première entrée de l'évêque: Réflexions sur son origine', *Revue historique*, 639 (March 2006), pp. 635-76.

32 Guenée, 'Liturgie et politique', pp. 428-31.

peace to the realm and support the common good.[33] Thompson argued that Parisian processions coincided with 'periods of political disturbance' and their frequency, nature and even record reflected changing socio-political attitudes, a point supported by the available data that indicates spikes during the military campaigns of 1412 and 1414, the transition to Lancastrian governance in 1420-22 and Jeanne d'Arc's 1429 campaign.[34]

The Bourgeois described around fifty extraordinary processions occurring between 1410 and 1450, of which twenty pertained to those undertaken to support the Burgundian siege of Bourges in 1412, vesting Parisians with a direct agency in the ongoing civil conflict.[35] However, when comparing the *Journal* to other narratives compiled in Paris, we find that over 150 extraordinary processions were actually omitted by the Bourgeois, while Guenée traced 110 processions in Notre-Dame's register alone for the period 1392-1422.[36] This discrepancy arises, in part, from the Bourgeois' exclusion of almost all of the processions organized under the Armagnac and Lancastrian regimes between 1413-18 and 1420-35. Examining other narrative sources, we can find an additional thirty-two known processions (to the Bourgeois' two) and eighty-five (to thirteen) that were omitted during these two respective periods. One of the few narrative Parisian sources for the period after 1436, the *Journal* emerges as a key source for propitiatory processions in the 1440s, with the Bourgeois accounting for sixteen of the twenty-three known processions.[37] Comparing these other chronicles with the *Journal* reveals the extent to which processions were essential for facilitating Parisian participation in and inculcating awareness of political events, but also the Bourgeois' agency in managing their presentation, often obfuscating the ties between Parisians, civic institutions and factional regimes.

The contrast is clear. For the first decades of the fifteenth century most of the extra-ordinary processions reported by the Bourgeois related to Burgundian interests: they evidently engaged members of his local community, while their relation correlated with the Halles' ties to Jean sans Peur. Where the 1412 processions were recorded in detail by the Bourgeois, they also formed the main focus of an anonymous, contemporary journal fragment for 1412-13, with both demonstrating the profound level of Burgundian influence at the parish level and the impact of this activity upon these authors' historiographical

---

33 Guenée, 'Liturgie et politique', p. 430; Anna Michalek-Simínska, 'Le rôle de processions *pro rege* en France sous Charles VI' in *Civitas Mentis*, vol. 1, ed. by Zbigniewa Kadłubka and Tadeusza Sławka (Katowice: Wydawnictwo Uniwersytetu Śląskiego, 2005), pp. 204-06.

34 Thompson, *Paris and its People*, pp. 180-81.

35 The best study of the 1412 processions remains Chiffoleau, 'Les processions parisiennes de 1412', pp. 37-76. See also Bernard Guenée, 'Le voyage de Bourges (1412). Un exemple des conséquences de la folie de Charles VI', *Comptes rendus des séances de l'Académie des Inscriptions et Belles-Lettres*, 140 (1996), p. 788.

36 This total, which is not exhaustive, is determined through a study of the journals of the Parlement *greffiers* Nicolas de Baye, Clément de Fauquembergue and their successors, the *Chronique du Religieux de Saint-Denis*, the so-called *Chronique des Cordeliers* and supplemented by the registers of the chapter of Notre-Dame. The methodological approach to Parisian processions was first proposed in Guenée, 'Liturgie et politique', pp. 426-31.

37 X^{1a} 1482 (December 1436 – November 1443), the Parlement register compiled by Clément de Fauquembergue's successors as *greffier*, Jean de Blois (beginning in December 1436) and Jean Cheneteau (after Jean de Blois' death) is understudied in this regard. A seventeenth-century copy of the register, Paris, Archives nationales, U 314 has been used for the following evidence.

interests.[38] While the Bourgeois repeatedly pointed to the organization of processions by parishioners 'autour de leurs parroisses',[39] the 1412-13 fragment was more specific, recording processions by the mercer apprentices around the cloister of Saints-Innocents, by the hosiers to Notre-Dame-des-Voûtes in the Cité and the *Grande confrérie aux bourgeois* in the Madeleine church.[40] Their similarities in style and content suggest that these were written by likeminded Parisian clerics invested in a record that could, perhaps, provide a framework for later devotional exercises. Subsequent mass demonstrations orchestrated by the Armagnac and Anglo-Burgundian regimes were unmentioned by the Bourgeois. In the rare instances that they were alluded to, the *Journal* focused upon their lay character, disguising the involvement of Parisian ecclesiastical institutions.

This is demonstrated by two examples. First, the Bourgeois avoided any reference to the general processions conducted by Paris' Armagnac governors in May 1414 to support and celebrate the conquest of Burgundian-held Soissons. These ceremonies emulated the Burgundian strategy in 1412, with general processions to Notre-Dame or Saint-Denis and a University procession to Sainte-Catherine-du-Val-des-Écoliers.[41] Instead, the *Journal* concentrates upon the celebrations held upon news of their victory at Soissons on 22 May, stressing the devastation wrought by the Armagnacs and implicitly juxtaposing civil conflict with notions of true, just war fought against Saracens. The governors 'firent faire les feus comme on fait a la Sainct Jehan [...] comme si ce eussent esté Sarazins ou mescreans que on eust destruis'.[42] No religious institutions were depicted as participating in these celebrations, rather 'vous eussiez veu a sesdits feuz [...] plus de iiij^M femmes, toutes d'estat, non pas d'onneur, toutes bandées et des hommes sans nombre'.[43] Likewise, when Paris' Lancastrian governors organized three general processions involving Notre-Dame and the parish church of Saint-Germain-l'Auxerrois to celebrate the English victory at Cravant (31 July 1423), the Bourgeois left out these elements of religious involvement in celebrations that potentially jeopardized Parisians' moral wellbeing.[44] Here, the comparison with other sources demonstrates the extent to which the Bourgeois manipulated the record of these ceremonies. As a member of the University of Paris, a clergyman and an inhabitant of the right bank, he would certainly have been aware of these processions and presumably participated in several of them. And yet, despite this, the Bourgeois appears to have deliberately avoided referencing connections that bound the city to factions that he opposed, and even went to great lengths to invert the moral overtones of Armagnac or Lancastrian successes.

---

38 The fragment of the anonymous journal for 1412-13 is found in Rome, Vatican, Reg. Lat. 1502, vol. 1, fols 103r-108v. The fragment was published by Alexandre Tuetey, 'Journal parisien des années 1412 et 1413', *MSHP*, 44 (1917), pp. 163-82. All quotations are sourced from the manuscript, hereafter Reg. Lat. 1502.
39 *Journal*, p. 20.
40 Reg. Lat. 1502, fol. 103r.
41 Baye, II, 185, 187; RSD, V, pp. 343-45.
42 Had fires lit as occurs on the feast of St. John [the Baptist] [...] as if it were Saracens or infidels that they had destroyed. *Journal*, p. 54.
43 You would have seen at the said bonfires [...] more than four thousand women, all of estate but not of honour, all *bandées*, and innumerable men. *Journal*, p. 54.
44 *Journal*, pp. 187-89; Fauquembergue, II, pp. 104-06. For the Bourgeois' reaction to Cravant see Chapter 2.

For Thompson, processions represented an essential medium for the inculcation of support during the Lancastrian dual monarchy.[45] While the evidence provided by administrative records certainly supports the conclusion that Paris' English governors attempted to harness the propagandistic potential of ceremonies, the absence of references to extraordinary processions performed under Lancastrian auspices in the *Journal* is conspicuous. Besides Cravant, the Bourgeois omitted as many as ten cycles of processions designed to elicit and manifest Parisian support for Lancastrian military endeavours. These include processions to support Henry V during his Loire campaign in August 1421 and his siege of Meaux in 1422, processions to publicize the English sieges of Montereau-fault-Yonne (4 July 1420), Pont-sur-Seine (27 May 1423), Le Mans (9 August 1425) and Pontorson (8 May 1427), and even those held during the summer of 1429 to counter Charles VII's advance.[46] The Bourgeois also avoided describing those religious events organized to articulate spiritual ties between the capital and the Lancastrian monarchy, including the ceremonies held for Henry V's and John, duke of Bedford's recovery from illness in July 1422 and August 1429, or the processions undertaken when Henry VI arrived in Calais in April 1430.[47]

Nor was the Bourgeois alone in nuancing responses to Lancastrian rule. Clément de Fauquembergue's description of these ceremonies also substantially changed after Charles VI's death in October 1422 and the advent of Lancastrian governance. In the Parlement *greffier*'s journal, at least eighteen processions *pro rege* are mentioned prior to this year, with all but two of these concerned with Charles VI's health.[48] Eight processions *pro rege* were recorded for 1422, including four for the siege of Meaux and Henry V's recuperation from the illness that the monarch suffered during the summer. However, during Bedford's regency, only one procession *pro rege* was related, in April 1430.[49] Excluding this example, after 1423 the mention of ceremonies *pro rege* disappears, replaced by 'pour le salut de ce royaume et de la cité de Paris'.[50] Where the Bourgeois ignored processions in order to obfuscate the ties between the capital and the Lancastrian regime, Fauquembergue similarly recorded these processions as taking place specifically for peace and for the city, circumventing endorsements of the Lancastrian monarch.

The tentativeness with which chroniclers recorded Lancastrian processions underscores their communicative role, conditioning relations between the royal centre and the capital. By beseeching God for His intercession in human affairs, participants acquired a degree of agency in the kingdom's politics, their power drawn from Parisian liturgical and saintly traditions that assumed a national character.[51] Relics, therefore, played an essential role in the success of these processions while reinforcing collective action and

---

45 Thompson, *Paris and its People*, pp. 191-99.

46 These processions are detailed in the following sources. Fauquembergue, I, 376; II, pp. 24, 39, 42, 98, 183; Paris, Archives nationales, LL 253, p. 42; LL 113, pp. 170, 179.

47 Fauquembergue, II, p. 52; III, pp. 338-39; Paris, Archives nationales, LL 113, p. 170.

48 Fauquembergue, I, pp. 207, 209, 265, 289, 300, 346, 376, 386; II, pp. 14, 33, 39, 42, 44, 52, 54, 55.

49 Fauquembergue, II, p. 338.

50 For the salvation of the kingdom and the city of Paris. Fauquembergue, II, p. 90.

51 As demonstrated by the prominence of St. Denis in Parisian ceremony. Colette Beaune, *The Birth of an Ideology: Myths and Symbols of Nation in Late-Medieval France*, trans. by Susan Ross Huston, ed. by Fredric L. Cheyette (Oxford: University of California Press, 1985), pp. 46-63.

identity, focusing the community through the repetition of specifically *Parisian* narratives that underscored the city's enduring Christian centrality.[52] Nicolas Confrant, possibly the *Journal*'s author, would certainly have been aware of the procession's importance. During the Valois siege of Meaux in 1439, the constable Arthur de Richemont had instructed the monks of Sainte-Geneviève to perform a procession with their relics every Friday. When the procession conflicted with the feast of St. Germain d'Auxerre, Confrant assisted Jean Chuffart in redirecting the Sainte-Geneviève procession to Saint-Germain-l'Auxerrois. The monks consented, 'eu égard à la nécessité du temps'.[53] Juxtaposing an image of ordered society within the city with the impression of the disordered world without, processions structured an idealized microcosm of society. Moreover, they accentuated Paris' status as an important pillar for the success of royal policy, spiritually tying king, capital and God into a greater French whole.[54]

This tripartite communication is clearly demonstrated by the explosion of Parisian ceremonies in the summer of 1412 during the siege of Armagnac-held Bourges.[55] The anonymous author of the journal fragment for 1412-13 explicitly viewed these processions as a medium that bound Paris to Charles VI, with his narrative alternating between events at Bourges and Paris, perhaps in tandem with the arrival of news. For example, the author interrupted his account of processions on 13 June to relate the beginning of the siege on 9 June, including rumours of the defenders' plot to murder Jean sans Peur and capture Charles VI, before returning to the processions on 14 June.[56] The author constructed an implicitly causal relationship between Parisian devotion and Charles VI's survival of the plot. As Parisians sought divine intervention, the cleric could remark that 'Notre Seigneur, qui tousjours a soustenu et secouru la noble fleur de lis, ne veult pas qu'ilz eschevassent leur tres deloyale entreprise'.[57] The Bourgeois followed a similar framework, reporting that when the Armagnac captain Raoul de Gaucourt's soldiers were captured outside Bourges, they 'recognurent qu'ilz cuidoient emmener le roy par force et tuer le duc de Bourgongne, mais Dieu les en garda celle foys'.[58]

The 1412-13 fragment presents Charles VI as being fully aware that his success was predicated upon Parisian support, with the author revealing the degree to which Parisians perceived the processions as conditioning reciprocity between crown and capital. When Charles VI heard of Paris' processions in his absence, he joined this devotional nexus:

---

52 Descimon, 'Le corps de ville' pp. 87-96. For the role of processions and relics in the affirmation of urban identities see Jacques Dubois and Laure Beaumont-Maillet, *Sainte Geneviève de Paris: la vie, le culte, l'art* (Paris: Beauchesne, 1997), p. 106; Moshe Sluhovsky, *Patroness of Paris: Rituals of Devotion in Early Modern France* (Brill: Leiden, 1998), pp. 160-61; Boone, 'Urban Space and Political Conflict', p. 632.

53 Given the necessity of the times. Pierre le Juge, *Histoire de saincte Geneviefve, patronne de Paris* (Paris: Henri Coyel, 1586), pp. 118-19; Alexandre Tuetey (ed.), *Journal*, p. 347, n. 3.

54 Descimon, 'Le corps de ville', pp. 86-7.

55 For this campaign, see Riccardo Famiglietti, *Royal Intrigue: Crisis at the Court of Charles VI, 1392-1420* (New York: AMS Press, 1986), pp. 105-10.

56 Reg. Lat. 1502, fols 103v-104v. This event was also reported by Monstrelet, II, pp. 274-75; RSD, IV, pp. 666-69.

57 Our Lord, who had always supported and aided the noble *fleur de lis* did not wish that they succeed in their disloyal enterprise. Reg. Lat. 1502, fol. 104r.

58 Admitted that they had hoped to capture the king by force and kill the duke of Burgundy, but God protected them this time. *Journal*, p. 25.

Il remercya tres haultement Notre Seigneur, en disant qu'il estoit plus tenuz a la bonne ville que a tout le monde, et que il tenoit et avoit ferme esperance que Notre Seigneur luy devoit victoire sur ses ennemis par le moyen de son loyal peuple plus que par aultre chose.[59]

The 1412-13 fragment rhetorically underscored Paris' centrality to the king's military successes. Every day, its author claimed, Charles VI and the Dauphin Louis, duke of Guyenne, wrote to the city 'en humblement la remerciant et priant de tousjours perseverer, comme bons et loyaulx'.[60] As such, an exchange of letters and news supplemented the spiritual connection. Michel Pintoin, who accompanied the Oriflamme to Bourges, related how news reached the king of Parisian ceremonies organized 'ut expedicionem bellicam'.[61] Pintoin also recognized the importance of propitiation to Charles' success and, by extension, the kingdom's salvation, describing how preachers reminded Paris that 'quoniam humilitate et non resistencia divina flectuntur'.[62]

In Pintoin's view, the successful binding of ruler and ruled depended upon the moral state of every participant. When the University processed

inter celebrandum divina omnibus subsequentibus publicari statuerunt quod sic incolumitatem regis, pacem lilia deferencium et regni transquilitatem erga auctorem et amatorem pacis Christum poterant procurerare.[63]

Moral purity was conditioned by the city's ecclesiastical institutions, with priests exhorting their congregations to confess their sins in order to secure divine mercy and consequently peace as an evident manifestation of Paris' connections to God and its inhabitants' agency as a support for royal authority. The French king's assertion of his 'most-Christian' status led to the extension of these claims to the kingdom's populace, 'assimilé au peuple d'Israel et le royaume de France à la terre sainte', with processions affording participants a role in the definition of this French, Christian community.[64] Through the *translatio studii*, Paris represented a microcosmic concentration of French society, encapsulating its religious and historical traditions.[65] If the king was sacralized in part through his ties to the capital, then the redirection of these traditions against a specific faction in the French civil conflict represented an important re-articulation of the boundaries of the Christian community that excluded the king's enemies from claims to moral right.[66] Religious symbolism

---

59 Very loudly thanked Our Lord, stating that he was more greatly indebted to the good city than anyone else, and that he maintained and had a firm hope that Our Lord should [grant him] victory against his enemies through the means of his loyal people more than in any other way. Reg. Lat. 1502, fol. 105r.

60 Humbly thanking the city and asking it to always persevere as good and loyal [subjects]. Reg. Lat. 1502, fol. 105r.

61 For the success of his war. RSD, IV, p. 658. On Pintoin, see Guenée, 'Le voyage de Bourges'.

62 [That] God's favour could be elicited through humility, not pride. RSD, IV, p. 658.

63 During the mass they invited all to pray to Christ, the author and lover of peace, to secure the king's safety and the concord of the lily and the tranquillity of the kingdom. RSD, IV, p. 660.

64 Assimilated to the peuple of Israel, with the French kingdom compared to the Holy Land. Jacques Krynen, *L'Empire du roi: Idées et croyances politiques en France, XIIIᵉ-XVᵉ siècle* (Paris: Gallimard, 1993), p. 365. See also Dominique Iogna-Prat, 'Constructions chrétiennes d'un espace politique', *Le Moyen Âge*, 1 (2001), pp. 59-60.

65 Serge Lusignan has traced Paris' central and royal status through the *translatio studii* in '*Vérité garde le roi': La construction d'une identité universitaire en France (XIIIᵉ-XVᵉ siècle)* (Paris: Publications de la Sorbonne, 1999), pp. 225-77.

66 A similar function to that seem at work in the elaboration of the anti-Armagnac stereotype. See above, Chapter 3.

was essential to manifesting this distinction, exemplified by the use of the Oriflamme, whose legendary origins lay in Charlemagne's own wars against Christendom's enemies.[67] Debates surrounding the Oriflamme's deployment against the Flemish at the Battle of Roosebeke in 1382 resulted in the conclusion that it could also be deployed against excommunicates, with Guillebert De Mets describing the banner as testimony to the French monarchs' status as the 'seulx principaulx protecteurs, champions et defenseurs de l'eglise'.[68] As such, in 1412 and 1414, with each side in the French civil conflict having excommunicated the other, the Oriflamme was used by the Burgundian and Armagnac factions respectively as a means of consolidating boundaries between moral right and wrong, and between French and Other.[69] The sermon preached upon the banner's collection for the Armagnacs' Soissons campaign in 1414 reminded Charles VI that French monarchs 'doivent avoir fiance es devotes prieres et oroisons de saincte eglise', since 'a la priere des devotes personnes plusieurs fois les princes ont obtenu victoire'.[70] The rhetoric surrounding the Oriflamme captured the conflation of French and Christian identities that also characterized Parisian processions, stressing the moral boundaries between the competing factions and reinforcing the Christian identity of those devoted to the king.

In Paris, this was extended through a series of relic traditions. On 5 June 1412, the Oriflamme, Holy Nail, Crown of Thorns and relics of St. Eustace were joined in procession to the Sainte-Chapelle.[71] Just as the processions themselves encouraged participation at the parish level, these ceremonies facilitated interaction between localized cults and those of the utmost Christian importance. Notably, the procession of St. Eustace's relics enabled the Halles' Burgundian partisans to manifest devotional ties to the overarching French cause, a politicization underscored by the Burgundian dukes' own investment in Saint-Eustache, located in the heart of the district.[72] Conflating the religious and the political, this procession assimilated a Burgundian ideological stance with notions of moral right, while transforming Paris into a sacred space structured by pious behaviour. The emphasis upon the ceremonies' heterogeneity underscored this unifying perspective. For

---

67 Franck Collard, 'Ranimer l'oriflamme. Les relations des rois de France avec l'abbaye de Saint-Denis à la fin du XVᵉ siècle' in *Saint-Denis et la royauté*, ed. by Françoise Autrand, Claude Gauvard and Jean-Marie Moeglin (Paris: Publications de la Sorbonne, 1999), pp. 563-81; Philippe Contamine, 'L'oriflamme de Saint-Denis aux XIVᵉ-XVᵉ siècles. Étude de symbolique religieuse et royale', *Annales de l'Est*, 25 (1973), pp. 179-244.

68 The uniquely principal protectors, champions and defenders of the Church. Guillebert De Mets, 'Description de la ville de Paris sous Charles VI' in *Paris et ses historiens aux XIVᵉ et XVᵉ siècles. Documents et écrits originaux*, ed. by Antoine le Roux de Lincy and Lazare-Maurice Tisserand,(Paris: Imprimerie impériale, 1867), pp. 149-51; Anne Lombard-Jourdan, *Fleur de lis et oriflamme* (Paris: Presses du CNRS, 1991), pp. 164-67. Debates about the relationship between the Oriflamme, mercy and the treatment of enemies were prevalent in the early fifteenth century. See Craig Taylor, *Chivalry and the Ideals of Knighthood in France during the Hundred Years War* (Cambridge: Cambridge University Press, 2013), pp. 187-92.

69 RSD, IV pp. 630-33,

70 Should have faith in the dedicated prayers of the holy Church, since through the prayers of the devoted people the princes have secured victory several times. 'Sermon de Philippe de Villette' ed. by Charles J. Liebman, Jr, 'Un sermon de Philippe de Villette, abbé de Saint-Denis, pour la levée de l'Oriflamme (1414)', *Romania*, 68 (1944), p. 463. See also Boris Bove, 'Un registre contre la crise, le "livre vert" de Saint-Denis (1411)', *BEC*, 172 (2014), pp. 355-56.

71 *Journal*, p. 21.

72 Werner Paravicini and Bertrand Schnerb, 'Paris, capitale des ducs de Bourgogne?', *Beihefte der Francia*, 64 (2007), pp. 473-75.

another procession on 10 June, 'une des plus honnourables que on eust oncques veue',[73] the 1412-13 fragment enumerates the relics of twelve saints involved, including Paris' patron St. Geneviève and parish relics such as St. Opportuna and the Holy Innocent.[74]

These local cults underpinned a popular political agency. Foremost among Parisian devotions were the city's patron saints, Denis and Geneviève, whose invocation marked significant political events. In 1431, the mystery of St. Denis' martyrdom greeted Henry VI during his pre-coronation procession; in 1429, Brother Richard poignantly preached at Montmartre, 'bien pres ou le glorieux martir monseigneur Sainct Denis avoit esté descollé'.[75] Evidently, the Bourgeois expected his audience to be familiar with these legends and to recognize their broader significance for the city. When conspiracies to betray Paris to the Valois were discovered in 1433, the Bourgeois envisioned Denis' protection of the capital, remarking that 'le glorieux martir monseigneur Sainct Denis ne volt pas souffrir qu'ilz feissent telle cruaulté en la bonne cité de Paris, qu'il a autres foys gardée de sa saincte priere de tel peril'.[76] Inversely, when the city was eventually reconquered by the Valois in April 1436, this too was rationalized in terms of saintly intercession. Two hours before the French had entered the city, the Bourgeois reported the soldiers' intention to pillage Paris and kill those who opposed them. However, the capital's good Christian inhabitants went to their churches and prayed to Mary and Denis for their aid:

> Et vraiement, bien fut apparant que monseigneur Sainct Denis avoit esté advocat de la cité par devers la glorieuse Vierge Marie, et la glorieuse Vierge Marie par devers Notre Seigneur Jhesu Crist, car quant ilz furent entrez dedens [...] ilz furent si meuz de pitié et de joye qu'ilz ne se porent oncques tenir de larmoier.[77]

During celebrations to mark the reassertion of Valois authority, Geneviève was portrayed as intervening to prevent the participants from falling ill as they processed in the pouring rain, just as 'par plusieurs foys elle a sauvé la bonne ville de Paris; l'une foys de cher temps, l'autre foys des grans eaues, et de plusieurs autres perilz'.[78] Through these miracles, the Bourgeois situated Paris at the centre of a divine hierarchy of prayer, implicitly reiterating Paris' status as the New Jerusalem and echoing the model found in Jean Gerson's *Opus Tripartum* that hierarchically distinguished prayers to God, the Virgin, angels and saints.

In short, participation in processions and religious ceremonies enabled Parisians to exert real political agency and assert a clear vision of Paris' centrality to both the French kingdom and enveloping Christian cosmology. Given the distances that separated the royal centre from the capital after 1436, as Charles VII and later Louis XI favoured the Loire towns, this religious dimension became integral to signalling Paris' cultural supremacy in

---

73 One of the most honourable that had ever been seen. *Journal*, p. 22.

74 Reg. Lat. 1502, fol. 103r.

75 Very close to the site where the glorious martyr my lord St. Denis had been beheaded. *Journal*, p. 237.

76 The glorious martyr my lord St. Denis would not suffer them to accomplish such cruelty in the good city of Paris, that he has protected at other times from such dangers through his holy prayer. *Journal*, p. 297.

77 And truly, it was clear that my lord St. Denis had been an intercessor for the city before the glorious Virgin Mary, and the glorious Virgin Mary had beseeched Our Lord Jesus Christ, for when they [the French] entered the city [...] they were so moved by pity and by joy that they could not keep themselves from crying. *Journal*, p. 317.

78 Many times she had saved the good city of Paris, sometimes from scarcity, other times from flooding and from many other perils. *Journal*, p. 321.

texts like the *Journal*. As the French gained the upper hand against their Lancastrian rivals in northern France throughout the 1440s, the gradual restoration of Paris' place within the kingdom could be communicated through descriptions of the return of relics to their traditional sites. In the mid- and late-1440s, the Bourgeois' record becomes a litany of spiritually symbolic events that signalled the French kingdom's restoration. Sandwiched between the account of the return of the Lendit fair in the city's suburbs for the first time since 1426 and the opening of the local porte Saint-Martin, the Bourgeois noted a procession that accompanied the relics of St. Clodoald – hidden in Saint-Symphorien on the Île-de-la-Cité 'pour les guerres bien avoit xvj ans ou environ' – back to their hometown of Saint-Cloud.[79] Likewise, it was only in 1445 that the Passion relics and coronation regalia were returned to the abbey of Saint-Denis, having been secreted away to Bourges by a monk 'a celle fin que les Anglois ne l'otassent de ladicte abbaie et l'emportassent en leur pais'.[80] The return provoked a series of carefully organized processions, moving from Notre-Dame-des-Champs to Paris' south through the city, resting at the abbey of Saint-Magloire on the rue Saint-Denis before continuing to the abbey in the city's suburbs. Their retrieval was inherently framed by a narrative shaped by Paris' struggles under English rule, but also a clear reconciliation with the Valois following almost two decades of resistance to Charles VII's own authority.

This realignment of Valois ideology with civic sensibilities was underscored by the ceremonies that marked Charles VII's successes during the same period, bringing together key spiritual sites and relic traditions to mark shifts in the French kingdom's political *status quo*. On 15 May 1444, a general procession was held to celebrate the conclusion of the Treaty of Tours between Charles VII and Henry VI. The Parisians processed first to Saint-Jean-en-Grève and then to the Billettes, in the process gathering the relics of the Eucharist and knife pertaining to the 'Miracle des Billettes', a Parisian legend of Host desecration in 1290. The miracle's centrality to the procession gave it a distinctly Parisian character, a fact best demonstrated by the performance that followed the relics, depicting 'le mistere du juif qui estoit en une charrecte lié, ou il avoit espines comme se on le menast ardoir'.[81] The prevalence of these Parisian traditions served to directly bind the city's experiences to the fate of the kingdom at large and the achievement of Valois successes, with the outpouring of devotional behaviour performed precisely 'pour ce que on avoit bonne esperance d'avoir paix entre le roy de France et d'Angleterre'.[82] Similar events marking the intimate connection between localized Parisian traditions and overarching royal goals can be seen at the *Journal*'s close, in 1449, when ceremonies again tied Parisian devotional practices to Charles VII's victories. For example, when the Seine fortress of Pont-de-l'Arche was captured by the French on 15 May 1449, the news was welcomed in Paris with processions to the royal Palais and the Sainte-Chapelle where the Passion relics were shown to the assembled populace for the first time since Pontoise had been reconquered by the French in 1441. On 13 October 1449, the children of Paris' schools

---

79 Sixteen years ago or thereabouts, because of the wars. *Journal*, p. 374.
80 In case the English removed them from the abbey and took them back to their country. *Journal*, p. 378.
81 The mystery of the Jew who was bound in a cart, with thorns as if he was being led to be burned. *Journal*, p 373.
82 Because people had high hopes of peace between the king of France and England. *Journal*, pp. 373-74.

processed together to the parish of the Saints-Innocents from where, after the Mass, they continued to Notre-Dame accompanied by the relics of the Holy Innocent to elicit divine favour for the French recovery of Normandy.[83] Two weeks later, the *Journal* concluded with 'la plus belle procession a Sainct-Martin-des-Champs que on eust veue puis cent ans devant', as the University, parishes and Parlement again processed with the Billettes relics to welcome the news that Charles VII had entered Rouen. This last ceremony's ties to the circumstances of French recovery were ultimately signalled by the performance of 'une tres belle histoire de paix et de guerre qui longue chose seroit a racompter'.[84] In doing so, the Parisians reclaimed divine grace for royal successes, and through performance signalled the sense of closure accompanying the recovery of Rouen after three decades of English occupation.

Through religious ceremonies bonds were formed between three poles: city, king and God. Chroniclers emphasized their reciprocity, with Parisians participating in processions to communicate their anxieties and, in the process, regaining a degree of control over political events. Rather than a unidirectional means of imposing messages upon Parisians, successful ceremonies were predicated upon the agency, moral probity and conformity of participants. Reasserting the city's Christian character, ceremonies juxtaposed the civic community with external threats. It is in this way that these rituals represented a crucial medium for political communication, reaffirming the community's ties in space and through tradition, articulating understandings of social order and according to participants a stake in civic and royal politics as an essential, spiritual resource for ruling regimes.

Political communication and urban ceremony

For royal, civic and religious authorities, processions were intended to harmonize the political perspectives of those involved and reinforce understandings of the city's complex socio-political hierarchy. Fundamentally, they were exercises in regaining control and instilling order at times of crisis, not only in civic politics, but also over the environment. In turn, processions represented a medium for the codification of urban ideology, itself the result of this constant underlying process of contest and consensus between Parisian bodies. They gave communities and individuals of all social strata a stake in the elaboration of civic identities. In these ceremonies, the city emerged as 'un espace agissant [...] le lieu d'accueil des différents groupes sociaux qui la structurent'.[85] As demonstrated above, through the connections between the temporal and the divine established by these ceremonies, ordinary Parisians arrogated the potential to directly influence the events

---

83 *Journal*, p. 329; 'Extraits des registres capitulaires de Notre-Dame' in *Chronique de Charles VII, roi de France, par Jean Chartier*, ed. by Auguste Vallet de Viriville, 3 vols (Paris: Jannet, 1858), III, pp. 329-30. See also Philippe Contamine, 'Rendre grâces, prier, faire mémoire: la "fête du roi", 14 octobre de l'année 1450 puis 12 aout de l'année 1451 et des années postérieures', *Bulletin de la Société Nationale des Antiquaires de France* (2009), pp. 343-44.

84 A very beautiful story of war and peace that would take a long time to relate. *Journal*, pp. 392-93.

85 An active space [...] welcoming the different social groups that structured it. Élodie Lecuppre-Desjardin, 'La ville. Creuset des cultures urbaines et princière dans les anciens Pays-Bas bourguignons' in *La cour de Bourgogne et l'Europe. Le rayonnement et les limites d'un modèle culturel*, ed. by Werner Paravicini (Ostfildern: Jan Thorbecke, 2013), p. 291.

around them, ranging from inclement weather and poor harvests to political strife and military campaigns Accordingly, religious ceremonies represented a crucial interface for the communication and interpretation of ideological messages. This section will explore these processes by examining the Bourgeois' descriptions of the roles performed by processions, public ceremonies and confraternities as a means of defining the civic community's political attitudes, assessing how these media encouraged both Parisian participation in and resistance to regimes' agendas.

Ecclesiastical institutions were central to the dissemination of factional messages that sought to redefine the boundaries of the Christian community, as demonstrated by the ceremonial pronouncement of excommunications in 1411 and 1417.[86] Principally, the involvement of religious bodies enabled both the Burgundian and Armagnac governors to assert a legitimate basis to factional action, masking the political intent underwriting the sentences of excomunication and evoking papal support for specific factional stances. When the bishop Gérard de Montaigu excommunicated Armagnac leaders in November 1411, his involvement in the sentence alongside the University deflected attention from the message's real status as an element of Burgundian propaganda. The *Journal* offers an insight into the sentence's articulation:

> la devant tout le peuple fut maudicte et excommuniée toute la compaignie des Arminaz et tous leurs aidans et confortans, et furent nommez par nom tous les grans signeurs de la maldicte bande [...] et furent excommuniez de la bouche du Saint Pere, tellement qu'ilz ne povaient estre absoulz par prebstre nul, ne prelat, que du Sainct Pere et en article de mort.[87]

As propaganda, the success of this messaging was founded upon Jean sans Peur's ability to insinuate his own aims through an appropriation of religious channels and papal authority to condition its acceptance as by Parisian audiences.[88]

In the Bourgeois' reconstruction of the ceremony this was achieved, either consciously or unconsciously, by the obfuscation of the real degree of Burgundian influence over the excommunication. This was conveyed as a papal act, with an implicit reference to the bull of 1367 that was read to the audience, and which had originally excommunicated men-at-arms and members of the *Grandes Compaignies* who had assembled against the king.[89] Indicative of the means by which ceremonies guided and shaped audience reactions, the Bourgeois' own agency in interpreting this ceremony and disguising the extent of

---

86 This is indicated in the discussion of sermons in Chapter 2. See also Emily Hutchison, 'Winning Hearts and Minds in Early Fifteenth-Century France: Burgundian Propaganda in Perspective', *French Historical Studies*, 35 (2012), pp. 21-2.

87 All of the Armagnacs' company, and their supporters and sympathizers, were cursed and excommunicated before all of the people, and all of the lords of the cursed *bande* were identified by name [...] and they were excommunicated by the mouth of the Holy Father, such that they could not be absolved by any priest or prelate, save by the Holy Father in the hour of death. *Journal*, pp. 16-17. See also Monstrelet, II, pp. 210-11.

88 Emily Hutchison has persuasively demonstrated how these excommunications can be considered prime examples of 'black propaganda', whereby information is credited to a false authority to creatively deceive. Emily Hutchison, "'Pour le bien du roy et de son royaume': Burgundian Propaganda under John the Fearless, Duke of Burgundy, 1405-19", PhD Thesis, University of York, June 2006, pp. 17-18; Garth Jowett and Victoria O'Donnell, *Propaganda and Persuasion*, Seventh Edition, (Thousand Oaks, CA: SAGE, 2018), p. 18.

89 *Ordonnances des rois de France*, IX, pp. 652-53.

Burgundian influence over the excommunication's declaration is demonstrated by the *Journal*'s divergence from Pintoin's own identification of the ceremony as an example of Burgundian propaganda. For Pintoin, the excommunication resulted from a small group of royal councillors who collaborated with 'professores excellentissimos in sacra pagina in utroque jure doctores, qui duci Burgundie favebant'.[90] Although taking Pintoin's chronicle as his source, the later Ursins compiler (who was sympathetic to the Valois) omitted any reference to a sentence of excommunication against the Armagnac leaders, simply stating that they had been 'bannis et leurs biens declares confisqués, et furent lesdits bannissemens et confiscations publiés'.[91] By comparison, the Bourgeois normalized the ceremony, stressing its repetition and confirmation: 'ij ou iij foys devant avoit esté faicte a Paris'.[92] As a result, the *Journal*'s very language stressed the excommunication's consolidation of the moral boundaries distinguishing Parisian from Armagnac, insisting upon the tyrannical qualities of those excommunicated such as 'le faulx conte d'Arminac' or 'frere Jacques le Grant, Augustin qui le pis conseilloit de tous'.[93] The impact of such ceremonies upon Parisian conceptions of the civil conflict was lasting, and in January 1418 a Parisian labourer, Jean Jourdain, was pardoned for venturing that he would never respect the dukes of Berry or Orléans because they were 'excommeniez'.[94]

The dating of Jourdain's remission letter suggests that his comments may have been a direct response to the similar sentences of excommunication delivered by Paris' Armagnac governors. In November 1417 Pintoin described a parallel ceremony of excommunication, this time emphasizing a decision made 'consultu Parisiensium in trino statu'.[95] Pintoin listed the offenses attributed to Jean sans Peur and his supporters, the parvis of Notre-Dame 'assistentibus similibus soliis summe auctoritatis civibus, magistratris et doctoribus Universitatis'.[96] As in 1411, the Saint-Denis monk stressed the consensus that underpinned an ecclesiastical involvement in politics, while accentuating the illicit nature of Jean sans Peur's march upon Paris by complementing his account with the report of a failed attempt by Burgundian supporters to betray the city, 'sed, divina gracia mediante, juxta ethereum cytaristam, cogitaverunt consilia que non potuerunt stabilire'.[97] Through rhetorical juxtaposition, Pintoin presented the impression of a city united in faith against those excluded from the Christian community, and it was this devotion which ensured Paris' continued security, demonstrating the place of these excommunications in defining the city's religious and civic identities.

---

90 Most worthy professors of theology and doctors in both laws, who supported the duke of Burgundy. RSD, IV, p. 532.

91 Banished and their goods declared confiscate, and these banishments and confiscations were proclaimed. *Histoire de Charles VI*, p. 467.

92 Two or three times this had been done before in Paris. *Journal*, p. 17.

93 The false count of Armagnac; brother Jacques le Grant, an Augustinian who was the worst of their advisors. *Journal*, p. 16.

94 Paris, Archives nationales, JJ 170, fols 122r-v.

95 Through the consultation of Paris' three estates. RSD, VI, p. 156. The bull mentioned by the Religieux for the 1417 excommunication was the same as that used in 1411. See also *Histoire de Charles VI*, p. 537.

96 Surrounded by the most notable bourgeois, masters and doctors of the University. RSD, VI, p. 158. The Ursins Compiler described those responsible for the excommunication as 'notables clercs'. *Histoire de Charles VI*, p. 537.

97 But they could not accomplish their plan for the grace of the heavens and the reaction of the holy prophet. RSD, VI, p. 160. The Ursins Compiler also noted the failed coup, *Histoire de Charles VI*, pp. 537-38.

Omitting any reference to Jean sans Peur's excommunication or the failed coup that followed, the Bourgeois instead focused upon the Armagnac governors' exploitation of processions as a means of communicating *evident* propaganda. As the duke of Burgundy marched upon the capital in August 1417, the Bourgeois described how Jean sans Peur declared the abolition of taxes in the king's name, echoing the manifesto issued by the duke at Hesdin on 25 April that year:

> dont les gouverneurs de Paris prindrent si grant haine contre lui qu'ilz faisoient faire processions, et faisoient prescher qu'ilz savoient bien de vrray qu'il voulloit estre roy de France, et que par lui et que par son conseil estoient les Engloys en Normendie.[98]

Here, a calculated effort to distract from an original, Armagnac source by channelling propaganda through an ecclesiastical framework was unsuccessful. By emphasizing the governors' control over the ceremonies, the Bourgeois signalled their deprivation of ritual value. Failing to inculcate the sense of a negotiated or collectively formulated message representative of more general Parisian opinions, the *Journal* articulated a dissonance between the anti-taxation rhetoric espoused by Burgundy and largely supported by Parisians, and the anti-Burgundian rhetoric that had been disseminated upon Armagnac orders.[99] This juxtaposition struck at the heart of the notions of good and evil government that had characterized Charles VI's reign. Jean sans Peur's commitment to a reduction in taxation was explicitly presented as the defence of the 'noble chose publique de ce royaulme, dissipée et despoullée', the protection of the poor and the tempering of princely cupidity, decrying those who 'obtiennent par voyes innumerables les finances de ladicte chose publique et icelle applicquer a leur prouffit particulier'.[100] In contrast, the Bourgeois' vision of an aggressive Armagnac response placed an emphasis upon the governors' motivation by a more personal hatred. Armagnac domination of the media used to spread their messages concurrently underscored a lack of sincerity or agency for those religious institutions participating in their diffusion. Rather, the governors controlled these ceremonies, as those who 'faisoient faire' processions and 'faisoient prescher' sermons. Lastly, the Bourgeois obfuscated the fact that processions in the autumn 1417 reached a frequency similar to that recorded in 1412. By omitting references to these processions, the Bourgeois countered their influence, implying their ritual hollowness and disguised Parisian support for the Armagnac regime.[101] With Armagnac propaganda laid bare, the Bourgeois mitigated its ability to inculcate anti-Burgundian feeling.

Consequently, the excommunications of 1411 and 1417 demonstrate the conflation of religious and political rhetoric designed to frame popular understandings of the Armagnac-Burgundian conflict. These sentences had a long-term impact. Like Jean Jourdain above,

---

98 Because of which the governors of Paris had such hatred for him that they organized processions and had it preached that they knew to be truth that he [Jean sans Peur] wanted to be king of France, and that because of him and his aid the English were in Normandy. *Journal*, p. 79. For the Hesdin manifesto, see Monstrelet, III, pp. 196-206.

99 The effectiveness of this rhetoric is demonstrated in Bertrand Schnerb, *Les Armagnacs et les Bourguignons*, 177; Maurice Rey, *Le domaine du roi et les finances extraordinaires sous Charles VI, 1388-1413* (Paris: SEVPEN, 1965), pp. 336-40.

100 The noble public good of this kingdom that has been dissipated and despoiled; obtain through innumerable means the finances of the said public good and employ them for their own personal profit. 'Manifeste de Jean sans Peur, duc de Bourgogne. Hesdin (25 April 1417)'. Paris, Archives nationales, AE II 435.

101 For these processions see Alexandre Tuetey (ed.), *Journal*, p. 79, n. 1.

four years after the Armagnacs' excommunication in 1411 the Bourgeois referred to Bernard, count of Armagnac as a 'personne escommeniée, comme devant est dit'.[102] Writing from Paris in 1445, Jean du Bois suggested that French souls had been endangered because the supporters of both factions had been excommunicated, 'en les pronunçant et getant, a sains sonnans et a chandelles ardans, en plusieurs eglises en ceste cité de Paris'.[103] The combination of processions and sermons facilitated the transmission of ideas from the confines of royal or aristocratic courts, where they were debated by counsellors and theologians, into the wider public sphere. Underscored by elements such as the soundscape, light and packed crowds involved, 'campane pulsarentur et accense extinguerentur candele', the identification of the moral and political boundaries separating 'Armagnac' from 'Burgundian' reiterated the ideological unity of Paris and the city's collective identity through its juxtaposition with an external threat, simultaneously aligning the populace with the sense of moral right propounded through the combination of a papal bull with royal authority.[104]

The proliferation of factional confraternities during the 1410s further demonstrates how religious discourse was essential to the distinction of Armagnac and Burgundian identities. Confraternities involved participation at the parish level, with their success determined by compromises reminiscent of those that framed city-wide ceremonies.[105] Authorities were aware of their subversive potential, contrary to Colette Beaune's assertion that they possessed 'almost no political power at all'.[106] Indeed, Anthony Black has argued that medieval guilds and confraternities occupied a central place in the development of urban political culture.[107] Through their promotion, the parish church emerged as a space where ideological perspectives were negotiated and propaganda transmitted. In fifteenth-century France, like much of medieval Europe, parish confraternities could be relatively open, functioning as a form of civil society that facilitated engagement with civic politics, the exhibition and accumulation of social capital, and the consolidation of political identities.[108] Like processions, they accorded participants agency in political events and enabled Parisians to shape public life. During the civil conflict, Charlotte Denoël has highlighted how their establishment represented a vital means of inculcating grassroots

---

102 An excommunicated person, as stated previously. *Journal*, p. 68.
103 By pronouncing them and expelling them, with ringing bells and burning candles, in several churches in this city of Paris. Jean du Bois, 'Conseils et prédictions adressés à Charles VII en 1445 par un certain Jean du Bois', ed. by Noël Valois, *Annuaire-Bulletin de la Société de l'histoire de France*, 46 (1909), p. 219. Jean du Bois encouraged Charles VII to send clerics to Pope Eugene IV to request absolution for those excommunicated on both sides of the conflict.
104 The bells ringing and with the candles being extinguished. RSD, VI, p. 158.
105 Catherine Vincent, *Les confréries médiévales dans le royaume de France, XIIIᵉ-XVᵉ siècle* (Paris: Albin Michel, 1994), pp. 180-83; André Vauchez, 'Les confréries au Moyen Âge: esquisse d'un bilan historiographique', *Revue historique*, 275 (1986), pp. 474-76.
106 Beaune, *The Birth of an Ideology*, 118.
107 Anthony Black, *Guilds and Civil Societies in European Politics Thought from the Twelfth Century to the Present* (Ithaca, NY: Cornell University Press, 1984).
108 Paul Trio, 'Les confréries comme expression de solidarité et de conscience urbaine aux Pays-Bas à la fin du Moyen Âge', *Beihefte der Francia*, 55 (2003), pp. 133-35, 141. See also Sarah Long, *Music, Liturgy and Confraternity Devotions in Paris and Tournai, 1300-1550* (Woodbridge: University of Rochester Press, 2021). The key sociological work on confraternities and social capital remains Robert Putnam, *Making Democracy Work: Civic Traditions in Modern Italy* (Princeton, NJ: Princeton University Press, 1993), pp. 121-36.

support through a 'parcellisation du sacré' that facilitated an 'enchevêtrement du politique et du religieux'.[109] In this respect, the Bourgeois portrayed the Armagnac governors who instituted a confraternity dedicated to St. Laurent on 3 August 1414 as saying 'que ce estoit la confrarie des vrays et bons catholiques envers Dieu et leur droit signeur', in an attempt to validate the faction's moral status.[110] Nevertheless, the confraternity's success depended upon the governors' ability to elicit institutional cooperation. Comparable to the 1417 processions, when the feast was celebrated at the Quinze-Vingts hospital in 1416 the Bourgeois emphasized the compulsion underlying its organization that inherently invalidated its ritual aims and negated the participants' agency: 'firent chanter lesdits bandez aux XV^{xx}, fut tort ou droit, et y avoit commissaires et sergens qui faisoient chanter devant eulx telz prebstres qu'ilz vouloient, malgré ceulx dudit lieu'.[111] The Quinze-Vingts' opposition to the feast's celebration followed a dispute involving the hospital, supported by the bishop of Paris and the royal *procureur*, after the transgression of the church's immunity when Châtelet officers arrested 'pluseurs malfecteurs' seeking asylum, having opposed the Armagnac governors.[112] When the Paris Parlement forced a resolution and ordered the Quinze-Vingts to resume its suspended offices on 30 May, the ensuing ceremonies signalled the faction's reestablishment of its authority over Parisian space.

The Bourgeois' description of the St. Laurent confraternity contrasts with its Burgundian equivalent, the confraternity dedicated to St. Andrew established in the Saint-Eustache parish church in June 1418 following the Burgundian capture of the capital.[113] Compared to the perceived exclusionary nature of the Armagnac confraternity, the Bourgeois stressed that St. Andrew's was instigated by members of the parish themselves: 'le peuple s'advisa de faire en la parroisse Sainct-Huitasse la confrarie Sainct-Andry', without any allusion to the influence of civic authorities.[114] This aspect was underscored by the confraternity's popularity: 'tant s'i mist de gens de Paris que les maistres de la confrarie disoient et affermoient qu'ilz avoient fait faire plus de lx xij^{es} de chappeaulx, mais avant qu'il fust doze heures les chappeaux furent failliz'.[115] Catherine Vincent has argued that the impact of these confraternities upon the political attitudes of the Parisian populace 'se laisse difficilement percevoir', but there can be no doubt that *Journal*'s portrayal of the St. Andrew confraternity's popularity was tellingly juxtaposed with the exclusionary

---

109 A parcelling out of the sacred; an entanglement of political and religious spheres. Charlotte Denoël, *Saint André: Culte et iconographie en France (V^e-XVe siècles)* (Paris: École des chartes, 2004), p. 93

110 That this was the confraternity for true and good Catholic before God and their rightful lord. *Journal*, p. 55.

111 The *bandez* had the mass sung at the Quinze-Vingts, whether rightly or wrongly, and there were officers and sergeants there who made any priests that they wished sing before them, despite the objections of the Quinze-Vingts. *Journal*, p. 73.

112 Baye, II, pp. 253-54; Alexandre Tuetey (ed.), *Journal*, p. 74, n. 2; Léon Le Grand, 'Les Quinze-Vingts depuis leur fondation jusqu'à leur translation au faubourg Saint-Antoine, XIIIe-XVIIIe siècles, *MSHP*, 13 (1886), pp. 135-36.

113 Denoël, *Saint André*, p. 93; Simona Slanicka, 'Male Markings: Uniforms in the Parisian Civil War as a Blurring of the Gender Order (AD 1410-20)', *The Medieval History Journal*, 2 (1999), pp. 232, 241; Emily Hutchison, 'Partisan Identity in the French Civil War, 1405-18: Reconsidering the Evidence of Livery Badges', *Journal of Medieval History*, 33 (2007), p. 273.

114 The people decided to establish the St. Andrew confraternity in the parish of Saint-Eustache. *Journal*, p. 95.

115 So many Parisians went to the church that the confraternity's masters stated and affirmed that they had made more than forty dozen hats, but before midday they had run out. *Journal*, p. 95.

St. Laurent feast to convey widespread Parisian support for the Burgundian coup.[116] The parishioners of Saint-Eustache certainly viewed the establishment of a confraternity as essential to promoting harmony during this politically turbulent era, with devotional concord securing the salvation of souls alongside the 'paix et tranquilité confermée, ire et envie temperée, noises et riotes appaisiées, amour et charité engendrées' that underpinned the foundation of two other confraternities in the church in September 1418 and July 1419.[117] Assembling to celebrate St. Andrew, the Parisians of the Halles region affirmed their identity as Burgundian supporters tied to the new regime, implicitly elevated to the status of a neighbourhood patron.

Moreover, as with the light and sound associated with processions, the Bourgeois stressed the confraternity's sensory elements. The distribution of rose garlands among the members of the St, Andrew confraternity meant that Saint-Eustache 'sentoit tant bon au moustier, comme s'il fust lavé d'eau rose'.[118] Famously considering these scents in the context of the concurrent Parisian massacres, Huizinga concluded that medieval people vacillated 'tusscen duistere haat en de meest goedlachse goedmoedigheid leeft het in uiter-sten'.[119] However, the Bourgeois deliberately evoked scent to legitimate Parisian behaviour, having explained several passages previously how heavy rain had washed the bodies of suspected Armagnacs piled in the streets such that 'ne sentirent nulle malle odeur, mais furent lavez par force de la pluie leurs plaies que au matin n'y avoit que sang bete, ne ordure sur leurs plaies'.[120] Conflating the absence of putrefaction with the sweet-smelling roses, the Bourgeois inferred a divine endorsement of the city's moral purification, with the confraternity tying the populace to their Burgundian saintly intercessor through sanctifying ritual. The sweetness involved in this process evoked the association of good smells with moral and saintly qualities, accentuating the positive veneration that spiritually bound Parisians to the Burgundian faction and retrospectively legitimated the massacres. In short, it becomes apparent that Armagnac and Burgundian regimes alike capitalized on the local function of confraternities to encourage political support, exploiting religious rhetoric and symbolism.

With the ascendance of Lancastrian power in 1422, John, duke of Bedford also endeavoured to make effective use of civic and religious ceremonies for the dissemination of propaganda.[121] Yet, as demonstrated above, most rituals and processions undertaken under

---

116 Vincent, *Les confréries*, pp. 169-70.
117 Peace and tranquillity ensured, anger and envy tempered, murmurs and quarrels appeased, love and charity encouraged. Paris, Archives nationales, JJ 170 fol. 181r; JJ 171, fol. 86r. Unlike later confraternities, these did not require a Châtelet sergeant to be present at their assemblies, with the Saint-Eustache confraternities even permitted to use a 'clochete' to cry their feasts throughout the city. Warnings against conspiracies and the monitoring of later confraternities by Châtelet sergeants in Lancastrian-governed Paris are demonstrated by the letters of institution issued after 1421. See Auguste Longnon (ed), *Paris pendant la domination anglaise (1420-36)* (Paris: Champion, 1876), pp. 14-15, 46-8, 284-85, 310-11, 353-55.
118 It smelled so sweetly in the church, as if it had been washed with rosewater. *Journal*, 95.
119 Between dark hatred and cheerful conviviality, living in extremes. Johan Huizinga, *Herfsttij der middeleeuwen*, ed. L. Brummel in Verzamelde werken, vol. 3, (Haarlem: H.D. Tjeenk Willink & Zoon, 1949), p. 28.
120 Did not emit any bad smell, but their wounds were washed by the heavy rain such that there was nothing but congealed blood, no foul matter at all. *Journal*, p. 91.
121 Thompson, *Paris and its People*, pp. 191-97; Ralph Griffiths, *The Reign of King Henry VI* (Stroud: Sutton, 2004), pp. 220-21.

Lancastrian auspices were omitted by the Bourgeois, obfuscating Parisian complicity in English military successes. One exception to this rule was the assembly organized in response to Charles VII's resurgence in the spring and summer of 1429. On 14 July, the Parisians undertook a general procession to Notre-Dame, where a 'moult bel sermon' was preached, before proceeding to the royal Palais.[122] There, the text of the Treaty of Pouilly-le-Fort agreed between the Dauphin Charles and Jean sans Peur on 11 July 1419 was read to the audience, stressing the sanctified oaths of mutual aid and protection that had been sworn between the two princes, vows subsequently ruptured by the latter's murder at Montereau-fault-Yonne, especially given 'comment ilz receurent le precieulx corps Notre Seigneur ensemble'.[123] Following this, the Bourgeois emphasized the description of Jean sans Peur's murder as the reading's climax: 'lequel duc de Bourgongne lui estant a genoulx devant le Dalphin fut ainsi traitreusement murdry, comme chacun scet'.[124]

The procession to Notre-Dame and thence to the Palais provided the necessary backdrop to a public demonstration of the historical developments that explained and justified Paris' continued opposition to Charles VII. Essential to this process was the revival of the memory of Jean sans Peur's assassination, depicted as an element of the common knowledge of those Parisians assembled before the Palais. The *Journal* reveals the profound emotional impact the reading was perceived to have upon the Parisians:

> Apres la conclusion de ladite lettre, grant murmure commenca, et telz avoit grant aliance aux Arminalx qu'ilz les prindrent en tres grant haine. Apres la murmure, le regent de France et duc de Bedfort fist faire silence, et le duc de Bourgongne se plaint de la paix ainsi enfrainte, et en apres de la mort de son pere, et adoncques on fist lever les mains au peuple, que tous seroient bons et loyaux au regent et au duc de Bourgongne, et lesdits signeurs leur promistrent par leurs foys garder la bonne ville de Paris.[125]

The preceding procession had functioned as an emotional transformer. The proclamation capitalised upon the heightened mood, with 'competing feelings driven out by the main group feeling' leading to a sense of solidarity 'through emotional coordination'.[126] Asserting the principal motivation for continued resistance to Charles VII, the Bourgeois' description of the declaration demonstrates that, for Parisians, Lancastrian authority was fundamentally predicated upon the continuation of the Anglo-Burgundian alliance and the emotional ties that bound the capital to Philippe III le Bon, duke of Burgundy through Jean sans

---

122 *Journal*, p. 241.

123 How they had taken the precious body of Our Lord together. *Journal*, p. 124. For the treaty of Pouilly-le-Fort, see Gaston du Fresne de Beaucourt, *Histoire de Charles VII*, 6 vols (Paris: Librairie de la Société bibliographique, 1881-91), I (1881), pp. 145-49; Paul Bonenfant, *Du meurtre de Montereau au traité de Troyes* (Brussels: Académie royale de Belgique, 1958), p. 14.

124 The duke of Burgundy then kneeling before the Dauphin was treacherously murdered, as everyone knows. *Journal*, p. 124.

125 After they had finished reading the letter, a great murmur arose, such that those who had once been fervent supporters of the Armagnacs regarded them with great hatred. After the murmuring had subsided, the regent of France and duke of Bedford had everyone be quiet, and the duke of Burgundy complained of the peace thus broken and subsequently of his father's death; and then the people were asked to raise their hands [and swear] that they would be good and loyal to the regent and the duke of Burgundy, and the said lords promised the people in turn that upon their faith, they would protect the good city of Paris. *Journal*, p. 124.

126 Randall Collins, *Interaction Ritual Chains* (Princeton, NJ: Princeton University Press, 2004), pp. 107-15.

Peur's memory. This approach reveals the very complexity with which Parisians perceived Lancastrian authority. Not only did the Bourgeois make no reference to Henry's genealogical right at a moment when Charles VII was days away from his coronation at Reims on 17 July 1429, but the very text of the Treaty of Pouilly-le-Fort would have reminded the assembled Parisians of France's historic conflict with the English and their status as conquerors, rather than straightforward heirs to the throne. The peace had been concluded with an explicit view to fighting the English, 'nostrorum antiquorum hostium', accused of 'usurping' Charles VI's kingdom.[127] The mixed attitudes that resulted from this political communication might be detected in the case of the Parisian mason, Pierre Thoroude, who in July 1429 had jestingly asked one of Philippe le Bon's followers, 'que venoit faire le duc de Bourgogne a Paris, et s'il vouloit empeschier que le Dauphin ne feust sacré?'.[128] For his implicit acknowledgement of Charles VII's right and the insinuation of Philippe le Bon's conflicted loyalties, Thoroude was pilloried at the Halles. In this climate, it is perhaps less surprising that the Bourgeois, too, avoided references to Charles' coronation.

Moreover, both procession and declaration evidence the importance of oaths for political stability.[129] If Charles VII's betrayal of the promises sworn in 1419 could subsequently validate the Treaty of Troyes, then the 1429 declaration likewise stressed that a Parisian betrayal of the same treaty would entail the city's exclusion from the realm's body politic.[130] These ties were reinvigorated with religious rhetoric through the procession, reiterating the notion that Charles VII had committed an irredeemable sin. Such moves echoed other instances of propaganda, including the Burgundian poet Laurent Calot's stress upon the Dauphin Charles' responsibility for Jean sans Peur's murder, and his resulting disinheritance, in the poem that he had compiled under Bedford's instruction in 1423.[131] Through the emotionally-charged atmosphere resulting from the collective procession and especially the sermon preached in Notre-Dame, the Bourgeois underscored the power of ceremony to substantially alter the perspectives of those who participated, encouraging his audience to reflect upon the narrative of the Dauphin's treachery in a similar way.[132] Through this same framework, the Bourgeois cemented the sincerity of the oaths that bound Parisians to the two dukes, establishing an essential bond presided over by God to defend the

---

127 RSD, VI, pp. 334-44.

128 What the duke of Burgundy had come to Paris to do, and if he wanted to prevent the Dauphin from being crowned. Paris, Archives nationales, JJ 174, fol. 145r.

129 Corinne Leveleux-Teixeira, 'Des serments collectifs au contrat politique? (début du XVᵉ siècle)' in *Avant le contrat social: Le contrat politique dans l'Occident médiéval, XIIIᵉ-XVᵉ siècle*, ed. by François Foronda (Paris: Éditions de la Sorbonne, 2011), pp. 274-82.

130 The Treaty of Troyes had stressed the direct involvement and commitment of the people of France to upholding the tenets of the agreement between Henry V, Philippe III le Bon, duke of Burgundy and Charles VI, when it included a term where 'il est accordé que les grans signeurs, barons et nobles, et les estatz dudit royaulme tant espirituelz comme temporeulz, et aussi les cités et nobles comunes, les citoyens et bourgois des villes dudit royaulme a nous obeissans, pour le temps, feront les seremens'. The treaty's terms were transcribed into manuscript copies of the *Journal*. Rome, Vatican MS Reg. Lat. 1923, fols 66v-70v. See also Anne Curry, 'Two Kingdoms, One King: The Treaty of Troyes (1420) and the Creation of a Double Monarchy of England and France' in *'The Contending Kingdoms': France and England, 1420-1700*, ed. by Glenn Richardson (London: Routledge, 2008), p. 37.

131 Laurent Calot's poem is published in R. Rodière and C. de la Charie (ed.), *Archives de la famille de Beaulaincourt*, 2 vols (Lille: Lefebvre-Ducrocq, 1911), I, pp. 334-37.

132 Paul Zumthor, *Essai de poétique médiévale* (Paris: Éditions du Seuil, 1978), p. 73; Guenée and Lehoux, *Les Entrées royales*, p. 8.

city's common good when confronted by inveterate sinners. Consequently, the processions rendered the relationship between the Estates and rulers determined by the Treaty of Troyes tangible, instilling a sense of mutual interdependence essential to the survival of the Anglo-Burgundian regime. Contrasted with the murmurs that the Bourgeois had described as welcoming Bedford's assumption of power in 1422, in this moment of political necessity procession and propaganda constructed a binding sense of civil community and stressed the loyalty imperative to resisting Charles VII.[133]

The *Journal* reveals the extent to which Parisian authorities manipulated elements of religious ceremony to secure their political objectives. As moments that assembled swathes of the Parisian population in an emotionally heightened atmosphere, these messages were communicated both more immediately and effectively. They were, therefore, integral to shaping political attitudes in fifteenth-century Paris, providing the city's inhabitants and political commentators alike with the symbolic and religious discourses through which they (re)conceptualized the boundaries of Christian, moral society and rationalized their political stances. Nevertheless, such ceremonies also enabled Parisians to insert themselves within the wider socio-political hierarchy through a religious framework that connected the devotional practices of the elite to the very localized level of parish confraternities, enabling them 'to share in events that were otherwise outside their experience'.[134] This was further determined by the complicity necessary for the success of these politico-devotional exercises. In the *Journal*, the apparent effectiveness of these strategies was ultimately defined by the Bourgeois' narrative selectivity, enabling the author to control the impression of a Parisian endorsement of specific factions through the religious framework that consistently defined the boundaries distinguishing Parisians from their enemies.

Royal entries and funerals

During the fourteenth century, royal ceremonies emerged as a crucial medium for the communication of both royal and civic ideologies, encapsulating a 'théatralisation' of authority.[135] In France, from Jean II's reign (1350-64) the king's first entry to Paris following his coronation at Reims became a 'constitutive ritual' legitimizing his power.[136] This presentation of authority was inherently contractual – entries articulated royal duties, adherence to which legitimated the king's rule and the limits to his power imposed by civic and royal institutions.[137] In doing so, the entry also underscored Paris' centrality to royal politics. Through the conflation of institutional prerogatives, the *jocundus adventus*

---

133 *Journal*, p. 241.
134 Thompson, *Paris and its People*, p. 198.
135 Marc Boone, 'Les pouvoirs et leurs représentations dans les villes des anciens Pays-Bas (XIVᵉ-XVᵉ siècle)' in *Villes de Flandre et d'Italie (XIIIᵉ-XVIᵉ siècles) les enseignements d'une comparaison*, ed. by Élodie Lecuppre-Desjardin and Elisabeth Crouzet-Pavan (Turnhout: Brepols, 2008), p. 187. See also Joël Blanchard, 'Le spectacle du rite: les entrées royales', *Revue historique*, 305 (July 2003), p. 475; Claire Sponsler, *The Queen's Dumbshows: John Lydgate and the Making of Early Theatre* (Philadelphia, PA: University of Pennsylvania Press, 2014), pp. 116-31.
136 Giesey, 'Inaugural Aspects', pp. 40-1.
137 Lawrence Bryant, *The King and the City in the Parisian Royal Entry Ceremony: Politics, Ritual and Art in the Renaissance* (Geneva: Droz, 1986), p. 92.

exhibited competing ideological perspectives concerning the nature of royal power, civic authority and corporate rights while restating notions of French socio-political hierarchy. As such, the entry framed competing understandings of the *auctoritas* underpinning royal *potestas*, the former being the 'moral authority' and 'faculty of shaping things creatively and in a binding manner' fundamental to the legitimation of royal government.[138] Moreover, the ceremony functioned as a forum for negotiation between overlapping and interleaving groups, contrary to conclusions that have focused predominantly upon dialogue between city and king. Urban institutions and communities jostled for precedence in ways that exhibited shifting hierarchies and conceptions of the civic community. The effervescent bubbling beneath the surface of ceremony culminated in a momentary image of the civic community presented to outsiders, subject to constant pressures and changes. This brief fixity found meaning in the king's tacit confirmation of the order presented before him and, in this way, the partnership and place of ruler and ruled, king and city, were mutually reinforced through the ceremony.

The importance of the royal entry to contemporary understandings of French kingship is evidenced by the increasing detail with which historiographers recorded these ceremonies during the fourteenth century, with the entry of Isabeau de Bavière in 1389 being particularly vivid.[139] Protocol, tradition and repetition were essential to an authoritative ritual, guaranteeing these rulers' legitimacy and their ties to Paris. In the later fifteenth century, the illuminator Jean Fouquet depicted this emulation through his illustration of a manuscript copy of the *Grandes chroniques*, BNF fr. 6465, where the beginnings of the reigns of Jean II and Charles V were portrayed through their parallel Parisian entries through the porte Saint-Denis.[140]

Royal ceremonies often expressed this simultaneity of dynastic rupture and traditional permanence, evidencing the importance of Ernst Kantorowicz's notion of the 'king's two bodies' that underlined the eternal continuity of the office of kingship despite each ruler's own mortality.[141] Paul Strohm has similarly stressed the momentary unification of the ruler's natural and symbolic persons in the funerary effigy that 'secures the symbolic legitimacy of the king's reign, but also marks its end; it images the *dignitas* of which

138 James Muldoon, 'Auctoritas, Plenitas and World Order' in *Plenitude of Power: The Doctrines and Exercise of Power in the Middle Ages*, ed. by Robert C. Figuiera (Aldershot: Ashgate, 2006), p. 125.

139 *Les Grandes Chroniques de France: Chronique des règnes de Jean II et de Charles V*, ed. by Roland Delachenal, 4 vols (Paris: Renouard, 1910-20), I (1910), pp. 27-8; II (1916), pp. 3-4; Guenée and Lehoux (ed.), *Les entrées royales*, pp. 47-58; Jean Froissart, 'Chroniques' in *Œuvres de Froissart*, ed. by Joseph Kervyn de Lettenhove, 28 vols (Brussels: Devaux, 1867-77), XIV, pp. 5-25; RSD, I, pp. 32-31; II, pp. 610-17; *Histoire de Charles VI*, pp. 326, 367-68. Entries from the close of the fourteenth century into the sixteenth century have been surveyed by Lawrence Bryant, 'La cérémonie de l'entrée', pp. 514, 524, 534. See also Tracy Adams, 'Isabeau de Bavière, le don et la politique de mécénat', *Le Moyen Âge*, 118 (2011), pp. 483-86.

140 BNF Fr. 6465, fol. 378v, 417r. See Anne D. Hedeman, 'Les perceptions de l'image royale à travers les miniatures: L'exemple des *Grandes chroniques de France*' in *Pratiques de la culture écrite en France au XVᵉ siècle*, ed. by Monique Ornato and Nicole Pons (Louvain-la-Neuve: Fédération internationale des instituts d'études médiévales, 1995), p. 543; Anne D. Hedeman, *The Royal Image: Illustrations of the Grande Chroniques de France, 1274-1422* (Berkeley, CA: University of California Press, 1991), p. 180.

141 Ernst Kantorowicz, *The King's Two Bodies* (Princeton, NJ: Princeton University Press, 1997), pp. 7-9; Bernard Guenée, *L'Occident aux XIVᵉ et XVᵉ siècles: Les États* (Paris: Presses Universitaires de France, 1971), pp. 86-8.

he was possessor, but announces its eligibility for transfer'.[142] According to this duality, royal power permeates throughout society. Where the king's lived body was temporally and spatially fixed, his figurative body – through its manifestation in written and spoken formulae, documents and symbols – was pervasive. Through this juridico-discursive power, the sovereign arrogated authority as an 'irrational' function of power that presented authority and legitimacy as possessions. However, an analysis of the *Journal* demonstrates how, rather than filtering simply *downwards* as proposed by Habermas' notion of 'repräsentativen Öffentlichkeit', the symbols and ideological bases of authority were also negotiated by heterogeneous socio-political groups through forums such as ceremonies that defined the overarching ideals embodied by the king. A medieval appreciation of this mutually constructed public entity is demonstrated by Jean Gerson's reflections concerning the king's status within the body politic upon the escalation of tensions in France in 1405:

> pour tant ung roy n'est pas une personne singuliere, maiz est une puissance publique ordonnée pour le salut de tout le commun, ainsi comme de chief descent et despand la vie par tout le corps; et ad ce furent ordonnés les roys et lez princes du commencement par commun accort de tous, et en telle maniere doivent parseverer.[143]

Gerson's thought followed the fourteenth-century Italian jurisprudent Baldus de Ubaldis, for whom *dignitas* was 'something intellectual, lasting forever miraculously, though not corporeally'.[144] In fifteenth-century France, this notion of an undying kingship was articulated through ceremonies that inculcated a sense of dynastic permanence. During royal funerals, *dignitas* became exposed at its point of transition from one ruler to another. Death marked a 'transition, a change in status, but not an end', and Ralph Giesey pointed to the importance of the royal effigy for the maintenance of a fiction whereby *dignitas* remained with the late king until his successor's coronation.[145] The shifting political circumstances in France during the first decades of the fifteenth century are particularly significant in this respect. Due to Lancastrian influences, the royal effigy was first used in France for Charles VI's funeral in November 1422, demonstrating ceremony's character as 'le lieu d'appropriations divers, de déchiffrements et d'interventions multiples' whereby competing notions of authority and legitimacy emerge.[146] Charles VI died on 21 October 1422 and, unlike his predecessors, his body lay in state until 7 November as the Paris Parlement awaiting John, duke of Bedford's arrival to determine the funeral proceedings.[147] In the

---

142 Paul Strohm, *England's Empty Throne: Usurpation and the Language of Legitimation, 1399-1422* (London: Yale University Press, 1998), pp. 102-03.

143 For the king is not a single person, but a public power ordained for the salvation of all of society, just as life descends from the head and spreads throughout the body; and it is for this reason that kings and princes were originally instituted by common accord, and for this reason their institution should endure. Jean Gerson, 'Pour la réforme du royaume: Vivat Rex, Vivat Rex, Vivat Rex' in *Œuvres complètes*, ed. by Palémon Glorieux, vol. 7, pt. 2 (Paris: Desclée, 1960), p. 1155.

144 Joseph Canning, *The Political Thought of Baldus de Ubaldis* (Cambridge: Cambridge University Press, 2003), p. 216.

145 Ralph Giesey, 'Models of Rulership in French Royal Ceremonial' in *Rites of Power: Symbolism, Ritual and Politics since the Middle Ages*, ed. by Sean Wilentz (Philadelphia, PA: University of Pennsylvania Press, 1999), p. 48.

146 The site of various appropriations, of deciphering and multiple interventions. Boureau, 'Les cérémonies royales françaises', p. 1257. See also Colette Beaune 'Mourir noblement à la fin du Moyen Âge' in *Mourir noblement à la fin du Moyen Âge*, ed. by Colette Beaune (Strasbourg: Librairie Istra, 1975), pp. 128-30.

147 *Journal*, pp. 177-78; Fauquembergue, II, pp. 67-70.

context of Paris' transition from Valois to Lancastrian rule ritual innovations assumed a significant symbolic importance for observers, as evidenced by the *Journal*.

The Bourgeois' description of Charles' funeral procession reveals profound anxieties associated with this transition and suggests Bedford's failure to fully convince Parisian audiences that Henry VI had assumed the French royal *dignitas*. Fundamentally, the Bourgeois perceived the communication of royal legitimacy through the emulation of ritual. This phenomenon was articulated through the record of Parisians comparing their memories of the ceremonial appearances of Charles V and Charles VI in conversation:

> disoient aucuns anciens qu'ilz avoient veu son pere [Charles V] venir du sacre, et vint en estat royal, c'est assavoir, tout vestu d'escarlatte vermeille, de housse, de chapperon fourré, comme a estat royal appartient; et en telle maniere fut porté enterrer a Sainct-Denis. Et aussi, comme on disoit, avoit esté cestuy roy [Charles VI] a son sacre ainsi ordonné de souliers d'asur semés de fleur de lis d'or, vestu d'un manteau de drap d'or vermeil, fourré d'arminez, et comme chacun le pot veoir; mais plus noble compaignie ot a son sacre qu'il not a son enterrement. Et son pere ot aussi noble compaignie ou plus a son enterrement que a son sacre, car il fut porté enterrer de ducz et de contes, et non d'autre gent, qui tous estoient vestuz des armes de France, et y avoit plus de prelaz, de chevaliers et d'escuiers de renommée qu'il n'y avoit a compaigner ce bon roy a ces darrains jours de toutes gens, de quelque estat que ce fust.[148]

Evidently, ceremonies provoked public reflection regarding the nature of French kingship, encapsulating the 'officializing strategies' designed to transmute royal goals into 'collective, publicly avowable interests'.[149] These underscored the importance of the king's physical image for popular understandings of royalty and the juridico-discursive power that that vision captured. The allusion to 'anciens' is also significant, evoking the idea of a generational memory that enabled the Bourgeois' personal experiences to intersect with an overarching Parisian narrative. These memories were reinforced by social determinants that accentuated the impact of the event in question. Conversations among those affected, recorded in the *Journal*, were engendered as a reaction to the emotions experienced in social contexts because of the event, with this mnemonic sharing reinforcing a sense of community through an emphasis upon the memory's collective appeal. In conveying the memories of these 'anciens', the Bourgeois asserted his own ability to compare the French kings over time and consider the symbolic manifestations of their legitimacy.

Fundamentally, the *Journal* depicts these living custodians of Parisian memory as recognizing an uncomfortable disconnect when contrasting the two kings' coronations and

---

148 Some elderly people described how they had seen his father return from his coronation, and how he had arrived in royal state, that is, dressed entirely in scarlet, in hose and a furred hood as is appropriate for a king; and in that same guise he was carried to his burial at Saint-Denis. Moreover, they said that this king, at his coronation, had been dressed in blue slippers sewn with gold fleurs-de-lis, wearing a red cloth-of-gold cloak furred with ermine as everyone could see; but he was more nobly accompanied at his coronation than at his funeral. And his father was just as nobly accompanied, or better, at his funeral than at his coronation, because he was carried to his grave by dukes and counts who all bore the arms of France, and not by others; and there had been more prelates, knights and squires of renown than there were of any kind of people whatsoever who accompanied this good king in his last days. *Journal*, p. 181.

149 Pierre Bourdieu, *Outline of a Theory of Practice* (Cambridge: Cambridge University Press, 1977), p. 54. See also Paul Strohm, *Theory and the Premodern Text* (Minneapolis, MN: University of Minnesota Press, 2000), p. 42.

funerals. The comparison of the two monarchs was a common strategy in contemporary political commentary. The theologian Jean Courtecuisse had similarly juxtaposed the reigns of Charles V and Charles VI in his sermon *Bonum michi*, delivered before Charles VI at the height of the Cabochien revolt on 29 May 1413, which asserted that if Charles V were to return to life, 'com seroit-il esmerveillié et esbahy de veoir la tres miserable face et la grant immutacion qui est ou royaulme, de veoir la grant distraction et dissipacion des biens et des richesses qu'il vous laissa'.[150] Collective memory – even nostalgia – framed significant ideological discussions, and in the case of 1422 the ideas of royal power's immutability, its ties to Paris and French symbolism were vital to Parisian rationalizations of dramatic political change.[151] Indeed, the discussion related by the Bourgeois highlighted a crucial means by which contemporary observers questioned authority, exhibiting distances between Parisian understandings of French royalty and the realities of Lancastrian domination.

It is perhaps not uncoincidental that the Bourgeois introduced these conversations immediately after his remark that, upon Bedford's return to Paris carrying the royal sword, 'le peuple murmuroit fort'.[152] These murmurs echoed the serious attempts to betray Paris to the Dauphin that occurred during the autumn of 1422. Already in June 1422, Monstrelet, the Bourgeois and the Cordelier had reported how a plot to deliver Paris to the Dauphin Charles was discovered, with letters brought to the city by the wife of an unnamed royal armourer, provoking Henry V's swift return to Paris.[153] In the winter of 1422, the Cordelier reported a second plot, whereupon 'furent prins plusieurs grans bourgois et manans de Paris pour souspechon de vouloir ladicte ville livrer aux Armignas', with the conspiracy organized by a member of the *Chambre des comptes*, Michel de Laillier, who fled to the Burgundian court.[154] These repressive moves were echoed by the Bourgeois in February 1423, when he reported that Parisians were compelled to swear an oath of fealty to the Lancastrian regime and how, day and night, the authorities continued to imprison those suspected of harbouring sympathies for Charles VII.[155] In this context, the Bourgeois' and his community's stress upon the materiality of kingship underscores Armand Strubel's argument that 'l'exhibition des symboles de la souveraineté [...] rappellent qu'au-delà de la personne royale, ce qui est en jeu ici, c'est la royauté en tant que tradition'.[156] The *Journal*

---

150 How he would be astonished to see the very miserable appearance and the profound changes of the kingdom, to see the extensive dispersion and dissipation of the goods and riches that he left to you. Giuseppe Di Stefano, 'Un sermon français inédit de Jean Courtecuisse, *Justum adiutorium*', *Romania*, 85 (1964), p. 422.

151 Paul Connerton, *How Societies Remember* (Cambridge: Cambridge University Press, 1989), pp. 36-9; Jacques Le Goff, *History and Memory*, trans. by Steven Randall and Elizabeth Claman (New York: Columbia University Press, 1992), p. 8.

152 The people murmured loudly. *Journal*, p. 180.

153 *Journal*, pp. 174-75; Monstrelet, IV, pp. 104-05; Cordeliers, p. 318.

154 Many important bourgeois and inhabitants of Paris were captured upon suspicion of conspiring to betray the city to the Armagnacs. Paris, BNF Fr. 23018, fol. 432r. Michel de Laillier would return to office in the Lancastrian Parlement at Paris during the 1420s, but later played a leading role in facilitating the Valois reconquest of the capital in April 1436, becoming the city's *prévôt des marchands* that year.

155 *Journal*, pp. 182-83.

156 The exhibition of the symbols of sovereignty [...] recalls that beyond the royal person at stake is the royalty as a tradition. Armand Strubel, 'Le "chevauchier" de Charles V: Christine de Pizan et le spectacle de la majesté royale' in *Penser le pouvoir au Moyen Âge (VIIIᵉ-XVᵉ siècle)*, ed. by Dominic Boutet and Jacques Verger (Paris: Éditions Rue d'Ulm, 2000), p. 390.

reveals the extent to which political commentary surrounding ceremony extended beyond the event itself as observers moulded the symbols they perceived into coherent narratives of civic and royal identity. Ultimately, the unavoidable *otherness* characterizing Charles VI's funeral procession inherently invalidated Henry VI's assumption of the royal *dignitas*.[157]

The Bourgeois' use of rhetorical juxtaposition as a mode of political analysis is further demonstrated by his description of the funeral processions of Henry V and Charles VI, presented upon the same folio in the Vatican manuscript.[158] Depicting Henry's death at Vincennes on 31 August 1422, the Bourgeois obviated his audience's expectations. Henry's body 'fut porté a Sainct-Denis, sans entrer a Paris', a version of events supported by the accounts of Fauquembergue and Jean Chartier's continuation of Michel Pintoin's chronicle.[159] The emphasis upon the cortege's bypassing of Paris is significant when compared with Burgundian narratives, with Monstrelet and the anonymous Cordelier reporting that Henry's body 'fut mené en grant triumphe a Paris et mis dedens l'église Nostre-Dame'.[160] It is worth noting, however, that there is no reference to Henry's death or burial in Notre-Dame's register (in comparison to Charles VI's obsequies).[161] Where the Burgundian chroniclers felt it necessary to portray Henry's funeral procession as anticipating the due form of Charles VI's burial, Parisian records actively distanced the capital from any association with the monarch. For English authors, the movement of Henry's cortege from France to Westminster represented a reassertion of his English dynastic ties, and likewise for the Bourgeois Henry's transferral from Saint-Denis to England, *away* from an ideological centre of French authority, highlighted the disparity between Lancastrian and Valois royal traditions, especially in such close proximity to Charles VI's funeral.[162] As a matter of fact, Charles VI's own funeral procession had seen him move through Parisian space to Saint-Denis, before his burial 'empres son pere et sa mere'.[163] Through this juxtaposition, therefore, the Bourgeois presented to his audience the fractured foundations of Bedford's regency, with no ideological centre and no physical body within the Saint-Denis necropolis, indicating the role symbolic 'othering' performed in the reinforcement of French and Parisian identities at a moment of acute political change.

---

157 Strohm, *England's Empty Throne*, p. 2.

158 Reg. Lat. 1923, fols 88r-88v.

159 Without entering Paris. *Journal*, p. 176. Fauquembergue, II, 58; RSD, VI, pp. 481-85.

160 Was brought in great triumph to Paris and placed inside Notre-Dame cathedral. Monstrelet, IV, pp. 112-13; Cordeliers, p. 323.

161 Paris, Archives nationales, LL 112, pp. 386-88; Georges Grassoreille, 'Histoire politique du chapitre de Notre-Dame de Paris pendant la domination anglaise, 1420-37', *MSHP*, 9 (1882), p. 151, n. 1.

162 For Middle English accounts of Henry V's death and return to England, see the appendices to Friedrich Brie (ed.), *The Brut or the Chronicles of England*, Pt. 2 (London: Kegan Paul, Trench, Trubner and Co., 1908): 'Appendix D, *Galba E. VIII*', p. 430; 'Appendix E, *MS Egerton 650*', p. 449; 'Appendix G, *Addit. MS., Brit. Mus. 10,099, leaf 181*', pp. 493-96; 'Appendix H, Extracts from Harleian MS 53', p. 563. See also *Ingulph's Chronicle of Croyland with the continuations by Peter of Blois and anonymous writers*, ed. and trans. by Henry T. Riley (London: Henry Bohn, 1854), p. 391; 'Julius B II' and 'Cleopatra C IV' in *Chronicles of London*, ed. by Charles Lethbridge Kingsford (Oxford: Clarendon Press, 1905), pp. 74-5, 128; *The Historical Collections of a Citizen of London in the Fifteenth Century*, ed. by James Gairdner (London: Camden Society, 1876), p. 148; 'Lambeth MS 306' in *Three Fifteenth-Century Chronicles*, ed. by James Gairdner (London: Camden Society, 1880), p. 58.

163 Beside his mother and father. *Journal*, p. 180.

Consequently, ceremonies embedded memories which structured ideological continuity, blurring the distinction between individual kings and developing collective understandings of French kingship and identity. These events were encapsulated by symbols, monuments, conversations and celebrations that consistently brought royal power to the minds of Parisians. In this light, royal entries and funerals represented one of the 'modes opératoires' presented by Paul Ricœur as facilitating the passage from a *mémoire privée* (that of the king or royal family) to a *mémoire publique* shared by the wider civic and national community.[164] The potential of ritual to communicate political legitimacy inherently relied upon 'collective memory', evoking the methods through which communities express and maintain impersonal memories and create an artificial, public sphere that frames personal experience.[165] Joël Blanchard has described royal ceremony as a 'fictionnalisation de l'histoire' that necessitates active narrative strategies on the part of commentators.[166] Collective memories are set within social, cultural and political frames of reference that enable participants to draw meaning from past experience, with this memory externalized in 'symbols such as texts, images, rituals, landmarks and other "lieux de mémoire"'.[167] The diverse symbols displayed through or the placement and participation of groups in civic ceremony represent this 'mémoire bricolée', a social fact through which Parisian society, and France more generally, invented its common past.[168] In doing so, it simultaneously presented a foundation for the affirmation of the community's identity and offered a referential context that helped Parisians to envisage and rationalize the political realignment taking place in 1422. Regarding Charles VI's funeral, the *Journal* reveals Parisians imagining an idalization of royal ceremony in the very absence of such a performance, demonstrating the importance of participants' responses for the legitimation of the French king, framed by the conflation of expectations and memories. The account demonstrates that the establishment of this memory was not unilateral. It depended upon the consensus of heterogeneous participants contributing to a public transcript that accorded Parisians a stake in the definition of French royal ideology, and the very determination of 'Frenchness', in the early fifteenth century.

---

164 Paul Ricoeur, *Histoire, Mémoire, Oubli* (Paris: Seuil, 2000), p. 52.

165 Maurice Halbwachs, *La mémoire collective* (Paris: Presses universitaires de France, 1967).

166 Blanchard, 'Les entrées royales', pp. 4-9.

167 Jan Assmann, 'Globalization, Universalism and the Erosion of Cultural Memory' in *Memory in a Global Age: Discourses, Practices and Trajcetoreis*, ed. by Aleida Assmann and Sebastian Conrad (New York: Palgrave Macmillan, 2010), p. 122; Brigitte Bedos-Rezak, 'Civic Liturgies and Urban Records in Northern France, 1100-1400' in *City and Spectacle in Medieval Europe*, ed. by Barbara A. Hanawalt and Kathryn L. Reyerson (Minneapolis, MN: University of Minnesota Press, 1994), pp. 42-6.

168 Roger Bastide, 'Mémoire collective et sociologie du bricolage', *L'année sociologique*, 21 (1970), pp. 65-108; Patrick Boucheron, 'La mémoire disputée: le souvenir de saint Ambroise, enjeu des luttes politiques à Milan au XVᵉ siècle', *Beihefte der Francia*, 55 (2003), pp. 205-08; James J. Fentress and Chris Wickham, *Social Memory: New Perspectives on the Past* (Oxford: Blackwell, 1992), p. 7.

Negotiation between king and city: Henry VI's Parisian entry, 1431

A consequence of the role accorded to Paris in the definition of royal ideology was the emphasis that Parisians could in turn place upon the city's centrality to the French kingdom. The dialogue between ruler and ruled was accentuated during Henry VI's entry into Paris on 2 December 1431 before his coronation as king of France, once identified by Ralph Griffiths as a prime example of Lancastrian propaganda.[169] In contrast, Thompson has described the ceremony as 'something closer to a Parisian monologue', and the Bourgeois' account reveals how Parisians perceived the entry to communicate the city's centrality to French history and identity.[170] For onlookers in the city, the pre-coronation ceremony underscored the Lancastrian dual monarchy's contractual character, signalling the mutual dependence of capital and king. This Parisian perspective appears when the Bourgeois' account is compared with three other surviving narratives describing the entry. First, an anonymous Burgundian account that served as Monstrelet's source, and which may have functioned similarly to the 'publicum instrumentum' circulated following Charles VII's 1437 entry.[171] The second is a French report copied into London, Letter Book K by John Carpenter, London's common clerk from 1417 to 1435.[172] Finally, a previously overlooked Middle English eyewitness account present in two of the *Brut* continuations known as the 'London Chronicles' presents several significant deviations from these Middle French sources.[173]

Henry VI's pre-coronation entry is well known for the series of displays produced by the Parisians that were designed to remind the monarch of the capital's centrality, its importance to the maintenance of the dual monarchy, but also its relative independence.[174] Theatrical halts punctuated processional movement for heightened effect, presenting Henry and his English entourage with messages that 'inscribed social and political relations onto the terrain of the city'.[175] The Bourgeois' reconstruction of the ceremony underscored

---

169 Griffiths, *Henry VI*, p. 192. See also J.W. McKenna, 'Henry VI of England and the Dual Monarchy: Aspects of Royal Political Propaganda, 1422-32', *Journal of the Warburg and Courtauld Institutes*, 28 (1965), p. 158.

170 Thompson, *Paris and its People*, p. 203. See also Kristin Bourassa, 'The Royal Entries of Henry VI in a London Civic Manuscript', *Journal of Medieval History*, 42 (2016), pp. 481-83; Jean-Philippe Genet, 'Le roi de France anglaise et la nation française au XVe siècle', *Beihefte der Francia*, 39 (1997), pp. 52-3.

171 This text was published as the 'Joyeuse entrée de Henri VI, roi d'Angleterre et prétendant au trône de France, en la ville de Paris' in *Archives de la famille de Beaulaincourt*, I, pp. 332-37. It is possible that the original manuscript was lost when the archives in Arras' Palais de Saint-Vaast burned down in 1915. Its status as Monstrelet's source is demonstrated by a comparison of the two accounts. Monstrelet, V, pp. 1-4. For the 'publicum instrumentum', see Guenée and Lehoux (ed.), *Les entrées royales*, pp. 79-86.

172 London, London Metropolitan Archives, Archives of the Corporation of London, MS Letter Book K, fols 101v-103r. The account has been published twice, in Jules Delpit (ed.), *Collection générale des documents français qui se trouvent en Angleterre*, vol. 1 (Paris: Dumoulin, 1847), pp. 239-44; Guenée and Lehoux, *Les entrées royales* pp. 62-70. See also Harry, *Constructing a Civic Community*, pp. 78-80.

173 The account is found in its most complete form in Cambridge, Trinity College, MS O.9.1, fols 208r-212r. A related version is found in Cambridge, University Library, MS Hh.6.9. The former is published as Appendix F in *The Brut or The Chronicles of England*, ed. by Friedrich W.D. Brie (London: Paul, Trench, Trubner, 1908), pp. 458-65. See also Sponsler, *The Queen's Dumbshows*, pp. 139-40; Mary-Rose McLaren, *The London Chronicles of the Fifteenth Century: A Revolution in English Writing* (Woodbridge: D.S. Brewer, 2002), pp. 54-8. The following references are sourced from MS O.9.1.

174 Bourassa, 'The Royal Entries', p. 479; Harry, *Constructing a Civic Community*, p. 81.

175 Sponsler, *The Queen's Dumbshows*, p. 117.

this Parisian emphasis, reordering the pageantry for rhetorical effect. For instance, in the *Journal*, the first symbols that Henry VI encountered were the city's arms, displayed above the porte Saint-Denis and 'si grant qu'il couvroit toute la maconnerie de la porte'.[176] City gates represented significant points of tension: weak points in the city's defences, they also constituted a fiscal, political and social boundary.[177] The ship featured upon the arms was large enough to hold several men depicting Parisian civic society, with the ship itself the symbol of the municipality. Municipal badges from the 1430s exhibited this same imagery, with one particular example stating on the obverse 'Sur toutes cités Paris prise' and on the reverse, 'Car sa nef figure église'.[178] Where the Bourgeois spoke of three men and Letter Book K of 'three estates' evoking a tripartite social division, the Burgundian account specified six individuals stood within the ship 'dont l'un estoit en guise d'evesque, l'autre en guise de l'Université, l'autre en guise de bourgois, et les III autres comme sergens'.[179] If this is to be believed, then it suggests that in funding and organizing the display, the *prévôté des marchands* conveyed a specifically civic symbolism that at once avoided references to Lancastrian kingship and underscored the predominance of Paris' officials.[180] The coat of arms' significance as a symbol of autonomy in 1431 is further indicated by its *absence* when Charles VII returned to the city in 1437. Unmentioned by the Bourgeois, on this occasion the French king was greeted by angels carrying a shield bearing the fleur-de-lis above a notice that read that 'les manans de vostre cité vous repcoivent en tout honneur et très grande humilité', the use of royal symbolism indicating conciliatory attitudes in response to the reassertion of Valois authority which Paris had resisted for almost two decades.[181]

The Bourgeois accentuated this focus upon Paris by altering the pageants' order, situating the city's arms as the first display encountered by Henry, followed by a description of the Nine Worthies located within the city when, in fact, the Worthies had greeted Henry beyond Paris' walls.[182] While Neil Murphy has argued that extramural encounters represented the most important elements in the dialogue between city and king, this reordering notably emphasized Paris' importance at Henry VI's expense.[183] The Nine Worthies' role in the ceremony as a means of articulating Parisian identity supports this conclusion, following their description in the other sources. Letter Book K portrays the Worthies'

---

176 So great that it covered all of the gate's masonry. *Journal*, p. 274.

177 Daniel Jutte, 'Entering a City: On a Lost Early Modern Practice', *Urban History*, 41 (2014), p. 210.

178 Of all cities Paris is the most worthy, because its ship symbolises the church. Jules Rouyer, 'Jetons municipaux de la ville de Paris au XVᵉ siècle', *Mémoires de la Société impériale des Antiquaires de France*, 4 (1869), pp. 126-27.

179 Of which one was dressed as a bishop, another as a member of the University, another dressed as a bourgeois, and three others as sergeants. 'Joyeuse entrée de Henri VI', p. 333; Monstrelet, V, p. 3. This division of society was common to contemporary authors. Kate Langdon Forhan, *The Political Theory of Christine de Pizan* (Aldershot: Ashgate, 2002), p. 58; Donald Perret, 'The Meaning of the Mystery: From *Tableaux* to Theatre in the French Royal Entry' in *Moving Subjects: Processions Performance in the Middle Ages and the Renaissance*, ed. by Kathleen Ashley and Wim Husken (Amsterdam: Rodopi, 2001), p. 203.

180 The *prévôté des marchands* had been responsible for the decoration of the porte Saint-Denis, paying in total 57l. 14s. 8d. for various decorations. As such, it appears unlikely that the three 'sergents' would have been Châtelet officials, but rather those belonging to the *prévôté des marchands*. Paris, BNF NAF 3423, fols 3r-3v.

181 The inhabitants of your city receive you in all honour and profound humility. Monstrelet, V, p. 302; Gilles le Bouvier, *Les chroniques du roi Charles VII par Gilles le Bouvier dit le héraut Berry*, ed. by Henri Courteault and Léonce Celier (Paris: Klincksieck, 1979), p. 191.

182 Letter Book K, fol. 101r; 'Joyeuse entrée de Henri VI', pp. 332-33; Cambridge, Trinity College MS O.9.1, fols 208r-v.

183 Murphy, *Ceremonial Entries*, p. 24.

as being escorted by Fama, meeting with Henry VI beyond the porte Saint-Denis, with the city forming the backdrop to their encounter. Dismounting before Henry, a herald introduced the pageant:

> Les preux jadiz et Renommée
> Tendoient qui est figuré
> Ci en dame, et vous represente
> Paris, qui de tout s'entente,
> Sire, vous recoit humblement,
> Gardez-la amoureusement,
> Car cele ville ainsi famée
> Est digne d'estre bien gouverné.[184]

The Worthies encapsulated the *translatio imperii* underscoring Paris' historical renown, echoing literature that portrayed Paris as an earthly paradise and its king as David or even, in Henry VI's case given his entry during Advent, as a Christ-king – imagery that was also common in Lancastrian displays.[185] Other pageants reiterated this paradisical impression, particularly the fountain of milk and wine at the Ponceau Saint-Denis or the mystery of Christ's birth portrayed along the rue Saint-Denis.[186] Furthermore, the employment of the Worthies to signal France's heritage and related conceptions of kingship echoed similar themes developed by Eustache Deschamps in two ballads that asserted that rulers should always uphold truth and 'parfaicte charité', avoiding the cupidity that moved men to cruelty and 'font perdre royaume et herité'.[187] In *Contre les vices du temps*, Deschamps had introduced the Nine Worthies to juxtapose a present state of decline with past glories.[188] This didactic role clarifies the messages the Parisians may have intended to communicate to their Lancastrian governors in 1431. Firstly, as the site of *translatio*, Paris – not the Lancastrian monarch –, embodied the *fama* of past heroes. Their display

---

184 I present to you the ancient Worthies and Renown, portrayed here as this lady, and Paris which as one, sire, receives you humbly; guard her lovingly, because this city is of such fame that it is worthy of being well governed. Letter Book K, fols 101v-102r.

185 Gordon Kipling, *Enter the King: Theatre, Liturgy and Ritual in the Medieval Civic Triumph* (Oxford: Oxford University Press, 1998), pp. 63-4, 72-3, 85-6; Beaune, *The Birth of an Ideology*, pp. 180-81, 343-44; *Le Songe du Vergier édité d'après le manuscrit royal 19 C IV de la British Library*, ed. by Marion Schnerb-Lièvre, 2 vols (Paris: Éditions du CNRS, 1982), I, Book 1, Chapter 156, 17, p. 328. Similar themes characterized the London celebrations organized for Henry V's return from Agincourt. *Gesta Henrici Quinti*, ed. and trans. by F. Taylor and J. S. Roskell (Oxford: Clarendon Press, 1975), 101-13. See also Nicola Coldstream, '"Pavillon'd in Splendour": Henry V's Agincourt Pageants', *Journal of the British Archaeological Association*, 165 (2012), pp. 155-57.

186 *Journal*, p. 276. The Ponceau Saint-Denis refers to a small bridge that covered a drain on the rue Saint-Denis, south of the street's fountain. On the importance of fountains to later entries see David Gilks, 'The Fountain of the Innocents and its Place in the Paris Cityscape, 1549-1788', *Urban History*, 45 (2018), pp. 51-55.

187 Quoted from 'Qualités que doit avoit un roi' (Ballad 338, *c.* 1381) in *Œuvres complètes d'Eustache Deschamps*, Queux de Saint-Hilaire, 11 vols (Paris: Firmin Didot, 1878-1903), I (1878), pp. 86-7, lines 21-25.

188 'Contre les vices du temps', *Œuvres complètes*, III (1882), p. 87, lines 21-2. This theme was reprised in several of Eustache Deschamps' poems, including 'Si les héros revenaient sur la terre, ils seraient étonnés' (Undated), *Œuvres complètes*, III (1883), no. 403, pp. 192-94 and 'Il est temps de faire la paix' (*c.* 1387-96), *Œuvres complètes*, I (1878), no. 93, pp. 199-200. On Eustache Deschamps' development of the Nine Worthies theme, see Anne Salamon, 'Les Neuf Preux: Vie d'une liste à la fin du Moyen Âge', *Cahiers de recherche des instituts néerlandais de langue et de littérature française (CRIN)*, 65 (2018), pp. 157-74.

highlights heroism's status as a site of ideological competition during the period.[189] Second, the Worthies encapsulated a dissonance between the idealized historical eras that they represented and the reality of Paris' present destitution. If, as Anne Salamon has argued, 'dans le contexte troublé de la Guerre de Cent Ans [...] l'évocation des Neuf Preux permet de faire rajaillir leur gloire passée sur l'époque contemporaine', an inverse articulation of difference was also possible.[190] Consequently, the final line of the Parisian Fama's poem assumes greater significance as the impression of a duty upon the Lancastrian regime to govern the city well and forestall further hardships. By implicitly situating this exchange within the city walls rather than without, the Bourgeois articulated a sense of contractual obligation between Paris and the Lancastrians predicated upon the former's independence and historical identity.

These messages were most clearly communicated by the pageant that awaited Henry VI at the end of the rue Saint-Denis before the Grand Châtelet, which depicted a boy-king wearing two crowns, flanked by Burgundian and English aristocrats. Where J.W. McKenna, Jean-Philippe Genet and Sarah Hanley have argued that the Châtelet pageant represented a clear example of Lancastrian propaganda, Thompson pointed to its organization by the royally-appointed *prévôt* Simon Morhier and it is clear that, even here, a Parisian emphasis upon independence was exhibited.[191] The ideal of the dual monarchy presented through the pageant stressed Paris' centrality to the Treaty of Troyes' settlement while delineating English and French prerogatives. The pageant was divided between two stages. On the first, Burgundian and English lords supported the arms of France and England on either side of the king, figuratively demonstrating their support for Henry's dual monarchy. This ordering emulated iconography common to other examples of Lancastrian propaganda, best demonstrated by the juxtaposition of the English and French arms on contemporary coinage or the dynastic branches of the Valois and Plantagenet houses joined by Henry VI in the well-known genealogy found in the Talbot-Shrewsbury Book, gifted by John Talbot to Henry VI's wife, Margaret Beauchamp, in 1445.[192]

Heralding Henry's dependence upon the aristocracy of the two kingdoms, the pageant's simple iconography also conveyed that Henry's authority was based upon the concerted support of the people of Paris, depicted below him on a second stage.[193] Here, countering the *prévôté des marchands'* likely prominence at the porte Saint-Denis, an actor representing the Parisian *prévôt* took centre stage, one hand gesturing towards the arrangement of Parisian society behind him, the other presenting to the king 'un escript [...] par maniere

189 Jacqueline Cerquiligni-Toulet, 'Fama et les preux: nom et renom à la fin du Moyen Âge', *Médiévales*, 24 (1993), p. 37.

190 In the troubled context of the Hundred Years War [...] the evocation of the Nine Worthies enabled their past glory to spill over into the present. Anne Salamon, 'Les Neuf Preux: entre édification et glorification', *Questes*, 13 (2008), p. 48.

191 McKenna, 'Henry VI of England and the Dual Monarchy', pp. 157-60; Genet, 'Le roi de France anglaise', p. 52; Sarah Hanley, *The Lit de Justice of the Kings of France: Constitutional Ideology in Legend, Ritual and Discourse* (Princeton, NJ: Princeton University Press, 1983), p. 30; Thompson, *Paris and its People*, p. 202.

192 'Joyeuse entrée de Henri VI', 334; Letter Book K, fol. 102v. For Lancastrian coins, see McKenna, 'Henry VI of England and the Dual Monarchy', pp. 146-51. For Henry VI's genealogy see Anne D. Hedeman, 'Collecting Images: The Role of the Visual in the Shrewsbury Book (BL Ms. Royal 15 E. vi)' in *Collections in Context: The Organization of Knowledge and Community in Europe*, ed. by Karen Fresco and Anne Hedeman (Columbus, OH: Ohio State University Press, 2011), pp. 99-114.

193 Perret, 'The Meaning of the Mystery', p. 193.

de requeste'.[194] The *prévôt's* gesture invited the king to observe the depicted Parisians who gazed up at the pageant's boy king, 'son honneur et prouffit'.[195] In this instance, Letter Book K highlighted the 'self-consciousness of vision in the drama' whereby the *prévôt's* figure acted as a conduit between pageant, real-life king and Parisian audience, establishing a prism that accorded the *prévôté* significant control over the determination of their relationship. Pointing to the lower stage, the figurative *prévôt* indicated the centrality of the city's estates as an essential foundation for the dual monarchy. And yet, Greg Walker has suggested that such gestures invite audiences 'to judge the veracity of the message expounded on the strength of their own observation', rendering the relationship between king and city open to multiple readings, as demonstrated by the Bourgeois' own refashioning of the pageant's integral message.[196]

The extent to which the Bourgeois' account of the Châtelet pageant diverges from what may actually have been performed can only be discerned by this comparison with other extant accounts, revealing ways in which the display's apparently unilateral meaning could be revised and redirected as commentary and critique. Where Letter Book K and the Burgundian account identify those lords holding the French shield as prominent Burgundians, the Bourgeois instead stated that there:

> estoit tout le sanc de France, c'est assavoir, tous les grans seigneurs de France comme Anjou, Berry, Bourgongne, etc., et ung pou loing de eulx estoient les clercs, et apres les bourgois, et a senestre estoient tous les grans signeurs d'Angleterre qui tous faisoient maniere de donner conseil au jeune roy, bon et loyal.[197]

This description of the pageant distorted its idalization of Lancastrian rule, bringing to light a powerful dissonance between the ideals and realities of France's government in 1431.[198] Mention of the dukes of Anjou and Berry highlighted the real absence and exclusion of French aristocrats from Anglo-Burgundian government, a phenomenon frequently remarked upon by the Bourgeois since Charles VI's death.[199] As a result, the Bourgeois' rendition of the pageant articulated an impossible ideal. Regarding these French lords, he would have known that the Angevin dynasty was tied to Charles VII following his 1422 marriage to Marie d'Anjou, to whom Charles had been betrothed since 1413.[200] The Angevin house's commitment to the Valois cause was all but confirmed in the aftermath

---

194 A document in the form of a petition. London, Letter Book K, fol. 102v.

195 His honour and profit. London, Letter Book K, fol. 102v.

196 Greg Walker, *Plays of Persuasion: Drama and Politics in the Court of Henry VIII* (Cambridge: Cambridge University Press, 1991), pp. 11-13, n. 17.

197 Were [portrayed] all of the French princes of the blood, that is, all of the great lords of France like Anjou, Berry, Burgundy, etc., and a little further beyond them were the clerics, and after them the bourgeois; and to the left there were all of the great lords of England and together they acted as if giving advice to the king. *Journal*, p. 276. The Middle English account ambiguously states that alongside Burgundy appeared 'alle the oder lordes of Fraunce in theire degree knelyng and offering up their armes', Cambridge, Trinity College MS O.9.1, fol. 209v.

198 The dangers of semiotic misrecognition in entry pageants has been demonstrated by Anne-Marie Lecoq, 'La symbolique de l'État: Les images de la monarchie des premiers Valois à Louis XIV' in *Les lieux de mémoire*, vol. 2, Part. 2, ed. by Pierre Nora (Paris: Gallimard, 1986), p. 150.

199 *Journal*, pp. 178, 185, 192.

200 Malcolm Vale, *Charles VII* (London: Methuen, 1974), pp. 22-4; David Green, *The Hundred Years War: A People's History* (London: Yale University Press, 2014), p. 190.

of the Battle of Bulgnéville on 2 July 1431, when René d'Anjou, claimant to the duchy of Lorraine, was defeated by his rival Antoine de Vaudémont who enjoyed Burgundian and English support and was, later, invited to attend Henry VI's coronation by John, duke of Bedford.[201] Meanwhile, John, duke of Berry, had died on 15 June 1416, with his apanage first passing to the Dauphin Jean de Touraine and then to Charles VII, with the duchy of Berry representing a key Valois power base. Considering this context, the Bourgeois' description of the pageant evoked a quintessentially French model of government, implicitly recalling the ordinances of 1374 and 1393 that had envisioned regency governments entrusted to French lords including the dukes of Orléans, Berry and Burgundy.[202] In the *Journal*, this ideal of French governance that had gradually evolved since the 1370s was juxtaposed with the fact that Henry VI's minority was conditioned by English convention and the circumstances of the Treaty of Troyes.[203] The account again implies the importance of nostalgia in historical reflection. As Adam Fox has argued, 'there could be something inherently subversive about popular perceptions of the past', as men and women divorced from official narratives employed their own interpretations and memories to make sense of the world.[204] Just as the Bourgeois had relied upon the memories of 'anciens' to interpret Charles VI's funeral and Bedford's rise to the French regency, the evocation of Charles V's children evidenced a nostalgic notion of France distanced from the political realities of 1431, accomplishing ideological work matched by that condensed within the symbolism of the Nine Worthies, illustrating the differences between an idealized past and uncomfortable present.

Instead of referring to Anjou and Berry, Letter Book K and the Burgundian account note the portrayal of the Burgundian lords Philippe III le Bon, duke of Burgundy, Charles, count of Nevers (mistakenly described as the duke's brother in both sources), the Lancastrian chancellor Louis de Luxembourg, bishop of Thérouanne, and Jean de Luxembourg-Ligny.[205] For these writers, the pageant exemplified the Anglo-Burgundian alliance, visibly stressing Burgundian ties to the dual monarchy through Philippe le Bon's presentation of the French arms to the infant king. Where Ralph Griffiths argued that this focus upon Burgundy was intended as 'a reminder to duke Philippe that his best interests lay with Lancaster', the pageant in fact suggests the inverse: that Henry VI's legitimacy depended directly upon continued Burgundian support. In doing so, it echoed the declaration pronounced before the assembled Parisians at the Palais in 1429, and its Burgundian focus was again accentuated by the absence of any reference in the surviving accounts to Henry's genealogical right to rule, a core component of other Lancastrian

---

201 Richard Vaughan, *Philip the Good: The Apogee of Burgundy* (Woodbridge: Boydell, 2002), pp. 70-1. For the letter to Vaudémont, see below.

202 *Ordonnances des rois de France*, VI, pp. 45-55; VII, pp. 530-38. See also Jacques Krynen, '"Le mort saisit le vif": Genèse médiévale du principe d'instantanéité de la succession royale française', *Journal des savants* (1984), pp. 196-202; Craig Taylor, 'The Salic Law, French Queenship, and the Defence of Women in the Late Middle Ages', *French Historical Studies*, 29 (2006), pp. 557-58.

203 Ralph A. Griffiths, 'The Minority of Henry VI, King of England and France' in *The Royal Minorities of Medieval and Early Modern England*, ed. by Charles Beem (New York: Palgrave Macmillan, 2008), pp. 162-65.

204 Adam Fox, *Oral and Literate Culture in England, 1500-1700* (Oxford: Clarendon Press, 2000), p. 222.

205 'Joyeuse entrée de Henri VI', p. 332; Letter Book K, fol. 102v.

propaganda efforts.[206] For instance, two Jesse trees depicting Henry's ancestry appeared in his corresponding entry to London in 1432.[207] Finally, like the Bourgeois' allusions to a distinctly *French* mode of governance, the emphasis upon Burgundy must have been jarring given the duke's own absence, having concluded a six-year truce with Charles VII on 13 December, leaving the Châtelet's depiction of the dual monarch bereft of meaning.[208]

Lastly, the pageant's potential as a medium for negotiation between king and city is further demonstrated by the *cedule* delivered by the figurative *prévôt* to Henry's entourage, 'escript en grosse lettre' and visible to all.[209] The poetic petition emphasized the contractual nature of the dual monarchy, reminding Henry to uphold Justice since 'par elle, ont royaumes durée', while asserting that the Parisian people

> de toute sa puissance
> a moult peine d'entretenir
> la ville en votre obeisance
> si vous en vueills souvenir.[210]

The message was clear. Henry VI's authority could only be maintained through his fulfilment of the Treaty of Troyes' obligations: the protection of each kingdom's respective rights; the maintenance of justice; and, finally, due recognition of Paris' loyalty to the Lancastrian regime.[211] These same principles were later recapitulated by Jean Juvénal des Ursins in *Audite Celi* (1435) as conditions for good government 'fondée sur IIII choses' within Paris, namely, 'la demourance des seigneurs [...] la justice souveraine qui y estoit de tout le royaume et le Chastelet [...] l'University [et] la marchandise'.[212] Henry's failure to meet these conditions would equate to the forfeiture of his right to rule. If the king ignored Paris' central status, the capital could, implicitly, withdraw its essential support for the Anglo-Burgundian regime. As such, through the implicit comparison of an idealized dual monarchy with the realities of Lancastrian rule, the Châtelet pageant established the conditions of Paris' continued loyalty and, in doing so, signalled the capital's centrality as a pillar of Lancastrian authority in northern France by reiterating the interdependence of ruler and ruled. The contractual character of 1431 is again underscored by its difference when compared with the iconography presented upon Charles VII's entry six years later,

---

206 Griffiths, *Henry VI*, p. 220; McKenna, 'Henry VI of England and the Dual Monarchy', pp. 156-62; Peter S. Lewis, 'War, Propaganda and Historiography in Fifteenth-Century France and England', *Transactions of the Royal Historical Society*, 15 (1965), pp. 8-10.

207 Letter Book K, fols 103v-104v; Kipling, *Enter the King*, pp. 63-4; Harry, *Constructing a Civic Community*, pp. 84-5.

208 Joseph Stevenson (ed.), 'Letter from the duke of Burgundy to Henry the Sixth respecting a truce with France (12th December 1431)' in *Letters and Papers illustrative of the Wars of the English in France during the reign of Henry the Sixth, King of England*, vol. 2, Pt. 1 (London: Longman, Green, 1864), pp. 196-202.

209 Letter Book K, fol. 102v. In the Middle English source this petition was described as 'dyvers scriptures þat all they require the kyng of rightwisnesse'. Cambridge, Trinity College, MS O.9.1, fol. 209v.

210 Through her [Justice], kingdoms have endured; you should remember that [the people of Paris] with all of their power have great difficulty keeping the city in your obedience. London, Letter Book K, fol. 103r.

211 Curry, 'Two Kingdoms, One King', pp. 26-8.

212 Founded upon four things: seigneurial residence, the sovereign justice found there for all of the kingdom and the Châtelet, the University and trade. Jean Juvénal des Ursins, 'Audite celi' in *Écrits politiques de Jean Juvénal des Ursins*, ed. by Peter S. Lewis, 3 vols (Paris: Klincksieck, 1978-93), I (1978), p. 257.

with the Bourgeois once more glossing this imagery. In 1437 the *prévôt*'s place was supplanted by Valois imagery and a concentration upon royal, rather than civic, justice. The *lit-de-justice* presented to Charles VII encapsulated natural, divine and human law – the latter embodied by the king in medieval political theory – while alongside the pageant was depicted the Final Judgement, presided over by the Valois patron St. Michael.[213] The Bourgeois' decision to instead describe the pageants of 1437 as being performed 'comme on fist pour le petit roy Henry', obfuscated this counterbalancing of Paris' ideological centrality and its renewed submission to royal power in the wake of the city's reconquest by the Valois.[214]

The contrast between norm and reality is further demonstrated by the Bourgeois' commentary upon other events taking place in December 1431. As Paul Strohm has persuasively demonstrated, the selective reconstruction of ceremony in chronicle narratives constitutes a significant medium for criticism, particularly through the detailing of *failed* ceremonies – the 'negation of the success-criteria that every reader […] would have borne in mind'.[215] Primarily, the Bourgeois indicated the failure to meet these success-criteria by highlighting Henry's avoidance of Notre-Dame cathedral during the pre-coronation entry, one such moment that drew attention to a Lancastrian deviation from an expected format. Where the Valois *adventus* typically followed a set route along the rue Saint-Denis to Notre-Dame cathedral, the Bourgeois poignantly noted that Henry 'n'ala point a Notre-Dame celle journée'.[216] In other contexts, the alteration of an entry route was a sign of princely power. For example, when Philippe le Bon entered Ghent in 1458 following the town's rebellion between 1449 and 1453, the Burgundian duke followed an entirely different trajectory to that traditionally followed by Ghent's rulers (entering from the west through the porte de Bruges, rather than the south) and deliberately avoided sites of civic power such as the town hall, thereby asserting a monolithic princely authority on urban space.[217] However, it is unlikely that Henry VI's avoidance of Notre-Dame can be read in the same light, not least considering the more conciliatory character of the relations between the Lancastrian administration and the city. Given the cathedral's constitutional role in previous ceremonies as the site where Valois monarchs repeated their coronation oath as a 'legal act which brought a bit of the coronation ceremony to Paris', Notre-Dame's omission was poignant, particularly when compared with Charles VII's subsequent entry six years later.[218] In 1437 the royal oath formed the climax of the Bourgeois' account, when 'le roy jura comme roy qu'il tendroit loyalment et bonnement tout ce que bon roy faire

213 Monstrelet, V, p. 303; Gilles le Bouvier, *Les chroniques du roi Charles VII*, p. 193.

214 'As was done for the little king Henry'. *Journal*, p. 336.

215 Paul Strohm, 'Interpreting a Chronicle Text: Henry VI's Blue Gown' in *London and the Kingdom: Essays in Honour of Caroline M. Barron. Proceedings of the 2004 Harlaxton Symposium*, ed. by Matthew Davies and Andrew Prescott (Donington: Shaun Tyas, 2008), pp. 335-37.

216 *Journal*, p. 276.

217 Marc Boone and Thérèse de Hemptinne, 'Espace urbain et ambitions princières: les présences matérielles de l'autorité princière dans le Gand médiéval (12ᵉ siècle-1540)' in Werner Paravicini (hg.), *Zeremoniell und Raum, 4. Symposium der Residenzen-Kommission der Akademie der Wissenschaften in Göttingen*, ed. by Werner Paravicini (Sigmaringen: Thorbecke, 1997), pp. 297-300; Élodie Lecuppre-Desjardin, 'Parcours festifs et enjeux de pouvoirs dans les villes des anciens Pays-Bas bourguignons au XVᵉ siècle', *Histoire urbaine*, 9, 1 (2004), pp. 40-3.

218 Bryant, *The King and the City*, p. 71.

devoit'.[219] The significance of this oath is underlined by its emergence as a contentious aspect of the 1437 ceremony, with other sources mentioning Charles VII's refusal to swear until his counsellors had verified the oath's content and precedent.[220] Neil Murphy has argued that this hesitancy was deliberately intended to display the limits of Parisian authority precisely as Charles reasserted his power over the capital.[221] The repeated transcription of the original oath sworn by Jean II in 1350 in the chapter's register of acts in the months prior to the 1437 entry suggests that the canons may have had similar concerns about Charles' potential refusal to swear the oath and uphold Notre-Dame's constitutional role.[222] The attention paid to the oath in 1437 reveals its fundamental place in the Valois *jocundus adventus*, and it is particularly telling that while the Bourgeois was content to summarize the detail of Charles VII's entry by evoking the Lancastrian ceremony in 1431, here he drew his audience's attention to the constitutionally foundational moment that was absent from his earlier description of Lancastrian ceremony.

Accordingly, the *Journal*'s emphasis upon Henry VI's avoidance of Notre-Dame in 1431 rendered the novelty of Lancastrian ceremony palpable, highlighting the regime's deviation from the established ritual norms that articulated Paris' ties to the Valois monarchy. The issues of authority preventing Henry's direct travel through Paris emulated those that the chapter had already experienced regarding the bishop's *jocundus adventus*. In 1422 Jean de la Rochetaillée was compelled to request the chapter's permission to reside in the episcopal palace on the Île-de-la-Cité prior to his formal first entry into the city. While he was permitted to do so, the chapter warned that 'il n'entrera pas dans l'église parisienne ni dans la ville jusqu'à ce qu'il doive faire son entrée solenelle'.[223] Henry VI's entry engendered similar constitutional issues, with the king engaging in a ceremony that, according to tradition, should only have taken place after his coronation. The fact that it ran counter to wider expectations is underscored by the Middle English account of the entry that, perhaps deliberately mitigating this symbolic dissonance, related that following the Châtelet pageant Henry 'rode forth to Oure Lady Chirche and made his offryng'.[224]

John, duke of Bedford's own awareness of this constitutional issue is illustrated by the letter in Henry VI's name inviting Antoine de Vaudémont to the coronation, with the regent clearly anticipating doubts regarding the decision to host the ceremony at Paris. The letter addressed the problem directly, asserting that

> ne se doit aucun esmerveiller se ainsi faire le desirons [...] que par loy, constitucion ou ordonnance n'ont esté noz predecesseurs roys de France, ne sommes aussi obligez

---

219 The king swore, as king, that he would uphold everything that a good king should loyally and well. *Journal*, p. 336.

220 Guenée and Lehoux, *Les entrées royales*, pp. 84-5.

221 Murphy, *Ceremonial Entries*, p. 95

222 Paris, BNF Latin 17740, fols 41r-41v and 49r-49v. The oath has been published in Guenée and Lehoux, *Les entrées royales*, pp. 48-55.

223 He will not enter the Parisian church nor the city until he should perform his solemn entry. Julerot, 'La première entrée de l'évêque', pp. 648-49.

224 Cambridge, Trinity College MS O.9.1, fol. 209v.

ne astrains que ne puissions prendre nosdiz sacre et couronnement en tel lieu de notre royaume de France qu'il nous plaira.[225]

The claim was supported by examples of royal coronations held elsewhere besides the traditional site of Reims, such as Charlemagne's crowning at 'Soissons' (in fact at Noyon, in 768) and Louis VI's coronation at Orléans (1108), drawn from 'les anciennes et nouvelles croniques et istoires de France'.[226] Nevertheless, the Bourgeois' testimony suggests that Bedford's justification was unsuccessful in alleviating the dissonance provoked by the entry's redirection, undermining the established formula of the royal entry and implicitly calling into question Lancastrian legitimacy. Paradoxically, there was no way Henry could fulfil these expectations prior to his coronation, thereby highlighting a crucial conflict between the Lancastrian entry and French tradition. Typically, the entry route symbolized an important rite of passage that momentarily accorded Parisian space an important role in the confirmation of the rights of the newly crowned bishop or the king over the capital. Here, alterations to space's use provoked an awareness of political tensions.[227]

The issues surrounding the entry route also highlight a significant element in the Bourgeois' account overlooked by other narratives, namely the participation of Paris' corporations. The *Journal*'s description of the series of pageants was framed by a concentration upon the corporations who escorted the king, focusing on each halt and their relay of the canopy that they carried, 'tout en la fourme et maniere c'om fait a Notre Seigneur a la Feste Dieu'.[228] When Henry VI passed through the porte Saint-Denis and entered the city, the city's *échevins* placed the canopy over the king's head. For the ceremony they were distinguished by the luxurious new robes that they had received, along with the *prévôt des marchands* Guillaume Sanguin and the municipal clerk Jean Falle, at a total cost of some 300 *livres parisis*.[229] Likewise, ninety-six 'chapeaux dorez' had been produced for the 'bourgeois notables' who would accompany the king.[230] As Henry VI processed through the city, representatives of the city's seven leading corporations escorted him, each taking up the canopy in turn after the *échevins*.

For Bryant, these corporations 'Groupés ainsi autour du roi [...] offrent une image de la solidarité qui règne entre les dirigeants de la ville aussi bien qu'entre la ville et le roi'.[231] However, a specific role appropriated by the butchers indicates how the ceremony

---

225 None should be surprised if we desire to do this [...] because our predecessors the kings of France were not so obliged nor compelled by [any] law, constitution or order, and nor are we, that we cannot receive our unction and coronation in any place that pleases us within our kingdom of France. Vienna, Staatsarchiv, AT-OeStA/HHStA LHA 98-1.

226 The ancient and recent chronicles and histories of France. Vienna, Staatsarchiv, AT-OeStA/HHStA LHA 98-1.

227 Claire Billen, 'Dire le Bien Commun dans l'espace public. Matérialité épigraphique et monumentale du bien commun dans les villes des Pays-Bas, à la fin du Moyen Âge' in *De Bono Communi: The Discourse and Practice of the Common Good in the European City (13th-16th centuries)*, ed. by Elodie Lecuppre-Desjardin and Anne-Laure Van Bruaene (Turnhout: Brepols, 2010), p. 82; Blanchard, 'Le spectacle du rite', pp. 486-92.

228 Just as in the form and manner that is done for Our Lord at Corpus Christi. *Journal*, p 274. For the history of the canopy, Guenée and Lehoux, *Les entrées royales*, pp. 13-20.

229 Paris, BNF NAF 3243, fol. 4r.

230 Paris, BNF NAF 3243., fol. 3r. At a total cost of 5l. 8s.p.

231 Grouped around the king [...] present an image of the solidarity that reigns among the city's governors as well as between the city and king. Bryant, 'La cérémonie de l'entrée', p. 523.

confirmed their rise to municipal power under the Lancastrian regime.[232] After 1418, the butchers had played an essential role in maintaining Anglo-Burgundian authority in Paris, with at least five butchers serving as municipal *échevins*.[233] Typically, the butchers were responsible for presenting pageants on the rue Saint-Denis, organizing a hunt near the Saints-Innocents and, in 1431, presenting Henry VI with a stag adorned with the 'armez de France et d'Angleterre' at the Grand Pont before the king crossed the Seine to reach the Palais.[234] Additionally, that year they secured the responsibility for escorting the king along the rue Saint-Antoine to his Parisian residence, the Hôtel des Tournelles, another element of invented Lancastrian tradition since, usually, the French monarch would have returned to the Palais on the Île-de-la-Cité after visiting Notre-Dame cathedral.[235] Through their new-found place in the entry, the butchers cemented their growing influence within the city by embracing novel elements of Lancastrian ceremony, articulating their proximity to the king at the entry's most intimate point as he proceeded to his residence. The corporation's stake in the Lancastrian regime is comparatively demonstrated by its decline following Paris' reconquest in 1436, when the Grande Boucherie's master Jean de Saint-Yon was compelled to leave with the English governors.[236] By the time that the Bourgeois recorded Charles VII's entry in November 1437, his focus had shifted dramatically. Instead of describing the roles performed by each corporation in turn, the *Journal* only stated initially that: 'a l'entrée les bourgoys luy mirent ung ciel sur sa teste [...] et ainsi le porterent jusques a la porte aux Paintres dedens la ville'.[237] Considering the Bourgeois' enthusiasm for the butchers since the 1413 Cabochien revolt, his omission of any reference to the corporations' presence in 1437 obfuscated the butchers' political deterioration with the return of Valois power.

Finally, the celebrations held after Henry VI's coronation on 16 December were also open to interpretation. Where the entry ceremony's pageants had at least ostensibly presented the ideal of a harmonized, hierarchically ordered Parisian community, the Bourgeois rhetorically inverted this image through his description of the coronation feast held at the Palais.

Il n'y avoit nulle ordonnance, car le commun de Paris y estoit entré des le matin, les ungs pour veoir, les autres pour gourmander, les autres pour piller ou pour desrober viandes ou autre chose [...] si grant presse y ot pour le sacre du roy que l'Université, ne le Parlement, ne le prevost des marchans, ne eschevins n'osoient entreprendre de

---

232 On the political volatility of guild participation in urban administration, Black, *Guilds and Civil Society*, pp. 67-9.

233 The five known fifteenth-century *échevins* were Michel Thibert, Marcelet Testart, Jean de Saint-Yon, Garnier de Saint-Yon and Henri Aufroy. Both Testart and Aufroy were serving as *échevins* upon Henry VI's entry in 1431. See Thompson, *Paris and its People*, pp. 57-62.

234 Letter Book K, fols 102v-103r; Cambridge, Trinity College, MS O.9.1, fol. 209v. The French sources only mention the hunt, 'Joyeuse entrée d'Henri VI', p. 334; *Journal*, p. 275.

235 As was the case for Philip VI, Charles V, Charles VI, Charles VII and Louis XI. Guenée and Lehoux, *Les entrées royales*, pp. 47, 55, 57, 75, 78, 92. By 1531, the next detailed description of the corporations involved in the ceremony, the butchers had been replaced in the procession by the *bonnetiers*. Bryant, 'La cérémonie de l'entrée', p. 521; Guillaume Bochetel, *L'entrée de la Royne en sa ville and Cité de Paris* (Paris: Geoffroy Tory, 1531).

236 *Journal*, pp. 318-19.

237 Upon the king's entry the bourgeois placed a canopy over his head [...] and thus they escorted him to the porte aux Paintres inside the city. *Journal*, pp. 335-36.

monter amont pour le peuple, dont il y avoit tres grant nombre. [...] Neantmoins s'assirent-ilz aux tables qui pour eulx ordonnées estoient, mais ce fu avec savetiers, moustardiers, lieux ou vendeurs de vin de buffet, aidez a macons, que on cuida faire lever, mais quant on se faisoit lever ung ou deux il s'en asseoit vj ou viij d'autre costé.[238]

Not for the first time, the Bourgeois' account presents a direct contrast with other narratives that evoked the success of Henry's feast. The author of the Middle English account stressed that after the coronation, 'the kyng was brought ageyn to his palyse and there set to mete with all delicacye of metes and drynkes þat myght be ordeyned, and open fest to all men þat wold com bothe pore and riche'.[239] Although other Middle English accounts are far briefer, they commonly stress the 'gret fest holden at Paris'.[240] Indeed, the London chronicle attributed to William Gregory demonstrates how feasts presented a medium for effective ideological communication, describing the symbolic foodstuffs at Henry VI's 1429 Westminster coronation, accompanied by poetry evoking Henry's common descent from saints Edward the Confessor and Louis IX.[241] Similarly, Monstrelet provided a detailed account of the order of Henry's Parisian feast, identifying the dignitaries in attendance and noting the sumptuous courses: 'quand est parler des divers mes, de vins et de viandes [...] ilz seroient trop longz a racompter'.[242] The Bourgeois' divergence suggests that the feast's disorganization represented a significant point of contention, an insult to Lancastrian honour obfuscated by Anglo-Burgundian narratives that instead underlined the Paris feast's magnificence.

In the *Journal*'s Vatican manuscript, the description of the ordered Châtelet pageant and disastrous coronation feast unfold over a single folio, with the events' incongruity striking.[243] Where the Bourgeois had portrayed the Parisians depicted by the pageant as 'bon et loyal', the feast's description betrayed the real absence of such loyalty to the Lancastrian monarch. 'La besongnoient les larrons', cutting purses and stealing 'plus de lx chapperons', while the commons pushed back the dignitaries who attempted to take their seats, now occupied by artisans.[244] This calamity again underscored the dissonance between norm and reality, evoking Parisian ambiguity towards the Lancastrian claim to

---

238 There was no order whatsoever, because the Parisian commons had entered the hall from the morning, some to look around, others to indulge themselves, others to pillage and steal the meats or other things [...] [and] there was such a dense crowd for the king's coronation that neither the members of the University of Paris, nor the *prévôt des marchands*, nor the *échevins* dared to try and make their way through the people because there were so many of them. [...] Nevertheless, [eventually] they sat down at the tables that had been prepared for them, but they sat alongside cobblers, mustard-sellers, wine-stall keepers or masons' apprentices. When they were told to move from the benches one or two would get up only for another six or eight to sit down on the other side. *Journal*, pp. 277-78.

239 Cambridge, Trinity College MS O.9.1, fol. 210r.

240 'Appendix G: Addit. MS, Brit. Mus. 10,099' in *The Brut or The Chronicles of England, edited from MS Rawl. B 171, Bodleian Library, etc.*, ed. by Friedrich W.D. Brie, vol. 1 (London: Kegan Paul, Trench, Trubner and Co., 1906), pp. 501-02. See also 'William Gregory's Chronicle of London' in *The Historical Collections of a Citizen of London in the Fifteenth Century*, ed. by James Gairdner (London: Camden Society, 1876), p. 173; *The Chronicle of Iohn Hardyng*, ed. by Henry Ellis (London, 1812), p. 395.

241 'William Gregory's Chronicle', pp. 168-69; Robert Epstein, 'Food and Text in the Coronation Banquet of Henry VI', *Journal of Medieval and Early Modern Studies*, 36 (2006), pp. 361-67

242 As for relating the various courses, wines and meats [...] it would take me too long to tell of them. Monstrelet, V, pp. 5-6.

243 Rome, Vatican MS Reg. Lat. 1923, fols 136r-v.

244 There the brigands were at work; more than sixty hoods. *Journal*, pp. 277-78.

France. The criticism was accentuated through satire. Contrary to Monstrelet's vision of the feast's quality, the Bourgeois poignantly described the meat as having been cooked the previous Thursday, with the result that those in attendance were 'si mal servis que personne nulle ne s'en louait'.[245] Moreover, just as the Westminster coronation's feast integrated symbols that communicated Henry's dynastic right, the Bourgeois conveyed the Parisian feast as a demonstration of English and French difference, evoking popular opinion. The cooking 'moult sembloit estrange chose aux Francoys, car les Anglois estoient chefz de la besongne, et ne leur challoit quelle honneur il y eust'.[246] Even 'les malades de l'Ostel-Dieu' would not praise their food, implying the impression that the Lancastrian governors had failed to reward the Parisians for their joyous welcome as an element of the contractual obligations binding ruler and ruled.[247] In the end, this breakdown of reciprocity was revealed by the Bourgeois upon Henry VI's departure from the capital on 26 December, underscoring a Lancastrian failure to inculcate popular enthusiasm:

> ledit roy se departy de Paris sans faire aucuns biens a quoy on s'atendoit, comme delivrer prinsonniers, de faire cheoir malles toutes, comme imposicions, gabelles, iiij[es] et telles mauvaises coustumes qui sont contre loy et droit, mais *oncques personnes, ne a secret ne en appert, on n'en ouy louer*. Et si ne fist oncques a Paris autant de honneur a roy comme on lui fist a sa venue et a son sacre.[248]

The Bourgeois' assessment inverted the relationship presented through the Châtelet pageant, with Henry VI failing to meet the legal and judicial expectations voiced by the figurative *prévôt*. Justice, stressed in the petition, was undermined by the continued imposition of taxes 'contre loy et droit', while the Bourgeois' alleged that no pardons were issued. This criticism encapsulated widespread dissatisfaction with the English entry among Parisians, and this in spite of the actual publication of a raft of remission letters 'en reverence de notre sacre et couronnement'.[249] Likewise, the privileges of the city and University of Paris were to all intents and purposes confirmed with the latter's exemption from taxes promulgated 'pour contemplacion de nostre sacre et couronnement' as well as to 'acroistre et multiplier a l'exaltacion de nostre dicte foy et du bien publique de toute chrestienté'.[250] Notwithstanding these attempts to reward Parisian loyalties, a letter sent by the *prévôté des marchands* to Henry VI in March 1432 complements the Bourgeois'

---

245 So poorly served that none praised the food. *Journal*, p. 278.

246 Which seemed a very strange thing to the French, because the English were in charge of the organization and they did not care for the honour of the ceremony. *Journal*, p. 278.

247 The sick of the Hôtel-Dieu. *Journal*, p. 278.

248 The king left Paris without according any of the concessions that were expected, such as the release of prisoners, a reduction in indirect taxes such as imposts, the salt tax, fourths on wine and other evil customs that are contrary to the law and right. Not a person, neither secretly nor openly, was heard praising him, and yet Paris had done more honour to him for his entry and coronation. *Journal*, p. 279.

249 In reverence for our unction and coronation. Archives nationales, JJ 175, fol 10v. Other examples from this register include the letters found on fols 10r-v, 18r and 26r-v. See also Longnon (ed.), *Paris pendant la domination anglaise*, pp. 313-20, Nos. 154, 157 and 158.

250 In regard for our consecration and coronation; increase and multiply the exaltation of our faith, the common good and for all Christendom. Paris, Archives nationales, JJ 175, fols 11r, and 103v-104r. Longnon (ed.), *Paris pendant la domination anglaise*, pp. 324-27, nos 155, 156.

perspective and reveals the degree to which the *Journal* rhymed with broader sentiments in the city, warning that it

> semble a la plusgrant partie du povre peuple que vous le ayez habandonnez et de tous poins laissez, par ce qu'ilz n'ont point eu par votre tresdesirée et joyeuse venue aucun alegement de leurs douleurs et tresgrief maulx qu'ilz ont longuement enduré paciemment et endurent de jour en jour.[251]

The *prévôté des marchands'* assumption of popular complaint suggests that the municipality may have shared these more widespread concerns. It is not insignificant that the *prévôt des marchands* Guillaume Sanguin and some among the *échevins*, such as Marcelet Testart, were intimately tied to the community and corporations of the Halles – precisely those Burgundian sympathizers upon whom Lancastrian authority relied.[252] Similar notions of abandonment were brought to the fore by the Parisian complaint poems compiled in 1434 and 1435 examined in the previous chapter. The first of these, whose appeal to Bedford in England enables it to be dated to 1434, was copied into a different hand at the end of the account of Henry's Parisian entry in Letter Book K. The poem lamented Paris' state, warning Bedford that

> Fortune m'a virer ma chance,
> mettez moy hors de celle dure serre,
> ou vous perdrez Paris et toute France.[253]

The second poem produced the following year emulates this complaint's imagery, addressing the city and stating that Paris:

> as perdu tous ces biens,
> tu n'a plus riens,
> fors misere, peine et douleur.[254]

Both poems reiterated the *prévôté des marchands'* emphasis upon the contractual character of Parisian support for the dual monarchy, the investment that Paris was owed as the capital of Henry's French kingdom and, by 1434-35, the Lancastrian failure to reinforce the city. In this context, the Bourgeois' selective reconstruction of events echoed wider criticism of Henry VI. His presentation of the coronation encapsulated the failure of dialogue between Lancastrian centre and French capital, highlighting cultural differences: 'espoir c'est pour ce que on ne les entend point parler, et que ilz nous entendent point'.[255] The Bourgeois

---

251 It seemed to the greater part of the poor people that you had abandoned them and in every point left them, because following your most desired and joyful entry they did not receive any alleviation of their pains and the great hardships that have patiently endured for a long time, and continue to endure day by day. Letter Book K, fol. 96v.

252 For these connections, see Chapter 1.

253 I have lost Fortune's favour, deliver me from this trepidation, or you will lose Paris and all of France. Letter Book K, fol. 103r.

254 [Paris, you] have lost all of these goods, you have nothing more besides misery, suffering and pain. Paris, BNF Fr. 5332, fol. 82r.

255 The hope is that this is because we do not understand what they say, and they do not understand us. *Journal*, p. 279. The point underscores the wider argument that national identities were developing during the late Middle Ages. See David

presented English practices, Lancastrian ideals of authority and the invention of tradition as incompatible with pre-existing Parisian conceptions of French royalty and identity. The result was a profound sense of disparity that laid bare English *otherness* and articulated Lancastrian illegitimacy before the Parisian community upon which the Anglo-Burgundian regime sorely depended.

In short, interpretations of Henry VI's entry and coronation as 'the zenith of English political propaganda in France' ignore important evidence that demonstrates how Parisians themselves interacted with these messages and their own involvement in their production.[256] Among surviving accounts, the *Journal* remains the sole example of commentary beyond courtly circles and, as such, represents an essential source for examining how Parisians themselves interacted with these messages. Through the comparison with other surviving narratives, it becomes clear that the Bourgeois deliberately structured his description of Henry VI's entry and coronation with an emphasis upon the Parisian reaction it engendered to question the legitimate bases of the Lancastrian dual monarchy and highlight the settlement's dependency upon the continued support of the capital, itself predicated upon the continued satisfaction of its demands, confirmation of its privileges and recognition of its precedence for the Lancastrian monarch.

Conclusion

The examination of civic and religious ceremony in the *Journal* reveals the extent to which these represented essential forums for dialogue between ruled and ruled, structured by and structuring ideological communication through symbolic and visual forms, elements over which the Bourgeois exerted his own authority in writing. Most studies of late medieval civic and royal ceremony have examined their performance and development either through an empirical delineation of the events taking place or an assessment of the meaning that they sought to impose. In contrast, the *Journal* exposes how Parisian audiences themselves interpreted these messages. Through their reconstruction in writing, the Bourgeois presents an embodied perspective that strove to understand the symbolism evoked by civic and royal ceremony but that also witnessed the deployment of narrative authority to redefine this meaning from a perspective that suited the author, his audience and their wider community.

In this light, the Bourgeois' selective reconstruction of ceremony and his focus upon popular agency in their unfolding demonstrates ritual's centrality to the medieval public sphere as a forum for the symbolic negotiation of the legitimate bases of authority, within the city and for the overarching French royal polity.[257] Like rumour, these ceremonies

---

Green, 'National Identities and the Hundred Years War' in *Fourteenth Century England VI*, ed. by Chris Given-Wilson (Woodbridge: Boydell, 2010), pp. 115-30; Rees Davies, 'Nations and National Identities in the Medieval World: An Apologia', *Revue belge d'histoire contemporaine*, 35 (2004), pp. 567-79.

256 McKenna, 'Henry VI of England and the Dual Monarchy', p. 180.

257 Kathleen Daly, '"Centre", "Power" and "Periphery" in Late Medieval French Historiography: Some Reflections' in *War, Government and Power in Late Medieval France*, ed. by Christopher Allmand (Liverpool: Liverpool University Press, 2000), p. 125.

worked by affording each of their participants a sense of agency in the definition of ideological principles. Concentrating upon ceremony, the Bourgeois signalled the continuing perception of Paris' ideological centrality for the French kingdom and the dual monarchy alike during an era when the capital's status was challenged on numerous fronts – from the development of rival political centres including Rouen, Caen or Lille, Bourges, Poitiers and even London, to the fragmentation of allegiances within the capital and the absence of its rulers from 1422.[258] These public ceremonies revealed the manifold and complex relationships that emerged for fifteenth-century Paris between these centres and peripheries. Having arrogated a position of political and constitutional centrality in the previous century, the vicissitudes of the first decades of the fifteenth century saw an increased Parisian effort to secure and confirm this status. Ultimately, the Bourgeois used Henry VI's 1431 entry and coronation to signal the contractual underpinnings of the dual monarchy and the conditional character or Parisian support for Lancastrian rule in France, thereby defining the bases for English legitimacy in profoundly Parisian terms.

Besides direct dialogue with rulers, the *Journal* evidences the propagandistic potential of religious and civic ceremonies. Again, the Bourgeois' narrative authority determined the perceived influence of these events for his immediate community, with a large number of politically oriented processions omitted from the *Journal*. Paradoxically, perhaps, where ceremonies that represented a forum for interaction between Parisians and their rulers reiterated the city's centrality to royal policy, the Bourgeois was at pains to obfuscate the extent of Parisian institutions' involvement in and support for Lancastrian or Armagnac regimes. The ties between the city's inhabitants, divine judgement and royal authority were only made explicit when this suited his vision of the capital's prerogatives. Finally, ceremonies represented a forum for Parisian participation but, most of all, they were rhetorically malleable elements prone to alteration, reconstruction and manipulation in narratives such as the *Journal* that sought to emphasize Parisian identity and centrality when this was most threatened, stressing a collective memory of tradition, stability and power contrasted with the real political turbulence of the fifteenth century.

---

258 Bernard Guenée, 'Espace et État dans la France du Bas Moyen Âge' in *Annales. Histoire, Sciences Sociales*, 23 (1968), p. 758.

Conclusion

> Item, le jour Sainct Simon et Sainct Jude, fut faicte la plus belle procession
> a Sainct-Martin-des-Champs que on eust veue puis cent ans devant, car
> ceulx de Nostre-Dame acompaignez de toute l'Université et de toutes
> les parroisses de Paris allerent querre le precieulx corps Nostre Seigneur
> a Sainct-Jehan-en-Greve, acompaignez de bien L mil personnes, tant de
> Parlement que d'autres, et parmy les rues ou ilz passerent, les firent
> encourtinez comme le jour du Sainct Sacrement. Et fut fait en la grant
> rue Sainct-Martin, devant la Fontaine Maubué ou pres, ung moult bel
> eschaffaut ou on fist une tres belle histoire de paix et de guerre qui long
> chose seroit a racompter, que pour ce on delaissa.[1]

The *Journal d'un bourgeois de Paris* concludes with this passage describing the celebrations undertaken in anticipation of Lancastrian-occupied Rouen's surrender to Charles VII on 28 October 1449. News had already reached the capital that the Valois monarch had entered the city proper on 19 October, and the day after this Parisian procession Edmund Beaufort, duke of Somerset would sign the treaty declaring the English garrison's surrender of Rouen's castle. Rouen's capitulation effectively ended over three decades of the English presence in northern France that had begun with Henry V's victory at Agincourt in 1415 and subsequent invasion in 1417. In the space of six months English resistance in Normandy crumbled, culminating in the devastating defeat of the English forces at the Battle of Formigny on 15 April 1450.

As with the other sieges that had marked this period, the Bourgeois depicted Paris' population as having a clear stake in the Valois enterprise of reconquest. Converging upon the place de Grève to acquire the relics of the miraculous Billettes Eucharist – a Parisian case of Host desecration – Parisian institutions and inhabitants alike situated themselves as spiritual agents in the French kingdom's fate. Much like the processions performed in favour of the Burgundian siege of Bourges in 1412 or with Henry VI's pre-coronation

---

1 Item, on the feast of St Simon and St Jude the most beautiful procession was undertaken to Notre-Dame-des-Champs that people had seen for a century. The clergy of Notre-Dame, accompanied by all of the University and by all of the parishes of Paris went to collect the precious body of Our Lord at Saint-Jean-en-Grève, accompanied by fifty thousand people, as much from the Parlement as others. All of the streets through which they passed were decorated as if it were Corpus Christi. And in the *grand rue* Saint-Martin, before the Maubuée fountain (or nearby), there was a great stage with a very appealing presentation of peace and war which would take a while to describe, and so it has been left out. *Journal*, pp. 392-93.

entry in December 1431, the Bourgeois focused upon those specifically Parisian traditions that concurrently signalled the city's spiritual, political and historical pre-eminence and, by extension, its unique, hallowed ties to the French monarchy. Fundamentally, through this account the *Journal* conveyed to an important degree the sense that these people, their opinions and their prayers played a central role in the political and salvific history of France, a view that had long been inculcated in the Bourgeois' writing for almost five decades.

Also apparent here is a sense of the Bourgeois' fatigue. The Parisian unity and devotion shown in the final throes of the Hundred Years War stand in marked contrast to precisely that 'histoire de paix et de guerre' that the *Journal* itself encapsulated. The author's career – and his writing – had spanned this entire period, from the escalation in tensions between Jean sans Peur and Louis d'Orléans in 1405, through the civil conflict of the 1410s, Lancastrian occupation in the 1420s and the reassertion of Valois authority after 1436. The theologian, Notre-Dame canon and priest of the Saints-Innocents parish, Nicolas Confrant, a candidate for the author's identification, was certainly unwell by this date, reported as suffering from leprosy in June 1448. His replacement as a canon by the doctor in medicine Enguerrand de Parenty on 5 September 1451 was preceded by months of regular absences from capitulary assemblies, such that the slow decline of Confrant's health closely parallels the increasingly brief and intermittent passages recorded within the *Journal* during the late 1440s.[2]

Reflections upon the Bourgeois' life and career underpin this assessment of the *Journal*, as an endeavour to breathe new life into a text that has rarely been given the necessary space for historical analysis on its own merit. Beginning with Claude Fauchet in 1555, for almost a century the *Journal* circulated among Parisian bibliophiles and historians who took a lively interest in the text, incorporating sections into early publications that included Étienne Pasquier's *Recherches de la France* (1596) and Denis Godefroy's edition of the *Histoire de Charles VI* attributed to Jean Juvénal des Ursins (1653).[3] And yet, despite this long-standing interest, with three scholarly editions and translations produced since 1881, the *Journal* has never been the subject of its own, focused study. As a result of the intense research regarding the historiographical foundations and enterprises of the French monarchy, scholars following in the footsteps of Bernard Guenée have overlooked the potential for Parisians to develop their own, independent historical culture. Consequently, as the first concentrated historical analysis of the text, this book has endeavoured to interrogate the *Journal*'s purpose and authorship, but also the potential audience, communities and institutions that informed the Bourgeois' writing. Most importantly, we should move away from viewing the *Journal* as an isolated reflection of Parisian events and opinions. Rather, it is fascinating because of the historiographical experimentation that it evidences, and because of its place within a broader and more intriguing collaborative process that framed intersections between the Bourgeois' own views and his audience's horizon of expectations.

---

2   For this decline, see Luke Giraudet, 'Nicolas Confrant, author of the *Journal d'un bourgeois de Paris*?', *Romania*, 139 (2021), p. 138.

3   Étienne Pasquier, *Les Recherches de la France, reveues et augmentées de quatre livres* (Paris: Mettayer and l'Huillier, 1596); Denis Godefroy (ed.), *Histoire de Charles VI, roy de France* (Paris: Imprimerie royale, 1653).

In countering the Bourgeois' awkward isolation in current histories of fifteenth-century Paris and late medieval historical writing more generally, the central premise of this book has been that the *Journal* captures these exchanges, with the text emerging as an interface between the Bourgeois' authorial intent and his audience's perspectives. As such, the *Journal* represents an especially fruitful basis for examining public opinion during one of the most chaotic eras in Parisian history. Twenty years ago, Bernard Guenée suggested that long-held assumptions regarding the Bourgeois' bias invalidated the *Journal* as a source for interrogating the nature of medieval public opinion, but this book has been motivated by the impression that it is precisely the Bourgeois' direct engagement with the political struggles, perspectives, and attitudes of a subsection of Parisian society that renders his *Journal* integral to envisioning the late medieval Parisian public sphere. Counterbalancing Guenée's concentration upon the *Chronique du Religieux de Saint-Denis*, the *Journal* captures a community that was closely involved in ongoing debates concerning the common good, taxation, warfare and the city's own place in the kingdom that preoccupied Parisians during the first decades of the fifteenth century. As this community navigated and negotiated the circumstances of the Armagnac-Burgundian conflict, Lancastrian occupation and their subsequent reabsorption into the Valois polity, the Bourgeois' sentiments, opinions and animosities similarly shifted. In the process, the *Journal* reveals how Parisians made adept use of common and established political repertoires and discourses to participate in the public transcript of political life and voice their own vision of the realm.

Theoretically, these conclusions add weight to the arguments put forward by medievalists in the past fifteen years who have substantially nuanced Jürgen Habermas' early, idealized notion of the public sphere, countering the grand narrative that has situated the birth of public political critique in the early modern period. In tandem with research on fifteenth- and sixteenth-century politics that has recently warned against an overemphasis upon print's revolutionary significance, the *Journal* points to the imaginative and tentative ways in which people employed manuscripts as a support to participation in overarching political cultures. In turn, this book's analysis of the public sphere through the lens of the Bourgeois' writing has sought to venture beyond the folios of the *Journal*'s surviving manuscripts. The Bourgeois brought to life the multivalent discursive, gestural, and performative repertoires through which everyday Parisians participated in political culture. Then, as in the eighteenth-century coffeehouses, people could and did gather to discuss political issues that they rationalized and evaluated according to commonly held and often assumed moral and politically normative systems that underpinned and framed their vision of the body politic. Fundamentally, the *Journal* presents the efforts of a single individual to record this negotiation of values by integrating Parisian complaint and rumour into an ongoing and shared commentary about political society.

Political communication was the driving force of the Bourgeois' narrative. Through the selective privileging of urban events and perspectives, the *Journal* underscored the reality of Parisian talk, rumour and opinion regarding the city's constantly changing circumstances. Recording instances of political and historical significance for Paris, the Bourgeois was also concerned with delineating how his community considered and responded to these same events. It is in this respect that reactions to official media, emotional rhetoric, the circulation of rumour, the appropriation of spaces and presence in civic ceremony consistently emerged in the *Journal* as sites of mediation and contest. These were the pivotal arenas within which Parisians staked their claim to act as dynamic members of the body politic, joining in a public transcript that balanced the competing views of royal authority, civic officials, Parisian institutions, artisans and commons. Codifying this public transcript in his writing, the Bourgeois arrogated authority through the delineation of the exchanges between ruler and ruled, with the *Journal* itself becoming a tool through which he and his audience could read relations of power, decry authority and validate a more representative less well-considered participation in public politics. Assessing the blurred and fluid boundaries between official and unofficial or verbal and written communication through the Journal has prompted important insights into how Parisians themselves accepted, contested and rejected political information in an effort to assert their own power or identity and arrogate for themselves a role in political developments and decision-making.

A conclusion highlighting the growing agency and claims of the Parisian artisanal classes and clergy alike in the political realm of fifteenth-century France also points to the broader significance of this study. An ever-growing historiography for late medieval political culture has clearly demonstrated that the circulation of news created more socially diverse, informed publics in Renaissance Europe – particularly in urban centres –, and that we should be alive to the subtle ways in which heterogenous groups removed from society's upper echelons reflected upon and even hoped to shape government. Indeed, the later Middle Ages was a time when subjects became increasingly prepared to participate in and critique rule, appropriating and manipulating political discourse to this end. However, studies of Valois France have tended to envision centralization and state-building as a singular site of power, wherein the monarchy stage-managed opinion. The major tensions within this perspective on the medieval past have been those between the French monarchy and the kingdom's leading aristocrats – a fact demonstrated most acutely by the very circumstances of the Hundred Years War and the monarchy's struggles with the houses of Navarre, Brittany and Burgundy. Less well-documented is the role that urban political culture played in these same struggles. Through a close reading of the Bourgeois' *Journal* and other examples of fifteenth-century urban historiography like it, I propose that there is another, very different kind of story to be told about royal power in late medieval France. Just as the inhabitants of the *bonnes villes* became more vocal in their responses to the acute taxation, economic hardship and military devastation that they experienced during the course of the Hundred Years War, texts like the *Journal* reveal how Parisians finely attuned to the monarchy's public responsibilities engaged in everyday urban politics, with the city an arena where ideas of good government were discussed, debated, played out and even inverted.

Ultimately, this points to the dangers of oversimplifying, negating, and ignoring those texts that escape neat, established generic classifications. This research challenges the habitual interpretations of the *Journal* by undoing our perception of the Bourgeois' stance as a mirror onto his world, situating the author as an individual who participated in active and diverse institutions and communities, negotiating the conflict that marked his era and informing his audiences in the process. The wealth of information supplied by the *Journal* invites a comparative re-evaluation of other fifteenth-century urban texts, not simply those produced in Paris such as the journals of Jean de Roye and Jean Maupoint, but also looking beyond the capital to the historiographical traditions of other northern French towns. Moreover, the methods proposed in this book for examining texts like these and discerning the opinion communities of which they formed a part invite parallel studies of the events and traditions known to be in development in other European centres. Bringing urban conversation to light, such studies are bound to give social depth to understandings of the public sphere before early modernity, redirecting our attention away from monarchies and centralized instances of historiographical production to reveal how urban inhabitants articulated and codified their agency in national politics.

Bibliography

Unpublished Primary Sources

Aix-en-Provence, Bibliothèque Méjanes, MS 432 (316).
Brussels, Bibliothèque royale de Belgique, MS 9559-64.
Cambridge, Trinity College, MS O.9.1.
London, College of Arms, MS 9.
London, London Metropolitan Archives, Archives of the Corporation of London, Letter Book K.
Paris, Archives nationales, AE II 435.
Paris, Archives nationales, JJ 86.
Paris, Archives nationales, JJ 170.
Paris, Archives nationales, JJ 171.
Paris, Archives nationales, JJ 172.
Paris, Archives nationales, JJ 173.
Paris, Archives nationales, JJ 174.
Paris, Archives nationales, JJ 175.
Paris, Archives nationales, K 950A.
Paris, Archives nationales, L 570.
Paris, Archives nationales, L 656.
Paris, Archives nationales, LL 112.
Paris, Archives nationales, LL 113.
Paris, Archives nationales, LL 116.
Paris, Archives nationales, LL 434-B.
Paris, Archives Nationales, MC ET XXXIII 24, no. 34.
Paris, Archives nationales, U 314.
Paris, Archives nationales, X 1^a 8603.
Paris, Archives nationales, Y 2.
Paris, Archives nationales, Z 1^b 286.
Paris, Bibliothèque de l'Arsenal, MS 3523.
Paris, Bibliothèque historique de la ville de Paris, 4-MS-RES-10 (527).
Paris, Bibliothèque nationale de France MS Fr. 23138.
Paris, Bibliothèque nationale de France, MS Dupuy 275.
Paris, Bibliothèque nationale de France, MS Fr. 10303.
Paris, Bibliothèque nationale de France, MS Fr. 10468.
Paris, Bibliothèque nationale de France, MS Fr. 1278.
Paris, Bibliothèque nationale de France, MS Fr. 14416.
Paris, Bibliothèque nationale de France, MS Fr. 14989.
Paris, Bibliothèque nationale de France, MS Fr. 20685.

Paris, Bibliothèque nationale de France, MS Fr. 22935.

Paris, Bibliothèque nationale de France, MS Fr. 23018.

Paris, Bibliothèque nationale de France, MS Fr. 24432.

Paris, Bibliothèque nationale de France, MS Fr. 24726.

Paris, Bibliothèque nationale de France, MS Fr. 4437.

Paris, Bibliothèque nationale de France, MS Fr. 4487.

Paris, Bibliothèque nationale de France, MS Fr. 5332.

Paris, Bibliothèque nationale de France, MS Fr. 6465.

Paris, Bibliothèque nationale de France, MS Fr. 8220.

Paris, Bibliothèque nationale de France, MS Latin 17740.

Paris, Bibliothèque nationale de France, MS Latin 18014.

Paris, Bibliothèque nationale de France, MS Latin 4641-B.

Paris, Bibliothèque nationale de France, MS Moreau 1161.

Paris, Bibliothèque nationale de France, MS Moreau 1162.

Paris, Bibliothèque nationale de France, MS Nouvelles acquisitions françaises 3423.

Paris, Bibliothèque nationale de France, MS Nouvelles acquisitions françaises 6221.

Rome, Vatican Library, Reg. Lat. 1389.

Rome, Vatican Library, Reg. Lat. 1502 (Volume 1).

Rome, Vatican Library, Reg. Lat. 1923.

Rome, Vatican Library, Reg. Lat. 753.

Vienna, Staatsarchiv, AT-OeStA/HHStA LHA 98-1.

Printed Sources

Aquinas, Thomas. *On the Government of Rulers*, ed. and trans. by James M. Blythe (Philadelphia, PA: University of Pennsylvania Press, 1997).

Archives de la famille de Beaulaincourt, ed. by R. Rodière and C. de la Charie, 2 vols (Lille: Lefebvre-Ducrocq, 1911).

Aristotle. *The Politics of Aristotle*, ed. and trans. by Peter L. Phillips Simpson (Chapel Hill, NC: University of North Carolina Press, 1997).

Basin, Thomas. *Histoire des règnes de Charles VII et de Louis XI*, ed. by Jules Quicherat, 4 vols (Paris: Renouard, 1855-59).

Baye, Nicolas de. *Journal de Nicolas de Baye, greffer du Parlement de Paris, 1400-17*, ed. by Alexandre Tuetey, 2 vols (Paris: Renouard, 1885-88).

Blondel, Robert. 'Robert Blondel, *Desolatio regni francie*, un poème politique de soutien au futur Charles VII en 1420', ed. and trans. by Nicole Pons and Monique Goullet, *Archives d'histoire doctrinale et littéraire du Moyen Âge*, 68 (2001), pp. 297-374.

Bochetel, Guillaume. *Lentrée de la Royne en sa ville and Cité de Paris* (Paris: Geoffroy Tory, 1531).

Bois, Jean du. 'Conseils et prédictions adressés à Charles VII en 1445 par un certain Jean du Bois', ed. by Noel Valois, *Annuaire-Bulletin de la Société de l'histoire de France*, 46 (1909), pp. 201-38.

Bourgeois of Paris. *A Parisian Journal 1405-49, translated from the anonymous* Journal d'un bourgeois de Paris, ed. and trans. by Janet Shirley (Oxford: Clarendon Press, 1968).

Bourgeois of Paris. *Journal d'un bourgeois de Paris 1405-49*, d'après les manuscrits de Rome et de Paris, ed. by Alexandre Tuetey (Paris: Champion, 1881).

Bourgeois of Paris. *Journal d'un bourgeois de Paris de 1405 à 1449*, ed. and trans. by Colette Beaune (Paris: Librairie Générale Française, 1990).

Chartier, Alain. *Le Quadrilogue invectif*, ed. by E. Droz (Paris: Champion, 1923).

Chartier, Jean. *Chronique de Charles VII, roi de France, par Jean Chartier*, ed. by Auguste Vallet de Viriville, 3 vols (Paris: Jannet, 1858).

Chartularium Universitatis Parisiensis, ed. by Heinrich Denifle, 4 vols (Paris: Delalain, 1889-97).

'Complainte sur les misères de Paris, composée en 1435', ed. by L. Auvray, *BSHP*, 18 (1891), pp. 84-87.

Chronicles of London, ed. by Charles Lethbridge Kingsford (Oxford: Clarendon Press, 1905).

Chronique de la Pucelle ou Chronique de Cousinot suivie de la Chronique normande de P. Cochon, ed. by Auguste Vallet de Viriville (Paris: Adolphe Delahays, 1859).

Collection générale des documents français qui se trouvent en Angleterre, ed. by Jules Delpit, vol. 1 (Paris: Dumoulin, 1847).

De Mets, Guillebert. *Description de la ville de Paris, 1434*, ed. and trans. by Evelyn Mullally (Turnhout: Brepols, 2015).

Deschamps, Eustache. *Œuvres complètes d'Eustache Deschamps*, ed. by Auguste-Henry-Edouard, le marquis de Queux de Saint-Hilaire, 11 vols (Paris: Firmin Didot, 1878-1903).

Épitaphier du vieux Paris. vol. 4, Saint-Eustache – Sainte-Geneviève-la-Petite, ed. by Émile Raunié (Paris: Imprimerie nationale, 1914).

Epitaphier du Vieux Paris: vol. 6, Les Saints-Innocents, ed. by Hélène Verlet (Paris: Comité des Travaux Historiques de la Ville de Paris, 1997).

Escouchy, Mathieu d'. *Chronique de Mathieu d'Escouchy*, ed. by Gaston du Fresne de Beaucourt, 3 vols (Paris: Renouard, 1863-64).

Fauquembergue, Clément de. *Journal de Clément de Fauquembergue, greffier du Parlement de Paris, 1417-35*, ed. by Alexandre Tuetey, 3 vols (Paris: Renouard, 1903-15).

Froissart, Jean. *Œuvres de Froissart*, ed. by Joseph Kervyn de Lettenhove, 28 vols (Brussels: Devaux, 1867-77).

Gaguin, Robert. *Roberti Gaguini, epistole et orationes. Texte publié sur les éditions originales de 1498*, ed. by Louis Thuasne, 2 vols (Paris: Bouillon, 1903-05).

Gerson, Jean. *Joannis Gersonii Opera Omnia*, ed. by Louis Ellies Dupin, vol. 5 (Antwerp: Peter de Hondt, 1728).

——. *Œuvres complètes*, ed. by Palémon Glorieux, 10 vols (Paris: Desclée, 1959-73).

Gesta Henrici Quinti, ed. by F. Taylor and J.S. Roskell (Oxford: Clarendon Press, 1975).

Gruel, Guillaume. *Chronique d'Arthur de Richemont, connétable de France, duc de Bretagne (1393-1458)*, ed. by Achille le Vavasseur (Paris: Renouard, 1890).

'Histoire de Charles VI, roy de France par Jean Juvénal des Ursins' in *Choix de chroniques et mémoires relatifs à l'histoire de France*, ed. by Jean Alexandre C. Buchon (Orléans: Herluison, 1875), pp. 323-573.

Histoire et recherches des antiquités de la ville de Paris, ed. by Henri Sauval, 3 vols (Paris: Moette and Chardon, 1724).

Ingulph's Chronicle of Croyland with the continuations by Peter of Blois and anonymous writers, ed. and trans. by Henry T. Riley (London: Henry Bohn, 1854).

Inventaire analytique des livres de couleur et bannières du Châtelet de Paris, ed. by Alexandre Tuetey, 2 vols (Paris: Imprimerie nationale, 1899-1907).

'Journal parisien des années 1412 et 1413', ed. by Alexandre Tuetey, *MSHP*, 44 (1917), pp. 163-82.

Juvénal des Ursins, Jean. *Écrits politiques de Jean Juvénal des Ursins*, ed. by Peter S. Lewis, 3 vols (Paris: Klincksieck, 1978-93).

'La Chronique dite "des Cordeliers"' in *La Chronique d'Enguerran de Monstrelet en deux livres avec pièces justificatives, 1400-44*, ed. by Louis Douët-d'Arcq, VI (Paris: Jules Renouard, 1862), pp. 191-327.

'La Complainte de Paris en 1436', ed. by Raynaud Gaston, *BSHP*, 27 (1900), pp. 36-41.

le Bouvier, Gilles. *Les chroniques du roi Charles VII par Gilles le Bouvier dit le héraut Berry*, ed. by Henri Courteault and Léonce Celier (Paris: Klincksieck, 1979).

le Fèvre de Saint-Remy, Jean. *Chronique de Jean le Fèvre, seigneur de Saint-Remy*, ed. by François Morand, 2 vols (Paris: Renouard, 1876-81).

le Juge, Pierre. *Histoire de saincte Geneviefve, patronne de Paris* (Paris: Henri Coyel, 1586).

Le Ménagier de Paris, ed. by Georgine Brereton and Janet Ferrier (Oxford: Oxford University Press, 1981).

Le procès de condamnation de Jeanne d'Arc, ed. and trans. by Pierre Tisset and Yvonne Lanhers, 3 vols (Paris: Klincksieck, 1960-71).

Le Songe du vergier édité d'après le manuscrit royal 19 C IV de la British Library, ed. by Marion Schnerb-Lièvre, 2 vols (Paris: Éditions du CNRS, 1982).

'Le Songe véritable, pamphlet politique d'un parisien du XVe siècle', ed. by Henri Moranvillé, *MSHP*, 17 (1890), pp. 217-438.

Lectures françaises de la fin du Moyen Âge: Petite anthologie commentée de succès littéraires, ed. by Frédéric Duval (Geneva: Droz, 2007).

Les contribuables parisiens à la fin de la guerre de Cent ans. Les rôles d'impôt de 1421, 1423 et 1438, ed. by Jean Favier (Geneva: Droz, 1970).

Les Entrées royales françaises de 1328 à 1515, ed. by Bernard Guenée and Françoise Lehoux (Paris: Éditions du CNRS, 1968).

Les Grandes Chroniques de France: Chronique des règnes de Jean II et de Charles V, ed. by Roland Delachenal, vols 1 and 2 (Paris: Renouard, 1910-16).

'Les journées parisiennes de mai-juin 1418: d'après des documents des archives de la couronne d'Aragon', ed. by Aznar Pardo de la Casta and J. Vieillard, *BSHP*, 76 (1940), pp. 125-53.

Les Ordonnances royaux sur le faict et jurisdiction de la prevosté des marchands et eschevinage de la ville de Paris (Paris, 1556).

Letters and papers illustrative of the wars of the English in France during the reign of Henry the Sixth, King of England, ed. by Joseph Stevenson, vol. 2, Pt. 1 (London: Longman, 1864).

Li Livres du Gouvernement des Rois; a XIIIth Century French Version of Egidio Colonna's Treatise De 'Regimine Principum', ed. by Samuel Paul Molenaer (London: Macmillan, 1899).

Maupoint, Jean de. 'Journal parisien de Jean Maupoint, prieur de Sainte-Catherine-du-Val-des-Écoliers (1437-69)', ed. by Gustave Fagniez, *MSHP*, 4 (1877), pp. 1-114.

Monstrelet, Enguerran[d] de. *La Chronique d'Enguerran de Monstrelet en deux livres avec pièces justificatives, 1400-44*, ed. by Louis Douët-d'Arcq, 6 vols (Paris: Jules Renouard, 1857-62).

Nicot, Jean. *Thresor de la langue francoyse, tant ancienne que moderne* (Paris: David Douceur, 1606).

Ordonnances des rois de France de la troisième race, ed. by Eusèbe Jacob de Laurière and Denis François Secousse, 21 vols (Paris: Imprimerie royale, 1723-1849).

Oresme, Nicole. *Le livre de Ethiques d'Aristote*, ed. by Albert Douglas Menut (New York: Stechert, 1940).

———. *Maistre Nicole Oresme: Le livre de Politiques d'Aristote*, published with the text of the Avranches manuscript 223 with a critical introduction and notes, ed. by Albert Douglas Menut (Philadelphia PA: American Philosophical Society, 1970).

Paris et ses historiens aux XIVᵉ et XVᵉ siècles. Documents et écrits originaux, ed. by Antoine le Roux de Lincy and Lazare-Maurice Tisserand (Paris: Imprimerie impériale, 1867).

Paris pendant la domination anglaise (1420-36), ed. by Auguste Longnon (Paris: Champion, 1878).

Pintoin, Michel. *Chronique du Religieux de Saint-Denys contenant le règne de Charles VI, de 1380 à 1422*, 6 vols (Paris: Crapelet, 1839-52).

Pizan, Christine de. 'Christine de Pizan's "Ditié de Jehanne d'Arc" (Part I)', ed. by Angus Kennedy and Kenneth Varty, *Nottingham Medieval Studies*, 18 (1974), pp. 29-55.

———. *Le livre de l'Advision Christine*, ed. by Christine Reno and Liliane Dulac (Paris: Champion, 2001).

———. *Le livre du corps de policie*, ed. by Angus J. Kennedy (Paris: Champion, 1998).

———. *The 'Livre de la paix' of Christine de Pizan*, ed by Charity Cannon Willard (The Hague: Mouton, 1958).

Procès de condamnation et de réhabilitation de Jeanne d'Arc dite la Pucelle, ed. by Jules Quicherat, 5 vols (Paris: Jules Renouard, 1841-49).

Registre criminel du Châtelet de Paris, du 6 septembre 1389 au 18 mai 1392, ed. by Henri Dulpes-Agier, 2 vols (Paris: Lahure, 1861-64).

Registre des causes civiles de l'officialité épiscopale de Paris, 1384-87, ed. by Joseph Petit (Paris: Imprimerie nationale, 1919).

Registre des délibérations du bureau de la ville de Paris, ed. by François Bonnardot and others, 16 vols (Paris: Imprimerie nationale, 1883-1927).

Rigord, *Œuvres de Rigord et de Guillaume le Breton, historiens de Philippe Auguste*, ed. by H. François Delaborde, 2 vols (Paris: Renouard, 1882-85).

Roye, Jean de. *Journal de Jean de Roye connu sous le nom de Chronique scandaleuse 1460-83*, ed. by Bernard de Mandroit, 2 vols (Paris: Renouard, 1894-96).

———. *Chronique Scandaleuse: Journal d'un Parisien au temps de Louis XI*, ed. and trans. by Joël Blanchard (Paris: Pocket, 2015).

Taylor, Craig (ed. and trans.). *Joan of Arc: La Pucelle* (Manchester: Manchester University Press, 2006).

Testaments enregistrés au Parlement de Paris sous le règne de Charles VI, ed. by Alexandre Tuetey (Paris: Imprimerie nationale 1880).

The Brut or the Chronicles of England, ed. by Friedrich Brie, Pt. 2 (London: Kegan Paul, Trench, Trubner and Co., 1908).

The Historical Collections of a Citizen of London in the Fifteenth Century, ed. by James Gairdner (London: Camden Society, 1876).

Three Fifteenth-Century Chronicles, ed. by James Gairdner (London: Camden Society, 1880).

'Un sermon français inédit de Jean Courtecuisse, *Justum adiutorium*', ed. by Giuseppe di Stefano, *Romania*, 85 (1964), pp. 417-54.

'Un sermon de Philippe de Villette, abbé de Saint-Denis, pour la levée de l'Oriflamme (1414)', ed. by Charles J. Liebman Jr., *Romania*, 68 (1944), pp. 444-70.

Venette, Jean de. *The Chronicle of Jean de Venette*, ed. and trans. by Jean Birdsall and Richard Newhall (New York: Columbia University Press, 1953).

Villon, François. *François Villon: Lais, Testament, poésies diverses*, ed. by Jean-Claude Mühlethaler (Paris: Champion, 2004).

Secondary Literature

Adams, Tracy and Rechtschaffen, Glenn. 'The Reputation of the Queen and Public Opinion: The Case of Isabeau of Bavaria', *Medieval Feminist Forum*, 47 (2011), pp. 5-31.

———. *Christine de Pizan and the Fight for France* (University Park, PA: Pennsylvania State University Press, 2014).

———. 'Feuding, Factionalism and Fictions of National Identity: Reconsidering Charles VII's Armagnacs', *Digital Philology*, 1 (2012), pp. 5-31.

———. 'Isabeau de Bavière, le don et la politique du mécénat', *Le Moyen Âge*, 117 (2011), pp. 475-86.

———. 'The Armagnac-Burgundian Feud and the Languages of Anger' in *Writing War in Britain and France, 1370-1854*, ed. by Stephanie Downes, Andrew Lynch and Katrina O'Loughlin (London: Routledge, 2018), pp. 57-72.

———. *The Life and Afterlife of Isabeau of Bavaria* (Baltimore, MD: John Hopkins University Press, 2010).

———. 'The Political Significance of Christine de Pizan's Third Estate in the *Livre du corps de policie*', *Journal of Medieval History*, 35 (2009), pp. 385-98.

Ailes, Marianne. 'Literary Responses to Agincourt: The Allegories of *Le Pastoralet* and the *Quadrologue Invectif*', *Reading Medieval Studies*, 41 (2015), pp. 1-26.

Allmand, Christopher. 'Alan Kirketon: a clerical royal councillor in Normandy during the English occupation in the fifteenth century', *The Journal of Ecclesiastical History*, 15, 1 (1964), pp. 33-39.

———. *Henry V* (London: Methuen, 1992).

———. *Lancastrian Normandy, 1415-50: The History of a Medieval Occupation* (Oxford: Clarendon Press, 1983).

Allport, Gordon and Postman, Leo. 'An Analysis of Rumor', *The Public Opinion Quarterly*, 10 (1946-47), pp. 501-17.

Althoff, Gerd. 'Demonstration und Inszenierung. Spielregeln der Kommunikation in mittelalterlicher Offentlichkeit', *Frühmittelalterliche Studien*, 27 (1993), pp. 27-50.

———. 'Du rire et des larmes. Pourquoi les émotions intéressent-elles les médiévistes?', *Écrire l'histoire*, 2 (2008), pp. 27-39.

———. 'The Variability of Rituals in the Middle Ages' in *Medieval Concepts of the Past: Ritual, Memory, Historiography*, ed. by Gerd Althoff, Johannes Fried and Patrick J. Geary (Cambridge: Cambridge University Press, 2002), pp. 71-87.

Ambühl, Rémy. 'Henry V and the Administration of Justice: The Surrender of Meaux (May 1422)', *Journal of Medieval History*, 43 (2017), pp. 74-88.

Andress, David. 'Popular Violence in the French Revolution: Revolt, Retribution and the Slide to State Terror', in *Cultures of Violence: Interpersonal Violence in Historical Perspective*, ed. by Stuart Carroll (London: Palgrave Macmillan, 2007), pp. 175-91.

Anthias, Floya. 'The material and the symbolic in theorising social stratification', *The British Journal of Sociology*, 52 (2001), pp. 367-90.

Appleford, Amy. *Learning to Die in London, 1380-1540* (Philadelphia, PA: Pennsylvania University Press, 2015).

Arnade, Peter, Howel, Martha and Simons, Walter. 'Fertile Spaces: The Productivity of Urban Space in Northern Europe', *The Journal of Interdisciplinary History*, 32 (2002), pp. 515-48.

———. 'City, State and Public Ritual in the Late-Medieval Burgundian Netherlands', *Comparative Studies in Society and History*, 39 (1997), pp. 300-18.

Ashley, Kathleen. 'Introduction: The Moving Subjects of Processional Performance' *in Moving Subjects: Processional Performance in the Middle Ages and the Renaissance*, ed. by Kathleen Ashley and Wim Husken (Amsterdam: Rodopi, 2001), pp. 7-34.

Assmann, Jan and Czaplicka, John. 'Collective Memory and Cultural Identity', *New German Critique*, 65 (1995), pp. 125-33.

———. 'Globalization, Universalism and the Erosion of Cultural Memory', *Memory in a Global Age: Discourses, Practices and Trajectories*, ed. by Aleida Assmann and Sebastian Conrad (New York: Palgrave MacMillan, 2010), pp. 121-37.

Attreed, Lorraine. 'Urban Identity in Medieval English Towns', *The Journal of Interdisciplinary History*, 32 (2002), pp. 571-92.

Autrand, Françoise. *Charles VI: La folie du roi* (Paris: Perrin, 1986).

———. 'Journal d'un bourgeois de Paris' in *Lexikon des Mittelalters*, vol. 5, ed. by Robert Auty (Stuttgart: Metzler, 1999), 639.

———. *Naissance d'un grand corps de l'État: Les gens du Parlement de Paris 1345-1454* (Paris: Publications de la Sorbonne, 1981).

Bailey, Michael D. and Peters, Edward. 'A Sabbat of Demonologists: Basel, 1431-1440', *The Historian*, 65 (2003), pp. 1375-95.

Bakhtin, Mikhail. *L'œuvre de François Rabelais et la culture populaire au Moyen Âge et sous la Renaissance*, trans. by Andrée Robel (Paris: Gallimard, 1970).

———. *Rabelais and His World*, trans. by Helene Iswolsky (Bloomington, IN: Indiana University Press, 1984).

———. *The Dialogic Imagination: Four Essays*, ed. and trans. by Michael Holquist (Austin, TX: University of Texas Press, 1981).

Bakir, Vian, Herring, Eric, Miller David, and Robinson, Piers. 'Organised persuasive communication: A new conceptual framework for research on public relations, propaganda and promotional culture', *Critical Sociology*, 45 (2018), pp. 311-28.

Bardsley, Sandy. 'Sin, Speech and Scolding in Late Medieval England' in Fama*: The Politics of Talk and Reputaton in Medieval Europe*, ed. by Thelma Fenster and Daniel Lord Smail (London: Cornell University Press, 2003), pp. 145-64.

Barkun, Michael. 'Les théories du complot comme connaissance stigmatisée', trans. by Brigitte Rollet, *Diogène*, 249-50 (2015), pp. 168-76.

Barthes, Roland. 'L'effet de réel', *Communications*, 11 (1968), pp. 84-89.

———. *Essais critiques* (Paris: Seuil, 1964).

Bastide, Roger. 'Mémoire collective et sociologie du bricolage', *L'année sociologique*, 21 (1970), pp. 65-108.

Bastine, Pascal. *Une histoire de la peine de mort. Bourreaux et supplices, 1500-1800* (Paris: Seuil, 2011).

Battifol, Louis. 'La prévôté des marchands de Paris à la fin du XIVᵉ siècle', *BEC*, 52 (1891), pp. 269-84.

Beaune, Colette. 'Costume et pouvoir en France à la fin du Moyen Âge: les devises royales vers 1400', *Revue des sciences humaines*, 55 (1981), pp. 125-46.

———. 'La rumeur dans le Journal du Bourgeois de Paris' in *La circulation des nouvelles au Moyen Âge: XXIVᵉ Congrès de la S.H.M.E.S., Avignon, Juin 1993* (Paris: Publications de la Sorbonne, 1994), pp. 191-203.

———. 'L'utilisation politique du mythe des origines troyennes en France à la fin du Moyen Âge' in *Lectures médiévales de Virgile. Actes du colloque de Rome (25-28 octobre 1982)* (Rome: École française de Rome, 1985), pp. 331-55.

———. 'Mourir noblement à la fin du Moyen Âge' in *Mourir noblement à la fin du Moyen Âge: Actes des congrès de la Société des historiens médiévistes de l'enseignement supérieur public*, ed. by Colette Beaune (Strasbourg, 1975), pp. 124-43.

———. 'Raoul de Presles et les origines de Paris' in *Penser le pouvoir au Moyen Âge (VIIIᵉ-XVᵉ siècle)*, ed. by Dominique Boutet and Jacques Verger (Paris: Presses de l'Ecole normale supérieure, 2000), pp. 17-32.

———. *The Birth of an Ideology: Myths and Symbols of Nation in Late-Medieval France*, trans. by Susan Ross Huston, ed. by Fredric L. Cheyette (Oxford: University of California Press, 1991).

Béchu, Claire, Greffe, Florence and Pebay, Isabelle (ed.). *Minutes du XVᵉ siècle de l'étude XIX, inventaire analytique* (Paris: Archives nationales, 1993).

Bedos-Rezak, Brigitte. 'Civic Liturgies and Urban records in Northern France, 1100-1400' in *City and Spectacle in Medieval Europe*, ed. by Barbara A. Hanawalt and Kathryn L. Reyerson (Minneapolis, MN: University of Minnesota Press, 1994), pp. 34-55.

Beik, William. 'The Violence of the French Crowd from Charivari to Revolution', *Past & Present*, 197 (2007), pp. 75-110.

Bell, Catherine. *Ritual Theory, Ritual Practice* (Oxford: Oxford University Press, 1992).

Benveniste, Henrietta. 'Dead Body, Public Body: Notes on Death by Execution in the Middle Ages', *Law and Critique*, 4 (1993), pp. 21-42.

Berland, Florence. 'Access to the Prince's Court in Late Medieval Paris' in *The Key to Power? The Culture of Access in Princely Courts, 1400-1750*, ed. by Dries Raeymaekers and Sebastiaan Derks (Leiden: Brill, 2016), pp. 17-39.

Bernstein, Hilary J. *Historical Communities: Cities, Erudition and National Identity in Early Modern France* (Leiden: Brill, 2021).

Billen, Claire. 'Dire le Bien Commun dans l'espace public. Matérialité épigraphique et monumentale du bien commun dans les villes des Pays-Bas, à la fin du Moyen Âge' in *De Bono Communi: The Discourse and Practice of the Common Good in the European City (13th-16th centuries) / Discours et pratique du bien commun dans les villes d'Europe (XIIIe au XVIe siècle)*, ed. by Elodie Lecuppre-Desjardin and Anne-Laure Van Bruaene (Turnhout: Brepols, 2010), pp. 71-88.

Black, Anthony. *Guilds and Civil Society in European Political Thought from the Twelfth Century to the Present* (London: Meuthen, 1984).

Blanchard, Joël. 'Le spectacle du rite: les entrées royales', *Revue historique*, 305 (2003), pp. 475-519.

Bloemendal, Jan and Van Dixhoorn, Arjan. 'Literary Cultures and Public Opinion in the Early Modern Low Countries' in *Literary Cultures and Public Opinion in the Low Countries, 1450-1650*, ed. by Jan Bloemendal and Arjan van Dixhoorn (Leiden: Brill, 2011), pp. 1-35.

Blumenfeld-Kosinski, Renate. 'Two Responses to Agincourt: Alain Chartier's Livre des quatre dames and Christine de Pizan's Epistre de la prison de vie humaine' in *Contexts and Continuities: Proceedings of the IVth International Colloquium on Christine de Pizan (Glasgow, 21-27 July 2000)*, ed. by Angus J. Kennedy, Rosalind Brown-Grant, James C. Laidlaw and Catherine M. Muller (Glasgow: University of Glasgow Press, 2002), pp. 75-85.

Bonenfant, Paul. *Du meurtre de Montereau au traité de Troyes* (Brussels: Académie royale de Belgique, 1958).

Boone, Marc and Dumolyn, Jan. 'Les officiers-créditeurs des ducs de Bourgogne dans l'ancien comté de Flandre: aspects financiers, politiques et sociaux', *Publications du Centre Européen d'Études Bourguignonnes*, 39 (1999), pp. 225-41.

———— and Hemptinne, Thérèse de. 'Espace urbain et ambitions princières: les présences matérielles de l'autorité princière dans le Gand médiéval (12e siècle-1540)' in Werner Paravicini (hg.), *Zeremoniell und Raum, 4. Symposium der Residenzen-Kommission der Akademie der Wissenschaften in Göttingen*, ed. by Werner Paravicini (Sigmaringen: Thorbecke, 1997), pp. 279-304.

————. *Gent en de Bourgondische hertogen ca. 1384 – ca. 1453: Een sociaal-politieke studie van een staatsvormingsproces* (Brussels: Paleis der Academïen, 1990).

————. 'Les pouvoirs et leurs représentations dans les villes des anciens Pays-Bas (XIVe-XVe siècle)' in *Villes de Flandre et d'Italie (XIIIe-XVIe siècles): les enseignements d'une comparaison*, ed. by Élodie Lecuppre-Desjardin and Elisabeth Crouzet-Pavan (Turnhout: Brepols, 2008), pp. 175-206.

————. 'The Dutch Revolt and the Medieval Tradition of Urban Dissent', *Journal of Early Modern History*, 11 (2007), pp. 351-75.

————. 'Urban Space and Political Conflict in Late Medieval Flanders', *The Journal of Interdisciplinary History*, 32 (Spring 2002), pp. 621-40.

Bordier, Henri Léonard. 'La confrérie des Pèlerins de Saint-Jacques et ses archives', *MSHP*, 2 (1876), pp. 330-97.

Boucheron, Patrick and Offenstadt, Nicolas. 'Introduction générale: une histoire de l'échange politique au Moyen Âge' in *L'espace public au Moyen Âge: débats autour de Jürgen Habermas*, ed. by Patrick Boucheron and Nicolas Offenstadt (Paris: Presses Universitaires de France, 2011), pp. 1-21.

————. 'La mémoire disputée: le souvenir de saint Ambroise, enjeu des luttes politiques à Milan au XVe siècle', *Beihefte der Francia*, 55 (2003), pp. 203-23.

Bouchet, Florence. 'Dire l'horreur: les relations du massacre des Armagnacs à Paris (juin 1418)' in *L'horreur au Moyen Âge*, ed. by Jean-Claude Faucon (Toulouse: Éditions universitaires du Sud, 2000), pp. 7-22.

Bouhaïk-Gironès, Marie. 'À qui profite l'auteur? Théâtre, responsabilité de la parole et fonction-auteur à la fin du Moyen Âge', *Parlement[s], Revue d'histoire politique*, 8 (2012), pp. 27-37.

Boquet, Damien and Nagy, Piroska. 'L'historien et les émotions en politique: entre science et citoyenneté' in *Politique des émotions au Moyen Âge*, ed. by Damien Boquet et Piroska Nagy (Florence: Edizioni del Galluzzo, 2010), pp. 5-32.

———. 'Pour une histoire des émotions. L'historien face aux questions contemporaines' in *Le sujet des émotions au Moyen Âge*, ed. by Piroska Nagy and Damien Bouqet (Paris: Beauchesne, 2008), pp. 15-52.

——— and Smagghe, Laurent. 'L'émotion comme désir de vie' in *L'Odeur du sang et des roses: Relire Johan Huizinga aujourd'hui*, ed. Élodie Lecuppre-Desjardin (Villeneuve d'Acq: Presses Universitaires du Septentrion, 2019), pp. 195-214.

Bouquet, Henri. *L'Ancien collège d'Harcourt et le Lycée Saint-Louis* (Paris: Delalain, 1891).

Bourassa, Kristin. 'The Royal Entries of Henry VI in a London Civic Manuscript', *Journal of Medieval History*, 42 (2016), pp. 479-93.

Bourdieu, Pierre and Wacquant, Loïc J. D. *An Inivitation to Reflexive Sociology* (Cambridge: Polity Press, 1992).

———. *Language and Symbolic Power*, ed. by John B. Thompson, trans. by Gino Raymond and Matthew Adamson (Cambridge, MA: Harvard University Press, 1991).

———. *Outline of a Theory of Practice*, trans. by Richard Price (Cambridge: Cambridge University Press, 1977).

———. *Practical Reason on the Theory of Action* (Stanford, CA: Stanford University Press, 1998).

Boureau, Alain. 'Les cérémonies royales françaises entre performance juridique et compétence liturgique', *Annales. Économies, sociétés, civilisations*, 46 (1991), pp. 1253-64.

Bove, Boris, Le Maresquier, Yvonne-Hélène, Bourlet, Caroline, Descamps, Benoît, Gironès-Bouhaïk, M. 'Du proche au lointain: essais de restitution de l'espace vécu à Paris à la fin du Moyen Âge', *BSHP*, 134-35 (2007-08), pp. 7-47.

———. 'Alliance ou défiance? Les ambiguïtés de la politique des Capétiens envers leur capitale entre le XIIe et le XVIIe siècle' in *Les villes capitales au Moyen Âge. XXXVIe Congrès de la SHMES (Istanbul, 1er-6 juin 2005)* (Paris: Éditions de la Sorbonne, 2006), pp. 131-54.

———. 'Aux origines du complexe de supériorité des parisiens: les louanges de Paris au Moyen Âge' in *Être Parisien*, ed. by Claude Gauvard and Jean-Louis Robert (Paris: Éditions de la Sorbonne, 2004), pp. 423-43.

———. 'Deconstructing the Chronicles: Rumours and Extreme Violence during the Siege of Meaux (1421-22)', *French History*, 24 (2010), pp. 501-23.

———. *Dominer la ville: Prévôts des marchands et échevins parisiens de 1260 à 1350* (Paris: Comité des Travaux historiques et scientifiques, 2004).

———. 'L'élite bourgeoise de Paris et l'expression de sa notabilité entre 1200 et 1400' in *Marquer la prééminence sociale*, ed. by Jean-Philippe Genet and E. Igor Mineo (Paris: Éditions de la Sorbonne, 2014), pp. 95-114.

———. 'Les joutes bourgeoises à Paris, entre rêve et réalité (XIIIᵉ-XIVᵉ s.)' in *Le tournoi au Moyen Âge*, ed. by Nicole Gonthier (Lyon: Centre d'histoire médiévale, 2003), pp. 135-63.

———. 'Un registre contre la crise, le "livre vert" de Saint-Denis (1411)', *BEC*, 172 (2014), pp. 323-72.

———. 'Y'a-t-il un patriciat à Paris sous le règne de Philippe le Bel (1285-1314)' in *Construction, reproduction et représentation des patriciats urbains de l'antiquité au XXᵉ siècle*, ed. by Claude Petitfrère (Tours: Presses universitaires François-Rabelais, 1999), pp. 47-63.

Briand, Julien. 'Foi, politique et communication en Champagne au XVᵉ siècle', *Revue historique*, 653 (2010), pp. 59-97.

Briquet, Charles Moïse. *Les Filigranes: Dictionnaire historique des marques du papier*, 4 vols (Paris: Alphonse Picard, 1907).

Broomhall, Susan. 'Introduction: Authority, Gender and Emotions in Late Medieval and Early Modern England' in *Authority, Gender and Emotions in Late Medieval and Early Modern England*, ed. by Susan Broomhall (Basingstoke: Palgrave Macmillan, 2015), pp. 1-17.

Brown, Andrew. 'Charisma and Routine: Shaping the Memory of Brother Richard and Joan of Arc', *Religions*, 3 (2012), pp. 1162-79.

———. *Civic Ceremony and Religion in Medieval Bruges, c. 1300-1520* (Cambridge: Cambridge University Press, 2011).

———. 'Civic Religion in late Medieval Europe', *Journal of Medieval History*, 42 (2016), pp. 338-56.

———. 'Liturgical Memory and Civic Conflict: The Entry of Emperor Frederick III and Maximillian, King of the Romans, into Bruges on 1 August 1486', *Publications du Centre européen des études bourguignonnes*, 52 (2012), pp. 129-48.

Brown, D. Catherine. *Pastor and Laity in the Theology of Jean Gerson* (Cambridge: Cambridge University Press, 1987).

Brown, Elizabeth A.R. 'Jürgen Habermas, Philippe le Bel et l'espace public' in *L'espace public au Moyen Âge: débats autour de Jürgen Habermas*, ed. by Patrick Boucheron and Nicolas Offenstadt (Paris: Presses Universitaires de France, 2011), pp. 193-204.

Brown-Grant, Rosalind. 'Narrative Style in Burgundian Chronicles of the Later Middle Ages', *Viator*, 42 (2011), pp. 233-81.

Bruna, Denis. 'De l'agréable à l'utile: le bijou emblématique à la fin du Moyen Âge', *Revue historique*, 301 (1999), pp. 3-22.

———. *Enseignes de pèlerinage et enseignes profanes* (Paris: Réunion des musées nationaux, 1996).

Bryant, Lawrence. 'La cérémonie de l'entrée à Paris au Moyen Âge', *Annales ESC*, 41 (1986), pp. 513-42.

———. *Ritual, Ceremony and the Changing Monarchy in France, 1350-1789* (Farnham: Ashgate, 2010).

———. *The King and the City in the Parisian Royal Entry Ceremony: Politics, Ritual and Art in the Renaissance* (Geneva: Droz, 1986).

Buc, Philippe. 'Pouvoir royal et commentaires de la Bible (1150-1350)', *Annales. Economies, sociétés, civilisations*, 44 (1989), pp. 691-713.

———. *The Dangers of Ritual: Between Early Medieval Texts and Social Scientific Theory* (Princeton: Princeton University Press, 2001).

Butter, Michael and Knight, Peter. 'Combler le fossé. L'avenir des recherches sur les théories du complot', trans. by Nicole G. Albert, *Diogène*, 249-50 (2015), pp. 21-39.

Buylaert, Frederik and Haemers, Jelle. 'Record-Keeping and Status Performance in the Early Modern Low Countries', *Past & Present*, Supplement 11 (2016), pp. 131-50.

Camille, Michel. 'Signs of the City: Place, Power and Public Fantasy in Medieval Paris' in *Medieval Practices of Space*, ed. by Barbara Hanawalt and Michal Kobialka (Minneapolis, MN: University of Minnesota Press, 2000), pp. 1-36.

Canning, Joseph. *The Political Thought of Baldus de Ubaldis* (Cambridge: Cambridge University Press, 2003).

Carlson, Marla. 'Painful Processions in Late Medieval Paris', *European Medieval Drama*, 6 (2003), pp. 65-81.

Carolyn Muessig, 'Sermon, Preacher and Society in the Middle Ages', *Journal of Medieval History*, 28 (2002), pp. 73-91.

Carrier, Hubert. 'Si vera est fama. Le retentissement de la bataille d'Othée dans la culture historique au XVe siècle', *Revue historique*, 303 (2001), pp. 639-70.

Carroll, Stuart. 'Thinking with Violence', *History and Theory* 55 (2017), pp. 23-43.

Cassidy-Welch, Megan. 'Testimonies from a Fourteenth-Century Prison: Rumour, Evidence and Truth in the Midi', *French History*, 16 (2002), pp. 3-27.

Cayley, Emma. 'Polyphonie et dialogisme: espaces ludiques dans le recueil manuscrit à la fin du Moyen Âge. Le cas de trois recueils poétiques du XVe siècle' in *Le recueil au Moyen Âge: La fin du Moyen Âge*, ed. by Tania Van Hemelryck and Stafania Marzano (Turnhout: Brepols, 2010), pp. 40-60.

Cazaux, Loïc. 'Le connétable de France et le Parlement: la justice de guerre au royaume de France dans la première moitié du XVe siècle' in *Justice et guerre de l'Antiquité a la première guerre mondiale*, ed. by Marie Houllemare and Philippe Nevet (Amiens: Encrage, 2011), pp. 53-62.

———. 'Les fonctions politiques de la foule à Paris pendant la guerre civile (1407-20)', *Hypothèses*, 14 (2011), pp. 65-76.

Cazelles, Raymond. 'La Jacquerie fut-elle un mouvement paysan?', *Comptes rendus des séances de l'Académie des Inscriptions et Belles-Lettres*, 122 (1976), pp. 654-66.

———. *Société politique, noblesse et couronne sous Jean le Bon et Charles V* (Geneva: Droz, 1982).

———. 'Une exigence de l'opinion depuis Saint Louis: la réformation du royaume', *Annuaire-Bulletin de la Société de l'histoire de France* (1962-63), pp. 91-99.

Cerquiligni-Toulet, Jacqueline. 'Fama et les preux: nom et renom à la fin du Moyen Âge', *Médiévales*, 24 (1993), pp. 35-44.

Certeau, Michel de. *The Practice of Everyday Life*, trans. by Steven Rendall (Los Angeles: University of California Press, 1988).

Challet, Vincent and Forrest, Ian. 'The Masses' in *Government and Political Life in England and France c. 1300-c. 1500*, ed. by Christopher Fletcher, Jean-Philippe Genet and John Watts (Cambridge: Cambridge University Press, 2015), pp. 279-316.

———. '"Morayn, los traidors, morayn": Cris de haine et sentiment d'abandon dans les villes languedociennes à la fin du XIVe siècle' in *Emotions in the Heart of the City (14th-16th century)*, ed. by Anne-Laure Van Bruaene and Élodie Lecuppre-Desjardin (Turnhout: Brepols, 2005), pp. 83-92.

———. 'La révolte des Tuchins: banditisme social ou sociabilité villageoise?', *Médiévales*, 34 (1998), pp. 101-12.

———. 'Violence as a Political Language: The Uses and Misuses of Violence in late Medieval French and English Popular Rebellions' in *The Routledge Handbook of Medieval Revolt*, ed. by Justine Firnhaber-Baker and Dirk Schoenaers (London: Routledge, 2017), pp. 279-91.

Champion, Pierre. 'Liste des tavernes de Paris d'après des documents du XVe siècle', *BSHP*, 39 (1912), pp. 259-67.

Chevalier, Bernard. 'Les boucheries, les bouchers et le commerce de la viande à Tours au XVe siècle' in *Commerce, finances et société, XIe-XVIe siècles*, ed. by Bertrand Schnerb, Philippe Contamine and Thierry Dutour (Paris: Presses de l'Université de Paris-Sorbonne, 1993), pp. 157-69.

———. *Les bonnes villes de France du XIVe au XVIe siècle* (Paris: Aubier Montaigne, 1982).

Chiffoleau, Jacques. 'Les processions parisiennes de 1412: Analyse d'un rituel flamboyant', *Revue historique*, 284 (1990), pp. 37-76.

Claustre, Julie. *Dans les geôles du roi. L'emprisonnement pour dette à Paris à la fin du Moyen Âge* (Paris: Éditions de la Sorbonne, 2007).

———. 'La prééminence du notaire (Paris, XIVe et XVe siècles)' in *Marquer la prééminence sociale*, ed. by Jean-Philippe Genet and E. Igor Mineo (Paris: Éditions de la Sorbonne, 2014), pp. 75-91.

Cobban, Allan B. 'The Role of Colleges in the Medieval Universities of Northern Europe, with special reference to England and France', *Bulletin of the John Rylands Library*, 71 (1989), pp. 49-70.

Cockshaw, Pierre. *Prosopographie des secrétaires de la cour de Bourgogne (1384-1477)* (Ostfildern: Jan Thorbecke Verlag, 2006).

Cohen, Esther. 'Symbols of Culpability and the Universal Language of Justice: The Ritual of Public Executions in Late Medieval Europe', *History of European Ideas*, 11 (1989), pp. 407-16.

———. *The Crossroads of Justice: Law and Culture in Late Medieval France* (Leiden: Brill, 1993).

Cohen, Meredith, Madeline, Fanny and Iogna-Prat, Dominique. 'Introduction', *Space in the Medieval West: Places, Territories and Imagined Geographies*, ed. by Meredith Cohen and Fanny Madeleine (Farnham: Ashgate, 2014), pp. 1-17.

Cohn, Samuel K. Jr. 'The Topography of Medieval Popular Protest', *Social History*, 44 (2019), pp. 389-411.

Coldstream, Nicola. 'Pavillon'd in Splendour': Henry V's Agincourt Pageants', *Journal of the British Archaeological Association*, 165 (2012), pp. 153-71.

Coleman, Janet. *Ancient and Medieval Memories: Studies in the Reconstruction of the Past* (Cambridge: Cambridge University Press, 1992).

Collard, Franck. 'Meurtres en famille. Les liens familiaux à l'épreuve du poison chez les Valois (1328-1498)' in *Familles royales: Vie publique, vie privée aux XIVe et XVe siècles*, ed. by Christine Raynaud (Aix-en-Provence: Presses universitaires de Provence, 2010), pp. 185-96.

———. 'Ranimer l'oriflamme. Les relations des rois de France avec l'abbaye de Saint-Denis à la fin du XVe siècle' in *Saint-Denis et la royauté*, ed. by Françoise Autrand, Claude Gauvard and Jean-Marie Moeglin (Paris: Publications de la Sorbonne, 1999), pp. 563-81.

———. '*Rex abhorret a sanguine?* De l'effusion à l'abstinence, Charles VII et le sang versé', *Revue historique*, 693 (2020), pp. 109-29.

Collins, Randall. 'Social Movements and the Focus of Emotional Attention' in *Passionate Politics: Emotions and Social Movements*, ed. by Jeff Goodwin, James M. Jaspers and Francesca Polletta (London: University of Chicago Press, 2001), pp. 27-44.

———. *Interaction Ritual Chains* (Princeton University Press, 2004).

Colson, Justine and Van Steensel, Arie. 'Cities and Solidarities: Urban Communities in Medieval and Early Modern Europe' in *Cities and Solidarities: Urban Communities in Pre-Modern Europe*, ed. by Justin Colson and Arie van Steensel (London: Routledge, 2017), pp. 1-24.

Connell, Charles. *Popular Opinion in the Middle Ages: Channelling Public Ideas and Attitudes* (Berlin: De Gruyter, 2016).

Connerton, Paul. *How Societies Remember* (Cambridge: Cambridge University Press, 1989).

Contamine, Philippe. *Guerre, État et société à la fin du Moyen Âge: études sur les armées des rois de France, 1337-1494*, 2 vols (Paris: Mouton, 1972).

———. 'L'oriflamme de Saint-Denis aux XIVe-XVe siècles. Étude de symbolique religieuse et royale', *Annales de l'Est*, 25 (1973), pp. 179-244.

———. 'Les chaînes dans les bonnes villes de France (spécialement Paris), XIVe-XVIe siècle' in *Guerre et société en France, en Angleterre et en Bourgogne XIVe-XVe siècle*, ed. by Maurice Keen, Charles Giry-Deloison and Philippe Contamine (Lille: Publications de l'Institut de recherches historiques du Septentrion, 1991), pp. 293-314.

———. 'Les compagnies d'aventure en France pendant la guerre de Cent ans', *Mélanges de l'École française de Rome*, 87 (1975), pp. 365-96.

———. 'Naissance d'une historiographie. Le souvenir de Jeanne d'Arc, en France et hors de France, depuis le "procès de son innocence" (1455-56) jusqu'au début du XVIe siècle', *Francia*, 15 (1987), pp. 233-56.

———. 'Rendre grâces, prier, faire mémoire: la "fête du roi", 14 octobre de l'année 1450 puis 12 aout de l'année 1451 et des années postérieures', *Bulletin de la Société Nationale des Antiquaires de France* (2009), pp. 338-53.

———. 'Une chronique pour un prince? Le "Geste des nobles Francois"', *Pariser Historische Studien*, 47 (1998), pp. 231-41.

Cottingham, Marci. 'Theorizing Emotional Capital', *Theory and Society*, 45 (2016), pp. 451-70.

Courroux, Pierre. 'History, Verse and *Chanson de Geste* in French Chronicles around 1400', *Nottingham Medieval Studies*, 62 (2018), pp. 111-36.

———. *L'écriture de l'histoire dans les chroniques françaises (XIIe-XVe siècle)* (Paris: Classiques Garnier, 2016).

Courtemanche, Danielle. *Œuvrer pour la postérité: les testaments parisiens des gens du roi au début du XVe siècle* (Paris: L'Harmattan, 1997).

Courtenay, William J. *Rituals for the Dead: Religion and Community in the Medieval University of Paris* (Notre Dame, IN: University of Notre-Dame Press, 2019).

Couzy, Hélène. 'L'église des Saints-Innocents à Paris', *Bulletin Monumental*, 130 (1972), pp. 279-302.

Coville, Alfred. 'Le véritable texte de la justification du duc de Bourgogne par Jean Petit (8 mars 1408)', *BEC*, 72 (1911), pp. 57-91.

———. *Jean Petit. La question du tyrannicide au commencement du XVe siècle* (Paris: Picard, 1932).

———. *Les Cabochiens et l'ordonnance de 1413* (Paris: Hachette, 1888).

———. 'Recherches sur Jean Courtecuisse et ses œuvres oratoires', *BEC*, 65 (1904), pp. 469-529.

Coyecque, Ernest. *Recueil d'actes notariés relatifs à l'histoire de Paris et de ses environs au XVIᵉ siècle*, 2 vols (Paris: Imprimerie nationale, 1905-23).

Crane, Susan. *The Performance of Self: Ritual, Clothing, and Identity during the Hundred Years War* (Philadelphia, PA: University of Pennsylvania Press, 2002).

Crooks, Peter. 'State of the Union: Perspectives on English Imperialism in the Late Middle Ages', *Past & Present*, 212 (2011), pp. 3-42.

Croq, Laurence. 'Droit, société et politique: La confusion des concepts et des identités pendant la période pré-révolutionnaire à Paris' in *Être parisien*, ed. by Claude Gauvard and Jean-Louis Robert (Paris: Publications de la Sorbonne, 2004), pp. 63-80.

Cuffel, Alexandra. *Gendering Disgust in Medieval Religious Polemic* (Notre-Dame, IN: University of Notre-Dame Press, 2007).

Curry, Anne. 'Representing War and Conquest, 1415-29: The Evidence of College of Arms Manuscript M9' in *Representing War and Violence, 1250-1600*, ed. by Joanna Bellis and Laura Slater (Woodbridge: Boydell, 2016), pp. 139-58.

———. 'Soldiers' Wives in the Hundred Years War' in *Soldiers, Nobles and Gentlemen: Essays in Honour of Maurice Keen*, ed. by Peter Coss and Christopher Tyerman (Woodbridge: Boydell, 2009), pp. 198-214.

———. 'The Military Ordinances of Henry V: Texts and Contexts', in *War, Government and Aristocracy in the British Isles, c. 1150-1500*, ed. by Christopher Given-Wilson, Ann Kettle and Len Scales (Woodbridge: Boydell and Brewer, 2008), pp. 214-49.

———. 'The coronation expedition and Henry VI's court in France, 1430-32' in *The Lancastrian Court*, ed. by Jenny Stratford (Donnington: Shaun Tyas, 2003), pp. 29-52.

———. 'Two Kingdoms, One King: The Treaty of Troyes (1420) and the Creation of a Double Monarchy of England and France' in *The Contending Kingdoms: France and England, 1420-1700*, ed. by Glenn Richardson (Aldershot: Ashgate, 2008), pp. 23-41.

Cuttler, S.H. *The Law of Treason and Treason Trials in Later Medieval France* (Cambridge: Cambridge University Press, 1981).

d'Avray, David. *Medieval Marriage Sermons: Mass Communication in a Culture without Print* (Oxford: Oxford University Press, 2005).

Daly, Kathleen. '"Centre", "Power" and "Periphery"' in Late Medieval French Historiography: Some Reflections' in *War, Government and Power in late Medieval France*, ed. by Christopher Allmand (Liverpool: Liverpool University Press, 2000), pp. 124-44.

Dauphant, Léonard. '*Si grant charté a Paris… par defaulte du roy*: Governmental practice and the customary geography of the absence and presence of the king in France (1364-1525)' in *Absentee Authority across Medieval Europe*, ed by Frédérique Lachaud and Michael Penman (Woodbridge: Boydell and Brewer, 2017), pp. 153-70.

Davies, Rees. 'Nations and National Identities in the Medieval World: An Apologia', *Revue belge d'histoire contemporaine*, 35 (2004), pp. 567-79.

Davis, Natalie Zemon. *Fiction in the Archives: Pardon Tales and their Tellers in Sixteenth-Century France* (Stanford, CA: Stanford University Press, 1987).

———. 'The Rites of Violence: Religious Riot in Sixteenth-Century France', *Past & Present*, 59 (1973), pp. 51-91.

De Weerdt, Hilde, Holmes, Catherine and Watts, John. 'Politics, *c.* 1000-15000: Mediation and Communication', *Past & Present*, 238, Supplement 13 (2018), pp. 261-96.

Delcorno, Carlo. 'Medieval Preaching in Italy (1200-1500)' in *The Sermon*, ed. by Beverley Mayne Kienzle (Turnhout: Brepols, 2000), pp. 449-560.

Deligne, Chloé, Billen, Claire and Kusman, David. 'Les bouchers bruxellois au bas Moyen Âge. Profils d'entrepreneurs' in *Patrons, gens d'affaires et banquiers: Hommages à Ginette Kurgan-van Hentenryk*, ed. by Serge Jaumain and Kenneth Bertrams (Brussels: Timperman, 2004), pp. 69-92.

Demets, Lisa. *Onvoltooid verleden: De handschriften van de 'Excellente Cronike van Vlaenderen' in de laatmiddeleeuwse Vlaamse steden (1440-1500)* (Hilversum: Verlorem, 2020).

———— and Dumolyn, Jan. 'Urban Chronicle Writing in Late Medieval Flanders: The Case of Bruges during the Flemish Revolt of 1482-1490', *Urban History*, 43 (2016), pp. 28-45.

Denoël, Charlotte. *Saint André: Culte and iconographie en France (V^e-XVe siècles)* (Paris: École des Chartes, 2004).

Desan, Suzanne. 'Crowds, Community and Ritual in the Work of E.P. Thompson and Natalie Davis' in *The New Cultural History*, ed. by Lynn Hunt (Los Angeles: University of California Press, 1989), pp. 47-71.

Descamps, Benoît. 'La destruction de la grande boucherie de Paris en mai 1416', *Hypothèses*, 7 (2004), pp. 109-18.

————. 'La toile [sociale] et la trame [urbaine]: la place des bouchers parisiens au Moyen Âge', accessed on 05/10/2019, *Anthropology of Food*, 13 (2019), http: journals.openedition.org/aof/9814.

Descimon, Robert and Nagle, Jean. 'Les quartiers de Paris du Moyen Âge au XVIIIe siècle. Évolution d'un espace', *Annales. Histoire, sciences sociales*, 34 (1979), pp. 956-83.

————. 'Le corps de la ville et les élections échevinales à Paris aux XVIe et XVIIe siècles. Codification coutumière et pratiques sociales', *Histoire, économie et société*, 13 (1994), pp. 507-30.

————. 'Le corps de ville et le système cérémoniel parisien au début de l'âge moderne' in *Statuts individuels, statuts corporatifs et statuts judiciaires dans les villes européennes (Moyen Âge et temps modernes)*, ed. by Marc Boone, Maarten Prak (Leuven: Garant, 1996), pp. 73-128.

Destemberg, Antoine. *L'honneur des universitaires au Moyen Âge. Étude d'imaginaire social* (Paris: Presses Universitaires de France, 2015).

————. 'Morts violentes et lieux de mémoire. Les réparations faites à l'Université de Paris à la fin du Moyen Âge', *Traverse. Zeitschrift für Geschichte*, 2 (2008), pp. 37-50.

Devaux, Jean. 'Le genre médiéval du journal et les chemins de mémoire: l'exemple de Jean de Roye', in *La mémoire à l'œuvre*, ed. by Caroline Cazenave, (Besançon: Presses universitaires de Franche-Comté, 2014), pp. 337-50.

Dickinson, Jocelyne. *The Congress of Arras 1435: A Study in Medieval Diplomacy* (Reprint. New York: Biblio and Tannen, 1972).

Diefendorf, Barbara. *Paris City Councillors in the Sixteenth Century: The Politics of Patrimony* (Princeton, NJ: Princeton University Press, 1983).

Dorez, Léon and Fournier, Marcel. *La Faculté de décret de l'Université de Paris au XVe siècle*, vol. 3 (Paris: Imprimerie nationale, 1908).

Douglas, Mary. *Purity and Danger: An Analysis of Concepts of Pollution and Taboo* (New York: Routledge, 2001).

Dubois, Jacques and Beaumont-Maillet, Laure. *Sainte Geneviève de Paris: la vie, le culte, l'art* (Paris: Beauchesne, 1997).

Dudash, Susan J. 'Christinian Politics, the Tavern, and Urban Revolt in Late Medieval France' in *Healing the Body Politic: The Political Thought of Christine de Pizan*, ed. by Karen Green and Constant J. Mews (Turnhout: Brepols, 2005), pp. 35-59.

Dufournet, Jean. 'L'épanouissement de l'histoire au quinzième siècle', *Fifteenth Century Studies*, 34 (2009), pp. 64-80.

Dumolyn, Jan and Haemers, Jelle. '"A Bad Chicken was Brooding": Subversive Speech in Late Medieval Flanders', *Past & Present*, 214 (2012), pp. 45-86.

———— and Lecuppre-Desjardin, Élodie. 'Propagande et sensibilité: la fibre émotionnelle au cœur des luttes politiques et sociales dans les villes des anciens Pays-Bas bourguignons. L'exemple de la révolte brugeoise de 1436-1438' in *Emotions in the Heart of the City*, ed. by Elodie Lecuppre-Desjardin and Anne-Laure van Bruaene (Turnhout: Brepols, 2005), pp. 41-62.

———— and Van Bruaene, Anne-Laure. 'Introduction: Urban Historiography in Late Medieval and Early Modern Europe' in *Urban History Writing in North-Western Europe (15th-16th Centuries)*, ed. by Bram Caers, Lisa Demets and Tineke Van Gassen (Turnhout: Brepols, 2019), pp. 7-24.

————, Oosterman, Johan, Snijders, Tjanmke and Villerius, Stijn. 'Rewriting Chronicles in an Urban Environment. The Dutch "Excellent Chronicle of Flanders" Tradition', *Lias*, 41 (2014), pp. 85-116.

————. 'Political Communication and Political Power in the Middle Ages: A Conceptual Journey', *Edad Media*, 13 (2012), pp. 33-55.

————. 'Urban Ideologies in Later Medieval Flanders: Towards an Analytical Framework', in *The Languages of Political Society: Western Europe, 14th-17th Centuries*, ed. by Andrea Gamberini, Jean-Philippe Genet and Andrea Zorzi (Rome: Viella, 2011), pp. 69-96.

Eco, Umberto. *A Theory of Semiotics* (Bloomington: Indiana University Press, 1976).

————. *The Limits of Interpretation* (Bloomington: Indiana University Press, 1994).

Eersels, Ben and Haemers, Jelle (ed.). *Words and Deeds: Shaping Urban Politics from Below in Late Medieval Europe* (Turnhout: Brepols, 2020).

Elias, Norbert. *The Civilizing Process: Sociogenetic and Psychogenetic Investigations*, Revised Edition, trans. by Edmund Jephcott, ed. by Eric Dunning, Johan Goudsblom and Stephen Mennell (Oxford: Blackwell Publishing, 2000).

Ellul, Jacques. *Propaganda*, trans. by Konrad Kellen and Jean Lerner (New York: Vintage, 1973).

Epstein, Robert. 'Food and Text in the Coronation Banquet of Henry VI', *Journal of Medieval and Early Modern Studies*, 36 (2006), pp. 355-77.

Eyerman, Ron. 'How Social Movements Move: Emotions and Social Movements' in *Emotions and Social Movements*, ed. by Helena Flam and Debra King (London: Routledge, 2005), pp. 42-56.

Fabris, Cécile. *Étudier et vivre à Paris au Moyen Âge: Le Collège de Laon (XIVe-XVe siècles)* (Paris: École des Chartes, 2005).

Famiglietti, Richard C. *Royal Intrigue: Crisis at the Court of Charles VI, 1392-1420* (New York, NY: AMS Press, 1982).

Fargette, Séverine. 'Rumeurs, propagande et opinion publique au temps de la guerre civile (1407-20)', *Le Moyen Âge*, 113 (2007), pp. 309-34.

Favier, Jean. *Le bourgeois de Paris au Moyen Âge* (Paris: Tallandier, 2012).

———. 'Les rôles d'impôt parisiens du XVᵉ siècle (à propos d'un article récent)', *BEC*, 130 (1972), pp. 467-91.

———. *Paris au XVᵉ siècle, 1380-1500* (Paris: Hachette, 1974).

———. 'Une ville entre deux vocations: la place d'affaires de Paris au XVᵉ siècle', *Annales ESC*, 28 (1973), pp. 1245-79.

Favreau, Robert. 'Les changeurs du royaume sous le règne de Louis XI', *BEC*, 122 (1964), pp. 216-51.

Fein, David A. 'Acts of Nature and Preternatural Acts in the *Journal d'un bourgeois de Paris (1405-49)*', *Fifteenth Century Studies*, 20 (1993), pp. 65-75.

Fenster, Thelma and Smail, Daniel Lord. 'Introduction' in *Fama. The Politics of Talk and Reputation in Medieval Europe*, ed. by Thelma Fenster and Daniel Lord Smail (London: Cornell University Press, 2003), pp. 1-11.

Fentress, James J. and Wickham, Chris. *Social Memory: New Perspectives on the Past* (Oxford: Blackwell, 1992).

Firnhaber-Baker, Justine. 'The Eponymous Jacquerie: Making revolt mean some things' in *The Routledge History Handbook of Medieval Revolt*, ed. by Justine Firnhaber-Baker and Dirk Schoenaers (Abingdon: Routledge, 2017), pp. 55-75.

———. *The Jacquerie of 1358. A French Peasants' Revolt* (Oxford: Oxford University Press, 2021).

———. 'The Social Constituency of the Jacquerie Revolt of 1358', *Speculum* 95 (2020), pp. 689-715.

———. 'Two Kinds of Freedom: Language and Practice in Late Medieval Rural Revolts', *Edad Media. Revista de Historia*, 21 (2020), pp. 113-52.

Flam, Helena. 'Anger in Repressive Regimes. A Footnote to *Domination and the Arts of Resistance* by James Scott', *European Journal of Social Theory*, 7 (2004), pp. 171-88.

Flanigan, C. Clifford. 'The Moving Subject: Medieval Liturgical Processions in Semiotic and Cultural Perspective' in *Moving Subjects: Processional Performance in the Middle Ages and the Renaissance*, ed. by Kathleen Ashley and Wim Husken (Amsterdam: Rodopi, 2001), pp. 35-51.

Flannery, Mary C. *John Lydgate and the Poetics of Fame* (Woodbridge: Boydell and Brewer, 2012).

Fletcher, Christopher D. 'News, Noise, and the Nature of Politics in Late Medieval English Provincial Towns', *Journal of British Studies*, 56 (April 2017), pp. 250-72.

——— 'Rumour, Clamour, mumur and rebellion: Public opinion and its uses before and after the Peasants' Revolt (1381)' in *La Communidad medieval como esfera publica*, ed. by Hipólito Rafael Oliva Herrer, Vincent Challet, Jan Dumolyn and María Antonia Carmona Ruiz (Sevilla: Universidad de Sevilla, 2014), pp. 193-210.

——— 'What Makes a Political Language? Key Terms, Profit and Damage in the Common Petition of the English Parliament, 1343-1422' in *The Voices of the People in Late Medieval Europe: Communication and Popular Politics*, ed. by Jan Dumolyn, Jelle Haemers, Hipólito Rafael Oliva Herrer and Vincent Challet (Turnhout: Brepols, 2014), pp. 91-106.

Forgeais, Arthur. *Collection de plombs historiés trouvés dans la Seine*, vol. 3 (Paris: Aubry, 1864).

Forhan, Kate Langdon. *The Political Theory of Christine de Pizan* (Aldershot: Ashgate, 2002).

Foucault Michel. 'Qu'est-ce qu'un auteur?' in *Dits et écrits*, vol. 1 (Paris: Gallimard, 1994), pp. 789-821.

———. *Power/Knowledge: Selected Interviews and Other Writings, 1972-77*, ed. and trans. by Colin Gordon (London: Harvester Press, 1980).

———. *Surveiller et punir. Naissance de la prison* (Paris: Gallimard, 1975).

Fox, Adam. *Oral and Literate Culture in England, 1500-1700* (Oxford: Clarendon Press, 2000).

———. 'Rumour, News and Popular Political Opinion', *The Historical Journal*, 40 (1997), pp. 597-620.

Fraioli, Deborah. *Joan of Arc: The Early Debate* (Woodbridge: Boydell, 2000).

———. 'Why Joan of Arc never became an Amazon' in *Fresh Verdicts on Joan of Arc*, ed. by Bonnie Wheeler and Charles Wood (London: Garland, 1996), pp. 189-204.

Fraser, Nancy. 'Rethinking the Public Sphere: A Contribution to the Critique of Actually Existing Democracy', *Social Text*, 25/26 (1990), pp. 56-80.

Fremaux, Henri. 'La famille d'Étienne Marcel, 1250-1397', *MSHP*, 30 (1903), pp. 175-242.

Fresne de Beaucourt, Gaston du. *Histoire de Charles VII*, 6 vols (Paris: Librairie de la Société bibliographique, 1881-91).

Fritsch-Pinaud, Laurence. 'La vie paroissiale à Saint-Jacques-de-la-Boucherie au XVᵉ siècle', *MSHP*, 33 (1982), pp. 7-97.

Froissart, Pascal. 'Historicité de la rumeur: La rupture de 1902', *Hypothèses*, 4 (2001), pp. 315-26.

Gauvard, Claude and Labory, Gillette. 'Une chronique rimée parisienne écrite en 1409: les aventures depuis deux cents ans' in *Le métier d'historien au Moyen Âge: études sur l'historiographie médiévale*, ed. by Bernard Guenée (Paris: Centre de recherches sur l'histoire de l'Occident médiéval, 1977), pp. 183-231.

Gauvard, Claude. 'Aux origines de la chronique judiciaire: l'exemple du royaume de France aux derniers siècles du Moyen Âge', *Histoire de la justice*, 20 (2010), pp. 13-24.

———. *Condamner à mort au Moyen Âge: Pratiques de la peine capitale en France, XIIIᵉ-XVᵉ siècle* (Paris: Presses Universitaires de France, 2018).

———. *'De Grâce especial': Crime, état et société en France à la fin du Moyen Âge*, 2 vols (Paris: Publications de la Sorbonne, 1991).

———. 'Fama explicite et fama implicite: Les difficultés de l'historien face à l'honneur des petites gens aux derniers siècles du Moyen Âge' in *La légitimité implicite*, ed. by Jean-Philippe Genet (Paris: Éditions de la Sorbonne, 2015), pp. 39-55.

———. 'Introduction' in *La rumeur au Moyen Âge: du mépris a la manipulation, Vᵉ-XVᵉ siècle*, ed. by Maité Billoré and Myriam Soria (Rennes: Presses Universitaires de Rennes, 2011), pp. 23-32.

———. 'Justification and Theory of the Death Penalty at the *Parlement* of Paris in the late Middle Ages' in *War, Government and Power in Late Medieval France*, ed. by Christopher Allmand (Liverpool: Liverpool University Press, 2000), pp. 190-208.

———. 'La *Fama*: une parole fondatrice', *Médiévales*, 24 (1993), pp. 5-13.

———. 'Le roi de France et l'opinion publique à l'époque de Charles VI' in *Culture et idéologie dans la genèse de l'État moderne. Actes de la table ronde de Rome (15-17 octobre 1984)* (Rome: École française de Rome, 1985), pp. 353-66.

———. 'Les révoltes du règne de Charles VI: Tentative pour expliquer un échec' in *Révolte et Société: Actes du IVᵉ Colloque d'Histoire au Présent*, 2 vols (Paris: Publications de la Sorbonne, 1989), I, pp. 53-61.

———. 'Mémoire du crime, mémoire des peines. Justice et acculturation pénale en France à la fin du Moyen Âge' in *Saint-Denis et la royauté*, ed. by Françoise Autrand, Claude Gauvard and Jean-Marie Moeglin (Paris: Éditions de la Sorbonne, 1999), pp. 691-710.

———. 'Rumeur et gens de guerre dans le royaume de France au milieu du XVᵉ siècle', *Hypothèses*, 4 (2001), pp. 281-92.

———. 'Rumeur et stéréotypes à la fin du Moyen Âge' in *La circulation des nouvelles au Moyen Âge: XXIVᵉ Congrès de la S.H.M.E.S., Avignon, Juin 1993* (Paris: Publications de la Sorbonne, 1994), pp. 157-77.

———. *Violence et ordre public au Moyen Âge* (Paris: Picard, 2005).

Geertz, Clifford. *Available Light: Anthropological Reflection on Philosophical Topics* (Princeton: Princeton University Press, 2000).

———. *The Interpretation of Cultures* (New York: Basic Books, 1973).

Genet, Jean-Philippe, Idabal, Hicham, Kouamé, Thierry, Lamassé, Stéphane, Priol Claire, and Tournieroux, Anne. 'General Introduction to the "Studium" Project', *Medieval Prosopography*, 31 (2016), pp. 161-70.

———. 'Compte rendu. Jean Guérout, Fiscalité, topographie et démographie à Paris au Moyen Âge', *Annales ESC*, 31 (1976), pp. 1162-63.

———. 'Histoire et système de communication au Moyen Âge' in *L'histoire et les nouveaux publics dans l'Europe médiévale (XIIIᵉ-XVᵉ siècles): Actes du colloque international organisé par la Fondation européenne de la Science a la Casa de Velasquez, Madrid, 23-24 avril 1993*, ed. by Jean-Philippe Genet (Paris: Publications de la Sorbonne, 1997), pp. 11-29.

———. 'Le roi de France anglaise et la nation française au XVᵉ siècle', *Beihefte der Francia*, 39 (1997), pp. 39-58.

Geremek, Bronisław. *The Margins of Society in Late Medieval Paris*, trans. by Jean Birrell (Cambridge: Cambridge University Press, 1987).

Gert, Joshua. 'Disgust, Moral Disgust and Morality', *Journal of Moral Philosophy*, 12 (2015), pp. 33-54.

Giesey, Ralph. 'Inaugural Aspects of French Royal Ceremonials' in *Coronations and Early Modern Monarchic Ritual*, ed. by Janos M. Bak (Los Angeles: University of California Press, 1990), pp. 35-45.

———. 'Models of Rulership in French Royal Ceremonial' in *Rites of Power: Symbolism, Ritual and Politics since the Middle Ages*, ed. by Sean Wilentz (Philadelphia: University of Pennsylvania Press, 1999), pp. 41-64.

Gilks, David. 'The Fountain of the Innocents and its Place in the Paris Cityscape, 1549-1788', *Urban History*, 45 (2018), pp. 49-73.

Giraudet, Luke. 'Nicolas Confrant, author of the *Journal d'un bourgeois de Paris?*', *Romania*, 139 (2021), pp. 115-41.

Girault, Pierre-Gilles. 'Les procès de Jeanne-Claude des Armoises' in *De l'hérétique à la sainte. Les procès de Jeanne d'Arc revisités*, ed. by François Neveux (Caen: Presses universitaires de Caen, 2012), pp. 197-210.

Glorieux, P. 'La vie et les œuvres de Gerson: Essai chronologique', *Archives d'histoire doctrinale et littéraire du Moyen Âge*, 18 (1950-51), pp. 149-92.

Gonthier, Nicole. *Cris de haine et rites d'unité: La violence dans les villes, XIIIᵉ-XVIᵉ siècle* (Turnhout: Brepols, 1992).

Gorochov, Nathalie. 'L'université recrute-t-elle dans la ville? Le cas de Paris au XIIIe siècle' in *Les universités et la ville au Moyen Âge: cohabitation et tension*, ed. by Patrick Gilli, Jacques Verger and Daniel Le Blévec (Leiden: Brill, 2007), pp. 257-96.

——. 'La mémoire des morts dans l'Université de Paris au XIIIe siècle', *Beihefte der Francia*, 55 (2003), pp. 117-29.

——. *Le collège de Navarre de sa fondation (1305) au début du XVe siècle (1418): histoire de l'institution, de sa vie intellectuelle et de son recrutement* (Paris: Champion, 1997).

Gransden, Antonia. *Historical Writing in England. Volume 2, c. 1307 to the Early Sixteenth Century* (Ithaca, NY: Cornell University Press, 1982).

Grassoreille, Georges. 'Histoire politique du chapitre de Notre-Dame de Paris pendant la domination anglaise, 1420-1437', *MSHP*, 9 (1882), pp. 109-92.

Green, David. 'National Identities and the Hundred Years War' in *Fourteenth Century England – VI*, ed. by Chris Given-Wilson (Woodbridge: Boydell, 2010), pp. 115-30.

——. *The Hundred Years War: A People's History* (London: Yale University Press, 2014).

Grévy-Pons, Nicole. 'Jean de Montreuil et Guillebert de Mets', *Revue belge de philologie et d'histoire*, vol. 58, no. 3 (1980), pp. 565-87.

Griffiths, Ralph A. 'The Minority of Henry VI, King of England and France' in *The Royal Minorities of Medieval and Early Modern England*, ed. by Charles Beem (New York, NY: Palgrave Macmillan, 2008), pp. 161-94.

—— *The Reign of King Henry VI* (Stroud: Sutton, 2004).

Guenée, Bernard. 'Espace et État dans la France du Bas Moyen Âge', *Annales. Histoire, sciences sociales*, 23 (1968), pp. 744-58.

——. *L'Occident aux XIVe et XVe siècles: Les états* (Paris: Presses Universitaires de France, 1971).

——. *L'opinion publique à la fin du Moyen Âge d'après la chronique de Charles VI du religieux de Saint-Denis* (Paris: Perrin, 2002).

——. 'Le voyage de Bourges (1412). Un exemple des conséquences de la folie de Charles VI', *Comptes rendus des séances de l'Académie des Inscriptions et Belles-Lettres*, 140 (1996), pp. 785-800.

——. 'Les *Grandes chroniques de France*, le *Roman aux Roys* (1274-1518)' in *Les lieux de mémoire*, vol. 2: *La nation*, ed. by Pierre Nora (Paris: Gallimard, 1986), pp. 189-213.

——. 'Liturgie et politique. Les processions spéciales à Paris sous Charles VI' in *Un roi et son historien: vingt études sur le règne de Charles VI et la Chronique du Religieux de Saint-Denis* (Paris: Boccard, 1999), pp. 427-54.

——. 'Paris et la cour du roi de France au XIVe siècle' in *Villes, bonnes villes, cités et capitales. Études d'histoire urbaine (XIIe-XVIIIe siècle) offertes à Bernard Chevalier*, ed. by Monique Bourin (Tours: Publications de l'Université de Tours, 1989), pp. 259-65.

——. *Un meurtre, une société. L'assassinat du duc d'Orléans, 23 novembre 1407* (Paris: Gallimard, 1992).

——. '*Scandalum inter antiquos et juvenes theologos*. Un conflit de générations à la Faculté de théologie de Paris au début du XVe siècle?' in *Un roi et son historien: Vingt études sur le règne de Charles VI et la Chronique du religieux de Saint-Denis* (Paris: Boccard, 1999), pp. 357-64.

Guerout, Jean. 'Fiscalité, topographie et démographie à Paris au Moyen Âge', *BEC*, 130 (1972), pp. 33-129.

Guittonneau Pierre-Henri. 'Entre pratique et discours: les villes de la région parisienne face au secret au début du XVe siècle', *Questes*, 16 (2009), pp. 12-24.

Guyot-Bachy, Isabelle. 'Culture historique et lecture de l'histoire: Nicolas de Lespoisse et son exemplaire des chroniques de Guillaume de Nangis (BNF Fr. 23138)', in *Humanisme et politique en France à la fin du Moyen Âge*, ed. by Carla Bozzolo, Claude Gauvard et Helene Millet (Paris: Éditions de la Sorbonne, 2018) pp. 39-56.

Habermas, Jürgen. 'Further Reflections on the Public Sphere', trans. by Thomas Burger in *Habermas and the Public Sphere*, ed. by Craig Calhoun (Cambridge, MA: MIT Press, 1992), pp. 421-61.

———. *The Structural Transformation of the Public Sphere: An Inquiry into a Category of Bourgeois Society*, trans. by Thomas Burger and Frederick Lawrence (Cambridge, MA: MIT Press, 1991).

Hablot, Laurent. 'Les signes de l'entente. Le rôle des devises et des ordres dans les relations diplomatiques entre les ducs de Bourgogne et les princes étrangers de 1380 à 1477', *Revue du Nord*, 84 (2002), pp. 319-41.

Haemers, Jelle. 'Filthy and Indecent Words: Insults, Defamation and Urban Politics in the Southern Low Countries, 1350-1550' in *The Voices of the People in Late Medieval Europe: Communication and Popular Politics*, ed. by Jan Dumolyn, Jelle Haemers, Hipólito Rafael Oliva Herrer and Vincent Challet (Turnhout: Brepols, 2014), pp. 247-67.

———. 'Social Memory and Rebellion in Fifteenth-Century Ghent', *Social History*, 36 (2011), pp. 443-63.

Hamilon, Tom. 'Contesting public executions in Paris towards the end of the Wars of Religion' in *Cultures of Conflict Resolution in Early Modern Europe*, ed. by Stephen Cummins and Laura Kounine (London: Routledge, 2017), pp. 179-202.

———. *Pierre de l'Estoile and his World in the Wars of Religion* (Oxford: Oxford University Press, 2017).

Hanawalt Barbara and Kobialka, Michal. 'Introduction' in *Medieval Practices of Space*, ed. by Barbara Hanawalt and Michal Kobialka (University of Minnesota Press, 2000), pp. ix-xviii.

Hanawalt, Barbara. *Ceremony and Civility: Civic Culture in Late Medieval London* (New York: Oxford University Press, 2017).

———. 'The Host, the Law and the Ambiguous Space of Medieval London Taverns' in *Medieval Crime and Social Control*, ed. by Barbara A. Hanawalt and David Wallace (Minneapolis, MN: University of Minnesota Press, 1999), pp. 204-23.

Hanley, Sarah. *The Lit de Justice of the Kings of France: Constitutional Ideology in Legend, Ritual and Discourse* (Princeton, NJ: Princeton University Press, 1983).

Harding, Vanessa. 'Medieval Documentary Sources for London and Paris: A Comparison' in *London and Europe in the Later Middle Ages*, ed. by Julia Boffey and Pamela King, (Turnhout: Brepols, 1995), pp. 35-54.

———. 'Space, Property and Propriety in Urban England', *Journal of Interdisciplinary History*, 32 (2002), pp. 549-69.

———. *The Dead and the Living in Paris and London* (Cambridge: Cambridge University Press, 2002).

Harry, David. *Constructing a Civic Community in Late Medieval London: The Common Profit, Charity and Commemoration* (Woodbridge: Boydell, 2019).

Harsin, Jill. *Policing Prostitution in Nineteenth-Century Paris* (Princeton, NJ: Princeton University Press, 1985), pp. 59-60.

Hartrich, Eliza. *Politics and the Urban Sector in Fifteenth-Century England* (Oxford: Oxford University Press, 2019).

Harvey, Margaret. *England, Rome and the Papacy, 1417-64: The Study of a Relationship* (Manchester: Manchester University Press, 1993).

Havet, Julien. 'Maître Fernand de Cordoue et l'Université de Paris au XVe siècle', *MSHP*, 9 (1882), pp. 193-222.

Hedeman, Anne D. 'Les perceptions de l'image royale à travers les miniatures: L'exemple des *Grandes chroniques de France*' in *Pratiques de la culture écrite en France au XVe siècle: Actes du colloque international du CNRS, Paris, 16-18 mai 1992 organisé en l'honneur de Gilbert Ouy*, ed. by Monique Ornato and Nicole Pons (Louvain-la-Neuve: Fédération internationale des instituts d'études médiévales, 1995), pp. 539-49.

Harding, Vanessa. *The Royal Image: Illustrations of the* Grandes chroniques de France, *1274-1422* (Berkeley, CA: University of California Press, 1991).

———. *Authorship and Publicity before Print: Jean Gerson and the Transformation of Late Medieval Learning* (Philadelphia, PA: University of Pennsylvania Press, 2009).

Hobbins, Daniel. 'The Schoolman as Public Intellectual: Jean Gerson and the Late Medieval Tract', *The American Historical Review*, 108 (2003), pp. 1308-37.

Hodges, Elisabeth. *Urban Poetics in the Renaissance* (Aldershot: Ashgate, 2008).

Hoogvliet, Margriet. 'Encouraging Lay People to Read the Bible in the French Vernaculars: New Groups of Readers and Textual Communities', *Church History and Religious Culture*, 93 (2013), pp. 239-74.

Howell, Martha C. 'Citizen-clerics in Late Medieval Douai' in *Individuals, Corporations and Judicial Status in European Cities*, ed. by Marc Boone and Maarten Prak (Leuven: Garant, 1996), pp. 11-22.

——— 'The Spaces of Late Medieval Urbanity' in *Shaping Identity in Late Medieval Europe*, ed. by Marc Boone and Peter Stabel (Leuven: Garant, 2000), pp. 3-23.

Huisman, Georges. *La juridiction de la municipalité parisienne de Saint Louis à Charles VII* (Paris: Ernest Leroux, 1912).

Huizinga, Johan. *Herfsttij der Middeleeuwen*, ed. L. Brummel in *Verzamelde werken*, vol. 3, (Haarlem: H.D. Tjeenk Willink & Zoon, 1949).

Hutchison, Emily. 'Knowing One's Place: Space, Violence and Legitimacy in Early Fifteenth-century Paris', *The Medieval History Journal*, 20 (2017), pp. 38-88.

———. 'Partisan Identity in the French Civil War, 1405-18: Reconsidering the Evidence of Livery Badges', *Journal of Medieval History*, 33 (2007), pp. 250-74.

———. 'Passionate Politics: Emotions and Identity Formation among the *Menu Peuple* in the Early Fifteenth-Century France' in *Affective and Emotional Economies in Medieval and Early Modern Europe*, ed. by Andreea Marculescu and Charles-Louis Morand Métivier (London: Palgrave Macmillan, 2018), pp. 19-49.

———. 'Winning Hearts and Minds in Early Fifteenth-Century France: Burgundian Propaganda in Perspective', *French Historical Studies*, 35 (2012), pp. 3-30.

Iogna-Prat, Dominique. 'Constructions chrétiennes d'un espace politique', *Le Moyen Âge*, 1 (2001), pp. 49-69.

Jamieson, Kathleen Hall and Kenski, Kate. 'Political Communication: Then, Now and Beyond' in *The Oxford Handbook of Political Communication*, ed. by Kate Kenski and Kathleen Hall Jamieson (Oxford: Oxford University Press, 2017), pp. 3-11.

Jan, Plamper. 'The History of Emotions: An Interview with William Reddy, Barbara Rosenwein and Peter Stearns', *History and Theory* 49 (2010), pp. 237-65.

Jasper, James M. 'Emotions and Social Movements: Twenty Years of Theory and Research', *Annual Review of Sociology*, 37 (2011), pp. 285-303.

———— 'The Emotions of Protest: Affective and Reactive Emotions in and around Social Movements', *Sociological Forum*, 13 (1998), pp. 397-424.

Johnson, Tom. *Law in Common: Legal Cultures in Medieval England* (Oxford: Oxford University Press, 2020).

————. 'The Preconstruction of Witness Testimony: Law and Social Discourse before the Reformation', *Law and History*, 12 (2014), pp. 127-47.

Jones, Chris. 'Perspectives from the Periphery: French Kings and their Chroniclers' in *The Medieval Chronicle X*, ed. by Ilya Afanasyev, Juliana Dresvina and Erik Kooper (Leiden: Brill, 2015), pp. 69-94.

Jowett, Garth and O'Donnell, Victoria. *Propaganda and Persuasion*, Seventh Edition (Thousand Oaks, CA: SAGE Publications, 2018).

Julerot, Véronique. 'La première entrée de l'évêque: Réflexions sur son origine', *Revue historique* 639 (2006), pp. 635-76.

————. 'Les chanoines cathédraux au parlement de Paris: Entre service de l'État et intérêts personnels' in *Église et état, église ou état? Les clercs et la genèse de l'État moderne*, ed. by Christine Barralis, Jean-Patrice Boudet, Fabrice Delivré and Jean-Philippe Genet (Paris: Éditions de la Sorbonne, 2014), pp. 87-100.

————. *Y a ung grant desordre: Élections épiscopales et schismes diocésains en France sous Charles VIII* (Paris: Publications de la Sorbonne, 2006).

Jutte, Daniel 'Entering a City: On a Lost Early Modern Practice', *Urban History*, 41 (2014), pp. 204-27.

Kaçar, Hilmi and Dumolyn, Jan. 'The Battle of Nicopolis (1396), Burgundian Catastrophe and Ottoman Fait Divers', *Revue belge de philologie et d'histoire*, 91 (2013), pp. 905-34.

Kaluza, Zénon. 'Nouvelles remarques sur les œuvres de Gilles Charlier', *Archives d'histoire doctrinale et littéraire du Moyen Âge*, 47 (1973), pp. 149-91.

Kantorowicz, Ernst. *The King's Two Bodies: A Study in Mediaeval Political Theory* (Princeton, NJ: Princeton University Press, 1997).

Kapferer, Jean-Noël. 'Le contrôle des rumeurs. Expériences et réflexions sur le démenti', *Communications*, 52 (1990), pp. 99-118.

————. *Rumors: Uses, Interpretations and Images*, trans. by Bruce Fink (New Brunswick, NJ: Transaction Publishers, 1990).

Karila-Cohen, Pierre. 'Introduction. Apologie pour un pluriel: de l'opinion aux opinions' in *S'exprimer en temps de troubles. Conflits, opinion(s) et politisation du Moyen Âge au début du XXe siècle*, ed. Laurent Bourquin, Philippe Hamon, Pierre Karila-Cohen and Cédric Michon (Rennes: Presses Universitaires de Rennes, 2012), pp. 15-22.

Karras, Ruth Mazo. 'The Regulation of Sexuality in the Late Middle Ages: England and France', *Speculum*, 86 (2011), pp. 1010-39.

Kempshall, M.S. *The Common Good in Late Medieval Political Thought* (Oxford: Clarendon Press, 1999).

Kerby-Fulton, Kathryn. 'The Clerical Proletariat: The Underemployed Scribe and Vocational Crisis', *Journal of the Early Book Society*, 17 (2014), pp. 1-34.

Kinch, Ashby. *Imago Mortis: Mediating Images of Death in the Medieval Culture* (Leiden: Brill, 2013).

King, Peter. 'Aquinas on the Emotions' in *The Oxford Handbook of Aquinas*, ed. by Brian Davies and Eleonore Stump (Oxford: Oxford University Press, 2012), pp. 209-26.

———. 'Emotions in Medieval Thought' in *The Oxford Handbook of Philosophy of Emotion* (Oxford: Oxford University Press, 2012), pp. 167-88.

Kipling, Gordon. *Enter the King: Theatre, Liturgy and Ritual in the Medieval Civic Triumph* (Oxford: Oxford University Press, 1998).

Kirbe, Pearl. *Scholarly Privileges in the Middle Ages: The Rights, Privileges and Immunities of Scholars and Universities at Bologna, Padua, Paris and Oxford* (London: Medieval Academy of America, 1961).

Knapp, Robert H. 'A Psychology of Rumor', *The Public Opinion Quarterly*, 8 (1944), pp. 22-37.

Kralik, Christine. 'Dialogue and Violence in Medieval Illuminations of the Three Living and the Three Dead' in *Mixed Metaphors: The* Danse Macabre *in Medieval and Early Modern Europe*, ed. by Sophie Oosterwijk and Stefanie Knöll (Newcastle-upon-Tyne: Cambridge Scholars Publishing, 2011), pp. 133-54.

Kristeva, Julia. *Powers of Horror. An Essay on Abjection* (New York, NY: University of Columbia Press, 1982).

Krynen, Jacques. *Idéal du prince et pouvoir royal en France à la fin du Moyen Âge, 1380-1440* (Paris: Picard, 1981).

———. *L'Empire du roi: Idées et croyances politiques en France, XIIIᵉ-XVᵉ siècle* (Paris: Gallimard, 1993).

———. '"Le mort saisit le vif": Genèse médiévale du principe d'instantanéité de la succession royale française', *Journal des savants* (1984), pp. 187-221.

———. '*Rex Christianissimus*: A Medieval Theme at the Roots of French Absolutism', *History and Anthropology*, 4 (1989), pp. 79-96.

La Martinière, Jules de. 'Frère Richard et Jeanne d'Arc à Orléans, mars-juillet 1430', *Le Moyen Âge* 44 (1934), pp. 189-98.

La Selle, Xavier de. *Le service des âmes à la cour: confesseurs et aumôniers des rois de France du XIIIᵉ au XVᵉ siècle* (Paris: École Nationale des Chartes, 1995).

Laitinen, Riita and Cohen, Thomas. 'Cultural History of Early Modern Streets – An Introduction' in *Cultural History of Early Modern European Streets*, ed. by Riita Laitinen and Thomas Cohen (Leiden: Brill, 2009), pp. 1-10.

Lambertini, Roberto. 'Political Thought' in *A Companion to Giles of Rome*, ed. by Charles F. Briggs and Peter S. Eardley (Leiden: Brill, 2016), pp. 255-74.

Landi, Sandro. 'Beyond the Public Sphere: Habermas, Locke and Tacit Consent', *Revue d'histoire modern et contemporaine*, 59 (2012), pp. 7-32.

Krynen, Jacques. 'Opinions et conflits. Une relecture des *Histoires de Florence* (Istorie fiorentine) de Machiavel' in *S'exprimer en temps de troubles. Conflits, opinion(s) et politization du Moyen Âge au début du XXᵉ siècle*, ed. Laurent Bourquin, Philippe Hamon, Pierre Karila-Cohen and Cédric Michon (Rennes: Presses universitaires de Rennes, 2012), pp. 25-49.

Lange, Tyler. *Excommunication for Debt in Late Medieval France: The Business of Salvation* (Cambridge: Cambridge University Press, 2016).

Lantschner, Patrick. 'Revolts and the Political Order of Cities in the late Middle Ages', *Past & Present*, 225 (2014), pp. 3-46.

Lapina, Elizabeth. '*Nec signis nec testibus creditur…*: The Problem of Eyewitnesses in the Chronicles of the First Crusade', *Viator*, 38 (2007), pp. 117-39.

Larivière, Claire Judde de. 'Du Broglio à Rialto: cris et chuchotements dans l'espace public à Venise (XVIe siècle)' in *L'espace public au Moyen Âge. Débats autour de Jürgen Habermas*, ed. by Patrick Boucheron and Nicolas Offenstadt (Paris: Presses Universitaires de France, 2011), pp. 119-30.

Lassalmonie, Jean-François. *La boîte à l'enchanteur: Politique financière de Louis XI* (Paris: Comité pour l'histoire économique et financière, 2002).

Le Goff, Jacques. *History and Memory*, trans. by Steven Randall and Elizabeth Claman (New York, NY: Columbia University Press, 1992).

le Grand, Léon. 'Les Quinze-Vingts depuis leur fondation jusqu'à leur translation au faubourg Saint-Antoine, XIIIe-XVIIIe siècles', *MSHP*, 13 (1886), pp. 107-260.

le Maresquier-Kesteloot, Yvonne-Hélène. 'Le voisinage dans l'espace parisien à la fin du Moyen Âge: bilan d'une enquête', *Revue Historique*, 299 (1998), pp. 47-70.

———. *Les officiers municipaux de la ville de Paris au XVe siècle* (Paris: Commission des travaux historiques de la ville de Paris, 1997).

———. 'Un conflit de voisinage devant le Parlement de Paris au XVe siècle' in *Un Moyen Âge pour aujourd'hui*, ed. by Julie Claustre, Olivier Mattéoni and Nicolas Offenstadt (Paris: Presses Universitaires de France, 2010), pp. 239-46.

Lebigue, Jean-Baptiste. 'L'ordo du sacre d'Henri VI à Notre-Dame de Paris (16 décembre 1431)' in *Notre-Dame de Paris, 1163-2013*, ed. by Cédric Giraud (Turnhout: Brepols, 2013), pp. 319-63.

Lecoq, Anne-Marie. 'La symbolique de l'État: Les images de la monarchie des premiers Valois à Louis XIV' in *Les lieux de mémoire*, ed. by Pierre Nora, vol. 2, Part 2 (Paris: Gallimard, 1986), pp. 145-92.

Lecuppre-Desjardin, Elodie and Toureille, Valérie. 'Servir ou trahir. La réaction des grands féodaux face aux innovations étatiques, au temps de la Praguerie', *Publications du Centre européen d'études bourguignonnes*, 60 (2020), pp. 7-14.

Lecuppre-Desjardin, Élodie. 'La ville. Creuset des cultures urbaines et princière dans les anciens Pays-Bas bourguignons' in *La cour de Bourgogne et l'Europe, Beihefte der Francia*, 73 (2013), pp. 289-304.

———. *La ville des cérémonies: Essai sur la communication politique dans les anciens Pays-Bas bourguignons* (Turnhout: Brepols, 2004).

———. 'Parcours festifs et enjeux de pouvoirs dans les villes des anciens Pays-Bas bourguignons au XVe siècle', *Histoire urbaine*, 9, 1 (2004), pp. 29-45.

Lefebvre, Henri. *The Production of Space*, trans. by Donald Nicholson-Smith (Oxford: Blackwell, 1991).

Lefevre-Pontlais, Germain. 'Épisodes de l'invasion anglaise. La guerre de partisans dans la Haute Normandie, 1424-29 (suite et fin)', *BEC*, 97 (1936), pp. 102-30.

Lenoir, Remi. 'Pouvoir symbolique et symbolique du pouvoir' in *La légitimité implicite*, vol. 1, ed. by Jean-Philippe Genet (Paris: Éditions de la Sorbonne, 2015), pp. 49-58.

Lepore, Jill. 'Historians Who Love Too Much: Reflections on Microhistory and Biography', *The Journal of American History*, 88 (2001), pp. 129-44.

Leproux, Guy-Michel. 'L'église des Saints-Innocents' in *Les Saints-Innocents*, ed. by Michel Fleury and Guy-Michel Leproux (Paris: Délégation à l'action artistique de la ville de Paris, Commission du Vieux Paris, 1990), pp. 75-83.

Léthenet, Benoît. 'Selon les nouvelles que vous me ferez savoir'. Essai sur le renseignement au Moyen Âge', *Revue du Nord*, 402 (2013), pp. 837-57.

Lett, Didier and Offenstadt, Nicolas. 'Les pratiques du cri au Moyen Âge' in *Haro! Noël! Oyé! Pratiques du cri au Moyen Âge*, ed. by Didier Lett and Nicolas Offenstadt (Paris: Publications de la Sorbonne, 2003), pp. 5-41.

Leurquin-Labie, Anne-Françoise. 'La Somme le roi: de la commande royale de Philippe III à la diffusion sous Philippe IV et au-delà' in *La moisson des lettres: L'invention littéraire autour de 1300*, ed. by Hélène Bellon-Méguelle, Olivier Collet, Yasmina Foehr-Janssens, and Ludivine Jaquiéry (Turnhout: Brepols, 2011), pp. 195-212.

Leveleux-Teixeira, Corinne. 'Des serments collectifs au contrat politique? (début du XVe siècle)' in *Avant le contrat social: Le contrat politique dans l'Occident médiéval, XIIIe-XVe siècle*, ed. by François Foronda (Paris: Éditions de la Sorbonne, 2011), pp. 269-89.

Lévi-Strauss, Claude. *The Savage Mind* (London: Weidenfeld and Nicholson, 1968).

Lewis, Peter S. 'Some Provisional Remarks upon the Chronicles of Saint-Denis and upon the [Grandes] Chroniques de France in the Fifteenth Century', *Nottingham Medieval Studies*, 39 (1995), pp. 146-81.

———— 'War Propaganda and Historiography in Fifteenth-Century France and England', *Transactions of the Royal Historical Society*, 15 (1965), pp. 1-21.

Liddy, Christian D. *Contesting the City: The Politics of Citizenship in English Towns, 1250-1530* (Oxford: Oxford University Press, 2017).

———— 'Cultures of Surveillance in late Medieval English Towns: The Monitoring of Speech and the Fear of Revolt' in *The Routledge Handbook of Medieval Revolt*, ed. by Justine Firnhaber-Baker and Dirk Schoenaers (London: Routledge, 2017), pp. 311-29.

Little, Lester K. 'Pride Goes before Avarice: Social Change and the Vices in Latin Christendom', *The American Historical Review*, 76, (1971), pp. 16-49.

Lombard-Jourdan, Anne. 'Fiefs et justice parisiens au quartier des Halles', *BEC*, 134 (1976), pp. 301-88.

————. *Fleur de lis et oriflamme* (Paris: Presses du CNRS, 1991).

————. 'La ville étudiée dans ses quartiers: autour des Halles de Paris au Moyen Âge', *Annales d'histoire économique et sociale*, 7 (1935), pp. 285-301.

————. *Les Halles de Paris et leur quartier (1137-1969)* (Paris: École des Chartes, 2009).

————. *Paris, genèse de la ville: La Rive Droite de la Seine des origines à 1223* (Paris: Éditions du CNRS, 1978).

Long, Sarah. *Music, Liturgy and Confraternity Devotions in Paris and Tournai, 1300-1500* (Woodbridge: University of Rochester Press, 2021).

Longnon, Auguste. 'Conjectures sur l'auteur du journal parisien de 1409-1449', *MSHP*, 2 (1876), pp. 310-29.

Luce, Siméon. *La France pendant la guerre de Cent Ans: épisodes historiques et vie privée aux XIVe et XVe siècles*, 2 vols (Paris: Hachette, 1890-93).

———. 'Les menus du prieur de Saint-Martin-des-Champs en 1438 et 1439', *Comptes rendus des séances de l'Académie des Inscriptions et Belles-Lettres*, 26 (1882), pp. 111-17.

Lurie, Guy. 'Citizenship in Late Medieval Champagne: The Towns of Châlons, Reims, and Troyes, 1417-c. 1435', *French Historical Studies*, 38 (2015) pp.

Lusignan, Serge. *Essai d'histoire sociolinguistique. Le français picard au Moyen Âge* (Paris: Classiques Garnier, 2012).

———. 'L'enseignement des arts dans les collèges parisiens au Moyen Âge' in *L'enseignement des disciplines à la Faculté des Arts (Paris et Oxford, XIIIᵉ-XVᵉ siècles), actes du colloque international*, ed. by O. Weijers et L. Hort (Turnhout: Brepols, 1997), pp. 43-54.

———. 'Le français et le latin aux XIIIᵉ-XIVᵉ siècles: pratique des langues et pensée linguistique', *Annales. Économies, sociétés, civilisations*, 42 (1987), pp. 955-67.

———. *Parler vulgairement: les intellectuels et la langue française aux XIIIᵉ et XIVᵉ siècles*, Second Edition (Paris: Vrin, 1987).

———. *'Vérité garde le roy': La construction d'une identité universitaire en France (XIIIᵉ-XVᵉ siècle)* (Paris: Éditions de la Sorbonne, 1999).

Lusset, Elisabeth. 'La *fama* et l'*infamia* des clercs réguliers d'après les suppliques adressées à la pénitencerie apostolique au XVᵉ siècle' in *Faire jeunesses, rendre justice*, ed. by Antoine Destemberg, Yann Potin et Émile Rosenblieh (Paris: Publications de la Sorbonne, 2015), pp. 25-35.

Lutz, Catherine A. and Abu-Lughod, Lila. *Language and the Politics of Emotion* (Cambridge: Cambridge University Press, 1990).

Magnússon, Sigurður G. and Szijártó, István. *What is Microhistory? Theory and Practice* (London: Routledge, 2013).

Mah, Harold. 'Phantasies of the Public Sphere: Rethinking the Habermas of Historians', *The Journal of Modern History*, 72 (2000), pp. 153-82.

Mairey, Aude. 'Les langages politiques au Moyen Âge (XIIᵉ-XVᵉ siècle)', *Médiévales*, 57 (2009), pp. 5-14.

Mandrot, Bernard de. 'Quel est le véritable auteur de la Chronique anonyme de Louis XI dite la Scandaleuse?', *BEC*, 52 (1891), pp. 129-33.

Marchandisse, Alain and Schnerb, Bertrand. 'La bataille du Liège' in *Écrire la guerre, écrire la paix*, ed. by Simone Mazauric (Paris: Éditions du CTHS, 2013), pp. 29-41.

Martin, Olivier (ed.). 'Sentences civils du Châtelet de Paris (1395-1505), publiées d'après les registres originaux. (Suite)', *Nouvelle revue historique de droit français et étranger*, 38 (1914), pp. 61-104.

Martinescu, Elena, Janssen, Onne and Nijstad, Bernard A. 'Gossip and Emotion' in *The Oxford Handbook of Gossip and Reputation*, ed. by Francesca Giardini and Rafael Wittek (New York, NY: Oxford University Press, 2019), pp. 152-69.

Masschaele, James. 'The Public Space of the Marketplace in Medieval England', *Speculum*, 77 (2002), pp. 383-421.

Massoni, Anne. *La collégiale Saint-Germain l'Auxerrois de Paris (1380-1510)* (Limoges: Presses Universitaires de Limoges, 2009).

———. 'Les collégiales parisiennes, "filles de l'évêque" et "filles du chapitre" de Notre-Dame' in *Notre-Dame de Paris 1163-2013: Actes du colloque scientifique tenu au Collège des Bernardins, à Paris, du 12 au 15 décembre 2012*, ed. by Cédric Giraud (Turnhout: Brepols, 2013), pp. 251-63.

McKenna, J.W. 'Henry VI of England and the Dual Monarchy: Aspects of Royal Political Propaganda, 1422-1432', *Journal of the Warburg and Courtauld Institutes*, 28 (1965), pp. 145-62.

McLaren, Mary-Rose. 'Reading, Writing and Recording. Literacy and the London Chronicles in the Fifteenth Century' in *London and the Kingdom: Essays in Honour of Caroline M. Barron. Proceedings of the 2004 Harlaxton Symposium*, ed. by Matthew Davies and Andrew Prescott (Donington: Shaun Tyas, 2008), pp. 346-65.

———. 'The Aims and Interests of the London Chroniclers of the Fifteenth Century' in *Trade, Devotion and Governance: Papers in Later Medieval History*, ed. by Dorothy J. Clayton, Richard G. Davies and Peter McNiven (Stroud: Sutton, 1994), pp. 158-76.

———. *The London Chronicles of the Fifteenth Century: A Revolution in English Writing* (Woodbridge: D.S. Brewer, 2002).

McLoughlin, Nancy. *Gerson and Gender: Rhetoric and Politics in Fifteenth-Century France* (Basingstoke: Palgrave Macmillan, 2015).

McNiven, Peter. 'Rebellion, Sedition and the Legend of Richard II's Survival in the Reigns of Henry IV and Henry V', *Bulletin of the John Rylands University Library of Manchester*, 76 (1994), pp. 93-117.

McSheffrey, Shannon. 'Place, Space, and Situation: Public and Private in the Making of Marriage in Late-Medieval London', *Speculum*, 79 (2004), pp. 960-90.

Melve, Leidulf. '"Even the Very Laymen Are Chattering about It": The Politicization of Public Opinion, 800-1200', *Viator*, 44(2013), pp. 25-48.

———. *Inventing the Public Sphere: Public Debate during the Investiture Contest (c. 1030-1122)* (Leiden: Brill, 2007).

———. 'Public Debate, Propaganda and Public Opinion in the Becket Controversy', *Viator*, 48 (2017), pp. 79-102.

Menache, Sophia. *The Vox Dei: Communication in the Middle Ages* (Oxford: Oxford University Press, 1990).

Métivier, Charles-Louis Morand. 'Narrating a Massacre: The Writing of History and Emotions as Response to the Battle of Nicopolis (1396)' in *Affective and Emotional Economies in Medieval and Early Modern Europe*, ed. Andreea Marculescu and Charles-Louis Morand Métivier (London: Palgrave Macmillan, 2018), pp. 196-202.

Metzler, Irina. *A Social History of Disability in the Middle Ages: Cultural Considerations of Physical Impairment* (London: Routledge, 2013).

Meyer, Paul. 'Paris sans pair', *Romania*, 11 (1882), pp. 579-81.

Michalek-Simínska, Anna. 'Le rôle de processions *pro rege* en France sous Charles VI' in *Civitas Mentis*, vol. 1, ed. by Zbigniewa Kadłubka and Tadeusza Sławka (Katowice: Wydawnictwo Uniwersytetu Śląskiego, 2005), pp. 197-211.

Mileson, Stephen. 'Sound and Landscape', *The Oxford Handbook of Later Medieval Archaeology in Britain*, ed. by Christopher Gerrard and Alejandra Gutiérrez (Oxford: OUP, 2018), pp. 713-27.

Miller, Anne-Hélène. 'Revisiting Urban Encomia in Fourteenth-Century Paris: Poetics of Translation, Universalism and the Pilgrim City', *Viator*, 45 (2014), pp. 193-210.

Miller, William Ian. *The Anatomy of Disgust* (Cambridge: Harvard University Press, 1997).

Millet, Hélène. 'Un bouillon de culture pour l'opinion publique: le temps du Grand Schisme d'Occident' in *Un Moyen Âge pour aujourd'hui*, ed. Julie Claustre, Olivier Mattéoni and Nicolas Offenstadt (Paris: Presses Universitaires de France, 2010), pp. 347-55.

Mills, Robert. *Suspended Animation: Pain, Pleasure and Punishment in Medieval Culture* (London: Reaktion, 2005).

Mirot, Léon. 'L'enlèvement du dauphin et le premier conflit entre Jean sans Peur et Louis d'Orléans (1405)', *Revue des questions historiques*, 51 (1914), pp. 329-55 and vol. 52 (1914), pp. 47-88, 369-419.

———. 'Le procès du Boiteux d'Orgemont. Épisode des troubles parisiens pendant la lutte des Armagnacs et des Bourguignons (Suite et fin). Quatrième partie: La vie politique et le procès du Boiteux d'Orgemont', *Le Moyen Âge*, 25 (1912), pp. 353-410.

———. *Les d'Orgemont. Leur origine, leur fortune – le Boiteux d'Orgemont* (Paris: Champion, 1913).

———. *Les insurrections urbaines au début du règne de Charles VI (1380-83). Leurs causes, leurs conséquences* (Paris: Fontemoing, 1905).

Moeglin, Jean-Marie 'La vérité de l'histoire et le moi du chroniqueur' in *La vérité: Vérité et crédibilité: construire la vérité dans le système de communication de l'Occident (XIIIe-XVIIe siècle)*, ed. by Jean-Philippe Genet (Paris: Éditions de la Sorbonne, 2015), pp. 521-38.

———. 'Réécrire l'histoire de la Guerre de Cent Ans. Une relecture historique et historiographique du traité de Troyes (21 mai 1420)', *Revue historique*, 664 (2012), pp. 887-919.

Mollat, Michel and Wolff, Philippe. *Ongles bleus, Jacques et Ciompi: les révolutions populaires en Europe aux XIVe et XVe siècles* (Paris: Calman-Lévy, 1970).

Morsel, Joseph. 'Communication et domination sociale en Franconie à la fin du Moyen Âge: l'enjeu de la réponse' in *L'espace public au Moyen Âge: Débats autour de Jürgen Habermas*, ed. by Patrick Boucheron and Nicolas Offenstadt (Paris: Presses Universitaires de France, 2011), pp. 353-65.

Muir, Edward. 'The Eye of the Procession: Ritual Ways of Seeing in the Renaissance', *Ceremonial Culture in Pre-Modern Europe*, ed. by Nicholas Howe (Notre Dame: University of Notre Dame Press, 2007), pp. 129-53.

———. *Ritual in Early Modern Europe* (Cambridge: Cambridge University Press, 1997).

Muldoon, James. '*Auctoritas, Plenitas* and World Order' in *Plenitude of Power: The Doctrines and Exercise of Power in the Middle Ages*, ed. by Robert C. Figuiera (Aldershot: Ashgate, 2006), pp. 125-39.

Murphy, Neil. *Ceremonial Entries, Municipal Liberties and the Negotiation of Power in Valois France, 1328-1589* (Leiden: Brill, 2016).

———. 'Ceremony and Conflict in Fifteenth-Century France: Lancastrian Ceremonial Entries into French Towns, 1415-1431', *Explorations in Renaissance Culture*, 39 (2013), pp. 113-33.

Nadrigny, Xavier. 'Espace public et révolte à Toulouse a la fin du Moyen Âge (v. 1330-1444)', pp. 321-36.

———. *Information et opinion publique à Toulouse à la fin du Moyen Âge* (Paris: École des Chartes, 2013).

———. 'Rumeur et opinion publique à Toulouse à la fin du Moyen Âge', *Annales du Midi*, 121 (2009), pp. 23-36.

Naegle, Gisela. 'Armes à double tranchant? *Bien commun* et *chose publique* dans les villes françaises du Moyen Âge' in *De Bono Communi. The Discourse and Practice of the Common Good in the European City (13th-16th c.) / Discours et pratique du Bien Commun dans les villes d'Europe (XIIIe au XVIe siècle)*, ed. by Élodie Lecuppre-Desjardin and Anne-Laure Van Bruaene (Turnhout: Brepols, 2010), pp. 55-70.

Nederman, Cary J. 'The Living Body Politic: The Diversification of Organic Metaphors in Nicole Oresme and Christine de Pizan' in *Healing the Body Politic: The Political Thought of Christine de Pizan*, ed. by Karen Green and Constant J. Mews (Turnhout: Brepols, 2005), pp. 19-33.

Nirenberg, David. *Communities of Violence: Persecution of Minorities in the Middle Ages* (Princeton, NJ: Princeton University Press, 2015).

Noelle-Neumann, Elisabeth. 'The Spiral of Silence a Theory of Public Opinion', *Journal of Communication*, 24 (1974), pp. 43-51.

Nora, Pierre. 'Between Memory and History: *Les Lieux de Mémoire*', *Representations*, 26 (1989), pp. 7-24.

Novák, Veronika. 'Cérémonies problématiques: les pratiques des rencontres au sommet à la fin du Moyen Âge et la visite de Sigismond de Luxembourg à Paris en 1416' in *'M'en anai en Ongria'. Relations Franco-Hongroises au Moyen Âge*, ed. Attila Györkös and Gergely Kiss (Debrecen: Kapitális, 2017), pp. 105-25.

———. 'L'espace du cri à Paris aux XIVe-XVIe siècles: recherches sur les 'lieux accoutumés', *Revue historique*, 696 (2020), pp. 61-86.

———. 'La source du savoir. Publication officielle et communication informelle à Paris au début du XVe siècle' in *Information et société a la fin du Moyen Âge* (Paris: Publications de la Sorbonne, 2004), pp. 151-63.

———. 'Le corps du condamné et le tissue urbain. Exécution, pouvoir et usages de l'espace à Paris aux XVe-XVIe siècles', *Histoire urbaine*, 47 (2016), pp. 149-66.

———. 'Places of Power: The Spreading of Official Information and the Social Uses of Space in Fifteenth-Century Paris' in *Towns and Communication*, vol. 1, ed. by Neven Budak, Finn-Einar Eliassen and Katalin Szende (Akron, OH: University of Akron Press, 2011), pp. 47-66.

Offenstadt, Nicolas. *Faire la paix au Moyen Âge: discours et gestes de paix pendant la guerre de Cent Ans* (Paris: Odile Jacob, 2007).

———. 'Guerre civile et espace public à la fin du Moyen Âge. La lutte entre des Armagnacs et des Bourguignons' in *La politisation. Conflits et construction du politique depuis le Moyen Âge*, ed. by Philippe Hamon and Laurent Bourquin (Rennes: Presses Universitaires de Rennes, 2010), pp. 111-29.

Oosterwijk, Sophie. 'Death, Memory and Commemoration: John Lydgate and "Macabrees Daunce" at Old St Paul's Cathedral, London' in *Memory and Commemoration in Medieval England. Proceedings of the 2008 Harlaxton Symposium*, ed. by Caroline M. Barron and Clive Burgess (Donington: Shaun Tyas, 2010), pp. 185-201.

———. 'Of Dead Kings, Dukes and Constables: The Historical Context of the *Danse Macabre* in Late Medieval Paris', *Journal of the British Archaeological Association*, 161 (2008), pp. 131-62.

Orlandi, Eni. 'Rumeurs et silences: Les trajets des sens, le parcours du dire', *Hypothèses*, 4 (2001), pp. 257-66.

Oschema Klaus. 'Die Öffentlichkeit des Politischen' in *Politische Öffentlichkeit im Spätmittelalter*, ed. by Martin Kintzinger and Bernd Schneidmüller (Ostfildern: Thorbecke, 2011), pp. 41-86.

———. 'Espaces publics autour d'une société de cour: l'exemple de la Bourgogne des ducs de Valois' in *L'espace public au Moyen Âge: débats autour de Jürgen Habermas*, ed. by Patrick Boucheron and Nicolas Offenstadt (Paris: Presses Universitaires de France, 2011), pp. 159-78.

———. 'Nouvelles de Perpignan en France et Bourgogne (1415) – un non-lieu historique?' in *Perpignan 1415. Un sommet européen à l'époque du Grand Schisme en Occident*, ed. by Aymat Catafau, Nikolas Jaspert and Thomas Wetzstein (Zurich: Lit Verlag, 2019), pp. 29-58.

Owens, Margaret E. *Stages of Dismemberment: The Fragmented Body in Late Medieval and Early Modern Drama* (Newark, DE: University of Delaware Press, 2005).

Paravicini, Werner and Schnerb, Bertrand. 'Les "investissements" religieux des ducs de Bourgogne à Paris', *Beihefte der Francia*, 64 (2007), pp. 185-218.

———. 'Paris, capitale des ducs de Bourgogne?', *Beihefte der Francia*, 64 (2007), pp. 471-77.

Pastoureau, Michel. 'Emblèmes et symboles de la Toison d'Or' in *L'ordre de la Toison d'Or de Philippe le Bon à Philippe le Beau (1430-1505). Idéal ou reflet de la société?*, ed. by C. Van den Bergen-Pantens (Turnhout: Brepols, 1996), pp. 99-106.

Pendergrass, Jan. 'Lettres, poèmes et débat scolaire de Germain Maciot, étudiant parisien du XVe siècle. MS. Latin 8659 de la Bibliothèque nationale de France', *Bulletin du Cange: Archivum Latinitatis Madii Aevi*, 55 (1997), pp. 177-270.

Perret, Donald. 'The Meaning of the Mystery: From Tableaux to Theatre in the French Royal Entry' in *Moving Subjects: Processional Performance in the Middle Ages and the Renaissance*, ed. by Kathleen Ashley and Wim Husken (Amsterdam: Rodopi, 2001), pp. 187-211.

Pettegree, Andrew. *The Invention of News: How the world came to know about itself* (London: Yale University Press, 2014).

Phythian-Adams, Charles V. 'Ceremony and the Citizen: The Communal Year at Coventry, 1450-1550', in *Crisis and Order in English Towns, 1500-1700*, ed. by Peter Clark and Paul Slack (London: Routledge and Kegan Paul, 1972), pp. 57-85.

Picot, Georges. 'Recherches sur les quartiniers, cinquanteniers et dixainiers de la ville de Paris', *MSHP*, Vol. 1 (1875), pp. 132-66.

Pile, Steve. *The Body and the City: Psychoanalysis, Space, and Subjectivity* (London: Routledge, 1996).

Plancher, Urbain. *Histoire générale et particulière de Bourgogne avec les preuves justificatives*, 4 vols (Dijon: Frantin, 1739-81).

Pocock, J. G. A. 'Historiography as a Form of Political Thought', *History of European Ideas*, 37 (2011), pp. 1-6.

Pollack-Lagushenko, Tim. 'Le parti Armagnac: nouveaux modèles de violence politique dans la France du bas Moyen Âge', *Annales du Midi*, 118 (2006), pp. 441-46.

Pollmann, Judith. 'Archiving the Present and Chronicling for the Future in Early Modern Europe', *Past & Present* (2016), Supplement 11, pp. 231-52.

Pons, Nicole. 'Honneur et profit. Le recueil d'un juriste parisien au milieu du XVe siècle', *Revue historique*, 645 (2008), pp. 3-32.

———. 'Information et rumeurs : quelques points de vue sur des événements de la Guerre civile en France (1407-20)', *Revue historique*, 297 (1997), pp. 409-34.

———. 'Mémoire nobiliaire et clivages poli tiques: le témoignage d'une courte chronique chevaleresque (1403-22)', *Journal des Savants* (2002), pp. 299-348.

———. 'Un exemple de l'utilisation des écrits politiques de Jean de Mon treuil: Un memorandum diplomatique rédigé sous Charles VII' in *Préludes à la Renaissance: Aspects de la vie intellectuelle en France au XVe siècle*, ed. by Carla Bozzolo et Ezio Ornato (Paris: CNRS, 1992), pp. 243-64.

———. 'Un traité inédit de bon gouvernement: le Trialogue Quiéret (1461)' in *Un Moyen Âge pour aujourd'hui: Mélanges offerts à Claude Gauvard*, ed. by Julie Claustre, Olivier Mattéoni and Nicolas Offenstadt (Paris: Presses Universitaires de France, 2010), pp. 160-68.

Porter, Lindsay. *Popular Rumour in Revolutionary Paris, 1792-94* (Basingstoke: Routledge, 2017).

Potin, Yann. 'Les rois en leur Palais de la Cité' in *Le Paris du Moyen Âge*, ed. by Boris Bove and Claude Gauvard (Paris: Belin, 2018), pp. 77-94.

Prétou, Pierre. 'Clameur contre fureur: Cris et tyrannie à la fin du Moyen Âge' in *Violences souveraines au Moyen Âge*, ed. by François Foronda, Christine Barralis and Bénédicte Sère (Paris: Presses Universitaires de France, 2010), pp. 271-80.

Putnam, Robert. *Making Democracy Work: Civic Traditions in Modern Italy* (Princeton, NJ: Princeton University Press, 1993).

Rawcliffe, Carole. *Urban Bodies: Communal Health in Late Medieval English Towns and Cities* (Woodbridge: Boydell and Brewer, 2013).

Raymond, P. 'Enquête du prévôt de Paris sur l'assassinat de Louis, duc d'Orléans (1407)', *BEC*, 26 (1865), pp. 215-49.

Reddy, William M. *The Navigation of Feeling: A Framework for the History of Emotions* (Cambridge: Cambridge University Press, 2001).

——— 'Emotional Liberty: Politics and History in the Anthropology of Emotions', *Cultural Anthropology*, 14 (1999), pp. 256-88.

Rees Jones, Sarah. 'Emotions, Speech and the Art of Politics in Fifteenth-Century York: House Books, Mystery Plays and Richard, Duke of Gloucester', *Urban History*, 44, 4 (2017), pp. 586-603.

Reddy, William M. 'Public and Private Space and Gender in Medieval Europe' in *The Oxford Handbook of Women and Gender in Medieval Europe*, ed. by Judith Bennett and Ruth Karras (Oxford: Oxford University Press, 2013), pp. 246-61.

Regalado, Nancy Freeman. '*Effet de réel, effet du réel*: Representation and Reference in Villon's *Testament*', *Yale French Studies*, 70 (1986), pp. 63-77.

Reumaux, Françoise. 'Traits invariants de la rumeur', *Communications*, 52 (1990), pp. 141-59.

Rey, Maurice. *Le domaine du roi et les finances extraordinaires sous Charles VI, 1388-1413* (Paris: SEVPEN, 1965).

Reyerson, Kathryn. 'Le procès de Jacques Cœur' in *Les procès politiques, XIVe-XVIIe siècle*, ed. by Yves-Marie Bercé (Rome: École française de Rome, 2007), pp. 123-44.

Richard, Olivier. 'Le jeu des aveugles et du cochon. Rite, handicap et société urbaine à la fin du Moyen Âge', *Revue historique*, 675 (2015), pp. 525-56.

Richards, Barry. *Emotional Governance: Politics, Media and Terror* (Basingstoke: Palgrave MacMillan, 2007).

Riché, Philippe et Verger, Jacques. *Des nains sur des épaules de géants: Maîtres et élèves au Moyen Âge* (Paris: Taillandier, 2006).

Ricoeur, Paul. *La mémoire, l'histoire, l'oubli* (Paris: Seuil, 2000).

————. *Time and Narrative*, vol. 1, trans. by Kathleen McLaughlin and David Pellauer (Chicago, IL: University of Chicago Press, 1984).

Rimé, Bernard. 'Les émotions médiévales. Réflexions psychologiques' in *Politique des émotions au Moyen Âge*, ed. by Damien Boquet an d Piroska Nagy (Florence: SISMEL, 2010), pp. 309-32.

Rollo-Koster, Joelle. *Raiding Saint Peter: Empty Sees, Violence and the Initiation of the Great Western Schism (1378)* (Leiden: Brill, 2008).

Rosenwein, Barbara. *Emotional Communities in the Early Middle Ages* (London: Cornell University Press, 2007).

————. 'Emotion Words' in *Le Sujet des émotions au Moyen Âge*, ed. by Piroska Nagy and Damien Boquet (Paris: Beauchesne, 2008), pp. 93-106.

————. *Generations of Feeling: A History of Emotions, 600-1700* (Cambridge: Cambridge University Press, 2016).

————. 'The Political Uses of an Emotional Community: Cluny and its Neighbours, 833-965' in *Politique des émotions au Moyen Âge*, ed. by Damien Boquet and Piroska Nagy (Florence: SISMEL, 2010), pp. 205-24.

Rosier-Catach, Irène. 'Communauté politique et communauté linguistique' in *La légitimité implicite*, ed. by Je an-Philippe Genet (Paris: Éditions de la Sorbonne, 2015), pp. 225-43.

Roux, Simone. 'L'habitat urbain au Moyen Âge: le quartier de l'Université à Paris', *Annales (ESC)*, 2 (1969), pp. 1196-1219.

————. *La rive gauche des escholiers* (Paris: Éditions chrétiennes, 1992).

————. 'Les bouchers et les juges à Paris à la fin du Moyen Âge' in *Un Mo yen Âge pour aujourd'hui: Mélanges offerts à Claude Gauvard*, ed. by Julie Claustre, Olivier Mattéoni and Nicolas Offenstadt (Paris: Presses Universitaires de France, 2010), pp. 270-77.

————. 'Modèles et pratiques en histoire urbaine médiévale: L'espace parisien à la fin du Moyen Âge', *Histoire, économie et société*, 13 (1994), pp. 419-25.

Rouyer, Jules. 'Jetons municipaux de la ville de Paris au XVᵉ siècle', *Mémoires de la Société impériale des Antiquaires de France*, 4 (1869), pp. 113-31.

Rowe, B.J.H. 'A Contemporary Account of the Hundred Years War from 1415 to 1429', *The English Historical Review*, 41 (1926), pp. 504-13.

Roye, Lyse. 'Histoire d'une université régionale: l'Université de Caen au XVᵉ siècle', *Paedagogica Historica*, 34 (1998), pp. 403-19.

Salamon, Anne. 'Les Neuf Preux: entre édification et glorification', *Questes*, 13 (2008), pp. 3 8-52.

————. 'Les Neuf Preux: Vie d'une liste à la fin du Moyen Âge', *Cahiers de recherche des instituts néerlandais de langue et de littérature française (CRIN)*, 65 (2018), pp. 157-74.

Sankovitch, Anne-Marie. 'Intercession, Commemoration, and Display: The Parish Church as Archive in Late Medieval Paris' in *Demeures d'éternité: églises et chapelles funéraires aux XVᵉ et XVIᵉ siècles*, ed. by Jean Guillaume (Paris: Picard, 2005), pp. 247-68.

Scanlon, Larry. *Narrative, Authority and Power: The Medieval Exemplum and the Chaucerian Tradition* (Cambridge: Cambridge University Press, 1994).

Schnerb, Bertrand. 'Jean sans Peur, Paris et l'argent', *Beheifte der Francia*, 64 (2007), pp. 263-98.

———. 'La croix de Saint-André, *ensaigne congnoissable* des Bourguignons' in *Signes et couleurs des identités politiques du Moyen Âge à nos jours*, ed. by Denis Turrel, Martin Aurel and Laurent Hablot (Rennes: Presses universitaires de Rennes, 2008), pp. 45-55.

———. *Les Armagnacs et les Bourguignons: la maudite guerre* (Paris: Perrin, 1988).

Scordia, Lydwine. *'Le roi doit vivre du sien': La théorie de l'impôt en France (XIIIe-XVe siècles)* (Paris: Institut d'Études Augustiniennes, 2005).

Scott, James C. *Domination and the Arts of Resistance: Hidden Transcripts* (New Haven, CT: Yale University Press, 1990).

Scott, James C. 'Infrapolitics and Mobilizations: A Response by James C. Scott', *Revue française d'étude américaines*, 131 (2012), pp. 112-17.

Scribner, Robert. 'Oral Culture and the Diffusion of Reformation Ideas', *History of European Ideas*, 5 (1984), pp. 237-56.

Singer, Julie. 'Eyeglasses for the Blind: Redundant Therapies in Meschinot and Villon', *Fifteenth Century Studies*, 35 (2010), pp. 112-31.

Sizer, Michael. 'Murmur, Clamor and Tumult: The Soundscape of Revolt and Oral Culture in the Middle Ages', *Radical History Review*, 121 (2015), pp. 9-31.

———. 'The Calamity of Violence: Reading the Paris Massacres of 1418', *Journal of the Western Society for French History*, 35 (2007), pp. 19-39.

Skoda, Hannah. *Medieval Violence: Physical Brutality in Northern France, 1270-1330* (Oxford: Oxford University Press, 2013).

———. 'Student Violence in Fifteenth-Century Paris and Oxford' in *Aspects of Violence in Renaissance Europe*, ed. by Jonathan Davies (Farnham: Ashgate, 2013), pp. 17-40.

Skupien, Raphaële. 'La cathédrale transfigurée: Notre-Dame de Paris dans les images de la fin du Moyen-Âge (XVe-XVIe siècle)', *Livraisons d'Histoire de l'Architecture*, 38 (2019), pp. 23-37.

Slanicka, Simona. 'Male Markings: Uniforms in the Parisian Civil War as a Blurring of the Gender Order (AD 1410-20)', *The Medieval History Journal*, 2 (1999), pp. 209-44.

Sluhovsky, Moshe. *Patroness of Paris: Rituals of Devotion in Early Modern France* (Brill: Leiden, 1998).

Smagghe, Laurent. *Les émotions du prince. Émotion et discours politique dans l'espace bourguignon* (Paris: Classiques Garnier, 2012).

Smail, Daniel Lord. 'Hatred as a Social Institution in Late-Medieval Society', *Speculum*, 76 (2001), pp. 90-126.

Small, Graeme. 'The Making of the Autumn of the Middle Ages I: Narrative Sources and their Treatment in Huizinga's Herfsttij' in *Rereading Huizinga: Autumn of the Middle Ages, a Century Later*, ed. by Peter Arnade, Martha Howell and Anton van der Lem (Amsterdam: Amsterdam University Press, 2019), pp. 169-210.

Spiegel, Gabrielle M. 'History, Historicism and the Social Logic of the Text', *Speculum*, 65 (1990), pp. 59-86.

——— *Romancing the Past: The Rise of Vernacular Prose Historiography in Thirteenth-Century France* (Berkeley, CA: University of California Press, 1995).

Stabel, Peter. 'The Market Place and Civic Identity in Late Medieval Flanders' in *Shaping Identity in Late Medieval Europe / L'apparition d'une identité urbaine dans l'Europe du bas Moyen Âge*, ed. by Marc Boone and Peter Stabel (Leuven: Garant, 2000), pp. 43-64.

Stewart, Laura A.M. 'Introduction: Publics and Participation in Early Modern Britain', *Journal of British Studies*, 56 (2017), pp. 709-30.

Stock, Brian. *Listening for the Text: On the Uses of the Past* (London: John Hopkins University Press, 1990).

———. 'Medieval Literacy, Linguistic Theory and Social Organization', *New Literary History*, 16 (1984), pp. 13-29.

———. 'The Self and Literary Experience in Late Antiquity and the Middle Ages', *New Literary History*, 25 (1994), pp. 839-52.

Straker, Scott-Morgan. 'Propaganda, Intentionality and Lancastrian Lydgate' in *John Lydgate: Poetry, Culture and Lancastrian England*, ed. by Larry Scanlon and James Simpson (Notre Dame, IN: University of Notre Dame Press, 2006), pp. 98-128.

Stratford, Jenny. *The Bedford Inventories: The Worldly Goods of John, Duke of Bedford, Regent of France (1389-1435)* (London: The Society of Antiquaries of London, 1993).

Strauss, Claudia. *Making Sense of Public Opinion: American Discourses about Immigration and Social Programs* (Cambridge: Cambridge University Press, 2012).

Strayer, Joseph. 'France: The Holy Land, the Chosen People and the Most Christian King', in *Medieval Statecraft and the Perspective of History: Essays by Joseph Strayer* (Princeton, NJ: Princeton University Press, 1971), pp. 300-14.

Strohm, Paul. *England's Empty Throne: Usurpation and the Language of Legitimation, 1399-1422* (London: Yale University Press, 1998).

———. *Hochon's Arrow: The Social Imagination of Fourteenth-Century Texts* (Princeton, NJ: Princeton University Press, 1992).

———. 'Interpreting a Chronicle Text: Henry VI's Blue Gown' in *London and the Kingdom: Essays in Honour of Caroline M. Barron. Proceedings of the 2004 Harlaxton Symposium*, ed. by Matthew Davies and Andrew Prescott (Donington: Shaun Tyas, 2008), pp. 335-45.

———. *Theory and the Premodern Text* (Minneapolis, MN: University of Minnesota Press, 2000).

Strubel, Armand. 'Le "chevauchier" de Charles V: Christine de Pizan et le spectacle de la majesté royale' in *Penser le pouvoir au Moyen Âge (VIIIᵉ-XVᵉ siècle)*, ed. by Dominique Boutet and Jacques Verger (Paris: Presses de l'École normale supérieure, 2000), pp. 385-99.

Sullivan, Thomas. *Parisian Licentiates in Theology, AD 1373-1500. A Biographical Register. vol. II, The Secular Clergy* (Leiden: Brill, 2011).

Swift, Helen. *Representing the Dead: Epitaph Fictions in Late-Medieval France* (Brewer: Cambridge, 2016).

Symes, Carol. *A Common Stage: Theatre and Public Life in Medieval Arras* (London: Cornell University Press, 2007).

———. 'Out in the Open in Arras: Sightlines, Soundscapes and the Shaping of a Medieval Public Sphere' in *Cities, Texts and Social Networks, 400-1500: Experiences and Perceptions of Medieval Urban Space*, ed. by Caroline Goodson, Anne Elisabeth Lester and Carol Symes (Farnham: Ashgate, 2010), pp. 279-302.

———. 'Popular Literacies and the First Historians of the First Crusade', *Past & Present*, 235 (2017), pp. 37-67.

————. 'Review: Leidulf Melve, *Inventing the Public Sphere: The Public Debate during the Investiture Contest (c. 1030-1122)*', *American Historical Review*, 114 (2009), pp. 468-69.

Tabbagh, Vincent. 'Les assesseurs du procès de condamnation de Jeanne d'Arc' in *De l'hérétique à la sainte. Les procès de Jeanne d'Arc revisités*, ed. by François Neveux (Caen: Presses Universitaires de Caen, 2012), pp. 111-26.

————. 'Les chanoines de la fin du Moyen Âge étaient-ils au service de l'État?' in *Église et État, Église ou État? Les clercs et la genèse de l'État moderne*, ed. by Christine Barralis, Jean-Patrice Boudet, Fabrice Delivré and Jean-Philippe Genet (Paris: Éditions de la Sorbonne, 2014), pp. 149-51.

Taithe, Bertrand and Thornton, Tim. 'Propaganda: A Misnomer of Rhetoric and Persuasion?' in *Propaganda: Political Rhetoric and Identity, 1300-2000*, ed. by Bertrand Taithe and Tim Thornton (Stroud: Sutton, 1999), pp. 1-24.

Taylor, Craig. *Chivalry and the Ideals of Knighthood in France during the Hundred Years War* (Cambridge: Cambridge University Press, 2013).

————. '*La maleureuse bataille*: Fifteenth-Century French Reactions to Agincourt', *French History*, 33, 3 (2019), pp. 355-77.

————. 'The Salic Law, French Queenship, and the Defence of Women in the Late Middle Ages', *French Historical Studies*, 29 (2006), pp. 543-64.

Taylor, Jamie K. *Fictions of Evidence: Witnessing, Literature and Community in the Late Middle Ages* (Columbus, OH: Ohio State University Press, 2013).

Thompson, E.P. 'The Moral Economy of the English Crowd in the Eighteenth Century', *Past & Present*, 50 (1971), pp. 76-136.

Thompson, Guy Llewelyn. *Paris and its People under English Rule: The Anglo-Burgundian Regime, 1420-36* (Oxford: Clarendon Press, 1991).

Timbal, Pierre-Clément and Metman, Josette. 'Evêque de Paris et chapitre de Notre-Dame: la juridiction dans la cathédrale au Moyen Âge', *Revue d'histoire de l'Église de France*, 50 (1964), pp. 47-72.

Toureille, Valérie. 'Pillage ou droit de prise. La question de la qualification des écorcheurs pendant la guerre de Cent Ans' in *La politique par les armes. Conflits internationaux et politisation (XVᵉ-XIXᵉ siècles)*, ed. by Laurent Bourquin, Philippe Hamon, Alain Hugon and Yann Lagadec (Rennes: Presses universitaires de Rennes, 2013), pp. 169-82.

Tournier, Laurent. 'Jean sans Peur et l'Université de Paris', *Beihefte der Francia*, 64 (2007), pp. 299-318.

Tournier, Laure nt. 'L'Université de Paris et Charles de Savoisy: Une affaire d'honneur et d'état', *BSHP*, pp. 122-24 (1995-97), pp. 71-88.

Trani, Camille. 'Les magistrats du grand conseil au XVIᵉ siècle (1547-1610)', *Paris et Île-de-France, Mémoires publiés par la fédération des sociétés archéologiques de Paris et de l'Île-de-France*, 42 (1991), pp. 61-218.

Trexler, Richard C. *Public Life in Renaissance Florence* (London: Cornell University Press, 1980).

Trio, Paul. 'Les confréries comme expression de solidarité et de conscience urbaine aux Pays-Bas à la fin du Moyen Âge', *Beihefte der Francia*, 55 (2003), pp. 131-41.

————. 'The chronicle attributed to "Oliver van Diksmuide": A misunderstood town chronicle of Ypres from late medieval Flanders' in *The Medieval Chronicle V*, ed. by Erik Kooper (Amsterdam: Rodopi, 2008), pp. 211-25.

Tuetey, Alexandre. *Les Écorcheurs sous Charles VII. Épisodes de l'histoire militaire de France au XVe siècle d'après des documents inédits* (Montbéliard: Barbier, 1874).

Ungeheuer, Laurent. 'La Danse macabre du cimetière des Saints-Innocents et celle de deux livres d'heures contemporains: propositions de liens, de sources et de commanditaires', *Annales de Bourgogne*, 92, 3-4 (2020), pp. 25-38.

Vale, Malcolm. *Charles VII* (London: Methuen, 1974).

Vallet de Viriville, Auguste. 'Notes sur deux médailles de plomb relatives à Jeanne d'Arc et sur quelques autres enseignes politiques ou religieuses, tirées de la collection Forgeais (Suite)', *Revue Archéologique*, Nouvelle Série, 3 (1861), pp. 425-38.

Vallet de Viriville, Auguste. *Histoire de Charles VII, roi de France, et de son époque 1403-1461*, 3 vols (Paris: Jules Renouard, 1862-65).

Valois, Noël, *La France et le Grand Schisme d'Occident*, 4 vols (Paris: Alphonse Picard, 1896-1902).

———. 'Un nouveau témoignage sur Jeanne d'Arc: Réponse d'un clerc parisien à l'apologie de la Pucelle par Gerson (1429)', *Annuaire-Bulletin de la Société de l'histoire de France*, 43, 2 (1906), pp. 161-79.

Van Bruaene, Anne-Laure. 'L'écriture de la mémoire urbaine en Flandre et en Brabant (XIVe-XVIe siècle)' in *Villes de Flandre et d'Italie (XIIIe-XVIe siècles): les enseignements d'une comparaison*, ed. by Élodie Lecuppre-Desjardin and Elisabeth Crouzet-Pavan (Turnhout: Brepols, 2008), pp. 149-64.

———. 'S'imaginer le passé et le présent: conscience historique et identité urbaine en Flandre à la fin du Moyen Âge', *Beihefte der Francia*, 55 (2003), pp. 167-80.

Van Houts, Elisabeth M.C. *Local and Regional Chronicles* (Turnhout: Brepols, 1995).

Van Nierop, Henk. '"And ye shall hear of wars and rumours of wars". Rumour and the Revolt of the Netherlands' in *Public Opinion and Changing Identities in the Early Modern Netherlands. Essays in Honour of Alastair Duke*, ed. by Judith Pollmann and Andrew Spicer (Leiden: Brill, 2006), pp. 69-86.

Vanwihnsberghe, Dominique and Verroken, Erik. *'A l'Escu de France': Guillebert de Mets et la peinture de livres à Gand à l'époque de Jan van Eyck (1410-50)* (Brussels: Institut royal du Patrimoine artistique, 2017).

Vasina, Augusto. 'Medieval Urban Historiography in Western Europe (1100-1500)' in *Historiography in the Middle Ages*, ed. by Deborah Deliyannis (Leiden: Brill, 2003), pp. 317-52.

Vauchez, André. 'Les confréries au Moyen Âge: esquisse d'un bilan historiographique', *Revue historique*, 275 (1986), pp. 467-77.

Vaughan, Richard. *John the Fearless: The Growth of Burgundian Power* (London: Longmans, 1966).

———. *Philip the Good: The Apogee of Burgundy* (Harlow: Longmans, 1970).

Veenstra, Jan. *Magic and Divination at the Courts of Burgundy and France: Text and Context of Laurens Pignon's Contre les Devineurs (1411)* (Leiden: Brill, 1998).

Verger, Jacques. 'La mobilité étudiante au Moyen Âge', *Histoire de l'éducation*, 50 (1991), pp. 65-90.

———. 'Prosopographie et cursus universitaire' in *Medieval Lives and the Historian: Studies in Medieval Prosopography*, ed. by Neithard Bulst and Jean-Philippe Genet (Kalamazoo: Medieval Institute Publications, 1986), pp. 313-32.

Véronique Julerot, 'La première entrée de l'évêque: Réflexions sur son origine', *Revue historique*, 639 (2006), pp. 635-75.

Villain, Étienne. *Essai d'une histoire de la paroisse de Saint-Jacques-de-la-Boucherie* (Paris: Praolt, 1758).

Vincent, Catherine. *Les confréries médiévales dans le royaume de France, XIIIᵉ-XVᵉ siècles* (Paris: Albin Michel, 1994).

Viola, Paolo. 'Violence révolutionnaire ou violence du peuple en révolution?' in *Recherches sur la Révolution*, ed. by M. Vovelle and A. de Baecque (Paris: La Decouverte, 1991), pp. 95-107.

Vissière, Laurent. 'Goûter la ville. Réflexions sur la poésie ambulatoire de Paris au Moyen Âge' in *Les œuvres littéraires au Moyen Âge aux yeux de l'historien et du philologue*, ed. by Ludmilla Evdokimova and Victoria Smirnova (Paris: Classiques Garnier, 2014), pp. 277-92.

———. 'La bouche et le ventre de Paris', *Histoire urbaine*, 16 (2006), pp. 71-89.

Vivo, Filippo de. *Information and Communication in Venice: Rethinking Early Modern Politics* (Oxford: Oxford University Press, 2007).

Vondrus-Reissner, Jean-Georges. 'Présence réelle et juridiction ecclésiastique dans le diocèse de Paris (fin XVème-1530)', *Histoire, économie et société*, 7 (1988), pp. 41-53.

Vulliez, Charles. 'Les maîtres orléanais (*doctores*) au service de l'Université, de l'Eglise et des pouvoirs séculiers au temps de Charles VI' in *Saint-Denis et la royauté. Études offertes à Bernard Guenée*, pp. 78-90.

Walker, Greg. *Plays of Persuasion: Drama and Politics in the Court of Henry VIII* (Cambridge: Cambridge University Press, 1991).

Walker, Simon. 'Rumour, Sedition and Popular Protest in the Reign of Henry IV', *Past & Present*, 166 (2000), pp. 154-82.

Walshaw, Jill Maciak. *A Show of Hands for the Republic: Opinion, Information and Repression in Eighteenth-Century Rural France* (University of Rochester Press, 2014).

Walters, Lori J. 'Constructing Reputations, *Fama* and Memory in Christine de Pizan's *Charles V* and *L'Advision Cristine*' Fama: *The Politics of Talk and Reputaton in Medieval Europe*, ed. by Thelma Fenster and Daniel Lord Smail (London: Cornell University Press, 2003), pp. 118-42.

Watts, John. 'Popular Voices in England's Wars of the Roses, c. 1445-c. 1485', in *The Voices of the People in Late Medieval Europe: Communication and Popular Politics*, ed. by Jan Dumolyn, Jelle Haemers, Hipólito Rafael Oliva Herrer and Vincent Challet (Turnhout: Brepols, 2014), pp. 107-22.

———. 'The Pressure of the Public on Later Medieval Politics', in *The Fifteenth Century IV: Political Culture in Late Medieval Britain*, ed. by Linda Clark and Christine Carpenter (Woodbridge: Boydell, 2004), pp. 159-79.

Weidenfeld, Katia. 'Le contentieux de la voirie parisienne à la fin du Moyen Âge', *Revue historique*, 301 (1999), pp. 211-36.

Wetters, Kirk. *The Opinion System: Impasses of the Public Sphere from Hobbes to Habermas* (New York: Fordham University Press, 2008).

Wickham, Chris. 'Gossip and Resistance among the Medieval Peasantry', *Past & Present*, 160 (1998), pp. 3-24.

Wijsmann, Hanno. 'Un Manuscrit de Philippe le Bon et la *Danse macabré* du cimetière des Saints-Innocents', *Le Moyen Age*, 127, 1 (2021), pp. 59-80.

Woltjer, Juliaan. 'Public Opinion and the Persecution of Heretics in the Netherlands, 1550-59' in *Public Opinion and Changing Identities in the Early Modern Netherlands. Essays in Honour of Alastair Duke*, ed. by Judith Pollmann and Andrew Spicer (Leiden: Brill, 2006), pp. 87-106.

Wood, Andy. 'Collective Violence, Social Drama and Rituals of Rebellion in Late Medieval and Early Modern England' in *Cultures of Violence: Interpersonal Violence in Historical Perspective*, ed. by Stuart Carroll (London: Palgrave Macmillan, 2007), pp. 99-116.

————. 'Fear, Hatred and the Hidden Injuries of Class in Early Modern England', *Journal of Social History*, 39 (2006), pp. 803-26.

Zumthor, Paul. *Essai de poétique médiéval* (Paris: Seuil, 1972).

————. *La Mesure du monde. Représentation de l'espace au Moyen Âge* (Paris: Éditions de Seuil, 1993).

Zwierlein, Cornel. 'Conspiracy theories in the Middle Ages and the early modern period' in *The Routledge Handbook of Conspiracy Theories*, ed. by Michael Butter and Peter Knight (London: Routledge, 2020), pp. 542-54.

Unpublished Theses

Berland, Florence. 'La Cour de Bourgogne à Paris (1363-1422)' (unpublished doctoral thesis, Université de Lille 3 Charles-de-Gaulle, 2011).

Brabant, Annick. 'Un pont entre les obédiences: expériences normandes du Grand Schisme d'Occident (1378-1417)' (unpublished doctoral thesis, Université de Caen Basse-Normandie, 2013).

De-Vries, Jenneke. '"Nothing but Mayors and Sheriefs, and the deare yeere, and the great frost". A study of written historical culture in late medieval towns in the Low Countries and England' (unpublished doctoral thesis, University of Durham, 2019).

Hutchison, Emily. '"Pour le bien du roy et de son royaume": Burgundian Propaganda under John the Fearless, Duke of Burgundy, 1405-1449' (unpublished doctoral thesis, University of Durham, (unpublished doctoral thesis, University of York, 2006).

Kralik, Christine. '"A Matter of Life of Death": Forms, Functions and Audiences for "The Three Living and the Three Dead"' in Late Medieval Manuscripts' (unpublished doctoral dissertation, University of Toronto, 2013).

Leteux, Sylvain. 'Liberalisme et corporatisme chez les bouchers parisiens (1776-1944)' (unpublished doctoral thesis, Université de Lille 3 Charles-de-Gaulle, 2005).

Index

treason 85-86, 105, 110-11, 118, 152, 165,
    198, 205, 210, 248-49
treaties
    Treaty of Brétigny (1360) 164
    Treaty of Pontoise (1413) 58
    Treaty of Pouilly-le-Fort (1419) 248-49
    Treaty of Saint-Maur (1418) 98, 149
    Treaty of Tours (1444) 98, 240
    Treaty of Troyes (1420) 16, 71-72, 76,
        87, 98, 129, 160, 195, 249-50, 260,
        262-63
Trésor des Chartes 88
Trois Morts et Trois Vifs 68-73
Troy 99, 214, 217
Troyes, Jean de 58, 210
Tuetey, Alexandre 11-12, 18 n., 26, 28, 39,
    87, 89
tyranny 17, 38, 69, 108, 127, 147, 152-57,
    160, 163, 182, 243

Ubaldis, Baldus de 252
University of Paris 17, 20, 26-29, 36-37, 46,
    51-53, 76-77, 82-90, 108, 114-16, 124-25,
    150, 168, 197, 199-200, 210, 216, 225-26,
    234, 237, 241-42, 258, 263, 267-69, 273
Urban V, Pope 164
Ursins Compiler 22, 105 n., 106, 108 n., 110,
    154-55, 193, 196, 209, n., 210, 243, 274
Ursins

Jean Jouvenel des *garde de la prévôté des
    marchands* 53
Jean Juvénal des 22, 127, 216, 263

Vaillant, Jean 57
Valois, Catherine of 87, 157, 160
Valois, Marie de Prioress of Poissy, 102
Vatican MS Reg. Lat. 1923 see *Journal d'un
    bourgeois de Paris*
Vaudémont, Antoine de, Count of
    Vaudemont 262, 265
Vauru
    Bâtard de Vauru 154-56
    Denis de 154-58, 160, 163
Vignier, Guillaume 87
Villette, Philippe de 162
Villon, François 39, 73
Vincennes 214, 255
Vivat Rex 17, 118, 252

Westminster 255, 268-69
William Gregory's *Chronicle* 268, see also
    London Chronicles
women 112, 157, 159, 161, 165, 168, 175,
    183-85, 195, 208, 234

York 146
Ysbarre, Augustin 64 n., 198
    Ysbarre family 68 n.